PRINCIPLES OF TAX POLICY

Second Edition

Stephanie Hunter McMahon

Professor of Law
University of Cincinnati College of Law

CONCISE HORNBOOK SERIES™

**WEST
ACADEMIC
PUBLISHING**

© 2018 LEG, Inc. d/b/a West Academic
© 2018 LEG, Inc. d/b/a West Academic
      444 Cedar Street, Suite 700
      St. Paul, MN 55101
      1-877-888-1330

Printed in the United States of America

ISBN: 978-1-64242-058-6

To Darcy

Preface

The Tax Cuts and Jobs Act of 2017 was enacted five days after the first edition of this book was published. My first thought on learning that the law had passed was self-pity. I knew that I needed to update the newly published book to address the many changes to the Internal Revenue Code adopted in late December 2017. These changes permeated how the tax system operates for families with children, for investors, for businesses, and for those operating internationally. The changes were wide-ranging, so that almost every chapter was revised to incorporate new law.

My second thought was frustration at how to present this material when new complexity replaced old and the short-term nature of many of these changes means that in the next eight years the old provisions are likely to be back. This major legislative change was not a simplifying law. The structure of new provisions was often complicated, and, with hurried drafting, it is not always clear how the law will be interpreted when these provisions end up in court.

On a deeper level, I am troubled that the current partisan environment in Washington DC and throughout the country makes it difficult for people to discuss these changes specifically and tax policy in general in an open-minded way. With the hardening of positions, less effort is made to persuade because it has become too easy to berate. Policymakers and the public think less deeply about issues when their partisan identification dictates responses to policy questions. This has not always existed and, I hope, will be a short-lived blip in our nation's political history.

Despite the political rancor, tax policy issues remain. As a nation we need to find a way to discuss these issues coolly and rationally. Hopefully this book can be a step to that end by providing readers a common vocabulary and an understanding of what we know and what we do not know about tax policy.

Stephanie Hunter McMahon

May 2018

Summary of Contents

PART E. USES OF TAXATION

Table of Contents

PART C. WHERE TO TAX

PRINCIPLES OF TAX POLICY

Second Edition

Introduction

All governments spend money. What they spend it on is a political choice far beyond the parameters of this book. This book focuses on an equally fundamental subject: How does the government raise the revenue that it spends? This question is one of the most important questions policymakers face. Although in the short term not all revenue has to come from taxes, ultimately taxes are necessary to finance government spending. The amount the government can raise affects the choice of how large or small the government will be. This makes tax policy a critical set of decisions for policymakers.

But the impact of tax policy is far greater than the amount of revenue that can be raised. An enacted tax's form affects the distribution of its burden and its benefits. Taxes can be structured to impose its least, or greatest, burden on any particular group within society. Taxes can contain many special provisions to encourage or to discourage targeted behavior. Taxes can try to minimize their evasion or tacitly accept that some people will not willingly pay them.

Because of its importance, one might assume that everyone understands and appreciates the tax system. Sadly, that is not the case, which is the reason for this book. The tax system's size and complexity plus a long-standing, widely held acceptance that our system is incomprehensible causes many people not to closely examine these issues.

However, tax policy is not much, if any, more complicated than other areas of social and economic policy. Taxes are statutory creatures that must tell taxpayers precisely what is and is not taxed, which at times necessitates complicated language, but that complexity can be separated from the statute's underlying goals. Complicated language largely responds to those who would exploit ambiguities in statutory language to their own advantage, and that reaction to taxation is one facet of tax policy. In this way, most of tax policy is much easier to grasp than its language—such as what should the government expect of human nature and economic forces. The concepts of tax policy can be broken down to pieces and assembled to make our national tax system.

This breaking down and rebuilding requires mental work, despite politicians' ability to reduce tax policy issues to sound bites. Whether a tax is susceptible to abuse, whether the taxpayer can shift the burden of taxes to someone else, or whether taxes are regressive in application are questions not always apparent on a statute's face.

1

Multi-faceted and unintended responses abound when the government changes the tax law. Consequently, policymakers must think deeply about the intended and unintended consequences of tax legislation that is as much about human behavior as the statutory language.

For those making these hard choices in tax policy debates, tax policy requires making political, economic, and social tradeoffs. Because it is impossible to fully predict human behavior or economic responses, the most that can be said on each issue (although it is a lot) is what the most important influences and results are likely to be. To this end, this student aid looks at both sides of what are often highly partisan debates and lists the unknown facts and open questions that policymakers would need to know to fully resolve the issue. By defining the arguments that will perplex the nation for years to come, this book admits that there are no easy answers, only tough questions and lots of arguments.

A fuller understanding of tax policy concepts and where the ambiguity lies helps policymakers frame tax laws in a way that is fairer, simpler, and more efficient. When the concepts are combined, Congress can create a good if imperfect tax system. As Alexander Hamilton, a chief architect of the federal government's fiscal system, once wrote:

> There is no part of the administration of government that requires extensive information and a thorough knowledge of the principles of political economy, so much as the business of taxation. The man who understands those principles best will be least likely to resort to oppressive expedients, or sacrifice any particular class of citizens to the procurement of revenue.[1]

People must understand the policy tradeoffs in order to get the results they desire. And if knowledge of history is necessary so that we are not doomed to repeat it, knowledge of tax policy is necessary to be able to finance it fairly in the first place.

Putting the policy to work in practice as on paper requires applying these concepts with legal skill. Even then, if policymakers do everything in their power to fully account for tax policy tradeoffs, they would still produce imperfect legislation because of its very nature. There is no perfect solution to taxing issues in this imperfect world. Every tax choice has drawbacks; the issue is often who suffers the drawbacks and how bad they will be. The most we can hope for is the best, not the perfect.

---

[1]   THE FEDERALIST NO. 35 (Alexander Hamilton).

The need to illustrate the pros and cons of choices is what drove me to write this book and to frame it as I have. Even when frustration at Washington is deserved, they are not the reason the tax system is imperfect. Congress and the president have yet to create the "reform" everyone seems to promise because any reform will hurt some group of Americans. This makes all choices difficult.

The hard choices to find the best compromise are ultimately Congress's responsibility. Political trade-offs are made in the halls of Congress, although the President must sign the final legislation making his opinion important. Despite the IRS being well known for enforcing federal taxes, it has little power in the creation of those taxes. Within Congress the process is far from simple. Because of the difficulty of the subject matter, responsibility for tax legislation is delegated to specialists within Congress and Congress uses special rules to ensure tax legislation is enacted. Nevertheless, even that process has been usurped in the heavily partisan debates of recent years. This book aims to shed light on what the specialists know so that their decisions, and those of partisan leaders, can be evaluated fairly and openly, without the filtering of someone seeking a donation or a vote.

Those not in Congress need to understand the issues so they can evaluate the sound bites they hear in the press and, if they are so inclined, to participate in public debates to change the policies that distribute the nation's tax burden. Writing to those who want to engage in this analysis, I pose many questions throughout this book; my research assistant complained it was too many. The reason is not that the Socratic method is my preferred teaching style, although it is, but to encourage readers to formulate their own answers to the many questions of tax policy that have yet to be answered definitively. My answers are for me alone. Thus, part of my objective is to direct readers to the questions and let readers formulate their own answers.

Despite the open-ended questions of policy choice, individual facets of the tax system are relatively straightforward. For example, payroll taxes, income taxes, or estate taxes raise questions for which people simply do not agree on the answers but at least the questions are clear. More complicated is the interaction of the many parts of the system, and this book only grazes the surface of these deeper questions. This deeper level requires comparing how choices affect different parts of the system at the same time. How does a change in international taxation affect payroll tax revenue? How does the double taxation of corporate income affect the estate tax? By the end of the book, these questions will make sense but readers are likely to still be grappling with their answers because, in truth, no one can fully answer them.

Thus, one can think of the tax system as a complex and huge puzzle with some bent and torn pieces. The puzzle has federal, state, local, and international pieces. It touches every part of Americans' lives. Although we often focus on parts of the puzzle—the income tax, Social Security, Medicare—they really need to be recognized as parts of a whole. This book discusses the pieces and urges readers to keep in mind the web the choices create.

The structure of the book sometimes hides this larger picture because it aims to clear up the easy questions first. I introduce many topics in tax policy by first defining the substantive rules as they exist. The book then examines arguments for and against different policy choices. Thus, the examination is of issues as a policy matter rather than the details necessary to implement the law. By necessity these discussions do not exhaust any one topic or idea.[2] There are entire books available on any one of these topics. Consequently, this book will not give you mastery over a particular issue, but it will introduce you to both sides of tax debates.

The book's goal is to familiarize the reader with current political debates but without the book getting political. Though I am sensitive to the range of arguments and how politicians often use them, I do not tag them by the political party associated with an idea. I almost never refer to the parties and only rarely to politicians because I fear partisanship muddles rather than clarifies the issues. No party is monolithic, and people see politicians differently, which is all well beyond the scope of this book. It is my hope, perhaps a naïve one, to avoid fights over politicized, but not directly tax, matters. At times I have loosely grouped ideas or think tanks along a spectrum from the more "conservative" and to the more "liberal," although I have tried to avoid even that except when a finding or research approach might have been influenced by political ideology. As much as possible, I leave it to readers to put ideas on their own political spectrum.

Therefore, perhaps most importantly, this book is not a work of advocacy, other than it advocates for all readers to grapple with the yet unresolved debates covered in this book. It does not offer a

---

[2]   Although I could have included many additional worthy citations, I made the choice to limit footnotes for readability. As for statistics, the IRS maintains its statistical records included in a Databook at https://www.irs.gov/statistics; the Joint Committee on Taxation maintains prior publications at https://www.jct.gov/publications.html; and the Office of Management and Budget maintains historical records at https://www.whitehouse.gov/omb/budget/Historicals.

solution to these taxing problems.[3] Tax policy questions are open for debate because there is no objectively correct answer. The most politicians and pundits can hope for is to find the best answer given the available information. The more information one has on these topics the better the answer that can be developed, but nothing is conclusive. With that understanding, readers should make their own determination of tax policy.

In this book, I do not assume readers have any prior knowledge, so I apologize in advance if parts cover too much basic policy for some. The book evolved from handouts I created for my students with definitions and an overview of arguments when I discovered that not everyone came to the table with background knowledge of economics, government, or behavioral psychology. My goal was, and is, to ensure that everyone knows the vocabulary and the range of arguments so that they can delve as deeply as they want into any particular issue. It is a difficult balance of defining every term concisely enough to save space (and attention) for delving into the issues. I can only hope that I have struck the appropriate balance.

I aim for precision and clarity in my language. Although a reference to the Treasury Department includes the IRS as a bureau within the Treasury Department, I refer to each separately. At times this is clunky but it helps underscore differences between their missions. Only with respect to the Internal Revenue Code and gender have I taken license. Technically, current tax law resides in the Internal Revenue of 1986, as amended. For simplicity, I refer to it as the Internal Revenue Code or, if the context is clear, the Code. Additionally, although the Internal Revenue Code is written for a "he," which is defined to include a "she," I split my references between the two terms for ease of readability and a sense that everyone is subject to tax.

Finally, I hope that you find this book as informative and enjoyable as I found writing it. Spelling out ideas in detail has been challenging. I struggled with concepts and arguments as I hope readers do. I refined my own thoughts, also as I hope readers do. The nation is always at the cusp of some major tax change; therefore, it is always a good time to think about tax policy.

---

[3]   The book also does not teach how to be a tax lawyer because that is for law school and years of legal practice, and it does not compare the U.S. system to those of other nations because doing so would take too long.

Part A

TAX POLITICS

Chapter 1

HOW LAW IS MADE

Table of Sections

The Internal Revenue Code is a complex, oft revised statute. It contains the income tax, which has thousands of provisions, hundreds of which are newly enacted or amended each year. The Code also holds many other taxes operated by the federal government. In addition to the income tax, there are payroll taxes (for Social Security, Medicare, and unemployment benefits), estate taxes, fees for services (such as entrance to national parks, airline tickets, and phone service), and tariffs on imported goods (including most consumer items and agricultural products).

All federal taxes are statutory, which means that they must be enacted through Congress and do not exist in the common law or in the state of nature. In the 1970s, *Schoolhouse Rock* sang about how a bill becomes a law.[1] First, a congressperson proposes a bill that goes to a congressional committee. If the bill emerges from that committee, the two branches of Congress must each vote to pass the bill. Then the president must sign the bill into law. If a tax bill does not complete the process, there is no tax. But this process is never simple, and taxation is an especially complex and controversial political issue.

§ 1.01   Tax as Legislation

Every year the federal government enacts numerous tax provisions. For example, in the twenty years between 1986 and 2005, there were almost 15,000 changes to the tax code, or more than two per day.[2] Some new provisions and some revisions of old provisions are part of major pieces of legislation. Other changes are technical revisions correcting only typographical errors in prior laws. Each piece of enacted legislation, whether big or small, follows much the

---

1   *I'm Just a Bill*, Schoolhouse Rock! (1976).
2   REPORT OF THE PRESIDENT'S ADVISORY PANEL ON FEDERAL TAX REFORM, SIMPLE, FAIR, AND PRO-GROWTH, at viii (2005).

same process but with vastly different amounts of congressional or popular attention. Thus, the Code that operates today evolved from a web of legislation.

When a tax bill becomes a law, the new law most often becomes an amendment to the Internal Revenue Code, published as Title 26 of the United States Code. That taxes are in the U.S. Code simply means that Congress has given this area of law a cohesive structure, and the structure tends to change little over time. Since the codification of the tax law in 1919, three times Congress has enacted a "restated" Code, which was a new law with many changes to the structure of the statute but that nonetheless included significant parts of the prior law. The most recent restatement was in 1986. Since then, Congress has continued to amend the Internal Revenue Code of 1986.

Additional tax provisions may be found outside of the Internal Revenue Code. These include when the tax law interacts with bankruptcy and the Tax Court, which are found in their own respective titles of the U.S. Code. Finally, some special tax provisions are not codified at all, which makes them harder to locate. These provisions are still enacted laws, but they are not organized for posterity. For example, section 530 of the Revenue Act of 1978 provides a safe harbor for employers hiring independent contractors versus employees.[3] This provision still applies even though it is not part of the Internal Revenue Code. Similarly, some of the Affordable Care Act's industry fees are off-Code revenue provisions.[4] Anyone operating in these areas of law needs to know the relevant provisions, despite the fact they are not found in the Code.

(a) Legislative Process

The creation of tax legislation requires a complex interplay between the executive and legislative branches of government because taxation is tied to the creation of the federal budget, due as of the beginning of each fiscal year on October 7.[5] The president's role in this process is limited, but the president often starts the dialogue over tax legislation. Pursuant to federal law, the president must submit a budget to Congress before the first Monday of each February. The Treasury Department's Office of Tax Policy (OTP), the office within the Department responsible for developing executive branch tax policies and programs, largely crafts the president's

---

[3]   Revenue Act of 1978, Pub. L. No. 95–600, 92 Stat. 273, 2885–86, § 350 (1978).

[4]   JOINT COMM. ON TAXATION, JCX–6–13, PRESENT LAW AND BACKGROUND RELATING TO THE TAX-RELATED PROVISIONS OF THE AFFORDABLE CARE ACT (Mar. 4, 2013).

[5]   31 U.S.C. § 1105.

package of taxing and spending proposals. The president's budget does not bind Congress, but in many years it is the first step in creating the federal budget.

Although the president often (but not always) begins the debate about tax legislation, the Constitution requires that all tax legislation originate in Congress's House of Representatives because the House was to be the more popular, as opposed to the more elite, house of Congress.[6] Nevertheless, the Constitution also gives the Senate authority to amend tax bills, and in some cases the Senate has amended legislation so much that many would say it was starting anew. For example, in 1911, the Supreme Court permitted the Senate's substitution of a corporate excise tax for an inheritance tax.[7] Moreover, the Origination Clause's limit only applies if the bill's purpose is to raise revenue to support the government generally as opposed to funding a particular program.[8] The Senate is constitutionally free to initiate targeted taxes to provide revenue for a program.

In the House of Representatives, any member can initiate a bill by placing it in the "hopper" after which it is assigned a number and sent to the appropriate House committee to consider its content. Within the House, tax legislation has been delegated to the House Committee on Ways and Means, a large committee of thirty-nine members. In addition to taxes, the Committee on Ways and Means also oversees Social Security, Medicare, and Temporary Assistance for Needy Families (TANF, a federal welfare program). Traditionally this was a prestigious and occupying commitment, so that members were not allowed to serve on other committees without a waiver from their party's leadership.

However, committees have declined in importance with an increase in political partisanship.[9] Today political parties are more ideological and cohesive than in prior decades, giving their leaders tremendous power over the shape of legislation.[10] In the process, the House's Ways and Means Committee's role has declined. This has resulted in new members working on the committee and it having less influence over tax legislation in the full House.[11] This is

---

[6] U.S. CONST., art I, sec. 7.

[7] Flint v. Stone Tracy Company, 220 U.S. 107 (1911).

[8] United States v. Munoz-Flores, 495 U.S. 385 (1990).

[9] See Elizabeth Garrett, *The Congressional Budget Process: Strengthening the Party-in-Government*, 100 COLUM. L. REV. 702, 706–707 (2000).

[10] BARBARA SINCLAIR, UNORTHODOX LAWMAKING 166 (5th ed. 2017).

[11] George Yin, *Of Geodesic Domes and Mud Huts: Constructing Tax Legislation in a Highly Polarized Congress* (2017).

evidenced by the committee's limited role in developing recent tax legislation.[12]

Despite the substance of tax legislation being framed in the Committee on Ways and Means, the House Committee on Rules has tremendous power over the fate of tax legislation because it sets the parameters of debate in the full House. The Rules Committee can either set a closed rule, so the bill must be accepted or rejected in its entirety, or a modified closed rule, permitting specific amendments and limiting the hours of debate. For example, the Rules Committee limited debate on the Tax Cuts and Jobs Act of 2017 to four hours.[13] Therefore, the Rules Committee determines whether Representatives can filibuster in the House, whereby a group of Representatives talk on the floor of the House to delay or defer a vote on a bill.

Once the House agrees on a draft bill, the bill goes to the Senate for the Senate's consideration. The Senate's committee comparable to Ways and Means is the Senate Committee on Finance, with twenty-six members. The Senate's Rules Committee is not as powerful as its House counterpart. In the Senate, a vote for cloture, the procedure to end debate and call the measure to vote, is normally required to end a filibuster. Cloture requires a three-fifths vote of the Senate (or 60 Senators) and, if passed, allows for thirty hours of additional debate followed by a vote on the bill.

The possibility of a Senate filibuster of tax legislation threatens the federal budget. Because neither political party may have sufficient votes for cloture in the Senate, in 1974 Congress created a mechanism to get budget legislation to a vote called the reconciliation process. Reconciliation is begun with a concurrent resolution by both houses of Congress, and it limits debate on budget bills to twenty hours in each house. Although the reconciliation rules apply in the House of Representatives, its Rules Committee often imposes more limiting restrictions. Therefore, reconciliation helps ensure budgeting legislation can make it out of the Senate without a super-majority vote. Under current rules, only one general reconciliation bill can be passed each year.

The reconciliation process is supplemented by the Byrd Rule, introduced in the Senate in 1985 and named after Senator Robert Byrd (D-WV). The Byrd Rule establishes a point of order against Senators amending the reconciliation bill with unrelated provisions. An unrelated provision includes any amendment to a reconciliation

---

[12]   *See* H.R.1, Actions Overview, Congress.gov, https://www.congress.gov/bill/115th-congress/house-bill/1/all-actions?overview=closed.

[13]   H.Res. 619, 115th Cong. (Nov. 15, 2017).

bill that decreases federal revenue after the ten-year period begun by the concurrent resolution starting the reconciliation process. The point of order strikes the extraneous provision but retains the rest of the bill. For example, in debates over the Tax Cuts and Jobs Act of 2017, the Senate Parliamentarian blocked the repeal of the Johnson amendment, which would have allowed 501(c)(3)s including churches to endorse candidates, as not having a budgetary impact. A supermajority vote of Senators is required to retain the offending provision. The Byrd Rule is applicable only in the Senate, but the House's Rules Committee can set equivalent rules in its discretion.

The fate of much tax legislation hangs on the Byrd Rule's limit on amendments and the permissive majority vote of reconciliation. Without these rules, much tax legislation would fail. For example, neither the Economic Growth and Tax Relief Reconciliation Act of 2001 and the Jobs and Growth Tax Relief Reconciliation Act of 2003, popularly referred to collectively as the Bush tax cuts, nor the Tax Cuts and Jobs Act of 2017 would have passed with a supermajority requirement to stop a filibuster.[14]

If the House of Representatives and Senate do not initially agree on the same version of a tax bill but do pass bills of the same number, a conference is formed. That conference is formed of Representatives and Senators from the Committees on Ways and Means and Finance. The conference can only consider disputed parts of the bill. If the conference reaches a compromise, the compromise bill then goes to each house for a vote. If approved by each house of Congress, the approved bill goes to the president for the president's signature.

Once Congress submits a bill for the president's signature, the president chooses whether or not to sign it. With a presidential signature, the bill becomes a law. If the president vetoes the bill, only a two-thirds vote of both houses of Congress overrides the president and the bill becomes a law. If the president neither signs nor vetoes the bill within ten days, the status of the bill depends upon whether Congress is in session. If Congress is in session, the bill becomes law without a signature. If Congress is not in session, the bill is vetoed (the pocket veto).

This process demonstrates that tax legislation is inherently a political compromise both within Congress and to win the president's support. There are complaints that this process slows, or even prevents, reform of the tax system. Legislative change occurs incrementally rather than holistically because of the need to build

---

14 Jobs and Growth Tax Relief Reconciliation Act of 2003, Pub. L. No. 108–27, 117 Stat. 752; Economic Growth and Tax Relief Reconciliation Act of 2001, Pub. L. No. 107–16, 115 Stat. 38; Pub. L. No. 115–97, 131 Stat. 2054. The 2017 law passed in the House by 227–205 (52.5%) and in the Senate by 51–48 (51.5%).

support throughout the government. *The Federalist Papers* described this consensus building as the purpose of the separation of powers.[15] It is purposefully hard to change federal laws.

(b) Structural Limitations

Although the Committees on Ways and Means and Finance are delegated the responsibility for drafting tax legislation, they do not have free reign to do so. The process for creating new tax legislation is bound by structural limitations in order to reduce the size of the federal budget deficit. In particular, the reconciliation process, which limits debate in the Senate, is often used to pass tax legislation but requires a given amount of tax revenue as dictated by the budget committees. Thus, reconciliation limits the size of the deficit by linking taxing and spending.

With the concurrent resolution calling for reconciliation, the House Committee on the Budget (which includes, among others, members of the Committees on Ways and Means, Appropriations, and Rules) establishes the aggregate amount of revenue to be raised as part of the reconciliation process. The Ways and Means Committee must raise at least that much tax revenue. With that revenue floor, the tax committees are able to structure tax provisions as they like subject only to getting the final provisions through the full houses and signed by the president. By setting the target, however, the reconciliation process limits the tax committees' freedom to enact or revise tax legislation if potential changes are not within revenue targets. This is a simplified description of reconciliation in practice; the process is more complicated because of the interplay between taxing and spending programs in a budget bill.

Congress created the reconciliation process and several other structural requirements for revenue bills as part of a decades-long effort to control its own spending power. Although there is no federal constitutional requirement for a balanced budget, federal legislation and congressional rules often require partially balanced budgets. The Budget Control Act of 2011, followed by the Bipartisan Budget Act of 2013, and pay-as-you-go (PAYGO) as operated in the House of Representatives and the Senate are all attempts to make the budget revenue neutral.[16] They generally require the estimated budget effects of any new or augmented spending program or tax expenditure be offset with revenue increases. However, all of these

---

[15] THE FEDERALIST NO. 47 (James Madison).

[16] Pub. L. No. 112–25, 125 Stat. 240 (Aug. 2, 2011); Pub. L. No. 113–67, 127 Stat. 1165 (Dec. 26, 2013); Rule 21, Rules of the House of Representatives, 114th Cong., Jan. 6, 2015; S. Con. Res. 11, 114th Cong.

self-imposed limits permit exceptions if there is a sufficiently large vote. The limits also have exceptions for emergency spending.

Limits are also suspended through political action. In 2017, the Senate Budget Committee Chairman called for the Finance Committee to create a revenue bill, eventually enacted as the Tax Cuts and Jobs Act, to cost no more than $1.5 trillion over ten years.[17] Because the tax reduction was not coupled with spending cuts, the government knew this would create a deficit.

As the budget system currently operates, the balancing is over a ten-year budget period.[18] Thus, the federal budget is measured over ten years, and not on an annual basis, in recognition of the ebbs and flows of the economy. It is over this ten-year period that federal expenditures are to equal, or be less than, the revenue the government raises.

The structural and political need to balance the budget is counterbalanced by the political difficulty of doing so. Therefore, demands to balance the budget encourage political manipulation. As one means to manipulate the tax system, Congress adopts tax provisions set to expire, which reduces their cost. For example, most of the individual tax cuts in the Tax Cuts and Jobs Act of 2017 are set to expire, generally at the end of 2025. Early expiration has a favorable budgeting effect.

When Congress frames a tax preference to last a number of years, it costs less than a preference that will exist indefinitely, even if everyone expects the preference to be reenacted. A vibrant debate rages over the pros and cons of expiring tax provisions and the effect they have on the federal budget.[19] The provision itself cost less, and any increase in revenue over the ten-year budget window can be used to offset the provision's shorter-term cost. At the same time, expiration provides Congress the opportunity to review the provision and minimizes the difficulty of repealing tax preferences by allowing them to lapse. In the last few years, the use of short-term tax extenders for expiring provisions has left more than fifty provisions waiting to be renewed at the end of each year, increasing taxpayer uncertainty.

In addition to short-term tax cuts, politicians can speed up revenue for purposes of the budget so that more revenue counts

---

[17]   H. Con. Res. 71, § 1101, 115th Cong. (2017).

[18]   For more on the parts of the budget, see Chapter 18.01.

[19]   Rachelle Holmes Perkins, *Breaking the Spell of Tax Budget Magic*, 6 COLUM. J. TAX L. 1 (2014); Rebecca Kysar, *Lasting Legislation*, 159 U. PA. L. REV. 1007 (2011); George Yin, *Temporary-Effect Legislation, Political Accountability, and Fiscal Restraint*, 84 N.Y.U. L. REV. 174 (2009); Jacob Gersen, *Temporary Legislation*, 74 U. CHI. L. REV. 247 (2007).

within the ten-year budget window. Speeding up the inclusion of revenue allows Congress to spend money earlier. Generally this technique does not actually increase government revenue, it is simply a game of timing. For example, changing the date tax payments are due causes money to come in earlier but does not change the amount of revenue, except for any interest to be earned.

Congress can also push revenue loss until after the close of the budget window. This strategy could be challenged with the Byrd Rule in the Senate or by requiring a longer budget window (the ten-year window used to be only one year and then five years). Nevertheless, Congress has pushed the cost of some tax preferences into the future. Consider the Roth IRA, which is an individual retirement account that allows people to invest money that has been taxed, accumulate tax-free returns, and receive tax-free distributions from the account.[20] There is no current revenue lost with the creation of the Roth IRA, but tremendous revenue is lost when distributions are made because appreciation on the account is never taxed. For most taxpayers this is far in the future.

These political maneuvers complicate the Internal Revenue Code, make the budgeting process more opaque, and reduce its value in balancing spending with revenue. By blurring information about how much money is being raised and spent, policymakers cannot truly know whether the budget is balanced. Moreover, given political incentives, an obscured budget is likely to lead to greater deficit spending. Deficit spending, unless coupled with economic growth, raises questions of equity for future generations and the federal government's long-term ability to fund its desired projects.[21]

However, tying Congress's hands with respect to the budget is not without risks. Economists agree that there are times when deficits are useful for the nation. Much as individuals do not always balance their budgets but they may take out loans, governments can wisely borrow and engage in deficit spending. The questions for individuals and the government are what the money is used for and how much borrowing is too much.[22]

Any measure of how much can be spent at a given time is made difficult because government spending tends to be cyclical with the economy. The government tends to spend more when its tax revenues are reduced. For example, more unemployment is paid in a bad economy when there are fewer jobs. The Congressional Budget Office (CBO) once estimated that for the year 2000 each additional

---

[20]   I.R.C. § 408.

[21]   For more on spending tax revenue, see Chapter 18.

[22]   For more on the national debt, see Chapter 18.02.

percentage point of unemployment produced an almost $90 billion increase in the deficit.[23]

Additionally, it is easier to build a budget surplus when the economy is doing well. With tax rates held constant, the system raises more income tax during economic upturns because more income is earned. When a taxpayer earns more money, the taxpayer may also be pushed into higher tax brackets, raising more revenue from each additional dollar earned. Even without the higher brackets, more income taxed at the same rate produces more tax revenue. That bump in revenue has been used to justify reducing tax rates in good times. However, during economic downturns, the same tax rates will yield less tax revenue because less income is earned. This effect gives income taxes some degree of an automatic counter-cyclical effect.

Deficit spending also means that the nation's current residents as a whole receive more from the government than they give to the government, and curtailing that receipt is politically difficult. Moreover, eliminating the deficit would risk shrinking the nation's purchasing power and the amount that is consumed. This is likely to have a ripple effect on the nation's economy. Not only is this likely to reduce economic growth to the extent growth is driven by consumption, it is likely to hurt state and local governments. If the federal government reduces its spending, states and localities may be forced to spend more.[24] With many potential unintended consequences, a balanced budget is properly placed within a larger analysis of the proper role of government in society and the economy.

Finally, structural limits requiring a balanced budget are not constitutional requirements, although in the last century many attempts have been made to adopt a balanced budget amendment. The limits that exist are weak constraints on political actors who respond to the revenue demands of their constituents. Much as a bill of rights was described in *The Federalist Papers* as a parchment barrier to a federal government that wanted to abridge rights, congressional limits on the budget are only useful as political rhetoric.[25] Modern balanced budget requirements may even thwart this objective if the public believes the requirements effectively limit spending.

---

[23]   CONG. BUDGET OFFICE, ECONOMIC AND BUDGET OUTLOOK: FISCAL YEARS 1996–2000, at 79 (1995).

[24]   For more on state and local budgeting, see Chapter 13.02(b).

[25]   THE FEDERALIST No. 48 (James Madison).

(c) Legislative History

When taxpayers and the courts read a tax statute, its meaning does not have to be confined to the words in the statute. Particularly in tax, legislative history has long been revered as a source of the law. Legendary tax scholar Boris Bittker claimed, "Tax lawyers routinely invoke 'legislative intent,' which, as you probably know is to statutory law what 'original intent' is to constitutional law. . . . In fact, someone once said that they look at the Internal Revenue Code only if the committee reports are ambiguous."[26] Non-specialist courts do not always accept this role for tax's legislative history, adding to the confusion over what a tax statute really means.

Whether tax legislation's legislative history must receive more deference than that of other statutes is open to debate. The difficulty of deciphering statutory language by most people, including many politicians, argues in favor of increased deference to what members of Congress thought they were enacting. The Code's complexity and that it has grown incrementally over more than one hundred years perhaps demands a coherent and lengthy legislative history. On the other hand, it may be unreasonable to expect taxpayers to consider legislative history when they are interpreting this complex statutory regime. If Congress wants to tax something, is it too much to ask that Congress make the language clear?

Use of legislative history to interpret tax statutes may be more reasonable because, unlike with other legislation, congressional committees generally do not use proposed statutory language as the basis of their discussion of tax bills. The statutory language that will later raise questions for the Treasury Department in the tax's implementation can be drafted late in the legislative process, although it is drafted earlier now than in the past. Instead, debate over most tax legislation proceeds from narrative descriptions that focus on the concepts.[27] These "one-pagers" describe legislative proposals and are written by the Joint Committee on Taxation (JCT). The staff of the JCT, acting in the same way as outside attorneys to a client, translates technical jargon and legal concepts to the lay Congress, who often vote based on these descriptions.

---

[26]   Boris I. Bittker, *The Bicentennial of the Jurisprudence of Original Intent: The Recent Past*, 77 CAL. L. REV. 235, 249–50 (1989).

[27]   The Senate Committee on Finance uses conceptual markups; however, in the House of Representatives, Newt Gingrich as Speaker of the House changed the rule so that the Committee on Ways and Means examines statutory language. When the House shifts to Democrats, this rule is usually suspended and debate reverts to conceptual documents. DANIEL BERMAN & VICTORIA HANEMAN, MAKING TAX LAW 264 (2014).

That Congress uses conceptual descriptions in tax matters means that members of Congress may never read the tax laws that they create. However, the use of one-pagers might be the best method for assuring that members understand what they are voting on. Because much of tax law is created through amendments to the Internal Revenue Code, statutes are often fragments adding clauses or isolated sentences to existing provisions that are not set forth in the bill. If the Code is difficult to read, changes to individual subsections within broad-reaching statutes are even more so. The larger context of each change is supplied only in the conceptual descriptions. Without those descriptions, policymakers who may not be attorneys and may not be versed in reading and applying tax statutes risk misconstruing disjointed phrases and clauses added to the Code.

Although these conceptual discussions provide greater clarity to members of Congress voting on tax legislation, one-pagers carry little weight as part of the legislative history when courts interpret the law. Despite likely being all that most members of Congress read about the bills they vote on, one-pagers are not the law. The law is formed when members of the congressional Office of Legislative Counsel, being managed by members of the JCT, draft the statutory language.

The House's Ways and Means and Senate's Finance Committees are then responsible for drafting their committee reports, which are the strongest form of legislative history. Committee reports have been growing longer as the tax committees use this form of legislative history to explain the statute. In the process, they arguably usurp administrative and judicial functions by specifying how the statute should be interpreted. Tax is again unique in that it is not these committees' staffs who draft their reports; the JCT drafts committee reports. Although committee members may review the reports drafted by the JCT, reports are not directly amendable by the congressional committees.

Perhaps because they are drafted outside the committees, these reports are unusually cohesive with significantly fewer minority responses than with most non-tax committee reports. If a committee member objects to the report, the member generally makes the objection known by putting the objection into the *Congressional Record*. However, the *Congressional Record* has less weight as part of the legislative history than the report itself.

Thus, the JCT is very important in the creation of tax statutes as well as their legislative history. The chairpersons of the Committees on Ways and Means and Finance chair the JCT on a rotating basis and some of their members populate the JCT.

However, the JCT seldom meets as a committee but allows its staff to perform its delegated functions. Thus, the JCT is primarily a repository for a staff of economists, lawyers, and analysts.

The JCT's staff is nonpartisan. In this context, nonpartisan means that politics is not a criterion for hiring, not that members are required to abdicate personal political positions.[28] Nevertheless, the JCT must regularly respond to a broad group of legislators from many political persuasions with heterogeneous interests. Doing so may force the JCT to remain higher above politics than other groups in the legislative process in order to maintain its responsibility and funding.

After legislation has been enacted, the JCT creates a "Bluebook," or General Explanation, of the relevant piece of enacted legislation. The General Explanation is published with a blue cover, hence its popular name. Bluebooks are compilations of committee reports and relevant statements on the floor of Congress. Notably, the JCT often adds its own chronological guidance of the bill's legislative process. Because this is added after the bill has been signed, this portion of the Bluebook is not properly termed legislative history and should not be given judicial deference. Nonetheless, Bluebooks provide coherence not present in most other areas of statutory law. Additionally, the same group within the Committees on Ways and Means and Finance, Treasury Department, and IRS review both the JCT-drafted committee reports and the annotated information.

As a result of Bluebooks' convenience and information, many courts and lawyers rely on them in their interpretation of statutory language, although that reliance is not universally accepted. Some courts do so while others do not. This reliance came to a head when the interpretive value of Bluebooks arose before the Supreme Court in 2013. In *United States v. Woods*, the taxpayer relied on the Bluebook for his interpretation of a provision imposing a tax penalty.[29] The Court stated that Bluebooks are not legitimate tools of statutory interpretation and are relevant only to the extent they are persuasive. Since 2013, this interpretive source is really no less valuable in figuring out what the words in the statute mean; however, taxpayers now rely on them at their peril.

(d) Statutory Interpretation

Judge Learned Hand wrote, "In my own case the words of such an act as the Income Tax, for example, merely dance before my eyes in a meaningless procession: cross-reference to cross-reference,

---

[28]   George Yin, *Legislative Gridlock and Nonpartisan Staff*, 88 NOTRE DAME L. REV. 2287 (2013).

[29]   571 U.S. 31 (2013).

exception upon exception—couched in abstract terms that offer no handle to seize hold of. . ."[30] The Supreme Court itself determined that "[t]he true meaning of a single section of a statute in a setting as complex as that of the revenue acts, however precise its language, cannot be ascertained if it be considered apart from related sections, or if the mind be isolated from the history of the income tax legislation of which it is an integral part."[31] In recognition of the complexity of the tax code, some courts read tax statutes with an eye to the statute's objective, whereas other courts expect greater clarity from so finely tuned a statute.

The complexity also raises questions regarding the role of non-tax judges in interpreting the statutory language and the legislative history. The Code's interrelation between sections and use of terms of art makes it difficult for the public and even judges who are rarely specially trained in tax law to understand the intent and larger meaning of statutory provisions. Professor William Blatt argues that the JCT and members of the Treasury Department should especially influence how the Code is interpreted because many lawyers and judges fail to master tax.[32] When interpreting this law, Blatt argues that judges should recognize the importance of the policy community and refer to the views of that community.

In the interpretation of tax statutes, the proposition accepted early in the income tax's history that the tax law "must be resolved against the government and in favor of the taxpayer" was short-lived.[33] Today, courts try to figure out the meaning of ambiguous statutory language without giving either party a presumptive advantage.[34] When a statute is ambiguous, Congress either intended a particular result but its drafting was unclear or Congress had no particular intent and left the subject for the agency to resolve. The first is a question of law for which the agency can look to the text of the statute and the legislative history for clarification. The second is Congress's conferral of discretion on the agency, and its result, as long as there is adequate procedure, should be given significant judicial deference.

To answer the first question, the theories of statutory interpretation apply in the tax context as with other laws. Four methods of statutory interpretation are generally identified: intentionalism, purposivism, textualism, and practical or dynamic

---

[30]   Learned Hand, *Thomas Walter Sawn*, 57 YALE L.J. 167, 169 (1947).

[31]   Helvering v. Morgan's, Inc., 293 U.S. 121, 126 (1934).

[32]   William S. Blatt, *Interpretive Communities*, 95 NW. U. L. REV. 629, 642 (2001).

[33]   United States v. Merriam, 263 U.S. 179, 188 (1923).

[34]   White v. United States, 305 U.S. 281, 292 (1938). *But see* United Dominion Indus., Inc. v. United States, 532 U.S. 822, 839 (2001) (Thomas, J. concurring).

reason.[35] Intentionalism seeks what Congress intended the statute to mean by examining legislative history, namely committee reports and floors statements, even when the statutory language is clear. Purposivism seeks the statute's purpose at enactmnet but as a reasonably intelligent and informed reader of the statute would have interpreted it at that time. Textualism reads only the statutory language with the aid of dictionaries, case law, and, possibly, treatises. Finally, practical reasoning or dynamic interpretation accepts the former use of evidence, without any one source of evidence trumping the others, and that evidence is applied to the statute with a presentist purpose to meet contemporary circumstances. Because of the Internal Revenue Code's complexity and its unique legislative process, the choice of method affects the meaning given to its terms.

In many tax cases, judges interpret the statutory language without defining their underlying theory. In one empirical study regarding judicial interpretation of the Code, Professor Daniel Schneider found that judges were "broad minded, applying all methods and frequently combining them in a way that defies scholarly purity."[36] Professors James Brudney and Corey Ditslear found that most judges do not interpret statutes in a one-size-fits-all manner and that the subject matter influences which types of interpretative skills are used.[37] By comparing tax cases with workplace cases, these professors discover different uses for legislative history (in workplaces cases to identify and elaborate the legislative bargain; in tax cases to borrow expertise) and different use of interpretive canons (structural canons are used more often in tax cases). Professor Nancy Staudt found that the Supreme Court's interpretation of tax cases has changed significantly over the years, first using its own precedent, then relying more heavily on legislative documents and administrative guidance, and more recently curtailing reliance on administrative documents.[38]

The tension over interpretive methods is often greatest when tax shelters are involved.[39] Those who dislike tax shelters may argue

---

[35]   William N. Eskridge, Jr. & Philip P. Frickey, *Statutory Interpretation as Practical Reasoning*, 42 STAN. L. REV. 321, 324–25 (1990).

[36]   Daniel M. Schneider, *Empirical Research on Judicial Reasoning*, 31 N.M. L. REV. 325, 326 (2001).

[37]   James J. Brudney & Corey Dislear, *The Warp and the Woof of Statutory Interpretation*, 58 DUKE L.J. 1231, 1234 (2009). Justice Harry Blackmun had expertise in tax law and used legislative history extensively. Since his retirement, tax cases have used less legislative history. *Id.*, at 1237,1270–75.

[38]   Nancy Staudt et al., *Judging Statutes*, 38 LOY. L.A. L. REV. 1909 (2005).

[39]   *See* Steven A. Dean & Lawrence M. Solan, *Tax Shelters and the Code*, 26 VA. TAX REV. 879 (2007); Shannon Weeks McCormack, *Tax Shelters and Statutory Interpretation: A Much Needed Purposive Approach*, 2009 U. ILL. L. REV. 697, 699

that there is an exceptional need to disavow textualism with respect to tax shelters. For example, Professors Noel Cunningham and James Repetti argue that an acceptance of textualism, or focusing strictly on the words of tax statutes, increases the likelihood that attorneys opine for and courts uphold tax shelters.[40]

When the words of the statute do not say what courts want, some judges have moved beyond the statute by creating judicial doctrines. For example, in *Gregory v. Helvering*, an early tax case, the Supreme Court took a nonliteral interpretation of the Code in order to deny taxpayer savings.[41] Creating the business purpose doctrine, the Court interpreted the Code in a broad, extra-statutory manner dismissing the earlier trial court's observation that a "statute so meticulously drafted must be interpreted as a literal expression of taxing policy."[42] Although the Supreme Court did not incorporate legislative history in its decision, its business purpose and other judicial doctrines extend the law beyond statutory language to reach the result that courts deem consistent with what the statute intended.

§ 1.02   Sources of Information

Members of Congress do not work alone to create tax legislation but rely heavily on others. That reliance is more than in the drafting of the statute's language. Members of Congress need information to evaluate the pros and cons of legislation and to win support for a particular bill. This information comes from many sources, some of which are inside the government and some are not. Although these sources provide politicians more information than much of the public has about tax proposals, politicians do not have complete information regarding a bill's potential impact. The real impact of legislative change can only be known after its enactment.

(a) Government Sources

The federal government funds a personal staff for each member of Congress and a majority party and minority party staff for each committee. Additionally, the government has created agencies to provide Congress and the president information upon request. These sources are important to the success of tax policy because members of Congress may know nothing about taxation before their

---

(2009). *See also* Joseph Bankman, *Tax Enforcement*, 31 OHIO N.U. L. REV. 1, 3–5 (2005).

[40]   Noel Cunningham & James Repetti, *Textualism and Tax Shelters*, 24 VA. TAX REV. 1 (2004).

[41]   293 U.S. 465 (1935).

[42]   22 B.T.A. at 225. *See* Daniel M. Schneider, *Use of Judicial Doctrines in Federal Tax Cases Decided by Trial Courts, 1993–2006*, 67 CLEV. ST. L. REV. 35 (2009).

appointment to a tax committee. Political appointments to the tax committees occur for a range of reasons that may not include expertise.

A congressperson can most readily obtain information from their personal and committee staffs. These staffs are partisan, meaning that they reflect the political leanings of the politician or the relevant political party. While personal staffs attend only to the Congress member, each committee's two staffs assist the majority and the minority party on the committee. However, staffs have larger jobs than gathering information and evaluating proposals. For example, committee staffs must coordinate among the committee members and between members and their constituents.

The staffs of the tax committees include specialist tax attorneys employed to assess proposed legislation. The Ways and Means Committee tends to use Inside the Beltway lawyers for this task whereas the Committee on Finance tends to use attorneys from outside of politics.[43] Producing discussion drafts and soliciting information, these committee staffs have grown in size and importance. In recent years, as these staffs have increased their ability to provide information, their influence has grown compared to other government sources.

Additionally, members of Congress can turn to the JCT or CBO, also government sources, for detailed information on the impact of tax proposals. The JCT was formed in 1926 and is the principal adviser to congressional tax-writing committees. The JCT's power has diminished in recent decades because of the proliferation of other sources of information, namely committee staffs and lobbyists. The CBO was created in 1974 to serve congressional budget committees rather than tax committees. Focusing on the budget, the CBO analyzes overall spending and revenue. Unlike committee staffs, which are partisan, these agencies are expected to compile information for policymakers of both political parties and in both houses of Congress, perhaps straining their rules of confidentiality.

The president of the U.S. obtains equivalent information from the Treasury Department and the Office of Management and Budget (OMB). The Treasury Department's Office of Tax Analysis (OTA) is the executive branch's counterpart to the JCT. The OTA houses economists and legal advisors for the Secretary of the Treasury and handles most of the executive branch's tax and tax-related planning. For example, the OTA prepares position papers on the effects of tax proposals, provides revenue estimates for the president's budget, and determines whether the president has to sequester funds as a result

---

[43]   BERMAN & HANEMAN, *supra* note 22, at 262.

of automatic spending reductions. Finally, the OMB is the executive branch's counterpart to the CBO, but it rarely deals directly with tax matters.

These different government sources create tables to explain the revenue and distributional consequences of various proposals. They try to predict how much revenue will be raised or lost and from which group of taxpayers will the money come from or go to. They create economic models based on assumptions about how people respond to changes. However, these sources struggle to make correct predictions, and no one estimate is perfect and no method infallible. Thus, advisors cannot precisely predict the effects of policies on the distribution of income and wealth. Despite their imperfections, these estimates are as scientific as possible. The specialists who create budget estimates are highly trained in taxation and economics.

Notwithstanding their best efforts, these sources are notorious for not interpreting proposals' effects in similar ways. For example, the JCT expected President George Bush's proposed reduction of capital gain rates to lose $11.4 billion in federal revenue over five years, but the OTA expected it to increase revenue by $12.5 billion.[44] These two very different predictions resulted from different assumptions regarding how people would respond to changed rates. Thus, estimates are inconsistent because there is no Magic 8 Ball telling policymakers how the public will react to a proposed change and different agencies make different assumptions. This is a simple way of saying that because of the importance of the human factor, there is some amount of subjectivity in their analysis. Nonetheless, the validity of these estimates is critical to the budget process.

That different organizations produce different estimates causes confusion, even though the estimates explicitly define what each purports to show and the assumptions on which they are based. Professor Michael Graetz complains that policymakers frequently do not understand the differences between the various estimates or what information each one lacks.[45] The differences are fundamental, going to different economic premises including different predicted reactions and start from different baselines. For example, the baseline may or may not assume that expiring tax provisions will be extended, and definitions and measurements of income may vary, all of which affect the distributional results. Similarly, tables may include people who are not tax return filers or else be limited to

---

[44]   JOINT CTTE TAX'N, JCX–5–90, ESTIMATE OF ADMINISTRATION PROPOSAL FOR A REDUCTION IN TAXES ON CAPITAL GAINS OF INDIVIDUALS (1990); CONG. BUDGET OFFICE, THE DISTRIBUTION OF BENEFITS FROM A REDUCTION IN THE TAX RATE ON CAPITAL GAINS (1989).

[45]   Michael J. Graetz, *Paint-by-Numbers Tax Lawmaking*, 95 COLUM. L. REV. 609 (1995).

taxpayers. With all of the differences, it is no wonder agencies rarely reach the same conclusion.

The House of Representatives recently changed its requirements for formulating estimates. Since 2015, House rules require that the CBO use dynamic scoring on legislation with a sufficiently large projected impact and budget resolutions have similarly required dynamic scoring.[46] Dynamic scoring is an economic forecasting model. This model evaluates the impact a proposal would have on the aggregate economy, including secondary effects. These newly considered secondary effects include increases or decreases to labor supply or investment. As a result, dynamic scoring is hoped to present a more complete estimation of a bill's effects.

A Republican Congress adopted dynamic scoring, but as a rule it is only as permanent as its supporters' control of Congress. Dynamic scoring is expected to make the passage of tax cuts easier by reducing their revenue impact. If people respond to a tax cut by working harder and earning more, their increased earnings would be subject to tax that, with dynamic scoring, offsets the initial cost of the tax cut. Critiques of dynamic scoring include that such projections are uncertain and are prone to political manipulation. The risk of inaccuracies may be greater the more nuanced the projections of how taxpayers will respond.

Additional complexities arise with projections because of the mismatch of time frames for budgeting and appropriations. Agencies generally conform their estimates to the time period that Congress requires for its budgeting process. Therefore, most estimates examine the cost of spending programs and the revenue raised from tax provisions over a ten-year period. On the other hand, appropriations are made on an annual basis even if the budget implications are longer. Therefore, although the federal government's budget must balance over a ten-year period, an agency must operate year-to-year without assurance of the next year's funding. This may make planning difficult for agencies and programs and may reduce the soundness of projections.

Distortion also plays out in the accounting of the Social Security system, the largest entitlement program in the U.S.[47] Unlike the federal budget as a whole, Social Security is accounted for on a cash-flow basis. Therefore, contributions are offset annually with disbursements to beneficiaries. Although analyses are made of the long-term viability of Social Security, the annual budget examines a fixed 365-day period. Even for this limited period, different people

---

[46]   Res. 5, 108th Cong. (2003); S Con. Res. 11, 114th Cong. (2015).

[47]   For more on the Social Security program, see Chapter 10.02.

can accurately say the Social Security system has a surplus and a deficit; it depends upon whether the speaker includes funds from the Social Security Trust Funds.[48] The use of these terms—budget, surpluses, and deficits—is highly nuanced in this area of law. Policymakers and the public may not always grasp how the nuance is being used.

As with questions of Social Security's long-term viability, it might be useful to look more generally at revenue and spending for longer time horizons than the current ten-year budget window. For example, generational accounting focuses on the impact of today's taxing and spending choices on those who are currently children.[49] Generational accounting examines whether policymakers are making commitments that will be funded with future tax dollars, thereby hiding the cost of the promises being made.

The study of the fiscal gap has even longer horizons than generational accounting. Introduced by economists Laurence Kotlikoff and Alan Auerbach, the fiscal gap is the difference between the present value of projected governmental obligations (such as future Medicare and Social Security payments and interest on government debt) and the present value of future tax and government income:

$$\text{present value of all future obligations} - \text{present value of all future revenue} = \text{fiscal gap}$$

This concept is similar to generational accounting in that it lengthens the budget period, but the fiscal gap also broadens the data that is considered. Because of unfunded future obligations, the fiscal gap creates a much larger burden than existing national debt. The fiscal gap was $222 trillion in 2012 and is compounding rapidly.[50]

The difficulty with these academic estimates, as with government estimates, is their inability to predict the future. With all estimates it is necessary to predict how people will respond or to assume that there will be no response. Correct analysis would also need to predict wars, famines, and financial bubbles bursting. Estimates also tend to focus on isolated projects or parts of the government as opposed to focusing on the government and national

---

[48]   Social Security Administration, *Trust Funds Operations*, https://www.ssa.gov/history/tftable.html (last visited May 1, 2018).

[49]   For one of the earliest works on generational accounting, see Alan Auerbach et al., *Generational Accounting: A Meaningful Way to Evaluate Fiscal Policy*, 8 J. ECON. PERSPECTIVES 73 (1994).

[50]   Laurence Kotlikoff & Scott Burns, *Blink! U.S. Debt Just Grew by $11 Trillion*, BLOOMBERGBUSINESS, Aug. 8, 2012.

welfare as a whole. As such, the information on which Congress bases its tax policy choices remains imperfect.

(b) Lobbyists and Think Tanks

Lobbyists and think tanks are private actors that supply members of Congress information in the hopes of shaping the law. Lobbyists do so to advantage their clients. Think tanks do so for the greater good, or at least their interpretation of the greater good. Policymakers generally like these sources of information because they do not have to pay cash for it. Nevertheless, policymakers do pay with their attention, a limited resource that these groups covet.

As with all statutory laws, there is a risk of lobbyists exercising undue influence shaping the law. In the tax context, lobbyists can attempt to influence the decisions of policymakers both in Congress and in the Treasury Department. Individuals or businesses can lobby these government officials directly. However, professional lobbyists may prove more effective.

Lobbyists can seek influence in many ways.[51] Many lobbyists bundle money from different clients to give as contributions to political campaigns so that the larger amount of money has greater influence.[52] Additionally, lobbyists provide free research and services to policymakers, likely personalized and responsive to their concerns. These services are not out of the goodness of lobbyists' hearts but are intended to facilitate a relationship in which a lobbyist receives benefits. The benefits may be specific tax legislation or access when their clients have a problem or want to voice an opinion.

Not everyone can become an effective lobbyist. It requires certain skills as well as strong contacts in Washington D.C. In fact, many lobbyists are former members of Congress. Because of their potential influence, lobbyists are required to register and comply with regulations so that the public can know who is lobbying and how much money is being spent.[53] However, there are ambiguities within the registration requirements, and staying within those areas many people do not register despite engaging in lobbying-like behavior.

The power of lobbyists raises concerns regarding fairness. People who use lobbyists may have greater influence compared to those not able to hire a lobbyist to represent their interests. Criticism of any unfairness may be particularly troubling in taxation because

---

[51]   For more on lobbying, see TIMOTHY LAPIRA, REVOLVING DOOR LOBBYING (2017); Richard Hasen, *Lobbying, Rent Seeking, and the Constitution*, 64 STAN. L. REV. 191 (2012); Lloyd Hitoshi Mayer, *What is This "Lobbying" That We Are So Worried About?*, 26 YALE L. & POLY REV. 485 (2008).

[52]   For more on rent-seeking by politicians, see Chapter 6.02(c).

[53]   2 U.S.C. § 1601 et seq.

the objective is often to reduce a small group's tax burden even if doing so requires raising taxes on everyone else. If lobbying for tax policy is effective, policymakers may care less about the most fair and efficient tax or even raising revenue than receiving the largest contributions from lobbyists.

On the other hand, there are lobbyists on both sides of many issues, even if greater amounts of money tend to be spent on one side than the other of different issues.[54] At times lobbyists defend politically unpopular positions and ensure that issues are properly vetted. And while the use of lobbyists may make it more likely legislation will be considered, it does not excuse policymakers from making final choices. As constitutionally protected free speech, there is nothing to prevent the continuation of lobbying.

Members of congressional tax committees are well known for their receipt of lobbyists' dollars.[55] The Sunlight Foundation, a self-described nonpartisan group seeking open government, drew a complicated web that connects industry sectors with specific tax bills on which the industry lobbied.[56] In total lobbying, there was $733 million in reported lobbying spending in 2011–2012 with respect to over 1,454 total legislative bills. The Sunlight Foundation found that 16% of lobbying organizations and almost 50% of registered lobbyists lobbied on at least one tax issue. Its study also showed that lobbying reduced taxes or at least was correlated to that reduction. The ten Fortune 100 companies that lobbied on at least 25 bills paid an average tax rate of less than 18%. The remaining companies paid an average tax rate of 26%. That lobbying and lower taxes was correlated does not prove causation.

Similar to lobbyists, although with different motives, think tanks and research centers seek to influence tax legislation. Numerous organizations could fit into this category. Some organizations are specialized around targeted issues, such as the Earth Institute or the Belfer Center for Science and International Affairs, and some cover broad agendas, such as the Rand Corporation or the American Enterprise Institute. These organizations often make proposals and are not simply educational.

For example, the Tax Policy Center is a joint venture of the Urban Institute and the Brookings Institution. Aiming to provide independent analyses of tax proposals and longer-term tax issues,

---

[54]   OPENSECRETS.ORG, TOP SPENDERS, https://www.opensecrets.org/lobby/top.php?indexType=s (last visited May 1, 2018).

[55]   ALAN MURRAY & JEFFREY BIRNBAUM, SHOWDOWN AT GUCCI GULCH (1988).

[56]   Lee Drutman & Alexander Furnas, *Untangling the Webs of Tax Lobbying*, Apr. 15, 2013, https://sunlightfoundation.com/blog/2013/04/15/tax-lobbying/ (last visited May 1, 2018).

the Center has numerous experts with government and academic ties. They model revenue and distribution estimates in much the same ways as government sources but may be quicker in doing so. Because they use their own modeling based on their own assumptions, they may come to different conclusions. For example, the organization's website lists a long list of research and commentary that focuses on issues such as "Taxes and Income Inequality" and "How Would Repeal of the State and Local Tax Deduction Affect Taxpayers Who Pay the AMT?"[57]

Although most think tanks purport to be nonpartisan, they often fall in recognizable ways on the political spectrum. For example, although the Tax Foundation purports to be nonpartisan, it can be identified as pro-business or conservative in orientation. Similarly, the Center on Budget and Policy Priorities purports to be nonpartisan but tends to be left leaning. Not all affiliations are hidden. For example, the Heritage Foundation embraces its conservative role. Finally other organizations, such as the National Bureau of Economic Research (NBER), are more successful about avoiding the partisan taint. NBER is likely successful in doing so because it is a diverse group of researchers joining on particular projects.

Although many tax policy think tanks focus on economic theory, legal analyses also play a part. For example, lawyers created the Shelf Project to devise enactment-ready revenue-raising proposals for Congress. The stated goal is to prevent Congress from enacting shortsighted or ill-thought-out proposals simply to create a balanced budget.[58] Additionally, lawyers and law professors submit research, comments, and feedback in their individual capacities in response to individual or general requests from the Treasury Department and Congress. Their objective may at times be partisan but generally have less potential for personal gain than lobbyists or think tanks.

§ 1.03   Isolating Taxes from Spending

Tax is one part of the federal budget. Consequently, for those within Congress and the executive branch, tax is rarely considered in isolation but as part of a system. Therefore, tax policy goals may not truly be the tax system's equity nor efficiency but specific revenue effects over a budget period because of the link between taxing and spending. Even if the public wants tax fairness, Congress has to act

---

[57]   Frank Sammartino, *Taxes and Income Inequality*, and *How Would Repeal of the State and Local Tax Deduction Affect Taxpayers Who Pay the AMT?*, TAX POLICY CENTER (Jun. 15, 2017).

[58]   Calvin H. Johnson, *The Shelf Project: Revenue-Raising Projects that Defend the Tax Base*, TAX NOTES 1076 (Dec. 10, 2007).

within the constraints of the budget deficit. In other words, Congress is limited by the effects of existing and proposed spending for the next ten years in its decisions on specific tax legislation. This link shapes the tax system.

(a) It's All Political

The link between taxing and spending is not a constitutional requirement but the result of political exigency. Because of the political reality that governments want to spend money more than they want to raise it, discussing tax law and tax policies in isolation may not be productive. Should Congress create an optimal tax system in isolation and whatever amount of revenue the system raises determine the amount to be spent? Or should Congress make the tax system respond to higher or lower revenue demands? Fundamentally, must the discussion of taxation be tied to a discussion of spending the revenue that is, or could be, raised? And is a like or dislike of those expenses the appropriate basis for evaluating the tax system?

Of course, in practice when policymakers question how to raise taxes, they are also questioning how much the government should spend. Professor Jeffrey Kwall once wrote:

> If a need for revenue did not constrain tax reform, efforts to further equity and efficiency logically would lead to the elimination of all taxes. The realistic reform goal, therefore, is to minimize on a system-wide basis the adverse impact on equity and efficiency of a tax system required to generate a given amount of revenue.[59]

Kwall suggests that taxes are inherently bad and without revenue demands taxes would be abolished. The government needs revenue so the tax system should be judged for meeting, or not, that need. However, the link between tax and spending can be used to ratchet tax rates up or down. The argument can be used to demand more revenue from the tax system if the person values the spending or to cut spending if the person dislikes taxes.

In particular, the link between taxing and spending has been used to try to force reductions in government spending. If Congress greatly reduces tax revenue then government expenditures must be comparably reduced or so the argument goes. In this way, taxes are a cap on the amount that can be spent. Note that this argument refers to the size of the tax system and not its composition. The best tax system might differ depending upon the amount of revenue to be

---

[59]   Jeff Kwall, *Uncertain Case Against the Double Taxation of Corporate Income*, 68 N.C. L. REV. 613, 616 (1990).

raised, but requiring that a smaller amount be spent does not determine how it should be raised. Perhaps surprisingly, however, cutting taxes has historically been associated with increased spending rather than the reverse.[60]

Although historically spending preceded taxing analytically, that is not always the case today. As the government spends more revenue, the tax system must raise more revenue if the government is to contain the deficit and national debt.[61] However, the Tax Cuts and Jobs Act of 2017 was an example of tax cuts driving budgetary policy. Matching spending cuts were not made and ultimately the debt ceiling was suspended. Before the suspension, the country had a two-day government shut down and an overnight funding gap. If we, as a nation, conclude that a perfect tax system can generate only so much in revenue, should perfection be sacrificed to meet the demands of government spending?

It is also possible to connect taxing and spending as part of a closed system of fiscal policy. Fiscal policy is the use of taxes and government spending to manage the economy. Ever since World War II, the federal government has assumed responsibility for regulating the economy through its use of fiscal policy.[62] Thus the government expects to manage unemployment, inflation, and economic slowdowns with its taxing and spending powers. The concept of fiscal policy is consistent with Keynesian economics in that aggregate demand for goods and services, funded in part by government spending, can improve the economy in times of distress. However, in recent years economists have become less certain that they are able to manage the economy with government's limited tools.[63] Regardless of fiscal policy's actual power, it is impossible to engage in an active fiscal policy and be committed to a balanced budget; a government cannot use fiscal policy and keep its budgets balanced when there is insufficient revenue.

Practically, the modern budget process links taxing and spending in a way that cannot be severed without changing budgeting. The result is significant pressure for tax-raising provisions that are politically palatable. Because reconciliation often requires revenue neutrality, revenue-losing proposals must be coupled with revenue-increasing proposals. This can also necessitate

---

[60]   Christina Romer & David Romer, *Do Tax Cuts Starve the Beast?*, BROOKINGS PAPERS ON ECONOMIC ACTIVITY 139 (2009).

[61]   For more on the deficit and debt, see Chapter 18.02(a).

[62]   *See* Employment Act of 1946, codified at 15 U.S.C. § 1201.

[63]   *See* Paul Krugman, *How Did Economists Get it So Wrong?*, N.Y. TIMES MAG., Sep. 2, 2009; Peter Ferrara, *Progressive Keynesian Myths Debunked*, FORBES, Apr. 14, 2013.

political tradeoffs and the consideration of subpar choices to fund a compromise.

And legislators must protect their ideas for revenue rather than share them for the greater good. Representative Frank Guarini (D-NJ), while on the Committee on Ways and Means, learned this lesson the hard way. With the assistance of the JCT, Guarini created an attractive offset to pair with a revenue-losing proposal he wanted. Guarini's first revenue-losing proposal was not adopted, and yet he described the revenue-raising offset he had created as its pair. A Representative then stole the offset to pair with his own revenue-losing proposal. Since that time, having one's revenue offset used by another Member is known as "being Guarini-ed."[64]

(b) Impact on Code's Complexity

One consequence of combining taxing and spending has been the gradual spreading of spending into the tax system. Today the Internal Revenue Code is used to accomplish many non-revenue objectives. Pamela F. Olson, former Assistant Secretary for Tax Policy, lamented that the Code now incorporates "policies aimed at the environment, conservation, green energy, manufacturing, innovation, education, saving, retirement, health care, child care, welfare, corporate governance, export promotion, charitable giving, governance of tax exempt organizations, and economic development to name a few."[65] This expansion of policies beyond revenue-raising increases the Code's complexity, and this spending is largely uncapped, unverified, and unverifiable.[66]

Moving non-revenue policies into the tax code also risks other costs. The expansion of the Code potentially opens tax committees to similar interest group pressures currently faced by the committees dealing with the relevant substantive law. These pressures may lead to the capture of the tax committees by those seeking tax advantages.[67] Moreover, the IRS has no particular expertise determining the eligibility for, or distributing the benefits of, such diverse projects. Thus, there is no reason to assume that these projects would be better run in a tax system possibly ill equipped to manage them.

Not everyone accepts that these costs should be dispositive. Some argue that the tax system should be used to further non-revenue objectives because of the Code's structural benefits. For

---

[64]   BERMAN & HANEMAN, *supra* note 22, at 125.

[65]   Pamela F. Olson, *And then Cnut Told Reagan . . . Lessons from the Tax Reform Act of 1986*, 38 O.N.U. L. REV. 1, 12–13 (2010).

[66]   For more on tax preferences, see Chapter 17.01.

[67]   For more on regulatory capture, see Chapter 6.03(b).

example, funneling benefits through the Code reduces any stigma associated with receiving benefits, and operating the programs in this way may be administratively easier than through independent agencies. Professor Tony Infanti argues that we should accept that tax is part of a larger sociolegal structure and not an isolated construct.[68] As a result, policymakers should accept that the tax system might be the best means of accomplishing objectives and should focus their attention on how to prevent abuse of this political tool.

The political choice to use the tax system to accomplish non-revenue objectives is influenced by tax's unusual legislative process. Congress's procedures for enacting tax legislation as a part of the budget make it easier to enact social policies through the Code rather than as direct spending.[69] Congress is able to extend economic benefits to select taxpayers without the oversight required of a direct appropriation. For example, Amtrak was given $2.323 billion in tax refunds at a time when direct appropriation was unlikely.[70] Thus, it may be simpler to enact benefits and to fund programs through the tax system than the traditional appropriation process.

Upset that the tax system may be losing its focus on raising revenue, tax purists would prefer to create the tax system isolated from considerations of how the revenue is spent. Instead of focusing on the budget, purists ask: What is the most equitable form of taxation? How simple should a tax be? How can the tax be made more administrable? This approach focuses on how to raise revenue separated from political debates over how much money is to be raised or how the money is to be spent. This perspective allows its proponents to concentrate on creating the most equitable, efficient, and simple tax system.

One reason to desire tax purity is the recognition that the budgeting process may limit the creation of good tax policy. When tax legislation is enacted as part of a budget package, the Ways and Means and Finance Committees are required to raise a certain amount of revenue unless a super-majority approves a departure from that rule. Therefore, the Committees' ability to use their expertise to create the best tax package is diminished. Additionally, consideration in conjunction with spending makes it harder to undertake fundamental reform of the tax system because the parts of the budget are so intertwined.

---

[68]   Anthony Infanti, *Tax Reform Discourse*, 32 VA. TAX REV. 205, 250–51 (2012).

[69]   *See* Susannah Camic Tahk, *Everything is Tax*, 50 HARV. J. ON LEGIS. 67, 82 (2013).

[70]   Christopher H. Hanna, *The Magic in the Tax Legislative Process*, 59 SMU L. REV. 649, 666 (2006).

The argument for separating taxing and spending is supported by the federal government's ability to borrow to fund its spending. To the extent that the government can borrow to finance expenditures, taxation does not need to be dictated by expenditures. If money is available from another source, one could think of the government raising revenue (from taxes and loans) to buy ingredients, making a pie, and then distributing the slices as hunger dictates. This view is different from the alternative view of tax policy as Congress promising slices of pie and then desperately raising the money to finance the promised slices. The former permits the separate evaluation of tax policy whereas the latter sees tax as merely reacting to revenue demands.

Regardless of whether taxing and spending policies should be linked, tax policy faces conflicting imperatives caused by this implicit linkage. First, there is the goal of creating a perfect tax system as judged by tax norms. We want a fair, efficient, and simple tax system.[71] Second, there is the reality of creating the best tax system that meets the demands of spending. If the perfect tax does not raise sufficient revenue, it has no chance of being enacted. Finally, there is the need to understand that tax is part of the overall economic system. The unintended consequences of tax policies may ripple through the larger system in ways that no one can predict or even fully understand.

---

[71]   For more on tax values, see Chapter 4.

Chapter 2

HOW TAX LAW IS ENFORCED

Table of Sections

In an ideal tax system, the government might assess tax liabilities based on what each person could afford to pay calculated according to some metric the American people all accept. This type of system might allow consideration of personal factors that are not recognized in our modern tax system. As part of a government of laws, the federal government instead creates a generally applicable tax system. In this system, the assessment of tax, which is the legal creation of a tax liability, ignores many personal factors that might affect a taxpayer's ability to pay taxes. On the other hand, the collection of taxes contains several opportunities for consideration of an individual's situation. This raises questions whether the imposition of tax should allow more individualized consideration and whether tax collection should be more automatic.

To enforce the tax law, the federal government's three branches interact repeatedly. After Congress creates a tax bill, the president signs the bill making it a statute, and the executive branch's Treasury Department must operationalize and enforce the law. Lawyers from the Treasury Department and the Department of Justice argue tax cases before courts often using legislative history crafted by the legislative branch. The judiciary interprets the statute and oversees the Treasury Department's enforcement. The most commonly used court for tax cases is not an Article III court (governing the federal judiciary) but the Tax Court, an Article I court (giving Congress the power to create inferior courts). Congress potentially responds to courts' interpretation and the Treasury Department's enforcement with new legislation.

§ 2.01   Creation of Tax Guidance

Although the administration and enforcement of laws is generally an executive branch function, a strict separation of the federal branches does not occur in practice, especially in the creation of tax guidance. The executive understands that the judiciary will interpret its conclusions and may overturn its decisions and that the legislature reviews its activities and may enact new laws in response. This creates a judicial and political check on how the tax system is administered.

The Freedom of Information Act (FOIA) ensures that much of the work behind the scenes in the executive agencies that operationalize the tax system is made public, although as a check on the exercise of power it may be slow.[1] FOIA requires that the Treasury Department disclose most of its internal documents, and this information can inform taxpayers as to the agency's position on various tax matters. Although it is the agency that creates this guidance, it is created with an eye to the other federal branches of government and the public.

(a) Role of the Treasury Department

On a day-to-day basis, the Treasury Department is tasked with administering the federal tax system as laid out in statute. To do so, the Department creates a tremendous amount of guidance for its own employees and for the public, explaining and operationalizing statutory language. The Treasury Department is an executive department headed by a presidential appointee. The president nominates the Secretary of the Treasury Department, currently Steven Mnuchin, and the Senate consents (or not) to the appointment. The Secretary's job is more than overseeing the tax system. The Secretary is the principal economic advisor to the president and responsible for many of the government's economic decisions. For example, the Secretary is to determine how much government debt to issue and buy back, how much money to print, and how to run the Social Security and Medicare trust funds.

The Treasury Department comprises bureaus and offices: bureaus are assigned specific tasks and offices are responsible for specific policy areas. The Treasury Department designates to the Office of Tax Policy (OTP), headed by the Assistant Secretary of Tax Policy, currently David Kautter, the job of crafting the executive's tax policy; and the Assistant Secretary reports directly to the Secretary. Consequently, it is the Assistant Secretary of Tax Policy and the OTP that creates the president's tax plan that is submitted to Congress in the process of developing tax legislation.

It is also the Treasury Department's job to create regulations implementing the Internal Revenue Code, having been given the authority to "prescribe all needful rules and regulations for the

---

[1]   Congress extended FOIA to tax in 1996. 5 U.S.C. § 552; 26 C.F.R. § 601.702.

enforcement" of the Code.[2] Despite the Legislative Counsel's efforts in crafting statutory language, regulations are necessary to interpret its often-complicated language. Moreover, try as Congress might, statutes are never complete. Ambiguities in the application of tax statutes arise because the application of the law depends upon the facts and circumstances of millions of transactions. Despite clear need for guidance, the Trump administration's position is to reduce the production of tax regulations.[3] This can have a signficant impact on taxpayers. In at least one case the Tax Court has sided with taxpayers for "mistakes of law in a complicated subject area that lacks clear guidance."[4]

The Secretary delegates the task of creating draft regulations to the Assistant Secretary of Tax Policy. Because of limited resources, the Department uses a Priority Guidance Plan created with the public's input to decide what guidance has precedence. This plan permits the quantification of the Department's successes and failures in creating guidance, but doing so risks causing the Department to frame its agenda around what is more likely to be completed rather than what would be most useful to IRS employees and the public.

The Treasury Department is required to comply with the Administrative Procedure Act (APA) when creating guidance unless Congress specifically carves out a particular item from the APA.[5] Created in 1946 as a generally applicable system, the APA was Congress's response to the growth of federal agencies' power over the public through the promulgation of agency rules. The APA "afford[s] parties affected by administrative powers a means of knowing what their rights are and how they may be protected."[6] Unless specifically carved out, all agencies that create guidance are required to follow a procedure laid out in the APA popularly referred to as notice and comment.

Notice and comment generally requires that agencies publicly post proposed language to provide notice of the proposal and wait for a public comment period prior to rules' finalization. This means that the public must be given notice, generally in the *Federal Register*, of proposed regulatory language and be given a reasonable comment period, often thirty to sixty days, to provide written comments to the agency. Because of judicial review of this procedure, agencies are

---

[2]   I.R.C. § 7805(a).

[3]   Exec. Order 13,789.

[4]   Simonsen v. Comm'r, 150 T.C. No. 8 (2018).

[5]   Administrative and Procedure Act, Pub. L. No. 70–404, 60 Stat. 237 (1946).

[6]   S. Rep. No. 752, 79th Cong., 1st Sess. 7 (1945); H.R. Rep. No. 1980, 79th Cong., 2d Sess. 16 (1946).

required to include a statement with the final regulations that responds to all but nonfrivolous comments that an agency receives.

Notice and comment is a time-consuming and costly process that, according to some administrative law experts, leads to delay in creating guidance.[7] As a result, many agencies attempt to issue guidance that does not go through notice and comment. The APA recognizes this as sometimes being in the public's best interest and has a number of exceptions, including for interpretive guidance or public policy statements that do not create law but merely explain how the agency interprets the law. There is also an exception for good cause, if notice and comment is "impracticable, unnecessary, or contrary to the public interest." These exceptions are generally interpreted narrowly.

The Treasury Department uses approximately 3.5% of its enforcement budget to create tax regulations, its most authoritative form of tax guidance.[8] The IRS's *Internal Revenue Manual* describes the method for drafting proposed regulatory language.[9] The IRS holds the pen in drafting regulations but receives guidance from the OTP because the OTP makes policy decisions and provides the Secretary its analysis. Before being proposed to the public, draft language is submitted to various constituents within the Treasury Department in order to have widespread internal acceptance of its content. Only when the language reaches the highest level of internal review is input received from outside the Department. If the Assistant Secretary for Tax Policy signs off on the proposed language, it becomes a proposed regulation to be published. This first internal step takes from months to years.

To speed up the process of issuing tax guidance, the Treasury Department often claims reliance on an exception to notice and comment in order to issue binding temporary regulations while simultaneously issuing proposed regulations that begin the notice and comment process. Temporary regulations are legally binding but can only be effective for three years.[10] Therefore, the Treasury Department creates guidance the public and IRS personnel can rely on as it goes through the potentially slow process of notice and comment.

---

[7]   Stephen M. Johnson, *Good Guidance, Good Grief!*, 72 MO. L. REV. 695, 695 (2007); Mark Seidenfeld, *Playing Games with the Timing of Judicial Review*, 58 OHIO ST. L.J. 85 (1997); Richard Pierce, Jr., *Seven Ways to Deossify Agency Rulemaking*, 47 ADMIN L. REV. 59, 82–86 (1995); Jerry Mashaw, *Improving the Environment of Agency Rulemaking*, 57 LAW & CONTEMP. PROBS. 185, 188 (1994).

[8]   U.S. DEP'T OF THE TREAS., THE BUDGET IN BRIEF 13–14 (2016).

[9]   The Internal Revenue Manual, or IRM, is available online at https://www.irs.gov/irm/.

[10]   I.R.C. § 7805(e).

When issued as proposed regulations, the public is given a chance to submit written comments. After the public comment period has lapsed and assuming no major changes are required in response to comments, the regulations can be finalized. If major changes are required, the notice and comment period must be restarted so that the public has the opportunity to comment on the revisions. This process, even assuming no major changes, can take months or years in addition to that taken before its publication as a proposal.

Once tax regulations are signed, they generally become effective after a 30-day waiting period, although regulations can have an earlier effective date of (1) the date the final regulation is published in the *Federal Register*, (2) the date any notice substantially describing the proposed, temporary, or final regulation is published, or (3) in case of a final regulation, the date the proposed or temporary regulation to which it relates is published.[11] In a few cases, for example regulations issued within 18 months of the enactment of the statute, regulations can be retroactive. Additionally, regulations that relate to statutes enacted before 1996 are sometimes permitted to be retroactive.[12]

Many academics and some judges currently critique the Treasury Department's process for issuing tax regulations on the grounds that it fails to comply with the APA.[13] In 2011 in *Mayo Foundation for Medical Education and Research v. United States*, the Supreme Court declared that tax would not be granted special exemption from administrative law.[14] Thereafter, what compliance with the APA requires has received a lot of attention. With the threat that tax regulations will be invalidated, taxpayers are learning that if they cannot succeed on the merits, they should challenge the procedure.

A difficulty in determining the requisite amount of procedure is the interface of tax guidance with the exemptions built into the APA. The Treasury Department argues that tax regulations can be legislative or interpretive; the former intended to have the force of law and the latter to provide guidance of how the Department

---

[11]   Taxpayer Bill of Rights II, P.L. 104–168, § 1001, 110 Stat. 1452, 1468–69.

[12]   Clendenen Inc. v. Comm'r, 207 F.3d 1071, 1074 (8th Cir. 2000); Esden v. Bank of Boston, 229 F.3d 154, 172 (2d Cir. 2000).

[13]   *See* Altera Corp. v. Comm'r, 145 T.C. No. 3 (2015); Kristin Hickman, *Unpacking the Force of Law*, 66 VAND. L. REV. 565 (2013); Shannon Weeks McCormack, *Tax Abuse According to Whom?*, 15 FLA. TAX REV. 1 (2013). *But see* Stephanie Hunter McMahon, *The Perfect Process Is the Enemy of the Good Tax: Tax's Exceptional Regulatory Process*, 35 VA. TAX REV. 553 (2016); James Puckett, *Structural Tax Exceptionalism*, 49 GA. L. REV. 1067 (2015); Lawrence Zelenak, *Maybe Just a Little Bit Special, After All?*, 63 DUKE L.J. 1897, 1901 (2014).

[14]   Mayo Found. for Med. Educ. & Res. v. U.S., 562 U.S. 44 (2011).

interprets the law. Interpretive guidance is not required to go through notice and comment. Additionally, the Treasury Department may have good cause to forego notice and comment. It remains for the courts or Congress to decide if the Department appropriately relies on these exemptions from notice and comment and whether tax guidance should bind taxpayers.

Failing to satisfy notice and comment procedures might cause the guidance to be invalidated in judicial review. Courts worry that without this enforcement agencies would fail to achieve the value of notice and comment, which is to gain input from many sources to improve the quality of final rules. At times comments should change how the agency views an issue. The process also increases public respect for guidance and makes it more likely that the public will comply with its dictates. The APA is also legally binding law, and failure to follow its dictates opens guidance up to a time-consuming and costly challenge based on the procedure for the rule's issuance.

On the other hand, the APA has exceptions for a reason. Procedure is not the final goal but the means of improving guidance that is produced with public input. By increasing the cost to the Treasury Department of creating guidance, notice and comment might decrease the amount of guidance available to IRS personnel and the public, making it harder for the IRS to do its job well and for the public to pay its taxes. Challenges based on procedural grounds may also threaten long-established guidance that has proven useful both to the government and taxpayers. These negative effects reduce consistency in the application of the law and increase the chances of tax evasion. With a 1% audit rate, binding tax guidance may be necessary to maximize compliance, and the need for revenue in the budget process may demand guidance's speedy production.

A complicating factor for determining appropriate levels of procedure is the potential deference courts will later give to the final guidance. Under *Chevron U.S.A., Inc. v. Natural Resources Defense Council, Inc.*, courts are to defer to agency guidance interpreting ambiguous statutory language.[15] This deference, when applicable, would all but force taxpayers to follow final regulations even if the taxpayer thought the regulations were not the correct interpretation of the law or that the procedures used to create them are questionable. Possibly fearing this result, in several cases courts have refused to find statutory language ambiguous in order to avoid deferring to tax regulations they do not like.[16] Thus, the issue of deference is far from settled, but it does argue for the Treasury

---

[15]   467 U.S. 837 (1984).

[16]   U.S. v. Home Concrete & Supply, LLC, 566 U.S. 478 (2012); King v. Burwell, 576 U.S. ___, 135 S.Ct. 2480 (2015).

Department creating a record of procedural compliance and taking public comments seriously.

A second complicating factor derives from the timing of challenges to the Treasury Department's procedures: They generally cannot be challenged until after a taxpayer has been audited. Congress enacted provisions permitting the Treasury Department defer most challenges to tax guidance and the collection of tax until after a taxpayer is audited, found to owe tax, and completed the appeals process. This deferral is unusual; most other agencies face pre-enforcement challenge whether on substantive or procedural grounds.[17] Additionally, sovereign immunity and standing doctrine discourage or prohibit most pre-enforcement challenges.[18] Although the extent of these limitations remains unclear, they operate to reduce the number and type of attacks the Treasury Department faces and, therefore, isolate the executive agency from judicial review.

Excluding the public from the creation of tax guidance may be particularly troubling when the Department's interpretation or enforcement of a tax provision is politically charged. However, in these circumstances the Treasury Department is likely to forego issuing guidance because of political risks. In the past, when the Department moved to issue politically unpopular regulations, Congress issued a moratorium to prevent the issuance. However, some issues only become politically charged after the guidance is issued. In those instances, the interaction between the branches of the government can become heated.

For example, the interaction over 501(c)(4) status for Tea Parties has been a hot political topic.[19] Several Tea Parties gained headlines for challenging the slow consideration of their section 501(c)(4) tax-exempt status.[20] The issue involved the organizations' level of campaign activities and whether their levels violated requirements for civic associations. The complaints prompted an investigation by

---

[17]   The Tax Anti-Injunction Act and the Declaratory Judgment Act isolate Treasury Department rules from pre-enforcement litigation. I.R.C. § 7421; 28 U.S.C. § 2001(a) (2000). *See* Stephanie Hunter McMahon, *Pre-enforcement Litigation Necessary for Taxing Procedures*, 92 WASH. L. REV. 1317 (2017). *But see* Chamber of Commerce v. IRS, Cause No. 1:15-CV-944-LY (W. Dist. Tx. 2017).

[18]   E. Ky. Welfare Rights Org. v. Simon, 370 F.Supp. 325 (D.D.C. 1973), *rev'd sub nom.* E. Ky. Welfare Rights Org. v. Simon, 506 F.2d 1278 (D.C. Cir. 1974), *vacated,* 426 U.S. 26 (1976); Allen v. Wright, 480 F.Supp. 790 (D.D.C. 1979), *rev'd sub nom.* Wright v. Regan, 656 F.2d 820 (D.C. Cir. 1981), *rev'd sub nom.* Allen v. Wright 468 U.S. 737 (1984).

[19]   For more on 501(c)(4) organizations, see Chapter 14.06.

[20]   Zachary Goldfarb & Karen Tumulty, *IRS Admits Targeting Conservatives for Tax Scrutiny in 2012 Election,* WASH. POST, May 10, 2013; Doug McKelway, *IRS Releases List of Groups Targeted in Scandal—3 Years Later,* FOX NEWS, Jun. 6, 2016.

the FBI (an executive agency) and the House Oversight Committee (a congressional committee). Lawsuits have been initiated from both sides of the isle, some of which have been settled in the Tea Parties' favor.[21]

(b) Role of the IRS

The IRS is the Treasury Department's largest bureau. The IRS is under the direction of a Commissioner, appointed by the president with the consent of the Senate for a five-year non-renewable term. The Commissioner reports to the Secretary of the Treasury Department through the Deputy Secretary of the Treasury. The current Commissioner is John Koskinen; the position of Deputy Secretary is currently vacant. The IRS is tasked with administering the Internal Revenue Code.

In its role as administrator of the tax system, the IRS creates a tremendous amount of guidance to facilitate consistent audits and to aid taxpayers in meeting their taxpaying obligations. This guidance is issued with less formal procedures than regulations, and the IRS receives less feedback in its issuance from either the Treasury Department or the public. Additionally, this guidance is given little deference by most courts. Nevertheless, it offers a snapshot of the IRS's perspective and gives the bureau the opportunity to make its arguments publicly known. These are also public as a result of FOIA.

There are many types of this informal guidance, and the IRS labels guidance to indicate its intended function.[22] Revenue rulings and revenue procedures apply the law to particular factual situations and can be used as precedent by both taxpayers and the IRS. Either explaining substantive law or administrative procedures, these forms of guidance give information to specific groups of targeted taxpayers. Public notices are viewed by the IRS as equivalent to rulings but tend to be issued more quickly in response to emerging public concerns. Private letter rulings are issued to particular taxpayers seeking guidance for proposed transactions, and numerous types of guidance lumped together as chief counsel advice are issued to IRS agents in the process of audits or on particular matters. These latter guidance are public documents but not truly intended for general application and are often given only local internal vetting.

According to Professor Michael Asimow, these informal forms of tax guidance are important tools to meet the public need for

---

[21]   Emily Cochrane, Justice Department Settles with Tea Party Groups After IRS Scrutiny, N.Y. TIMES, Oct. 26, 2017.

[22]   For the IRS's description, see IRS, *Understanding IRS Guidance-A Brief Primer*, at https://www.irs.gov/uac/understanding-irs-guidance-a-brief-primer (last visited May 1, 2018).

information. Nevertheless, their issuance is "quite sensitive to the bureaucratic costs of adopting them."[23] For example, the number of published revenue rulings declined between 1974 and 1984 by 70% because of their cost, the review process creating delays and bottlenecks, and the need to divert guidance personnel to higher urgency tasks.

The IRS is required to provide some amount of tax guidance as part of the Taxpayers' Bill of Rights. Most recently in 2014, the IRS renewed its Taxpayer Bill of Rights explaining ten fundamental taxpayer rights vis-à-vis the agency, partially in response to a 2012 survey that found only 46% of respondents recognized they had any rights before the IRS.[24] Legislation protecting these rights was enacted along with a general restructuring of the IRS in 1998.[25] For example, Congress shifted the burden of proof to the IRS in limited circumstances, expanded attorney-client confidentiality, and barred the IRS from using the term "illegal tax protester" for people who fail to file tax returns because they contest the validity of the Sixteenth Amendment.

To pay for the creation of guidance and to audit for compliance, the IRS depends upon congressional appropriations. The IRS is funded in the same way as other agencies, largely from discretionary spending that is subject to spending caps. Notwithstanding the IRS's importance to the federal government, it is widely accepted as true that "[n]o member of Congress ever got a single vote by telling his constituency that he got more resources for the IRS."[26] From its budget Congress expects the IRS to provide services to the public, audit returns, and collect revenue. At the same time, Congress adds new, non-revenue initiatives to the IRS's burdens, such as monitoring taxpayer identity theft, reviewing foreign holdings through the Foreign Account Tax Compliance Act (FATCA), and implementing the credits and mandate portion of the Patient Care and Affordable Care Act.

The IRS is concerned about its budget because the agency operates under an almost constant threat of budget cuts. These cuts occur despite estimates that for every $1 spent on the IRS, the government brings in $6 of taxes that are owed.[27] The IRS's budget has had a 12% reduction over the last ten years when adjusted for

---

[23]   Michael Asimow, *Nonlegislative Rulemaking and Regulatory Reform*, 1985 DUKE L.J. 381, 406.

[24]   NAT'L TAXPAYER ADVOC., ANNUAL REPORT TO CONGRESS 2013, at 14–15 (2013).

[25]   Taxpayer Bill of Rights III, Pub. L. 105–206, 112 Stat. 685 (Jul. 22, 1998).

[26]   George Guttman, *The IRS's Fiscal 2004 Budget: More or Less*, 98 TAX NOTES 486, 488 (2003) (quoting Larry Levitan).

[27]   U.S. DEP'T OF TREAS., THE BUDGET OF THE UNITED STATES GOVERNMENT, FY 2017, at 1051 (2016).

inflation (although the nominal budget has increased modestly).[28] The following chart is in nominal dollars and does not reflect inflation; with inflation the decrease in funding would be starker.

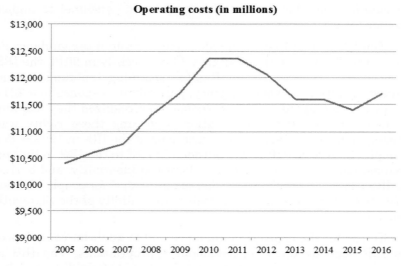

Operating costs (in millions)

IRS, Data Book 2016, table 29 (2017).

Because of the IRS's decreased funding, there have been substantial staff reductions in auditing and collection (11.9% and 21.4%, respectively). Notwithstanding the cuts, the number of tax returns has increased (individual returns are up 11% and business returns up 23%).

The IRS could be funded other than through direct appropriations. For example, Congress could permit the IRS to retain a percentage of its collections. The increased revenue could be targeted to creating guidance or further enforcement activities. However, this funding mechanism would encourage the IRS to aggressively seek collections, possibly too aggressively in the collection process.

§ 2.02   Individual Enforcement

Once the Treasury Department and the IRS decide upon an interpretation of the Internal Revenue Code, taxpayers must apply that law to their individual circumstances. Guidance is a first step in assisting taxpayers comply with the law, but even without guidance

---

[28]   Jeremy Temkin, *Internal Revenue Service Budget Cuts Spell Trouble*, 253 NEW YORK L.J. (Jan. 22, 2015) (in nominal terms, the 2005 budget was $10.2 billion and 2015 budget was $10.9 billion).

taxpayers are required to pay their taxes. They must file annual income tax returns in which they calculate their own taxes.[29] However, to ensure that taxpayers meet that requirement, Congress has empowered the IRS with the authority to audit and, if necessary, collect the taxes that taxpayers owe.

(a) Assessment

Before taxes can be collected, they must be assessed. It is the assessment that creates the legal obligation to pay a certain amount to the government. Although taxpayers file individual returns stating the amount they owe, it is the IRS who formally records the tax liability to create the assessment. Most taxpayers who file their tax returns and never hear from the government about those returns, other than possibly receiving a refund, are unaware of this step. Nevertheless, it is only when the IRS accepts the return or after requesting information that the IRS records the determination of tax, becoming the assessment of taxes owed.

If a taxpayer reports taxes as owed but does not remit payment to the government, the IRS may summarily assess the tax liability. If the IRS believes that additional taxes are owed but not reported by the taxpayer, the IRS makes such a determination and then audits the taxpayer in order to assess a tax deficiency. For most taxpayers who hear from the IRS about a determination involving their tax returns, a government computer is asking them to prove a deduction or income to complete the assessment process.

The window of time during which the IRS can challenge a taxpayer's return is not unlimited. The statute of limitations for assessment is generally three years from when the return is filed.[30] The statute of limitations is extended to six years for substantial understatements of income, meaning by more than 25%, and indefinitely if a return is filed fraudulently or no return is filed. This period tolls, meaning the time limit is paused, if the taxpayer appeals to the Tax Court for judicial review, and during that tolling the assessment of the tax is postponed until the Tax Court issues its final decision.

In the determination of a tax liability, the IRS has extraordinary powers as a backstop to what is generally viewed as a voluntary tax system. These powers make it only partially accurate to say that taxpayers' annual tax returns calculate their taxes or that paying

---

[29]   I.R.C. § 6012.
[30]   I.R.C. § 6501.

taxes is voluntary.[31] The IRS has the authority to contest the tax return and to demand taxes that are neither reported nor paid.

The rules of audit are laid out for IRS personnel in the *Internal Revenue Manual*, but the *Manual*'s instructions and guidelines do not give taxpayers substantive rights.[32] When IRS employees violate the *Manual*, it does not have legal effect. For example, in one case, although the *Manual* told IRS employees not to record conversations, an employee did so and the tape was admissible in a criminal trial against the taxpayer.[33] Despite this significant limitation on the information the *Manual* contains, it provides taxpayers an idea of how an audit will progress.

There are three ways that the IRS selects returns for audit. First, some returns are randomly selected based on a statistical formula that is not publicly available. This formula is the basis for the claim that certain deductions or reported items are red flags that increase a taxpayer's chance of being audited.[34] Second, returns are audited when there is a mismatch between filed documents. For example, when W-2s (regarding wages) or Form 1099s (reporting royalties, rents, prizes, etc.) do not match what is reported on a tax return, the IRS requests additional information, and that request is technically an audit. Finally, returns may be selected for audit if they involve transactions or issues with other taxpayers who are in audit. For example, one business partner may trigger the audit of another partner if something is discovered on the first's return.

Despite the three ways to be selected, few returns are selected for audit. In 2016, although almost 1.2 million returns were audited, this was only 0.6% of tax returns.[35] However, this rate is misleading for different economic groups. Those claiming the earned income tax credit experience an audit rate of 1.7%, as compared to 0.6% of similarly economically situated taxpayers who do not. The result is that almost 40% of audits are on those in the lowest income bracket. Similarly, those with more than $10 million of income have almost a 35% chance of being audited. Except at the ends of the income spectrum, few Americans are likely to ever face an audit.

What constitutes an audit for this statistic does not need to be an hours long questioning in the bowels of a cinderblock IRS building. Audits can either be in person or via correspondence. The vast

---

[31]   I.R.C. § 6001; Treas. Reg. § 601.103(a).

[32]   IRS, INTERNAL REVENUE MANUAL, Part IV, available at https://www.irs.gov/irm/part4 (last visited May 1, 2018).

[33]   United States v. Caceres, 440 U.S. 741 (1979).

[34]   *See e.g.*, Kay Bell, *How to Avoid an Audit by the IRS: These Red Flags May Invite an IRS Examination*, BANKRATE.COM (2017).

[35]   IRS, *Enforcement: Examinations*, Table 9a, DATA BOOK (2017).

majority is conducted via correspondence and the government's side of the audit is all computer-generated, often the result of forms not matching. In 2016, for tax audits of individuals' returns, over 75% were via correspondence, leaving only 243,722 with a field audit.[36] The different forms of audit yield different amounts per return, with field audits yielding on average over $12,355 more than correspondence audits.

During an audit to determine whether additional taxes are owed, the IRS has greater powers over the taxpayer compared to other creditors, although the IRS is not the only government agency with such broad powers. The IRS can investigate any taxpayer at any time, even when there is no probable cause or reason to think that the taxpayer has not complied with the law. During an audit, the IRS is expected to first ask for information, but the IRS has the statutory authority to compel the production of records and information. In the event of a court challenge, IRS determinations have a presumption of validity, and taxpayers bear the burden of proof except in limited circumstances. Moreover, statutorily created benefits, namely deductions and credits, are defined narrowly; income is defined broadly.

Some powers the IRS enjoys are shared by other agencies. For example, one power, also enjoyed by the Securities and Exchange Commission, is the power to initiate joint criminal and civil investigations. This joint investigation raises questions regarding the proper procurement and admissibility of evidence under different criminal versus civil law standards. The IRS's summons power coupled with the Tax Court's willingness to allow its use after cases have begun is unusual.[37]

Professor Bryan Camp defends these special powers as necessary for the tax system's inquisitorial process to function properly.[38] Because U.S. taxation is an inquisitorial system, an impartial evidence-gatherer/decision-maker is to find the taxes that are truly owed, not those that can be collected or that are reasonable. In an adversarial system, on the other hand, as occurs in other areas of American litigation, the roles of evidence-gather and decision-maker are separated. In that type of system, a negotiated or inaccurate amount is acceptable. The question remains whether an

---

[36]   *Id.*

[37]   David Hyman, *When Rules Collide*, 71 TUL. L. REV. 1389, 1405 (1997); Leo Martinez, *The Summons Power and the Limits of Theory*, 71 TUL. L. REV. 1705 (1997).

[38]   Bryan Camp, *Tax Administration as Inquisitorial Process and the Partial Paradigm Shift in the IRS Restructuring and Reform Act of 1998*, 56 FLA. L. REV. 1, 3 (2004).

inquisitorial tax system is better or whether an adversarial system better protects taxpayers' rights.

The stages after audit involve a lot of paperwork. The paperwork is intended to protect taxpayer rights, but it may confuse taxpayers. Following an audit or if the taxpayer ignores the audit request, the IRS sends the taxpayer a letter, popularly called the 30-day letter, with the proposed amount owed in taxes. The taxpayer can appeal the IRS's proposed deficiency within 30 days to an Appeals Office that is a separate part of the IRS. If the taxpayer does not respond or following an unsuccessful appeal to the Appeals Office, the taxpayers receives a Statutory Notice of Deficiency, or the 90-day letter or stat notice, that starts a 90-day window to petition the Tax Court. Alternatively, the taxpayer can pay the amount the IRS says is due and sue for a refund in the District Court or Court of Claims. If the taxpayer loses or does nothing, the IRS moves to collections.

The amount of detail the IRS puts in these letters differs widely. One taxpayer claimed that a notice of deficiency must provide an APA-style, reasoned explanation that includes findings of fact because the notice functions as a final agency action, but the Fourth Circuit disagreed.[39] Not only does the Code define the content of these notices, the letters come after an audit when issues are fleshed out or the taxpayer has proven uncooperative. It remains to be seen if the Supreme Court or other circuits agree. Faced with IRS budget pressures and a declining audit rate, standing on procedural formality might all but eliminate tax audits.

There are organizations that help taxpayers navigate the rules of tax filing and tax assessment. The Voluntary Income Tax Assistance (VITA) program is a long-standing IRS program that offers free services helping low-income taxpayers prepare their tax returns. Typically housed in community and neighborhood centers, libraries, and schools, VITA's objective is to help taxpayers comply with their initial filing obligation. In order for people to volunteer and receive liability protection, they must register and complete an IRS on-line exam. In addition to VITA, the IRS has established a Tax Counseling for the Elderly program that offers free tax help for all taxpayers, particular those 60 years and older.

Once a taxpayer has received notice from the IRS of a deficiency, low-income taxpayers or those who speak English as a second language may go to a Low-Income Taxpayer Clinic (LITC), of which there are 139 in 2017.[40] LITCs represent qualifying individuals in

---

[39] Qinetiq US Holdings, Inc. v. Comm'r, 845 F.3d 555 (4th Cir. 2017). Qinetiq has petitioned for certiorari.

[40] A list of available clinics is available at: https://www.irs.gov/pub/irs-pdf/p4134.pdf.

disputes with the IRS, such as audits, appeals, or collections. LITCs perform this representation for free or at a nominal cost. Although LITCs are independent of the IRS, many of them receive funding through an IRS program created in 1998. The LITC program provides matching grants of up to $100,000 per year to organizations who meet its qualifications and win some of the total $10 million in federal funds that are available. In 2015, through LITCs, almost 1,800 volunteers represented almost 19,000 taxpayers and gave advice to another 19,000.[41]

Finally, taxpayers may contact the Taxpayer Advocate Service (TAS), an independent organization within the IRS created in 1979.[42] The TAS's job is to advocate for taxpayers to ensure that they are treated fairly and understand their rights. To that end, the organization has the authority to issue Taxpayer Assistance Orders if taxpayers are suffering or about to suffer significant hardships because of the administration of tax laws. These orders direct the IRS to take or refrain from taking specific actions as determined by the TAS, such as to release a levy or to reconsider a determination. Long-standing TAS leader Nina Olson also advocates for the protection of taxpayer rights before Congress and in semi-annual reports.

Assistance preparing tax returns and going through the audit process can help improve outcomes for taxpayers and the government. Taxpayers often need an advocate and to be taught of their rights and the legal process. The receipt of representation makes taxpayers nearly twice as likely to receive a positive outcome compared to unrepresented taxpayers.[43] Because many people are daunted by the tax system, these organizations fulfill a mediating role that increases accuracy, compliance, and taxpayer trust in the system. From the government's perspective, assistance increases timely compliance and improves taxpayer responsiveness.

There are limits on what these programs can do. First, running this type of organization is not cheap and available federal grants are capped, limiting the size and manpower the organizations can achieve. Some organizations defray costs by using volunteers, and those operated through schools can offer school credit instead of paychecks. Additionally, federal funding limits these organizations' activities because of statutory restrictions on activities that can be funded from federal sources. For example, LITCs are limited in their

---

[41]   IRS, *Program Report and 2017 Publication 4134, Low Income Taxpayer Clinic List*, IRS–2017–56.

[42]   IRS, Taxpayer Advocate Service, https://www.irs.gov/advocate.

[43]   NATIONAL TAXPAYER ADVOCATE, ANNUAL REPORT TO CONGRESS 2007 vol. 2 93–116 (2007); Janene R. Finley & Allan Karnes, *An Empirical Study of the Effectiveness of Counsel in United States Tax Court Cases*, 16 J. AM. ACAD. OF BUS. 1 (2010).

ability to engage in the notice and comment process for regulations or to lobby for legislative change.[44] Even if consistent with the organization's underlying mission, advocacy can rise to the level of prohibited lobbying.

Of course, not all taxpayers need low-cost representation because some are in the position to engage in pricey tax planning. For example, the government works closely with some corporations to determine their assessment. The IRS traditionally used about 20% of its examination budget on the Coordinate Industry Case program (CIC), started in the late 1960s. In a CIC examination, the IRS established workrooms in taxpayers' offices to perform continuous audits of targeted taxpayers. The CIC process raised about two-thirds of the IRS's collected revenue.[45] However, as of February 2016, the IRS began moving away from this total business audit to focus more on issues across businesses.[46]

Although many corporate taxpayers like the shift away from continuous auditing, some corporations worry about its effect on the resolution of their tax matters. Traditional corporate audits usually start months or years after a tax return is filed and can take years to complete. Therefore, corporations have years of uncertainty about their actual tax liabilities. That uncertainty must be reflected on financial statements.

To speed up the process of corporate audits and to facilitate the filing of correct returns, the IRS piloted the Compliance Assurance Process (CAP) in 2005 that continues today for 181 taxpayers.[47] In CAP, IRS examiners and participating large corporations work to reach agreement on how to report tax issues before tax returns are filed. If corporations complete the process, they are generally subject to shorter and narrower audits. To the extent CAP works as intended, taxpayers should achieve tax certainty sooner and with less administrative burden.

Because of budgeting concerns, the IRS is not expanding the number of corporations that can use CAP as of 2017.[48] Concerns have also been raised regarding CAP's effectiveness. The Senate Committee on Appropriations and the Treasury Inspector General

---

[44]   For more on the LITC grant application process, see LITC 2018 Grant Application Package and Guidelines, IRS Publication 3319.

[45]   INTERNAL REVENUE MANUAL, § 4.1.21.2.2.1.1; PRACTICAL LAW INST., IRS PRACTICE AND PROCEDURE DESKBOOK § 7.2.2 (4th ed. 2010).

[46]   Timothy McCormally & Lawrence Mack, *"Needs Must": IRS Launches Compliance Campaigns for Large Corporate Examinations*, BNA NEWS (Apr. 3, 2017).

[47]   IRS, COMPLIANCE ASSURANCE PROCESS, https://www.irs.gov/businesses/ corporations/compliance-assurance-process (last visited May 1, 2018).

[48]   *Death of the Compliance Assurance Program?*, NAT'L L. REV. (Apr. 13, 2016).

for Tax Administration recommended that the IRS develop an evaluation plan for CAP because of a worry about its cost efficiency. The hourly revenue rate of audit in the CAP program is only $2,939 compared to the non-CAP $8,448.[49] If CAP works as intended, initial revenue should be greater for participating corporations because they should be taking fewer aggressive tax positions that are overturned on audit. Although the reduced revenue might reflect greater compliance, a concern is that large corporations have captured the process and agreements unreasonably favor their tax reduction.

(b) Litigation

Over twenty-five years ago, Professor William Popkin argued that the courts and Congress were collaborators in developing the meaning of tax statutes, adopting a form of practical reasoning for tax interpretation.[50] This reasoning over statutory language is unusual for many reasons. Tax statutes were generally written after Congress agreed on conceptual descriptions of the new law and, even today, members of Congress may rarely review statutory language. Everything authoritative in tax legislation, from the statute to the legislative history, is written by non-committee staff.[51] However, even beyond the statute itself, tax litigation is unusual because of reversed roles of the parties and the optional use of a specialized tax court.

(i) Structure of Tax Litigation

Tax litigation's structure pits a plaintiff seeking to protect property from claims of the defendant, instead of the more regular plaintiff seeking property from the defendant. This reversal of roles causes some procedural anomalies. For example, despite being the plaintiff and bringing suit in the Tax Court, taxpayers often challenge the court's subject-matter jurisdiction. Thus, the taxpayer argues that the court does not have jurisdiction over the matter even though the taxpayer initiates the litigation. If the taxpayer wins on a substantive inaccuracy or a technicality regarding the IRS's notice to the taxpayer of the tax deficiency, the Tax Court must dismiss the case for lack of jurisdiction to hear the case. Once the case is bounced from the Tax Court, the IRS can mail the taxpayer a new notice, but the three-year statute of limitations for assessment has likely lapsed because it is not tolled by bad notice. Consequently, the dismissal on

---

[49]   TREAS. INSPECTOR GEN. FOR TAX ADMIN., 2013–30–021,THE COMPLIANCE ASSURANCE PROCESS HAS RECEIVED FAVORABLE FEEDBACK, BUT ADDITIONAL ANALYSIS OF ITS COSTS AND BENEFITS IS NEEDED (2013).

[50]   William D. Popkin, *The Collaborative Model of Statutory Interpretation*, 61 S. CAL. L. REV. 541 (1988).

[51]   For more on the legislative process, see Chapter 1.01.

jurisdiction, although without prejudice, often ends any possibility of tax collection.

Tax litigation is also unusual because of the number of possible forums: the Tax Court, the appropriate District Court, the Court of Federal Claims, and, at times, the Bankruptcy Court.[52] Taxpayers choose their forum based on many factors. One factor is the requirement to prepay the taxes due in order to litigate for a refund in the District Court or the Court of Federal Claims. A taxpayer is able to challenge assessments in the Tax Court without prepaying the liability. Tax issues also arise in bankruptcy litigation but only if the taxpayer is in bankruptcy. Second, Tax Court judges have more specialized tax knowledge and can hear cases earlier in the process because Congress granted the Tax Court specific jurisdiction to hear cases earlier in the assessment-collection process. Studies show that more than 90% of tax litigation, with an aggregate tax deficiency of $4.66 billion, occurs in the specialized Tax Court.[53]

(ii) Tax Court

The Tax Court hears most tax litigation but still its status as a court is unsettled. The specialized Tax Court is not a traditional federal court or part of a federal agency.[54] The Tax Court is not subject to the APA or FOIA, both of which apply to agencies, nor the Administrative Office of the United States Courts, the Judicial Conference, or the Rules Enabling Act, which apply to federal courts. The result is that the Tax Court has less transparency and accountability than other courts and must handle all of its own administrative matters, such as budget requests or arrangements to visit cities to hear cases.

Debates over the Tax Court's position within the government have arisen several times. Congress created this court as the Board of Tax Appeals within the Treasury Department in 1924 to provide independent review of IRS determinations. The Tax Court was separated from the Treasury Department in 1969 when it was changed from an administrative court to a full judicial court under Article I of the Constitution. The court's trials are bench trials (not being part of the judicial branch there is no right to a jury) in front of

---

[52] For more on choices between forums, see Thomas Greenaway, *Choice of Forum in Federal Civil Tax Litigation*, 62 TAX LAW. 311 (2009).

[53] Leandra Lederman, *Restructuring the U.S. Tax Court*, 99 MINN. L. REV. 1 (2014).

[54] For debate over the Tax Court's status, see *id.*; Stephanie Hoffer & Christopher Walker, *The Death of Tax Court Exceptionalism*, 99 MINN. L. REV. 221 (2014); Danshera Cords, *Administrative Law and Judicial Review of Tax Collection Decisions*, 52 ST. LOUIS U. L.J. 429 (2008); Henry Dubroff, *United States Tax Court: An Historical Analysis, Parts I–IV*, 40–41 ALB. L. REV. 1, 53, 253 (1975–1977).

one of sixteen judges as of early 2018 (nominations are pending before the Finance Committee, consistent with the statute providing for nineteen judges). As presidential appointees, Tax Court judges are Article I judges who do not enjoy lifetime appointment but are appointed for fifteen-year renewable terms and do not have salary guarantees. This Article I status is generally accepted as constitutional.

The Tax Court's constitutional position in one of the three branches arose in 2014 because of the president's ability to remove Tax Court judges.[55] The right of removal is an issue of the separation of powers between the three branches of the federal government. Article III judges are appointed for life and can only be impeached from office for crimes and misdemeanors. The concern was that the threat of removal of an Article I judge might affect a judge's decision-making capacity. Nevertheless, the D.C. Circuit Court placed the Tax Court in the executive branch and upheld the removal power.

Although most accept the existence of the Tax Court as a good thing, many question the court's lack of procedural transparency. For example, the Tax Court has based judgments on secret reports that could not later be produced and permitted collaboration among judges who were supposed to remain separate.[56] Annoyed that the Tax Court fails to follow its own stated policies, the Supreme Court has demanded that there be "at the very least, full and fair statement in the Tax Court's own Rules."[57] More transparency could be accomplished by requiring the Tax Court comply with either federal courts' procedural rules or agencies' procedural law. However, consigning the Tax Court to either would have collateral consequences, possibly altering the level of deference the court must give to the IRS and the process by which its litigation proceeds.

Within Tax Court trials, the rules and procedure used are modeled after the Federal Rules of Civil Procedure and the Federal Rules of Evidence.[58] Nevertheless, there are oddities in Tax Court procedure: The IRS's formal answer to the petition is generally its only official pleading; parties are required to stipulate evidentiary facts and the application of law to the facts to the fullest extent possible; the parties generally do not file briefs until after trial. Unless contrary to statute, stipulations are treated as conclusive admissions by the parties. The process works imperfectly because omitted facts may later be found relevant or stipulations may be

---

[55] Kuretski v. Comm'r, 755 F.3d 929 (D.C. Cir. 2014).

[56] *Ballard v. Commissioner* and *Estate of Kanter*, 544 U.S. 40 (2005).

[57] 544 U.S. at 46–47.

[58] Rules of Practice and Procedure of the United States Tax Court, 60 T.C. 1057 (1973); Tax Ct. R. 143; I.R.C. § 7463.

ambiguous. On the whole, however, there is relatively less fact-finding for the Tax Court than other courts because of its procedures.

Additionally, the Tax Court has an unusual small tax case procedure if the amount at issue is no more than $50,000.[59] Approximately half of the cases docketed in the Tax Court elect this status. The small tax case permits simplified evidentiary rules, and the procedure may be considered beneficial to taxpayers. However, tax cases using these procedures are before special trial judges, appointed by the Chief Judge of the Tax Court and not the president with the approval of the Senate, and the results are not appealable to a higher court. This exceptional process, and the extent to which it is exceptional, receives little discussion.

Some question Tax Court judges' potential bias in favor of the government.[60] Judges may be sympathetic to the government because many are appointed from government service. However, little empirical evidence supports the court's capture by either the government or taxpayers. Tax Court judges appear more ideological than are judges in other courts in their holdings on tax matter. This may be because the specialized judges are less reliant on the litigants to explain the issues and can more easily apply their own ideology.

(iii) Appellate Review

Tax decisions, including those from the Tax Court except for small tax cases, are subject to appellate review. Appeals are to the applicable federal Circuit Court that has jurisdiction over the taxpayer.[61] Although the Board of Tax Appeals's decisions could initially be collaterally attacked in federal court, today appeals follow generally applicable procedures. Proposals have been advanced for having tax cases be appealed to a specialized appeals court. This would eliminate all general federal court review. For example, a proposal was made in the Senate in 1979 and one by the Federal Courts Study Committee in 1990.[62] A specialized appellate tax court

---

[59]   I.R.C. § 7463.

[60]   For debates over potential Tax Court bias, see Michael J. Bommarito et al., *An Empirical Survey of the Population of U.S. Tax Court Written Decisions*, 30 VA. TAX REV. 523 (2011); Banks Miller & Brett Curry, *Expertise, Experience, and Ideology of Specialized Courts*, 43 LAW & SOC'Y REV. 839 (2009); Leandra Lederman, *Tax Appeal: A Proposal To Make the United States Tax Court More Judicial*, 85 WASH. U. L. REV. 1195, 1216 (2008); Nancy Staudt et al., *The Ideological Component of Judging in the Taxation Context*, 84 WASH. U. L. REV. 1797 (2006); Daniel M. Schneider, *Using the Social Background Model to Explain Who Wins Federal Appellate Tax Decisions*, 25 VA. TAX REV. 201 (2005); Robert Howard, *The Federal District Court Versus the Tax Court*, 26 JUSTICE SYSTEM J. 135 (2005).

[61]   Dobson v. Comm'r, 320 U.S. 489 (1943); Leandra Lederman, *Unappealing Deference to the Tax Court*, 63 DUKE L.J. 1835, 1851–54 (2014).

[62]   Deborah Geier, *The Tax Court, Article III, and the Proposal Advanced by the Federal Courts Study Committee*, 76 CORNELL L. REV. 985 (1991).

would consolidate appellate review of tax cases into one specialized tribunal. Practitioners speaking in the lone Senate hearing on the topic opposed the idea, while most Treasury Department officials supported it.

One objective of specialized appellate review would be to provide greater consistency and earlier decisions on tax matters. Judge Roger Traynor complained of the delay of tax cases winding their way through the IRS and then courts.[63] Since the Supreme Court only hears about 20 to 25% of the petitions filed, it slows the development of tax law. The varying rules created by the different districts, Court of Claims, Bankruptcy Court, and Tax Court delay the establishment of final rules because each Circuit Court can reach its own conclusion.

The overarching argument against a specialized appellate court is that tax involves too many other areas of law, often local in nature, to vest near final authority and guidance in a federal court of no specific circuit jurisdiction. Moreover, this could risk judicial capture, potentially tainting the interpretation of tax statutes. Finally, by consolidating the voices interpreting the tax law into a single, specialized court, it may make it harder for those without specialized training, including most taxpayers, to understand the tax's development.

One alternative to an appellate court is greater deference to the Tax Court, which hears 95% of tax litigation. This would provide one important benefit of a specialized appellate court, namely greater uniformity in decisions. Furthermore this recognizes the expertise of tax specialists and the Internal Revenue Code's complexity. This can work for or against the IRS by providing an educated check on the reasonableness of the government's position. However, there might be value to incorporating generalist judges in tax matters, in part to reduce its insularity and stereotyping.

(c) Collection

Once tax is assessed, most people pay the taxes they owe. Nevertheless, there was a $458 billion annual gross tax gap of taxes owed but unpaid for 2008 through 2010.[64] Of this amount 84% came from taxpayers underreporting their income, 9% from taxpayers underpaying their taxes, and 7% from taxpayers not filing tax returns. Of the tax gap, $65 billion was collected through enforcement and late actions. This collection process is cost effective: In 2016, the IRS spent on average 35¢ to collect $100 in revenue.[65]

---

[63]   Roger Traynor, *Administrative and Judicial Procedure for Federal Income, Estate, and Gift Taxes*, 38 COLUM. L. REV. 1393, 1393 (1938).

[64]   IRS, TAX GAP ESTIMATES FOR TAX YEARS 2008–2010, Pub. 1415 (2016).

[65]   IRS, DATA BOOK 63 (2017).

Nevertheless, that leaves $385 billion in lawfully owed taxes that is never paid.

The government has ten years following assessment to collect the assessed taxes.[66] In that collection process, the IRS has fewer restrictions on its tax collection powers than other creditors. For example, it is constitutional to require taxpayers pay the tax before they can sue for a refund even if the taxpayer does not actually owe the taxes assessed.[67] Most procedures enacted to restrict the IRS's collections are not constitutional requirements; and Congress generally can change them in its discretion. Nevertheless, despite the IRS's power, there remain significant safeguards to protect the public.

After the IRS assesses a tax liability, the IRS can pursue three avenues for collecting the taxes owed: (1) issue a tax lien, (2) levy taxpayer property, and (3) offset refunds or other amounts received from the government.[68] Each collection method has safeguards to protect taxpayer rights. For example, tax liens arise automatically; however, in order for the IRS's lien to be perfected, and take priority over competing creditors to the extent that it can, the IRS must file a Notice of Federal Tax Lien.[69] Thus, a lien attaches by operation of law to all property but has limited value without further action as to specific property. For property to have a perfected lien, the taxpayer must receive notice of the IRS's intent. Moreover, the Code requires that the IRS give the taxpayer notice of its intent to use its levy power to seize property, and certain types of property are exempt from the IRS's power to levy.[70] Finally, except in limited circumstances, if the IRS does not complete its collection within ten years, the authority to pursue these avenues lapses.

To encourage taxpayers to timely pay the taxes they owe, Congress imposes interest on taxes that are not paid.[71] Interest on the unpaid balance of taxes compounds daily from the due date of the return until payment is made. The interest rate is the federal short-term rate plus 3%. This rate is set every three months. In the second quarter of 2018, the rate increased to 5% for individual taxpayers.[72]

---

[66]   I.R.C. § 6502.

[67]   Murray's Lessee v. Hoboken Land & Improvement Co., 59 U.S. 272, 282 (1855).

[68]   I.R.C. § 6212; § 6321; § 6331; § 6402.

[69]   I.R.C. § 6323. Without perfection, tax liens take precedence over all creditors but for purchasers for value, mechanics lienors, holders of security interests, and judgment lien creditor.

[70]   I.R.C. § 6331(d).

[71]   I.R.C. § 6601; § 6621; § 6622.

[72]   IRS, IR–2018–43, INTEREST RATES INCREASE FOR THE SECOND QUARTER OF 2018 (2018).

Rates are different for corporate taxpayers, in which case underpayments are charged 7% in interest until paid.

Additionally, Congress has enacted more than 100 kinds of civil penalties as part of the Internal Revenue Code. Most penalties are calculated as a percentage of the taxes owed, although some are flat rate amounts. Penalties generally compound and, when applicable, become a large percentage of what delinquent taxpayers owe.

For example, penalties are automatically imposed on those who fail to file tax returns or to pay their taxes. The failure to file tax returns penalty is up to 25% of the amount of the tax that should have been reported; the failure to file penalty is also up to 25% of the amount of the tax that should have been paid.[73] If both penalties are owed, a maximum penalty of 47.5% of the tax owed can be incurred. The IRS may abate these penalties if taxpayers have reasonable cause for their failure and the failure was not due to willful neglect.

Other penalties may be incurred if taxpayers act unreasonably in filling out their tax returns. Penalties of 20% of any underpaid tax are imposed if the taxpayer negligently disregarded the Treasury Department's or IRS's rules and regulations.[74] These civil penalties are not imposed if the taxpayer believes that the government's interpretation of the law is incorrect and either has a realistic possibility of winning in court or discloses the position on the return and it has at least a 5% chance of winning in court.[75] The objective is to encourage compliance while giving taxpayers an out if they reasonably disagree with the government's interpretation of the statute.

To discourage abusive transactions, Congress imposes a 40% penalty on transactions that lack economic substance.[76] The economic substance doctrine was a common law doctrine until Congress codified it in 2010. Under the new statutory provision, a transaction is respected for having economic substance only if it passes a two-prong test. If either prong is not met, the penalty is imposed. First, the transaction must change the taxpayer's economic position in a meaningful way apart from any federal income tax effects. Second, the taxpayer must have a substantial purpose for entering into the transaction other than the federal income tax effects. Thus, federal tax savings alone are not enough to justify a transaction.

---

[73]   I.R.C. § 6651.

[74]   I.R.C. § 6662.

[75]   Treas. Reg. § 1.6662–3(b)(2).

[76]   I.R.C. § 7701(*o*).

Penalties' value as a deterrent and as compensation for the cost of detecting evasion is debated.[77] It is unknown whether penalties increase or decrease tax compliance.[78] Their rates may be prohibitively high, especially when combined with interest, amounting to confiscation and frightening people from disagreeing with the IRS. Their high rates, however, are coupled with permissive excuses, allowing people to avoid penalties. With a less than 1% audit rate, the likelihood of financial penalties may be so low that taxpayers engaging in risky tax behavior do not fear them while their existence may lessen compliant taxpayers' moral sense of obligation to pay taxes.

Criminal prosecution under the Internal Revenue Code is even less likely than the imposition of civil penalties. Criminal tax evasion is a felony defined as the willful attempt to evade or defeat the income tax.[79] Therefore, tax crimes require an affirmative act constituting evasion and willfulness. Although juries are not always instructed that a "bad purpose" or "evil purpose" is necessary for criminal evasion, a good faith misunderstanding of tax law is a defense, and the Supreme Court has held that this understanding need not be objectively reasonable.[80] Negligence, even gross negligence, does not establish the willfulness necessary for criminal tax evasion. In 2016, 3,721 investigations were completed, resulting in 2,761 accusations of criminal charges and 2,672 convictions.[81]

Although much of the tax system is designed to encourage collection, the system also recognizes that some people are just not able to pay. For example, the offer-in-compromise ("OIC") program offers taxpayers the ability to pay some amount less than the full amount of the tax that is owed based on the taxpayer's income, expenses, and asset equity. For an OIC to be accepted by the IRS, there must be doubt as to the liability, doubt as to its collectability, or a claim that it aids "effective tax administration." The latter is code that the collection would create an economic hardship or be unfair and inequitable. Professor Shu-Yi Oie argues that not only does this program maximize government revenue but functions as a form of

---

[77]   Michael Doran, *Tax Penalties and Tax Compliance*, 46 HARV. J. ON LEGIS. 111 (2009); Alex Raskolnikov, *Crime and Punishment in Taxation: Deceit, Deterrence, and the Self-Adjusting Penalty*, 106 COLUM. L. REV. 569 (2006); Eric Zolt, *Deterrence Via Taxation: A Critical Analysis of Tax Penalty Provisions*, 37 UCLA L. REV. 343 (1989).

[78]   The federal government rarely targets taxpayers with other penalties, such as public shaming. For more on shaming, see Chapters 5.02(b) and 12.02(c).

[79]   I.R.C. § 7201.

[80]   Cheek v. U.S., 498 U.S. 192 (1991).

[81]   IRS, *Criminal Investigation Program*, Table 18, DATA BOOK (2017).

social safety net.[82] In 2016, 27,000 of 63,000 OIC applications were approved.[83]

A second means of relief are installment agreements, of which the TAS received 3,943 cases in 2016.[84] Installment agreements require full payment of the taxes that are owed but over a longer period of time than normally allowed. Under the Fresh Start provisions set up in 2011, taxpayers who owe up to $50,000 in taxes can pay over a 72-month period.[85] For those owing more in tax or who need more time, installment agreements are only entered into when taxpayers are financially unable to pay their tax debts immediately. Finally, penalties and interest continue to accrue until the tax balance is paid in full, which can make this a costly option.

If taxpayers agree on the amount of the liability but cannot pay it, they can use the collection due process ("CDP") system to challenge the IRS's method of tax collection with an appeals officer not previously connected to the taxpayer's case.[86] CDP can be used to fight a tax lien or levy. Within thirty days of the completion of this review process, the taxpayer can seek further review by the Tax Court. The CDP system is intended to ensure that the IRS is not an abusive collector by applying rule of law principles to prevent arbitrary collections processes. Nevertheless, there are critiques of the system.[87] The CDP program uses a significant amount of government resources and, in part because of its frequent use by tax protestors who argue the Sixteenth Amendment is unconstitutional, few taxpayers win their claims.

The CDP program was one of many changes enacted in 1998 when Congress restructured the IRS.[88] With a new focus on increasing taxpayer protection and facilitating compliance, a significant amount of the IRS's budget, over 20%, is spent on

---

[82]　Shu-Yi Oei, *Getting More By Asking Less*, 160 U.PA. L. REV. 1071, 1094–97 (2012).

[83]　IRS, *Delinquent Collection Activities*, Table 16, DATA BOOK (2017).

[84]　*Id.*, at Table 20.

[85]　IRS, IR–2012–31, IRS OFFERS NEW PENALTY RELIEF AND EXPANDED INSTALLMENT AGREEMENTS TO TAXPAYERS UNDER EXPANDED FRESH START INITIATIVE (2012).

[86]　I.R.C. § 6330. Form 12153 is required to dispute the IRS's proposed collection action.

[87]　For debate over the CDP program, see Leslie Book, *The Collection Due Process Rights*, 41 HOUS. L. REV. 1145, 1187 (2004); Bryan Camp, *Tax Administration as Inquisitorial Process and the Partial Paradigm Shift in the IRS Restructuring and Reform Act of 1998*, 56 FLA. L. REV. 1, 122 (2004); Steve Johnson, *The 1998 Act and the Resources Link Between Tax Compliance and Tax Simplification*, 51 U. KAN. L. REV. 1013, 1060–62 (2003); Diane L. Fahey, *The Tax Court's Jurisdiction Over Due Process Collection Appeals*, 55 BAYLOR L. REV. 453 (2003).

[88]　Internal Revenue Service Restructuring and Reform Act of 1998, Pub. L. No. 105–206, 112 Stat. 685 (1998).

customer-based activities.[89] Nevertheless, in the 2016 tax-filing season the IRS answered only 73% of its calls, but that is significantly more than the 37% answered in 2015.[90]

Alternative processes for administering an income tax might ease administration for taxpayers, if not the government. The United Kingdom has a Pay As You Earn (PAYE) system in which the government does not withhold on behalf of taxpayers but collects taxes currently from each paycheck. The government determines the amount to collect through a coding system. Each taxpayer is assigned a code, and that code determines the taxes due. As a result, most British taxpayers do not file tax returns but, instead, trust that the government correctly collected taxes throughout the year. However, one study found that 37% of the codes the British government used were incorrect.[91] For a PAYE system to work, significantly fewer public policies can be operated through the tax system than currently exist in the U.S. because these policies increase the complexity of the coding system.

At the other end of the spectrum of alternatives is the privatized collection of tax revenue. Some countries have used tax farms in which the government licenses to private parties the right and obligation to raise a designated amount of revenue.[92] Tax farming is a speculative business for the entrepreneur who has to make up any debts that are not collected. Less speculative is hiring collection agencies that only profit if they collect but do not owe for failure to collect. In December 2015, Congress instructed the IRS to resume use of third party collectors to collect on delinquent taxes, as it did between 1996 and 1997 and again between 2006 and 2009. Previously, private collection agencies' methods were found objectionable and their return not what was expected, and they were discontinued. In fact, the TAS found that between 2006 and 2009, the IRS collected about twice as much as the private collectors.[93] Nevertheless, the JCT estimates that private collectors could bring in $2.4 billion by 2025.[94]

---

[89]   IRS, *IRS Budget & Workforce*, § 8, DATA BOOK (2017).

[90]   IRS, IR–2016–97, NATIONAL TAXPAYER ADVOCATE REVIEWS FILING SEASON (2016).

[91]   Patrick Collinson, *Tax Codes Tax HMRC's Experts*, THE GUARDIAN (Oct. 26, 2013).

[92]   Peter Stella, *Tax Farming: A Radical Solution for Developing Country Tax Problems?*, IMF WORKING PAPER No. 92/70 (1992).

[93]   Nat'l Taxpayer Advoc., *The IRS Private Debt Collection Program*, ANNUAL REPORT 97 (2013).

[94]   IRS, PRIVATE DEBT COLLECTION, https://www.irs.gov/businesses/small-businesses-self-employed/private-debt-collection (last visited May 1, 2018).

Altogether, the collection process contains many sticks to ensure compliance but also carrots to make paying more palatable. The system incorporates an analysis of individuals' personal economic circumstances in determining whether or not to enforce payment. Unlike the inquisitorial assessment process that seeks the correct amount of taxes owed, collections looks to the amount a taxpayer can reasonably pay of the amount owed.

§ 2.03   Public Response to Taxes

The American tax system is largely voluntary, even though one could debate the voluntariness of a withholding-based system. Despite widespread bickering about the tax system, the U.S. has one of the highest levels of tax morale in the world.[95] In a 2014 survey, 74% of taxpayers reported they were satisfied with their personal interaction with the IRS, although this is a decline from recent years.[96] One study found that about one-third of those surveyed like completing their taxes, largely because they expected a tax refund.[97] Views about the IRS are divided along political lines: 62% of Democrats have a favorable rating of the IRS, 30% of Republicans, and only 15% of those identifying with the Tea Party.[98]

Gallup Polls[99]				
	Too high (%)	About right (%)	Too low (%)	No opinion (%)
Do you consider the amount of federal income tax you have to pay as too high, about right or too low?	45	48	3	3
	Fair (%)	Not fair (%)	No opinion (%)	
Do you regard the income tax which you have to pay this year as fair?	61	36	3	

---

[95]   James Alm & Benno Torgler, *Culture Differences and Tax Morale in the United States and in Europe*, 27 J. ECON. PSYCHOLOGY 224 (2006).

[96]   NAT'L TAXPAYER ADVOC., ANNUAL REPORT TO CONGRESS 24 (2014).

[97]   Seth Motel, *5 Facts on How Americans View Taxes*, PEW RESEARCH CENTER (Apr. 10, 2015).

[98]   *Id.*

[99]   Gallup, *Taxes*, Apr. 2, 2018, http://www.gallup.com/poll/1714/taxes.aspx (last visited May 1, 2018).

	Fair share (%)	Too much (%)	Too little (%)	No opinion (%)
Do you think lower-income people are paying their fair share in federal taxes?	32	49	16	2
Do you think middle-income people are paying their fair share in federal taxes?	51	42	6	1
Do you think upper-income people are paying their fair share in federal taxes?	26	10	62	2
Do you think corporations are paying their fair share in federal taxes?	24	7	66	3

Regardless of individuals' perception of taxation, American compliance with taxes in the period between 2008 and 2010 was at 81.7%, the highest in the world.[100] Within the U.S.'s larger compliance rate lies deep division depending upon the ease with which taxpayers can evade their obligation. Reporting compliance is about 99% for income subject to withholding at the source, namely wages (because taxpayers must file fraudulent W-4s or request a refund to evade tax); 93% for income subject to third-party information reporting such as interest and dividends (in part because computers can easily detect omissions); but less than 40% for self-employment income that is not subject to third-party reporting.[101] This latter group has the easiest time evading taxes, and significant numbers do so.

How people perceive and understand taxes is a psychological matter, so people's views of the tax system are not always rational, despite most debates assuming an economically rational public.[102] For example, how policymakers frame tax policies influences public perception of the policies' value. Empirical studies find that people are more receptive to fees than to taxes, to taxes expressed in percentages rather than as dollar amounts, and to hidden taxes rather than to salient ones. To the extent the public can be manipulated by the framing of tax policies, policymakers have the power to spin their preferred choice by altering the optics of proposals rather than their content.

---

[100]   IRS, THE TAX GAP, *supra* note 61.

[101]   Theodore Black et al., *Federal Tax Compliance Research: Tax Year 2006 Tax Gap Estimation*, IRS RESEARCH, ANALYSIS & STATISTICS WORKING PAPER (2012).

[102]   For more on behavioral economics, see Chapter 6.02(b).

One reason for the power of perception is people's bounded rationality; people simply cannot process information about everything at all times. Studies of bounded rationality show that decision-making is limited by the information people have and their ability to use it. In response to these limits, people create heuristics, or rules of thumb, rather than pouring through the complex information that is available.[103] Heuristics are strategies or tools that require little information to make complicated decisions. Streamlining the process of decision-making, these rules of thumb or first principles make choices easier and more effective. If people have good heuristics about taxes, they will make better tax-related decisions.

Another factor in how people respond to taxes depends on how aware they are of the tax or how salient the tax is. Salience is the state of being prominent or noticeable. The more salient a tax is the more taxpayers are aware of the tax. Only if a tax is salient will taxpayers adjust their demand of the taxed activity in response to changes in the after-tax price. Studies on the salience of taxes have found that even if people know of an applicable tax, the tax may not be salient in that it fails to affect their behavior. For example, Professor Raj Chetty and his coauthors performed an experiment in a grocery store and, without changing the applicable tax, found that posting signs including the sales tax reduced demand by 8%.[104] Even when people correctly identified their local sales tax without the sign, the posting changed their behavior by making the tax more salient.

If tax salience affects behavior and people have strong reactions to the framing of tax policies, a question is how salient should a government's revenue system be? The answer determines how to raise revenue without distorting behavior and how democratic a tax system should be. Lower salience taxes reduce consumers' tendency to substitute away from the taxed good but, at the same time, cause consumers to err when choosing how much of a good to purchase. The best level of salience may be influenced by the amount of revenue that is needed, and the best result might be a compilation of highly salient and low salience taxes.

---

[103] Anuj Shah & Daniel Oppenheimer, *Heuristics Made Easy*, 134 PSYCHOLOGICAL BULL. 207 (2008).

[104] Raj Chetty et al., *Salience and Taxation*, 99 AM. ECON. REV. 1145 (2009).

Chapter 3

HISTORY OF AMERICAN TAXATION

Table of Sections

The American tax system did not simply appear. It began before the nation's founding as it, along with our political system, arose from a colonial past. The tax system has changed dramatically in the last 200 years. Change occurs because the tax system is the product of politics and has evolved in response to many demands. Politicians, taxpayers, interest groups, producers, and consumers all play a part in shaping the evolution of the system. Their disagreements and compromises determine what is taxed and what goes untaxed.

§ 3.01   Evolution of Taxation in the U.S.

The American colonials did not have an advanced tax system, and they did not raise much tax revenue.[1] Disliking taxes, they fought a revolution largely over the power to tax. The colonials complained of the ability of the British Parliament, in which they had no direct representation, to impose and enforce taxes to fund the Seven Years War, often ignoring that the war produced significant benefits for the colonies. In the Boston Tea Party, Americans destroyed more than $1.5 million (in current dollars) worth of tea to avoid taxes. George Washington, and many other colonials, reacted negatively to this destruction of private property and urged Boston to pay restitution, if not the tax.[2]

The American Revolution and most other government activities necessitate taxes, reinforcing the tension between needing revenue and resenting taxation. On one hand, the majority of the American public has often understood the value of taxation and enjoyed what the revenue can provide. On the other hand, the majority has also resisted increases in tax rates or the elimination of targeted tax

---

[1]   For more on colonial and pre-Civil War taxation, see ROBIN EINHORN, AMERICAN TAXATION, AMERICAN SLAVERY (2006).

[2]   HARLOW GILES, AMERICAN TEMPEST: HOW THE BOSTON TEA PARTY SPARKED A REVOLUTION 183 (2011).

reduction.[3] Throughout the nation's history, a pendulum has swung between appreciating spending and hating the taxes that fund it.

(a) Constitutional Limitations

Before the U.S. had the Constitution, the federal government operated under a much weaker Articles of Confederation.[4] A primary reason for the failure of the Articles was that the federal government could not tax the people of the states. Instead, the federal government had to requisition revenue from the states and the states were to raise the revenue from their own citizenry. That process failed because states would not raise the requested revenue. Two attempts to amend the Articles of Confederation so that the federal government could tax imports into the country failed because of the Articles' requirement that the states unanimously agree to the change. The Constitution was to eliminate these limitations.

Under the Constitution, Congress has the power to impose and collect federal taxes directly from the citizens of the states pursuant to the Taxing and Spending Clause in Article I.[5] The Taxing and Spending Clause requires taxation to be for the general welfare. Early in the nation's history, the Supreme Court limited the power to tax when the tax's objective was clearly other than to raise revenue for the general welfare.[6] That limitation has largely been read out of the Constitution. Today, any revenue-raising provision is likely to qualify as a tax under the Taxing and Spending Clause.

There are a few limits on Congress's taxing power. The Constitution requires taxes be applied uniformly throughout the U.S.[7] In practice, the Uniformity Clause only requires that a tax apply with "the same force and effect" across the country.[8] Congress cannot discriminate geographically in favor of, or targeting, particular states, although it can tax resources or activities, such as oil and filmmaking, that are disproportionately housed in a limited number of states.[9] Despite changes that might have occurred, uniformity does not require taxes be prospective. Uniformity and due process concerns do not prevent Congress from enacting retroactive

---

[3]   For more on the psychology of taxation, see Chapters 2.03 and 6.02.

[4]   ARTICLES OF CONFEDERATION OF 1781.

[5]   U.S. CONST. art. I, § 8, cl. 1.

[6]   For more on the history of taxes as penalties, see Chapter 7.02.

[7]   U.S. CONST. art. I, § 8, cl. 1.

[8]   Edye v. Robertson, 112 U.S. 580 (1884).

[9]   The Supreme Court allowed an exclusion from tax for oil produced above the Arctic Circle, which could only apply in the state of Alaska. U.S. v. Ptasynski, 462 U.S. 75 (1983).

taxes as long as taxing prior choices or activities is a rational means to accomplish a legitimate legislative purpose.[10]

Facially, a stricter limit on the power to tax is the limit on direct taxes.[11] The Constitution requires that direct taxes be apportioned between the states. This means that each state must bear the tax equal to its share of the national population, and states with more people owe more tax even if those states have less wealth. This results in different tax rates in different states, making them politically unlikely. At the founding, newer states' populations were high relative to their taxable property, so that apportioned taxes would have created higher rates of taxation per capita in new states, favoring the original colonies. What direct taxes included, however, was unclear. When Gouverneur Morris introduced the phrase in the Constitutional Convention, Rufus King asked what it meant. No one answered.[12]

Additionally, the Constitution requires tax legislation originate in the House of Representatives, although the Senate may amend a bill originating in the House.[13] The Origination Clause stemmed from English parliamentary practice requiring revenue bills be first read in the House of Commons before being sent to the House of Lords. This process ensures that the masses have a greater voice in tax legislation. Although this limitation arguably applies to both tax increases and decreases, courts sometimes dodge the issue by asserting it is a political question, by raising issues of standing, or by invoking other doctrines.[14]

The Origination Clause was also part of the Connecticut Compromise between large and small states. After the issue of representation almost derailed the Constitutional Convention, the different states accepted two houses of Congress, one with proportional representation (favoring large states) and one with equal representation (favoring small states). Thereafter, the parties fought over what tasks were assigned to each house. In this instance, the large states won having the house in which they had greater representation originate tax legislation.

---

[10]   United States v. Carlton, 512 U.S. 26, 28–31 (1994).

[11]   U.S. CONST. art I, § 2, cl. 3; art. I, § 9, cl. 4.

[12]   The history was developed extensively in Pollock v. Farmers' Trust, 157 U.S. 429, 562–8 (1895).

[13]   U.S. CONST. art. I, § 7, cl. 1. For more on the legislative process, see Chapter 1.01.

[14]   These cases were very popular in the mid-1980s. *See* Moore v. U.S. House of Representatives, 733 F.2d 946 (D.D. Cir. 1984), cert. denied, 469 U.S. 1106 (1985); Texas Ass'n of Concerned Taxpayers v. U.S., 772 F.2d 163 (5th Cir. 1985); Armstrong v. U.S. 759 F.2d 1378 (9th Cir. 1985).

Although the Origination Clause has little impact today, it could develop teeth. In *United States v. Munoz-Flores*, the Supreme Court rejected the argument that origination claims are not justiciable.[15] Refusing to delegate this issue to the political branches, the Court held that the plaintiff could have the standing to pursue the claim. However, based on the particular facts, the Origination Clause did not apply because the law providing users' fees was not "a bill for raising revenue." Therefore, it was not a tax law subject to the Origination Clause.

A provision that receives little press today but still applies is the ban on export taxes.[16] Therefore, the federal government cannot tax goods as they leave the U.S., although it can tax goods as they enter. The South demanded this prohibition in the Constitutional Convention because they feared that the North would tax exports of cotton in its attempt to eliminate slavery or to decrease the power of the South. The South thought that with a power to tax exports Congress would be able to tax slavery out of existence by making cotton exports uncompetitive in the world market. This Northern concession was given to persuade the South to stop demanding a supermajority vote for commercial legislation.

Some constitutional tax compromises have thankfully been repealed. The three-fifths clause regarding representation and taxation arose from battles over the allocation of power between the North and the South.[17] Following the Connecticut Compromise, the Constitutional Convention had to decide how or if slaves were to be counted for the house of Congress apportioned according to population. The debate could have continued forever; there was no consensus. Then came another compromise, one that had been proposed as an amendment to the Articles of Confederation: the three-fifths clause. Direct taxes and voting would both be apportioned counting three-fifths of a slave. As a quid pro quo, slaves were counted as three-fifths of a person for determining both direct tax rates and representation; however, few direct taxes were to be imposed and so it won little for the North.[18]

Today, despite questions of direct taxation reappearing periodically, constitutional limits to the taxing power have been marginalized. The nation no longer relies on their limits in the making of modern tax policy. This may largely result from the vast

---

[15]   495 U.S. 385 (1990).

[16]   U.S. CONST., art. I, § 9.

[17]   U.S. CONST., art I, § 2, § 9.

[18]   The three-fifths clause altered early elections. The election of 1800 was so close in the Electoral College that Thomas Jefferson needed that three-fifths to win the presidency.

differences in the economies of the 21st and 18th centuries. It may also be because of the evolution in tax theory and administrative capacity, which together permit the imposition of taxes unthinkable at the time of the American Revolution.

(b) Founders' Taxation

Following the Constitutional Convention, the Founding Fathers expected to fund the government through well-established revenue-raising tools, namely tariffs and excises. Tariffs are taxes on imported goods and services; excises are taxes on licenses for particular activities and on goods or commodities produced within the country. The income tax was not only foreign to an American people wary of taxation, it had not yet been operated in its modern form.[19] Thus, the American Revolution did not attempt to revolutionize tax policy.

Despite the limited sources of federal tax revenue, the federal government paid off a sizable amount of state debt it had assumed following the American Revolution. Other than this debt, there was little federal spending. Between 1796 and 1811, there were thirty-two budget surpluses and four deficits.[20] In 1792, federal taxes raised $4.6 million; in 1900, taxes raised $577.2 million; the projected amount for fiscal year 2017 is over $3.3 trillion. Of early republic revenue, tariffs of about 20% were imposed on imported goods and raised as much as 95% of total federal revenues. There was not even a federal excise tax on alcoholic liquors between 1817 and the Civil War began in 1861.[21]

There was some debate over the imposition of direct taxes in the country's early years. Needing revenue in 1794, Congress imposed a non-apportioned tax on carriages. Whether this was an unconstitutional direct tax came before the Supreme Court. In *Hylton v. United States*, the Court held that the tax was not direct and, according to some interpretations, the case limited the definition of direct taxes to capitation and land taxes.[22] However, the Secretary of the Treasury Department took no notice of the Court's opinion in his report, "Direct Taxes," issued nine months after the decision was handed down.[23] The issue of direct taxation was not litigated in the Supreme Court again until *Pollock v. Farmers' Loan & Trust Co.* in

---

[19]   The modern income tax was first introduced in Great Britain in 1798 during the Napoleonic Wars.

[20]   WHITE HOUSE, HISTORICAL TABLES, Table 1.1, https://www.whitehouse.gov/omb/budget/Historicals (last visited May 1, 2018).

[21]   For more on the Whiskey Rebellion as an early exercise of government power, see Chapter 17.02(c).

[22]   3 U.S. 171, 175 (1796).

[23]   OLIVER WOLCOTT, SEC. OF TREAS., DIRECT TAXES, H.R. Doc. No. 4–100 (1796).

1895 doomed part of the 1893 income tax.[24] *Hylton* was again used as precedent in upholding the Affordable Care Act's healthcare mandate in 2012.[25]

For most of the pre-Civil War era, tax theory was a matter of political philosophy. Philosophers, such as Adam Smith and John Stuart Mill, developed and debated conceptions of taxation. But with little taxation in the era, much of this theoretical debate was not tested in practice. These authors' copious writings have been interpreted as supporting both progressive and flat rate taxation; redistribution and laissez faire freedom. Ideas developed and redeveloped through political debate as people struggled with the idea of justice and what justice required of the tax system. Most philosophers influential in the U.S. generally accepted that a free and open economy was the best means of securing justice, although philosophers' views of what constituted a free economy was not always well defined.

The free and open economy was not to extend beyond national borders. Most American policymakers of the era did not seek free trade vis-à-vis other countries but used tariffs on imports to raise revenue and to protect local markets. Alexander Hamilton, who largely shaped the early U.S. fiscal system, argued that the U.S. could not be independent until it was self-sufficient.[26] Therefore, Hamilton pushed President George Washington to create a strong federal government capable of developing the nation's industry. Thereafter, dominant thought in Congress accepted some version of these Hamiltonian ideas.

Reliance on tariffs gave rise to protective tariffs based largely on a belief in mercantilism, or that it was important to maintain a positive trade balance and thereby increase the nation's international power. Policymakers wanted the nation to export more than it imported. To that end, Congress enacted protective tariffs, which were high taxes imposed on imported goods to make imports comparatively more expensive than domestically produced goods. Protectionists wanted to protect the domestic market for domestic manufacturers and to maintain a positive trade balance.

Protective tariffs became the bread and butter of the federal government. Only the South regularly opposed protectionism and supported free international trade because of its dependence on exporting cotton and its need for imports. Despite this resistance,

---

[24]   157 U.S. 429 (1895).

[25]   Nat'l Fed'n of Indep. Bus. v. Sebelius, 567 U.S. 519, 570 (2012).

[26]   ALEXANDER HAMILTON, REPORT ON THE SUBJECT OF MANUFACTURERS, Dec. 5, 1791.

federal tariffs developed into a vibrant tariff regime that lasted from 1816 until World War II, when free trade finally supplanted the mercantilist philosophy. At times, however, protectionism returns in debates and policies. The cost of protecting American producers was largely borne by American consumers who paid the price in the form of more expensive imported goods.[27]

(c) Civil War and the Panic of 1893

The Civil War was difficult to finance, both because of the added expense of fighting and the loss of revenue from the Confederate states. National credit was weak, and it was hard to raise taxes with already high tariffs. Over the course of the war, government spending jumped from less than 2% of gross national product (GNP) to an average of 15%. To fund the Union's war effort, Congress borrowed, doubled tariff rates, sold public lands, created new and increased rates of existing excise taxes, and enacted the government's first income tax.[28]

Policymakers never expected the income tax to become a big revenue source, and the public cared little about it. The first flat rate income tax was quickly amended to have slightly graduated rates of 3% to 5% for incomes in excess of $600 and $10,000, respectively.[29] However, even with several progressive additions during the Civil War, the income tax did not provide a significant portion of federal revenue.[30] Moreover, the income tax was not even a campaign issue in the 1864 presidential election, the contested last election before the end of the war. The national debt, not taxation, was the main fiscal issue. Of all taxes, tariffs and excises most captured public attention as the primary source of tax revenue for the federal government.

When the Civil War ended, so did the federal deficit. Resistance to the income tax and various excises spread as the government

---

[27] Tariffs are a targeted form of consumption tax. Tariffs are regressive in that they tend to consume a larger portion of lower-income people's income because lower-income people consume a larger portion of their income. For more on consumption taxes, see Chapter 8.

[28] Civil War taxes were so sweeping that when one Senator remarked that everything was taxed except coffins, another quipped, "Don't say that to [Senate Finance Chair John] Sherman or he will have them on the tax list before night." JOHN SHERMAN, RECOLLECTIONS OF FORTY YEARS IN THE HOUSE, SENATE, AND CABINET: AN AUTOBIOGRAPHY 304 (1895).

[29] Act of August 5, 1861, ch. 45, 12 Stat. 292, 309–11; Revenue Act of 1862, ch. 119, sec. 89–93, 12 Stat. 432, 473–75.

[30] Sixty-five percent of the Union's war efforts were financed with debt; 21% was from taxes but mainly excises. Annual receipts from the income tax topped out at almost $61 million in 1865 based on 1864 incomes, when annual spending was over $1 billion. For more on American financing during wars, see STEVEN BANK ET AL., WAR AND TAXES (2008).

reduced its expenditures and the fear of inflation receded. But the greatest opposition to the income tax arose from supporters of protective tariffs. Protectionists feared that the income tax would raise sufficient revenue to force Congress to reduce tariffs with the aim of easing burdens on consumers. The income tax lapsed without fanfare in 1872.

It took time for supporters of the income tax to spread support for the tax in the peace following the Civil War. Most of the tax's advocates were scattered across the nation, and it was never a rallying issue for advocates of social reform. Then, during a major recession begun in 1893, proponents of the income tax again included an income tax in a larger revenue bill. The Democratic Senate had made hundreds of amendments to the House version of the tariff bill raising tariff rates. Raising tariff rates angered consumers, and Democrats needed to enact some legislation to offset this betrayal of its electorate. The income tax was their fig leaf.

While the 1894 income tax passed easily, not even being voted on separately in the Senate, the tax was weaker than its Civil War progenitor.[31] It taxed incomes above $4,000 at a flat rate of 2% and was set to expire in five years. As with the Civil War income tax, the 1894 tax was not intended to be a large revenue raiser, and the members of Congress did not devote significant resources to craft its statutory language.[32]

In the winter of 1894, legal challenges to the income tax climbed to the Supreme Court. Reversing an 1881 decision, the Court invalidated the new income tax five months after its enactment in a case in which neither the U.S. nor any of its officers were parties.[33] Charles Pollock sued his trust company on the grounds that the company was about to commit a breach of trust by paying an unconstitutional tax. Although the Court's decision was narrow, the majority's dicta took a broader and more hostile view toward income taxation, arguing that "[n]othing can be clearer than that what the Constitution intended to guard against was the exercise by the general government of the power of directly taxing persons and property within any State through a majority made up from the other States."[34]

As a result of *Pollock v. Farmers' Loan and Trust Co.*, at the turn of the century the federal tax system looked much the same as it had

---

[31]   Wilson-Gorman Tariff of 1894, ch. 349, § 73, 28 Stat. 570.

[32]   Stephanie Hunter McMahon, *A Law with a Life of Its Own: The Development of the Federal Income Tax Statutes Through World War I*, 7 PITT. TAX REV. 1 (2009).

[33]   Pollock v. Farmers' Loan and Trust Co., 157 U.S. 429 (1895); Springer v. United States, 102 U.S. 586 (1881).

[34]   157 U.S. at 582.

at the time of the American Revolution. The nation had acquired more debt during the Civil War, but the country was still reluctant to adopt deficit spending except in national emergencies. The power of the federal government had grown and there was greater dependence upon the federal government throughout the economy. Nevertheless, the tools to care for the economy remained limited.

(d) Progressive Era and the New Deal

The end of the nineteenth century, called the Gilded Age because a thin gold gilding hid serious social and economic problems, witnessed extreme extravagance by the fabulously wealthy and a competing rise of progressivism. As part of the progressive response to excess, reformers advocated for an income tax for its redistributive potential, although the amount of redistribution was small by today's standards. Nevertheless, whereas politicians of earlier generations had despised redistributive taxation as an unjust taking of another's property and a threat to economic development, Progressives saw something noble in this taking from the haves to give to the have nots.

With significant public anger directed at excess, most politicians of both political parties took up the call for an income tax if for differing reasons. Despising debt, Republican presidential candidate William Howard Taft accepted the idea of an income tax in 1908 as part of a package of tax increases necessary to pay the government's debts. Then the new administration and a group of Senators forged a political compromise, which traded away congressional consideration of an individual income tax for the current imposition of a 4% corporate income tax plus a congressional resolution calling for a constitutional amendment authorizing an individual income tax. That amendment became the Sixteenth Amendment.

Many advocates for the income tax were professors at the nation's first research universities, including Johns Hopkins formed in 1876 but also Columbia University, University of Wisconsin-Madison, and the University of Michigan. These universities' scholars were able to develop new theories in emerging disciplines that reshaped issues of their day. Many influential proponents of the 1913 income tax were political economists trained in Germany, leading the U.S.'s intellectual movement for a progressive tax built on taxpayers' ability to pay taxes, which was a relatively new idea in the U.S. They shifted majority opinion away from the idea that the person who benefited from something should pay for it, which had justified tariffs.

This new crop of experts supported social progressivism by attacking classical economics, which advocates that markets function best without government intervention. These new economists, including Edwin R.A. Seligman, Richard T. Ely, and Henry Carter Adams, sought to use taxation to address the social problems they argued were created by laissez-faire capitalism.[35] As scientists who were to operate above the political fray, they argued that their findings were objective and apolitical. By no means the only voice in academia, this small band of economists challenged the established view that there were immutable laws of economics and resisted the benefit theory that limited the tax system's capacity to redistribute wealth.

These proponents of Progressive Era redistributive taxation challenged classical economists who argued for equality and uniformity in taxation. Equality in taxation, according to the classical view, improved the economy by permitting markets to move toward their natural equilibrium. Classical political economists of the era, such as William Graham Sumner, argued that reallocating income to the poor through taxation harmed everyone, including those Progressives sought to help.[36] Instead, treating everyone equally permitted the best to rise through natural selection. These theorists often combined evolution and economics into social Darwinism, a theory reaching its height in the Gilded Age. In economics, as in the wild, the fittest should survive.

Another group of theorists of the period were more extreme in their redistributive tax policy than most scholars at universities. For example, Henry George sought to tax land as the ultimate source of monopoly and to eliminate other forms of taxation. In 1879, George advocated a single tax on land to curtail land speculation and radical tax reform because, according to George, land was the source of all wealth.[37] Viewing land as a source of power, George sought to tax it as common property ultimately owned by all even if used by a few.

At the same time, socialism was growing dramatically in America, although less as an academic movement than a political one. Eugene V. Debs won 900,000 votes in the 1912 presidential election, in part aided by Jack London and Upton Sinclair who popularized theories of redistribution and equality.[38] The Socialist movement focused less on taxation, however, than on the redistribution of property and wages. Because taxation had

---

[35]   For more on the intellectual and theoretical developments, see AJAY MEHROTRA, MAKING THE MODERN AMERICAN FISCAL STATE (2013).

[36]   WILLIAM GRAHAM SUMNER, WHAT THE SOCIAL CLASSES OWE TO EACH OTHER (1883).

[37]   HENRY GEORGE, PROGRESS AND POVERTY (1879).

[38]   JACK LONDON, THE IRON HEEL (1908); UPTON SINCLAIR, THE JUNGLE (1906).

historically been tariffs, recognized as disproportionately taxing the poor, taxes were not a radical's tool to change social dynamics.

Along the spectrum of popular political views in the early 20th century, the economists advocating the income tax were not seen as radicals but as moderate advocates of ameliorative change. They influenced political debates by talking to legislatures and writing in popular journals, attempting to educate voters and leaders on their theories. For a period they succeeded, culminating in the passage of the Sixteenth Amendment.

The Sixteenth Amendment was ratified in 1913. Most people of the era had thought the income tax amendment would not be ratified by the states. The public's level of interest in the income tax was low relative to the other concerns of the day. As a result, this change to the Constitution took 3½ years to ratify, more than had been required to obtain the necessary votes for any previous amendment, and was regional, beginning in the South and West. Throughout ratification, few social groups or special interests lobbied in support of the Sixteenth Amendment.

Not everyone accepts that the Sixteenth Amendment was properly ratified, leading to the "tax protestor" movement.[39] Some argue that the amendment's capitalization, spelling of words, or punctuation marks as proposed by Congress was not the same as that ratified by various states. Others argue that the Sixteenth Amendment does not grant the underlying power to tax labor or income from labor, it merely removes the apportionment requirement for taxes for which there is constitutional power. Still others argue that Ohio, counted as one of the ratifying states, was not actually a state from 1803 when Congress passed a public law recognizing its admission into the union but only became a state in 1953 when Congress passed an official proclamation doing so. These arguments have all been dismissed by federal courts.[40]

In President Woodrow Wilson's 1913 inaugural address before ratification was completed, he did not mention the income tax. Instead, President Wilson called for tariff reform. Many expected

---

[39]   This is not the only argument made by protesters of the constitutionality of the income tax. For example, some argue that the tax itself is not problematic, but that tax filing is a violation of the Fifth Amendment's privilege against self-incrimination and still others argue that the tax imposes involuntary servitude prohibited by the Thirteenth Amendment. Congress legislated the IRS cannot label anyone an "illegal tax protester" in 1998. Internal Revenue Service Restructuring and Reform Act of 1998, Pub. L. 105–206, 112 Stat. 685 (1998).

[40]   For example, Knoblauch v. Comm'r, 749 F.2d 200 (5th Cir. 1984), *cert. denied*, 474 U.S. 830 (1985); U.S. v. Porth, 426 F.2d 519 (10th Cir. 1970), *cert. denied*, 400 U.S. 824 (1970); Swallow v. U.S., 307 F.2d 81 (10th Cir. 1962), *cert denied* 371 U.S. 950 (1963), *rehearing denied*, 372 U.S. 924 (1963).

Wilson to use the income tax to make up revenues lost when tariff reform reduced government receipts. Then, after the ratification of the Sixteenth Amendment, President Wilson called a special congressional session, and the House Committee on Ways and Means reported a bill less than a week later. The Underwood-Simmons Tariff of 1913 applied a graduated tax on individual incomes above a $3,000 exemption for individuals or $4,000 for married couples.[41] These exemptions were high when the mean adult male income was only $578.[42] The proposed tax differed from earlier income taxes because it was not seen as a temporary measure for the purpose of securing revenue for short-term purposes but as a permanent part of the revenue system.

Many scholars who examine the early history of the federal income tax describe its adoption and development as progressive in intention. They argue that the income tax was adopted to further ideals of social justice.[43] Others, however, note the dearth of interest groups participating in the income tax's creation and see the adoption of the income tax more as a defensive measure, a means to preserve the status quo and protect the elite from more radical class legislation or social change.[44] More recently scholars have situated the income tax within the framework of fiscal policy or broader economic objectives of the era.[45] In this view, the tax system cannot be isolated from larger policy objectives and social movements.

At first the revenue generated by the income tax was minimal, in 1914 yielding only $28 million, or 2.4% of federal revenue. In 1913, only 1.5% of all households paid federal income taxes, and only 2% of the labor force paid income taxes each year from 1913 through 1915. The tax's yield grew at a faster rate than the number of taxpayers but remained relatively small until 1917 and World War I. In 1915, the federal income tax raised $41 million, when the top rate was 7%, and nearly $68 million in 1916 when the top rate was raised to 15%.[46]

---

[41]   Revenue Act of 1913, ch. 16, 38 Stat. 114 (1913).

[42]   ROBERT STANLEY, DIMENSIONS OF LAW IN THE SERVICE OF ORDER: ORIGINS OF THE FEDERAL INCOME TAX, 1861–1913, at 249 (1993).

[43]   See, e.g., JOHN D. BUENKER, THE INCOME TAX AND THE PROGRESSIVE ERA (1985); SIDNEY RATNER, TAXATION AND DEMOCRACY IN AMERICA (1967); RANDOLPH E. PAUL, TAXATION IN THE UNITED STATES (1954); ROY G. AND GLADYS C. BLAKEY, THE FEDERAL INCOME TAX (1940).

[44]   See, e.g., STANLEY, supra note 42; JOHN F. WITTE, THE POLITICS AND DEVELOPMENT OF THE FEDERAL INCOME TAX (1985).

[45]   See, e.g., W. ELLIOTT BROWNLEE, FEDERAL TAXATION IN AMERICA: A SHORT HISTORY (2004); STEVEN R. WEISMAN, THE GREAT TAX WARS (2002); ROBERT HIGGS, CRISIS AND LEVIATHAN (1987).

[46]   W. Elliott Brownlee, Historical Perspective on U.S. Tax Policy Toward the Rich, in DOES ATLAS SHRUG? 29, 41–42 (Joel Slemrod ed., 2000); WITTE, supra note 44, at 79.

The $177 million budget deficit caused by World War I caused Congress to increase tax rates and lower personal exemptions. By the end of 1918, the U.S.'s daily average war expenditure almost doubled that of Great Britain and was far greater than in any other combatant nation. To fund the nation's participation in the war, more than $1 billion was raised by the federal income tax, with exemptions reduced from $4,000 for heads of families and $3,000 for single individuals to $2,000 and $1,000 respectively, and top rates raised to 67% in 1917 and 77% in 1918.[47]

The changes enacted during World War I meant that the income tax's impact on wealth was more similar to the current income tax than the Civil War tax. Before World War I, 90% of federal revenues came from regressive excise taxes or tariffs. By 1918, the income tax accounted for almost 68% of the federal government's revenue. The war on shipping and decreased wartime demand for goods had drastically reduced tariff revenue; the income tax, primarily that on corporations and excess profits, largely filled the void. Those shouldering the burden of the stiffer individual income tax remained a small percentage of the population. In 1918, approximately 15% of American families had to pay personal income taxes, and the wealthiest 1% paid 80% of the revenues raised. The average effective rates for this group increased from 3% in 1916 to 15% in 1918.[48]

Following World War I, the U.S. famously sought a return to normalcy and, in the process, experienced a backlash against the academic experts who had advocated for progressive taxation and income redistribution before the war. The political standing of advocates for reform faded. In their place, the third richest man in America, Andrew Mellon, was appointed Secretary of the Treasury Department. In the 1920s, the higher, more progressive tax rates of World War I were reduced but not eliminated. Mellon's vision of limited taxation to spur economic growth became the model for the 1920s.[49] He reacted to opposing considerations: that people engaged in tax planning to avoid highly progressive taxes, thereby reducing tax revenue, but simply eliminating progressivity would spur demands for more radical changes to capitalism. As a result, Mellon preserved a limited progressive tax.

Mellon's tax base was insufficient for President Franklin D. Roosevelt's plan to spend the country's way out of the Great Depression without deficit spending. Consequently, President

---

[47]   Act of Sept. 8, 1916, Pub. L. 64–271, c. 463, § 1(a), 39 Stat. 756; Act of March 3, 1917, Pub. L. 64–377, c. 159, 39 Stat. 1000.

[48]   BROWNLEE, FEDERAL TAXATION IN AMERICA, *supra* note 45, at 63.

[49]   Mellon published a book explaining his tax philosophy in 1924. ANDREW MELLON, TAXATION: THE PEOPLE'S BUSINESS (1924).

Roosevelt struggled to raise taxes, not all of which were progressive, to fund his spending programs. For example, the New Deal witnessed the advent of the Social Security system, a regressive tax, which has developed into the second largest revenue raising tax in the U.S. President Roosevelt's larger "soak the rich" plans did not win widespread political support.

The Great Depression challenged much of the nation's thinking about economics, although experts had little role initiating this change during the early New Deal. Early in the depression when faced with a massive deficit, President Roosevelt and Secretary of the Treasury Department Henry Morgenthau sought to close tax loopholes and prevent tax evasion. Morgenthau had studied architecture and agriculture in college but developed into an orthodox economist believing in balanced budgets and stable currency. Led by Morgenthau, the Treasury Department viewed taxes as a way to balance the budget rather than as a means to redistribute wealth. However, consistent with more popular theories, New Deal economics avoided taxing consumption and taxed savings to meet the needs of the times. This produced progressive income tax rates. A mini-recession in 1937–1938 made tax cuts, not reform, more widely popular.

By the end of the Great Depression, a rising voice in economics began to reestablish the prominence of academics in government. John Maynard Keynes was an English economist who challenged the classical idea that free markets would provide full employment if workers were flexible in their wage demands. Instead, Keynes argued that governments should use fiscal and monetary policies to mitigate economic recessions and depressions.[50] His seminal 1936 work, *The General Theory of Employment, Interest, and Money*, was the standard economic model for much of the post-World War II period.

Despite the focus on fiscal policy, early versions of Keynesian economics envisioned a relatively small role for taxation. The disregard for taxation was, in part, the result of the shape of the tax itself. Because of the income tax's limited reach as a tax on the elite and the limited progressivity of tax rates, a federal tax cut was viewed as a benefit only to the wealthy. Before World War II, the nation saw federal spending as the primary means to encourage economic growth.

---

[50]   Fiscal policy involves changing tax rates and government spending to influence aggregate demand in the economy; whereas monetary policy involves changing the interest rate and money supply to encourage the public to borrow or invest.

(e) Post-World War II

During World War II, President Roosevelt urged reform of the tax system; however, the need for revenue drove changes more than a widespread desire for reform in its own right. By the end of the war nearly 90% of the workforce was required to submit federal income tax returns and 60% paid some amount of income tax.[51] Tax rates were raised and made more progressive, ranging from 22% to 94%. The income tax raised $45 billion in 1945, which was about 54% of what the government spent that year on the war effort.[52] Since the war, tax rates have fallen and, with lower top rates, the tax is less progressive. Nevertheless, World War II had a profound impact on the tax system, converting the individual income tax into the bread and butter of the federal government and from a tax on elites to a tax on the masses.

World War II also changed many policymakers' perception of how best to stimulate the economy. With the expansion of the tax base and reduction of tax exemptions, tax policy was increasingly put ahead of spending policy to stimulate growth, both because it could help the middle class and because taxes contained greater built-in flexibility. With a tax that reached the masses, tax rate cuts would increase more people's disposable incomes so that their spending could stimulate the economy. Changes in taxes also have built-in flexibility; taxes raise more revenue in good economic times and less when the economy is bad because less income is earned. This responsiveness is an automatic countercyclical tool.

The acceptance of an active tax policy grew with the understanding of what taxation could do. Tax policy became a larger tool to the government because taxes raised significant revenue and changing withholding rates quickly impacted taxpayers' disposable incomes. Thus, Congress could increase or decrease revenue as it desired and restrict or free up the public's spending power. Additionally, the broad-based income tax ushered in an era of easy financing that permitted politicians to enact targeted tax cuts while also financing new expenditures. A professor at the Wharton School of Finance argued, "More and more, taxation is being related to the problems of the economy—to such objectives as increasing the national income, stabilizing the economy, maintaining high-level employment, encouraging investment, and increasing the flow of consumer purchasing."[53] Thus, tax policy, especially in the individual

---

[51]   WITTE, *supra* note 44, at 126.

[52]   Christopher Tassava, *The American Economy During World War II*, ECON. HIST. ASSN., https://eh.net/encyclopedia/the-american-economy-during-world-war-ii/ (last visited May 1, 2018).

[53]   Alfred G. Buehler, *Taxation and the Economy*, 3 NAT'L TAX J. 121 (1950).

income tax, was no longer an ancillary issue to tariffs but a central concern for policymakers.

The end of World War II and the resulting surplus in federal revenue focused the public's and policymakers' attention on tax cuts. Politicians sought tax cuts to stimulate investment and encourage consumer demand as the government decreased its own demand for war materials. However, at the same time the government feared inflation, and standard economic theory held that tax reduction would exacerbate inflation. This tension between growth and inflation reverberated through tax policy choices.

Initially, tax reduction trumped fears of inflation. From the time Republicans took control of both houses of Congress in 1946, tax reduction was their priority. They argued that if taxes were not reduced, the combined federal surplus for fiscal years 1948 and 1949 would be almost $16 billion. Taxes would crush initiative, destroy free enterprise, and possibly result in socialism or communism. On the other hand, Democratic President Harry Truman thought that the surplus would not last and should be used to fund the U.S.'s new international obligations, such as the Marshall Plan, which was over $12 billion of U.S. financial aid to Western Europe. A 1948 tax rate cut overcame three presidential vetoes when the rate cuts were combined with narrow preferences for diverse interest groups.[54]

Despite the fear of inflation and President Truman's concerns, in practice both political parties used tax reduction to stimulate the postwar economy. In the process, taxation was largely abandoned as an instrument to mobilize class interests for much of the second half of the 20th century. Notwithstanding this agreement, there was little consensus on the most effective form of tax cuts, both between and within the parties. The result was contradictory legislative changes. During the early 1950s, legislation widened loopholes, reducing taxes on the wealthy by approximately 25% even as top statutory rates rose.[55] Pressure for tax reduction mounted as the country experienced numerous minor recessions, but policymakers sought to keep the tax reduction hidden.

The underlying tension over tax's potential impact increased economists' influence because economists were thought able to predict the impact of legislative changes. Influenced by Keynes, New Keynesian Economics considered savings a virtue, not unexpected in an era of pent-up consumer demand and beset by fears of inflation. To achieve full employment, capital investment was thought more important than progressive taxation. Therefore, popular perceptions

---

[54]   Revenue Act of 1948, Pub. L. 80–471, §§ 301–303, 62 Stat. 110, 114–16 (1948).

[55]   Brownlee, *Historical Perspective, supra* note 46, at 29–73, 61.

of the best tax policy largely swung to encouraging savings and investment through targeted tax reduction and away from the New Deal focus on reducing wealth concentration.

Despite the majority re-envisioning the goals of tax policy, not all politicians or academics agreed with cutting taxes to stimulate growth. Political leaders enlisted the help of increasingly divided members of the economics academy to develop policies consistent with their ideals. Economists identified as either conservatives, supply-side liberals, or demand-side liberals vied for control over policy. Put simply, conservative economists advocated tax cuts on the theory that taxes distort the free market and threatened America's ability to compete against communism; supply-side liberal economists advocated reduced taxes on high incomes and corporations, with a goal to stimulate the economy and increase employment; and demand-side liberal economists did not accept the conservative and supply-side premise that high marginal rates would distort economic behavior or reduce economic growth and thought the revenue could be put to better use after being collected by the government.

The splintering in economics was coupled with a pervasive shift in theory away from the incorporation of social values into economic analysis. In the late 20th century it became less acceptable to discuss distributive justice or fairness as economic objectives. Instead, economists increasingly measured outcomes in terms of efficiency. Much as the nation was focused on economic growth, that too became the central goal in economics.

The focus on growing the economy resonated with the intensification of the Cold War. Government officials worried that, "[t]o a very substantial extent, the conflict between the East and West today is an economic one, a struggle between conflicting economic ideologies."[56] Policymakers argued that the federal government needed to cut taxes to stimulate national economic growth to compete with the Soviet Union. Economists were expected to help policymakers accomplish this growth.

As part of this developing, post-war focus, many scholars no longer supported, and some attacked, progressive taxation. Despite the income tax's origins as a progressive response to the Gilded Age, its power for redistribution lost influence. As scholars debated whether the American tax system was in fact progressive or even should be, Australian economist Colin Clark's warning in the popular *Harper's Magazine* that high levels of taxation, often interpreted as

---

[56]   J. ECON. COMM., FEDERAL TAX POLICY FOR ECONOMIC GROWTH AND STABILITY, 84th Cong. ix (Comm. Print 1955).

requiring progressive rates, would result in destructive inflation.[57] According to Clark's work, when taxation exceeds 25% of GNP, inflation is inevitable. The concern was the unintended consequences of progressive taxation.

The attack on progressive rates was also at the theoretical level. In 1952, Professors Walter Blum and Harry Kalven, Jr. published their essay, *The Uneasy Case for Progressive Taxation*.[58] Although personally supporting progressivity, they concluded that support for this form of income taxation could only be made on the grounds of income redistribution. Conservative political economist F.A. Hayek then argued that redistributive policies fostered class discrimination and threatened tyrannies of the majority.[59] These and other attacks on progressive taxation supported the new focus on growing the national economic pie instead of redistributing the slices.

Of course not everyone in the second half of the 20th century attacked progressivity, but the goal fell in political importance. For example, congressional hearings held in 1955 focused the tax on "enhanc[ing] the built-in stabilizing capacity of the Federal tax system" and "encourag[ing] the balanced growth of the economy."[60] Congress did not agree that an objective of the tax code was to increase fairness or to redistribute income. Some politicians used the accepted goals as justification to cut tax rates. Proposals circulated in Congress for a constitutional amendment to limit federal income and estate taxation to 25%.[61]

However, inflation remained a concern for those who wanted to cut taxes. The accepted wisdom was that cutting taxes would increase spending which would increase inflation; inflation occurs when prices rise without economic growth because the dollar's purchasing power declines. As people spend money without increasing production, they simply spend more for each purchase without getting more because more is not available. Consequently,

---

[57]   Colin Clark, *The Danger of High Taxes*, HARPER'S MAGAZINE 67 (1950). The academic basis of this work was published at *Public Finance and Changes in the Value of Money*, 55 ECON. J. 371, 376 (1945).

[58]   Walter J. Blum & Harry Kalven, Jr., *The Uneasy Case for Progressive Taxation*, 19 U. CHI. L. REV. 417 (1952).

[59]   F.A. HAYEK, THE ROAD TO SERFDOM (1944).

[60]   S. Rep. 84–1606, JOINT ECONOMIC REPORT, 105–08 (1956).

[61]   The idea was developed in 1937 by former Congressman Thomas W. Phillips, Jr. and had been introduced to Congress in 1939, 1945, 1947, 1951, and 1953 with variations as to implementation and percentages. *See* Erwin Griswold, *Can We Limit Taxes to 25 Percent*, 190 ATL. MONTHLY 76 (1952); Walter W. Heller & Irma A. Linse, *Implications of a Twenty-Five Percent Ceiling on Federal Income and Death Tax Rates*, 38 IOWA L. REV. 661 (1953). There was an exchange about the proposal in the American Bar Association Journal and the ABA created a Special Committee on Income Tax Amendment to study the issue. *See* 39 A.B.A.J. 25, 206, 883 (1953); 40 A.B.A.J. 35 (1954).

the government sought to increase production and limit spending to keep prices stable.

The tax battle against inflation came to a head in 1968 when President Lyndon Johnson enacted a 10% income tax surcharge after having signed two major tax cuts.[62] As the cost of the Vietnam War grew, coupled with the administration's desire to build a more comprehensive welfare state in his Great Society, President Johnson asked for the tax but only after advisors warned of war-borne inflation. The Great Society used federal spending in an attempt to end poverty and racial injustice and created Medicare and Medicaid that have grown to major components of the federal budget.[63] However, the temporary tax did little to curb consumer spending and little to stem double-digit inflation in the 1970s.

Despite the tax cuts and subsequent tax increase, tax policy fell in relative importance in the mid-1960s and 1970s as it was only tangentially involved in the growth of the Great Society. With most of the nation focused on economic growth and inflation, tax reform grabbed headlines only following major triggers. For example, in 1969 immediately before Richard Nixon's inauguration, the revelation that 155 people with adjusted gross incomes over $200,000, including twenty-one individuals with incomes over $1 million, paid no federal income tax triggered calls for reform.[64] Nevertheless, economic worries and a political split between Congress and the presidency limited the ability to enact changes to the tax system. The new Nixon administration responded with some tax simplification, a bit of tax reduction, and a host of targeted tax benefits.

Tax policy regained a prominent role in the 1980s, as a centerpiece of President Ronald Reagan's plan for revitalizing America. In the 1980s, as in 1948, congressional Republicans proposed across-the-board tax rate cuts, but the political process resulted in a broader bill that dispersed tax reduction among different groups. Republicans cut tax rates in 1981 from a statutory high of 70% in 1981 to 50% in 1982.[65] However, the revenue loss coupled with increased military spending necessitated restructuring and eliminating many of the cuts in 1982.[66]

---

[62]   Revenue and Expenditure Control Act of 1968, Pub. L. 90–364, 82 Stat. 251.

[63]   The Great Society resembled the New Deal in that spending addressed education, medical care, urban and rural problems, and transportation, among others.

[64]   *Treasury Secretary Warns of Taxpayers' Revolt*, N.Y. TIMES, Jan. 18, 1969, at 15.

[65]   Economic Recovery Tax Act of 1981, Pub. L. 97–34, 95 Stat. 172.

[66]   Tax Equity and Fiscal Responsibility Act of 1982, Pub. L. 97–248, 96 Stat. 324.

President Reagan's tax policy objectives coincided with a new group of supply-side economists, united behind a theory opposing Keynesian demand-side theorists prominent in the years following the Great Depression. Supply-siders argued that the way to achieve economic growth was through investing in capital and lowering barriers on the production of goods and services, which included taxes. This created a battle between experts as to which theory should dominate tax policy.

Supply-side economics did not prevent the revenue loss from tax cuts or the increased military spending. These two events necessitated restructuring and eliminating many of the earlier tax cuts in 1986.[67] Nevertheless, top tax rates were lowered from 50% to 28% and parts of the tax system were simplified. Codification of the Internal Revenue Code in 1986 solidified some of these changes. In the process, the tax burden shifted towards payroll taxes and investment taxes and away from capital gains and high-income earners.

That focus on growth has remained largely in place in the post-Reagan years, although the rhetoric changes, and the centrality of tax to political debates at times wanes. For example, tax policy was less significant in the 2016 than in the 2012 presidential election. When tax policy is a popular topic, much of modern debate is framed around tax deductions and credits as on rate reductions and increases.[68] This can be seen in 2000 when tax reduction was an important issue and took targeted form, namely as favorable rates for dividends and capital gains.[69] This newer movement has added many targeted tax preferences throughout the Code.

The new method of dispensing tax benefits is largely a result of budgeting constraints and the 1976 creation of the earned income tax credit. Congress learned that tax preferences could spread tax relief and do so with less budgetary conflict. The last decade has also seen tax credits framed as expiring provisions to further ease budgetary tensions. With the push to use the tax system to accomplish many goals beyond revenue raising, these new additions have increased the complexity of the tax system and isolated the system to bands of experts—lawyers, accountants, and economists—as tax policy has become increasingly specialized.

Increased partisanship throughout the nation and the resilience of the Tea Party movement has severely divided national debates on

---

[67]   Tax Reform Act of 1986, Pub. L. 99–514, 100 Stat. 2085.

[68]   For more on the distinction between deductions and credits, see Chapter 17.01(c).

[69]   For more on capital gains, see Chapter 7.03.

tax policy. Although debates often eschew compromise, because of the permissive political process encouraging tax legislation changes are nevertheless enacted. These changes, satisfying neither the goal of forging consensus or of any single group, illustrate a wider malady that seems to afflict the taxpaying public.

§ 3.02   Historical Rates of Taxation

There has been significant fluctuation over time in the percentage of a person's income that is paid in taxes as well as the total amount of revenue that is raised. Because of taxpayer privacy laws, it is impossible to determine how much any given person paid in taxes or the average amount an average person paid at any point in time. The IRS maintains composite data for the nation but is lawfully required to keep secret all information that might pinpoint a particular taxpayer. Therefore, the only information we have is on a national scale and not about individual people.

(a) Statutory Rates

Statutory tax rates are those enacted by Congress. These are the rates listed in the statute, but they are not the amount of people's gross incomes that they actually pay in tax. Statutory rates hide the tax's real impact because they say nothing of the availability of deductions or exceptions that limit the application of these statutory rates. Nevertheless, statutory rates often receive significant political and popular attention. Congress can change statutory rates although the political cost of doing so often means it is easier for Congress to change other aspects of the tax system that attract less attention in order to raise revenue or to provide targeted tax reduction.

Despite popular awareness of statutory rates, they are not always straightforward. For example, tariff rates on imported goods differ depending upon the type of good and from where the goods come. Despite an international movement for free trade, tariffs remain applicable unless tariff treaties reduce the tax or trade penalties increase them, the latter currently applicable only for Cuba and North Korea. Consider that goats taxed at 68¢ per head under the general statutory rate are not taxed from a listed group of countries and are taxed $3 per head if the goats come from Cuba or North Korea. And footwear with a protective metal toecap has a general 37.5% tax rate, but that rate is eliminated or reduced if from listed countries and is 75% if from Cuba and North Korea.[70]

The income tax's statutory rate is more complex because the tax is a progressive tax. Consequently, there are different statutory

---

[70]   U.S. INT'L TRADE COMM'N, HARMONIZED TARIFF SCHEDULE OF THE UNITED STATES (2017).

marginal rates at different income levels. For example, as of 2018 a single person's first dollar is taxed at 0% but $1 millionth dollar (assuming few deductions) is taxed at 37%, with seven rate brackets in between. The different rate brackets are the different marginal rates. Each marginal rate applies to some fragment of the taxpayer's total income. The top marginal rate is the rate applicable to the last dollar that is earned.

Individual Income Tax Top Marginal Tax Rate

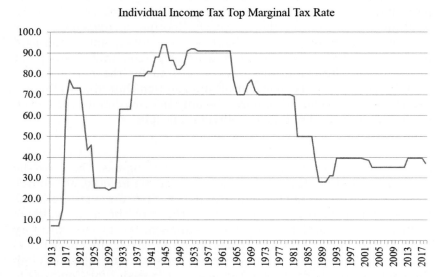

Based on IRS, SOI Tax Stats, Historical Table 23, https://www.irs.gov/uac/soi-tax-stats-historical-table-23.

Because top income tax rates only apply to a fragment of a taxpayer's income and much of a person's income can be offset with deductions, top rates are of limited usefulness in determining a person's total tax liability. For example, for the people of plenty in the early 1960s, although rates included 70%, 80%, and 90% brackets, wealthy individuals were actually paying an average of 48%.[71] The Chair of the House Committee on Ways and Means noted that the individual income tax is "borne principally by low and middle income groups because in most instances all their income is fully subject to tax."[72]

However, the top statutory rate is useful when taxpayers must decide whether to earn another dollar because the top marginal rate is the rate that applies to the next dollar earned. Therefore, the taxpayer's top statutory rate tells the taxpayer how much of the next

---

[71]   Stanley S. Surrey, *The Federal Income Tax Base for Individuals*, 58 COLUM. L REV. 815, 816 (1958).

[72]   Wilbur Mills, *Preface*, 44 VA. L. REV. 835, 836 (1958).

dollar earned the taxpayer can keep. If a person is in the 35% top tax bracket, the person will receive 65¢ of the next dollar earned, minus any payroll and state and local taxes owed on that dollar. Economists urge people to make choices at the margins and to consider only the marginal costs, including marginal taxes, when making economic decisions.

Unfortunately, not everyone understands the nuance in this analysis. Some interpret their top marginal tax bracket as the amount they pay in taxes. This overstates the amount of tax that is owed, often significantly. Some even think of the top statutory rate in the Code as the amount they pay even if that rate does not apply to any of their income. This is often wrong, as top marginal tax rates applied to fewer than 0.66% of U.S. taxpayers in 2014.[73]

Top statutory rates for all U.S. taxes have varied considerably throughout American history. For example, top rates in the individual income tax have ranged from 7% in 1913 to 94% in 1944. Spikes occurred in World War I and again from the Great Depression through World War II. Following the war, top rates only went below 50% in the late 1980s. What may be more surprising is the stickiness of rates; they do not change often—they have bounced between 39.6% and 35% for twenty-five years. Similarly, corporate income tax rates have varied significantly but are nonetheless relatively sticky. They began at 1% in 1909 and went up to 52.8% in 1968 and 1969 (still significantly lower than the top 70% individual income tax rates at the time). They remained at 35% for almost 25 years until 2017 when Congress cut the corporate income tax to a flat 21% rate.

Despite sometimes high rates, top statutory rates of either the individual or corporate income taxes often have limited applicability. Their application depends upon the amount of deductions that can reduce the income subject to tax. Additionally, the bracket structure means that top brackets may only apply to the highest levels of income. For example, in 1918, there were 56 different rate brackets, with the top rate applying to those earning over $15 million in 2013 dollars.[74] And during the three years from 1935 through 1937, the top income tax bracket only applied to a single person, John D. Rockefeller, Jr.[75] There has been political reluctance to reenact such a limited top statutory bracket. As of 2017, the top individual income rate applies to income over $500,000 for single individuals and

---

[73]   IRS, PUBLICATION 1304, Table 3.4 (2016).

[74]   TAX FOUNDATION, U.S. FEDERAL INDIVIDUAL INCOME TAX RATES HISTORY, 1862–2013, http://taxfoundation.org/sites/taxfoundation.org/files/docs/fed_individual_rate_history_adjusted.pdf.

[75]   MARK LEFF, THE LIMITS OF SYMBOLIC REFORM: THE NEW DEAL AND TAXATION, 1933–1939, at 292 (1984).

$600,000 for married couples, or approximately 900,000 households.[76]

(b) Average Rates

A taxpayer's average tax rate is also known as the taxpayer's effective tax rate. The average tax rate is the amount paid in taxes divided by the taxpayer's total income.

TAXES PAID ÷ TOTAL INCOME = AVERAGE TAX RATE

Average rates are useful because they explain how much a person pays of each dollar that is earned. Therefore, a progressive income tax will always have a lower average tax rate than the applicable top marginal rate, which is the tax rate applied to the last dollar earned. Historically, average rates received little popular attention but have gained traction with some politicians and economic leaders. For example, billionaire Warren Buffett pointed out that his secretary had a higher average tax rate than he did.[77] Buffett paid more in absolute tax dollars but because he had more deductions and income taxed at lower capital gain rates, she paid a higher percentage of her income to the government.

The average tax generally provides more information regarding how much taxpayers pay to the government. For example, in 1918 the top marginal rate was 77% but the average rate for taxpayers in that bracket was only 15%.[78] Congress's ability to carve out income that is subject to high tax rates makes top marginal numbers less useful when discussing the impact of taxes on most people. To understand how much a person pays in taxes, knowing the amount that comes out of each dollar is often more important than knowing how much comes out of the last dollar earned.

Not everyone agrees on average rates because the average tax rate depends upon how total income is defined. Consequently, it is important to understand what the effective tax rate purports to say. The JCT uses gross income, or income before any deductions, as the measure of total income to highlight the importance of tax deductions in the tax system. Alternatively, the accounting term "effective income rate" uses taxable income after deductions are claimed. By accepting deductions as a given, the accounting method generally has a larger effective tax rate than under the JCT's system. Some call the

---

[76]   Rev. Proc. 2016–55, 2016–45 I.R.B. 707.

[77]   Warren Buffett, *Stop Coddling the Super-Rich*, N.Y. TIMES, Aug. 14, 2011. Buffett included payroll and income taxes in his calculations.

[78]   BROWNLEE, FEDERAL TAXATION IN AMERICA, *supra* note 45, at 63.

effective rate used in tax the "average effective" as opposed to the "marginal effective" tax rate used in accounting. For a taxpayer with significant deductions, the differences are substantial.

Few studies examine the average impact of taxes because of the difficulty of knowing who pays what in taxes.[79] Any estimate of average taxes requires the government understand the interaction of all taxes on all people. The information is not collected because of the difficulty of doing so and because of taxpayer confidentiality laws. Comparing rates in 1979 and 2011, one estimate found that in 1979 the top 1% paid an average of 35% of their income in federal taxes but, as of 2011, the percentage paid was 29%.[80] For the lowest quintile, in 1979, the average paid was 7.5% but, in 2011, was 1.9%. From those numbers, the amount people have paid in taxes from each dollar earned has fallen across the board, although the decline in average taxes was greatest for the lowest quintile.

Focusing on the income tax as a component of federal taxes, the average amount of taxes paid fell from 1979 until 2011. For the lowest quintile, in 1979, the average individual income tax rate was 0% and, in 2011, was negative 7.5%. The number became negative because credits provide low-income taxpayers refunds. Even for the second quintile of taxpayers, the after-income tax rate was negative in 2011, in that people received back more than they paid. At the other end of the economic spectrum, for the top 1% in 1979 the after-income tax average rate was 22.7% and, in 2011, was 20.3%.

(c) National Tax Revenue

The federal government's revenue raised through taxes has been capped by the law and by the government's administrative capacity. Nevertheless, revenue has increased dramatically in absolute amounts since the second half of the 19th century.

---

[79]   For a discussion of the incidence of tax, see Chapter 4.02(d).

[80]   TAX POLICY CENTER, HISTORICAL AVERAGE FEDERAL TAX RATES FOR ALL INCOMES, http://www.taxpolicycenter.org/statistics/historical-average-federal-tax-rates-all-households.

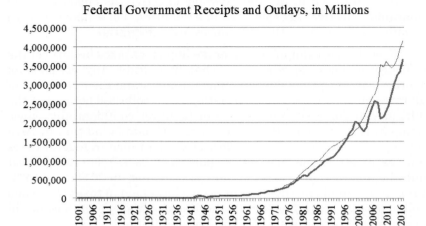

Office of Mgmt. & Budget, Historical Table 1.1—Summary of Receipts, Outlays, and Surpasses or Deficits.

However, part of the increase in both federal receipts and outlays is the result of inflation, which hides the real impact of taxes. With inflation, each dollar of tax revenue purchases less. As the cost of items rises because of inflation, it generally rises for all consumers, including the federal government.

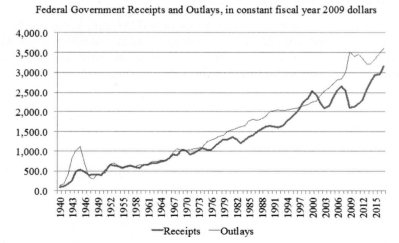

Office of Mgmt. & Budget, Historical Table 1.3—Summary of Receipts, Outlays, and Surpasses or Deficits, in current dollars, constant (FY 2009).

Although the amount of government revenue has increased dramatically even when controlling for inflation, this increase only tells part of the story. Despite the increase in tax revenue, that amount has not grown significantly as compared to the nation's gross domestic product (GDP). Until the mid-1900s, federal spending was consistently about 3% of GDP. Thereafter, despite changes in tax rates, tax revenues as a percentage of GDP has averaged just under 19%.[81] The reasons for this seemingly constant amount of revenue are unknown. It may be because taxpayers respond to changes in rates as economists predict. Alternatively, GDP may change as a result of changes in taxes or it may be that there is maximum amount that the government can absorb. Regardless, tax revenue as a percentage of the nation's economy has proven remarkably stable despite the dominant political party changing in Congress and the presidency.

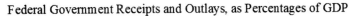

Federal Government Receipts and Outlays, as Percentages of GDP

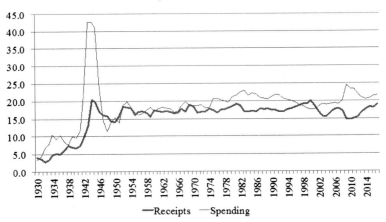

Office of Mgmt. & Budget, Historical Table 1.2—Summary of Receipts, Outlays, and Surpasses or Deficits, As Percentages of GDP.

Despite a relatively consistent amount of tax revenue as a percentage of GDP, the source of that revenue has changed significantly over the years. The types of taxes have changed as has reliance on the different types. Although tariffs could raise large amounts of revenue, there was counter-pressure in the form of reduced demand for goods with high tariffs. The introduction of the income tax and then payroll taxes were less susceptible to supply and demand. For example, even increased spending on Medicare and Medicaid did not result in a significant increase in tax revenue as a

---

[81]   W. Kurt Hauser, *There's No Escaping Hauser's Law*, WALL ST. J., Dec. 8, 2010.

percentage of GDP. What has changed is who is impacted the most because of the changing sources of tax revenue. Tariffs and payroll taxes tend to be more regressive than the income tax.

Percentage Composition of Federal Receipts By Source

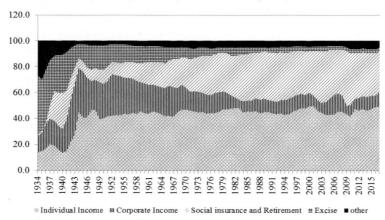

Office of Mgmt. & Budget, Historical Table 2.2—Percentage Composition of Receipts By Source: 1934-2021.

What we do know from historical records is that taxes spiked during World War II and never came back down. Even when war spending declined, the government had to repay its borrowing. Thereafter, larger social insurance obligations began to demand revenue. That revenue came from the individual income tax and payroll taxes. The change in the role of government and source of revenue has demanded a new and sustained role for revenue-raising tax policy.

Chapter 4

STANDARDS TO JUDGE
THE TAX SYSTEM

Table of Sections

Because people do not come to tax policy debates with the same background, they often bring to discussions widely different expectations. These differences may be hard to discern because people use shorthand to convey important values and understandings of various policies. They may think the shorthand is clear to everyone, but terms are rarely defined or universally understood. Therefore, to be able to decide on the "best" tax policy, it is first necessary to develop a rubric to judge proposals. This chapter discusses possible values for the rubric but does not purport to rank or definitively define them for the diverse American politic.

§ 4.01   Basic Tax Values

The three most common values used in evaluations of tax policy are fairness (also referred to as equity), efficiency, and simplicity. Thus, politicians routinely state that they want to create a "fair" tax system that is "efficient" and "simple."

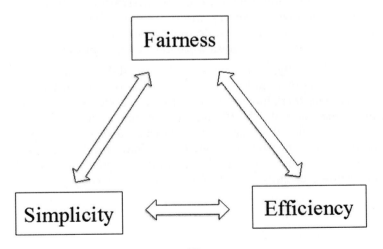

It is often hard for individuals to rank these values for themselves, and much harder for the nation to rank them. Part of the difficulty of ordering these values is that there is no universal definition of any of the terms. Moreover, these values may conflict so that prioritization is necessary. Does the public prefer a fairer system that reduces economic growth? Or does the public want a simple system even if it is less fair to individuals or raises their taxes? Or is economic growth worth a less fair distribution of taxes or a complex system to achieve the growth? If the tax system cannot accomplish everything, it must sacrifice some goals to achieve others; alternatively, the goals may reinforce each other.

In addition to the difficulty of defining and ranking these values, there may also be a political benefit in not doing so. It is easier to promise everything and say that the "tax system should be simple, fair, efficient, and pro-growth."[1] If politicians and policymakers probe constituents' values, they risk creating significant debate about the validity of the meanings and rankings of the values themselves. That debate would likely derail discussions of tax policies. By leaving open and ambiguous the meaning of tax values, policymakers also allow the public to see into the law the values they want to find.

(a) Fairness

The idea of fairness has a long and tortured history in philosophy, and most Americans do not become philosophers before discussing tax policy. Instead, politicians and the public generally use fairness as shorthand for less academic ideas of governmental and societal obligations of one person to another. That the notion of equity is multi-faceted and can be defined in many different ways makes determinations of fairness difficult. Additionally, a conception of fairness alone is insufficient; the administration of the tax system must make the law fair in operation. Complex economic and social factors might make it impossible to administer a tax system that is fair in practice, even if fairness were defined and put into statute.

More basically, comparing different definitions of fairness underscores the fact that what is fair to one person may not be fair to another. The term has yet to be defined in a way that the majority of the country accepts. Until that acceptance is reached, fairness's value in tax policy debates is more to raise awareness of potential problems than to provide solutions. That limited objective is valuable. The process of identifying unfair tax policies may help the nation create a broadly acceptable meaning of fairness.

---

[1]   Exec. Order 13789 (Apr. 21, 2017).

Different theories of fairness often lead to particular features in the tax system. For those who hold a stronger sense of obligation for others, fairness often demands a higher level of taxation. For those who have a stronger sense of independence and self-sufficiency, fairness often requires a lower level of taxation. If a person believes that it is only appropriate to tax based on how much a person benefits from the government, the person is more likely to support a tax on consumption than a tax on incomes. In this way, one's sense of equity can push towards, or be used to justify, a particular form of taxation.

(i) Ability to Pay

American debates about tax policy often invoke the theory that people should be taxed according to their ability to pay taxes. This concept has been popular since at least Adam Smith, and there remains something satisfying to most American politicians in saying that people should pay according to their ability.[2] Ability to pay generally implies some sense of progressive taxation because those with more income spend a smaller percentage on necessities and, therefore, can pay a larger percentage in taxes.

This concept might seem intuitive in a world of two people—a rich person and a destitute one. The rich person can certainly afford to pay more in taxes than the destitute person. However, as between a teacher, small business owner, and chef, who can afford to pay more? Should the determination be limited to their wages or include their investments and retirement savings? Should the government consider their obligations to provide for children or parents or charity? Should their lifestyle or education levels impact their ability to pay? These questions do not have definitive answers. Instead, each person can frame her own. Ultimately, political compromise develops answers for the country. Despite this complexity, all of these questions must be answered with the support of the taxpaying public to create a system based on taxpayers' ability to pay.

Although often used to support progressive taxation, ability to pay principles do not define the amount of progressivity in tax rates that is best. When coupled with a desire for small government, for example, the resulting progressivity may be limited.[3] Additionally, defining a person's "ability to pay" has proven impossible in any

---

[2]   ADAM SMITH, AN INQUIRY INTO THE NATURE AND CAUSES OF THE WEALTH OF NATIONS, Book V, ch. 2.25 (1776). For a review of the history of the ability to pay, see Joseph M. Dodge, *Theory of Tax Justice: Ruminations on the Benefit, Partnership, and Ability-to-Pay Principles*, 58 TAX L. REV. 399 (2005); Stephen Utz, *Ability to Pay*, 23 WHITTIER L. REV. 867 (2002).

[3]   Exemption levels, or some amount of income that is not subject to tax, creates a progressive tax even in an otherwise flat tax system. For more on flat rate taxation, see Chapter 4.02(b).

quantifiable sense. A purist may argue that ability should be measured with a subjective valuation: Each person determines what they can pay, including in their calculation nonmarket items such as leisure and psychic income. More mainstream advocates suggest an objective valuation of one's ability, looking to wages or the receipt of money or market items rather than a person's subjective utility.[4] In this latter interpretation, the ability to pay is limited to net income with limited incorporation of personal obligations or expenses.

(ii) Utilitarianism

A concept of tax fairness as old as the ability to pay is utilitarianism.[5] Utilitarianism is a broad category of philosophical theory that seeks to maximize utility, which may be defined as a measure of satisfaction or happiness. This desire to maximize happiness may permit the ends to justify the means of accomplishing it, so that any tax system that maximizes utility is a good thing. As applied to governments, utilitarianism generally holds that society should maximize utility, or maximize total benefit and reduce total suffering.

The act of paying taxes rarely, if ever, brings a person happiness; therefore, the goal for utilitarianism is to minimize the pain created from taxation. The person who should pay the most in a fair tax system is the person who suffers the least pain when doing so.

Coupled with this conception is the utilitarian principle of the declining marginal utility of income. Declining utility means that people derive less utility from each dollar as they have more dollars. Under this combined theory, Congress accomplishes the greatest good taking more from the wealthy than from the poor because there is less pain generated. This has been used to justify progressive tax rates.

---

[4]   E.R.A. SELIGMAN, PROGRESSIVE TAXATION IN THEORY AND PRACTICE 200 (1894).

[5]   JOHN STUART MILL, THE COLLECTED WORKS OF JOHN STUART MILL, vol. 10, at 258 (1963).

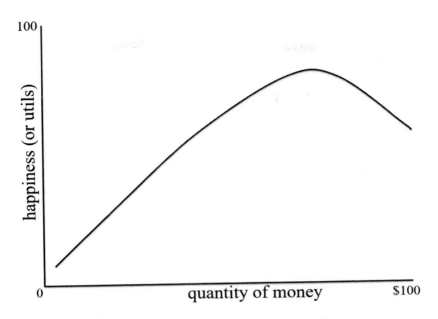

The main difficulty, and perhaps fatal flaw, of utilitarianism is the impossibility of quantifying utility. Most economists accept that different people have different marginal utilities. In other words, people with the same income may value an extra dollar differently. This can be trivialized with the case of unlimited pizza; people will value an extra slice of pizza differently. At some point a person does not want another slice, but that point differs for each person. More pertinently for students, the public values an extra year of education differently; some choose graduate school but others do not.

If utility is not the same for everyone, utility may not universally decline. For example, some wealthy individuals may value each additional dollar more than the previous dollar, perhaps because they seek a threshold or greater status. Even if an additional dollar is not valued more, the wealthy may value the dollar more than a less wealthy individual values it. Because of the variance in utilities and the difficulty of quantifying them, deciding how progressive a tax can be based on income's declining marginal utility is impossible.

This basic conception of utilitarianism also permits people's desires to override their intellect. If people take happiness from money, they should keep the money unless someone else values the money more, even if in the long-term there may be wiser uses of the money. It is for this reason that greed and other negative feelings may need to be carved out as components of utility.[6] However, moving to more lenient definitions of utility risks it becoming an infinitely malleable concept that provides little aid to policymakers.

(iii) Benefit Principle

The benefit principle posits only that people should contribute to the government according to the benefits they receive from the government. This principle justifies fees for government services and tariffs on consumed goods. Because the person paying the tax is the consumer, there is a direct link between tax and consumption. Under this theory, redistribution through taxation is unfair. If taxpayers are to pay taxes to the extent they receive government-provided goods and services, decreasing the taxes of the poor relative to wealthier taxpayers violates the fairness principle. Instead, benefit theory likely requires a flat rate unless there is proof that wealthier taxpayers benefit sufficiently more than poorer taxpayers for them to pay higher rates.

Similar to other theories of fairness, the benefit principle depends on many measurements that are difficult or impossible to obtain. It is difficult, if not impossible, to quantify how much anyone benefits from any particular government-provided good or service. For example, who benefits from the military, roads, and functioning markets and, if so, how much do they benefit? Because benefits cannot be valued or apportioned with precision, basing a system on the amount a person benefits is likely impossible. Additionally, this theory ignores any possibility that the incidence of the tax may be shifted. If incidence can be shifted, the person who ultimately bears the burden of the tax may not be the one who consumed the taxed item.[7] The ability to shift taxes undercuts the practicability of benefit taxation.

Although the benefit principle was initially thought to justify only limited government, the principle has been expanded by the notion that the government provides public goods. Public goods are those things everyone enjoys without paying for them directly, such as clean air and public education. As a result of the expansion of government-provided goods, even market outcomes are a benefit provided by the government. For instance, under this theory Mark Zuckerberg was able to amass his wealth only because of the services provided by the government ranging from military security to roads to functioning markets. With this broader notion of goods, it may be

---

[6]   See John C. Harsanyi, *Morality and the Theory of Rational Behavior*, in UTILITARIANISM AND BEYOND 39, 56 (1982).

[7]   For more on the incidence of taxation, see Chapter 4.02(d).

possible to justify taxation based on outcomes (such as wealth) rather than being limited to inputs (such as consumption).

(iv) Tax on Faculty

A final basis for taxation, described in 1888 as the ideal tax base, is a tax on "faculty, or native or acquired power of production."[8] Faculty taxation taxes what people can earn rather than what they choose to earn. For this method of taxation to work, the government must be able to discern how much a person could earn if the person applied effort. In doing so, faculty taxation values a person's choice not to apply that effort. This eliminates any financial penalty on those who work hard to earn a living and any reward to those who choose not to work. Taxing people on what they could earn rather than what they choose to earn eliminates the current "premium on self-indulgence in the form of indolence, the waste of opportunities, and the abuse of natural powers."[9]

Faculty taxation has sufficient practical difficulties to be impossible to administer. Nevertheless, equity may require practical tax regimes be measured against this ideal. In other words, does a particular regime reward those who squander opportunities or punish those who accomplish more than their abilities would provide. This version of fairness suggests that a government's actions should be measured against a perfect regime rather than a readily administered one.

(v) Morality Versus Ethics

Discussions of fairness and equity often employ the terms morality and ethics. While fairness has many definitions, morality and ethics generally have singular definitions but multiple ways to achieve them. Morals are the principles upon which an individual decides whether a choice is right or wrong. Ethics are societal principles of right conduct. Therefore, a person has a personal moral choice whether that person wants to engage in tax planning, but American society has declined to label lawful tax planning unethical. Society has determined that illegal tax evasion is unethical, at least for lawyers who can be disbarred for tax evasion.

(b) Efficiency

Other discussants of tax policy argue that efficiency should be the tax system's primary objective. Similar to fairness, however, the concept of efficiency can mean different things to different people. This difference sometimes occurs without people realizing that they

---

8   Francis A. Walker, *The Bases of Taxation*, 3 POL. SCI. Q. 1, 15 (1888).

9   *Id.*

are not discussing the same idea. Therefore, it is not sufficient to say you want an efficient tax; efficiency must be defined further. Despite different possible meanings, anyone using efficiency to analyze policy choices invariably incorporates some version of economic theory into the discussion, and the core objective of this economic analysis is to increase the material wealth of society.

A governing model in much economic theory is an unfettered free market exchange, long assumed to achieve an increase in societal wealth. Of course, not everyone accepts this as the best economic theory. Even those who use the free market model accept that the world is not so simple as to support this model. In the real world, there are negative externalities, transaction costs, and market failures that reduce the effectiveness of the unfettered free market.[10] In other words, without something to offset these market imperfections, society's wealth is inexorably decreased.

An underlying question for those incorporating economic theory into tax policy debates is whether taxation is a cause of, or a potential solution to, these market failures.[11] On one hand, to the extent taxation is a market failure itself, it creates a deadweight cost by distorting supply and demand. Therefore, taxes should be reduced as much as possible to minimize the cost. Furthermore, significant attention should be given to ensure that the taxes that must exist do not distort choices any more than necessary to permit the free market to operate as best as possible. On the other hand, to the extent taxation is a potential solution to market imperfections by causing taxpayers to internalize externalities or to equalize transactions costs, taxes can be adjusted to offset problems that arise from other causes.

Adopting the latter view, many people popularly use the term efficiency when they want the tax system to encourage economic growth in the least costly way. This idea has been used to accelerate depreciation deductions for the wear and tear of business equipment faster than it actually wears down or to increase research tax credits to encourage specific types of business growth. Using tax to encourage growth requires an active tax policy, viewing tax as a tool to accomplish other goals.

---

[10]   Negative externalities occur when individuals or firms do not have to pay the full cost of their decisions, often illustrated with pollution. Transaction costs are incurred in making an economic exchange, including search and information costs, bargaining costs, and pricing and enforcement costs. Market failures occur when the allocation of goods and services are not efficient, i.e., there is no Pareto optimal outcome, often associated with information asymmetries, non-competitive markets, and public goods.

[11]   For more on economic theory, see Chapter 6.

This pro-economic growth conception of efficiency may or may not be constrained by a notion of Pareto efficiency, an economic concept created by Vilfredo Pareto. Pareto efficiency requires society allocate resources in such a way that it is impossible to make any one individual better off without making at least one person worse off. Thus, a Pareto improvement reallocates resources to make at least one person better off without making anyone else worse off, generally by "growing the pie." This is an economic constraint to prevent exploitation of the few to benefit the majority.

For example, the government can take $100 from Rich A and directly or indirectly give the $100 to Poor B if doing so improves Rich A by more than $100, such as $101. This could be achieved by educating Poor B to be a specialized worker in Rich A's business, thereby improving both A's and B's quality of life. However, if Poor B is made $105 better but Rich A is only made better by $99, or $1 less than the $100 taken from Rich A, the redistribution is not Pareto efficient. Under this theory, the government should undertake the former plan but not the latter despite society being $3 worse off with $201 rather than $204. Unfortunately, implementing this constraint in practice is all but impossible because of the many unintended consequences that might occur.

Using efficiency in another sense, most economists claim that efficient taxes are those in which the tax system is neutral and does not influence individuals' choices. When taxes affect choices, taxes are likely to cause a misallocation of resources among differently taxed items. Therefore, according to this conception of efficiency, taxes should not interfere with the free market either by encouraging or discouraging particular economic activities but should leave a level playing field of choices. Consequently, tax incentives designed to encourage behavior, even if they lead to economic growth, are anathema to those focused on this strand of economic efficiency.

A reason economists urge this form of efficiency is because it is impossible to predict exactly how people will respond to taxes. Economists describe responses as the substitution effect or the income effect but cannot quantify either *a priori*. The substitution effect results when people change their behavior to adopt a low-taxed activity and give up a preferred high-tax activity. For example, instead of working and paying employment and income taxes on earnings, a person might substitute a low-tax activity like leisure. Alternatively, the income effect results when people react to taxes by increasing the taxed activity to produce the same after-tax result. For example, a person might increase overtime work when tax rates rise if the person wants to raise a targeted amount of income to pay for a child's private school.

Whether a person responds with the substitution effect or income effect depends upon the elasticity of the person's response. If a person's response is highly elastic, a small tax leads to a large change in behavior. If a person's response is inelastic, even a large tax does not affect the person's behavior. At this time, economists are unable to precisely predict elasticities. Therefore, elasticity is a good theoretical construct but of limited help to policymakers.

Optimal tax theory attempts to design a tax that minimizes its distortion of market choices. A neutral tax avoids distortion completely so an optimal tax is completely neutral. But what is neutral in this context sometimes produces unusual results. For example, because taxes discourage the taxed activity, progressive rates may discourage a taxpayer from working at her optimal production level. As the taxpayer earns more income, a greater percentage goes to taxes even as she is more likely to choose leisure for the substitution effect. A regressive tax in which rates go down with more income might offset this effect. Therefore, regressive taxes might be optimal.

Similarly, Professor Edward McCaffery argues that women should be taxed at a lower tax rate than men.[12] Because women's work efforts are more elastic than men's they are more likely to change their behavior because of tax rate changes. Consequently, Congress should impose lower tax rates on women than on men because women are more likely to leave work when their take-home pay is lower. Reducing women's rates will increase their work hours while men, with less elasticity in their work effort, will maintain their work hours with higher tax rates.

One proponent of optimal tax theory, Arthur Laffer, made famous the Laffer curve, although the theory of the curve had existed for many centuries. The Laffer curve demonstrates the optimal tax rate for revenue maximization (in the figure on the next page at 50%) and for growth maximization (in the figure at 30%). Increasing tax rates beyond the revenue maximization rate actually reduces government revenue by reducing taxpayers' incentive to earn more taxable income. Although tax rates are higher, there is less income to multiply against the higher tax rates.

---

[12]   Edward J. McCaffery, *Taxation and the Family*, 40 U.C.L.A. L. REV. 983, 1035–46, 1060 (1992).

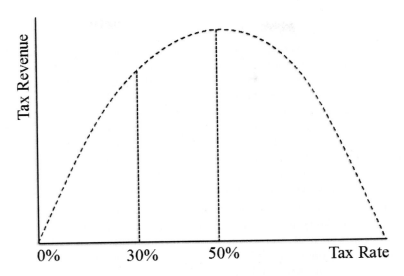

Unfortunately for tax policymakers, the shape of the real world Laffer curve is unknown, and the revenue maximization rate is disputed. Economists have predicted the peak at anywhere between 30% and 70%.[13]

To create a truly neutral tax would require predicting taxpayers' responses to various tax options. Policymakers would need to know people's elasticity and optimal tax rates. This would produce a tax that did not distort behavior, which in turn would allow the economy to create the "best" result. This view of efficiency depends on an underlying faith in the market to allocate resources. The pro-growth version of efficiency rejects that assumption because it accepts that some interference in the market is a good thing.

(c) Simplicity

Almost everyone would prefer the tax system be simpler. In the abstract it certainly sounds like a good idea. With the current Internal Revenue Code and Treasury Regulations containing over 9 billion words, a simpler system should be easier to comply with and to enforce. Complying with the tax code is estimated to require 6 billion hours and cost over $168 billion.[14] The Code's complexity costs taxpayer money and requires enforcement capability and taxpayer

---

[13]   Don Fullerton, *Laffer Curve*, in THE NEW PALGRAVE DICTIONARY OF ECONOMICS 839 (2d ed., 2008); Arthur Laffer, *The Laffer Curve*, HERITAGE FOUNDATION (2004).

[14]   *Hearing on President's Fiscal Year 2014 Budget Proposal before Ways and Means Committee*, 113th Cong., Apr. 11, 2013 (statement by Dave Camp).

compliance efforts. However, a simpler regime may not alleviate those problems.

Much of the Code's complexity applies only to subsets of taxpayers, and this concentrates the cost of complexity. For example, 15% of paper returns were Form 1040EZ, which is, by definition, an easy return.[15] For many taxpayers, their only income is wage income for which employers withhold, making much of tax filing simple unless taxpayers are seeking deductions and credits. Much tax complexity occurs for those with sufficient resources to plan to minimize their taxes. But not all complexity affects only those who can afford legal advice. For many reasons, including to control its cost and to prevent abuse, low-income taxpayers' earned income tax credit is one of the most complicated provisions in the Code.[16]

If simplicity for some or all is the goal, simplicity must first be defined. Simplicity may be a simple law or an administrable one in that taxpayers and the government can comply and enforce the statutory language easily. These differ because even a perfectly simple, fair, and efficient law that the IRS cannot apply or enforce would fail to achieve its objectives and would not be simple as taxpayers planned around it. Currently, complex language is drafted to simplify future implementation of the rules.

An alternative would be looser and easier to understand standards, which would often make the law itself simpler to understand. However, legal standards that give taxpayers discretion may not be simpler in operation. If taxpayers have to apply loose standards, they must decide if the rules apply to their particular situations, and people are unlikely to take consistent positions. For example, a definition of gross income that includes all income from whatever source is simply written but leaves open questions of whether it includes gifts, lottery winnings, or a treasure trove. Specific and detailed rules may be simpler in practice, such as an inclusive list of gross income so that if an item is not on the list it is not taxable.

Thus, a statute with few words may be simpler to create and to read; however, it might lead to more questions regarding the application of the tax to particular situations. It might also lead to increased tax avoidance and economic inefficiency to the extent taxpayers plan their activities in order to exploit ambiguities in a simple code. Consequently, simplicity in the law and in its application might be at odds.

---

[15]   Brett Collins, *Projections of Federal Tax Return Filings*, 131 STAT. INCOME BULL. 181 (2012).

[16]   For more on the EITC, see Chapter 16.02(b).

Second, simplicity may be used, intentionally or not, to mean other things. People may claim to desire a simple tax when what they really want is lower tax rates or lax enforcement. One may seek to eliminate tax rate brackets, which is often advocated by those seeking simplicity, but this is likely more for tax reduction than simplicity. It is doubtful these advocates would prefer flat, but higher, rates. Thus, advocates may have the hope that a simple tax will be better in any number of ways that are not necessary features of simplicity itself.

One test for the level of support for simplicity itself is what its advocates are willing to sacrifice for it. Reducing or eliminating tax credits and deductions, such as the earned income tax credit or deductions for medical expenses, state and local taxes, charitable giving, and business expenses, could most easily achieve simplicity. It is often the record keeping and substantiation of these expenses that creates much of the average taxpayers' complexity. However, eliminating the former removes a primary method of income redistribution and the latter items would create a gross, as opposed to a net, tax system. Their elimination also arguably decreases equity if the expenses reflect a real difference in people's ability to pay taxes. Alternatively, Congress could continue these credits and deductions but with an honor system for their reporting. Doing so would likely result in rampant tax evasion. It is dislike of these alternatives that often results in complex taxes.

Valuing simplicity as a means to achieve other things or as a component of a fair and efficient regime is different than valuing it for simplicity's sake. Reducing complexity is often for fear of what complexity does to the attainment of other tax values. Complex rules are inequitable because taxpayers with equal abilities to pay (or meet any other criteria of fairness) may have different tax burdens because of their unequal abilities to understand or manipulate the tax rules. Complex rules are inefficient because taxpayers must divert time and resources from other activities to comply and the government must maintain the department to interpret complex rules and ensure that taxes are correctly assessed. Therefore, policymakers might seek simplicity to facilitate either equity or efficiency.

At the same time, however, fairness and efficiency often require a more complex tax law. Differentiating the proper taxation of different items, such as excluding food from a consumption tax or limiting the ability to purchase tax shelters, requires drawing lines. For example, if the government wants to allow business deductions for working farms but not for a person's two pet chickens, the two situations must be differentiated in the Code or rules. Because all tax systems, no matter how simple, differentiate among behaviors, they must craft rules of inclusion and exclusion that risk influencing choice. Whether in the statute or in enforcement, complex rules provide the backdrop to minimize tax evasion, which itself is both unfair and inefficient.[17]

Another reason that it is difficult to reduce complexity is that there are at least three sources of complexity within the tax system: rule, compliance, and transaction. Rule complexity refers to the problems of understanding and interpreting the law. Rule complexity results from the statutes, regulations, and other sources of law being detailed and abundant. Compliance complexity is what one encounters when fulfilling the law's requirements. Thus, compliance complexity involves keeping records and filling out the appropriate forms. Transaction complexity arises when taxpayers organize their affairs to minimize taxes. Transaction complexity results any time the tax system treats similar economic transactions differently.

It is possible to target one element of complexity and not others, and it is possible that attempts to improve simplicity in one area would increase complexity in others. For example, a simple rule for tax rates may have only 0% and 50% brackets. Having only two brackets has less rule complexity than having many brackets. However, two brackets would likely create a significant amount of transaction complexity as taxpayers try to be in the 0% group, and the IRS would need to increase enforcement to preserve compliance.

Similarly, attempts to target a type of complexity might decrease complexity for some taxpayers but increase complexity for others. For example, the Obama administration proposed that the IRS submit to taxpayers completed or partially completed tax returns in lieu of taxpayers starting from scratch each year. This targets compliance complexity but would be of limited value to many Americans. Self-employed taxpayers would likely receive no help with this proposal or have to verify the IRS's assumptions each year. And the one-third of individual taxpayers who itemize their tax returns must compile information unavailable to the IRS but might be confused or dissuaded from claiming these deductions if other parts of the return were ready to file. Finally, other taxpayers with changed personal circumstances would need to recognize those changes and alter the partially completed return, such as the availability of child-based credits that depend upon agreements or custody of children. The amount of aid the IRS could provide to decrease this new complexity is minimal, and confusion or passively accepting incorrect information might be greater with this simplifying change.

---

[17]   For more on tax evasion versus tax avoidance, see Chapter 5.

Thus, simplicity is hard to define, particularly as it applies to real people complying with their tax obligations. Moreover, simplicity requires determining the proper tradeoff of simplicity and other values. The conflict of simplicity with other values means that it is rarely sought in the absolute. In fact, there has never been a cohesive constituency for tax simplification when simplicity threatens the other values in taxation, namely fairness or efficiency. To improve administration of the regime, Congress could stop enacting new tax legislation and allow the law to settle; however, that would require tremendous political restraint and would not guarantee the point of settlement is optimal.[18] Instead, it is easier to advocate for simplicity as a vague ideal than to achieve it or to admit that simplicity should be sacrificed for other goals.

§ 4.02   Fairness Between Taxpayers or Against the Government

Few people enjoy paying taxes, but most recognize that some amount of tax is required to pay for essential infrastructure and services. The extent to which the public feels that amount is raised fairly promotes voluntary compliance with the laws that raise the government's revenue.[19] Creating that sense of equity is not easy. It requires trust among taxpayers and between taxpayers and the government. Taxpayers' participation in the political process expressing how, and to what extent, they are taxed promotes acceptance but it is insufficient.[20]

As taxpayers engage in tax policy discussions, they focus not only on the tax system for themselves but also for others. To this end, taxation is framed as either taxpayer versus the government (in that one's tax burden is compared only with the government as a whole) or taxpayer versus taxpayer (in that one's tax burden must be examined as compared to other taxpayers' burdens). Under the former framing, increases or decreases in one taxpayer's tax obligation should be evaluated compared to the amorphous government's budget, and the amount a single taxpayer pays is generally trivial compared to the federal budget. Under the second

---

[18]   Professor Steve Johnson advocated a moratorium on changes to the tax system for "some" years. Steve Johnson, *The 1998 Act and the Resources Link Between Tax Compliance and Tax Simplification*, 51 U. KAN. L. REV. 1013, 1050–51 (2002).

[19]   Much work has been done on voluntary compliance. For example, J.T. Manhire, *What Does Voluntary Tax Compliance Mean?: A Government Perspective*, 164 U. PENN. L. REV. ONLINE 11 (2015); Brian Camp, *Tax Administration as an Inquisitorial Process*, 56 FLA. L. REV. 1 (2004); Leandra Lederman, *Tax Compliance and the Reformed* IRS, 51 U. KAN. L. REV. 971 (2003).

[20]   The discussion in this chapter uses the individual income tax as an example because the income tax is the federal government's largest revenue raiser, but similar issues apply with any tax.

framing, each taxpayer's burden is part of a collective decision among the public. In this sense, increases or decreases in one taxpayer's tax obligations are compared to increases or decreases in other taxpayers' obligations. The choice of comparison often determines acceptance or rejection of a particular choice.

(a) Horizontal and Vertical Equities

As discussed above, equity is one principle for evaluating the tax system. Although equity or fairness must be further defined, it sets parameters for analyzing whether the tax system should be progressive. Examining the issue of progressivity as an issue of equity, scholars have developed the concepts of horizontal and vertical equities. These two terms examine the treatment of taxpayers vis-à-vis other taxpayers to determine when it is justified to tax one taxpayer more or less than another.

First, American voters generally accept that similarly-situated taxpayers should be taxed the same. This focus on similarly-situated taxpayers is referred to in tax circles as horizontal equity. Horizontal equity requires that taxpayers with equal amounts of income (or property) pay the same amount of tax. In this formulation, the precept says only that taxpayers should not be arbitrarily discriminated against by the tax system.

One difficulty with horizontal equity is that no one has yet satisfactorily defined similarly-situated. Thus, the idea that similarly-situated taxpayers should be taxed equally requires criteria to determine who is similarly-situated and who is not. For example, taxpayers may have equal incomes but different personal obligations that may affect their abilities to pay taxes. As such, extenuating circumstances may affect taxpayers' disposable income but not their gross income. If the government considers factors other than income, horizontal equity may demand different levels of taxation because the taxpayers are not, in fact, similarly-situated. Thus, evaluating tax policy in terms of horizontal equity often leads to debate between adopting progressive and flat rate taxation. If everyone is considered similarly-situated, the system would favor flat rates or even a per person tax; otherwise differences might necessitate a range of tax results.

This leads to the second concept: vertical equity. Unlike horizontal equity, which focuses on similarity, vertical equity requires that differently-situated taxpayers be taxed differently. Debates over vertical equity often involve progressivity. If people are different because one has more than another, that person should pay more than the other. However, as with horizontal equity, no one has satisfactorily defined difference for this purpose or what it means to be taxed differently, whether it is an absolute amount or proportionately more.

Consider Anna and Ben. Anna owns $5,000,000 worth of investments, earns $75,000 on her investments while she relaxes by a pool on her multi-million dollar estate, and spends the $75,000 of earnings eating at fancy restaurants and throwing yacht parties. Ben owns $10,000 of non-investment assets (a used car), earns $75,000 of wages, and spends $75,000 paying off his law school loans and taking care of his terminally ill child. Are these two individuals similarly situated? Should they owe the same amount of tax because they both earn $75,000 and consume $75,000? Should the source or use of income matter? If Anna and Ben should be taxed differently, how differently?

Alternatively, consider Charlie and Danielle who also each earn $75,000. Charlie's wife died and he takes care of their five children; Danielle lives alone and has no support obligations. Do these taxpayers' personal responsibilities justify different rates of taxation? Are their personal choices something that should be recognized in the tax system? If Congress should recognize certain differences, how should they be treated?

These issues have been debated extensively, but no conclusive answers have been found. For example, there is academic argument whether horizontal equity is an independent principle or merely a necessary corollary of vertical equity.[21] According to the latter argument, the focus is rightly on those with different incomes being taxed different amounts; it follows that those with the same incomes must be taxed the same. Equal treatment then becomes only a necessary step to vertical equity. On the other hand, horizontal equity arguably applies even when vertical equity, in the sense of progressivity, does not. For example, a consumption tax likely permits higher-income taxpayers to pay a smaller percentage of their income in taxes than lower-income taxpayers, a violation of vertical equity. Nevertheless, it would presumably still be important that equal consuming taxpayers pay the same amount of tax.

Regardless of their relative supremacy, both horizontal and vertical equities demand a way of defining similarly-situated. Economist Richard Musgrave once wrote that in order to create a fair progressive tax "[a]n objective index of equality or inequality is

---

[21]   James Repetti & Diane Ring, *Horizontal Equity Revisited*, 13 FLA. TAX REV. 135 (2013); Richard Musgrave, *Horizontal Equity: A Further Note*, 1 FLA. TAX REV. 354 (1993); Louis Kaplow, *A Note on Horizontal Equity*, 1 FLA. TAX REV. 191 (1992); Richard Musgrave, *Horizontal Equity, One More Time*, 43 NAT'L TAX J. 113 (1990); Louis Kaplow, *Horizontal Equity: Measures in Search of a Principle*, 42 NAT'L TAX J. 139 (1989).

needed. . ."[22] To tax people in different situations differently, Congress must know what differences are worthy of different tax treatment, either heavier or lighter taxation. Formulating those criteria requires the use of some form of distributive justice, a first step in measuring equity. Instead of defining distributive justice, however, proponents of progressive taxation generally assume everyone accepts, and critics assume all reject, an unstated conception of distributive justice.[23]

Drawing the lines necessary for defining sameness or difference as required by horizontal and vertical equity has implications for efficiency and simplicity. First, taxing some choices or activities more heavily than others will motivate some taxpayers to adjust their behavior. They will opt for tax reduction rather than their otherwise preferred activities. Most economists critique this effect because it distorts the market. This adjustment might, or might not, foster economic growth; the impact on growth would depend upon how people respond.

Second, differentiating among behaviors and imposing progressive tax rates on select behaviors increases the tax system's complexity. The statute must be written to differentiate based on the differences Congress chooses to recognize and to ignore taxpayer behavior that hides similarities. For example, one popular means of tax avoidance is to shift income among family members or business entities to have income taxed to multiple people at lower rates or to use many people's tax exemptions. The goal is to make it impossible to accurately differentiate among taxpayers. To overcome this avoidance, Congress must define the appropriate tax unit in a way that a truly flat tax, one without exemptions or deductions, would not require. By creating these definitions, the government makes the tax system more complex.

Once the statute differentiates behaviors, the IRS must police transactions that seek to circumvent the rules. This policing occurs through the creation of complicated rules and procedures, more detailed tax filing, and audits of tax returns. The less the government differentiates behaviors, either permitting all evasion or taxing everything the same, the less cost and complexity is required to maintain lines around what is supposed to be taxed, what is properly deductible, and who should owe the tax on given income.

---

[22]   RICHARD A. MUSGRAVE, THE THEORY OF PUBLIC FINANCE 161 (1959).

[23]   For more on distributive justice, see Chapter 18.02(c).

(b) Flat Taxes, or Taxing Everyone at the Same Rate

What constitutes a flat tax is not always self-evident. It could mean that every person or every activity is taxed the same amount. However, unless the tax is only imposed on truly discretionary activities, this would require those without income to find a way to pay the government. Alternatively, the claim could mean that all income is taxed the same percentage, but this would require the elimination of the standard deduction so that the poorest earners would owe the same rate of tax as the wealthiest. However, many flat tax advocates do not go that far. Instead, flat tax proposals generally apply the same percentage to all income, goods, or activities above a threshold. Therefore, some progressivity is preserved. Additional key precepts of the tax remain to be defined.

As a theoretical matter, proponents of a flat tax reject the requirement of vertical equity that different income levels should be subject to different tax rates. Instead, they argue that everyone is similarly-situated, at least as it matters for tax rates. Consequently, flat tax proponents would impose a single marginal tax rate. If the tax base is broad enough, the tax could enjoy lower rates and raise the same revenue.

Flat rate taxes may also permit a simplified tax system, which would make compliance and enforcement easier. The primary savings is because a single rate that is generally applicable reduces the incentive to engage in tax avoidance and the amount of economic distortion. It is hoped that this would stimulate economic growth. For much the same reasons proponents argue for tax rate reduction, a flat rate tax could promote investment and growth followed by more tax revenue even though raised with lower rates. Moreover, the law itself would be shorter and the simplification could permit a smaller IRS and less government intervention in taxpayers' lives.

Opponents of flat rate taxation argue that a flat rate tax would likely be as complex as the current progressive income tax.[24] Congress could add loopholes, deductions, and exclusions to a flat rate tax because Congress determines the income against which the flat rate is multiplied. Alternatively, Congress could create a simple progressive system by removing existing preferential tax rates, deductions, and exclusions. In other words, there is nothing inherent in a rate system that demands complexity.[25]

---

[24]   *See* David Weisbach, *Ironing Out the Flat Tax,* 52 STAN. L. REV. 599 (2000).

[25]   The 1913 income tax return illustrates a significantly simpler progressive tax. Revenue Act of 1913, ch. 16, 38 Stat. 114 (1913).

Flat taxes are popular at the state level. Sales taxes imposed by U.S. states are flat taxes except for sales tax holidays that exempt purchases for designated items and designated times.[26] Several states have also adopted flat income taxes: Colorado, Illinois, Indiana, Massachusetts, Michigan, North Carolina, Pennsylvania, and Utah. However, even flat state income taxes have large exemptions, permissive deductions, or credits that create some degree of progressivity.

The many proposals for a federal flat tax have so far failed. In 1981, two economists, Robert Hall and Alvin Rabushka, proposed a flat tax on earnings at 19%.[27] The Kemp Commission, headed by former Secretary of Housing and Urban Development Jack Kemp, proposed a flat tax in 1996.[28] Bills were proposed in 2007 and 2009 but were not voted on in either session.[29] Republican presidential candidate Herman Cain proposed the "9-9-9 plan" in 2011 that would have replaced all current federal taxes with a 9% business transaction tax, a 9% personal income tax, and a 9% federal sales tax, and similar plans were supported by Carly Fiorina and Ted Cruz in 2016.[30]

Recently, advocates of flat taxes have focused on imposing flat rates at the higher end of the income spectrum. Warren Buffett, the billionaire chairman of investment firm Berkshire Hathaway, proposed a flat tax for the wealthy with his Buffett rule.[31] The Buffett rule's objective is to raise the tax rate on the wealthy by making it a broadly applicable flat tax. This addresses the fact that the current income tax system is regressive, with declining effective rates for wealthy taxpayers because of reduced rates for capital gains and dividends. In 2012, the Congressional Research Service found that

---

[26]   For more on sales taxes and sales tax holidays, see Chapter 13.01(c).

[27]   ROBERT HALL & ALVIN RABUSHKA, THE FLAT TAX (2007). Several countries, particularly those in Eastern Europe, have adopted flat tax systems. This format has generally been thought more successful, in part because of poor enforcement of the prior progressive systems. Michael Keen et al., *The "Flat Tax(es)": Principles and Evidence*, IMF WORKING PAPER NO. 06/218 (2006).

[28]   NATIONAL COMMISSION ON ECONOMIC GROWTH AND TAX REFORM, UNLEASHING AMERICA'S POTENTIAL: A PRO-GROWTH, PRO-FAMILY TAX SYSTEM FOR THE 21ST CENTURY (1996).

[29]   Taxpayer Choice Act, H.R. 3818, S. 2416 (2007, 2009).

[30]   Derek Thompson, *Herman Cain's 9-9-9 Tax Plan is Incredible! (Liberally)*, THE ATLANTIC, Oct. 12, 2011; Jeanne Sahadi, *Carly Fiorina Wants 3-Page Tax Code*, CNN MONEY, Nov. 11, 2015; Joseph Rosenberg et al., *An Analysis of Ted Cruz's Tax Plan* TAX POL'Y CTR (2016).

[31]   Warren Buffett, *Stop Coddling the Super-Rich*, N.Y. TIMES (Aug. 14, 2011).

roughly 94,500 millionaires face a lower effective tax rate than that faced by 10.4 million moderate-income taxpayers.[32]

Few flat tax proposals are fully developed and, therefore, most do not answer the countless questions necessary to put a tax regime into operation. One difficulty is defining the income against which the flat rate is to be applied. Under the U.S.'s existing tax regime, gross income is offset by deductions. Proponents of flat taxes have to decide whether they will retain the deduction-based system but doing so is not without complexity and political risk. To achieve simplicity and keep rates low, advocates of the flat tax may support a broader gross tax as opposed to a net tax.[33] A gross tax, unlike a net tax, does not permit deductions. Eliminating deductions is often expected to reduce existing political pressure around tax incentives and to reduce tax planning by taxpayers seeking to maximize their deductions.

Nevertheless, few proponents of flat rate taxation argue for the complete elimination of deductions because many deductions are for real costs in the production of income. For example, the 9-9-9 plan allowed businesses to deduct the purchase of machines and other capital assets but did not permit deductions for labor costs. The effect of this choice would likely have been to encourage businesses to buy machines rather than to hire employees, a choice with political and economic costs. Using the 1996 Kemp Commission report as a baseline, one accounting firm concluded that the report's inclusion of exemptions for homeownership, charitable contributions, investments, payroll taxes, and other preferences would require a 25% flat rate.[34]

If businesses are allowed deductions, the flat tax's tax base is as political as it is with a progressive tax. Congress must define and limit deductible expenses. Debates over accelerating depreciation, entertainment expenses, the reasonableness of salaries, among countless other policy choices can plague a flat tax in the same way as they plague a progressive one: Is a home office a legitimate business expense? What about dinner with clients? What about a shampoo manufacturer who purchases a bottle making company and an advertising agency: Are the purchases a deductible expense because the manufacturer would buy bottles and advertising or a nondeductible investment?

---

[32]   THOMAS L. HUNGERFORD, CONG. RESEARCH SERV., R42043, AN ANALYSIS OF THE "BUFFETT RULE," (2012).

[33]   For more on the distinction between a gross and net tax system, see Chapter 11.02.

[34]   Clay Chandler, *On the Road to a Flat Tax, A Curve, or Two*, WASH. POST, Jan. 21, 1996.

The presence of exemptions, deductions, or credits in an otherwise flat rate system creates some amount of progressivity or regressivity. For example, if the income tax has a flat 20% rate but a $20,000 standard deduction, the tax is, in fact, a progressive tax. There is a 0% rate for the first $20,000 of income and a 20% rate thereafter. Alternatively, if the income tax has a flat 20% rate but includes deductions for charitable donations, the tax may be progressive or regressive; it depends upon the relative wealth of those who claim the charitable donation deduction.

Finally, a move to a flat rate tax should not be considered in isolation but as part of a complex tax system. A flat rate income tax is only one of many taxes that taxpayers face. Some other components of the system are likely regressive, such as federal employment taxes and state and local taxes. Therefore, adding a flat rate income tax might exacerbate the regressivity of the system as a whole.

(c) The Negative Income Tax, Treating Them Truly Equally

Free-market economist Milton Friedman first proposed the negative income tax in 1962, as a flat tax with a fully refundable personal deduction for each taxpayer similar to today's exemptions.[35] The equal, fully refundable deduction makes the negative income tax a means of redistribution without the requirements imposed by modern tax credits. It creates a guaranteed minimum income for all tax filers. In the process, the negative income tax treats each person equally, whether they are rich or poor.

The personal deduction under most negative income tax proposals, often called a demogrant, is significantly larger than the existing personal exemption. When this deduction exceeds income, taxable income would become negative rather than being capped at zero. The flat tax rate is then applied to all taxable income, even to negative income. For those with a negative income, there would be a negative income tax that the government pays to the taxpayer.

Consider a system in which personal deductions are set at $20,000 per person and the flat rate is 20%. If the deduction is not refundable, the deduction makes the tax only mildly progressive. The first $20,000 of income is not taxable, with a 0% bracket for the first $20,000, and a 20% rate thereafter. However, those who earn nothing receive no benefit from the deduction.

With a negative income tax, even those who earn nothing benefit from the deduction. A married couple earning $50,000 would owe $2,000 in taxes calculated as $50,000 of earnings minus $40,000 in

---

[35]   MILTON FRIEDMAN, CAPITALISM AND FREEDOM (1962).

total deductions, for a net $10,000, times the 20% tax rate.[36] Alternatively, if the couple earned $30,000, they would owe a negative amount and receive a payment from the government. Their $30,000 of income minus their $40,000 of deductions produces a negative $10,000 of income. This negative $10,000 times the 20% tax rate produces a negative $2,000 to be paid by the government to the couple. Going further, if the couple earns no income, they would have negative $40,000 of income because of their $40,000 of deductions. Multiplying the negative $40,000 times the 20% rate produces a negative $8,000 to be paid by the government.

Everyone has the same deduction regardless of a person's work status. Therefore, some number of people would likely choose to live off of the refundable deduction rather than earn income. Thus, the guaranteed income amount could create for some recipients a disincentive to work.

To reduce the disincentive to work, Friedman wanted a progressive deduction. This would mean that a person without earnings would receive some lesser amount of deduction, for example $10,000 instead of the $20,000. Consequently, a person with no income would only receive the $10,000 deduction times the 20% rate, or a $2,000 payment from the government, rather than the $4,000 from a full $20,000 deduction. As more income was earned, the deduction would increase, for example if the person earned $5,000 the deduction would be $15,000. Therefore, the person would receive $2,000 from the government, or the $5,000 of earnings minus the $15,000 deduction times the 20%. This $2,000 government payment plus the $5,000 that was earned creates an incentive to earn that $5,000.

The numbers in the above examples were selected because they are nice round numbers. In a real system, the amount of deduction and its phase-down would need to be carefully calculated to encourage people to enter the labor force without leaving the poor destitute. This would not be easy because it relies on estimates of taxpayer behavior. Nevertheless, the initial choices of deduction size and phase-in are critical because these are likely to be sticky, so that they will be politically hard to change significantly.

The increase in consumer spending made possible with the refundable deduction may trigger inflation. Inflation results when people have more money to spend that is not accompanied by increases in their productivity. With this extra money, people engage in more competition for goods and hence higher prices. To the extent

---

[36] A negative income tax system would need to consider the impact of taxpayers' losses. If losses are recoverable in tax refunds, it would produce a tremendous incentive to fabricate losses.

that the purchasing power of money decreases because of the increase in the money supply, no one is better off. Moreover, to the extent the deduction triggers inflation, political pressure might mount to increase the amount of guaranteed income in order to offset inflation, possibly creating a cycle of increase, inflation, and increase again.

When not inflationary, the use of refundable deductions creates redistribution to the poor through the tax system. Its methodology, however, is different than used by the earned income tax credit (EITC).[37] Currently, as taxpayers earn more income subject to tax, they lose benefits, creating an economic disincentive. The disincentive caused by the loss of benefits is sometimes referred to as a cliff effect. For every additional dollar earned, the income is taxed plus benefits are lost, a double hit. For some benefits the cliff is abrupt because crossing a threshold of income results in a sharp decline or complete disallowance of benefits. The EITC has a gradual phase-out as people earn income, which creates less of a disincentive to work, although it still creates a disincentive once a person enters the phase-out range. The negative income tax, on the other hand, would apply universally, not be limited to earned income, and would provide an incentive to earning income because it does not phase out.

Because it does not contain a disincentive, a negative income tax arguably empowers those at the lower end of the income spectrum to make their own choices. Similarly, it removes the stigma of welfare and the poverty trap that may occur to the extent the EITC discourages additional work. However, the proposal requires trust that recipients of refunds will make wise economic choices. This is particularly true for the negative income tax as proposed by Friedman. Friedman expected the negative income tax to replace the EITC and other forms of federal redistribution, such as TANF (or food stamps) and Medicaid. People would be given money through the deduction that they would need to use to purchase the goods otherwise provided by the government.

A side effect of giving taxpayers the right to purchase their desired benefits is to reduce the size of the government that administers state-provided aid. An estimate by the conservative think tank Heritage Foundation found that the federal portion of America's welfare system cost $522 billion in 2008, or about $7,060 per person with incomes below 200% of the federal poverty level, administered through over 70 interrelated means-tested programs through four independent agencies and nine departments.[38] To the extent the negative income tax is not added to existing programs, the

---

[37]   For more on the EITC, see Chapter 16.02(b).

[38]   Robert Rector et al., *Obama to Spend $10.3 Trillion on Welfare*, HERITAGE FOUNDATION (2009).

bureaucracies associated with these other programs could be eliminated.

Friedman is not the only advocate of a negative income tax. For example, Bruce Ackerman and Anne Alstott argued that each person should be guaranteed $80,000 to underscore the importance of private property but in a more democratic and free way.[39] Their objective is to increase choices for lower-income Americans, not to change the economic system. On the other hand, Charles Murray suggests a $10,000 annual cash payment to everyone 21-years and older with a stipulation that $3,000 must go to health insurance and some other amount to retirement savings.[40] Murray attempts to dismantle the social safety net while empowering people.

Experiments in a negative income tax are being tried. Finland, for example, began a program guaranteeing a minimum income regardless of employment.[41] All Finns, the wealthy and the poor, would be eligible to receive about $600 per month, although the initial two-year test of a 2,000 person sample came from people receiving unemployment or an income subsidy. One objective of the Finnish experiment is to reduce the costly bureaucracy behind its complex welfare state.

At this time, providing all American tax filers a refundable deduction has proven politically untenable. To do so would require a broad acceptance of redistribution and the economic cost thereof.[42] Even if redistribution were accepted as a worthy goal, how that redistribution would best be accomplished would need to be debated. These two issues are entangled in policy debates over the negative income tax.

(d) Incidence of Taxes

Even if a tax statute names a particular taxpayer to be liable for a tax, that naming does not guarantee that the taxpayer is ultimately liable for the tax. The person ultimately responsible can be the person who pays the tax or some other person who pays the tax indirectly. In tax policy lingo, the incidence of a tax is the person who bears a tax's burden.[43] For example, if a tax is imposed on car manufacturers

---

[39]   BRUCE ACKERMAN & ANNE ALSTOTT, THE STAKEHOLDER SOCIETY (1999).

[40]   CHARLES MURRAY, IN OUR HANDS: A PLAN TO REPLACE THE WELFARE STATE (2006).

[41]   Heikki Hiilamo, *Finland May Have Found the Answer to Increasing Global Unemployment*, HUFFINGTON POST, Jan. 20, 2017.

[42]   For more on redistribution, see Chapter 18.02.

[43]   For more on the incidence of taxation, see Lily Batchelder & Surachai Khitatrakum, *Dead or Alive: An Investigation of the Incidence of Estate and Inheritance Taxes*, THIRD ANN. CONF. OF EMPIRICAL LEGAL STUDIES WORKING PAPERS (2008); Kimberly Clausing, *In Search of a Corporate Tax Incidence*, 65 TAX L. REV. 433

but manufacturers are able to raise prices to offset the cost of the tax, the tax is passed on to consumers who pay the tax in the form of more expensive cars. In this example, the tax is shifted from the person who is nominally responsible for the tax, the manufacturer, to the consumer who bears the burden of the tax. Thus, just because a person remits a tax payment to the government does not mean that the payment reduces that person's wealth or consumption.

Who bears the incidence of a tax is impossible to determine definitively because it would require a comparison of a world with the tax against a world without the tax. It is generally accepted by economists that the individual income tax, so far as it falls on wages and other earnings from services, is largely borne by labor. There is less consensus on the incidence of the corporate income tax and whether it is shifted to consumers, capital providers, or labor.

In the example of the car manufacturer, if manufacturers could negotiate lower wages to employees, the tax is borne by labor. Alternatively, if payment of the tax decreases investors' rate of return because purchasers will not pay more for cars, it is borne by capital providers. It is likely that the corporate income tax is borne by some combination of consumers, capital providers, and workers.

Because of uncertainty regarding the incidence of taxation, statutory tax rates determine the amount of revenue to be raised from a given amount of income or activity but not from whom. Thus, policymakers should understand that just because they tax a particular item or behavior does not mean the item or behavior actually bears the burden. The person who pays the tax is not always the person who bears the incidence of the tax. To understand a taxpayer's true tax bill, it is important to know whether the taxpayer is bearing taxes indirectly. If taxpayers are bearing taxes indirectly they have a higher, but hidden, average tax rate. Similarly, if taxpayers shift taxes onto others, their average tax rates decrease while retaining a higher statutory rate.

(2012); Philip Reny et al., *Tax Incidence Under Imperfect Competition*, 30 INT'L J. OF INDUST. ORG. (2011); Don Fullerton & Gilbert Metcalf, *Tax Incidence*, NBER WORKING PAPER NO. 8829 (2002).

Chapter 5

TAX PLANNING

Table of Sections

All that is required for something to constitute tax planning is for taxpayers to consider the tax consequences of their choices. Therefore, not all tax planning is unlawful; the federal government even encourages some tax planning. For example, when taxpayers choose to save for retirement through tax-advantaged plans, they are engaging in government-encouraged tax planning. This tax planning is tax avoidance, but tax avoidance that is considered socially useful. However, some tax planning goes beyond what the law permits and beyond what is merely tax avoidance. Tax evasion is illegal tax planning. Thus, it is tax evasion that is subject to financial penalties and possibly criminal sanctions whereas tax avoidance is not punishable under the law.

The term tax shelter is like tax planning in that it can constitute tax avoidance or tax evasion. Tax shelters are any method of reducing payments to tax collecting entities. Thus, tax shelters can minimize federal, state, or local taxes. They can work by decreasing gross income, increasing deductions or tax credits, or changing the timing of income. Tax shelters can be legitimate or illegitimate, legal or illegal. Only legal shelters and legal planning are tax avoidance; if shelters cross the line to illegal planning their use becomes tax evasion.

There is no measure of lawful tax avoidance because it is such a broad concept. On the other hand, studies estimate the revenue cost of tax evasion. In the years between 2008 and 2010, the annual gross tax gap—the gap between the amount taxpayers lawfully owed in taxes and what they paid—was $458 billion.[1] The gap is almost 150%

---

[1]   IRS, TAX GAP ESTIMATES FOR TAX YEARS 2008–2010 (2016). The IRS compiled this data by conducting an intensive individual income reporting compliance study, significantly more detailed than regular audits.

of the amount raised by the corporate income tax. The net tax gap, which includes revenue collected after late payments and enforced collection, was $406 billion. Because of the size of the U.S. economy and its manner of recording evasion, American tax evasion is a large number compared to other countries' evasion. Brazil has the second largest tax gap, at $280 billion.[2]

§ 5.01   Tax Avoidance

Lawful tax planning is technically tax avoidance, but the amount of money saved from tax is not included in the tax gap. It is often hard to measure tax avoidance as the activity tends to be as hidden or discrete as evasion. Nevertheless, classification as tax avoidance rather than tax evasion is important. At times tax avoidance is recognized as beneficial and, at others, is discouraged as wasteful. Although taxpayers have the right to engage in lawful tax avoidance, Congress can choose to limit the benefits of particular forms of tax avoidance by enacting statutory responses.

(a) Classifying Activities as Tax Avoidance

Because tax avoidance is generally not a public activity and cannot be audited for, there is no data on the amount of tax avoidance that occurs. Thus, no one knows definitively how much taxpayers save in taxes through lawful tax planning. Available substitutes for this information have significant faults. For example, the amount of revenue that corporations hold internationally and the cost of congressionally created tax incentives show only a portion of possible avoidance behavior. Moreover, it is unknown how much of this behavior would have occurred in a world without the tax savings. In other words, tax avoidance hinges on taxpayers' intent, and it is impossible to measure individual intent on a national scale.

Drawing the line between lawful tax avoidance and illegal tax evasion can be difficult. When taxpayers craft means of tax avoidance, they often play on the gray area between what the law intends and what is clearly illegal. Taxpayers use ambiguity in statutory language to their advantage. Moreover, some taxpayers engage in aggressive tax planning hoping to win what has been called the audit lottery because they know that few returns are audited. Therefore, avoidance that is actually evasion is not always identified as such. To catch those crossing the line beyond the gray area into tax evasion, the IRS must audit the tax return and detect the problem.[3] Taxpayers can try to make auditing difficult for the IRS by shrouding planning in complexity or secrecy, although doing so

---

[2]   Richard Murphy, *Tackle Tax Havens*, TAX JUSTICE NETWORK (2011).

[3]   For more on audits, see Chapter 2.02(a).

carries risks of increasing the punishment if the avoidance is actually evasion and it is discovered.

Americans may believe that use of the gray area to their advantage is their right and that tax statutes are interpreted to taxpayers' advantage. Therefore, they may believe that any uncertainty in the letter of the law or its application to a particular set of facts is interpreted in favor of taxpayers. A justification for this reasoning is that taxpayers should have a right to understand exactly what behaviors are taxed. In the early decades of the income tax, the Supreme Court agreed, concluding:

> In the interpretation of statutes levying taxes it is the established rule not to extend their provisions by implication, beyond the clear import of the language used, or to enlarge their operations so as to embrace matters not specifically pointed out. In case of any doubt they are construed most strongly against the Government, and in favor of the citizen.[4]

Thus, ambiguities were resolved in favor of the taxpayer.

However, this narrow interpretation of tax statutes no longer holds and has not for a long time. Instead, the Supreme Court has held that it is "not impressed by the argument that . . . all doubts should be resolved in favor of the taxpayer. It is the function and duty of courts to resolve doubts."[5] Today, tax statutes are generally interpreted in the same manner as other statutes and not in a pro-taxpayer manner. Some judges may remain more sympathetic to taxpayers, but there is no default form of interpretation in favor of the taxpayer over the government or vice versa.

(b) Benefits of Tax Avoidance

Tax avoidance is not only lawful and preserves money in the hands of taxpayers, in some instances Congress expects tax avoidance to benefit society as a whole. For example, Congress creates some means to avoid taxes by enacting tax breaks for taxpayers engaging in certain activities, such as saving for education and retirement or developing alternate fuels.[6] When adopting these tax provisions, Congress purposefully encourages taxpayers to change their behavior. If people do not respond with tax planning, the legislation fails to accomplish its goal.

---

[4]   Gould v. Gould, 245 U.S. 151, 153 (1917); *see also* U.S. v. Merriam, 263 U.S. 179, 188 (1923).

[5]   White v. U.S., 305 U.S. 281, 292 (1938); *see also* Interstate Transit Lines v. Comm'r, 319 U.S. 590, 593 (1943) (construing deductions in favor of the government).

[6]   For more on tax incentives, see Chapter 17.01.

At other times, tax planning results from legitimate business activities that may be encouraged by Congress but then used by taxpayers to accomplish unrelated goals. For example, mining and oil drilling businesses often take many years before they generate revenue. Before they generate revenue, these businesses incur significant expenses, which under normal income tax concepts would be deductible in increments over many years. Additionally, while costing lots of money to start operations, these businesses have a high risk of never becoming profitable. All together this downside of the business may deter investors. To persuade people to invest in mining and oil drilling, Congress enacted favorable deductions that permit these businesses to deduct their expenses currently rather than to capitalize them and deduct them over time.[7] Today, tax sensitive investors may choose to invest in these tax shelters in order to benefit from the early tax savings (and investors would later pay tax on any gain if the business is successful). The result is that more money flows into a business that Congress concluded would otherwise be underfunded.

Even tax avoidance planned by taxpayers without congressional sanction may benefit society. Taxes are said to create a friction that reduces otherwise useful or economically beneficial business transactions. The concern is that taxes prevent business transactions that would, but for the taxes, be profitable. Consequently, the taxes alone prevent the creation of a societal good of increased economic growth. To the extent this is true, tax avoidance reduces that friction by selectively reducing taxes. By avoiding these taxes, business transactions can occur. In this way, tax avoidance may be a form of price discrimination in that those who object to taxes the most take the greatest efforts to avoid paying them.

(c) Negative Consequences of Tax Avoidance

When people take steps to avoid taxes they are not creating new wealth but merely trying to appropriate a larger share of wealth that has already been created. This rent seeking is wasteful because its cost is lost wealth in society.[8] Therefore, all planning to minimize taxes creates some amount of deadweight loss for society. Deadweight loss is problematic because no one benefits from this cost, neither taxpayers nor the government. Although successful tax planners, their lawyers, and accountants enjoy reduced taxes and

---

[7]   For example, I.R.C. § 263(c) intangible drilling costs; I.R.C. §§ 611–617 permits a depletion allowance.

[8]   David Weisbach, *Ten Truths About Tax Shelters*, 55 TAX L. REV. 215, 222 (2002).

fees, resources are being spent to carve up the national pie rather than to grow it.

Moreover, tax avoidance is inefficient because people are taking actions they otherwise would not. The desire to reduce a person's tax burden alters the attractiveness of choices to the extent that some choices are taxed more than others. The degree of inefficiency depends upon the amount of planning a particular taxpayer is willing to undertake. For example, if a business owner prematurely transfers ownership of her business to her grandchildren to minimize estate taxes, this is inefficient if the owner would have preferred to retain ownership. If the goal of efficient taxes is to not influence behavior, the persistence of tax avoidance shows that the goal has yet to be achieved.

Tax avoidance also has distributional consequences in that avoidance tends to reduce the taxes of wealthier taxpayers more than it does lower income taxpayers. Because not everyone can avoid taxes to the same degree, some people benefit more from the existence of avoidance mechanisms than others. Tax planning often requires financial flexibility to buy into shelters or to shift behavior to lower taxed activities. Moreover, tax avoidance often requires financial acumen or financial advisors. Therefore, with only a subset of taxpayers benefiting from tax avoidance, taxes cannot be imposed evenly throughout society so that similarly-situated taxpayers are not taxed similarly.

The reduction in revenue caused by tax avoidance also risks more in hardship for lower-income taxpayers. To the extent that lower-income taxpayers are net recipients from tax revenue, they are more apt to suffer from reductions in that revenue. With less revenue, the government can provide fewer services or engage in less redistribution. That this harm remains immeasurable and is diffused across society makes it no less real.

Finally, tax avoidance poses a broader risk to the tax system than the immediate loss of revenue. Even lawful tax planning may undermine confidence in the tax system. If taxpayers become convinced that other taxpayers are planning their way out of their fair share of taxes, those unable to engage in lawful tax planning may choose to engage in tax evasion. Thus, tax avoidance may reduce overall taxpayer compliance. Decreasing the perception that others are paying taxes threatens to snowball noncompliance. Perhaps counter intuitively, this may mean that the IRS should keep tax avoidance out of the press and not broadcast successful prosecutions of evasion.[9]

(d) Right to Engage in Tax Avoidance

Judge Learned Hand wrote that "[a]nyone may so arrange his affairs that his taxes shall be as low as possible; he is not bound to choose that pattern which will best pay the Treasury; there is not even a patriotic duty to increase one's taxes."[10] What is forgotten is that in the case, *Gregory v. Helvering*, Hand sided with the government and created a doctrine requiring transactions have economic substance beyond saving taxes. Thus, the rhetorical support for the right to avoid tax is often tempered by a recognition that some taxpayers will do just about anything not to pay taxes.

Tax avoidance also raises issues of taxpayers' morality, even though avoidance is clearly legal. Different people come to different conclusions regarding all moral questions and tax is no exception.[11] However, at least according to the Kantian categorical imperative, an act is only moral if everyone can do the same.[12] Not only are some people unable to engage in tax avoidance, if only because they have too little income or only have income that cannot be avoided, if everyone engaged in tax avoidance the government's coffers would soon be depleted and its revenue would be raised unevenly.

On the other hand, tax avoidance may be moral to the extent that an individual's tax avoidance is not harmful. This argument is premised on the idea that immorality is conditioned upon imposing harm on others.[13] Accordingly, it may be possible that the tax avoidance of one taxpayer is properly weighted against the vast revenue the government, so that the cost of the one taxpayer's avoidance is insignificant to the whole. Contra the Kantian perspective, this view considers each person's morality as distinct from all others.

Similarly, because taxes are legal extractions and not voluntary contributions, one could argue that there is no moral obligation to refrain from reducing the forcible extraction of revenue. This argument is stronger if one accepts that people have a moral entitlement to their pre-tax incomes derived from a Lockean

---

[9]   *But see* Joshua Stark & Daniel Levin, *When Is Tax Enforcement Publicized?*, 30 VA. TAX REV. 1 (2010).

[10]   Helvering v. Gregory, 69 F.2d 809, 810 (2d Cir. 1934).

[11]   For more on the distinction between morality and ethics, see Chapter 4.01(a)(v).

[12]   IMMANUEL KANT, GROUNDING FOR THE METAPHYSICS OF MORALS 421 (James Ellington translator, 3d ed. 1993).

[13]   BERNARD GERT, COMMON MORALITY: DECIDING WHAT TO DO (2004).

conception of natural property rights.[14] According to this argument, tax avoidance to maintain pre-tax income merely protects what taxpayers otherwise own.

This Lockean view of property rights has been countered, although not definitively, by the Benthamian argument that the government creates property. If government is necessary to have property and taxes are necessary to support the government, then taxes are part of the creation of property, although Bentham would limit taxes to those necessary for vital services.[15] In other words, the state creates property rights and taxes are a condition upon which the state exists. Therefore, taxes are not a taking of what the person owns. Instead, taxes occur before a person has property rights, even if payment of the taxes occurs after property is acquired.

In the latter view, a given tax regime is merely one of many possible ways of funding the government that creates property rights. Nevertheless, without some type of tax regime there would be no property. Therefore, to avoid taxes is to take from the system that creates the property in the first instance. This might not make paying taxes a moral obligation, but it is an argument that avoiding taxes is immoral.

(e) Statutory Responses

Despite being lawful, Congress does not always respond favorably to tax avoidance. If Congress's reaction is strong enough, Congress may enact legislation to make particular tax avoidance measures unlawful, and hence it becomes tax evasion, or may limit the benefit derived from particular tax avoidance transactions. There are many of these types of statutory limits in the Code that may catch novice investors and business people unaware.

For example, Congress enacted the passive activity loss rules to prevent taxpayers from using deductions generated from investments they were not actively engaged in, such as tax shelter losses, to offset their active income, such as their wages or business income.[16] These rules limit most investment deductions and credits to offsetting investment income. Congress was concerned that taxpayers were investing in tax shelters, often in real estate, to

---

[14]   JOHN LOCKE, THE SECOND TREATISE ON GOVERNMENT, 287 ([1690], P. Laslett ed., 1991).

[15]   JEREMY BENTHAM, THE WORKS OF JEREMY BENTHAM, PUBLISHED UNDER THE SUPERINTENDENCE OF HIS EXECUTOR, JOHN BOWRING, vol. V, 416 (1838–43). *See also* LIAM MURPHY & THOMAS NAGEL, THE MYTH OF OWNERSHIP (2002).

[16]   I.R.C. § 469.

generate deductions in order to reduce their income from their regular businesses.[17]

Returning to the mining and drilling example, for most taxpayers, the deductions and credits associated with investments in mining and oil drilling are now limited by the passive activity loss rules. Therefore, passive investors can enjoy the deductions only to the extent that they also have income or gain from passive activities. Congressional concern with tax avoidance trumped its desire for increasing investment in these activities. On the other hand, if an investor is actively involved in drilling or mining, the expenses remain fully and currently deductible.

As illustrated by the passive activity loss rules, Congress rarely prohibits activities through the tax code but limits their usefulness to reducing taxpayers' taxes. Thus, Congress balances its desire to let taxpayers act in their own best interests with limits on taxpayers' ability to reduce their taxes below politically acceptable levels. That statutory limits on tax avoidance balance competing goals generally means that they are complex statutes. Congress faces the difficulty of crafting its statutes broadly enough to target the offending behavior but not so broadly as to discourage legitimate activities.

It is the desire to maintain the balance that prevents Congress from enacting a general anti-avoidance rule, popularly known as a GAAR. Many countries have GAARs that void tax planning when the planning has the purpose of tax avoidance. For example, the New Zealand GAAR, which evolved from one of the oldest GAARs, states, "A tax avoidance arrangement is void as against the Commissioner for income tax purposes."[18] This is further defined to be any agreement, contract, plan, or understanding, whether enforceable or not, to avoid, reduce, or postpone taxes.[19] Read literally a GAAR converts tax avoidance into evasion. However, few countries interpret their GAARs broadly on a regular basis because of the potential impact on useful tax planning.

Although the U.S. does not have a GAAR, the U.S. does have common law rules that may be invoked by courts to accomplish similar objectives.[20] Additionally, in 2010 Congress enacted a provision requiring transactions have economic substance in order for their tax treatment to be respected.[21] The limited U.S. economic

---

[17]   S.Rep. No. 99–313, at 732 (1986); H.R. Conf. Rep. No. 99–841, at II–147 (1986).

[18]   Income Tax Act 2007, s BG 1 (N.Z.). For more on New Zealand's GAAR, see John Prebble & Craig Elliffe, *General Anti-Avoidance Rules and Double Tax Agreements*, 19 REVENUE L.J. (2009).

[19]   *Id.* s YA 1.

[20]   For more on the common law rules of anti-avoidance, see Chapter 5.03.

[21]   I.R.C. § 7701(*o*).

substance doctrine converts affected planning into evasion. The primary difference between a statutory and common law regime is that statutory GAARs give legislative blessing for courts to examine the purpose of all transactions.

Although GAARs may reduce the amount of tax avoidance activity, their effectiveness has not been proven.[22] A difficulty for GAARs is that ambiguities arise in the application of a GAAR to particular facts. As a result, GAARs add uncertainty to the operation of the tax system. They effectively authorize courts to override statutory language when the results conflict with the law's intent, as defined by the court. This may negate a statute's specificity in ways that many Americans would find troubling.

§ 5.02   Tax Evasion

Because there is no natural law of taxation, statute determines what is taxed, and tax evasion is simply what the statute does not permit to reduce taxes. Therefore, tax evasion is the unlawful mitigation of taxes. Tax evasion occurs when taxpayers fail to file tax returns or deliberately misrepresent their income, deductions, or credits to reduce their tax liability. The latter offense may include dishonest tax reporting, such as overstating deductions or declaring less income, profits, or gains than the amounts actually earned. Taxpayers may buy into tax shelters to bolster their case for the tax reduction by creating a paper trail for the evasion even though the paper trail does not work as the taxpayer hopes.

(a) Classification as Evasion

Tax evasion is often defined to require an intent to illegally avoid taxes or at least an intent to take actions that are illegal. Under this standard, tax evasion is not merely making a mistake on a tax return, even if the mistake is ridiculous to an average taxpayer. To detect tax evasion, the IRS generally must audit taxpayers to determine whether an error was caused by evasion or mistake. Together evasion and mistakes comprise the tax gap, but the IRS must distinguish between the two for the imposition of penalties, despite their having the same effect on federal revenue. When intent is present, tax evasion may result in criminal prosecution but is more frequently handled with civil penalties.[23]

---

[22]   For more on GAARs, see Christophe Waerzeggers & Cory Hillier, *Introducing a General Anti-Avoidance Rule (GAAR)*, INT'L MONETARY FUND (2016); Graeme Cooper, *International Experience with General Anti-Avoidance Rules*, 54 SMU L. REV. 83 (2001).

[23]   For more on enforcement and penalties, see Chapter 2.2(c).

A simple kind of tax evasion occurs when people work off the books for cash and never report the income. Using cash and forgoing receipts allows the underreporting of income and the evasion of the income tax, sales tax, and employment taxes. The amount at issue is not trivial. It was estimated that in 2007 the U.S.'s informal economy was 8.4% of GNP, allowing a considerable amount of tax evasion, and that number has likely grown.[24] More recent estimates found that underreported income was 18% of taxable income (a smaller amount than GNP), which resulted in up to $537 billion of lost federal revenue.[25]

Not all tax fraud results in reduced tax revenue, although the tax system is ill prepared for tax fraud that produces greater tax revenue in the short-term. For example, between 1999 and 2001, WorldCom created faulty records to inflate its share price, so its underlying crime was securities fraud. However, to prevent the public from catching its securities fraud, WorldCom willingly filed false tax returns overstating its income.[26] To report different financials from tax returns requires reconciling the book-tax difference on a Schedule M-1 on its tax return. Therefore, WorldCom paid more in taxes than it needed to based on its actual business operations to artificially increase its share price.

After the fraud was detected, WorldCom filed amended tax returns and received over $300 million in tax refunds, including interest on its overpaid taxes.[27] Despite knowingly filing false returns, few penalties exist to punish the behavior because existing penalties focus on the failure to pay tax, not their overpayment. Although some argued that the money was rightfully WorldCom's shareholders, the false returns likely impacted the federal budget in the year the taxes were received and again when the refunds were paid. Moreover, refund suits are claims in equity, not statutory law, and arguably WorldCom had no equitable right to the repayments; although penalties would have most harmed the creditors of the bankrupted company. Congress considered denying the refund or imposing stiffer penalties but ultimately no action was taken to deny the refunds.

---

[24] Friedrich et al., *Shadow Economies All Over the World*, POLICY RESEARCH WORKING PAPER 5356, at 24 (2010).

[25] Richard Cebula & Edgar Feige, *America's Underground Economy*, 57 CRIME, L. & SOC. CHANGE 265 (2012).

[26] For more on WorldCom's overreporting, see Craig Boise, *Playing with "Monopoly Money": Phony Profits, Fraud Penalties and Equity*, 90 MINN. L. REV. 144, 148 (2005).

[27] Rebecca Blumenstein et al., *After Inflating Their Income, Companies Want IRS Refunds*, WALL ST. J., May 2, 2003.

(b) Perception of Evasion

Most Americans think that the tax system is too complex and hard to understand, but their views of tax evasion are less clear. One 2013 survey found that only 6% of Americans thought it is morally acceptable to underreport income on tax returns. But, in addition, 19% thought it is not a moral issue.[28] Unsurprisingly, when it is easy to evade taxes, people are more likely to do so; but evasion by convenience may reflect either a desire to break the law or evidence of a certain laxness in compliance.

Whether the average person is engaged in tax evasion is hard to know. Neighbors do not walk around with a scarlet E on their chest for evading taxes, although some have suggested public shaming in at least some contexts.[29] Taxpayers' tax filings are confidential unless a taxpayer chooses to pursue tax litigation, is criminally indicted, or faces a public collections process. Therefore, it is often impossible to know whether someone is filing her taxes and paying what she owes. This has not always been the case, although full disclosure of taxpayers' federal returns has been rare. To increase awareness, nearly two dozen states publish lists online revealing tax delinquents.[30] This public shaming can be effective in getting people to pay the taxes they owe but risks taxpayer privacy, alienating the public, and taxpayer morale. Moreover, shaming works only if evasion is detected, a difficult task for enforcement.

Tax evasion is more likely than tax avoidance to be perceived as immoral because tax evasion has an illegal element. For example, the Roman Catholic Church has a catechism that categorizes tax evasion as a sin.[31] If one accepts that there is a moral obligation to pay taxes, one could still debate whether tax evasion is *malum prohibitum* (something wrong because it is prohibited) or *malum in se* (wrong because it is evil in itself).[32] One view is that tax evasion draws its disapproval from its legal status; if there were no tax laws, there would be nothing to willfully defeat. Consequently, tax evasion is not bad in and of itself. Of course, even if tax evasion is only *malum*

---

28   Seth Motel, *5 Facts on How Americans View Taxes*, PEW RES. CTR (2015).

29   Joshua Blank, *Reconsidering Corporate Tax Privacy*, 11 N.Y.U. J.L. & BUS. 31 (2014); Joseph Thorndike, *The Thorndike Challenge*, 122 TAX NOTES 691 (2009); Marjorie Kornhauser, *Doing the Full Monty*, 18 CANADIAN J. L. & JURIS. 1 (2005); Stephen Mazza, *Taxpayer Privacy and Tax Compliance*, 51 U. KAN. L. REV. 1065, 11120–43 (2003); Marc Linder, *Tax Glasnost' for Millionaires*, 18 N.Y.U. REV. L. & SOC. CHANGE 951 (1990–1991).

30   Ricardo Perez-Truglia & Ugo Troiano, *Shaming Those Who Skip Out on Taxes*, N.Y. TIMES, Apr. 15, 2015.

31   Catechism of the Catholic Church, Revised, art. 2409, 2240.

32   Zoe Prebble & John Prebble, *The Morality of Tax Avoidance*, 43 CREIGHTON L. REV. 693, 729 (2010).

prohibitum, the lying and fraud necessary to accomplish tax evasion might be *malum in se.* On the other hand, there may exist a moral duty to contribute to society and failure to do so may be *malum in se.* Because of the complexity of society, the amount of the contribution is defined by law in the form of taxes, making evasion morally bad.

Alternatively, people may have a moral obligation to evade taxes if they disagree with how the government uses the money.[33] Whether contested spending is for war or abortion, the argument goes that taxpayers should not give money that will be used for things they find morally reprehensible. Proponents of this argument claim that because taxes are a compulsory taking of property, the taking must first be justified. Without the initial justification, resisting the taking is not wrong. This ignores that it is impossible to segregate funds between spending items, and most taxpayers accept that some spending in the budget is justified.

Morally tying evasion to spending also raises the question whether individuals should be allowed to judge the just nature of government spending outside of the democratic process. Arguably, the democratic system shifts the authority to make moral determinations regarding taxation and other laws from the public to elected officials. On the other hand, voter turnout in the 2016 presidential election was about 60% of the voting-eligible population but just under 55% of the voting-age population.[34] Off year elections have even lower turnouts; in 2014, turnout was 36.7% of the voting-eligible or 33.2% of the voting-age population. The low turnout possibly undermines democratic support for elected officials carrying the moral weight of taxation.

(c) Historic Role of Advisors in Evasion

Policymakers and the public are more apt to take issue with the role of tax practitioners in perpetuating tax evasion than tax avoidance. In 2002, a Senate subcommittee investigated the development, marketing, and implementation of evasive tax shelters by professional organizations. According to the subcommittee:

> The evidence also shows that respected professional firms [like major accounting firms, banks, investment advisory firms, and law firms] are spending substantial resources, forming alliances, and developing the internal and external infrastructure necessary to design, market, and implement hundreds of complex tax shelters, some of which are illegal

---

[33]   Robert McGee, *Is Tax Evasion Unethical,* 42 U. KAN. L. REV. 411 (1994).

[34]   UNITED STATES ELECTIONS PROJECT, 2016 NOVEMBER GENERAL ELECTION TURNOUT RATES, http://www.electproject.org/2016g (last visited May 1, 2018).

and improperly deny the U.S. Treasury of billions of dollars in tax revenues.[35]

The market for tax shelters has long existed but its marketing has become increasingly developed since the 1990s.

Marketing tax shelters generated a significant backlash against the tax practice of one of the nation's largest accounting firms, KPMG.[36] KPMG self-reported an inventory of over 500 active tax products designed to be offered to multiple clients for a fee. In the process, KPMG traded on its accounting reputation to establish a lucrative tax shelter practice. The government conducted case studies on four of the products: BLIPS, FLIP, OPIS, and SOS.[37] All four were found to be tax evasion and not avoidance. KPMG had sold these four tax products to more than 350 individuals from 1997 to 2001, and together the four had earned more than $124 million for KPMG. By the end of the government's investigation, KPMG had disbanded its tax shelter practice, replaced several high level partners, entered a deferred prosecution agreement, and paid a fine of nearly $500 million. Nine former partners were indicted. Most of the criminal cases were dismissed, although some partners pled guilty to tax evasion and fraud.[38]

The Son of BOSS ("Bond and Option Sales Strategy") transaction strategy, of which BLIPS and SOS are variants, is a good example of why the IRS considered these tax shelters evasive. The Son of BOSS was designed to offset capital gains with artificial capital losses. If it works, the strategy eliminates a taxpayer's reportable income so that no taxes are owed. To create the loss, the Son of BOSS creates artificial basis by using the since-amended partnership contingent liability rules.[39] Taxpayers love basis because it represents amounts that can be recovered tax-free.[40]

As a hypothetical to show the way the Son of BOSS works: A taxpayer sells a short (an agreement to sell something) for a $100,000

---

[35]　MINORITY STAFF OF THE PERMANENT SUBCOMM. ON INVESTIGATIONS OF THE COMM. ON GOVERNMENTAL AFFAIRS, 108TH CONG., REP. ON U.S. TAX SHELTER INDUS.: THE ROLE OF ACCT., LAW., AND FIN. PROF. FOUR KPMG CASE STUDIES: FLIP, OPIS, BLIPS, AND SC2 34 (Comm. Print 2003).

[36]　Tanina Rostain, *Travails in Tax: KPMG and the Tax-Shelter Controversy*, in LEGAL ETHICS: LAW STORIES (Deborah Rhode & David Luban eds. 2006).

[37]　Many tax shelters go by acronyms. BLIPS is Bond Linked Issue Premium Structure; FLIP is Foreign Leveraged Investment Program; OPIS is Offshore Portfolio Investment Strategy; and SOS is Short Option Strategy.

[38]　Press Release, IRS, IR–2005–83, KPMG to Pay $456 Million for Criminal Violations (Aug. 29, 2005).

[39]　These rules have since been changed, affecting all taxpayers, in order to prevent this tax shelter. *See* T.D. 9788, 81 Fed. Reg. 69,282 (Oct. 5, 2016); T.D. 9787, 81 Fed. Reg. 69,291 (Oct. 5, 2016).

[40]　For more on basis, see Chapter 7.01(b).

profit and buys a long (an agreement to buy something) for $101,000. The short is a contingent liability because no one may want to buy from the taxpayer at that price, but the long is an asset because the burden already exists. The net cost is $1,000. The taxpayer puts both instruments in a partnership and claims that the long is an asset with a $101,000 basis but that the short is only a contingent liability so it should not reduce his basis until, and if, the short is triggered.

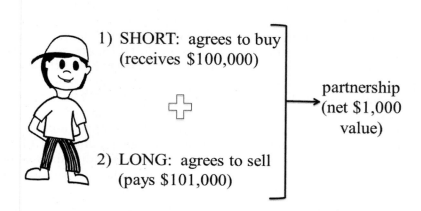

Then the taxpayer sells his interest in the partnership containing the two agreements for $1,000 because that is what the two contracts are really worth. Doing so, the taxpayer generates a $100,000 tax loss because of the $101,000 reported basis minus the $1,000 he receives. However, he has no economic loss because combined the two contracts are worth the same $1,000 he receives.

The Son of BOSS was designed and promoted in the late 1990s and 2000 by tax advisors in law firms and accounting firms, and, for a while, were highly successful for their purveyors. Son of BOSS schemes involved 1,800 people and cost the government an estimated $6 billion in lost revenue. The IRS has recovered more than one-half of that revenue since cracking down in 2000. Unless people came forward when the IRS offered amnesty from penalties, taxpayers using Son of BOSS suffered 40% penalties. By 2005, 1,165 people had settled Son of BOSS cases.[41]

The IRS came down heavily on the Son of BOSS shelters, and all cases decided on the facts held that Son of BOSS losses were invalid for federal income tax purposes. Courts accepted that to enter into a transaction that has no business purpose except for the reduction of

---

[41] Press Release, IRS, IR–2005–37, IRS Collects $3.2 Billion from Son of Boss (Mar. 24, 2005).

taxes violates common law and statutory economic substance doctrines.[42] Therefore, the tax loss should be disregarded for tax purposes and the income the Son of BOSS was intended to offset is taxable. However, despite the lack of business purpose, unless the transaction amounted to fraud, buying into a Son of BOSS transaction was not criminal so that its users faced only civil penalties.

In the only case regarding a Son of BOSS investment that came before the Supreme Court, *United States v. Home Concrete & Supply, LLC*, the Court ruled in favor of the taxpayer on the grounds that the statute of limitations had lapsed, preventing the government's recovery.[43] Normally there is a three-year statute of limitations after which the IRS cannot assess taxes, but the period is extended to six years when taxpayers understate their gross income by more than 25%.[44] Despite unpaid taxes totaling $6 million, the Court held that the taxpayer did not understate income by overstating its basis based on a 1958 precedent.[45] In response, Congress overruled the precedent and extended the statute of limitations for gross understatements of basis.[46]

Jenkins & Gilchrist's Chicago tax group were the lawyers who helped create and, more importantly, wrote tax opinions covering Home Concrete's tax shelters.[47] The lawyers had worked with tax advisors at Ernest & Young and earned $267 million from 1998 to 2003 in their work with this and other tax shelters. With their firm's implosion playing out in the press, Jenkins & Gilchrist faced lawsuits from clients and the IRS. The firm settled with the IRS for a $76 million fine plus approximately $80 million to former clients. The firm also agreed to cease practicing law immediately. In 2011, four of its partners were found guilty of tax evasion.

§ 5.03   Common Law Limits on Avoidance and Evasion

The Supreme Court accepts that "[t]he legal right of a taxpayer to decrease the amount of what otherwise would be his taxes, or

---

[42]   For more on common law and statutory limitations on tax evasion, see Chapter 5.03.

[43]   566 U.S. 478 (2012).

[44]   For more on the assessment of taxes, see Chapter 2.02(a).

[45]   Colony, Inc. v. Comm'r, 357 U.S. 28 (1958).

[46]   Surface Transp. & Veterans Healthcare Choice Improvement Act of 2014, Pub. L. 114–41, 129 Stat. 443.

[47]   Patricia Hurtado & Chris Dolmetsch, *Chicago Lawyer Daugerdas Found Guilty in Tax Shelter Trial*, BLOOMBERG, May 24, 2011; Lynnley Browning, *Inquiry into Tax Shelters Widens Beyond Audit Firms*, N.Y. TIMES, Feb. 4, 2006; *When Tax Avoidance Crosses a Line*, NEWSWEEK, Apr. 10, 2007.

altogether avoid them, by means which the law permits, cannot be doubted."[48] However, the American judicial system has created a vibrant common law that restricts tax avoidance. These judicial doctrines reach beyond the language of the Internal Revenue Code in order to minimize the economic rewards of tax avoidance by converting some planning into tax evasion.

The most fundamental of these doctrines is the sham transaction doctrine. As the name suggests, this doctrine requires that courts not respect transactions that have been created on paper but that never took place in fact. This is a threshold question for courts. A court should not inquire more deeply into the tax effect of a transaction until it determines that the transaction is bona fide and not a factual sham. If something is a factual sham, the transaction is ignored for tax purposes. For example, if a person claims a business deduction for dinner out with a client but no one went out to eat, the claim is a factual sham.

Second, the doctrine of substance-over-form permits courts and the IRS to examine the substance of a transaction instead of being bound by its legal structure. In other words, when the government analyzes the tax treatment of a transaction, the government can consider the practical purpose and effect of the transaction. Therefore, if the form appears to secure favorable tax treatment but the substance is really something else, courts will treat the transaction as it really is and ignore the legal form.

For example, if a corporation tries to structure a non-deductible dividend to a majority shareholder as a deductible interest payment, the IRS can classify the payment according to its economic reality rather than being limited by the labels given by the taxpayer. In an early case involving the substance over form doctrine, the Supreme Court ruled, "To permit the true nature of a transaction to be disguised by mere formalisms, which exist solely to alter tax liabilities, would seriously impair the effective administration of the tax policies of Congress."[49]

Third, the step transaction doctrine builds on the substance-over-form doctrine. It allows the government to combine a transaction's separate steps into a single, integrated transaction for the purpose of determining the transaction's appropriate tax treatment. The step transaction doctrine can apply even when each step is a formally distinct transaction. This prevents taxpayers from accomplishing in many steps what they would be prohibited from

---

48   Gregory v. Helvering, 69 F.2d 809, 810 (2d Cir. 1934), *aff'd*, 293 U.S. 465, 469 (1934) (citations omitted).

49   Comm'r v. Court Holding Co., 324 U.S. 331 (1945).

doing in one transaction. This often applies in mergers and acquisitions or the purchase of a business's assets, so that courts can examine the starting point and end result rather than accepting the independence of the steps in between.

Finally, the economic substance doctrine, also known as the business purpose doctrine or "shams in substance," requires that a transaction have an economic purpose aside from the reduction of tax liability. If no reasonable possibility of profit exists or if the taxpayer was not motivated by a bona fide purpose other than obtaining tax benefits, the transaction is not respected. This was often used in Son of BOSS cases.

The economic substance doctrine had a long and tortured common law history that has been codified. In 2010, Congress defined when a transaction would be deemed to have economic substance.[50] First, the transaction must change the taxpayer's economic position in a meaningful way. Second, the taxpayer must have a substantial purpose for entering into the transaction. Both prongs must be satisfied as a result of something other than the federal income tax effects of the transaction. If the taxpayer fails either prong, the transaction is ignored for tax purposes and any deductions generated or favorable tax rates imposed are lost.[51]

Despite years of litigation over these judicial doctrines' meaning and application, the common law of tax remains imprecise. Courts disagree on when and how to apply each of these doctrines. At times the doctrines are even applied interchangeably. The resulting webbed common law of anti-avoidance may change the tax treatment of a transaction that literally complies with the Code but is incompatible with its purpose. Prohibited tax shelters are often found to be in breach of one or more of these doctrines. It is the expectation that the existence of these doctrines, and their use by courts, will reduce tax avoidance and tax evasion.

Even if revenue is protected, applying common law rules in the tax system has drawbacks. The further judges go beyond the literal application of the statutory language to a given transaction or transactions, the more likely the taxpayer will owe the government. However, taxpayers have less ability to anticipate what courts will hold. Thus, common law makes the tax law more difficult to predict *a priori*. Revenue is raised, but only as judges decide that particular

---

[50]   Health Care and Educ. Reconciliation Act of 2010, Pub. L. No. 111–152, § 1409 124 Stat. 1029, 1067 (2010) (codified at I.R.C. § 7701(o) (2017)).

[51]   For individuals, economic substance only applies to transactions entered into in connection with a trade or business or an activity engaged in for the production of income; personal activities are not held to this standard, in part because they generate few deductions.

taxpayers are bad actors vis-à-vis the tax system. This also means the law is applied inconsistently to taxpayers, compounding the reality that some tax evasion avoids detection in the assessment process. Judges add an additional lawyer of inconsistency in the law's application when some taxpayers are held to higher common law standards.

Although taxpayers cannot know for certain if these extra-statutory initiatives will be applied to their activities, the doctrines are intended to stop tax evasion or when tax avoidance boarders the gray area with impermissible evasion. Consequently, taxpayers are likely aware that they are being aggressive with respect to their tax planning; they simply do not know if they will be caught or punished. Whether their knowledge that they are taking a position not favored by the government is sufficient to justify extra-statutory standards to punish the position is left to courts to decide. The influence these doctrines have in restraining taxpayer planning has yet to be measured.

§ 5.04   Advisors' Obligations

When advising clients on ways to minimize their tax burdens, most tax advisors, including attorneys and certified public accountants (CPAs), evaluate a range of tax proposals. This evaluation raises professional and personal questions of ethics and morals, particularly when advisors are faced with aggressive plans.[52] These questions may be particularly important if tax advisors have a greater duty to the tax system (one possibly unregulated by an external source) than other advisors who may run across tax issues from time to time.[53] How advisors respond to aggressive tax positions that are not quite tax evasion is a personal choice. Legally, the duty is limited to that laid out in the law and as set out by regulatory bodies. However, reputational effects should be considered because there is a risk of being tainted by proximity to tax evasive transactions. Thus, advisors have ethical, moral, legal, and reputational concerns that they must consider when deciding how to deal with their employers' or clients' tax planning.

Consider Michael Hamersley, a tax lawyer, who became a whistleblower at KPMG.[54] He reported on KPMG's tax shelter business to the IRS and Congress. As Hamersley describes events, he worked at KPMG in 2002 and was asked to sign off on the tax treatment of a transaction ultimately found to be tax evasion. He

---

[52]   For more on the difference between ethics and morality, see Chapter 4.01(a)(v).

[53]   For a discussion of attorneys' personal ethics, see Heather Field, *Aggressive Tax Planning & The Ethical Tax Lawyer*, 36 VA. TAX REV. (forthcoming 2017).

[54]   Rostain, *supra* note 36.

complained of significant financial pressure by the accounting firm to develop increasingly aggressive tax shelter strategies. In particular, lawyers at KPMG faced internal pressures to create strategies that would "more likely than not" be upheld in court, which the lawyers knew would be actively marketed to clients.

Despite the market pressure, over the last two decades, Congress and the Treasury Department have increasingly designated advisors as gatekeepers of the tax system in the hope of reducing tax evasion in general and the creation of tax shelters in particular. The rules Congress and the Treasury Department have created punish advisors for certain types of involvement with shelters. Thus, even if investing in tax shelters itself is not unethical, these rules make advising about the shelters punishable. Consequently, although advisors are permitted to help clients lawfully avoid taxes, they must navigate a web of ethical restrictions before doing so.

For example, in 2004 Congress enacted provisions that require advisors, including attorneys and CPAs, disclose information regarding so-called reportable transactions.[55] Even transactions that are entirely legitimate must be disclosed if they fall within broad categories of reportable transactions laid out in Treasury Regulations. These transactions are generally those that create large tax deductions and require confidentiality.

In addition to this disclosure, the Treasury Department imposes restrictions originally published as part of Circular 230 that apply to those who practice before the IRS or give tax advice.[56] These rules require that advisors do certain things that make it harder for taxpayers to benefit from tax shelters. Penalties may be imposed on advisors for their noncompliance. First, persons preparing returns or giving tax advice must disclose on returns all nonfrivolous tax positions (frivolous positions were already prohibited). This allows the IRS to more easily identify and assess possible tax shelter transactions.

Second, those giving tax advice must follow certain rules, although the rules were scaled back in 2014.[57] Today, written tax advice must be based on reasonable factual and legal assumptions and may not unreasonably rely upon representations made by the client or others. These requirements mean that someone writing a tax opinion must investigate before they sign the opinion, although

---

[55]　I.R.C. § 6011; Treas. Reg. § 1.6011–4.

[56]　Treas. Dept. Circular No. 230 (Rev. 6–2014), *Regulations Governing Practice Before the Internal Revenue Service*, Title 31 Code of Fed. Reg., Subtitle A, Part 10 (June 12, 2014).

[57]　T.D. 9668, I.R.B. 2014–27.

significantly less investigation is needed than had been required before 2014.

The development of advisors' gatekeeping function likely resulted from their position as members of accredited groups that purport to be leaders in the field of taxation. Moreover, because of their roles in tax matters, these advisors are in the best position to assess when tax avoidance crosses over into tax evasion. As a result, maybe they should have a special responsibility for reporting it. The perception that advisors are helping some, particularly wealthy, taxpayers evade their tax obligations may justify a heightened obligation if only to protect reputational interests. Practically, with the current low audit rates, without self-reporting by taxpayers or their advisors, much tax evasion will not be caught.

On the other hand, clients need to feel free to talk to their advisors about tax planning ideas to learn when something is evasive. Clients may be discouraged from having these conversations if they know that their advisors might report them. If clients know advisors will report their behavior, they may forego tax advice that might convince them to comply with the law.

In addition to government-imposed obligations, accountants have their own ethical obligations that govern their professional conduct. CPAs have two main governing bodies that enforce codes of conduct on their members: the American Institute of CPAs (AICPA) and state boards of accountancy. Most states have adopted a version of the AICPA Code of Professional Conduct.[58] The code is revised annually and establishes standards for auditor independence, integrity, and objectivity; responsibilities to clients and colleagues; and acts discreditable to the accounting profession.

As for lawyers, even if as individuals they feel no moral obligation to pay their taxes, state bar associations' ethical rules require lawyers to follow the law. One such law is the Internal Revenue Code. Because tax evasion is breaking the law, attorneys may not engage in tax evasion and may not assist clients in tax evasion, although they may engage in tax avoidance. Therefore, in addition to potentially facing IRS punishment, state bar associations police this ethical obligation, and lawyers may be sanctioned. Many lawyers embrace and advocate for this responsibility.[59]

Their responsibility as lawyers may be murky because of the unusual way tax matters are handled by the government. According

---

[58]   AMER. INST. OF CPAs, CODE OF PROFESSIONAL CONDUCT (2014), http://pub. aicpa.org/codeofconduct/ethicsresources/et-cod.pdf (last visited May 1, 2018).

[59]   *See generally* Tanina Rostrain, *Sheltering Lawyers*, 23 YALE J. ON REG. 77 (2006).

to the American Bar Association (ABA), the IRS is not a tribunal and, therefore, attorneys do not owe the same duty to the agency as they do to courts.[60] For example, attorneys are not required to volunteer information to the IRS in the way they must to tribunals. Instead, the ABA views the IRS as a unique type of adversary.

On the other hand, the Treasury Department's reporting obligations imposed on reportable transactions and in Circular 230 add unusual responsibilities. For attorneys, complying with the rules could violate attorney-client privilege. In a real sense the ethical rules imposed on lawyers to the tax system may create a conflict between representing a client and upholding the lawyer's obligations to the state. The government's interest, even if it is to find the correct amount of taxes owed, often conflicts with the client's desire to minimize taxes.

As a final concern regarding advisors' gatekeeping function, blaming advisors for the creation and adoption of tax shelters risks isolating blame for this behavior to one group. This blame implies tax shelter creators are relatively worse actors than tax shelter buyers. Instead, it may be better to share blame among those who create tax shelters, those who use the shelters to reduce their taxes, and the IRS who does not always catch the evasion thereby increasing their attractiveness. To the extent blame is shared, the scope of corrective actions may need to be broadened. If any group is absolved of responsibility, the incentives for the behavior are likely to continue.

Nevertheless, today, purchasers of tax shelters are often isolated from risk, ensuing that the market for shelters will continue. Malpractice suits allow many buyers of failed tax shelters to recover penalties owed to the government from their lawyers or accountants.[61] Therefore, taxpayers who owe taxes, interest, and penalties after buying into a failed tax shelter can seek to recover those costs, plus the cost of the shelter, from the people who sold them the shelter.[62] These civil lawsuits have yet to reduce the supply of tax shelters, although they may have driven up their cost.

Malpractice claims do create a new alliance that may make it easier to punish tax shelters once they are detected. No longer are taxpayers and advisors working together against the government

---

[60]   ABA COMM'N. ON ETHICS & PROF'L RESPONSIBILITY, FORMAL OP. 314 (1965); ABA COMM'N. ON ETHICS & PROF'L RESPONSIBILITY, FORMAL OP. 85–352 (1985).

[61]   Tax malpractice suits are a small percentage of legal malpractice claims; between 1985 and 2011 tax claims ranged between 1.2 and 1.6% of all malpractice suits. Tom Baker & Rick Swedloff, *Liability Insurer Data as a Window on Lawyers' Professional Liability*, 5 UC IRVINE L. REV. (2015).

[62]   Jay Soled, *Tax Shelter Malpractice Cases and their Implications for Tax Compliance*, 58 AM. U. L. REV. 267 (2008).

but, for a time, taxpayers and new advisors join the government against the old advisors. This levels the playing field between the IRS and private interests. The resource and information deficits the IRS faces compared to the advisors creating and marketing complex shelters is counterbalanced when private advisors join the side to punish old advisors.

But that alliance is weak and creates perverse incentives. Successful malpractice claims involving tax shelters reduce the risk of being caught in tax evasion, and thereby should increase taxpayers' aggressive positions. If taxpayers cannot lose, they have no incentive to eliminate the market for shelters. At the same time, these claims increase the risk for advisors in giving tax opinions and representing tax evasion. The latter effect may be weaker than the former because the claims only exist if a given tax shelter has been discovered and successfully challenged.

§ 5.05 Tax Patents

In the last few decades, people who create strategies to lawfully reduce taxes have sought government protection of their ideas. Much as with other potentially lucrative ideas, people sought to patent their ideas so that they could collect payments from people who used these strategies.[63] To the extent tax patents are respected, it encourages the creation of tax avoidance devices because of the opportunity to capture greater returns from an idea. Although permitted for a period, in 2011 Congress prohibited the Patent Office from issuing tax patents going forward.[64]

The basis for a claim for a tax patent is that it is a type of business method patent. Business method patents disclose and claim new methods of doing business, such as new types of e-commerce, insurance, and banking. For most of U.S. history these ideas have not been considered patentable; however, interpreting statutory changes enacted in 1952 in light of the advent of e-commerce, the U.S. Patent Office began issuing these types of patents and, in 1998, the Federal Circuit Court held that business methods are patentable under patent law.[65] The court reversed itself in 2008, although the Supreme Court would not accept that reversal.[66]

---

[63] For more on tax patents, see Linda Beale, *Tax Patents: At the Crossroads of Tax and Patent Law*, 1 U. ILL. J. L. TECH. & POL'Y 107 (2008); Dustin Stamper, *Tax Strategy Patents: A Problem Without Solutions*, 2007 TNT 78–3.

[64] Leahy-Smith America Invents Act, Pub. L. No. 112–29, § 14 (Sept. 16, 2011).

[65] State Street Bank & Trust Co. v. Signature Financial Group, Inc., 149 F.3d 1368 (Fed. Cir. 1998).

[66] Bilski v. Kappos, 561 U.S. 593 (2010), *aff'g*, 543 F.3d 943 (Fed. Cir. 2008).

By 2000, the number of tax patents was growing. In the mid-2000s, the Treasury Department reviewed existing patents and vetted many ideas regarding how to deal with the growing number but failed to formulate a response.[67] Thereafter, Congress eliminated the U.S. Patent Office's ability to grant patents for strategies for "reducing, avoiding, or deferring tax liability, whether known or unknown at the time of the invention or application for patent."[68] The legislation was prospective, so that the 161 tax patents previously issued remain in effect. It is uncertain how courts will respond to any attempts to enforce them.

It is possible that tax patents could be useful to the government because a patent application must explain the methodology used in the strategy. Instead of hiding a strategy behind confidential documents, to be patentable a strategy must be laid out in detail. By centralizing the information in the patent and possibly requiring advisors report use of tax patents to the IRS, the system could permit the IRS to focus resources on evaluating the strategy only once. Moreover, owners of the patent have a financial incentive to help police the market.

On the other hand, the issuance of tax patents requires tax and patent specialists learn each other's skills, a significant combination of two highly technical fields. Before tax advisors can help taxpayers comply with their tax obligations, they may have to evaluate patents' applicability. At the same time, to be worthy of a patent, an idea must be of patentable subject matter, novel, inventive or non-obvious, and have utility, which may be hard for patent specialists to evaluate. After undertaking some training in the area of tax law, the Patent Office created a classification of 705/36T for tax patents but the IRS refused to directly participate in the determination of a patent proposal's effectiveness or legitimacy. This isolation of patent law increased the risk that common tax strategies would appear novel and non-obvious. For example, someone won a patent for the strategy of purchasing an annuity contract to fund a charitable remainder trust despite the IRS previously issuing letter rulings on the idea.[69]

Similarly, in a well-reported case, a financial advisor, Robert Slane, received a patent for a type of grantor retained annuity trust (GRAT).[70] GRATs are creatures of federal tax law that allow

---

[67]   T.D. 9295, 71 Fed. Reg. 64, 458 (Nov. 2, 2006); Reg–129916–07, 26 C.F.R. § 1,301 (Sep. 26, 2007); *Issues Relating to the Patent of Tax Advice: Hearing Before the Subcomm. On Select Revenue Measures of the H. Comm. on Ways & Means*, 109th Cong. (2006).

[68]   Leahy-Smith America Invents Act, § 14(a), Pub. L. 112–29, 125 Stat. 284.

[69]   Jack Cathey et al., *Tax Patents Considered*, J. OF ACCOUNTANCY, Jul. 1, 2007.

[70]   Wealth Transfer Group v. Rowe, No. 3:2006cv00024; Steve Seindeberg, *Crisis Pending*, ABA J., May 1, 2007; *Tax Strategies?*, INS. IP BULL. (Oct. 15, 2006).

taxpayers to reduce federal gift taxes for gifts to family members of assets that grow substantially in value while held in the trust. The patent focused on Slane's funding mechanism, which was the contribution of unqualified stock options. Thus, Slane took an estate planning technique that Congress created for use with any asset and coupled it with a particular asset. Slane sued Dr. John Rowe, at the time President and CEO of Aetna U.S. Healthcare, for two trusts worth an estimated $28 million that were funded in this way. The suit was for treble damages, an injunction, and attorney fees. The case was ultimately settled.

Another downside of tax patents is that they appear to sanction a particular form of tax reduction. In other words, a patent might be interpreted as the government's seal of approval for tax avoidance, despite the Patent Office not including legality in its criteria for granting patents. Moreover, to the extent that patents are intended to grant short-term monopoly rights in order to encourage investment in new strategies, there is no reason to grant this protection for tax strategies. The creation of tax shelters is not in the public interest and they have flourished even when not given monopoly protection.

Chapter 6

ECONOMIC THEORY

Table of Sections

Many people debating tax policy incorporate economic concepts into their arguments. Although sometimes intimidating to the uninitiated, a PhD in economics is unnecessary to understand these concepts and to evaluate their application in a given context. The brief introduction below examines the interaction of economics and tax policy. One reason to incorporate economic theory into these debates is that economics is predictive. Therefore, a hope for economic theory is to estimate how changes in tax policy will change taxpayer behavior and uncover unintended consequences.

Although predictive, economic theories are often impossible to test empirically because doing so would require creating a counterfactual world. The only way to know for sure how an alternative tax regime would work is to have the alternative in place. Therefore, modern economists sometimes use mind-numbingly complex equations to mathematically prove their theories. These economic equations are only as good as their underlying assumptions. One common assumption in economic theory is that people are economically rational and utility maximizing. This requires people to have stable preferences, one of which is a preference for money, that are complete and transitive. This means that people are expected to understand how to maximize their preferences and will do so, all anecdotes and evidence to the contrary.

A final caveat is that economic theory is a diverse field with different specialties that can be applied to different questions in tax policy. Much of that diversity is glossed over in this chapter in the quest for simplicity. Generally, microeconomics examines parts of the economy, such as individuals or businesses, and macroeconomics studies the economy as a whole. For example, microeconomics might examine how an individual would respond to tax rate changes and macroeconomics might study how tax rate changes would affect the GDP or national economic growth. There is further specialization within each branch as economists refine theory to study particular questions of policy.

§ 6.01   Supply and Demand

One of the most basic tools of economic theory is the supply and demand curves. Supply and demand examines the interrelation of those who want to sell a given good or service and those who want to buy it. The depiction of that relationship is generally drawn as intersecting straight lines. Widgets is the classic economics example of an abstract product, one which does not exist, that is supplied and demanded.

The concepts are best described with a hypothetical market for widgets. In the hypothetical, 20 people are interested in buying widgets, and the price they are willing to pay varies from $1 to $20 because some people want the widgets more and are willing to pay more for them.[1] Consumers' demand for widgets creates a demand curve that shows the prices people are willing to pay. Additionally, suppliers are willing to sell up to 20 widgets at prices ranging from $1 to $20. This creates a supply curve illustrating the number of widgets to be sold at each price point. Because consumers are generally willing to pay less for each additional widget and suppliers are willing to supply more at higher prices, the lines go in different directions.

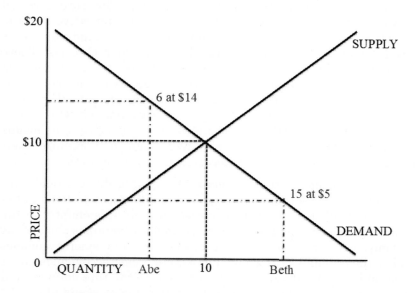

---

[1]   This problem has symmetrical numbers for ease of their depiction and not because it reflects the real world. The curves could be straight, curved, or uneven.

In the diagram, the demand curve is set so that people want, or demand, smaller quantities as the price increases, meaning the demand curve goes down to the right. The supply of goods increases as the price increases, meaning the supply line goes up to the right. The point at which the demand and supply curves intersect is the equilibrium point where the price is stable.

Economists call the price that a person is willing to pay the person's reservation price. In the diagram Abe has a reservation price of $14 per widget for 6 widgets, and Beth has a $5 reservation price for 15 widgets. The equilibrium point where the supply curve meets the demand curve for the 20 people and the 20 widgets is 10 widgets for $10. The equilibrium makes Abe happy because he pays less than he was willing to pay for his 6 widgets. Beth is unhappy because the widgets cost more than her reservation price so she buys no widgets.

Supply and demand are not static. For example, demand may change because something becomes more popular or goes out of fashion. Supply may change because of reduced manufacturing costs or a shortage of a critical input. When either line changes, the equilibrium point changes, so do the price and quantity of items sold.

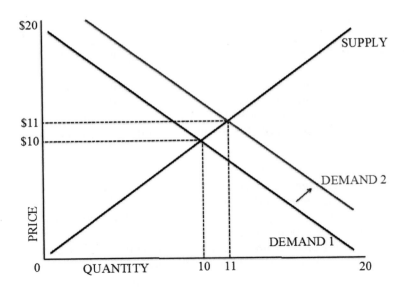

In the diagram, the increase in demand increases the price at equilibrium as more widgets are sold.

When the price settles at the equilibrium point, some people who would be happy to pay more for an item are able to pay less. This is because some demand on the demand curve is to the left of the equilibrium point. Abe would buy 6 widgets at $14 but now only has to pay $10. Similarly with the supply, some items are being sold for a higher equilibrium price than some sellers would otherwise require. Carol would have sold 2 widgets at $2 but is now able to charge $10. In the diagram, the extra each group of suppliers and purchasers receive is a surplus.

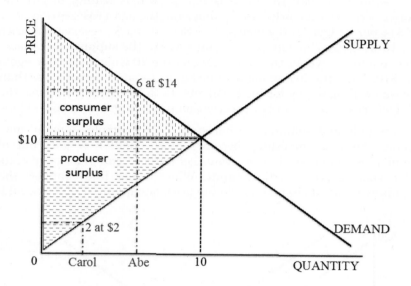

The surplus means that buyers and sellers are collectively better off by entering the market. These trades have made both buyer and seller better off than they would be without them, although one of the two may capture more of the surplus depending upon the slopes of the curves.

That buyers may capture a share of the surplus is one reason that sellers engage in price discrimination. Price discrimination occurs when a seller sells the same item at different prices in different markets. With price discrimination, those who are willing to pay more for an item are charged more, shifting the surplus above the equilibrium price from the buyer to the seller. The difficulty for sellers is to gauge buyers' relative willingness to pay and to enforce different prices for different markets. The opposing goal for some buyers becomes an arbitrage of buying low and selling high between markets to capture the surplus for themselves as a new middleman.

Taxes add complexity to this analysis, but taxes do not fundamentally change what the diagrams depict. Taxes are a cost of buying or selling goods that can affect either supply or demand by changing prices. The impact depends upon how the taxes are structured. Comparing how equilibrium prices are changed by taxes illustrates a more complete picture of tax policies.

If the seller has to pay the tax, such as with a value-added tax, the tax increases the seller's reservation price. By raising sellers' reservation prices, the supply curve shifts upward so that the same goods are offered at a higher price. For example, in the diagram below the $3 tax shifts the supply curve up by $2. The amount that the tax affects the supply curve depends upon the extent to which the seller is willing to internalize the cost of the tax as opposed to passing it on to consumers. In this example, the seller pays $1 of the tax himself by reducing his profits but passes on $2 to the consumer by increasing the price. Thus, the equilibrium point is not always adjusted by the face value of the tax.[2]

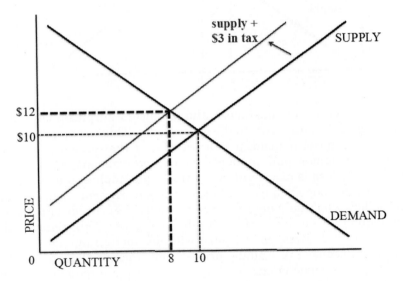

In this example, the new equilibrium point is at 8 widgets at $12 per widget. Buyers as a group pay $12 for 8 widgets but would have paid $10 for 10 widgets without the tax. Abe, who would have purchased 6 widgets at $14, is still willing to make the purchase because his reservation price was higher than the new equilibrium, but he has less surplus.

The change in the equilibrium point as a result of taxes produces government revenue but also reduces surpluses and creates a deadweight loss. In this example of the $3 tax, there is a $2 decrease in consumer surplus per widget and a $2 decrease in producer

---

2   For more on the incidence of taxes, see Chapter 4.02(d).

surplus per widget. Thus, based on these supply and demand curves, both surpluses are smaller as a result of the tax.

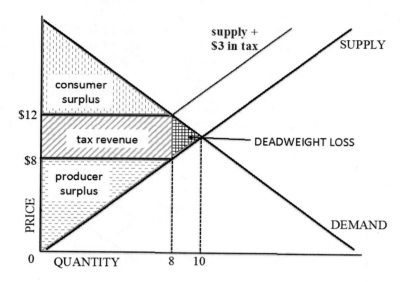

The reduction in the consumers' and producers' surpluses caused by the tax goes, in large part, to the government. This tax revenue is not a loss in welfare; instead, it is a transfer of that amount from the private consumer and producer to the government. However, a deadweight loss is also created. As the name implies, a deadweight loss does not benefit buyer, seller, or the government. Some buyers and sellers who would have entered the market at the lower price are not willing to do so at the tax-adjusted price. This reduces the consumer and producer surplus without increasing government revenue. Because taxes adjust prices, some amount of deadweight is always created when taxes are imposed as people respond to the new price.

If taxes are imposed on consumers rather than producers, such as with a sales tax, the demand curve is adjusted rather than the supply curve; but the same results hold. With the $3 tax applied to the consumer, the demand curve moves downward because people are willing to buy fewer widgets at the new higher post-tax price. If the demand curve only moves downward $2, it means the buyer is willing to assume the cost of $1 of taxes.

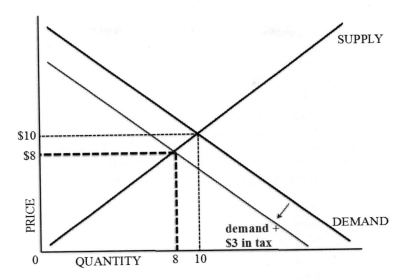

The new equilibrium is $8 for 8 widgets. The difference from the example when the seller paid the tax is who remits the revenue to the government and who bears the cost of any tax that cannot be shifted.

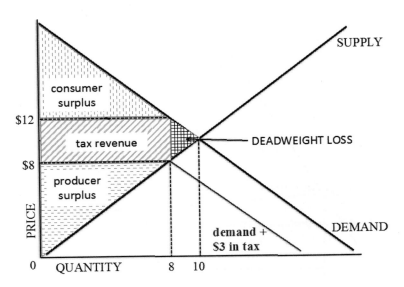

Because the curves in the example are equal, the government gets the same revenue and the same deadweight loss is created. This symmetry is unlikely to play out in the real world.

How the tax is structured determines whether the tax adjusts the supply curve or the demand curve. Nevertheless, these diagrams show that if the tax affects parties symmetrically it does not matter who the tax is imposed on, the economic results are the same. In other words, the amount of the surpluses and the government revenue is the same regardless of whom the statute taxes if supply and demand react equally to the tax.

Thus, the slopes of the supply and demand curves are the primary determinants of the size of the deadweight loss and the amount of surplus. A curve is steeper when supply or demand is more elastic because consumers or producers change their behavior more in response to changes in price. A curve is flatter and more inelastic if consumers or producers are less willing to change their behavior. The more responsive either party is to changes in price, the greater their elasticity and the greater an impact taxes will have on the equilibrium point.

Consider an inelastic demand curve showing that consumers barely reduce their purchases despite increases in price and a very elastic supply curve showing that producers supply a lot more with an increase in price. This demand curve could result if widgets are perceived as a necessity so that demand is largely fixed. The supply curve could be elastic because widgets are easily and cheaply made so that suppliers can enter the market quickly and at low cost.

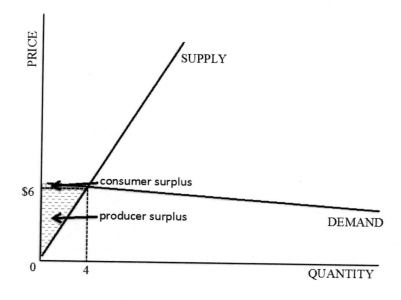

In this example, there is little consumer surplus and a lot of producer surplus. Thus, in this example, suppliers keep most of the extra benefit created by trade in widgets.

Imposing a $3 tax on the supplier would still shift the supply curve to the left, as in the prior example, but would also have a greater impact on the surpluses.

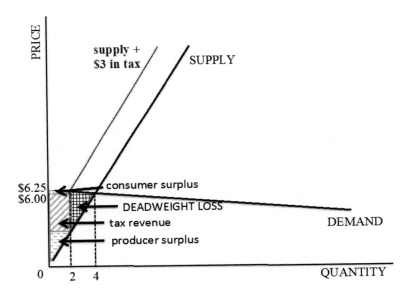

The slopes of the curves change the initial equilibrium and determine the impact on the quantity consumed and the after-tax price, but the slopes do not change the fundamental nature of the transaction. Without the tax, suppliers had a large surplus and consumers had a small surplus. With the tax, suppliers lose more than half of their surplus, but consumers are barely affected. Therefore, producers bear the burden of this tax because of their much greater elasticity. This elasticity had allowed suppliers to initially capture the surplus but thereafter bear the tax.

These supply and demand curves can be used to illustrate different types of markets. For example, to depict the labor market, workers are producers as they produce the hours of employment and employers are the consumer as the buyer of those hours.

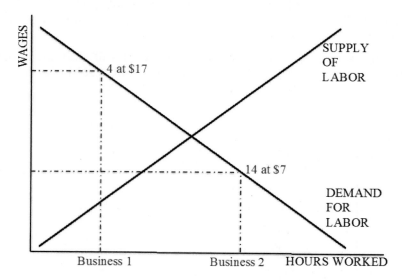

In the above diagram, among the many businesses making up the demand curve, Business 1 is willing to pay $17 per hour for 4 hours of work; Business 2 is willing to pay $7 per hour for 14 hours of work. Therefore, each labor hour is more valuable to Business 1 than it is to Business 2. However, instead of paying their reservation prices, the price of labor settles at the equilibrium.

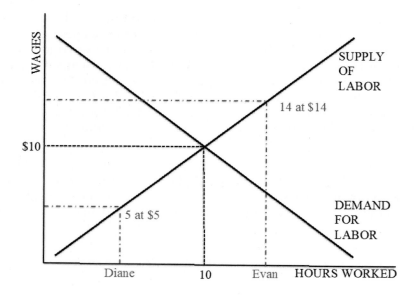

As for the supply of labor hours, among the many potential workers Diane is willing to work 5 hours at $5 per hour and Evan is willing to work 14 hours at $14 per hour.

In this example of the labor market, supply and demand meet at the equilibrium of $10 per hour for 10 hours of work. Without price discrimination Diane makes more per hour than she required to work her 5 hours, but Evan chooses to stay home because the equilibrium met at $10 and not his $14 per hour.

Because taxes reduce the amount workers retain of their wages, taxes have the same effect on the labor market as taxes did on the market for widgets.[3] If wage rates are held constant, as tax rates increase there should be a decrease in the number of hours people are willing to work. This change is at the margins, meaning that some people change some amount of hours that they are willing to work even though the bulk of labor remains available at the new equilibrium point.

One difficulty with supply and demand curves is that elasticity is unknown. As the price of labor increases, people may supply more labor but the extent to which they are willing to do so depends on people's response to wage changes. The more responsive they are to changes in wage rates the more elastic their behavior.[4] A further difficulty is the assumption that people have flexibility in the number of hours that they work. Many workers have little choice as to their hours. For people that do, the income effect causes them to respond to tax increases with increased labor in order to maintain the same lifestyle. A second response, the substitution effect, is for people to choose lesser-taxed substitutes, such as leisure, to higher taxed labor. The interaction of the income and substitution effects is generally unpredictable before a tax policy change.

Studies of the elasticity of labor led to discovery of the backward bending supply curve. When wages increase beyond a certain point, workers substitute leisure for work regardless of the wage rate. The rationale is that beyond a certain amount of wage income, a person needs an additional dollar less, so they substitute leisure for work. The result is that when wages go high enough, there is less labor available.

---

[3]   Income taxes and employment taxes on workers, as suppliers of labor, decrease the supply curve of labor; employment taxes on employers, as buyers of labor, decrease the demand curve for labor.

[4]   Studies have been undertaken, although not perfectly predictive. For example, one study in rural Pakistan found that girls' labor was inelastic whereas boys labor was elastic and contingent upon family poverty. The finding should influence the shape of Pakistan's policies targeted to childhood education. Sonia Bhalotra, *Is Child Work Necessary?*, 69 OXFORD BULL. OF ECON. & STAT. 29 (2007).

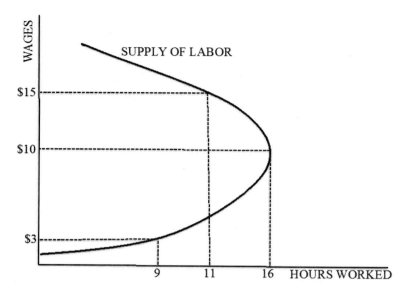

The diagram shows that this person's maximum hours worked is 16 at $10 per hour. If wages increase beyond $10 per hour, he will supply fewer hours. This labor-leisure trade-off varies by person depending upon their relative desire to substitute unpaid activities for paid activities. Moreover, the trade-off is generally not measurable so no one knows at what point workers will choose to stay home.

Differences between peoples' labor-leisure trade-off points are both individualized and systematic. For example, historically wives' calculations of their labor supply curves included their husbands' wages, whereas husbands only included their own wages.[5] This made wives' work commitment more elastic than their husbands' because only wives made labor-leisure decisions with combined marital earnings. Because of their elasticity, wives had greater market volatility than husbands who could be kept in the market at lower wages, and wives had lower bends in their backward bending supply curve. As wives began to see other benefits of paid employment or found less security in their husbands' wages, women's elasticity has lessened and they are less likely to think of the combined total when evaluating whether to work. Consequently, today women respond more like men to wages and have similar supply curves.

---

[5]   See Lora Cicconi, *Competing Goals Amidst the Opt-Out Revolution*, 42 GONZ. L. REV. 257, 263–64 (2007); Bradley T. Heim, *The Incredible Shrinking Elasticities: Married Female Labor Supply, 1979–2003*, 42 J. HUM. RES. 881 (2007).

§ 6.02   What Drives Choices?

Some choices might stand *ceteris paribus*, or all else being equal, but most choices depend on many variables. Some variables arise from the constraints that limit the quality of people's choices. Some of these constraints are financial; others are informational limits, tastes and preferences, and the effect of prior choices. Although some constraints focus a person's decision-making, many others hinder the rational evaluation of options. For example, a lack of financial literacy frustrates much decision-making, including the evaluation of tax policy.[6] Most people do not consider everything necessary to be truly rational economic actors if only because they lack the time or the inclination.

(a)   Costs and Future Values

People's choices are constrained by their budgets because even with borrowing there is an upper limit to what a person can choose. Economists would say that choices must be made within an opportunity set. For example, someone is limited by his budget when deciding whether it is possible to pay for a vacation or private education. By affecting prices or the size of a person's budget, taxes limit the opportunity set of what a person is able to do. Taxes' impact on choices and budgets is greater if people are conscious of their long-term and short-term budgets and use this information in their decision-making. However, because some taxes are hidden, even the most conscientious planners may not accurately incorporate taxes into their plans. Budget constraints also apply to the government, but taxes are not a constraint for the government. Instead, raising taxes reduces Congress's budget constraint, permitting it to spend more.

(i)   *Opportunity Costs*

Many individuals consider an item's cost as it directly affects their budget, but economists would also like them to consider other costs. In particular, most people ignore opportunity costs. An opportunity cost is the price of an alternative use of the money, time, or whatever is being measured. In other words, people should think about what else they could do with the money when they question whether something is too expensive because the choice is not made in isolation. For example, one opportunity cost of going to law school is the lost earnings from full-time wages for three years.

---

[6]   *See* Annamaria Lusardi & Olivia Mitchell, *Planning and Financial Literacy*, 98 AM. ECON. REV. 413 (2008); Victor Stango & Jonathan Zinman, *Exponential Growth Bias and Household Finance*, 64 J. FIN. 2807 (2009); van Rooij et al., *Financial Literacy and Stock Market Participation*, 101 J. FIN. ECON. 449 (2011).

Opportunity costs also apply in tax policy analysis. An opportunity cost of raising tax revenue is the loss of what taxpayers would do with the money. Conversely, an analysis of lowering taxes should consider the opportunity cost of what the government would have done with the revenue. Policy choice trade-offs in a world of finite resources are all about the opportunity costs of various options.

(ii) Sunk Costs

On the other hand, people often think too much about the sunk costs of their choices, which is another way of saying they focus on what they have already spent or invested in a choice. Economists argue that people should not include in future decisions amounts that they have already spent on something when that money is gone and cannot be recovered. Thinking retrospectively clouds people's judgment because they hate to admit a mistake. The result is they throw good money after bad.

For example, having invested $50,000 for one year of law school should not be a deciding factor in whether to continue with a legal education. After the first year, that money has been spent. When considering whether to continue into the second year, a student should look at prospective costs and the benefits therefrom, although the prospective costs are less since only two years of law school need be considered.

Sunk costs abound in tax policy choices. Prior government spending, the public's sunk cost, is funded with previously collected taxes, taxpayers' sunk costs. The spending may or may not have resulted from wise decisions, but now it is in the past. Those decisions should not affect how money is spent in the future. Thus, policymakers are urged to consider alternate uses of money going forward and not to focus on what was spent in the past. In some ways this thinking forces a clean mental slate.

However, not all prior decisions are to be ignored. Unlike a sunk cost that is in the past, transition costs arise because of prior choices but are not themselves old. Transitioning is part of a new decision that arises in response to an old decision. Thus, today's decision-making should incorporate assets created by prior spending and the costs of changing directions even as it ignores all other amounts that were spent before.

(iii) Time Value of Money

Costs often occur at different times, and comparisons between those times require special analyses. A dollar in one period is rarely of the same value as a dollar in another. Future costs must be discounted to present values for a true comparison of current and future costs. The difference in values is premised on the time value of money, which generally holds that a dollar today is worth more than a dollar tomorrow. Inflation and the opportunity for investment makes a dollar today worth some amount more than the same dollar tomorrow. For example, $100 saved by a 20-year-old worker should be worth more than $100 at the time the worker retires. A return on investing that $100 provides a larger dollar amount at retirement even though that larger amount is worth only $100 today.

To discount future amounts to present values requires an estimated rate of return. The rate of return, or return on investment (ROI), is the change in value an investment has over time and cannot be known beforehand with certainty. The number can also be positive or negative because assets can increase or decrease in value. To calculate a return, it is the increase or decrease in the investment's value plus any other amount the investment pays out. The percentage ROI is simply the amount received on the investment divided by the initial investment.

For example, an investor pays $10,000 for stock and owns the stock for one year. During that period, the investor receives $250 in dividends. If the investor sells the stock for $11,000, the investor has a $1,000 gain on the stock plus the $250 received in dividends, for a total return of $1,250. The rate of return on the stock is $1,250 divided by the $10,000 cost of the stock, or 12.5%.

The reasoning behind the time value of money and ROI might be intuitive to some; others may have to think about it. Because a dollar today could be invested, its future value is some amount more, which means that the time value of a set amount of money decreases over time because of the lost opportunity to earn interest or other appreciation if that money were received today. As a theoretical matter, this loss in value occurs even if a person chooses not to invest the money. And as a corollary, people prefer to pay taxes tomorrow instead of today because the dollar it takes to pay the tax tomorrow is worth less than the dollar needed to pay the tax today.

For example, if there is no inflation and a guaranteed 5% return, $100 invested for a year is worth $105 at the beginning of year 2 because $5 is earned in year 1. Therefore, a taxpayer should be indifferent as to having $100 now or $105 a year from now. Similarly, a taxpayer should be indifferent to paying $100 in taxes today or $105 at the beginning of year 2. However, if given the choice, the taxpayer should prefer to pay $100 in year 2 than $100 now. With that choice the taxpayer stands to earn the $5 return. This latter example is of tax deferral. Tax deferral occurs when taxpayers arrange their affairs so that they pay taxes later instead of now so they can capture the time value of money.

The time value of money worsens the fact that for most taxpayers in most situations, taxpayers' economic and tax incentives conflict. Although transactions, such as earning income and paying business expenses, have economic and tax consequences, peoples' perception of these consequences are almost opposite. For example, a business generates an expense to earn a profit. From an economic perspective, the business does not want to pay the expense. From a tax perspective, the deduction for paying the expense is useful. The business's preferred result is to claim the deduction today while only paying the expense in the future, something the Code often prevents. Accelerating the deduction is only wise for taxpayers if its tax savings is more than the economic cost. This analysis also highlights that decisions regarding tax policy affect non-tax considerations.

Taxes reduce most investments' ROI, but because taxes are not uniformly imposed on all investments their impact on ROI is not uniform. Therefore, ignoring taxes produces a false sense of higher returns and makes for inaccurate comparisons. Some investments are tax preferred, meaning that taxpayers can either deduct the initial investment or claim distributions without tax. Additionally, there are multiple levels and types of taxes that might impact investments differently. This could make comparing post-tax ROI complicated. It is important to know whether an investment is pre- or post-tax and whether the accumulation is subject to tax. Only the returns calculated after applying all taxes represent a real increase in value.

The time value of different choices is also affected by inflation.[7] Inflation is a general increase in prices that results in money's decreased purchasing power. Put most simply, inflation is the reason that a dollar can buy less stuff over time. Inflation rates vary over time due to many factors in the economy; however, if often occurs when monetary policy results in more dollars being printed than are backed by increases in productivity.[8] Therefore, people have more dollars to compete for the same amount of goods and services. This competition is really more demand without a corresponding increase in supply which pushes up the equilibrium price.

Almost always a portion of an investment's ROI is the product of inflation and is not reflected in an increase in purchasing power. In a period of high inflation, a larger part of an investment's return exists only because a dollar is worth less at the end of the period than

---

[7]   Deflation occurs when a dollar is worth more because of a reduction in prices. During the Great Depression, demand dropped sharply so that prices fell precipitously which, in turn, reduced national economic activity.

[8]   For a consumer price index inflation calculator, see the BUREAU OF LABOR STAT., CPI INFLATION CALCULATOR, https://data.bls.gov/cgi-bin/cpicalc.pl (last visited May 1, 2018).

it was worth at the beginning so the same value is paid in a larger number of bills. This means that investors and policymakers should discount returns with an assumed rate of inflation. Unfortunately, inflation can be estimated but not predicted with certainty.

Consider an investment that costs $10,000 and has a fixed return. The return is $2,000 of revenue per year for ten years before the investment becomes worthless. A potential investor must calculate the present value and applicable tax rate of each year's $2,000 to find out how much less it is worth today after-tax to see if the investment makes sense. To determine the present value of these future payments, an investor must assume a rate of inflation and rate of taxation, both of which have fluctuated widely over time. For example, in August 2017 inflation was only 1.94% but in 1980 was over 13%. Not believing that the low inflation rate will last, the investor might assume a higher discount rate, say 3%. The $2,000 earned in 10 years with a 3% discount rate is worth only $1,448.19 today.[9] If the sum of the discounted return for each year's receipt minus the amount spent for the investment and taxes paid on the investment is greater than $0, the investment is profitable and will make more than inflation and tax.

(iv) Response Times

The difficulty of accurately predicting inflation and rates of return is one reason it is difficult to compare short-term and long-term costs and opportunities. Additionally, costs incurred, and opportunities available, for a short period are harder to respond to because of the time it takes to adapt behaviors. In other words, people's choices are more constrained in the short-term than the long-term for which they can better adapt. For example, if the market for lawyers greatly improves, it would still require three years for people to enter the legal market because of the time to complete law school.

Taxpayers face similar constraints responding to changes in tax policies. Taxpayers are often unable to change their behavior in the short-term. They cannot adjust their behaviors immediately in response to increased or decreased rates or other tax changes. On the other hand, taxpayers can adjust their behavior for long-term policies, although possibly creating unintended consequences for policymakers. People may not enter a market immediately after Congress extends tax benefits to that market but, over some period, people will respond even if not always as Congress intends.

---

[9]   Excel does present value calculations as do a number of free on-line calculators that require only inputting a few facts. *See* Investopedia, *Present Value*, http://www.investopedia.com/calculator/pvcal.aspx (last visited May 1, 2018).

(v) Fixed, Variable, and Marginal Costs

Responsiveness to changing costs depends, in part, on the type of cost. Fixed costs are constant regardless of the quantity of goods or services that are provided. These costs, such as rents or salaries, are often fixed in the short-term so that government policy changes cannot readily affect them. Variable costs, on the other hand, vary with the level of output. For example, the cost of raw materials in produced goods is a variable cost. Policymakers can affect most variable costs in the short-term by changing government policies.

Marginal costs combine the fixed and variable costs associated with producing each additional item. Because marginal costs are focused on additional costs of the next good or item, they could be more or less than the sum of its component parts. Economists urge the decision to increase or decrease production be based on marginal costs and sales prices. However, policymakers can only quickly affect the variable cost component of marginal costs. Therefore, part of marginal cost is sticky and hard to change. When trying to affect the economy, policymakers need to think about what can be changed swiftly and what requires a long-term fix.

(b) Behavioral Responses and Game Theory

Behavioral economics is the study of how people make choices. In most of life's complex choices, including tax choices, people use heuristics, or rules of thumb, to guide their decisions. Heuristics provide a framework for making satisfactory decisions quickly. The goal of a good heuristic is to reduce the effort needed to make a decision by providing mental shortcuts. The thought that it is better to pay taxes later than today is one heuristic based on the time value of money. However, not all rules of thumb are accurate and few are accurate all of the time, and they are personal to each taxpayer.

Behavioral economists evaluate the heuristics that people bring to decision-making. They have found that people generally are myopic and innumerate; give greater weight to losses than gains; and have confirmation bias, hindsight bias, and optimism bias.[10] In other words, people are short-sighted; do not really understand numbers and math; hate losing something more than they enjoy gaining something new; interpret information to confirm what they already believe; remember things incorrectly; and believe they are less at risk of negative things happening to them as opposed to other people.

These patterns of thinking apply when making decisions regarding taxation as much as anything else. Professors Edward

---

[10]   *See generally* PETER DIAMOND & HANNU VARTIANINEN, BEHAVIORAL ECONOMICS AND ITS APPLICATIONS (2012).

McCaffery and Jonathan Baron observe systematic cognitive biases in a series of experiments involving tax and financial decision-making.[11] For example, they found that people react differently if taxes are listed in dollars as opposed to percentages and whether the amounts paid to the government are framed as taxes or as fees. These findings have been confirmed in many studies, and neither education nor work experience alters the result.[12] Even managers base financial decisions on salient information regarding taxes, such as average tax rates, rather than more accurate but less accessible information, such as marginal tax rates.[13] Thus, taxpayers take shortcuts in assessing the tax system, but the rules they adopt are not always accurate.

Focusing on tax, behavioral economists illustrate the importance of the framing effect (people care how taxes are presented), loss aversion (it hurts to part with hard-won earnings), and endowment affect (people value what they have more than what others have). Combined, these understandings often mean that tax rates are sticky in that it is hard to adjust rates and helps explain why Congress tries to increase or decrease effective taxation without adjusting tax rates. Policies are anchored in the public's minds at current rates, so that it is hard to enact large changes even if the current anchor is disfavored. So when policymakers propose new laws, they should establish the anchor close to where they hope to end up because it is hard to make large modifications from what is initially proposed.

Taxpayers also tend to isolate issues in tax and find it hard to integrate multiple factors, including multiple parts of the tax system. Therefore, when changes are made to one part of the tax system, its effect on other parts of the system or from offsetting changes to other parts are hard for people to assess together. For example, cutting benefits to lower-income groups provided through the tax system or through direct spending reduces the progressivity of the system as a

---

[11] Edward McCaffery & Jonathan Baron, *Framing and Taxation*, 25 J. ECON. PSYCHOL. 679 (2004); Edward McCaffery & Jonathan Baron, *The Humpty Dumpty Blues*, 91 ORG. BEHAV. & HUMAN DECISION PROCESSES 230 (2003).

[12] Harold Amberger et al., *Heuristics and Tax Planning: Evidence From a Laboratory Experiment* (2015), https://www.sbs.ox.ac.uk/sites/default/files/Business_Taxation/Events/conferences/2015/Doctoral_mtg_2015/amberger-paper.pdf; Alejandro Drexler et al., *Keeping It Simple*, 6 AM. ECON. J. 1 (2014); John Graham et al., *Tax Rates and Corporate Decision Making*, REV. FIN. STUD. (2017); Kay Balufus et al., *Decision Heuristics and Tax Perception*, 35 J. OF ECON. PSYCHOL. 1 (2013); John Scholz & Neil Pinney, *Duty, Fear, and Tax Compliance*, 39 AM. J. POL. SCI. 490 (1995); Michael Spicer & Rodney Hero, *Tax Evasion and Heuristics*, 26 J. PUB. ECON. 263 (1985).

[13] Graham et al., *supra* note 12; Claudia Townsend & Suzanne Shu, *When and How Aesthetics Influences Financial Decisions*, 20 J. of CONSUMER PSYCHOL. 452 (2010).

whole; however, most people segregate tax benefits from raising revenue and spending programs.

One result of the isolating effect is that many people are unaware of the federal budget as a whole. Although many Americans prefer lower taxes as well as the government running a surplus rather than a deficit, when asked to propose particular budget items to cut to raise the revenue, they find it difficult to do so.[14] One of the most common federal expenditures requested to be cut is foreign aid; however, it constitutes less than 1% of the federal budget, a tiny part compared to Social Security and Medicare, which together constitute 40%.

Similarly, how issues are framed matters greatly in how taxpayers understand them. In politics, preferred framing presents the facts in a way that defines a problem in need of the solution that favors policymakers' desired result. For matters that are framed successfully, only perspectives that politicians and their constituents favor are made salient. The more successfully framed the tax policy question, the more likely constituents will see the desired answer from the problem. This can be done with labels that frame issues to policymakers' advantage. Thus, the marriage penalty is more likely to lead to reduced tax rates than a single-earner bonus, although economically they have the same result. Even when one argument is the flip side of the other, the choice of terms matters.

As people review problems, whether or not properly framed, they tend to have optimism bias or short-term myopia that causes them to make poor choices for the long-term. If a person expects to become a millionaire, the person is going to have a different view of Social Security and the estate tax than someone who expects to end up lower- or middle-class. Tax policy can try to redress this bias but has had limited success. For example, Americans' low savings rate for retirement is often cited to justify tax-preferred savings plan; however, even tax benefits fail to overcome most people's myopia.

One way of testing behavioral responses is through the use of game theory. In its simplest form, game theory posits two people in a zero-sum world in which one person's gains result in the other person's losses. As a simple example, assume Evan and Felicity are deciding on tax policy. They each have a choice and there are two options.

---

[14]   Edward McCaffery & Jonathan Baron, *The Political Psychology of Redistribution*, 52 UCLA L. REV. 1745, 1780 (2005).

	Evan chooses option 1	Evan chooses option 2
Felicity chooses option 1	$10, $5	$2, $2
Felicity chooses option 2	$1, $2	$5, $10

If Evan and Felicity both choose option 1, Felicity receives $10 and Evan receives $5; if they both choose option 2, Felicity receives $5 and Evan receives $10. If they do not agree to the same choice, they both receive a lesser amount than with agreement. Thus, Evan and Felicity have every incentive to agree but because they have different relative benefits, it will be hard for them to reach agreement in a non-cooperative game.

Basic game theory is too simplistic to explain how tax policy is made in the real world. However, with mixed strategies, many parties, and the recognition that the game may or may not be zero sum, the game increasingly reflects reality. Tax bargains may be cooperative or non-cooperative; strategies may be symmetric or different for the various players; parties may make simultaneous choices or be sequential. There may or may not be informational deficiencies and repeat players. All of these factors play a role in how the game turns out and, for tax policy, what law is ultimately drafted.

These theories are tested mathematically and in experiments. Although some experiments occur in the real world or use real world data, many are laboratory experiments using paid volunteers. A difficulty with any of this testing, as with theories in general, is the impossibility of knowing whether the same results would hold true if we were able to test more broadly. Until better testing becomes possible, game theory remains good for explaining behavior but always with a caveat that it may contain flaws or unrecognized assumptions.

Game theories are used for modeling competing behaviors, including political behavior. Scholars use these tools to explain how voters, interest groups, and politicians have acted and to predict how they will act in the future. For example, Michael Graetz examines tax enforcement using game theory and finds that decision-making is not individual but also "depends upon and responds to the detection and punishment structure" in an interactive way.[15] He used game theory to illustrate the impact one person's choices can have on others in tax compliance. This understanding should push policymakers to think of potential reactions and the collective effects of proposed policy changes.

---

[15]   Michael Graetz et al., *The Tax Compliance Game: Toward and Interactive Theory of Law Enforcement*, 2 J. OF L., ECON. & ORG. 1, 3 (1986).

(c) Public Choice's Underlying Sensibilities

Public choice theory uses economic tools to examine political problems. In doing so, public choice theory assumes self-interested parties (either voters, businesses, politicians, or bureaucrats) and self-interested behavior. Therefore, much of public choice analysis treats government as a quid pro quo exchange. The main issue for public choice theorists is who makes the exchange and, as a normative matter, how can theorists make the exchange better for the nation or some group within it.

Public choice theorists often attempt to explain why political actors make the choices they do, particularly when political outcomes conflict with the general public's stated preferences. For example, the public states that it does not like pork barrel legislation, but preferences continue to be enacted. Some public choice theorists have studied pork's links with campaign contributions.[16] Those making campaign contributions and receiving the pork act rationally, but the result might be irrational for society as a whole. It is also rational that taxpayers rarely succeed in defeating pork legislation because taxpayers are diverse and the benefits any one taxpayer will receive from opposing the pork is small compared to what recipients enjoy. When costs are diffuse but benefits are concentrated, public choice theorists expect the minority to win.

The tax system is full of situations with targeted benefits and diffuse costs. The diffuse majority may have a harder time eliminating benefits because much of the public is unaware of the system's many parts. The income tax and the tax system as a whole are salient to the public; however, their component parts are not particularly salient. Some parts, such a tax rates, receive significant attention in the press; but other parts are ignored, no matter their import. This selective salience creates ripe ground for policymakers and interested parties to trade public and non-public issues to get what each wants.

For salient issues, the Treasury Department must find technically defensible and politically acceptable solutions to pressing problems. This salience allows the public to offset some of the pressure applied on the agency by special interests. On the other hand, the lack of salience for most issues makes it easier for special interests to dominate the discussion. Thus, in salient and complex fields there is pressure for both accountability and expertise but, as salience drops off, so does the push for accountability.

---

[16]   DAVID MACPHERSON, ECONOMICS: PRIVATE AND PUBLIC CHOICE 120–21 (2012).

Overcoming the public's lack of attention is particularly hard because of the public's self-interested responses, namely free rider problems and collective action problems.[17] Free riders are those who benefit from goods or services but who do not pay for them. For example, public goods such as public defense or a well-functioning tax system are available to everyone. The difficulty with free riders is that they lead either to the under-production of the public good (such as under-investment in defense or tax administration) or to excessive use of the resource. Consider for the latter public parks that might be overused because they are free for all.

Collective action problems occur when people fail to work together to achieve a common objective. Therefore, collective action is not always impossible but at times it is improbable. For example, when the cost of working together is high, people are less likely to do so. Moreover, diffuse benefits from some forms of collective action make it unlikely that any one group of people will assume the cost of securing those benefits, even if the benefits outweigh the costs in an absolute sense. On the other hand, concentrated benefits, even if less than the cost to society as a whole, are more likely to be won because those who receive the concentrated benefits have the incentive to work together.

Free rider and collective action problems help explain why tax reform has proven elusive. The benefit of eliminating specific tax benefits is a public good for all taxpayers because it raises general funds or permits the reduction of tax rates. On the other hand, a smaller group enjoys targeted tax benefits. When facing off against each other, the group enjoying the benefit often outweighs the diffuse group who gain from eliminating a benefit.

Another part of public choice theory focuses on politicians' rent seeking, explaining how politicians drive the development of tax legislation. The explosion in the last fifteen years of short-term tax legislation is arguably because Congress can secure campaign contributions every time an issue comes before it. Thus, short-term legislation gives members of Congress the ability to maximize their own revenue in the form of contributions by having tax legislation appear frequently.

Professors Edward McCaffery and Linda Cohen use tax to illustrate this rent-seeking behavior, finding that legislators were the predators and not the prey.[18] Examining the estate tax and calls for its repeal, they argue that legislators proactively solved coordination

---

[17] *See* MANCUR OLSON, THE LOGIC OF COLLECTIVE ACTION (1965).

[18] Edward J. McCaffery & Linda R. Cohen, *Shakedown at Gucci Gulch*, 84 N.C. L. REV. 1159 (2006).

and free-riding problems in order to extract campaign contributions from both sides of the issue. Politicians helped form the interest groups and then delayed legislation while looking busy debating the issue. In this way tax, legislators used the special interest groups that are commonly vilified for corrupting politics. These public choice issues are visible in other areas of the law, but as McCaffery and Cohen show in tax there are many opportunities to extract rent.

§ 6.03   When Should the Government Intervene?

Modern law and economics theory argues for limited government intervention in the market. Despite urging restraint, this school of thought would permit some involvement and is, therefore, a permutation of traditional laissez-faire analysis, which sought greater restraint on government involvement. Today, economists often urge that the primary, if not only, legitimate role of the government is to correct for failures in the market or in response to the capture of a portion of the government by interested parties. How these terms are defined these terms dictates the amount of permissible government activity.

(a) Market Failures

Accepting a law and economics perspective generally requires accepting two basic premises. First, when markets function reasonably well, markets achieve better results than the government. Second, most markets function reasonably well most of the time. Although it appears that market-based economies have relatively greater prosperity than centrally-planned economies, no one has proven or disproved that the planning dictated this outcome as opposed to some other cause, such as luck or natural resources.

Despite belief in the market, law and economic theorists accept that the free market does not work perfectly because of the existence of market failures. Market failures result when competition's invisible hand is unable to create the best outcome. In particular, market failures prevent the market from achieving a Pareto optimal outcome, in which no one is made better off without making someone else worse off.[19] In this conception, a market failure exists when the allocation of resources works against someone or some group within society. However, that an allocation is Pareto optimal does not mean that it is socially desirable or just, only that the result is not a market failure per se. For example, a Pareto optimal result might accept significant levels of poverty or inequality. Under law and economics,

---

[19]   For more on Pareto efficiency, see Chapter 4.01(b).

these are not market failures but issues of distributive justice, issues largely beyond the realm of modern law and economics.

There are several sources of market failure, only some of which can be addressed through the tax system. For example, imperfect market structures, such as monopolies, create market failures that are rarely addressed through taxation. A means to address imperfect market structures through the tax system is to use taxation to encourage the entry of other businesses into the market, such as by offering tax credits for competitors, to correct the failure.[20] Similarly, public goods, such as clean air or national defense, produce collective benefits by being collectively consumed but are often under-funded. Other than taxes for the use of some forms of public goods, such as admission to parks, the tax system only indirectly contributes to public goods' preservation or creation. Third, imperfect information on the part of buyers and sellers creates a market failure that cannot be addressed through the tax system.

Tax policy can target a fourth source of market failure more easily: the creation of costs or benefits that the producer of goods does not internalize without government intervention. These externalities exist when an activity creates costs or benefits that are not fully borne by the person or business engaging in the activity. These can be good or bad in that other people may enjoy or dislike the results.

The classic case of a negative externality is a business that produces pollution. The pollution is an externality burdening all of society. Because the business does not bear all of pollution's cost, the cost is not reflected in the price of the goods produced, and the goods may be overproduced or produced without the optimal level of environmental protection.

Alternatively, some activities produce positive externalities that the producer cannot fully capture. For example, research may produce social benefits beyond what the researcher can market herself. Because the benefits to everyone exceed the benefits received by the researcher, society is likely to under-invest in research.

Congress can correct for externalities by enacting tax credits or tax penalties intended to force the producer to internalize the cost.[21] The difficulty with this approach is setting the right rate of tax. To be most effective, the tax should offset the externality and no more. However, there is rarely an exact measure of the externality. Therefore, the tax result is a political compromise that may under- or over-compensate for the market failure.

---

[20]   For more on tax incentives, see Chapter 17.01.

[21]   For more on carbon tax proposals, see Chapter 17.02(d).

Optimal tax theory is the study of which tax features reduce inefficiency and distortion in the market under the given economic constraints. Therefore, optimal tax theory can seek the best tax to reduce or eliminate a particular market failure. Focusing on efficiency in the sense that taxes should not cause distortion, optimal tax theory looks for the most neutral tax regime. The result is generally higher taxes on inelastic goods and lower taxes on elastic ones. Although an interesting theory, there remains no definitive answer as to what is the optimal tax regime.

(b) Regulatory Capture

Regulatory capture is a form of government failure in which an agency fails to act in the public interest. Instead, if an agency is captured, the interested parties that dominate an industry also dominate the agency tasked with regulating the industry. Captured agencies, therefore, prioritize private interests over public interests in the creation of public policy. These agencies are reluctant to challenge the businesses they regulate and accept the businesses' claims.

The worry about regulatory capture is not new and quickly supplanted early studies that painted regulation idealistically. George Stigler's 1971 *The Theory of Economic Regulation* used empirical evidence to conclude that, "as a rule, regulation is acquired by the industry and is designed and operated primarily for its benefit."[22] Turning traditional regulatory thought on its head, that government regulation would rein in private actors, Stigler showed that private actors could capture regulators because they were groups or individuals with high stakes in an issue. By focusing their resources or energies in gaining policy outcomes, they could overcome diffuse members of the public who would fail to counter that focus.

The iron triangle is one theory of capture in which a relationship develops among congressional committees, the regulatory agency, and interest groups. Accepting that agencies seek to consolidate their own power base, these agencies work with interest groups to increase the agency's power and funding. In return, interest groups receive special favors and lower levels of regulation than public policy would otherwise dictate.

The pervasive influence of experts, whether economists or others with special training, increases the risk of agency capture. By centralizing information and decision making in experts, agencies may inadvertently make it easier to be influenced because there are smaller numbers to be influenced. This may occur even for issues in

---

[22] George Stigler, *The Theory of Economic Regulation*, 2 BELL J. OF ECON. & MGMT SCI. 3 (1971).

the public eye because the agency's use of information may distort what is reported to the public.

Tax is an area with significant reliance on experts who are far from the public eye. Because of tax's complicated law, interested parties use experts to help shape agency outcomes. They can frame the issues for policymakers or the perception of how the agency is performing, for example, by providing biased information or by lobbying against the agency for particular outcomes. Relatively little public pressure pushes back against expert analysis, which permits politicians to enact procedural or superficial changes instead of substantive reforms to appease the public. In doing so, politicians can show the public they are taking action but without grappling with the difficult issues the public is unable to properly self-assess.

Risks of regulatory capture raise hard questions for tax policy because much of tax law has been delegated to the Treasury Department or the IRS.[23] Because the agency interprets the law and enforces the tax, the risk of capture will always exist. Some taxpayers have high stakes in outcomes and theory shows they have a great ability to influence policy choices unless other pressures are brought to bear. However, there are few countervailing interest groups. Think tanks, academics, and elements of the press attempt to bring light to agency practices, but they have limited influence and are subject to diffuse personal motivations.

To reduce the threat of agency capture, Congress could create more bright line rules in tax statutes and minimize agency discretion. This would reduce the agency's influence interpreting the law. However, although removing discretion and rule-making from the agency decreases opportunities for abuse, it also minimizes use of the agency's expertise. This is also politically unlikely because of Congress's difficulty defining clear tax laws.

Another potential response is to reduce outside influence on the agency. Congress could try to prevent those leaving government employment from entering private practice or to make government service attractive enough to produce career-long employment. However, many high level employees are political appointees and necessarily have short terms. Those terms may be shortened by political pressure. Political attacks on the IRS in particular are popular as evidenced by House Republican attempts to impeach or censure former IRS Commissioner John Koskinen.[24] These attacks

---

[23]   For more on how tax law is made, see Chapter 1.

[24]   H.R. Res. 737, 114th Cong. (May 18, 2016).

threaten the IRS's ability to exercise independent judgment, opening it up to capture.[25]

Despite risks of agency capture, insulating an agency from new voices or even from partisan political review risks amplifying the problem if capture has been accomplished. A means of preventing capture is to shed light on the agency's policies. Therefore, insulating highly technical agencies may increase the risk of capture even as it gives agencies the power to resist pressure from interest groups.[26] Thus, there is always a balance that economic theory can help define but it takes politics to achieve.

---

[25]   Letter from American College of Tax Counsel to the House of Representatives, Jul. 13, 2016, http://www.actconline.org/wp-content/uploads/2014/05/ACTC-letter-to-Congressional-Leadership.pdf; Leandra Lederman, *Don't Impeach IRS Commissioner Koskinen,* https://surlysubgroup.com/2016/07/20/dont-impeach-irs-commissioner-koskinen/ (last visited May 1, 2018).

[26]   For example, James Hines & Kyle Logue, *Delegating Tax,* 114 MICH. L. REV. 234 (2015), argues that more of the creation of tax law should be delegated to the IRS.

Part B

WHAT TYPE OF TAX?

Chapter 7

INCOME TAXATION

Table of Sections

The federal government taxes individuals' and corporations' incomes. In addition, many states and localities tax this same base.[1] Federal rates are more progressive and higher than those imposed by the lower levels of government, and lower levels of government often piggyback off the federal tax return by making only minor adjustments to federal filing. Almost 15.6% of individuals file the one-page Form 1040EZ and almost 30% use the only slightly more complicated Form 1040A.[2] For others, however, income tax returns can be hundreds of pages long.

The individual and corporate taxes that have evolved into the largest source of federal revenue initially raised relatively little in tax at a time when the government spent relatively little.[3] The 1913 individual income tax was a mildly progressive tax with rates ranging from 1% to 7%. It applied to less than 2% of the labor force. The 1909 corporate income tax was a 1% tax on corporate income above $5,000, but in 1913 the exemption was removed for several years, so that the tax applied to all of every corporations' net income. Although both taxes were adapted to raise more revenue in World War I, the biggest changes to the taxes were made in World War II. For example, in World War II, the individual income tax became a mass tax, meaning that it applied for the first time to the middle class.

Today, income tax rates are more progressive than they were in 1913 but significantly lower than they were during World War II. Brackets range from 10% to 37%, and the IRS receives almost 150

---

[1]   For more on taxation by state and localities, see Chapter 13.01.

[2]   IRS, SOI TAX STATS, INDIVIDUAL INCOME TAX RETURNS PUBLICATION 1304, Table A (2014) [hereinafter Publication 1304].

[3]   For more on the history of income taxation, see STEVEN A BANK, ET AL., WAR AND TAXES (2008); W. ELLIOTT BROWNLEE, FEDERAL TAXATION IN AMERICA: A SHORT HISTORY (3d ed., 2016).

million individual tax returns.[4] One accounting firm's study of countries' taxes on $100,000 of gross income found the U.S. 55th in terms of highest rates and, at $300,000 of gross income, the U.S. was 53rd.[5] The corporate income tax with, as of 2018, a single bracket of 21% applies to almost 6 million active corporations.[6] Federal income tax revenues are approximately 10% of GDP.

The individual and corporate income taxes both tax net income. Therefore, the tax base or what is taxed is only an increase in income as opposed to all earnings, all transactions, or overall wealth. Although a simple concept, significant complexity arises from taxing this base. Chapter 7.01 defines the structure of the income tax, or how the tax defines the tax base. This discussion is intended to provide the details necessary for a discussion of their policy implications; more detailed discussions can be found in books devoted to the income tax. Important policy choices for this tax base are discussed in Chapters 7.02 and 7.03.

§ 7.01   Structure of the Income Tax

People are more aware of tax rates than how Congress defines the taxable income to which the rate applies. However, the tax's base is important because how it is defined may make the nominal rates mean very little. The earliest income taxes were simple, with few deductions and credits, so that the nominal rate applied to most income. As the tax's importance to the federal budget increased, changes reduced the tax base and increased the complexity of the income tax. Compared to 1913, today the nominal ordinary income rate applies to a smaller portion of a person's total income.

Although there are broadly applicable rules for determining taxable income, taxable income differs slightly depending upon whether the taxpayer is an individual or an entity, and then depending upon the type of entity.[7] These differences create much of the rule complexity in the income tax system.

(a) Tax Unit

The first step in determining a taxpayer's federal income tax is to determine the appropriate tax unit, or whose income is included on a single tax return. In the federal income tax, there are several

---

[4]   For more on the history of the tax system, see Chapter 3.

[5]   Lia Mahapatra, *The Highest Effective Personal Tax Rates in the World*, BUS. INSIDER, Jan. 9, 2013.

[6]   For more on the corporate tax system, see Chapter 11.

[7]   For more on the taxation of various business entities, see Chapter 11.01.

categories for individuals.[8] An unmarried individual has only that person's income on the return and is either a single taxpayer, using the single payer tax brackets, or a head of household if the unmarried individual has a qualifying dependent, using the favorable head of household brackets. Married individuals have a choice either to file separately, each reporting one person's income and using the married filing separate rates, or to file jointly, combining their income and using favorable filing jointly rate brackets.[9] Favorability is defined in this context as wider tax brackets, which tax more income at lower tax rates, and larger standard deductions.

Some entities are taxed as separate entities from their owners. Most corporations are separate entities, taxed similarly to individuals on their corporate incomes. Therefore, these separate corporations are their own tax unit. For corporations with subsidiaries, the tax unit question is whether ownership is sufficiently integrated that subsidiaries qualify as an affiliated group and, if so, do they choose to file a single consolidated return for the group.

Other entities do not have a choice as to their tax unit. Partnerships, estates, and trusts are pass-through entities, which means that their income and deductions pass through to their owners. Therefore, the owners of pass-through entities report and owe tax on the entity's income and claim the entity's deductions on their individual tax returns. These latter entities are not separate taxable entities and are not considered separate tax units.

(b) Income

The second step for determining a taxpayer's tax liability is to calculate gross income. This calculation of income is largely the same regardless of the type of taxpayer. The Internal Revenue Code defines gross income as "all income from whatever source derived."[10] The Treasury Department and the courts interpret this provision broadly to include wages, annual bonuses, or fees for services.[11] Thus, gross income is all the stuff a taxpayer has to pay tax on, not yet offset by anything.

---

[8]   Individuals tax brackets are provided in I.R.C. § 1; however, after 2018 inflation adjusted numbers will be provided in an annually updated revenue procedure. For example, see Rev. Proc. 2016–55, 2016–45 I.R.B. 707.

[9]   For more on married couples filing statuses, see Chapter 15.01.

[10]   I.R.C. § 61.

[11]   For an interesting debate regarding the interpretation of gross income, see Alice Abreu & Richard Greenstein, *The Rule of Law as a Law of Standards*, 64 DUKE L.J. ONLINE 53, 88–92 (2015); Lawrence A. Zelenak, *Custom and the Rule of Law in the Administration of the Income Tax*, 62 DUKE L.J. 829 (2012); Alice Abreu & Richard Greenstein, *Defining Income*, 11 FLA. TAX REV. 295 (2011).

Gross income includes payments even if they are not in cash, so that payments in the form of stock, cars, free haircuts, or ice cream are likely to be gross income. Gross income also includes any fringe benefits one's employer provides unless Congress specifically excludes the benefit from gross income. Therefore, congressional exceptions for tax-free perks, such as employer-provided health insurance, employer-provided housing, and qualified employee discounts, are coveted forms of no-tax compensation.[12]

Thus, gross income is broad; most things that are recognized as improving a taxpayers' wellbeing are taxable. And Congress, the Treasury Department, and the courts have developed lots of rules to prevent taxpayers from minimizing their gross income. For example, if a taxpayer pays for services by performing services, the fair market value of the services the taxpayer receives must be included in income as compensation.[13] This provision prevents taxpayers from bartering for goods and services to avoid taxation, although this requirement is only so good as the IRS's ability to detect and prove the bartering.

Even having goods and services paid to someone other than the person doing the work does not change this result.[14] The assignment of income doctrine prevents taxpayers in higher tax brackets from shifting their income to family and friends in lower tax brackets. Generally, the person who earns income must pay tax on it.

But the reach of gross income is not all expansive. Taxpayers do not include in gross income the value of items they create for themselves. In tax lingo, this is "imputed income." Imputed income is a real economic gain, but the gain is not taxable. For example, cutting one's own lawn is a real value because the alternative is to pay someone else to do it with money that has been subject to tax. Congress does not force taxpayers to include this increase in value in gross income. Similarly, Congress does not force taxpayers to report items that do not have a monetary equivalent, such as the receipt of love or happiness.

Additionally, an asset's appreciation, meaning its increase in value over time, is only taxed when the taxpayer sells or otherwise disposes of the asset.[15] For example, by selling appreciated stock, the taxpayer triggers tax on the previously untaxed appreciation. Until that realization event, the taxpayer has increased wealth represented by the appreciated stock but owes no tax. When the stock

---

[12] I.R.C. §§ 105, 106, 118, and 132.

[13] Treas. Reg. § 1.61–2(d)(1).

[14] Lucas v. Earl, 281 U.S. 111 (1930).

[15] Eisner v. Macomber, 252 U.S. 189 (1920); Helvering v. Horst, 311 U.S. 112 (1940).

is disposed of, everything the taxpayer receives is unlikely to be taxable. Instead, the gain realized on a sale is the difference between the sales price and the amount of post-tax dollars invested in the asset. In tax, the amount invested in an asset is called its tax basis, although that basis may be adjusted over time. The taxpayer can receive an amount equal to the adjusted basis without owing tax on that amount. The adjusted basis prevents the double taxation of invested amounts because basis is recovered tax-free.

Most people are not taxed on income and gain until they are paid because individuals use the cash method of accounting. Under the cash method, people balance their books as cash comes in and cash goes out. However, individuals may also be taxed earlier if the Treasury Department and courts believe that they have a significant increase in wealth that is measurable. For example, taxpayers must report income if they constructively receive payment.[16] Taxpayers constructively receive income when a payment is available to them, but they asked for payment to be delayed in order to defer taxation. Similarly, individuals may currently have income if they become the beneficiary of an irrevocable trust.[17] In other words, rules have developed to prevent taxpayers from minimizing their gross income in most instances.

An alternative to the cash method of accounting is the accrual method of accounting. Accrual accounting is generally elective except for certain corporations, partnerships with corporations as partners, and tax shelters.[18] Under the accrual method of accounting, taxpayers must report income if they are legally entitled to receive a reasonably determinate amount of income. Therefore, corporations or other taxpayers using the accrual method may have to report gross income for tax purposes even though they have not received it and possibly will never receive payment.

Thus, rules regarding gross income operate to include most increases in a taxpayer's well being in amounts subject to tax. The rules are generally interpreted broadly, although not always so. Therefore, under current law, it is not an unreasonable rule of thumb to think Congress taxes anything it can with the income tax.

(c) Deductions

With some notable exceptions, taxpayers are not taxed on their gross income but on their net income. To calculate net income, gross income is reduced by deductions, most of which are for the expenses

---

[16]   Treas. Reg. § 1.461–1(a).

[17]   Rev. Rul. 60–31, 1960–1 C.B. 174.

[18]   I.R.C. § 441; § 448(a).

incurred in earning income. Other deductions reflect Congress's economic and social policies. Congress enacts deductions to encourage activities or in recognition of their personal or social importance. However, unlike gross income, which is interpreted expansively, deductions are a matter of legislative grace and are construed narrowly.[19] For every expense that might be deductible, a taxpayer must find a specific Code provision authorizing the deduction.

For individuals, but not corporations, partnerships, trusts, or other entities, adjusted gross income (AGI) is gross income less certain, listed deductions.[20] These favored deductions are above-the-line deductions, the "line" being AGI. These are not the only type of deductions individuals can claim; the other type of deductions is below-the-line deductions.[21] This distinction does not matter for corporations or other entities, which only have one type of deduction, so all deductions for entities are equally favored.[22]

Congress created the concept of AGI in 1944 to permit individuals to choose a new standard deduction instead of the less favored below-the-line deductions. Before 1944, all taxpayers had to itemize all of their deductions, which meant that they had to separately report them and maintain records substantiating the expense. When the tax began to apply to larger numbers of people during World War II, Congress allowed individuals to choose the standard deduction in place of itemizing some of their deductions. However, the standard deduction was not meant to replace tax-preferred, above-the-line deductions, which still must be separately reported but are always deductible.

The most common above-the-line deduction is for trade or business expenses.[23] For ongoing trades or businesses, taxpayers can deduct all ordinary and necessary expenses paid in carrying on that trade or business.[24] Other above-the-line deductions include deductions for losses on the sale of property or for contributions to certain retirement accounts.

---

[19]   White v. U.S., 305 U.S. 281 (1938).

[20]   I.R.C. § 63.

[21]   I.R.C. § 67.

[22]   Congress does not permit entities to claim the standard deduction; therefore, entities must incur expenses to have deductions and must itemize those expenses.

[23]   Trade or business expenses are also among the most litigated. *See* TAXPAYER ADVOCATE SERVICE, 2016 ANNUAL REPORT TO CONGRESS 474–81 (2017). Above-the-line deductions are listed in I.R.C. § 62(a).

[24]   As of 2018, a deduction is denied for nonreimbursed expenses paid by employees, which previously were an above-the-line deduction.

A subset of trade or business expenses is deductible above-the-line but only over time or on the sale or disposition of an asset. For example, the cost of land or stock in a corporation is not deductible except when the taxpayer disposes of the land or stock.[25] The cost of a building on the land is also not deducted in the year the building is purchased; however, if the building is used in a business, its cost can be deducted over a number of years through depreciation deductions.[26] Because the building will provide the business a benefit for many years, a current deduction of the full cost would distort the taxpayer's earnings and expenses when the deduction should be divided over the building's useful life. Similarly, start-up expenses for businesses that are not yet operational are not currently deductible but deducted over a number of years, which has the benefit of discouraging taxpayers from fabricating such expenses.[27]

Most personal expenses, even if incurred in order to work, are never deductible.[28] Thus, taxpayers are unable to deduct their commuting costs, most clothing expenses, or childcare expenses even if these expenditures are necessary to get to work, perform at work, or stay at work. The theory is that the choice of where one lives, how one dresses, or whether to have children is a personal decision that does not have to be included in the calculation of net income. Congress may extend targeted deductions or credits to cover these costs, but that is a result of congressional politics rather than to conform to Congress's sense of net income.

Because AGI only exists for individuals, only individuals have below-the-line deductions. As of 2018, each individual can claim two types of deductions below the line.[29] First, individuals may claim either the standard deduction or itemized below-the-line deductions. Second, individuals may claim a deduction to offset certain business-related income that they earn through sole proprietorships or pass-through businesses, but not if the payments are received as employees and not if received from entities taxable as corporations.[30] Therefore, individuals today can claim (1) above-the-line deductions plus (2) either the standard deduction or itemized below-the-line deductions and (3) between 2018 and 2025, an additional below-the-line deduction for certain business income.

---

25   I.R.C. § 263.

26   I.R.C. §§ 167; 168; 179.

27   I.R.C. § 195.

28   I.R.C. § 262.

29   Before 2018 and after 2025, taxpayers could also claim personal exemptions; however, personal exemptions and most below-the-line deductions phased down or out at higher income levels. For more on phase-outs, see Chapter 16.02(c).

30   For more on the Section 199A deduction, see Chapter 11.01(f).

Before 2018, less than one-third of taxpayers itemized their deductions and, after 2018, even fewer should itemize.[31] Instead, people choose the standard deduction, a fixed deductible set by Congress that is adjusted annually for inflation. In 2018, Congress raised the standard deduction for a married couple filing jointly from $12,600 to $24,000, double the $12,000 for single taxpayers (up from $6,300). If the standard deduction is greater than the aggregate amount of itemized below-the-line deductions, the taxpayer should claim the standard deduction. The standard deduction also saves taxpayers the need of keeping records of tax deductions. More than two-thirds of individual taxpayers claim the standard deduction rather than itemize.[32]

Not all itemized deductions are currently deductible. For the period between 2018 and 2025, Congress has denied deductibility for otherwise valid miscellaneous itemized deductions granted elsewhere in the Code. For example, if taxpayers have costs associated with their stock portfolio, which they hold for investment purposes, they are unable to deduct these costs.[33] The result is that Congress made these investments taxable on a gross, rather than a net, basis.

Because deductions are a matter of legislative grace, Congress can draw lines around what is deductible as it sees fit. For example, Congress permits below-the-line deductions for certain home mortgage interest, certain amounts of state and local taxes, certain medical expenses, and certain amounts of charitable contributions. However, Congress has limited the deductions for these expenses. Looking at taxes, business taxes are deductible above-the-line. Individuals can also deduct below-the-line up to $10,000 of non-business state and local real property taxes and either state and local sales or income taxes. To complete the web regarding taxes, federal taxes and non-business fees for services provided by the government are never deductible. Congress's lines create a maze.

Consider Elaine, who is single, and in 2018 earns $279,800 of gross income, has a $10,100 deduction from her trade or business, has a $5,250 § 164 deduction for taxes, a $2,300 § 213 medical deduction, and $8,750 of investment management expenses for her stock portfolio. First, the $10,100 deduction for trade or business expenses reduces her income as an above-the-line deduction, creating $269,700 of AGI. Second, Elaine cannot deduct her management expenses despite being a real cost of the investment. Therefore,

---

[31]   I.R.C. § 163.

[32]   PUBLICATION 1304, *supra* note 2, at Table 1.3.

[33]   I.R.C. §§ 162; 212. *See also* Higgins v. Comm'r, 312 U.S. 212 (1941); Moller v. U.S. 721 F.2d 810 (Fed. Cir. 1983); Purvis v. Comm'r, 530 F.2d 1332 (9th Cir. 1976).

Elaine can deduct only $7,550 of her below-the-line expenses. Because $7,550 is less than the $12,000 standard deduction, Elaine should claim the standard deduction and ignore the amount she spent on taxes and in medical bills.

The existence of deductions adds to the Code's complexity even as they make it more of a net income tax or further Congress's economic and social policies. Some people debate whether it is better to create a simpler income tax at the cost of these deductions. However, politics makes it hard to eliminate specific deductions because each deduction has its own supporters. For example, charities as well as donors champion the charitable contribution deduction, and states and high-tax taxpayers champion the state and local tax deduction. Therefore, attempts to eliminate specific deductions risk significant opposition.

For those entitled to deductions, the taxpayer's accounting method plays into when deductions can be claimed. For those who use the cash method of accounting, deductions are only claimed when taxpayers actually pay the deductible expense. For those taxpayers who use the accrual method of accounting, deductions are claimed when all of the events occur which establish a reasonably certain amount of liability and either party has performed its side of the obligation to set the liability.

In 2018, when Congress raised the standard deduction, it also eliminated personal exemptions and the phase-out of below-the-line deductions for the period between 2018 and 2025. Personal exemptions originally ensured that some amount of income is never subject to income tax, with a larger benefit to taxpayers with more dependents, whereas phase-outs denied the tax benefit to higher-income taxpayers. Unless additional changes are made to the law, these facets of the tax apply in 2026.

(d) Tax Liability

Taxable income is multiplied by progressive rates set by statute. The rates are adjusted annually for inflation, which has the effect of decreasing the amount of tax revenue generated each year from the same amount of income. This multiplication produces a taxpayer's tentative tax liability. For individuals, applicable tax rates are listed on schedules on Form 1040 as simple formulas to account for the progressive rates; as of 2018 corporations have a flat rate of 21%.[34] For businesses such as partnerships, estates, or trusts that are pass-through entities, their income is reported by their owners and taxed at their owners' tax rates.

---

[34] Forms incorporate the law from I.R.C. § 1. *See* note 8.

When Congress reduced individual tax rates in 2017, it did so on a temporary basis. Therefore, rates automatically increase in 2026 unless Congress extends the new rates. One reason for temporary legislation is to control the cost of tax reduction, which was estimated at over $1.2 trillion for the period in effect; it would have cost much more to make the tax cut permanent. That the rates are temporary means that the Internal Revenue Code currently has two sets of individual tax rate brackets. Subsections (a)–(e) contains post-2025 law and subsection (j) is current through 2025.

A hidden and permanent tax rate increase in the Tax Cuts and Job Acts of 2017 was a new method of calculating inflation adjustments. Both for rate brackets and other inflation-adjusted elements of the income tax, this new method is estimated to save the government $133.5 billion between 2018 and 2027. At issue was that the Bureau of Labor Statistics measured the consumer price index (CPI) as an indirect measure of inflation by only considering certain goods. The new system is a chained CPI intended to incorporate ripple effects through the economy and consumer purchasing patterns. Therefore, if a tested item increases in price but its market substitutes do not, the measure of inflation rises less.

Although chained CPI is likely a more accurate reflection of inflation, the result will be smaller adjustments. Therefore, rate brackets and tax credits will not increase as quickly, which generally disfavors taxpayers because rate brackets apply to smaller amounts and credits grow more slowly. Although as of early 2018 chained CPI is only used in the tax system, the new method may be extended to the nation's redistributive programs, including Social Security.

A taxpayer's preliminary tax liability may be more complicated than Form's tax bracket formulas for two reasons. First, some amount of income may be taxed at favorable rates. For example, as discussed more fully below in Chapter 7.03, individuals' capital gains are taxed at preferential tax rates that vary from 0% to 20%. The capital gain preference has a lot of limitations. For example, capital gain rates only apply to certain dividends or to the sale or exchange of certain assets held for more than one year.[35] That capital gains have a preferential rate means taxpayers must allocate their income into different buckets to be taxed at the appropriate rate.

In addition to capital gains, there are other favorable rates and characterizations of income, such as for collectibles and certain other stock holdings, which may reduce a taxpayer's liability.[36] These other characterizations have lower tax rates than ordinary income but

---

[35] I.R.C. § 1(h); § 1222.

[36] *See e.g.,* I.R.C. §§ 1(h)(5); 1202; 1250.

generally not as low as capital gains. Many people are unaware of the preferences' existence, so one could question how effective they are as incentives. These favorable rates may serve to offset other costs of these assets, such as the impact of inflation on their value; however, any benefit comes at the cost of complexity.

A second complication that requires adjusting preliminary tax liability is the potential application of offsetting tax credits that reduce the taxes owed. Credits are more valuable than deductions in that they reduce tax liabilities dollar for dollar whereas deductions reduce gross income and are worth their value times the taxpayer's top marginal tax rate.[37] For example, a $5,000 charitable contribution deduction reduces gross income by $5,000 and if the taxpayer's top marginal rate is 28%, this deduction saves $1,400 in taxes. If, however, the deduction were made a credit, a $5,000 credit would create a total reduction in taxes of $5,000. Consequently, credits are generally in smaller nominal amounts than deductions or apply some form of limiting percentage.

The most common credit is the credit for withholding.[38] Withholding really means that employers have prepaid employees' taxes on employees' behalf. Therefore, the amount withheld is properly credited against the taxes owed and, if there was a surplus withheld, it gets paid to the employee. The self-employed do not have withholding but are required to make estimated tax payments per quarter or else face penalties.[39] Taxpayers may also be entitled to other congressionally-created credits. For example, credits exist for childcare, certain solar-power-based home improvements, and certain education expenses.[40] Some credits phase out for taxpayers with higher levels of AGI.

The last step for individual taxpayers in determining their tax liability is to calculate whether they must pay an additional tax under the Alternative Minimum Tax (AMT).[41] In 2018, Congress repealed the corporate AMT and raised the exemption on the individual AMT so that fewer individuals would be subject to this additional tax. Although by this point taxpayers are likely tired, calculation of the AMT forces them to redo much of their analysis of their deductions, exemptions, and credits.

---

[37]   For more on the difference between deductions and credits, see Chapter 17.01(c).

[38]   I.R.C. § 31.

[39]   I.R.C. § 1401.

[40]   For more on childcare, see Chapter 15.02(b)(vi), and for more on incentives, see Chapter 17.01.

[41]   For more on the AMT, see Chapter 16.02(d).

§ 7.02   Income Tax Policy Choices

The income tax raises lots of sometimes big and sometimes small policy choices. Each policy choice affects taxpayers' tax liabilities and whether some group of taxpayers will engage in the taxed activity or substitute a lesser-taxed activity. Despite the effect, income taxes are often so incorporated into prices that people fail to register them. As Professor Herbert Stein pointed out, "In general, there is a tendency for the market to adjust to different tax treatment of incomes from different sources in such a way as to reduce the net effects on income after tax. . . . The economic system has adjusted to them so as to reduce discriminatory effect they might have had when first introduced."[42] Put simply, through no overt choice or action, the income tax was incorporated into prices and wages a long time ago. Consequently, most people never realize the tax's effect except when complaining generally of their taxes.

(a) Definition of Income

The U.S. has an overwhelmingly income-based tax system, and income taxes have tremendous revenue-raising potential. The individual income tax accounts for nearly 50% of all federal revenue. The corporate income tax, individual income tax, and Social Security tax combined, all of which are to a degree based on income, account for over 90% of federal revenue, and almost 16% of GDP.[43] This puts a tremendous amount of pressure on the definition of income.

The modern income tax originates with the Sixteenth Amendment, which is vague on what is meant by income:

> The Congress shall have power to lay and collect taxes on incomes, from whatever source derived, without apportionment among the several States, and without regard to any census or enumeration.

The language of the Sixteenth Amendment is generally accepted, if it does not actually require, that the U.S. federal income tax taxes net income.[44] Thus, the Supreme Court may require that people be permitted some form of offset for the costs of producing taxable income (although deductions are not provided in many flat tax proposals and are currently disallowed for some profit-seeking activities as a miscellaneous itemized deduction).[45]

---

[42]   Herbert Stein, *What's Wrong With the Federal Tax System?*, in TAX REVISION COMPENDIUM 5, 9 (1959).

[43]   U.S. OFFICE MGMT. & BUDGET, FISCAL YEAR 2016, HISTORICAL TABLES, Table 2.1 (2017).

[44]   Comm'r v. Tellier, 383 U.S. 687, 691–92 (1966).

[45]   For more on flat taxes, see Chapter 4.02(b).

During early income tax debates, Henry Simons, who was a public finance economist at the University of Chicago, published an influential book that defined income for purposes of taxation as: "the result obtained by adding consumption during the period to 'wealth' at the end of the period and then subtracting 'wealth' at the beginning."[46] One could restate this rather simplistically as the increase in the amount saved during a taxable period plus the amount that is consumed in the same period. Other advocates of this concept have largely been forgotten, at least in the U.S., except for Robert Haig. And now you have the Haig-Simons conception of income.

The Haig-Simons conception of income is a broad definition and is generally accepted as a governing theory in the U.S. Therefore, all increases in a taxpayer's net worth regardless of source are to be included in income per section 61 of the Internal Revenue Code. This is not the case for all countries' income taxes. For example, the United Kingdom does not consider lottery winnings to be income because these winnings result from neither labor nor capital investment.[47] Moreover, even in the U.S., not all increases in a taxpayer's net worth are actually taxed. For example, the receipt of gifts increases one's wealth but gifts are statutorily excluded from gross income.[48] There are a sufficient number of deviations from the Haig-Simons definition of income that it might be easier to redefine income than it is to list all the deviations.

The broad Haig-Simons sense of income is sometimes difficult for courts to apply. For example, in *Murphy v. United States*, the D.C. Circuit Court held that an employee awarded compensatory damages for emotional distress and loss of reputation did not owe income tax on the payment of these damages.[49] Despite the Internal Revenue Code excluding awards for physical injury from income, it does not carve out compensation for emotional distress and loss of reputation. Not having a statutory basis, the court narrowed the reach of the Sixteenth Amendment to not tax these payments of damages. Arguing that emotional well-being and a good reputation would not be taxed, compensation for their damage should not be taxable.

On rehearing, the court changed its mind. Instead, the court agreed that the ability to tax this compensation was within Congress's Article I, section 8 taxing power because the tax is not a direct tax and is imposed uniformly. The court concluded that

---

[46]   HENRY SIMONS, PERSONAL INCOME TAXATION 50 (1938).

[47]   Mark King, *Do You Have to Pay Tax on a Lottery Win?*, THE GUARDIAN, Sep. 10, 2012.

[48]   I.R.C. § 102.

[49]   460 F.3d 79 (D.C. Cir. 2006), *overturned on reh'g*, 493 F.3d 170 (D.C. Cir. 2007).

Congress may not make a thing income when it is not income but it can tax income that has a different label.

(b) Imputed Income

The current tax system creates an economic incentive for taxpayers to do things for themselves even when they would prefer to pay someone else to do it. Self-help, known in tax as imputed income, is not taxable whereas buying the same service in the market can only be with after-tax dollars. Thus, imputed income is real economic value created when a taxpayer owns and uses durable goods or exerts personal effort. It is a policy choice that this imputed income is not taxed despite the exclusion creating an economic distortion.

Classic examples of imputed income are owner-occupied housing (in other words, living in a house the taxpayer owns) or parent-provided childcare. If a taxpayer owns his own home, the taxpayer can live in the home without generating taxable income. On the other hand, to earn the money to pay rent for the home, the taxpayer owes tax as the income is earned, producing less after-tax dollars to spend. Similarly, if a taxpayer provides childcare for his own children, there are no tax consequences; however, if the taxpayer earns wages and pays someone else to provide childcare, the wages are taxed. It requires more pre-tax dollars to purchase after-tax services.

Adding numbers to the first example, consider Abby who is in the top 37% tax bracket. She can buy a house or rent an equivalent house for $5,000 per month. In order to pay the $5,000 per month, she must earn $7,937 before income taxes.[50] Thus, the rent does not really cost $5,000 but at least an additional $2,937 to be paid in taxes. Of course, this difference should not be Abby's only consideration in making the choice whether to rent or buy.

There are arguments for and against taxing imputed income. Taxing what a person does for himself would require the government exercise tremendous reach into taxpayers' daily lives. The administrative difficulty for taxpayers to track and the government to enforce this source makes it unlikely this income could ever be consistently taxed. On the other hand, not taxing imputed income creates economic distortions. Some people choose to do things for themselves simply for that reason, possibly eliminating the market or at least altering market outcomes. It is partly for this reason that Professor Nancy Staudt suggests housework be taxed to reduce the

---

[50] The equation is: $5,000 ÷ (1 − .37) = x; or $5,000 ÷ 0.63 = $7,397.

incentive for housework over wage work that disproportionately affects women.[51]

Some countries have taxed imputed income from owner-occupied housing. For example, between 1911 and 1917 Wisconsin taxed owner-occupied houses based on their estimated rental value.[52] Australia similarly taxed imputed rent from 1915 through 1923.[53] The Australian tax was abolished because it appeared to discourage homeownership and was difficult to administer. Austria, Finland, Germany, Sweden, and the United Kingdom have all taxed this form of imputed income at some point in the post-World War II era.[54]

An alternative to the taxation of imputed income is for Congress to enact a deduction or credit for the comparable after-tax spending. For example, people could deduct or claim a credit for the rent they pay. The rationale for creating this tax benefit would be that, because imputed income is tax-free, others should not have to use after-tax dollars to purchase the same as a matter of horizontal equity. The dependent care credit is one example that helps offset the cost of childcare for wage-earning parents. To the extent of the credit, taxpayers can use pre-tax dollars to make designated purchases.

However, if Congress enacted a credit for renting a residence, this alternative to taxing imputed income would not create equality between users of owner-supplied and rental properties. Homeowners are acquiring an asset with their spending that does not exist for renters. On the other hand, homeowners have nondeductible expenses for the upkeep of their homes that are deductible by rental properties' owners and should result in lower rents for equivalent housing. Thus, equality between imputed and non-imputed incomes is not always clear or easy to calculate.

(c) Realization

A fundamental issue for any income tax system is whether the tax system will tax all income, including accumulation and consumption, or only part of this total. An income tax can tax both parts while a consumption tax only taxes part.[55] A policymaker's

---

[51]   Nancy Staudt, *Taxing Housework*, 84 GEO. L.J. 1571 (1996).

[52]   Richard Goode, *Imputed Rent of Owner-Occupied Dwellings Under the Income Tax*, 15 J. FIN. 504, 504 (1960).

[53]   Barry Reece, *The Income Tax Incentive to Owner-Occupied Housing in Australia*, 51 ECON. RECORD 218, 219 (1975).

[54]   Steven Bourassa & William Grigsby, *Income Tax Concessions for Owner-Occupied Housing*, 11 HOUSING POL'Y DEBATE 521, 526–27 (2000).

[55]   Depending on the applicable deductions and credits, the income tax allows the government to reach accumulation and is more easily justified as assessing taxpayers' ability to pay taxes. Similarly, an income tax may (but also may not) alter work and

preference depends on the standard the policymaker uses to judge taxes.[56] If the policymaker believes taxpayers should only pay to the extent they directly benefit from the government, accumulation and dis-accumulation should not be taxed. Alternatively, if the policymaker wants to tax according to taxpayers' ability to pay, accumulation or dis-accumulation is an important factor. Today, the U.S. tax system does not take either as a pure approach but, instead, defers tax on accumulation.

More specifically, the U.S. income tax system generally taxes accumulation only when it is realized, a term of art in taxation. There is no definition of realization in the Internal Revenue Code or Treasury regulations. The concept developed largely in common law as a change in form. There must be some type of change, and a change recognized by the courts, to trigger taxation of appreciation or to entitle a taxpayer to deduct depreciation.

Realization is often easy to recognize because the change in form is obvious. Realization of wages occurs with the receipt of the wages. First the taxpayer had nothing and then the taxpayer had something—a check or deposit. Sales and exchanges of assets are realization events because one thing is traded for another thing, even when what is received is not cash. There was something and then there was something else. Other events, such as the abandonment of property, a tax forfeiture, or an involuntary foreclosure, are less obvious but also treated as realization events as a result of court decisions.[57] There was something and then there was nothing. Congress has also designated some events as realization events, such as securities becoming worthless or entering into a short sale of a security while retaining an identical security that has increased in value.[58] Still uncertain, however, is buying a security, such as a collar, that is the economic equivalent of selling any asset that is not a security and yet retaining title to the asset.

Henry Simons did not want the income tax to have a realization requirement.[59] Ignoring the problem of valuing assets, Simons argued that wealth increases with appreciation regardless of whether the wealth changes form. Simons was concerned that a realization requirement allows taxpayers to live a profitable life and

---

savings choices more than a consumption tax. For more on consumption taxes, see Chapter 8.

[56]   For more on standards to judge taxes, see Chapter 4.

[57]   Yarbro v. Comm'r, 737 F.2d 479 (5th Cir. 1984); Helvering v. Nebraska Bridge Supply & Lumber Co., 312 U.S. 666 (1941); Helvering v. Hammel, 311 U.S. 504 (1941).

[58]   I.R.C. § 165(g); I.R.C. § 1259.

[59]   HENRY C. SIMONS, FEDERAL TAX REFORM 65 (1950). A taxpayer could achieve the same result by borrowing against the gains because a loan does not produce taxable income.

accumulate wealth with minimal taxation. One example he provided was a taxpayer with diversified holdings who realized losses by selling depreciated investments, and so had cash but no taxable income. That taxpayer could hold onto appreciated investments until death so as not to trigger the taxable gains.

By ignoring the increase in wealth that exists with appreciation until there is a triggering event, the income tax resembles a tax on transactions more than a tax on incomes. Some taxpayers with real economic income are able to defer taxation, giving themselves an economic advantage over taxpayers of equal incomes who are unable to defer taxation. This arguably violates horizontal equity because those taxpayers who can defer taxation are in a better position than those who cannot. This advantage is not because of a difference in amount of income but because of the form of their income.

Additionally, a realization requirement makes the government a silent partner in profit-seeking activities. By deferring taxation until a triggering event, the government waits to collect its share of gain. The government may never receive its share of gain if there are subsequent declines before a triggering event. For example, if a taxpayer purchases an asset in year 1 for $100 and it appreciates to $200 by year 2, there is no tax consequence from the increase in value. If the taxpayer is in a 50% tax bracket, the government has $50 at stake in the appreciation but cannot collect it.

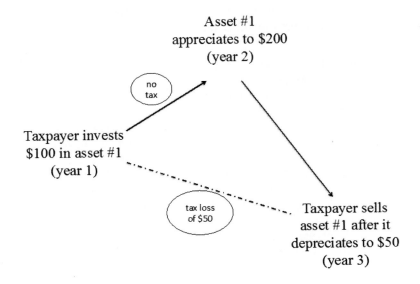

Then, if the asset declines in value in year 3 to $50 and the taxpayer sells the asset, the amount taxable is a negative $50. The taxpayer realizes a $50 tax loss as the difference between the amount invested in year 1 and the amount realized in year 3. The government's share of appreciation is lost. This same analysis applies no matter how long the asset is held.[60]

Moreover, taxpayers can use losses to offset gains in other assets, increasing the government's role as a silent investor. Because losses are deductible against gains, taxpayers can invest in high-risk endeavors knowing that they will not bear all of the loss. As long as taxpayers also have successful ventures to offset, any loss on bad investments times their tax rate is borne by the government through reduced tax revenue on their gains. Thus, the government bears a portion of the cost of risky investments and is slow to get paid on the profitable ones.

But there remain practical and theoretical problems with taxing unrealized income. First, taxpayers may not have the liquidity necessary to pay tax on unrealized appreciation. Some taxpayers might have to sell the appreciated asset just to pay the tax. And even if taxpayers desire to sell an appreciated item, there might not be a buyer available despite an increase in the item's value. Until there is an actual buyer, any paper gain may never be realized and is, therefore, a poor proxy for increased wealth. In other words, unrealized appreciation is really nothing but potential. The owner has the asset that was originally purchased plus, perhaps, the satisfaction of knowing that there may be gain on the disposition of the asset. Despite a potential increase in an abstract sense of wealth, until the asset changes form, it does not produce anything new for the owner.

Although the U.S. system generally requires realization, the tax system ignores realization in limited circumstances. For example, one could argue that the accrual method of accounting is a step away from realization because income must be reported when earned and not when received. More notably, marking assets to market is permitted for traders in securities and required of passive foreign investment companies (commonly referred to as PFICs).[61] Mark to market requires taxpayers value their assets and pay tax on any increase in value for each tax period whether or not the asset is disposed of during that period. This removes the realization requirement for taxation. Expansion of the mark to market system as proposed by some academics, including a system set out by Professor David Weisbach, extend only to assets that are subject to

---

[60]   Moreover, if the asset is held until death, any increase in value is never taxes. I.R.C. § 1014.

[61]   I.R.C. § 475; §§ 1291–1297.

valuation and are liquid, such as publicly traded stocks and bonds.[62] This limitation recognizes the practical problems of eliminating a realization requirement generally.

(d) Income Averaging

Congress originally adopted annual tax filing without debate. Since 1913, however, whether taxpayers should pay the income tax on an annual basis has been contested. An annual tax period provides a regular flow of revenue for government operations and allows taxpayers to understand their tax obligations with regularity. On the other hand, depending upon the nature of a taxpayer's earnings, an annual period might inequitably distort the taxpayer's income.

For example, an author might work unpaid on a novel for two or three years and then recognize huge gains the year when the rights are sold. This causes a bunching of income and the imposition of higher tax rates because of progressive taxation than would apply to more evenly distributed income. To reflect the author's uneven earnings, the annual system could be stretched out to two or three years or even a longer period. The most equitable income tax might be imposed on a taxpayer's entire life earnings to properly account for income's ebbs and flows.[63]

Historically, Congress adopted limited forms of income averaging that were optional so that the system operated only to reduce a taxpayer's income. If averaging worked to reduce a taxpayer's taxes, they could opt into the system; but, if averaging did not decrease taxes, taxpayers could use annual filing. Political pressure for this benefit has not been consistent. When tax rates are relatively flat, there is less theoretical demand for averaging because flatter rates reduce the cost of bunching income in higher brackets. However, even with flat rates, lower-income taxpayers may lose tax benefits if their income fluctuates and in some years is either too high or too low.

Today Congress only permits income averaging for certain fishermen and farmers.[64] This system allows qualifying taxpayers to average their income over a period of three years to reduce the impact of high marginal rates if the taxpayer has significant income in one

---

[62] David Weisbach, *A Partial Mark-to-Market Tax System*, 53 TAX L. REV. 95 (1999).

[63] Daniel Shaviro, *Permanent Income and the Annual Income Tax*, NYU Working Paper 61 (2006); Neil Buchanan, *The Case Against Income Averaging*, 25 VA. TAX REV. 1151 (2006).

[64] I.R.C. § 1301. A more extensive averaging provision was enacted in 1964 until major revision in 1986. Revenue Act of 1964, Pub. L. No. 88–272, § 232, 78 Stat. 19, 105–12 (1964) (codified at I.R.C. § 1301–05); Tax Reform Act of 1986, Pub. L. 99–514, § 141(a), 100 Stat. 2117 (1986).

year but little in the earlier, base years. Even in this limited form, averaging costs approximately $140 million per year.[65]

On the other hand, despite the claim that the U.S. has an annual income tax, the statutory requirement that taxpayers make quarterly payments (or more often for employees subject to withholding) arguably creates shorter periods for taxation.[66] If a taxpayer under-estimates their quarterly payments, penalties and interest accrue. This withholding ensures a larger number of taxpayers can pay their tax bills, rather than waiting until the end of the year, but practically it works to divide the tax year into many shorter periods. Once withholding is accepted, requiring quarterly payments from the self-employed similarly improves payment rates, increases government revenue, and improves equity between those with employer-based withholding and those without.

(e) Special Exclusions

Arguably, the Internal Revenue Code and notions of horizontal equity, or the maxim that similarly-situated taxpayers be treated similarly, demand that all income be subject to tax.[67] Nevertheless, the government excludes some amounts from income to achieve other policy objectives and for administrative need. For example, excluding contributions to health care savings accounts encourages such savings and excluding receipt of frequent flyer miles reduces administrative costs.

The structure of an exclusion may determine the exclusion's budgetary consequences, so that some forms of exclusion are cheaper for the government than others. Consider, for example, traditional and Roth individual retirement accounts, or IRAs. Traditional IRAs permit taxpayers to deduct contributions to qualified accounts, so income is excluded when the account is funded.[68] Thereafter the investment compounds tax-free until it is distributed, and then the entire amount of the distribution is included in income. The tax benefit of traditional IRAs is deferral of taxation so that taxpayers enjoy the time value of the money. Because of the current deduction, traditional IRAs immediately reduce government revenue for budgetary purposes.

On the other hand, contributions to a Roth IRA are included in current income for tax purposes, after-tax amounts compound tax-free, and the distribution of the investment's earnings is tax-

---

[65]   U.S. Dept. Treas., Tax Expenditures 21 (2017).

[66]   I.R.C. § 6654; IRS, Topic 306, Penalty for Underpayment of Estimated Tax (2017), https://www.irs.gov/taxtopics/tc306.html (last visited May 1, 2018).

[67]   I.R.C. § 61.

[68]   I.R.C. § 408.

exempt.[69] Thus, for the Roth IRA the tax benefit of the exclusion is at the time of the distribution of investment income. This structure means the Roth IRA has little current effect on the budget but reduces government revenue when distributions are made, a significant reduction in government revenue that is mostly outside the 10-year budget window. If all things are equal, such as the earnings rate and tax rates, the two investments are equivalent except for their impact on the government's budget.[70]

Statutory exclusions are often for public policy reasons whereas administrative exclusions often result from administrative necessity (the nightmare of valuing frequent flyer miles), because courts are likely to require it (such as the exclusion of imputed income), or from political interest (such as not enforcing the disallowance of losses when banks merged after the Great Recession). Policy rationales for each of these necessarily vary, although one could question whether exclusions should ever exist. Even exclusions for "good" things, such as education or housing, hide the benefit and its cost from those using the exclusion and the larger public. The same objective could be reached, but more visibly, by including the spending in income and providing a deduction or credit to encourage the behavior.

(f) Valuation

Because the tax system requires that taxpayers include items in gross income when the income is realized, even if what the taxpayer receives is not cash, taxpayers are required to value many types of items. Therefore, if Benjamin exchanges stock in a private corporation for Evelyn's land, Benjamin has to know how much the land is worth and Evelyn must know the value of the stock. If Carly performs legal services in return for David mowing her lawn, each must know the value of the services received to determine the amount of income. This fundamental question must be answered, but doing so is often difficult. Treatises are written on how to value something.[71] The practical difficulty of this valuation is one reason for the realization requirement itself.

Much of the tax system answers this question with an ambiguous answer: something is worth what a third party would pay in an arm's length transaction.[72] The arm's length standard is used throughout the Internal Revenue Code and Treasury regulations

---

[69] I.R.C. § 408A.

[70] For more on savings plans, see Chapter 17.01(e).

[71] JOHN BOGDANSKI, FEDERAL TAX VALUATION (2010); LEWIS SOLOMON & LEWIS SARET, VALUATION OF CLOSELY HELD BUSINESSES (1998).

[72] I.R.C. § 83(a); § 482; Treas. Reg. § 1.61–21(b)(2); § 1.482–1(a)(3); § 1.736–1(b)(1).

even though it is more of an idea than a real answer. Often there is no third party to ask; the government and the taxpayer can imagine answers but their answers can vary widely.

Tax abuse occurs when people try to play games with valuation, but sometimes taxpayers can be trusted to police themselves. In some scenarios taxpayers are opposing parties who will try to create an accurate valuation. For example, when Benjamin exchanges stock for Evelyn's land, Benjamin wants the land to be valued low in order to minimize his gain on the exchange. Evelyn, on the other hand, wants a high valuation of the land in order to minimize her later gain on a sale of the stock. In these cases, the parties' opposing interests can be used to keep them honest. This is one reason that Congress requires taxpayers acquiring a business's assets be bound by a joint statement of the value assigned to each asset.[73] Their competing incentives work to solve the valuation problem for the IRS.

At other times there is no competing third party because the opposing party does not owe taxes to the U.S. government. This may occur in transactions with a foreign taxpayer or a tax-exempt entity. In these instances, professional appraisals are generally required. For example, to claim a charitable contribution donation deduction when the value of a donated asset is greater than $5,000, the donor must obtain a qualified appraisal of the asset.[74] Regulations help define who is a qualified appraiser to provide a qualified appraisal. There are windows for how long an appraisal is valid before a contribution; the amount and type of fee the appraiser can receive; the types of details that must be disclosed. Although the appraiser is supposed to be disinterested, many within the appraisal industry understand what they are trading in—tax deductions.[75]

Similarly, valuation is frequently an issue for small businesses, particularly in transfers of control to avoid the estate or gift tax. Popular tax planning devices are family limited partnerships (FLPs) and family limited liability companies (FLLCs).[76] Despite legitimate nontax goals (such as protection from creditors, economies of scale, or transfer of control), many people see these devices as a way of decreasing the value of a taxable estate with limited gift tax consequences. FLPs, for example, permit an older family member to transfer a minority interest in the partnership to heirs. That interest

---

[73]   I.R.C. § 1060.

[74]   I.R.C. § 170(f)(11)(C).

[75]   Alan Breus, *Valuing Art for Tax Purposes,* J. OF ACCOUNT., Jul. 1, 2010; Reuven Avi-Yonah, *The Rise and Fall of Arm's Length,* 15 VA. TAX REV. 80 (1995).

[76]   Stephen Black, et al., *When a Discount Isn't a Bargain,* 32 U. MEM. L. REV. 245 (2002); Louis Mezzullo, *Successful Defense to an IRS Section 2036(a) Attack,* 6 BUS. ENTERPRISE 36 (2004).

is valued at significantly less than its share of the partnership's assets because the minority interest's owner has no control over the workings of the partnership and generally cannot sell the interest either because of a lack of marketability or because transfers are prohibited.[77] The discount has been sanctioned since the 1990s and today can reach as high as 50% of the underlying assets.

The Treasury Department proposed regulations that would have limited the discount available for interests in FLPs and FLLCs.[78] The Department balked at discounts when a partnership held marketable securities or other assets that could easily be valued or sold, but the proposed regulations applied to all family partnerships. This raised complaints from partnerships that held on-going, and hence hard to value, businesses. Although tax planners used these prospective regulations to drum up business, President Trump's general executive order forcing reconsideration of regulations that impose burdens on taxpayers led to the withdrawal of these proposed regulations.[79]

Thus, the myth of a fair valuation is a necessary part of the current tax system but it remains, nevertheless, a myth. Often relying on the arm's length standard, rules require taxpayers to estimate what a third party would pay when there is no third party. Despite the difficulties this valuation creates, no better alternative has been proposed. To simply ignore all transactions not in cash because of the difficulty of valuation would create a dangerous incentive for bartering that would be economically inefficient and threaten the federal budget.

§ 7.03   The Capital Gain Preference

Capital gains' preferential tax rate receives a lot of press.[80] Politicians, members of the press, think tanks, plus anyone else interested in tax policy hotly debate the value of continuing this long-standing tax preference. The capital gain preference is either the cure for the economy or another loophole for the wealthy. Many of the arguments supporting favorable rates are variations of the argument that the alternative produces more negative consequences than

---

[77]   I.R.C. § 2704.

[78]   81 Fed. Reg. 51, 413 (2016); Treas. Reg. § 25.2701–2; § 25.2704–1, –2, –3.

[79]   Exec. Order 13,794; Notice 2017–38, 82 Fed. Reg. 48,013; Paul Sullivan, *Treasury Wants to End Tax Deal for Some Family-Owned Businesses*, N.Y. TIMES, Aug. 19, 2016.

[80]   Tax Policy Center, *What is the Effect of a Lower Tax Rate For Capital Gains*, BRIEFING BOOK, http://www.taxpolicycenter.org/briefing-book/what-effect-lower-tax-rate-capital-gains (last visited May 1, 2018); David Block & William McBride, *Why Capital Gains are Taxed at a Lower Rate*, TAX FOUNDATION (2012); *Is It Fair to Tax capital Gains at Lower Rates than Earned Income?*, WALL ST. J., Mar. 1, 2015.

keeping the preference; that lower capital gain rates prevent inequities or inefficiencies that would result from taxing this type of income at the relatively higher ordinary income tax rates. Critics of the preference dispute this assertion.

(a) Structure of Preference

The capital gain preference only applies to gains on capital assets held by individuals for a long-term holding period.[81] The long-term holding period is currently more than one year. Therefore, not all capital gains are taxed at preferential rates. Individuals' short-term capital gains and all corporations' capital gains are taxed at ordinary income rates. The structure of the preference and the length of time that is required for preferential rates to apply have changed repeatedly over the years. For a period only a portion of capital gains had to be included in income, but that portion was taxed at ordinary rates. At other times, the definition of qualifying gain has changed. Thus, although some form of preference has almost always existed, the form of preference has changed.

(i) History[82]

Changes to the capital gain preference occur as Congress responds to political and economic pressures. However, until 1921, it was not clear if capital gains would be taxed at all. Then, in 1921, the Supreme Court ruled that capital gains were taxable.[83] For taxpayers who paid tax on gains before 1921, the gains would have been taxed at the same rate as ordinary income. Responding to the Court, that same year Congress set a maximum 12.5% rate for capital gains from assets held for at least two years compared to a top 73% income tax rate.

Thereafter, the structure of the capital gain preference has changed significantly and frequently. Beginning in 1934 through 1941, Congress enacted five graduated holding periods each providing some amount of exclusion but non-excluded gains were taxed at ordinary rates. In 1942, if a taxpayer's ordinary rate was more than 50%, the taxpayer was given a choice either to exclude 50% of the gain from capital assets held for six months and pay tax on the remaining 50% at ordinary rates or pay tax on all the gains at 25%. Capital gain taxes grew heavier and more complicated until the 1980s when, in 1986, Congress eliminated the preference as part of

---

[81]   I.R.C. § 1(h); § 1221.

[82]   For more on the history of the capital gains preference, see Ajay Mehrotra & Julia Ott, *The Curious Beginning of the Capital Gains Tax Preference*, 84 FORDHAM L. REV. 2517 (2016); Marjorie Kornhauser, *The Origins of Capital Gains Taxation*, 39 SOUTHWESTERN L. J. 869 (1985).

[83]   Merchants Loan & Trust Co. v. Smietanka, 255 U.S. 509 (1921).

its general tax rate reduction but without eliminating capital gain provisions from the Code.

The lack of a preference did not last long. Preferential rates were reintroduced in 1990 at 28% and reduced again in 2001 and 2003 when Congress cut the capital gains rates to 0% (if taxable income would otherwise be taxed at less than a 25% rate) and 15%. The Taxpayer Relief Act of 2012 added a 20% bracket for those taxpayers in the 39.6% ordinary income bracket. In 2017, for the period between 2018 and 2025, the link to tax brackets was replaced with income caps, so that the top of the 0% bracket in 2018 is $77,200 for joint filers and their bottom of the 20% bracket is $479,000. These rates no longer correspond exactly to rate brackets.

(ii) Capital Assets

In debates over the preference, its proponents and opponents rarely discuss what assets are, or should be, entitled to this preference. The Code defines capital assets by what is not a capital asset, most notably inventory or what a taxpayer sells or trades in.[84] This may differ from popular perception. The popular understanding of "capital gain" is likely the appreciation of investment property, such as stock or land. However, the proper characterization depends on what the person uses the property for; in other words, what is a capital asset for one person might not be a capital asset for another.

Although the broad outline of the rules appear clear, in practice which assets constitute capital assets for purposes of preferential rates is complicated. Corporate stock is often viewed as the quintessential capital asset, but stock accounts for only about 25% of all capital gains. At times even stock is not a capital asset, as dealers in stock hold it as inventory so that their gain is taxable as ordinary income.[85] Sometimes the rules are unpredictable in their complexity. For example, gain by inventors on the sale of their patents is capital gain per section 1235, although in 2017 patents were specifically carved out from listed capital assets in section 1221. Similarly, gain on the sale of copyrights is definitely ordinary, unless the copyright is for a musical composition in which case the taxpayer can choose the characterization.[86]

---

[84]   I.R.C. § 1221.

[85]   Publication 1304, *supra* note 2, at Table 1A, Table 1B. While corporate stock may be the archetypical capital asset, gain from the sale of stock of a "collapsible corporation," which is a temporary corporation formed with the intent of its termination, was for many decades taxed as ordinary income, although that requirement was temporarily repealed in 2002 and permanently repealed in 2012. I.R.C. § 341 (repealed).

[86]   I.R.C. §§ 1221(a)(3), (b)(3); 1235.

Not everyone holds an equal amount of capital assets. Instead, ownership of these assets tends to be concentrated in the hands of the wealthy. The bottom 90% of income earners have their principal residence as 60% of their assets and hold only 6% of the nation's financial securities and 8% of its business equity.[87] On the other hand, the top 1% has as their assets 65% of the nation's financial securities and 61% of its business equity and only 10% of their assets in their residence. It is the securities and business equity that is more likely to benefit from the capital gain preference.

(iii) Dividends

In addition to gain on the sale or other disposition of capital assets held for more than one year, qualifying dividends have been taxed at favorable capital gain rates since 2003. Qualifying dividends are defined as dividends from U.S. corporations (with some exceptions) and from certain non-U.S. corporations. There is a requirement that the taxpayer hold the stock for 60 days (90 days for certain preferred stock) before the dividends become qualifying in order to minimize taxpayers' ability to purchase stock at a higher price because of an imminent dividend issuance, claim the dividend, and then claim a capital loss on the sale of the stock. Favorable rates are not usual for dividends; before 2003 all dividends were taxed at ordinary income tax rates. Ordinary rates still apply to non-qualifying dividends.

Advocates of giving dividends preferential tax rates expected that it would increase the payout of dividends, as opposed to corporations retaining their earnings.[88] Studies are inconclusive whether this tax relief changed the amount of distributions or only accelerated the timing of distributions that would have been made without it.[89] Extending favorable rates to dividends has reduced a planning opportunity for taxpayers, thereby decreasing planning complexity. When dividends were taxed at higher rates than long-term capital gains available on the sale of stock held long-term, there was significant tax planning to convert dividend payments into sales of shares or the redemption of shares. Although there remain some

---

[87] G. Willian Donhoff, *Wealth, Income, and Power, Who Rules America?*, http://www2.ucsc.edu/whorulesamerica/power/wealth.html (last visited May 1, 2018).

[88] John McKinnon, *Tax Cuts on Dividends Paid to Individuals Gains Support*, WALL ST. J., Dec. 4, 2002; Mark Gongloff, *A Dividend for the Economy?*, CNN MONEY, Jan. 7, 2003; Gary Becker, *The Dividend Tax Cut Will Get Better With Time*, BUSINESS WEEK, Feb. 10, 2003.

[89] John L. Campbell et al., *Did the 2003 Tax Act Increase Capital Investments by Corporations*, 35 J. OF AM. TAX'N ASS'N 33 (2013); Steven Bank, *Dividends and Tax Policy in the Long Run*, 2007 U. ILL. L. REV. 533; Raj Chetty & Emmanuel Saez, *Dividend Taxes and Corporate Behavior*, 120 Q. J. OF ECON. 791 (2005).

advantages of capital gains over qualifying dividends for some taxpayers, the 2003 change has reduced those advantages.

(iv) Depreciation Recapture

Although historically most legislation has favored capital gains, not all legislation has done so. In the 1960s, Congress responded to taxpayers claiming capital gains on the sale of property for which the taxpayer had previously claimed depreciation deductions by enacting a depreciation recapture.[90] In other words, Congress narrowly denied certain taxpayers the benefit of capital gain rates if taxpayers had already claimed offsetting depreciation deductions.[91] Depreciation is an ordinary deduction available on certain capital assets. The deduction offsets ordinary income but also decreases the taxpayer's basis in the depreciated asset. Under prior law, if a taxpayer claimed deductions without equally reducing what a third party would pay for that asset, the taxpayer could claim an ordinary deduction and later a capital gain on the sale of the asset. The taxpayer received the best of both worlds—an ordinary deduction and capital gain. Congress's response taxed any gain attributable to previously claimed depreciation at ordinary income rates so that the ordinary deduction was offset with ordinary income. This new feature increases complexity in administering the tax but reduces complexity in planning.

(b) Limitation on Losses

Although capital gains are taxed preferentially, Congress limits taxpayers' ability to deduct capital losses. Limits on taxpayers' ability to claim loss deductions increase capital assets' tax burdens. One justification for these limits is that taxpayers control the realization of losses on the assumption that the sale of capital assets is relatively elastic. Therefore, taxpayers control the timing of their losses. Another justification is that without restrictions taxpayers will artificially inflate losses to reduce their taxes. Many tax shelters operate by increasing, shifting, or fabricating tax losses. On the other hand, as long as limits to losses exist, taxpayers must maintain records of their capital assets, even if preferential rates were to be repealed.

With its own complicated history, capital losses can now be deducted in full against capital gains but are limited against dividends or ordinary income.[92] In tax, this is called the basketing of

---

90   Calvin Johnson, *Gains and Losses on Business Depreciable Property*, 126 TAX NOTES 787 (2010).

91   I.R.C. §§ 1245 and 1250.

92   I.R.C. § 1211.

losses against gains, which limits the economic value of a loss deduction. Both individuals and corporations can basket capital losses against capital gains. Individuals, but not corporations, can also deduct $3,000 of capital losses against ordinary income. Capital losses that are not currently deductible can be carried back to prior tax years (for corporations only) or carried forward (for individuals and corporations) and basketed on those returns.[93] Corporations that experience capital losses might have their losses expire if they do not have sufficient gains to offset within an eight-year window; individuals have the ability to carry capital losses forward indefinitely.

Additionally, Congress has enacted several other limits that may prevent taxpayers from deducting losses. Limits on loss deductions arguably create a bias against risk-taking or, framed another way, curtail risky investments. Without the limits, when an investor loses, the losses offset other income and so the loss is shared with the government in the same way that successes are shared. However, sharing of the risk may encourage overly risky investments because investors know that they will not bear the full weight of bad investments. The ability to offset gains or income also creates an incentive to increase or even fabricate losses in the form of tax shelters.

As one example of a statutory limit on loss deductions, Congress enacted the wash sales rule in 1954 to prevent taxpayers from deducting losses on the sale of financial securities if a taxpayer repurchases a substantially identical security within a 60-day window around the sale.[94] The purpose of disallowing this loss is to prevent taxpayers from triggering losses for tax purposes when they do not suffer a loss economically. If there is no economic loss, Congress tries to deny the taxpayer the tax loss, although doing so is often difficult to enforce and adds complexity to the tax system.

The economic result of these limits on tax loss deductions can be substantial. Consider the case of a wealthy individual who invests $1 million in each of 100 different publicly traded stocks. Some portion declines in value. The individual then sells enough of the losing stock to offset any gain on the sale of appreciated stock while retaining the rest of the appreciated stock until death. This taxpayer owes nothing in income tax. Because of the taxpayer's ability to choose which stock to sell, the perception is of tax abuse because the taxpayer has money to live on without owing tax. On the other hand, consider a not-wealthy individual who invested heavily in one corporation. That stock generates a significant loss and, because of the limits on

---

[93]   I.R.C. § 1212.
[94]   I.R.C. § 1091.

deductibility, the not-wealthy individual who generates no capital gains is only able to deduct his loss in $3,000 increments each year.

These loss limitations remained in the Internal Revenue Code even in the short period in the 1980s during which Congress repealed the capital gain preference. Therefore, taxpayers remained limited in their ability to deduct their capital losses even though they owed tax on capital gains at ordinary income rates.

(c) Arguments in Favor of the Capital Gain Preference

The first, and often considered the strongest, argument in favor of the capital gain preference is that without favorable rates people lock-in their capital assets to avoid taxation.[95] The lock-in effect reduces the mobility of capital. Lock-in results from the realization requirement in taxation; if taxpayers had to mark-to-market their assets and pay tax annually on any gain, there would be no deferral of taxation and no lock-in. That taxpayers can wait until death, which eliminates any income taxation of the appreciation to either the decedent or heir, strengthens the lock-in effect.

Consider George, who holds land with a $100 basis and a $500 fair market value, hence $400 of untaxed appreciation. The land's expected yield in rent is 10%, or $50. George has the opportunity to invest in stock, which has an expected yield of 11%, so 1% more than the land. Assuming a 20% flat tax rate, if George sold the land, he would owe tax on $400 in net gain. The $400 gain times the 20% tax rate produces an $80 tax bill. That leaves only $420 of the land's $500 fair market value to invest in the stock. Because a $420 investment in the stock times the 11% rate yields only $46.20, instead of the $50 from the land, George should not change investments despite the higher yield in the new opportunity.

However, just because the lock-in effect burdens the individual does not necessarily mean that it burdens society as a whole. According to most economists, that George does not invest in the stock because the cost of selling the land is too high does not greatly impact the amount of stock outstanding. As long as the return is high enough, someone will invest in the stock even if George chooses not to do so. Lock-in thus affects the ownership of assets, not the deployment thereof. To the extent this is true, any loss is in individual welfare and not in society's welfare as a whole. Moreover, any level of tax would produce some amount of lock-in. The lower the tax rates, the lesser the amount of lock-in, so the natural argument

---

[95] Reuven Avi-Yonah & Dmitry Zelik, *Are We Trapped by Our Capital Gains?*, U. OF MICH. PUBLIC L. RESEARCH PAPER NO. 476 (2015).

for critics of lock-in is that tax rates should be reduced to 0% or as close to 0% as possible. Only the elimination of the tax eliminates the problem.

A second argument in favor of the capital gain preference is that there is a bunching of the gain into a single tax year. Because gain is only taxable when it is realized and because tax rates are progressive, the gain on the sale of a capital asset that has been held for a number of years is likely pushed into higher tax rate brackets than would have been applied if the tax had been imposed as the asset appreciated. A lower capital gain rate helps mitigate this bunching problem as a quasi-averaging device. However, other than the one-year holding period requirement for favorable rates, the preference has no link between the rate and the holding period. Thus, the same rate and the same rough averaging apply whether a capital asset is held for 1 or 100 years.

Third, much of capital gain is illusory because it results from inflation. The optimal solution to this illusory gain problem is not favorable tax rates but indexing an asset's tax basis to inflation rates so that the amount of gain itself would be adjusted with time. However, this fix is likely administratively impossible and too confusing for most taxpayers. Therefore, favorable rates may be a rough justice for inflation. On the other hand, as with bunching, there is no tie between favorable rates and the amount of inflation. Moreover, for assets held for a long period, the preference is arguably unnecessary because the taxpayer already enjoys the benefit of deferral from taxation; and for short periods, both deferral and inflation have little impact.

Fourth, taxing capital gains arguably disincentivizes saving and investing. Preferential rates reduce any disincentive. Moreover, the reduced rate of tax should encourage taxpayers to save and invest rather than consume as a result of the substitution effect. Economic theory argues taxpayers will substitute lower-taxed investing to higher-taxed consuming.[96] However, the Congressional Research Service has found no proof of this effect.[97]

Fifth, to the extent capital gains are from the sale of corporate stock, the preference arguably reduces the double tax that may inhibit economic development by taxing corporations when they earn

---

[96]   For more on economic theory of the substitution effect, see Chapter 6.01. It could also be argued that capital gain rates make a dollar from investment more attractive than a dollar from wages, stigmatizing work.

[97]   THOMAS HUNGERFORD, CONG. RESEARCH SERV., R40411, THE ECONOMIC EFFECTS OF CAPITAL GAINS TAXATION (2010). *But see* John Campbell et al., *Did the 2003 Tax Act Increase Capital Investments by Corporations*, 35 J. AM. TAX'N ASS'N 33 (2013).

income and shareholders when they receive distributions or dispose of their shares.[98] By reducing the taxation of gains on the sale of stock and dividends distributed from a corporation, the double tax regime does not bear the same tax burden as it would without preferential rates. Of course, this argument only applies for corporate stock, only one of a range of assets that benefit from capital gain rates.

Finally, there is the argument that taxes and tax preferences, including the capital gain preference, are priced into the market price of assets. Changing the tax regime to eliminate the capital gain preference would disrupt the market balance that has evolved since imposition of the tax. In other words, the price people are willing to pay for capital assets presupposes a reduced tax rate on the assets' appreciation. People pay more for capital assets than they otherwise would because of reduced tax rates. To the extent a preference creates a windfall of lower taxes to holders of capital assets, that windfall has long since been enjoyed. To remove the preference now may impose a disproportionate burden on current holders of those assets.

(d) Arguments Against a Capital Gain Preference

Despite the long life of the capital gain preference, not everyone supports the concept. One scholar wrote over half a century ago that "there is not the slightest basis for any distinction between a capital gain and any other form of income."[99] Arguably, because the economic benefit from a dollar of capital gain is the same as the economic benefit from wages, the burden of proof for a capital gain preference should be on its proponents. Nevertheless, opponents of the preference generally focus on one of four claims discussed below.

First, even if preferential rates provide the economic stimulus proponents of the preference claim, there remain issues of equity in providing a preference to one form of income over others. Through the capital gain preference, those who hold assets that are not depleted over time enjoy lower tax rates than those who earn their income from wages. Republican Secretary of the Treasury Department and fervent capitalist Andrew Mellon even argued that wages should be given a preferential rate compared to income from invested capital because wages can only be earned for a portion of a worker's life but capital investments can last forever.[100]

On the other hand, investments that generate economic growth are likely to stimulate higher wages for workers. Therefore, increasing investment can have a mutually beneficial result for

---

[98]   For more on the double taxation of corporate income, see Chapter 11.01(e).

[99]   Charles Lowndes, *The Taxation of Capital Gains and Losses Under the Federal Income Tax*, 26 TEX. L. REV. 440, 460 (1948).

[100]   ANDREW MELLON, TAXATION: THE PEOPLE'S BUSINESS (1924).

workers. This presupposes the connection between favorable capital gain rates and increased employment or increased investment, neither of which has been proven.[101] A difficulty with the linkage is that the nation may need little new private investment to fund sound investments, and there is no proof that higher taxes actually decrease investment. Lower taxes may only cause people to consume more and to stop saving because most individuals are not systematic in choosing their savings levels but instead target an amount of savings.[102] Once people reach their target, they stop saving; hence the falling savings rates over the past 30 years despite falling capital gain rates. Decreasing tax rates would allow people to reach their target sooner.

Another reason why tax rates may matter little to national economic growth is the role of those not subject to U.S. tax or not entitled to the preference. In 2010, institutions managed about 67% of publicly-held stocks.[103] Many of these institutions were tax-exempt investors, such as pension funds, were international investors and not subject to U.S. taxation, or did not expect the long-term holding period necessary for preferential rates, such as hedge funds. These sources of investment funds do not benefit from preferential rates.

Second, those benefiting from the capital gains preference already benefit from deferral. Because there is a realization requirement before tax is imposed, those holding capital assets for long enough to enjoy the favorable rate have already deferred paying tax for at least one tax year, possibly much longer. This benefit allows taxpayers to enjoy the time value of money.[104] Deferral of tax on appreciation benefits taxpayers by allowing them to accumulate more wealth. Deferral is further enhanced because the appreciation may never be taxed if the owner of the asset dies.[105] Thus the system already has many benefits for holders of capital assets in addition to preferential rates.

Third, opponents complain that primarily a few, wealthy taxpayers enjoy the preference. The CBO estimates that low rates on capital gains and dividends will cost the federal government $1.34

---

[101]   THOMAS HUNGERFORD, CONG. RESEARCH SERV. R42729, TAXES AND THE ECONOMY: ANALYSIS OF THE TOP TAX RATES SINCE 1945 (2012); Jane Gravelle, *Limits to Capital Gains Feedback Effects*, 51 TAX NOTES 363 (1991).

[102]   F. Thomas Juster et al., *The Decline in Household Saving and the Wealth Effect*, 88 REV. ECON. & STAT. 20 (2006).

[103]   Luis Aguilar, Commissioner of SEC, Remarks at Ga. St. Univ., Institutional Investors: Powers and Responsibilities (Apr. 19, 2013) (transcript at https://www.sec.gov/news/speech/2013-spch041913laahtm).

[104]   For more on the time value of money, see Chapter 6.02(a)(iii).

[105]   One argument made for the estate tax is that because appreciation is not taxed under the income tax the estate tax ensures there is no leakage from the tax system. For more on the estate tax, see Chapter 9.04.

trillion in revenue over the next ten years.[106] Taxpayers with incomes in the top 1% of the country will get 68% of that savings, while the bottom 80% will receive only 7%. As with deferral, this benefit is enhanced at death. Unrealized capital gains comprise 55% of the total value of estates worth more than $100 million and, upon the decedent's death, that gain is never taxed.[107]

Fourth, preferential capital gain rates add to the complexity of the Internal Revenue Code, moving Professor Boris Bittker to call the treatment of capital gains and losses "perhaps the single most complicating aspect of existing law."[108] Because preferential rates only apply to some categories of income, lines have to be drawn around those categories. As taxpayers structure their activities to convert ordinary income to capital gains, Congress responds by restricting the number of transactions that qualify for preferential treatment. Numerous rules have been enacted to keep the universe of capital gains contained. Some taxpayers, in turn, exploit loopholes in these rules. This complexity and tax planning violate the rules of efficiency and simplicity and, to the extent that only some can avoid tax, also violate horizontal equity.

(e) Lack of Evidence Either Way

Although many scholars and government agencies have tried, no one has been able to prove or disprove the capital gain preference's achievements. The difficulty is that proof requires a counterfactual of what people would have done but for the preference. Scholars have tried with time-series studies over long periods, cross section studies of a single year, panel studies of sample taxpayers, and pooled time-series cross sectional analysis.[109] The failure of empirical studies is well known, but no one knows how to fix the problem. Because it is impossible to predict how people would react to changes in the law, policymakers must guess about the effects.

Scholars often assume that without the preference all holders of capital assets would hold the assets until death, but that is unlikely. If the holder of a capital asset needs cash, the holder could borrow

---

[106] MARK BOOTH & JOSHUA SHAKIN, CONG. BUDGET OFFICE, PUB. NO. 4869, THE BUDGET AND ECONOMIC OUTLOOK: 2014 TO 2024 (2014).

[107] Robert Avery et al., *Estate vs. Capital Gains Taxation*, FED. RESERVE BOARD (2013).

[108] *Panel Discussions on General Tax Reform Before House Comm. on Ways and Mean*, 93d Cong. 118 (1973).

[109] Jon Bakija & William Gentry, *Capital Gains Taxes and Realizations*, NBER WORKING PAPER 13469 (2014); Matthew Eichner & Todd Sinai, *Capital Gains Tax Realizations and Tax Rates*, 53 NAT'L TAX J. 663 (2000); Gerald Auten et al., *Estimation and Interpretation of Capital Gains Realization Behavior*, 42 NAT'L TAX J. 353 (1989); Leonard Burman & William Randolph, *Measuring Permanent Responses to Capital Gains Tax Changes in Panel Data*, 84 AM. ECON. REV. 794 (1994).

using the asset as collateral and retain the asset, but that might not always be realistic. Moreover, holders know that the money invested in a capital asset remains at risk as long as the asset is held and that other opportunities may be lost. Both of these facts may motivate a sale. On the other hand, some people may not maximize national economic development because of their preference to avoid ordinary income tax rates. Until someone can predict what portion of the public would only sale with a tax advantage, it is impossible to know definitively to what extent the capital gains preference provides on its promise.

Chapter 8

CONSUMPTION TAXATION

Table of Sections

In early American history, most taxes were levied on consumption, such as stamp taxes, whiskey taxes, and taxes on tea. Early policymakers favored consumption taxes because they thought it was harder to raise consumption tax rates to "confiscatory" levels, however that is defined, because they are visible taxes.[1] Despite early support for consumption taxes, the trend has been away from such taxes since the adoption of the modern income tax in 1913. Nevertheless, there have been repeated calls for new consumption taxes, both at the state and federal level. Some calls are for national sales taxes and others for value-added taxes (popularly referred to as VATs). The proposals take many forms because there is no one model for consumption taxes. Not only do rates change among proposals, so do the items subject to the tax, the payer of the tax to the government, and the items excluded from taxation.

§ 8.01   Tax Base[2]

A consumption tax raises revenue from the sale of goods and possibly services; actual consumption is generally not required. For most consumption tax proposals, any income that is not consumed through a purchase is defined as saved or invested. More than four decades ago, Professor William Andrews advocated for the tax in terms of its fairness, economic efficiency, and simplicity.[3] However, each of these claims has been disputed. To date, there is no conclusive evidence that a consumption tax will, or will not, accomplish what its advocates propose. Nonetheless, it is certain that a consumption tax would narrow the tax base from that under a traditional income tax.

---

[1]   THE FEDERALIST No. 21 (Alexander Hamilton).

[2]   The tax base defines what is subject to tax. Thus, the income tax's base is income as defined in the Internal Revenue Code and a sales tax's base is sales.

[3]   William Andrews, *A Consumption-Type or Cash Flow Personal Income Tax*, 87 HARV. L. REV. 1113 (1974).

(a) How the Tax Base Works

By only taxing items that are consumed, a consumption tax redefines the proper base to be taxed. Unless no one saves anything, a consumption tax has a smaller amount subject to tax than taxing all of the income that taxpayers earn. How much the tax base is smaller depends upon the amount of savings and the structure of the income tax because Congress has carved some forms of savings out of the income tax, such as with 401(k) plans and IRAs. These provisions make the income tax operate similar to a consumption tax. The inverse is not true in that a consumption tax can never reach all forms of income.

Nevertheless, as a tax base, a consumption tax may achieve greater efficiency or neutrality between taxpayers' choices than can be achieved with an income tax. Arguably, an income tax distorts behavior because it first taxes income as it is earned (for example wage income is taxed) and, if that income is invested, it taxes earnings on the investment (such as dividends and interest).[4] This taxation of investments both before and after pushes some people to choose lesser taxed consuming than investing. It is also likely to induce some others to save less because the savings have a lower rate of return because they are post-tax. With a consumption tax, taxpayers are only taxed on the return on the investment so that people invest more and receive a higher return. This should increase the amount of national savings as people choose to consume less. Thus, with a consumption tax rather than an income tax, more money is available for investment and increased national growth, which benefits both the saver and the consumer.

In the process of narrowing what is subject to tax, the consumption tax is founded on a different premise than is income taxation. Unlike the income tax, which is often advocated because of its ability to raise revenue based on people's ability to pay taxes, a consumption tax generally focuses on what people take from society.[5] In this view, consumption more clearly reflects what is taken from society because consumption benefits the person who consumes the resources; an income tax taxes what is added to the nation's economy through work or savings.

Alternatively, one could argue that a consumption tax is based on ability-to-pay principles by defining ability-to-pay away from the possession of resources to current utility. Under this theory, the focus is on how much people use of society's resources. The Federal Reserve Bank of Cleveland stated that consumption is "clearly a better

---

4   For more on the income tax, see Chapter 7.
5   For more on the standards to judge tax systems, see Chapter 4.

measure of an individual's well-being than is his or her income."[6] If consumption indicates how well off someone is, so that those who consume more are better off than those who consume less, consumption-based taxation more accurately taxes their ability to pay. Along similar lines, horizontal equity, or treating people in similar circumstances the same, could be argued on a consumption basis as well as an income one.[7]

On the other hand, accumulating wealth may benefit a person even when the wealth is not spent, which a consumption tax ignores. Simply put, can money, not yet spent, bring a person happiness? If having wealth is a good thing because it increases prestige, financial security, or for any other reason, there is arguably an element of consumption even though nothing is purchased per se. These benefits increase a person's happiness in a way that the tax system perhaps should recognize. Moreover, people consume different items for different reasons so all consumption might not be equal for society's purposes. In other words, some consumption is socially useful and other is wasteful. Is consuming education the same as consuming video games? If the focus is on what people take from society, it is possible some forms of taking deserve higher taxation than others. Thus, consumption has philosophical questions Congress has not yet faced as it has with the income tax.

That the tax base is consumption does not define what is consumed. Consumption can be defined by what it is not. For administrative reasons, purchased consumables are assumed to be consumed even if they are not. But not all items are consumable and therefore taxable. Savings and investment are not consumed and savings are generally, but not always, invested. In practice, consumption tax proposals can define consumption to exclude savings or to require specific investments. The authors of a proposal make this distinction.[8] Certainly purchases of investments are generally excluded from the consumption tax.

However, some purchases have both savings and consumption elements, so that the purchase should theoretically be divided between the two. For example, when a person invests in a home, the house is not merely an investment but is consumption in the form of housing. Therefore, the house cannot properly be classified as all consumption or all savings, but the division between the two depends on the person as much as the asset.

---

[6]   LaVaughn Henry, *Income Inequality and Income-Class Consumption Patterns*, 2014 FED. RESERVE BANK OF CLEVELAND, ECON. COMMENT 18.

[7]   For more on horizontal equity, see Chapter 4.02(a).

[8]   For purposes of this chapter, savings and investment are used interchangeably.

In whatever way consumption is defined, a pure consumption tax is applied to all consumption, however defined, regardless of whether purchases are made with current income, borrowed funds, or previously saved funds. This means, however, that there is no exclusion from tax for purchases made with gifts or borrowed funds comparable to what currently exists in the income tax. Taxing consumption financed with borrowings is likely to raise political ire. For example, 100% of a car's purchase price would be taxable even if a person only had a down payment. This could also mean that the purchase of a home, with or without a home mortgage, and the purchase of education, with or without student loans, would be taxable as the buyers are consuming society's resources.

Congress could designate certain spending, such as a home or education, as an investment but this increases complexity because lines will have to be drawn—are books for education and is remodeling the home part of the investment? Doing so also changes the economic return for certain types of borrowing. For example, if housing and education are viewed as an investment and excluded from taxation on policy grounds, this leaves borrowing spent on the purchase of clothes, cars, or movie tickets to be currently taxable to the consumer, making it significantly more expensive. This increases the value of loans for the purchase of some goods and increases the return to those who can afford significant amounts of leverage for their investment purchases.

(b) Effect on Tax Rates

The tax base not only determines what is subject to tax, its size determines the tax rates necessary to fund government spending. The larger the tax base the lower the tax rate required to raise a given amount of revenue. For example, if the tax base (or what is subject to tax) is $12,000 and is subject to tax at 50%, the tax raises $6,000 in revenue. If the tax base is increased to $15,000, the same 50% tax raises $7,500 in taxes. And to raise $6,000 with the larger tax base, the rate can be reduced to 40%. Thus, all else being equal the smaller tax base for a consumption tax results in higher rates and, consequently, a larger amount of money spent on consumption being paid to the government.

Moreover, the higher tax rate that would apply to a smaller base is not necessarily applied evenly across all taxpayers. The distribution of the rate depends upon the distribution of the tax base. If consumption is not distributed evenly across society, those who consume more are disadvantaged by higher rates and those who consume less are advantaged. Politically, if a particular group has a lot of something that would escape taxation with a smaller tax base, it makes sense for the group to favor the narrower base even though it is taxed at a higher rate. And the inverse is true: If the group owns a lot of something that will remain taxed, it should want the broader base to reduce the rate that applies.

To be clear, an increase in rates would not necessarily be an increase in the amount that is paid to the government. Much of the rate increase is optics. Not only is the higher rate needed because of the smaller base, most consumption taxes are tax-exclusive rather than tax-inclusive, which requires a higher nominal tax rate. The tax-exclusive amount is calculated on a base that does not include the taxes paid. For example, if a $100 item has a 50% sales tax (a large percentage only to highlight the issue), the tax is imposed on the $100 and the final cost is $150, to raise $50 in taxes. A tax-inclusive amount includes the amount paid in tax in calculating the tax rate. For example, if Congress wants $150 of income to raise $50 in taxes, the rate would be only 33%. The 33% times the $150, produces the $50 in tax. Thus, a tax-inclusive rate is always lower than a tax-exclusive rate even when the economic result is the same.

That the tax rate must be higher to yield comparable government revenue is only accurate to the extent a move to consumption taxation does not generate more growth that is then consumed. Note that economic growth alone is insufficient; that growth must fuel additional consumption. That increase in consumption runs counter to the tax's incentive effects. The change in tax base is to encourage people to save, but it necessitates more consumption in order to raise equivalent revenue at equivalent rates. The consumption tax may not create sufficient savings for the savings to produce enough economic growth to yield new consumption to meet revenue demands.

Thus, a key question for any consumption tax is the amount of economic growth it can produce. It should produce some amount of growth if people respond to the incentive effects and if there are adequate worthy investments to use the additional savings. Even assuming flat rates of return, the exclusion of savings from tax allows taxpayers' invested assets to grow more quickly. Consider if in the absence of taxes, $1,000 of savings earns 10% interest compounded annually.[9] That $1,000 would grow to $17,449.40 after thirty years. At that time, a 40% tax would raise $6,979.76 in government revenue.

Now assume a 40% income tax rate applied before the investment. With current taxation, the $1,000 is reduced to about

---

[9]   If an investment earns compound interest, it earns interest on the interest previously earned. This results from reinvesting interest rather than cashing out the interest.

$600 so that only $600 is invested. Even assuming the same 10% yield is available despite the smaller investment, after thirty years the balance is $10,469.64. With the regime that taxes amounts saved, the cumulative tax revenue is the initial $400 plus $4,187.86 on the appreciation, or $4,587.86.

10% Compound Interest Comparison

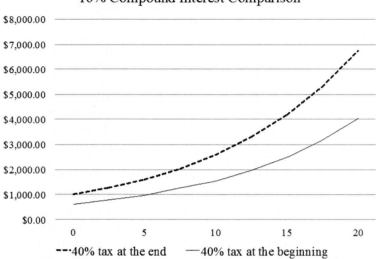

- - - 40% tax at the end —— 40% tax at the beginning

Thus, the timing when the tax is imposed creates a difference for both the taxpayers and the government. The taxpayer earns $6,979.76 ($17,449.40 minus $10,469.64) more before taxes under the consumption than the income tax. Additionally, the government receives $2,391.90 ($6,979.76 minus $4,587.86) more in revenue under the consumption tax. However, although a saver has less total growth under an income tax than a consumption tax, the difference does not have to be lost by the economy. As recipient of the tax proceeds, the government could earn the difference in interest if the government invested its tax revenue.

However, this example also illustrates a difficulty with consumption taxes. In this example the consumption tax raises $0 of government revenue for thirty years. It is unlikely that a government could survive with so little revenue for so long a time. Because an intended effect of consumption taxation is to discourage taxed activities, in the short-term revenue should be significantly reduced. Congress would likely need to rely on other forms of taxation in the early years of a consumption tax to provide necessary revenue.

(c) Regressivity

Although most consumption taxes apply equal tax rates to all taxpayers who consume, consumption taxes raise concerns that they are almost always regressive as between income levels. When comparing the two ends of the income spectrum, low-income taxpayers spend more of their income on subsistence consumption whereas high-income taxpayers have discretionary income to spend on luxury items or can choose to save the excess. Thus, when taxpayers become wealthier, consumption generally falls as a percentage of income and savings increase.[10] Evidence is not clear whether consumption inequality has increased more or less than income inequality in recent decades.[11]

The impact of consumption taxes on different income groups can be illustrated by looking at effective, or average, tax rates with a 20% consumption tax. Low income taxpayer, Abby, spends 100% of her $10,000 income on consumption for food and clothes for herself and her family. If these items are not exempted from tax, Abby can consume $8,000 worth of stuff and pays $2,000 in taxes. Abby's effective tax rate is 20%. A high-income taxpayer, Brad, with $100,000 of income saves half of his income. The result is that Brad consumes $40,000 of goods and services for himself and his family and pays $10,000 in consumption tax. Brad's effective tax rate is the $10,000 of tax divided by his $100,000 income, or 10%. In this example, the higher-income taxpayer's effective tax rate is half that of the lower-income taxpayer even though they have the same marginal tax rate on consumption.

Although the example uses fictitious numbers, any flat rate consumption tax is likely to constitute a larger percentage of the income of those struggling to make ends meet than of those taxpayers with disposable income to save. Because taxpayers' effective rate depends upon the percentage of their income that they consume, those who are unable to save, namely the poor, are likely to pay a larger percentage of their income in taxes. This is true for a consumption tax unless it is progressive as to income and not as to spending; this can be achieved with a cash flow consumption tax as discussed below.

Attempts to mitigate consumption taxes' regressivity often result in exempting some types of consumed items from the consumption tax. For example, most states exclude food and some

---

[10]   Karen Dynan et al., *Do the Rich Save More?*, 112 J. POL. ECON. 397 (2004).

[11]   Bruce Meyer & James Sullivan, *Consumption and Income Inequality and the Great Recession*, 103 AM. ECON. REV. 178 (2013).

value of clothing from the sales tax.[12] In states that tax food, for example Illinois, they generally tax it at lower rates. Doing so likely decreases the amount on which a poor person is required to pay tax. However, the exclusion requires drawing lines around favored and disfavored items, for example candy and alcohol are often excluded from the exemption and are therefore taxable. A 1979 proposal for a federal VAT would have imposed a general 10% rate; 5% rate on food, medical care, and residential housing; and 0% on charitable transactions, public and private nonprofit educational institutions, and mass transit.[13] For political reasons, if for no other, consumption items are unlikely to all be taxed at the same rate.

Carving consumption items out of the consumption tax, even if to address concerns regarding the tax's regressivity, further reduces the tax base. With the average household spending 50% of all that it spends on housing, education, food, and healthcare, not taxing these items would shift the tax onto a very narrow base of items.[14] One difficulty that arises from the narrow base is that it necessitates higher tax rates on those items that are taxed.

(d) Simplicity and Simple Evasion

The consumption tax may be simpler than an income tax. Its simplicity likely arises from two sources. First, consumption taxes may be relatively simpler for the government to administer. From the government's perspective, increased simplicity occurs if the tax reduces the number of entities that report and pay tax. For example, a VAT or sales tax is generally imposed only on sellers and not the more numerous consumers. Second, consumption taxes may be relatively simpler for taxpayers to pay. This is likely if a consumption tax eliminates most tax filings, although doing so would eliminate social and economic policies that are administered through the tax system.

From the government's perspective, the simplified structure of most consumption tax proposals makes it impossible for the government to use the tax to accomplish many of its non-revenue-raising policies. Today, numerous economic and social policies are accomplished through tax expenditures tied to the income tax.[15] Everything from economic stimulus to support for green energy are conducted, in part, through the tax system. Depending upon how

---

[12]   For more on state taxes, see Chapter 13.01(c).

[13]   *Hearing Announcement on Tax Restructuring Act of 1979 (H.R. 5665) Before H. Comm. on Ways and Means*, 96th Cong., 6–12 (1979).

[14]   Press Release, Bureau of Labor Statistics, Consumer Expenditures—2015 (Aug. 30, 2016), http://www.bls.gov/news.release/cesan.nr0.htm.

[15]   For more on tax expenditures, see Chapter 17.02.

Congress structures a consumption tax, it might be impossible to retain these incentives in the tax system. This does not necessarily mean incentives would no longer exist, it simply means they must be shifted out of the tax regime, possibly leading to greater or lesser bureaucracy and complexity.

From the taxpayer's perspective, the main argument for simplicity is a decreased cost of compliance compared to the current income tax. Representative Dave Camp once estimated that complying with the income tax costs Americans over $160 billion and 6 billion hours.[16] Moving to a tax system with fewer forms and compliance requirements, which is possible but not necessary with a consumption tax, would save these resources.

The simplicity in filing and compliance may only be theoretical; it may not exist in the real world. For example, most consumption taxes require significant differentiation between types of goods and services that are to be taxed at different rates. Drawing these lines increases the tax's rule complexity as well as transactional complexity to ensure that people are not evading the consumption tax. As one illustrative example under the British VAT, Jaffa Cakes fought to be classified as a 0%-tax rate cake rather than a 20%-standard-tax rate luxury biscuit.[17] Because the goodies had a chocolate glaze and an orange base, they were classified a 20% luxury item. Similar issues come up for catered or restaurant food, chewable vitamins, flavor enhancers, non-nutritional ingredients, and alcohol. Thus, the tax planning that exists under the income tax is unlikely to go away but would change forms.

Additionally, similar complexities regarding the timing and definition of consumption are likely to exist as with the timing and definition of income in an income tax system. For example, one consumption tax proposal made business meals fully deductible as a business expense.[18] With this proposal, Congress would need to import statutory and regulatory distinctions between business and personal meals and police the line between these two, much as it does today. There would likely be similar line-drawing for gifts, personal computers, home offices, and hobby farms in the attempt to define what is consumption and what is savings or for the purpose of savings.

---

[16] *Hearing on President's Fiscal Year 2014 Budget Proposal before Ways and Means Committee*, 113th Cong. (Apr. 11, 2013).

[17] GOV.UK, HMRC Internal Manual, VAT Foods, Excepted Items, available at https://www.gov.uk/hmrc-internal-manuals/vat-food/vfood6260 (last visited May 1, 2018). David Daly, *Cake or Biscuit? Case of the Jaffa Cakes Shows the Many Layers of VAT Law*, THE NAT'L, Apr. 8, 2017.

[18] ROBERT HALL & ALVIN RABUSHKA, THE FLAT TAX 106 (1995).

If complexity were diminished because a consumption tax eliminates tax filing, these taxes would likely be less salient to the taxpaying public. By permitting these taxes to be relatively hidden, people would respond less to tax changes, and taxes would come at a lower political cost.[19] This effect is slightly different than simplicity per se. Reduced salience comes from taxpayers not internalizing the cost rather than being confounded how to complete their returns. A simple tax can be salient if people are aware of the obligation. With a consumption tax, one saving is the psychic gain for those who pay the tax but forget that they are doing so.

Congress could also enact a simple consumption tax but total taxation be more complex as a result of its adoption. If the U.S. replaces the income tax with a consumption tax, Congress might reinforce other taxes to support the consumption tax, namely transfer taxes such as the gift and estate taxes. Because some taxpayers can amass so much wealth that they will never consume it all, relying heavily on a consumption-based system is likely to result in significant untaxed dynasties. Without transfer taxes, some wealth could accumulate without ever being taxed. However, transfer taxes have proven complex and difficult to administer and would need to be strengthened in order to limit the untaxed accumulation of wealth.[20] On the other hand, if one accepts that only wealth that is consumed matters, this accumulation may not be a problem. If society ignores wealth inequality on the theory that the wealth is being invested for the public good, these auxiliary taxes are as troublesome as the income tax.

That a consumption tax may be simple does not mean that there is no tax avoidance or tax evasion with consumption taxes. As for lawful tax avoidance, businesses can and do plan to minimize their consumption tax as they do their income tax. For example, in Maryland, a delivery charge is exempt from the sales tax when separately stated from handling and other taxable charges, so people design their invoices to separately state them. Thus taxpayers reduce the taxable portion of a sale transaction but not the amount paid.[21] This is not illegal but adds transactional complexity.

Tax evasion of consumption taxes also occurs.[22] Traders may underreport sales, collect tax but not remit it, or make false claims

---

[19]   For more on the optimal public awareness of taxes, see Chapter 6.02.

[20]   For more on transfer taxes, see Chapter 9.

[21]   Comptroller of Maryland, Frequently Asked Questions About the Sales and Use Tax #6, http://taxes.marylandtaxes.com/Resource_Library/Taxpayer_Assistance/ Frequently_Asked_Questions/Business_Tax_FAQs/Sales_and_Use_Tax/Sales_and_ Use_Tax_FAQs/6.shtml (last visited May 1, 2018).

[22]   For more on tax evasion, see Chapter 5.02.

for a credit or refund of taxes paid. Claims for a credit or refund can result in significant government outlays to tax evaders. In 2014, approximately 14% of total expected European Union VAT revenue was lost, but the disparity between countries was substantial with only 1.24% in Sweden but 37.89% in Romania.[23] The same incentive to cheat the tax system exists with consumption taxes as with other taxes. This necessitates enforcement activities if evasion is to be caught or discouraged.

(e) Impact on Savings

Because the consumption tax excludes from current taxation any income not consumed, savings are tax-deferred until they are consumed. This increases incentives to save and, consequently, the amount available for investment. Assuming people are economically rational, this exclusion should cause people to save more and increase the national savings rate as individuals shift some of their income from consumption to savings in order to reduce their personal taxes.

This incentive to shift away from consumption may be problematic to the extent one accepts Keynesian economic theory. According to traditional and new Keynesian theory, spending is a critical component of a healthy economy. Put in economic terms, output is more strongly influenced by demand than supply. With dampened consumption, there might not be enough demand to use the savings. This might ring true to those tired of calls for Black Friday spending in order to save the economy.[24] Therefore, if the nation depends upon consumption to propel economic growth, a tax that purposefully decreases consumption may negatively affect that growth.

The tax's focus on savings also ignores the possibility that there is a life-cycle pattern of saving, which the tax system cannot fully counteract. To the extent that people save more at different periods of their lives, a consumption tax may impose taxation at times when people are less able to compensate for the tax by altering their behavior. Although the life cycle of savings theory is difficult to prove empirically, it estimates that people consume more than earned in young adulthood; save during middle age; and consume savings during retirement. If this is the case, the consumption tax is imposed more when people are young or retired whereas an income tax is greater when people are in their prime earning years. People who consume more because they are raising children or are elderly may

---

[23] CENTER FOR SOCIAL AND ECONOMIC RESEARCH, TAXUD/2015/CC/131, STUDY AND REPORTS ON THE VAT GAP IN THE EU-28 MEMBER STATES: 2016 FINAL REPORT (2016).

[24] For example, see the aptly titled: Jill Schlesinger, *Will Black Friday Save the Economy?*, CBS MONEYWATCH, Nov. 19, 2012.

not be influenced by the tax, but it may be harmful to concentrate taxation during these times. Moreover, to the extent it is socially helpful for people to respond to taxation, the peaks of consumption are times when taxpayers are least able to respond with the income effect of earning more through increasing their workloads.

Instead, people may change behavior in ways less socially helpful. Most theories of saving suggest people desire a targeted amount of savings and change their behavior to get to that amount, no more and only reluctantly less. If this is the case, people may save a smaller percentage of their incomes with a consumption tax because they will hit their target savings earlier because it is not taxed. Alternatively, people may not have a plan with respect to savings in which case consumption taxation may have little impact on people's decision-making. A study of twenty-three nations with a VAT found no evidence of increased national savings.[25]

Therefore, although a consumption tax is designed to change choices' relative tax rates, and consequently people's incentives, the extent to which people respond depends upon their elasticity. Elasticity refers to how quickly or absolutely people change their behavior in response to changing conditions. People may not respond to a change in taxes if they have consumption patterns that are not affected by tax signals. Even those who are elastic and respond quickly to tax changes may have their response dulled over time as static taxes become less salient.

Moreover, there should be no expectation that the incentive effects will be distributed evenly across society. The consumption tax can have no incentive effect for the lowest income taxpayers who have no choice but to consume their income. When over 50% of Americans make less than $50,000 per year, a significant percentage consume all of their money. Instead, a consumption tax's incentive effect is targeted to those with discretionary income. For this latter group there is, arguably, a paternalistic goal of getting them to change their behavior in a way that helps themselves and society.

Because the benefit of a consumption tax is limited to those who save and are greatest for those who save large sums, a long-term consequence of a consumption tax regime is likely that some people amass a disproportionate amount of untaxed savings. This growth is accelerated for those who save big early because of the possibility of favorable returns on their investments, although not everyone will have favorable returns. Lower- and middle-income taxpayers may not have sufficient money to invest in those investments that yield

---

[25]   Ken Militzer, *VAT: Evidence from the OECD*, 47 TAX NOTES 207 (1990). *But see* Brigitte C. Madrian & Dennis F. Shea, *The Power of Suggestion: Inertia on 401(k) Participation and Savings Behavior*, 116 Q. J. OF ECON. 1149 (2001).

the highest returns but suffer lower rates of return than that available to wealthy savers. For example, to invest in private placements of potentially lucrative startups, a person must be an accredited investor with substantial means, currently defined to be $1 million net worth not including one's house, or a $200,000 annual income for the individual or a $300,000 annual income for a married couple.[26] Similarly, investment funds have different minimum investments; mutual funds often have relatively low thresholds from $50 to $3,000 but private equity funds generally start around $100,000 and the requirement can go up to millions of dollars.

The increased concentration of wealth at higher incomes occurs as the wealthy are able to compound their savings at a faster rate. If the wealthy invest in higher return investments that are not taxed, they enjoy all of the return as future investment capital. Wealth keeps growing and none is paid directly to the government until converted into consumption. Even if the same investment strategy works under the income tax, the initial investment was subject to tax for both wealthy and poor investors, reducing the advantage and compounding effect for higher income investors. It also ensures the frugal wealthy are contributing directly to their government.

(f) International Competitiveness

A consumption tax could increase American businesses' competitiveness by eliminating indirect taxes on exported items because most consumption tax proposals would tax goods only where they are consumed and not where they are produced. As a result, there are no tax consequences in the country where value is added but not consumed. This means that exported goods could be sold more cheaply abroad than they are sold at home, increasing export demand. Currently, the income tax is imposed on the producer of even exported goods.

However, the inverse statement is also true: Only those businesses that export would benefit from changing regimes; importers would suffer. This splits interests between producers and retailers. For American producers, a consumption tax would likely reduce their collective taxes if they export some goods. On the other hand, U.S. retailers that import goods would bear the full American tax. Thus, the consumption tax favors exports over consuming domestic production or importing for consumption. This is consistent with traditional mercantilist economics that favored exports over imports.

---

[26]   17 C.F.R. § 230.501(a) (2017).

Depending on the relative amount of imports versus exports and the ruling theory of international taxation, consumption taxes could increase the tax base. If the U.S. were to export more than it imports, the tax base would be smaller than it would be under an income tax, which would also tax profits from exports. Alternatively, if the U.S. were to import more than it exported, the tax base would be larger, possibly yielding more government revenue. Under an income tax, only the final retailer's profits are taxed whereas the full sales price can be taxed under a consumption tax. Of course, that increase would depend upon the structure of the consumption tax. In a world of both imports and exports, that most of the U.S.'s international tax treaties are framed for the income tax, and not a consumption tax, would necessitate significant and swift government action.

Furthermore, depending on any new treaties adopted between countries, a switch from an income to a consumption tax would likely decrease the number of people who file U.S. tax returns by defaulting to a territorial tax regime. Currently, the U.S. taxes all citizens and residents on their global income, offset with credits for any foreign taxes paid.[27] Under most proposals, this issue would no longer arise. Under a consumption-based system, only those consuming within the U.S. would owe tax. Citizens who consume abroad would not; all residents and visitors would, although visitors may receive an exemption for durable goods when the final consumption is not in the U.S. This would also decrease the desire to shift savings offshore because there would be no tax disincentive for retaining the money within the U.S.

§ 8.02   How a Consumption Tax Works

Advocating for a consumption tax voices support for one tax base rather than another. It does not state how consumption is to be taxed. In fact, there are many different consumption taxes. In the U.S., many states impose sales taxes, which is one form of consumption tax. Additionally, many countries have VATs. Finally, a theoretical consumption tax that does not yet operate in practice is the cash flow consumption tax.

(a) Sales Tax

Forty-five states plus the District of Columbia currently operate one type of consumption tax: the retail sales tax.[28] A retail sales tax imposes a flat-rate tax on amounts spent to purchase consumption items and (sometimes) services. Therefore, if a retail store sells a $100 cell phone to a consumer and there is a 20% sales tax, the

---

[27]   For more on international taxation, see Chapter 12.
[28]   For more on state sales taxes, see Chapter 13.01(c).

consumer owes $20 in tax on the sale, for a total price paid of $120. These tax-exclusive tax rates are imposed on consumption items at the point of final sale.

In the U.S., the sales tax is often itemized separately from the price of goods, and the pre-tax price is listed on the item. This may lessen the sales tax's salience to consumers. Consumers may not consider the tax, making it a more efficient tax because it has less impact on consumers' choices. Consumers may even know of the tax and its rates but not adjust their consumption patterns. One study compared sales over a three-week period when pre-tax versus post-tax prices were shown.[29] The study found that posting prices including the tax reduced demand by roughly 8% among the treated products relative to control products and nearby control stores. Additionally, the study found that state-level increases in excise taxes included in posted prices reduced aggregate alcohol consumption significantly more than increases in sales taxes that were added at the register.

Whether or not because of taxpayer salience, the country has a long history with sales taxes and only five states currently do not have general sales taxes: Alaska, Delaware, Montana, New Hampshire, and Oregon. Kentucky and Mississippi adopted the first broad-based, general sales taxes in the U.S. in 1930 during the Great Depression, but Kentucky repealed its sales tax in 1936. Forty-three states adopted general sales taxes between 1940 and 1969, including Kentucky re-enacting its sales tax in 1960. Vermont was the last to enact the tax in 1969.

The federal government has considered a national sales tax several times, perhaps most notably during the Great Depression.[30] Conservative leaders thought it would be a good source of revenue affecting those who had the resources to consume. Opponents, including President Franklin D. Roosevelt, thought the tax would be regressive for the poor. Since the Great Depression, some have called for a nationwide sales tax to fund certain expenses such as healthcare, but they have failed to gain traction in part because of concerns that a national tax would either eliminate the state tax (greatly reducing most states' revenue) or simply be added on top of state sales taxes (greatly increasing the cost of goods and decreasing consumption).

In theory, all goods sold are taxed under a sales tax with two big exceptions. First, the main exception is if the sale is not to an end

---

[29]　Raj Chetty et al., *Salience and Taxation*, 99 AM. ECON. REV. 1145 (2009).

[30]　For descriptions of early attempts, see U.S. TREAS. DEPT., HISTORY OF FEDERAL GENERAL SALES TAX PROPOSALS (1942).

consumer but part of the chain of production or if to tax-exempt consumers. In these instances, purchasers are exempt from the tax, generally providing paperwork to sellers proving their use or status. Second, states purposefully exclude some items from sales taxation, namely food and health care.[31] Eighteen states have experimented with tax-free sales weekends before the school year begins on clothes and school supplies. The University of Cincinnati Economics Center found that Cincinnati's first year of an August sales holiday on targeted items generated $4.7 million in additional sales tax revenue and saved taxpayers $3.3 million on $46.75 million worth of back-to-school supplies.[32]

The evasion of a state sales tax is easy in many instances. For example, people travel to another state to purchase jewelry or other high-ticket items and do not report the sale to their home jurisdiction.[33] Many people also pay for goods and services in cash in order to avoid paying sales taxes. In 2012, the underground economy in the U.S. was estimated to be $2 trillion.[34] This allows tax-evading businesses to undercut sales-tax-paying competitors. Moreover, some businesses that do collect the tax do not pay it over to the government. In some instances a state can detect the omission, for example by charging a sales tax when a car purchased out of state is registered in state. In most instances, however, enforcing the tax is impossible. Nevertheless, when merchants fail to pay sales taxes, U.S. consumers are generally obligated to report the tax due. Sales tax evasion can be misdemeanors or felonies depending upon the state and the amount that is evaded.

(b) Value-Added Tax

A VAT is a consumption tax that is similar to a retail sales tax; however, a VAT is collected along each step of the manufacturing and distribution process based on the value added in each step rather than a lump sum tax at the retail sale. Since France introduced the first VAT in 1954, VATs have grown to provide an estimated 20% of worldwide tax revenue and have been adopted by more than 140 countries, but not by the U.S.[35] Countries in Western Europe, especially in Scandinavia, have some of the world's highest VAT rates. Norway, Denmark, and Sweden have 25% VATs; Hungary has

---

[31] For more on states' exclusions from sales taxes, see Chapter 8.01(c).

[32] ECON. CTR. UNIV. OF CINCINNATI, ECONOMIC ANALYSIS ON THE EFFECTS OF BACK-TO-SCHOOL SALES TAX HOLIDAY IN OHIO (2016).

[33] For more on use taxes, see Chapter 13.01(c).

[34] Edgar Feige & Richard Cebula, *America's Underground Economy*, 57 CRIME, L. & SOC'L CHANGE 265 (2012).

[35] Alan Charlet & Jeffrey Owens, *An International Perspective on VAT*, TAX NOTES INT'L 943 (2010).

the highest at 27%. Reduced rates are used for some goods, such as for groceries, art, books, and newspapers. Of Organization for Economic Cooperation and Development (OECD) countries, only the U.S. does not have a VAT.

As an example of how a typical VAT works, reconsider the cell phone that sells for $100 to the final consumer. Hypothetically, the first step in the chain that gets the phone to the consumer is a producer removing $20 of raw materials from the earth, which are sold to a manufacturer. The second level of activity is the manufacturer combining personal services with the raw materials to produce a phone, which is sold to a wholesaler for $45. In step three, the wholesaler markets the phone to a retail store for $60. Finally, the retail store sells the phone to the consumer for $100. Assuming a 20% VAT rate, the value added at each stage is taxed as follows:

Activity:	Raw materials	Production	Wholesaler	Retailer
Change in price:	$0 → $20	$20 → $45	$45 → $60	$60 → $100
Value added:	$20	$25	$15	$40
VAT imposed:	**$4**	**$5**	**$3**	**$8**

The total tax is $20, or $4 plus $5 plus $3 plus $8. This is the same $20 result as if a 20% retail sales tax was applied to a $100 phone, but the tax is collected in bits and pieces at each stage.

Although the cell phone was listed to consumers at $100 in each case, the economic result in the VAT example is not the same as in the sales tax example. In the sales tax example, the $100 was a pre-tax amount; in the VAT, $100 was a post-tax amount. If the sales tax rate is the same as the VAT rate (20%) and the sales-tax phone was to cost a total of $100 instead of $120, the phone would cost $83.33 and the sales tax would be $16.66. The government receives $3.34 less in revenue. Thus, the sales tax rate must be higher than the VAT rate in order to raise the same amount of government revenue at the same after-tax price. If the sales tax rate was 25% and the final amount paid for the phone was $100, the government would receive $20 and the phone would cost $80, the same as under the 20% VAT.

Thus, because a VAT is tax-inclusive, the VAT can raise more revenue with a lower rate. This may be politically helpful to those seeking to raise more government revenue. There are political difficulties associated with high rates independent of the revenue that they raise. The perception is that a higher rate costs taxpayers more. Additionally, regardless of the starting tax rate, rates are sticky and hard to change, although they have changed at times in countries with VATs. The British standard VAT was imposed at 10% in 1973 but has been 20% since 2011.[36] The Japanese standard VAT was introduced in 1989 at 3% and, as of 2017, is 8% but set to increase to 10% in 2019.[37] These VATs raise more government revenue than a comparable 20% or 10% sales tax.

Because VATs are imposed during production, they are included in the sales price and not separately stated. This display likely reduces their particular salience more than a sales tax but increases the public's awareness of the final cost of the taxed item. In particular, if Congress adopts a VAT, the public would likely have considerable sticker shock as they see higher rates charged for goods, even if the VAT simply replaced the states' sales taxes. The psychological element, if only on transition, should not be ignored.

As a tax imposed at each step of production, the government can structure VATs in a number of ways in order to tax the value each business adds to the final item. One method offers taxpayers later in the line of production a tax credit for payments of VAT by producers earlier in the chain of production. A second method allows taxpayers to subtract from their sales the cost of their purchases and apply the VAT rate to the difference. A third method combines the components of wage, rent, interest, and net profit at each stage and multiplies that number times the VAT rate. These different methods may produce different amounts of VAT to be paid. They also affect the ease with which evasion of the VAT can be detected.

Each European Union (EU) country sets and enforces a VAT, but a common legal framework called the VAT Directive limits what EU countries can do.[38] The VAT is set at a minimum of 15%, although individual countries can impose a higher rate. To determine the amount subject to tax, countries in the EU use the credit method, and at each level of production the full value of the item is taxed at that country's VAT rate but then a credit is received for prior VAT payments on the same item. This method was chosen largely for compliance reasons since both buyers and sellers along the manufacturing cycle report the same income, creating a double check of reporting. Noncompliance by one party under the credit method is less likely to shrink the tax base because the item is reported multiple times.

Nevertheless, compliance remains a significant problem. The European Commission recently announced that, despite renewed

---

[36]   Harry Wallop, *General Election 2010: A Brief History of the Value-Added Tax*, TELEGRAPH, Apr. 13, 2010.

[37]   *Japan Delays Sales Tax Rise to 2019*, BBC NEWS, Jun. 1, 2016.

[38]   Council Directive 2006/112/EC, 2006 O.J. (L341) (EC).

compliance efforts, VAT revenue collection has not improved as they had hoped. Instead, a significant discrepancy of approximately €168 billion, or 15.2% of revenue, continues to exist between the expected VAT revenue and collections.[39] The gaps in VAT payments ranged from 4% in Scandinavia to 41% in Romania.

Despite being a major source of revenue for most countries, VATs have not been politically popular in the U.S. This may result from a sense that the VAT would be an additional tax on top of current taxes. Thus, the concern may be evidence of fears of taxation in general rather than of the VAT in particular. Additionally, VAT-specific concerns are that the VAT is a hidden tax that escapes public review, would rob states of their sales tax revenue base, and pushes more of the economy underground. Professor Michael Graetz suggests "another name will be necessary [to get a VAT in the U.S.]; call it a goods and services tax, a business sales tax, or simply a consumption tax."[40]

(c) Cash Flow Consumption Tax

A final variant of a tax on consumption is a cash flow consumption tax.[41] With this type of consumption tax, taxpayers would continue to file tax returns but could exclude any amount that is not spent on consumption. This reduces the tax's simplicity compared to the other consumption taxes. On the other hand, because taxpayers file tax returns, the tax is more likely to be salient to taxpayers, and Congress could continue its social and economic policies on the same tax form. Additionally, because a cash flow consumption tax is calculated at year-end unlike with the other consumption taxes, it could have progressive tax rates based either on income or on the amount consumed, as Congress chooses.

A cash flow consumption tax could be structured in several ways, but the easiest might be to keep the income tax. The government could require taxpayers report all wages and fee income currently but not report the income earned from investments. Thus, the government would exclude interest, dividends, and capital gains from taxation. This taxes income when it is earned. Alternatively, the government could tax individuals on their wages and fee income with

---

[39] CTR. SOC. & ECON. RES., TAXUD/2016/CC/131, STUDY AD REPORTS ON THE VAT GAP IN THE EU-28 MEMBER STATES: 2016 FINAL REPORT (2016).

[40] Michael Graetz, *The U.S. Income Tax: Should It Survive the Millennium?*, 85 TAX NOTES 1197, 1200 (1999).

[41] Many countries have considered a cash flow consumption tax. For example, Bolivia sought such a tax but the movement failed when the U.S. ruled that it was not an income tax eligible for the foreign tax credit. Charles McClure, Jr. & George Zodrow, *The Economic Case for Foreign Tax Credits For Cash Flow Taxes*, 51 NAT'L TAX J. 1 (1998).

a deduction for the money that is saved, thus carving saved money out of current taxation. Under this second approach, Congress would later tax the income from savings unless the income is reinvested. This taxes income when it is spent. These two methods are economically equivalent in terms of present value but have significantly different consequences post-investment.

For example, Abe earns $10,000 in wage income in 2018, purchases a stock for that $10,000 in 2018, and sells the stock for $11,000 in 2019. Finally, Abe consumes the proceeds in 2019. Also assume this 10% appreciation in the stock is the prevailing rate of return. Under the first method, Abe cannot deduct the purchase price of the stock so Abe is taxed in 2018 when he earns the original $10,000. He is not taxed on the sale of the stock, and he receives $1,000 tax-free. Under the second method, Abe deducts the $10,000 in 2018 and is taxed on the entire $11,000 proceeds in 2019. With the 10% discount rate, $11,000 in 2019 has a $10,000 present value in 2018, so Abe should be indifferent as to when he is taxed in this scenario.[42]

However, although the methods are equivalent when viewed before the investment is made, the timing difference is not equivalent when taxpayers consider investments' risk. Consider Abe and Betty who are otherwise completely equal in earnings and tax position. They each invest $10,000 to purchase common stock, but their two investments do not yield the same return. Abe's investment in Boohoo Inc. goes bankrupt, and Abe loses the principal amount of his investment. Betty's investment in Yippee Corp. is the next Google or Facebook, and she enjoys a much improved standard of living through Yippee's dividends and the eventual sale of her stock. The first method taxes both investments the same; the second method taxes Betty on her return and never recoups the deduction granted to Abe.

In order to structure a cash flow investment tax, Congress has to choose which perspective it favors. Arguments can be made in favor of each approach. Taxing each taxpayer because of their equal pre-investment income acknowledges the risks that each takes but allows the taxpayer to retain all growth beyond the prevailing rate of return, so that all major success is the taxpayer's alone. Taxing only the after-tax results recognizes the realities of the market and is consistent with other consumption taxes. However, focusing on after-tax results encourages investment in risky investments and initially narrows the tax base. Congress must weigh the costs and benefits of the methods of implementing a cash flow consumption tax and, in

---

[42]   For more on present value and the time value of money, see Chapter 6.02(a)(iii).

doing so, will face similar political pressure as it does when shaping the income tax.

This political pressure would likely ensure that a cash flow consumption tax retains the income tax's complexity. As a result, the cash flow consumption tax would simply slim down the existing regime by excluding those items that are preferred while retaining pre-existing preferences. This structure would likely favor some savers over others. The only way to ensure a pure regime is to transition to a new regime in a holistic way that might not be politically realistic.

§ 8.03   Transition Between Tax Regimes

Congress does not make tax policy choices on a blank slate. Instead, the government has a functioning tax system that must be altered or replaced with the adoption of a major tax change. Therefore, if Congress replaces the income tax with a consumption tax, it must consider the problems created by a transition, which would not occur if the country had no prior tax regime. These transition problems arguably would not exist if the income tax were retained, even in a significantly smaller form. Replacing the regime might pose greater transition problems than simply layering on a consumption tax.

Most consumption tax proposals ignore the problem of transitioning between regimes, even as they advocate for replacing the income tax with the consumption tax. Those that engage issues of conversion generally recognize that accumulated wealth that has already been subject to the income tax would be subject to the new consumption tax. Thus basis, representing invested amounts that have already been taxed under the income tax, would be taxed a second time when the investment or its proceeds are used to fund consumption. This result would be particularly harsh on retirees with little opportunity to benefit under the new tax regime by accumulating new untaxed savings.

This harsh reality can be mitigated; Congress might allow a carryover of post-income tax basis to reduce consumption taxes for lower-income taxpayers immediately or over a number of years. However, if Congress allowed everyone to use basis to fund tax-free consumption, the government might receive no revenue for several years because of the trillions of dollars of basis now in existence. It is unlikely the government could survive with so little revenue for so long a time. One method to balance equity and simplicity, proposed by Professor Michael Graetz provides limited transition relief for elderly taxpayers.[43] Everyone not in that category would suffer double taxation. With this limited relief, Graetz balances equity with economic reality. On the other hand, the elderly are some of the nation's biggest consumers, which is not surprising under the life cycle of savings. To exempt the elderly from the tax reduces the tax base and results in less revenue and higher rates.

Transitioning would also raise questions regarding borrowed money. Under the income tax system, borrowing is not currently taxed and therefore investments paid for with borrowed money are not taxed. Repayment of the borrowed money is not deductible so that borrowing has little effect under the income tax. On the other hand, if the nation transitioned to a consumption tax, repayment of the borrowings would likely generate a deduction because purchases with borrowed funds would be taxed. This disparate tax treatment creates a loophole during transition to allow some to avoid tax altogether and would potentially necessitate a complicated procedure to differentiate pre- and post-transition borrowing. However, any tracing is difficult because money is fungible. Nevertheless, without some limit, taxpayers would almost certainly game the system.

These points illustrate that Congress would need to work through numerous issues to create a workable and fair transition. In addition to being complicated, many requirements would be onerous for taxpayers who may not anticipate the issue. For example, because an intended effect of consumption taxation is to discourage consumption, Congress would likely need to raise other forms of taxation to offset revenue lost in the early years of a consumption tax. This supplemental tax revenue would be necessary because of the smaller tax base, regardless of how Congress comes out on the problem of already-taxed basis. This new tax might exacerbate any distortion caused by the new tax on consumption.

Additionally, under most consumption taxes Congress would need to rethink its policies on tax expenditures. Much could be retained with the more complex cash flow consumption tax but with most other consumption taxes these policies would no longer be administrable through the tax system. Non-revenue policies could be continued through other agencies; however, funding through the tax system would no longer work.

For example, consider that charities are funded with tax-deductible donations, which means that they are partially funded with money that would otherwise go to the government. Under the income tax, if a person in a 40% tax bracket donates $100,000 to a

---

[43] Michael Graetz, *Implementing a Progressive Consumption Tax*, 92 HARV. L. REV. 1575, 1653–58 (1979).

charity, $40,000 of the donation represents tax savings in the form of a deduction; the taxpayer only really suffers loss of $60,000 because $40,000 would go to the government if not to the charity. Even if donations were not considered consumption, an exclusion from a consumption tax would only remove the tax. A $100,000 donation that is not subject to a consumption tax costs the donor the full $100,000 because there is no deduction to offset other spending. Thus, a consumption tax would not permit the Treasury Department to allocate government revenue to the chosen charity. Of course, it would cost the donor more if the donation were also considered consumption, in which case the $100,000 would be subject to tax.

That transitioning between tax regimes would be difficult should be considered when enacting a new regime although not to deter the adoption of a better tax. The difficulty for policymakers is that it is impossible to mathematically weigh the benefits of a new regime with the costs of transition. Additionally, any consumption tax would need to complete the political process that might make it no less pristine following the enactment process than the tax it is to replace. This difficulty always exists when comparing an imperfect existing tax with an ideal theoretical alternative.

Chapter 9

GIFT AND ESTATE TAXATION

Table of Sections

People love to give and receive gifts and inheritances; but how often do people think about the tax consequences of these transfers? Under current law these transfers are only taxable pursuant to the gift and estate taxes, which are structured as transfer taxes on the gratuitous transfer of substantial amounts of wealth. Transfer taxes are essentially fees imposed on passing the title to property, including cash, from one person or entity to another. The Supreme Court has upheld these taxes as taxes on the transfer of property and not a tax on the property itself.[1] If Congress taxed wealth directly, the tax would likely face constitutional challenge as a direct tax not apportioned according to the population of the different states.[2] If Congress taxed these transfers with the income tax, doing so would contravene a long-standing tradition of excluding these items from income taxation.

§ 9.01   Estate Taxation

In the U.S., taxes on transfers made at death may be imposed at both the state and federal level. As of 2017, only seventeen states, the District of Columbia, and the federal government do so.[3] These taxes are either estate or inheritances taxes. The estate tax is on the transfer of a decedent's estate via will, intestacy, certain trusts, or the payment of certain life insurance benefits. Therefore, the estate tax is imposed on the decedent's estate and not on the recipient of the estate. Alternatively, the inheritance tax is imposed on recipients of transfers resulting from a death. Currently, the federal and most

---

[1]   Knowlton v. Moore, 178 U.S. 41, 78–79 (1900); Bromley v. McCaughn, 280 U.S. 124, 138 (1929).

[2]   U.S. Const., Art. I, § 9.

[3]   *Why More States Are Killing Death Taxes*, WALL ST. J., June 16, 2017.

states' taxes have large exemptions causing these taxes to apply to a small number of taxpayers.

(a) How the Tax Works

The federal estate tax applies to transfers of property, including cash, at a person's death. The top marginal estate tax rate is 40%, but the estate tax is nominally structured as a progressive tax, like the income tax, so that the first $10,000 is taxed at 18%.[4] However, Congress enacted a tax credit that offsets any estate tax owed at the lower rates, so the rate is effectively a flat 40% for those estates that are taxed.[5] In 2018, Congress more than doubled 2017 credits, so that the estate tax only applies to estates of greater value than $11.2 million for single taxpayers and $22.4 million for married couples, and those thresholds apply after excluding statutorily favored transfers. With the lower 2017 credits, the Tax Policy Center estimated that the effective federal estate tax rate for the estates subject to the tax is 16.6%; average tax rates will be significantly lower with the higher credit.[6]

The estate tax rate is tax inclusive, which means that the amount paid in tax is included in the calculation of the taxes owed. In this way the estate tax resembles the income tax but not the gift tax. The result is increased revenue at a particular rate. For example, if Charlie dies and his taxable estate above the credit is $100,000 and is subject to the 40% estate tax, Charlie pays $40,000 of tax to the government. In this hypothetical situation, $60,000 plus the amount below the credit is left for the beneficiaries of the estate, and the estate's effective tax rate is less than 40%.

Not all amounts that a decedent leaves in her estate are subject to the estate tax. Some amounts are excluded from estate taxation. For example, transfers to a spouse or to a charity are completely excluded from the estate for federal tax purposes. Additionally, as mentioned above, the unified tax credit offsets the tax, and the credited amount is adjusted annually for inflation. However, this credit is the same one that offsets the gift tax. Therefore, the unified credit is reduced by any amount that the decedent had used to offset taxable gifts under the gift tax.[7] Joining the gift and estate tax credits prevents taxpayers from circumventing the estate tax by giving property away before they die. If a spouse dies without using that

---

4   I.R.C. § 2001(c).

5   I.R.C. § 2010.

6   TAX POL'Y CTR, CURRENT LAW DISTRIBUTION OF GROSS ESTATE AND NET ESTATE TAX BY SIZE OF GROSS ESTATE, Table T13–0020 (2013).

7   The credit also applies to the generation-skipping tax discussed in Chapter 9.03.

spouse's full exclusion, the other spouse can claim the unused exclusion pursuant to a portability election.[8]

The exclusions work so that only the excess above the exclusion is subject to tax. For example, in 2018 at her death Diane owned a farm in Wyoming with 3,000 acres (larger than average) with a land value of $650 per acre (approximately average).[9] Diane owned the farm plus $1 million in farm tools, her total estate is worth $2,950,000. Even if there were no special rules for farms, Diane would not be subject to the estate tax unless she made taxable gifts worth millions of dollars because her unified credit is worth $8.25 million more than her estate. Alternatively, Evan's 50,000-acre farm at $650 per acre plus $1 million in farm tools produces a $32,500,000 estate. Assuming Evan has made no taxable gifts in his life, the excess above his $11.2 million credit, or $21.3 million, is his taxable estate. This $21.3 million is subject to tax at 40%, or $8.52 million. The excluded amount is not taxed.

However, Evan is unlikely to owe that much in estate tax because of rules favorable to farms and family-owned businesses. Congress enacted special rules that reduce the likelihood owners of farms and closely held businesses will owe the estate tax. If these businesses do owe estate tax, special rules help them finance their tax bill.[10] For example, special valuations apply to land that continues to be farmed for ten years after a death if one or more family members participates in managing the farm. Other discounts are also available for farms, and a provision of the Code permits the tax to be paid over 15 years at below market interest rates.

Of the fourteen states and the District of Columbia with estate taxes, their taxes mirror the federal estate tax, except that states often have their own tax rates and exempted amounts. For example, Washington has the highest maximum state estate tax rate at 20% and Maine and Connecticut have the lowest maximum at 12%. Most states have lower exemption thresholds than the federal government, which increases the number of taxable estates and the amount of each estate subject to the state tax, although Delaware, Hawaii, and Maine match the federal credit and several states are in the process of raising the amount exempted.

(b) Political Debate

The value of a federal estate tax has been debated since the nation's founding. The debate often centers on the amount of revenue

---

[8]   I.R.C. § 2010(c)(4).

[9]   U.S. DEPT. AGRIC, WYOMING AGRICULTURAL STATISTICS 2015, at 24–25 (2015).

[10]   I.R.C. § 2032A; 6166.

the tax raises as compared to the costs of administering the tax, the impact the tax has on the market and people's behavior, and the desire to break up estates or to permit their transmission between generations. To date there is no clear winner of the policy debate, and the debate is likely to continue. For example, in the 2016 presidential election Donald Trump proposed the tax's elimination while Hilary Clinton supported the tax, but even with disagreement it was not a salient political issue.[11]

(i)   Amount of Revenue Versus Cost of Administration

The existence of a federal estate tax dates back to the 18th century, although it has not been in effect continuously and its form has varied significantly.[12] In 1797, Congress imposed a stamp tax on bequests with significant exceptions. The amount of tax varied with the size of the bequest from 10¢ on inventories to $1 for each $500 bequeathed in excess of $500. Although the tax was not particularly controversial, this early tax was repealed in 1802. An inheritance tax, taxing the recipient rather than the estate, was enacted with a stamp tax to help fund the Civil War and lasted the duration of the war. So many things were taxed during the war, it is not surprising this tax attracted little attention. In the War of 1898, a precursor to the modern estate tax was enacted, and this short-lived tax was the first time the tax was hotly debated.

Thus, until the 20th century, the estate tax had short lives and was associated with funding wars. Then Congress enacted the modern estate tax in 1916, three years after the income tax, at a time when forty-two states had some form of transfer tax at death. Although rates and procedures have since varied, the estate has remained a source of federal revenue since 1916 until it was phased out beginning in 2001, was completely repealed in 2010 but with a caveat that people could opt into the estate tax, and then returned in 2011. Throughout this evolution, there has been a consistent low-level harangue against the estate tax, grown larger since being labeled the "death tax" in the 1940s.

The political debate over the estate tax often questions the amount of revenue the estate tax raises as a share of the federal budget. Although the percentage is relatively small, approximately 1%, the federal government would lose $269 billion over ten years

---

[11]   Gene Sperling, *Don't Cut the Estate Tax—Raise It*, THE ATLANTIC, Apr, 25, 2017.

[12]   Darien Jacobsen et al., *The Estate Tax: Ninety Years and Counting*, 27 STAT. INCOME BULL. 118 (2007).

without the federal estate tax.[13] The percentage of revenue has not always been so small. From 1935 until 1940, transfer taxes raised more than 6% of federal revenue, peaking in 1936 at 9.7%.[14] The decline in the estate tax's relative import to the budget resulted from the growth of the budget and an increase in income tax revenue rather than a decline in the estate tax itself.

Moreover, reviewing only the amount of federal revenue that has been raised may mislead as to the effectiveness of the estate tax as a source of revenue. Many states have had an estate tax, and the federal government permits a deduction from the federal estate for state estates taxes paid.[15] Before 2005, the federal government offered an even more favorable credit for state estate taxes. With the deduction, payments of a state-level estate tax reduce the amount owed to the federal government. Thus, federal revenue is purposefully reduced to protect the states' revenue source, and the credit reduced federal revenue dollar-for-dollar. However, with the deduction, as opposed to the credit, state taxes are not completely offset by a reduction in federal taxes. Consequently, many states have eliminated or are debating eliminating their state estate tax.[16] This elimination of tax may also signal an increase in state-level competition for wealthy residents.

Congressional changes in the estate tax's structure have also reduced the amount of revenue that it can raise. For example, in 1948, Congress first enacted a 50% deduction for property transferred to a spouse; this was expanded to a 100% exclusion in 1981.[17] In 2007, 60% of terminal wealth was given to a spouse, removing it from the estate.[18] Additionally, donations to charity have been excluded from the estate since 1918; and evidence shows this motivates some people to increase their donations to minimize their estate tax. In 2007, larger estates were more likely to report charitable bequests than smaller ones; and charitable bequests made up 12.7% of all taxable decedents' total gross estate. A 2004 report by

---

[13]   JOINT COMM. TAX'N, JCX–68–15, DESCRIPTION OF AN AMENDMENT IN THE NATURE OF A SUBSTITUTE TO THE PROVISIONS OF H.R. 1105, THE "DEATH TAX REPEAL ACT OF 2015" (2015).

[14]   David Joulfaian, *The Federal Estate Tax: History, Law, and Economics*, Table 6.1, OFF. TAX ANALYSIS (2013).

[15]   I.R.C. § 2058.

[16]   For example, New Jersey considered estate tax repeal in 2016. *See* Ashela Ebeling, *NJ Governor Chris Christie Bails On New Jersey Estate Tax Repeal*, FORBES, June 29, 2016.

[17]   Revenue Act of 1948, Pub. L. No. 80–471, 62 Stat. 110; Economic Recovery Tax Act of 1981, Pub. L. No. 94–455, 95 Stat. 172.

[18]   Brian Raub & Joseph Newcomb, *Federal Estate Tax Returns Filed for 2007 Decedents*, 31 STAT. INCOME BULL. 291 (2011).

the CBO found that eliminating the estate tax would reduce charitable giving by 6% to 12%.[19]

These exclusions and the large credit result in few people being subject to the estate tax. In 2015, there were only 11,917 estate tax returns filed of 2.6 million reported deaths, or less than 0.5%.[20] This is lower than most years, although the all-time low was less than 0.1% in fiscal year 2011. The number of estate tax returns was largest in 1977 when 248,000 returns were filed, although only 139,115 were taxable.[21] Those filing were nearly 8% of deaths. Regardless, only a small minority of wealthy taxpayers pays an estate tax. The widespread dislike of the tax may result from a sense that it unfairly targets a few or from people's irrational optimism that they will be subject to the tax.

Counter-balancing the tax's revenue is its administrative cost for taxpayers and for the government. Part of taxpayer' compliance cost is in planning to minimize the tax. Studies have found that compliance costs, including planning, were roughly equal to the amount of revenue raised, or nearly five times more costly per dollar of revenue than the income tax (although much of the income tax is raised from withholding on wages which cannot effectively be avoided).[22] However, tax planning for the estate tax is not all deadweight loss. Some planning is socially useful planning for the transition of family businesses that is initiated for tax purposes but would be needed regardless of the tax's existence.

The tax's timing also improves its administration. Because the tax is imposed after death, significant information regarding this tax base is compiled for non-tax purposes. Therefore, it is relatively harder to completely evade the estate tax if audited. Only 8.8% of all estate returns and 37.6% of estates worth more than $10 million were audited in 2015, and $789 million in additional tax was found to be owed.[23]

Nevertheless, significant administrative issues arise because taxpayers must determine property's fair market value even though

---

[19]   CONG. BUDGET OFFICE, THE ESTATE TAX AND CHARITABLE GIVING 1 (2004).

[20]   I.R.S., ESTATE TAX RETURNS FILED FOR WEALTHY DECEDENTS, 2006–2015 (2015).

[21]   JOINT COMM. TAX'N, JCX–52–15, HISTORY, PRESENT LAW, AND ANALYSIS OF THE FEDERAL WEALTH TRANSFER TAX SYSTEM (2015); David Joulfaian, *The Federal Estate Tax: History, Law, and Economics*, Table 4.1, OFF. TAX ANALYSIS (2013).

[22]   Henry J. Aaron & Alicia H. Munnell, *Reassessing the Role for Wealth Transfer Taxes*, 45 NAT'L TAX J. 119 (1992); Douglas Bernheim, *Does the Estate Tax Raise Revenue?* in 1 TAX POLICY AND THE ECONOMY 113–138 (1987); Alicia H. Munnell, *Wealth Transfer Taxation: The Relative Role for Estate and Income Taxes*, NEW ENGLAND ECO. REV. 19 (1988).

[23]   IRS DATABOOK 2016, at 23, 24 (2017).

the property is not being sold on the open market. Although the fair market value is the price at which the property would change hands between a willing buyer and seller, if those parties are not available the taxpayer must use rather complicated procedures to determine a fair market value.[24] Therefore, people planning for their estates often hire advisors to minimize valuation because, under the estate tax, reducing valuation maximizes the amount taxpayers can transfer without transfer taxation. Appraisers and surveyors may also be necessary, depending upon the size and type of property that is transferred. These valuation problems are not limited to the estate tax context.

The resulting complexity is often sorted out in litigation. For example, after Michael Jackson died in 2009, a tax battle ensued over the value of his name.[25] The IRS valued his name at $434 million; his estate says it was worth $2,105. The trial was completed in February 2017 and, in December 2017, the Tax Court barred the IRS from seeking the full amount of penalties the IRS initially sought because of procedural violations. The case is estimated to be worth more than $1 billion, due to interest and penalties. The executors of the estate have earned well more than their estimated value off of the name, one documentary grossed $261 million alone, but that is not the basis of valuation. Instead, valuation is what his name was worth at the time of his death, arguably with no deals in place.

(ii) Effect on the Economy

In addition to the estate tax's impact on government revenue, people debate the estate tax's impact on the economy as whole. Adam Smith objected to wealth transfer taxes as taxes on capital that take assets from productive uses.[26] Moreover, as a tax on accumulated savings, the estate tax should produce similar substitution and income effects as the income tax. Arguably the imposition of an estate tax disfavors saving for bequests. The conservative Tax Foundation concludes that eliminating the estate tax would lead to a 0.8% increase in the economy, a 2.2% increase in investment, and produce 139,000 new jobs.[27]

The estate tax may also negatively influence business decisions. Pending estate taxes might create disincentives for investment in an otherwise viable business if it would increase the taxes owed. One

---

[24]   Treas. Reg. § 20.2031–1.

[25]   Hannah Karp, *Michael Jackson's Estate Faces Demand for Big Tax Payment*, WALL ST. J., Feb. 5, 2017.

[26]   ADAM SMITH, AN INQUIRY INTO THE NATURE AND CAUSES OF THE WEALTH OF NATIONS 862 (Oxford U. P. 1976) (1784).

[27]   Andrew Lundeen, *The Estate Tax Provides Less Than One Percent of Federal Revenue*, TAX FOUNDATION (2015).

study conducted over two decades ago found that the 55% estate tax rate then in effect had roughly the same disincentive effect as doubling an entrepreneur's top marginal income tax rate.[28] Moreover, because some countries have lower estate taxes than the U.S., the disparity between rates encourages wealthy individuals to relocate, which moves the wealth and associated future revenue outside the U.S.[29]

On the other hand, estate taxes may have relatively less of a disincentive effect on earnings than other taxes. Therefore, if some amount of revenue must be raised, the estate tax may be the least distortionary option. Disincentives are reduced because the estate tax is imposed after income is earned. In fact, the estate tax might bolster earnings for the 0.2% of estates that owe the tax if people seek to leave a certain after-tax amount to their beneficiaries.[30]

Although both sides of the debate are plausible, without a counterfactual world it is impossible to know whether people save less because of the estate tax, spend more of their income as they age, or save more to compensate for the tax. Even though the tax might encourage the elderly to consume their earnings, this group is already a large consumer because of the cost of healthcare.

More specifically, however, the complaint that the estate tax forces people to sell the family farm or family business is overstated. No one has provided an example of this occurring, although some farmers have almost certainly had to sell acreage. From the data that is available, the Tax Policy Center estimates that only 50 small business and small farm estates will owe any estate tax in 2017, and an older 2005 CBO study found that the overwhelming majority of estates with farms and family businesses had liquidity to pay the estate tax without touching the farm or business.[31]

The farmer most likely to owe estate tax is one whose farmland has been surrounded by commercial land uses, so that the value of the land is greater for a non-farming purpose than it would be if retained for farming. Farmers in this situation may legitimately complain that they are land rich and cash poor, although this is the market indicating that their land is more valuable for another purpose. Nevertheless, responding to these complaints, for most active farms Congress permits a special valuation, additional

---

[28]   Patrick Fleenor & J.D. Foster, *An Analysis of the Disincentive Effects of Estate Tax on Entrepreneurship*, TAX FOUNDATION (1994).

[29]   For more on the cost of giving up citizenship, see Chapter 12.02(b)(v).

[30]   Chye-Ching Huang & Chloe Cho, *Ten Facts You Should Know About the Federal Estate Tax*, CTR ON BUDGET & POL'Y PRIORITIES (2017).

[31]   *Id.*; CONG. BUDGET OFFICE, EFFECTS OF THE FEDERAL ESTATE TAX ON FARMS AND SMALL BUSINESSES (2005).

discounts, and a fifteen-year installment period to minimize the impact of the estate tax. Thus, most of the approximately forty affected farms should be able to pay tax on their estate and retain their farm, despite there being higher value uses of the land.

Tax filings show the types of assets most likely a part of taxable estates. These estates are not predominately cash but are composed primarily of stock and real estate.[32] In 2007, publicly traded stock was the largest class of assets, at almost 25%; investment real estate was the next largest at 13.5%. Business assets, farms (but not farm land), and limited partnerships were 5% or less of gross estates. Although it is hard to be certain because of the lack of detailed public information, the value of stock in closely-held corporations as parts of taxable estates has likely grown over time. Nevertheless, for those with the largest estates, interests in small businesses make up less than 15% of the estate; for those with estates under $5 million small businesses make up just under 25%. Thus, the tax might require the sale of some assets to pay the taxes owed but much of these estates are liquid.

Moreover, that stock and real estate composed about half of decedents' assets means that a large amount of taxable estates are appreciable property. These types of assets are likely to have untaxed gains. Under current law, that untaxed gain would only be taxable through the estate tax. Any untaxed appreciation held at death is never taxed under the income tax. Therefore, without the estate tax there is a tremendous incentive for the elderly, in particular, to lock in their ownership of appreciated assets until death even if better alternative uses for the assets are available.

By reducing the tax advantage of accumulating large estates and diverting some of the estate to societal purposes, the estate tax also reduces unequal inheritances. In the process it can help equalize, if only to a limited degree, opportunities to participate in the economy. Although beneficiaries receive most inherited wealth after they have outgrown childhood, the tax revenue could be used to increase opportunities for less wealthy children. Family income has been shown a predictor of academic achievement; and differences in reading and math achievements between economic groups are larger than several decades ago.[33] Innate ability and luck may not be equalized, but most arguments that justify income or wealth disparities based on individual talents, efforts, or achievements do not support the same disparities resulting from inheritance.

---

[32]   Jacobson et al., *supra* note 12, at 127; Raub & Newcomb, *supra* note 19, at 291.

[33]   GREG DUNCAN & RICHARD MURNANE, RESTORING OPPORTUNITY: THE CRISIS OF INEQUALITY AND THE CHALLENGE OF AMERICAN EDUCATION (2014).

Reducing estates may even benefit the beneficiaries of those estates by encouraging them to be more productive members of society. Winston Churchill described large inheritances as creating a "race of idle rich," and Andrew Carnegie once stated that "[t]he parent who leaves his son enormous wealth generally deadens the talents and energies of the son, and tempts him to lead a less useful and less worthy life than he otherwise would."[34] Some research suggests that the more wealth that older people inherit, the more likely they are to leave the labor market.[35] According to this line of argument, taxing estates motivates or requires potential beneficiaries to contribute more to the economy that may, or may not, offset the disincentives created by taxing the money in their future estates.

(iii) Theoretical Arguments

Transfer taxes do not prevent the transfer of property between transferor and beneficiary, even though these taxes reduce the amount that the beneficiary receives. Proponents and critics of the estate tax disagree whether this is a good thing. One often-stated purpose of the estate tax is to break up estates for those whose estates surpass the cumulative credit. When the estate tax was reenacted after the Gilded Age in 1916, the tax was part of a concerted plan to reduce the large concentrations of wealth that progressives thought threatened democracy.[36] These theoretical debates pit the wealthy person's desire for unlimited giving to family and friends against one sense of social fairness.

Political theorists are not of one mind on the estate tax. John Locke in his *Two Treatises of Government*, a foundational text for early American leaders, argued that inheritance was the right of children because they were "born weak, and unable to provide for themselves."[37] On the other hand, one of America's Founding Fathers, Thomas Jefferson, argued that it was "self-evident" that the *"earth belongs to the living*: that the dead have neither powers nor rights over it. The portion occupied by an individual ceases to be his when himself ceases to be, and reverts to society."[38] Under the latter theory, taxing estates 100% would be permissible. Sir William Blackstone, possibly the leading 18th century English jurist, argued

---

[34]   ANDREW CARNEGIE, THE GOSPEL OF WEALTH (1891); M. GILBERT, WINSTON S. CHURCHILL, vol. V, Companion Part I, Documents: The Exchequer Years, 1922–29, at 297–8 (1979), Churchill to Lord Salisbury, 9 December 1924.

[35]   *The Case for Death Duties*, THE ECONOMIST, Oct. 27, 2007.

[36]   For more on the history of the tax system, see Chapter 3.01(d).

[37]   JOHN LOCKE, TWO TREATISES OF GOVERNMENT, bk. 1, § 88, at 206–07 (1988).

[38]   THOMAS JEFFERSON, THE PAPERS OF THOMAS JEFFERSON, vol. 15, 392–93 (1958) (emphasis in original).

that inheritance was merely custom turned into positive law[39]; and the Supreme Court agreed in 1898 that "[t]he right to take property by devise or descent is the creation of the law, and not a natural law."[40] As a creature of law, the tax can be changed with few constitutional or procedural limits.

Even if permissible, the death tax can be seen as a double tax on a person's earnings. The person earns income throughout his life, paying the income tax on those earnings, and then is taxed a second time on death. This may decrease the incentive to save or leave estates for his heirs. People may choose to consume any wealth above the exemption amount to avoid paying a share of it to the government a second time. In doing so, the estate tax arguably punishes people because they work hard, become successful, and want to pass on the fruits of their labor (or the inherited fruits of others' labor) to their children. Viewed in this way, the tax assumes that excess wealth should be taken away, but critics can claim that proponents do not define excess wealth or explain why it is undesirable if procured through legal efforts.

However, the double tax argument does not always apply. Death currently provides a step-up in basis under the income tax (discussed more fully below), which means any appreciation at the time of death is never taxed under the income tax. Therefore, if a decedent's appreciated property is not taxed at death under the estate tax, the federal government never taxes that component of wealth. Thus, for appreciation, the estate tax is not a double tax but a first and only tax.

Moreover, even for the portion of the estate that is not appreciation, double and triple taxation is common in other contexts through income, property, and sales taxes. In those instances, however, the second tax is on consumption in which a person removes an asset from society. An estate may later yield consumption, but the transfer of the estate merely changes who may undertake that consumption.

Different people will have different views as to the strongest theoretical arguments regarding the estate tax. The tax does partially offset an advantage large estates have under the income tax. Consequently, the transfer tax contributes to the progressivity of the overall tax regime; without it the tax system would be less progressive. Thus, an underlying issue with respect to estate taxes is whether progressivity is a desirable feature in a tax system.

---

[39]   WILLIAM BLACKSTONE, COMMENTARIES, Book 1, Part 1, Sec. II (1765–1769).

[40]   Magoun v. Illinois Trust & Sav. Bank., 170 U.S. 283, 288 (1898).

(c) Potential for Repeal

The federal government and some states have repealed the estate tax, at least for short periods. Repeal is consistent with international trends, as many countries, including Canada and Australia, have abolished their wealth transfer taxes.[41] The federal estate tax was repealed for 2010. The repeal lasted only one year and was optional for that year.[42] In 2010, estates had the choice of (1) applying the estate tax or (2) not applying the estate tax but recipients risked later being taxed under the income tax on appreciation from the pre-transfer period. Thus, large estates were given the choice of currently paying the estate tax or deferring income tax on any appreciation accrued before death until their beneficiaries sell or otherwise dispose of the assets.

It is likely that any repeal of the estate tax would continue trading off the estate tax for future income taxation of previous untaxed appreciation. As shown in 2010, Congress was unwilling to completely eliminate all tax on appreciation just because someone died, although Congress allowed up to $3 million to go untaxed. A difficulty with this approach is the need for maintaining records of basis (generally the original cost of something like stock), possibly over generations.

Ignoring the issue of untaxed appreciation, many states have permanently repealed their estate tax. For example, until 2013, Ohio imposed an estate tax on resident decedents or on Ohio assets of nonresident decedents.[43] The credit was much smaller than at the federal level, with the estate tax applying to estates worth more than $338,333. Until its repeal, the state retained 20% of the tax revenue and gave the rest to the decedent's township or municipality, a reason some municipalities lobbied against repeal when it was proposed in 2001.[44]

One alternative to repealing the tax would be to reinforce the estate tax so that it raises sufficient revenue to justify its administrative expense. Reducing either the credit or exclusions or increasing the rates would raise revenue. The first approach, however, would also increase the number of estate tax returns to be filed. Increasing rates might increase political attacks if they are made significantly higher than income tax rates. Finally, although

---

[41]   David Duff, *The Abolition of Wealth Transfer Taxes: Lessons from Canada, Australia, and New Zealand*, 3 PITT. TAX REV. 71 (2005).

[42]   Tax Relief, Unemployment Insurance Authorization, and Job Creation Act of 2010, Pub. L. 111–312, 124 Stat. 3296.

[43]   OHIO DEPT. TAX'N, ATTN: TAX CHANGE—OHIO ESTATE TAX HAS ENDED, http://www.tax.ohio.gov/estate.aspx (last visited May 1, 2018).

[44]   Ohio Dept. Tax'n, *Estate Tax,* 2014 ANNUAL REPORT 49 (2015).

likely the most difficult, reducing wealthy taxpayers' ability to shrink their estate through planning would significantly bolster the estate tax. With so much planning currently available, the tax may already be viewed as partially elective.

(d) Inheritance Tax as Alternative

Unlike an estate tax that taxes the transferor of an inheritance, an inheritance tax taxes the recipient. Nevertheless, inheritance taxes are often structured so that the estate pays the tax on behalf of recipients. This payment is similar to employers withholding taxes for employees. Despite this payment mechanism, the amount of tax that is due is computed by reference to each individual heir instead of the estate as a whole. Therefore, if an inheritance tax is progressive, its progressivity is determined per beneficiary.

Many states have had inheritance taxes, and six still do.[45] The structure of an inheritance tax need not be complicated and could be made to mirror many of the perceived benefits of an estate tax. In practice, however, many inheritance taxes are complicated structurally and do not break up large estates because they favor transfers to children and other family members. Thus, they impose different tax rates based on the relationship between decedent and beneficiary, and the closer the relationship, the lower the tax rate. Therefore, a decedent can avoid inheritance tax by leaving all of the estate to the decedent's children or spouse. This aspect of inheritances taxes is inconsistent with the objective of breaking up inherited wealth.

For example, since 1906 Kentucky has taxed the right to receive property from a decedent's estate if the property is located within Kentucky.[46] The tax rate and exemptions are based on the relationship of the beneficiary to the decedent. Close relatives, such as surviving spouses, parents, and children, do not owe the tax but cousins and friends may owe tax at a rate up to 16%. In 2015, the Kentucky inheritance tax raised $51 million, which is more than the state spent on its child care assistance program but was less than 1% of the state's general fund revenue. This tax has traditionally been coupled with an estate tax, but the estate tax was allowed to lapse in

---

[45]   Iowa, Kentucky, Maryland, Nebraska, New Jersey, and Pennsylvania. As of 2017, New Jersey and Maryland have both inheritance and estate taxes although New Jersey's estate tax is set to expire on January 1, 2018.

[46]   Ky. Dept. of Revenue, *Kentucky Inheritance and Estate Tax*, ANNUAL REPORT FY 2015–2016, at 76 (2017).

2005. In 1997, these two taxes together made up almost 2% of the state's tax revenue.[47]

Although an inheritance tax is a transfer tax, a rough equivalent would be repealing the exclusion from the income tax for the receipt of inheritances.[48] The repeal of this income tax provision would subject inheritances to the recipient's income tax, which might be higher than an inheritance tax. This change would mean that anyone, no matter the relationship, might be taxed on receipt of an inheritance depending upon his total income for the year. It would also mean receipt by wealthy people is taxed at higher rates than receipt by lower income taxpayers.

§ 9.02 Gift Tax

The gift tax applies to transfers during the gift giver's, also known as the donor's, life. The tax is collected from the donor, except in limited circumstances. For this transfer tax to apply, the donor must give away something of sufficiently large value with the proper donative intent and not receive full value in return. When applying the gift tax, the issue is often whether a transfer constitutes a gift and whether the item's value is above a congressionally designated threshold. If a transfer is subject to the gift tax, the gifted item is taken out of the donor's estate and is not thereafter subject to the donor's estate tax.

(a) How It Works

The gift tax on intervivos transfers, a fancy way of saying transfers during a donor's life, is currently taxed at a top rate of 40%.[49] Although the gift tax, like the estate tax, is structured as a progressive tax so that smaller gifts are taxed at lower rates, the unified tax credit offsets the taxes owed at lower rates.[50] Therefore, the gift tax and estate tax effectively have flat 40% rates. The same credit applies to both transfer taxes. Consequently, once a taxpayer has given gifts equal to the credited amount, all taxable gifts and estates are taxed at 40%.

The gift tax is cumulative and its rate is tax exclusive. Therefore, for determining whether a particular gift is taxable, all prior taxable gifts are added together, and the current year's tax depends on whether prior taxable gifts pushed the taxpayer past the credit. Additionally, gift tax rates are based on the amount received by the

---

[47] Anna Baumann, *Reinstating Kentucky's Tax on Extreme Wealth a Part of Making State Taxes Fair an Adequate*, KY. CTR FOR ECON. POL'Y (2015).

[48] I.R.C. § 102.

[49] I.R.C. § 2502.

[50] I.R.C. § 2001(c).

recipient and not the total amount given by the donor, which includes the tax. For example, if a donor has $10,000 to transfer and is subject to a 50% gift tax, he transfers $6,667 to the recipient and pays a 50% tax on that amount, or $3,333. Calculating gift tax's effective rate in the same manner as for the income tax, the donor's effective tax rate is the $3,333 tax divided by the $10,000, or only 33%.[51]

These special rules only apply to taxable gifts, and not all gifts are taxable. In other words, if a particular gift is below a congressionally defined threshold, it is ignored for all gift tax purposes, including future aggregation for thresholds and use of the unified credit. Two thresholds for the gift tax operate to make few gifts taxable. First, transfers in 2018 of $15,000 (this amount is adjusted annually for inflation) are not subject to the gift tax; this exemption was increased by only $1,000 from the 2017 level.[52] This threshold is calculated per recipient. Therefore, each year donors can give untaxed amounts below this threshold to as many people as they wish. If Charlie gives $15,000 to twenty people each year, Charlie can give away $280,000 per year without being subject to the gift tax; and if he wants to give to more people he can untaxed. However, if he increases the gift to any of these people, the excess above $15,000 per person is subject to gift tax if the excess is also in excess of the unified credit.

The second exclusion is the unified credit, but it applies only to gifts that exceed the annual threshold for a particular recipient. In 2018, donors have a lifetime credit for a total of $11.2 million of gifts (this amount is also adjusted annually for inflation); however, this credit applies for both the gift tax and estate tax. Use of this exclusion to eliminate the gift tax directly reduces the estate tax credit. Structured as a unified credit for the gift and estate taxes, this exclusion is personal to the donor. The credit applies whether the donor gives to one or one hundred recipients.

More rules apply, in addition to these exclusions, that can change the amount subject to gift tax. For example, married couples can give an unlimited amount to each other, but gifts to their children are subject to the statutory caps after which they become taxable.[53] Married donors can also pool their exemptions and give $30,000 per year to each recipient. Thus, married couples can give tax-free twice the amount one person can give. Several recipients are given special, tax-free status: namely charities, providers of medical services

---

[51]   Under the tax inclusive income and estate taxes, the tax liability would be $10,000 times the 50% rate, or $5,000, leaving only $5,000 to be given to the beneficiary.

[52]   Rev. Proc. 2016–55, sec. 37, 2016–45 I.R.B.

[53]   I.R.C. § 2523.

(regardless of the recipient), providers of education (regardless of the recipient), and political organizations.

Some rules make the tax hard to administer but are necessary if the country is to retain the gift tax. Similar to the estate tax, because exclusions and the amount of tax are tied to gifts' value, Congress requires donors report their fair market value. However, the value of a gift is rarely easy to define with precision. Therefore, compliance can be difficult even for the most conscientious.

Finally, because not all taxpayers respect the gift tax, Congress enacted some rules to minimize abuse. For example, for much of its history the gift tax had lower tax rates than the estate tax had, so some taxpayers attempted deathbed gifts to avoid the estate tax. To prevent deathbed gifts from reducing the estate and because of the general difficulty of policing these gifts, Congress mandated that gifts made three years before a decedent's death are included in the decedent's estate.[54] Similarly, because of the need for a fair market value and the application of caps in the annual exclusion, the exclusion only applies to gifts of present interests and not future interests.[55] Therefore, someone cannot give another a reversion interest and claim its present value is less than the annual exclusion. However, fearing this would discourage gifts to one's own children, Congress legislated that in some instances gifts of future interests to minors are treated as present interests for this purpose, facilitating the planning.[56]

(b) Political Arguments

There is significantly less political debate over the gift tax than the estate tax. It is possible that the gift tax is seen as part of the estate tax so that policymakers referring to the estate tax assume it includes the gift tax. If so, the assumption is incorrect. Despite the link created by the unified credit and tax rates, the gift tax is a separate tax. When the estate tax was repealed in 2010 for the year, the gift tax was retained.

The gift tax was initially enacted in 1924 to reduce avoidance of the estate tax.[57] Without the gift tax, people could give away all of their assets during their lives without the transfers being subject to tax. Nevertheless, the gift tax was repealed in 1926 and overhauled when reenacted in 1932. The 1932 House Committee Report stated that the tax was to "assist in the collection of the income and estate

---

[54]   I.R.C. § 2035.

[55]   I.R.C. § 2503(b)(1).

[56]   I.R.C. § 2503(c).

[57]   Much of the discussion on the gift tax derives from Jeffrey Cooper, *Ghosts of 1932*, 9 FLA. TAX REV. 875 (2010), and Joulfaian, *supra* note 22.

taxes and prevent their avoidance through the splitting of estates during the lifetime of a taxpayer."[58] Nevertheless, in the Great Depression the gift tax was given a 25% lower rate than the estate tax. Congress expressly encouraged avoidance of the estate tax to accelerate receipt of much needed revenue.

Despite its longevity, the gift tax has never been a major source of revenue. In the 1930s, when coupled with the estate tax, transfer taxes raised almost 10% of government revenue.[59] The more normal is for the transfer tax system to raise less than 2%. In 2013, the gift tax raised $4.7 billion, although that was partly in response to expectations that the gift tax credit would be reduced from over $2 million to $1 million after fiscal year 2013. In 2014, the gift tax raised $1.67 billion, or 0.1% of the federal government's gross tax collections.[60] Because of the unified credit, the gift tax should always raise less than the estate tax because the gift tax is the first to use the credit.

Who gives taxable gifts and the nature of their gifts is unsurprising. Wealthy people give taxable gifts and almost 87% of gifts were in the form of cash, real estate, and stock.[61] Over 73.6% of recipients were children and grandchildren. Most of those who make taxable gifts do not do so frequently. From one study, only 13% made three or more taxable intervivos gifts.[62] There is evidence that people give fewer gifts in response to increases in gift tax rates.[63] However, high short-term responses to gift taxation are less likely than changes over longer time horizons.

Measuring revenue and the gifts are easier than estimating how much is spent administering the tax. In 2016, 249,000 gift tax returns were filed, raising almost $2.3 billion.[64] This was out of more than 240 million total tax returns and supplemental documents processed in 2016. Only 0.8% of gift tax returns were audited, although all of those were in person field audits, recommending $302 million in additional taxes.[65]

Noncompliance with the gift tax is rampant. From one study conducted by the IRS Estate and Gift Tax Examinations team, 60%

---

[58]   H.R. REP. NO. 72–708, at 8 (1932).

[59]   Joulfaian, *supra* note 22, at 6–5.

[60]   IRS, SOI Tax Stats, Gift Tax Returns Filed in 2013; IRS, SOI Tax Stats, Gift Tax Returns Filed in 2014.

[61]   Melissa Belvedere, *2008 Gifts*, 30 STAT. INCOME BULL. 255, 259 (2011).

[62]   David Joulfaian, *The Federal Gift Tax: History, Law, and Economics*, U.S. DEPT. TREAS., OTA PAPER 100, at 22 (2007).

[63]   *Id.*, at 17–18, 29.

[64]   IRS, DATA BOOK 2016, at 3–4.

[65]   *Id.*, at 23–24.

to 90% of taxpayers making intrafamily real property transfers fail to file gift tax returns as required.[66] Another study found that roughly 20%, or approximately $200 million, of gifts are underreported.[67] This noncompliance with the gift tax may not actually reduce gift tax revenue because of the existence of the unified credit. However, if the transfers were reported and used some portion of the credit, they might affect later revenue from the estate tax.

The fate of the gift tax is almost inexorably tied to that of the estate tax. As a stand-alone tax, the gift tax has less justification than as part of a transfer tax system. Because of its annual exclusion and the unified credit, the gift tax only applies to large gifts to anyone not qualifying for an exclusion, such as spouses or charities. Therefore, alone the gift tax would likely only defer transfers of significant wealth. Repealing the estate tax but retaining the gift tax, as happened in 2010, would make transitioning some family businesses among generations more difficult. These businesses would have to choose either to pay tax for a current transfer of ownership or to wait until a prior generation dies for the ownership to be transferred tax-free by their estates.

§ 9.03 Planning Around Transfer Taxes

Many wealthy individuals plan in order to minimize their gift and estate taxes, especially in response to changes and anticipated changes in these taxes' rates. These planning techniques can range from early gifts of partnership interests in family businesses to creating complicated ownership structures of assets, possibly involving offshore entities. For example, many wealthy individuals create trusts, some with favorable statutory features, in order to reduce transfer taxes whereas others rely on favorable valuations.[68] These maneuvers are intended to reduce the value of the estate with minimal gift taxation.

Consider the case of Melvin Simon, former half owner of the Indiana Pacers. He transferred his interest to his brother, Herb, the owner of the other half of the Pacers.[69] The transfer was seven months before Melvin's September 2009 death. The terms of the deal

---

[66] Jay Soled et al., *Rethinking the Penalty for Failure to File Gift Tax Returns*, 141 TAX NOTES 757 (2013).

[67] Martha Briton Eller, *Audit Revaluation of Federal Estate Tax Returns, 1992*, 20 STAT. INCOME BULL. 100 (2000).

[68] For example, Grantor Retained Annuity Trusts (GRATs) permit wealthy donors to transfer a trust's excess earnings to a recipient without the application of the gift tax on that excess. I.R.C. § 2702.

[69] Kelly Philips Erb, *Widow of Former Pacers Owner Sues IRS for $21 Million*, FORBES, Apr. 28, 2015.

were not made public. In 2015, Melvin's wife, Bren, sued the IRS to overturn the agency's determination that the favorable terms of the deal made it an $83 million gift, which subjected the estate to a $21 million gift tax. She paid under protest and sued the IRS for a refund. Ultimately, she settled her lawsuit in 2017, but the terms have not been disclosed.

At least part of the Simons' transfer tax planning likely involved discounting the value of the gift in order to reduce the transfer tax. A study found that 35,000 returns reported valuation discounts that had the effect of reducing the size of the gift and accounted for almost 25% of gifts.[70] There were $3.7 billion in valuation discounts in 2008, on 102,608 gifts, with almost 70% of returns claiming discounts greater than 40%.[71]

Proper discounts can be achieved by placing restrictions on the gifted assets. For example, family limited partnerships (or FLPs) can be used to generate discounts for those willing to pool family businesses or investment assets. As a pool, these assets can be transferred among generations. By transferring minority interests in the FLP that lack control and marketability, these interests are often significantly discounted. In other words, transferors claim FLP interests are worth less than the fair market value of the underlying assets. Most FLP assets are real estate and stock; the stock can be either publicly traded or of closely-held corporations. Interestingly, in 2008 farm assets were only 8.42% of the total in FLPs and only 2.58% of all gifts.

Over time, Congress has responded to many forms of planning with legislation to reduce or discourage such planning. For example, Congress enacted the generation-skipping tax (GST) in 1976. The GST taxes transfers of more than $1 million that would otherwise avoid estate and gift taxes.[72] In an exceedingly complicated way but with tax rates and exemptions like the estate tax, the GST applies to gifts and transfers in trust to younger recipients. The tax applies if the recipient is related to the donor and is more than one generation younger than the donor or is not related to the donor and more than 37.5 years younger.

Without the GST, if a wealthy individual transferred property in a trust for one's children for life, then to his grandchildren for life, with a remainder to his great-grandchildren (as long as it avoids first year law students' bane: the rule against perpetuities), there would be only one level of gift tax. But if the person had simply left the

---

[70]   Joulfaian, *supra* note 62, at 23.

[71]   Belvedere, *supra* note 61, at 259.

[72]   Tax Reform Act of 1976, § 2006, Pub. L. 94–55, 90 Stat. 1520.

property to his children who left it to their children who, in turn, left it to their children, estate taxes could be due three times. Congress crafted the GST to prevent the tax avoidance of skipping generations of taxpayers; however, political compromise has made the GST one of the most complicated sections of the Code.

§ 9.04   Income Tax Effects

For most of the modern income tax's history, gifts and bequests have been carved out of the income tax. Therefore, these transfers are ignored under the income tax although they affect people's ability to pay taxes and economic incentives. The carve out may be justified because of the existence of the estate and gift taxes. However, the income tax consequences have infrequently been tied to transfer taxation and even then only in a limited sense.

(a) How It Works

The income tax consequences of gifts and estates are legally independent of any transfer taxes that might result from the transfer. Therefore, it is constitutionally permissible for both the donor and recipient to be subject to both income and transfer taxes on these transfers. Nevertheless, under current law there are no income tax consequences of these transfers, at least not at the time of the transfer. Notably, the earlier Civil War and 1894 income taxes did not exclude the receipt of gifts and inheritances from current taxation to the recipient. Although under current law neither donor nor recipient is taxed, giving gifts or estates is also ordinarily not deductible unless a gift is given to a charitable organization.

This exclusion may increase the attractiveness of gifting or devising certain assets. First, donors and decedents may prefer to transfer assets with built-in gain that has not yet been taxed under the income tax. Normally when property is transferred, any built-in gain becomes subject to tax. However, this appreciation is not taxable for gifted or inherited property. In *Taft v. Bowers*, the Supreme Court concluded that the donor does not realize income but the Court applied a standard of income that may no longer apply, so the result could change.[73] Without realization, nothing triggers current taxation to the donor.

For example, Mom and Dad purchased stock in 2000 at a cost of $10 per share and give it to their daughter this year when it has a fair market value of $100 per share. The fact that there is no

---

[73]   278 U.S. 470 (1929). Taft v. Bowers was decided under the more onerous Eisner v. Macomber, 252 U.S. 189 (1920), standard of realization than the modern Comm'r v. Glenshaw Glass, 348 U.S. 426 (1955).

realization means that Mom and Dad do not owe income tax on $90 of appreciation per share at the time they give the gift.

Additionally, Congress enacted a rule in the 1913 income tax that recipients are not taxed on the receipt of gifts or inheritances.[74] Congress created this income tax benefit for public policy and administrative reasons. The theory behind the exclusion is that most of these transfers are within the family and those relationships should not be burdened with taxes. Moreover, requiring people to keep track of all the gifts they receive, to accurately value those gifts, and to report all gifts on their returns would be an administrative nightmare both for taxpayers and the IRS. Congress has decided that the foregone revenue is less important than these other policy considerations.

While the exclusion for recipients appears very broad on its face, there are limits to this exclusion. For example, Congress legislated that income earned on excluded property is not itself excluded from gross income.[75] So if Grandma gives a shopping mall to her grandson, the income the mall generates is taxable to the grandson. If this were not the result, everyone living on the earnings of gifted or inherited wealth would never pay tax. Despite its limits, the existence of favorable income tax rules means that there are no income tax consequences for most gifts, and built-in gain in gifted or inherited property is not taxed to the donor or recipient at the time of the gift or bequest.

Moreover, with an inheritance any untaxed gain at the time of a bequest is never taxed. Congress currently requires taxpayers wipe out any pre-transfer appreciation or loss at the time of the owner's death. For future tax purposes, the recipient is treated as having bought the asset at its fair market value at the time of receipt, resulting in a step-up or step-down in tax basis.[76] The CBO estimates that the step-up in basis rule under the income tax will reduce federal revenues by $644 billion over ten years, with 21% going to the top 1% of income earners.[77] The highest quintile enjoys 60% of the benefit.[78] This is $375 billion more than the estate tax will raise. This beneficence does not extend to gifts. The recipient of a gift is generally taxed on appreciation when he disposes of the gifted asset, including

---

[74]   I.R.C. § 102.

[75]   I.R.C. § 102(b)(1). Similarly, gifts of the income from property are not excluded. I.R.C. § 102(b)(2).

[76]   I.R.C. § 1014.

[77]   CONG. BUDGET OFFICE, THE DISTRIBUTION OF MAJOR TAX EXPENDITURES IN THE INDIVIDUAL INCOME TAX SYSTEM (2013).

[78]   *Id.*

appreciation from when the asset was owned by the donor.[79] Therefore, gifted gain is eventually taxed to the recipient but inherited gain is never taxed to anyone under the income tax.

Using the above example, Mom and Dad did not owe tax on the $90 of appreciation in the stock when they give it to their daughter. Their daughter also does not owe income tax on the receipt of the stock. If the daughter takes a fair market value basis of $100 in the stock, the $90 of appreciation is never taxed. If Daughter takes her cost basis (the $0 she spent on the stock), the $10 Mom and Dad invested is never recovered. Not liking the result of either a fair market value or cost basis, Congress provides that in the case of a gift the daughter can recover her parent's investment tax-free and not owe tax on that $10. Therefore, if the daughter disposes of the stock for its $100 fair market value, she will owe income tax on the $90 of appreciation. However, if the daughter takes the property as a bequest, she takes the higher fair market value basis, and no one ever owes tax on the $90 of appreciation.

Because gifts do not erase gains, whether a gain exists must follow from the donor to the recipient. Therefore, for gifts the issue is determining the donor's investment, or basis, in the gifted property. Congress recognized this might be difficult and put the onus on the government. Congress provided that if the recipient cannot determine the basis, the IRS is to search for this information. If the information still cannot be found, the basis used for calculating gain or loss is the fair market value at the time the last taxpayer acquired the property in a taxable transaction.

Because of their value as exclusions from income taxation, the definition of what makes a transfer a gift, inheritance, devise, or bequest is critical to the preservation of the income tax. Despite its importance, this issue of what constitutes a gift or inheritance remains uncertain. For example, when talk show host Oprah Winfrey gave new cars to her audience, they soon learned that they owed tax on the receipt because the cars were not gifts.[80] Because of the

---

[79] The means of preserving the gain is by requiring the recipient take a transferred basis from the donor. I.R.C. § 1015. However, if a donor gives away property that has a built-in loss at the time of the transfer, a special rule can, but does not always, apply. Congress limits the recipient's ability to deduct donor-held losses to offset the recipient's future gain in that property. Congress worried that without this limit taxpayers would shift losses from low-income taxpayers to high-income taxpayers to reduce their collective tax obligations. A $100 loss deduction is worth $15 to a taxpayer in a 15% top marginal tax bracket but it is worth $30 to a taxpayer in a 30% top marginal tax bracket.

[80] Kelly Erb, *A Look Back at Oprah's Ultimate Car Giveaway*, FORBES, Sept. 13, 2016.

promotional value to Oprah, the transfers did not qualify as a gift for tax purposes.

The seminal case defining a gift for federal income tax purposes is *Commissioner v. Duberstein*.[81] In *Duberstein*, the Supreme Court focused on the donor's motive. The case's most famous phrase is that a gift must proceed from the donor's "detached and disinterested generosity." Whether detached and disinterested generosity exists is determined based on "the application of the fact-finding tribunal's experience with the mainsprings of human conduct to the totality of the facts of each case."[82] Thus a facts and circumstances test is applied to each gift. Similar concerns as to proper classification arise for transfers claiming to be bequests, devises, and inheritances. In *Wolder v. Commissioner*, the Court of Appeals for the Second Circuit held that when an attorney received stock under the terms of a client's will, it was not an excludible bequest but, instead, was taxable as compensation.[83]

(b) Political Arguments

Politicians often focus on the death tax, so that few are interested in the income tax consequences of these transfers. The result is favorable to taxpayers who give and receive gifts and estates. It decreases income taxes without costing those who benefit much political capital. Nevertheless, the income tax result can be viewed as a tax loophole. Under the theory of *Commissioner v. Glenshaw Glass*, gifts and bequests are an accession to wealth, clearly realized, over which the recipient has control and, consequently, the default should be that they are taxed.[84] This longstanding, often overlooked benefit provides its greatest return to those who give and receive large value gifts and bequests. These income tax benefits are significant, for example those for the donor alone are estimated to cost more than $624 billion in federal revenue between 2017 and 2026.[85]

The income tax benefits extend to anyone who gives or receives gifts and estates. Nevertheless, the tax benefit is larger for those with larger incomes to the extent that they are in higher tax brackets. Additionally, wealthier taxpayers are generally able to give larger gifts and bequests. Therefore, the exclusion permits wealthier people to defer tax and benefit more from the regime than lower-income taxpayers.

---

[81] 363 U.S. 278 (1960).

[82] *Id.*, at 289.

[83] 493 F.2d 608 (1974).

[84] 348 U.S. 426 (1955).

[85] U.S. TREAS. DEPT., TAX EXPENDITURES, Table 1, at 22 (2017).

In addition to its regressive benefit, the income tax exclusion creates some incentives not beneficial to society. For example, the eventual elimination of tax on previously untaxed gain only for property held until a person's death could produce a lock-in effect. Taxpayers, particularly those who are elderly or in poor health, may not dispose of assets they otherwise would because of the tax benefit their own death produces. The easiest way to eliminate this lock in effect would be to treat death as a realization event for the decedent. This would require decedents' estates pay tax on appreciation, possibly offset by any built-in losses in depreciated property. In the process, it would raise significant government revenue.

On the other hand, eliminating this loophole would require courts to accept that death is a realization event, something President Barack Obama proposed but failed to achieve.[86] Although the standards for realization have been loosened since the 1929 *Taft v. Bowers*, it is not certain that courts would accept that death creates a sufficient change for realization to occur. Moreover, this change of law is likely to be perceived by the public as punishing death. As long as a person lives, the person gets tax deferral. That deferral would be lost because of an unavoidable event of life, giving taxpayers a stronger claim than under the current estate tax it harms family farms and closely held businesses by taxing otherwise untaxed gain.

Moreover, making death or gift-giving a taxable event under the income tax would create significant administrative problems. For example, more property would need to be valued when there is no third party buyer, although a problem not unique to this context. Additionally, a rule would have to be created for built-in losses in transferred property, which under the present regime are generally never deductible. No result would satisfy everyone. Losses triggered on death could be carried back to be used in the decedent's or donor's prior taxable years, transferred to beneficiaries, or continue to be nondeductible. This debate would likely raise administrative as well as political tradeoffs.

Nevertheless, as long as gifts and estates are taxed differently under the income tax, taxpayers have incentives to choose the least-taxed option. This makes it more difficult for the government to enforce the income tax. The economic value of the exclusion of gifts that can occur at any point in a taxpayer's life mean that people have an incentive to structure other, taxable activities as tax-free gifts. This imposes a policing burden on the government to distinguish between gifts and non-gifts, particularly when the parties have a special relationship. For example, a gift might also be something else

---

[86] Sean McElroy, *A New Estate Tax: Eliminating the Step-Up in Basis at Death*, 148 TAX NOTES 985 (2014).

to families operating a family business, such as compensation, and the government is tasked with minimizing tax evasion.

Potential evasion of the income tax through mischaracterization of transfers caused Congress to limit taxpayer flexibility in defining their transactions. For example, because of the desire to use untaxed gifts in place of taxed compensation, Congress prohibits tax-free gift treatment for transfers between employer and employee.[87] Because this statutory prohibition denies gift status even for transfers among family members in a family business context, the Treasury Department clarified in Proposed Regulations that this statutory rule does not apply when an employer gives "extraordinary transfers" to those who would ordinarily receive gifts, such as family and friends.[88] The burden of proof is on the employee to show that the transfer was not in recognition of her employment. This facts and circumstances test requires the taxpayer prove that the "gift" was really a gift but in practice requires that the IRS detect and distinguish between types of payments.

Complexity for both taxpayer and the government arises if someone sells property to a buyer for less than its fair market value and gifts the remaining value. In the case of a part-gift, part-sale, the seller must divide the transfer so that some portion is an excludible gift and some portion is a taxable sale.[89] In this case, the seller-donor may owe tax on any gain but is prohibited from deducting any loss; and the buyer-recipient may later owe tax on any built-in gain that the seller-donor defers.[90] The result requires complicated record keeping and third-party valuation.

The economic benefit from the exclusion of gifts and bequests from the income tax, even with significant record keeping obligations, may justify transfer taxation. Because transfers are not subject to current income taxation, they may deserve to be subject to their own tax. If the public believes that the income tax ignores these transfers, the public is more likely to demand current taxation of large transfers among people.

However, except for appreciation on death, the income used to fund the gift or bequest has already been taxed, and gifted appreciation will be taxed by the income tax when the recipient disposes of the asset. Consequently, for many transferred assets, income and transfer taxation is a form of double taxation, once of the donor when the income is earned and again to the donor when the

---

[87]   I.R.C. § 102(c). *See also* H.R. REP. NO. 99–426, at 106 n. 5 (1985).

[88]   Prop. Reg. § 1.102–1(f)(2).

[89]   Different rules apply to part-gifts, part-sales to charities. *See* I.R.C. § 1011(b).

[90]   I.R.C. § 102; Treas. Reg. § 1.1001–1(e); § 1.1015–4.

transfer is made. An analogy could be made to a payment for personal services, which is taxed twice—once when the payer earns the income to buy the services and then to the recipient on receipt of the payment for providing services. The incongruity is that a gift or bequest does not consume society's resources as does personal services; consumption takes place in the future by the recipient. Therefore, transfer taxation in addition to the initial income tax on earning the funds to buy the asset is more accurately described as double taxation than in most other instances of American tax law.

§ 9.05   Other Transfer Taxes

Congress has discussed implementing transfer taxes on the transfer of legal title in other contexts than gifts or transfers of estates.[91] Transfer taxes are most often framed as a tax on particular types of transactions, for example on the sale of financial products or on mergers of businesses. Previously, the U.S. has taxed the sale or other transfer of stock. In 1914, Congress taxed these transfers at a rate of 0.2%.[92] The rate was doubled in the Great Depression, and it was phased out in 1966. Today, the objective is generally framed both to raise revenue and to reduce financial speculation that was thought to trigger the Great Recession.[93] Even at the low rates proposed by Representative Pete Defazio or Representative John Larson, such a tax could raise significant revenue, according to one estimate from $100 billion to $150 billion per year.

---

[91]   DealBook, *Transaction Tax Is Floated on Capitol Hill*, N.Y. TIMES, Oct. 16, 2009.

[92]   Act of Oct. 22, 1914, ch. 331, Pub. L. No. 63–217, 38 Stat. 745.

[93]   *See* Cong. Budget Office, *Impose a Tax on Financial Transactions*, OPTION 33 (2013); Josh Bivens & Hunter Blair, *A Financial Transaction Tax Would Help Ensure Wall Street Works For Main Street*, ECON. POL'Y INST. (2016).

Chapter 10

PAYROLL TAXES

Table of Sections

Payroll taxes are imposed on employees' wages to fund Social Security, Medicare, and unemployment insurance. These taxes currently raise 34% of federal revenue, more than any source other than the individual income tax.[1] Payroll taxes also constitute a major portion of most individuals' tax burden, particularly among lower-income taxpayers. One estimate is that 75% of taxpayers pay more in payroll taxes than they do in income taxes.[2]

Payroll taxes are usually calculated as a percentage of an employee's salary. Except for unemployment insurance, which is paid entirely by the employer, half of payroll taxes are paid by the employer and half are paid by the employee. Like the income tax, employees' portion of payroll taxes are withheld by employers from employees' wages and paid to the government on employees' behalf. Self-employed workers are required to pay an equivalent of both halves of these taxes and to perform the necessary administrative work because they are effectively both employer and employee.

These taxes originated in the Great Depression of the 1930s and the Great Society of the 1960s. Their statutory bases have been amended frequently, and their tax rates have risen significantly since their enactment. Starting with rates of less than 3%, the current tax rate for Social Security and Medicare taxes is more than 15%, with every indication that the rates will rise again.

Payroll taxes imposed by the Federal Insurance Contributions Act (FICA) pay a portion of the cost of Social Security, which provides

---

[1]   WHITE HOUSE, HISTORICAL TABLES, Table 2.1 (2017).

[2]   David Kamin & Isaac Shapiro, *Studies Shed New Light on Effect of Administration's Tax Cuts*, CTR ON BUDGET & POL'Y PRIORITIES (2004).

old age and disability insurance, and Medicare, which provides health insurance for the elderly, disabled, and children of deceased workers. Social Security and Medicare constituted almost 40% of federal expenditures in 2017.[3] Social Security alone is the largest single government program in the world. A separate payroll tax imposed by the Federal Unemployment Tax Act (FUTA) partially covers the federal government's 50% share of the cost of unemployment benefit programs operated by state governments.

§ 10.01 Progressivity

Payroll taxes are almost certainly regressive in that they constitute a larger share of lower-income earners' income than of higher-income earners' income.[4] The Tax Policy Center listed effective payroll taxes for different income groups, and, in 2010, the 60% to 90% income brackets have an effective payroll tax of 10.2% whereas the top 0.1% have an effective tax rate of 0.9%.[5] Payroll taxes clearly have regressive features, such as a flat (rather than progressive) rate structure, no standard deduction, and no exemption. The Social Security tax also caps the amount of earnings that are subject to tax. However, the Social Security system has progressive elements. When all the Social Security programs are examined together, the payout structure is progressive over a generation.[6] It is impossible to say with precision whether payroll taxes and accompanying benefits are regressive or progressive in practice.

As a tax levied on wages and salaries, payroll taxes are imposed on almost all the income of most low- and middle-income taxpayers but a much smaller proportion of high-income taxpayers' income.[7] This occurs in one obvious way and one less obvious way. First, the Social Security tax is not imposed on all wages but is capped so that the tax does not apply to the portion of an employee's wage income above the cap, which in 2018 is $128,400.[8] This means that employees with earnings that exceed the six-figure cap get a portion of their income "tax free" from payroll taxes while lower-earning employees have all their income subject to payroll taxes.

---

[3] WHITE HOUSE, HISTORICAL TABLES, Table 3.2 (2018).

[4] CTR ON BUDGET & POL'Y PRIORITIES, POLICY BASICS: FEDERAL PAYROLL RATES (2016).

[5] TAX POL'Y CTR, T11–0099—BASELINE TABLES: EFFECTIVE TAX RATES BY CASH INCOME PERCENTILE (2011).

[6] CONG. BUDGET OFFICE, IS SOCIAL SECURITY PROGRESSIVE? (2006).

[7] The income not subject to payroll taxes does not count towards eligibility for Social Security benefits.

[8] SOC'L SECURITY ADMIN., FACT SHEET 2017 SOCIAL SECURITY CHANGES (2017).

Second, payroll taxes are imposed on wages and salaries but not on income from things like rental properties, loans, stocks, and sales of investment property. Wealthy taxpayers generally derive a much larger portion of their income from sources free from payroll taxation than poorer taxpayers, again resulting in poorer taxpayers having a greater percentage of their incomes subject to payroll taxes than wealthy taxpayers do. For example, in 2014, for the taxpayers with the top 400 adjusted gross incomes, wages and salaries made up only 4.47% of their incomes, whereas wages and salaries made up 80% of the income of taxpayers with less than $50,000 of adjusted gross income.[9]

On the other hand, the receipt of tax revenue to fund these programs is not their only potential source of progressivity. For example, the payout structure of Social Security is progressive. As a result, Social Security recipients with lower lifetime average wages receive larger Social Security benefits both as a percentage of their lifetime average wage income and as a percentage of total Social Security benefits than do recipients with higher lifetime average wages. For people in the bottom fifth of the earnings distribution who pay into Social Security, the return they receive as compared to the taxes they pay is almost three times greater than that for the top fifth of earners.

Further shifting the benefit to lower-income recipients, Social Security benefits are excluded from taxable income only for lower-income recipients. For higher-income beneficiaries, Social Security payments are taxable under the income tax. Unlike for most phase-outs, thresholds are not high for tax inclusion. Single taxpayers who have more than $25,000 of annual income and joint filers with $32,000 potentially owe income tax on up to 85% of the benefits they receive.[10]

Although containing limited progressive elements, the receipt of benefits occurs later in people's lives than they pay payroll taxes. The money they pay earlier is worth more than the money they receive later because of the time value of money. Therefore, a proper evaluation of the cash flow of payroll taxes and benefits in different periods of time must be discounted, recognizing the amounts for particular people may be unknowable as they pay the taxes because they do not know their lifespans or whether they will need the disability insurance component of the system.

---

[9] IRS, SOI TAX STATS—TOP 400 INDIVIDUAL INCOME TAX RETURNS WITH THE LARGEST ADJUSTED GROSS INCOMES; IRS, SOI TAX STATS—BASIC TABLES, Table 1 (2015).

[10] I.R.C. § 86.

Finally, further confounding determinations of progressivity is the fact that the incidence of payroll taxes is not conclusively known.[11] It is unclear if the person who remits payroll taxes to the IRS ultimately bears their burden. It is likely that for most employees both the employee and employer's taxes are ultimately borne by the employee by reducing the amount paid to the employee. In some industries with a shortage of specialized employees, however, employees may be able to shift a portion of both employee and employer taxes onto the employer or the consumer of the goods they produce.

§ 10.02 Social Security Taxes

The employer and employee each pay half of the total Social Security taxes owed per worker. In 2018, employees pay a 6.2% tax on their first $128,400 of wages (this cap is indexed annually for inflation). This means the maximum Social Security tax an employee can pay in 2018 is $7,960.80, and any wages he earns in excess of $128,400 are not subject to Social Security tax. In addition, employers pay a tax of 6.2% on the wages they pay up to the cap of $128,400 for each employee. To the extent an employee has multiple employers, the employee receives a refundable credit for the employee's portion of Social Security taxes paid on wages in excess of the cap. However, each employer must always pay its full portion, which can result in an employee's employers collectively paying more than the $7,960.80 per employee maximum amount.

(a) Development

Social Security was introduced in the 1930s as a New Deal insurance program.[12] The choice to fund the program with a payroll tax was for political as much as for financial reasons. President Franklin D. Roosevelt is said to have explained:

> We put those pay roll contributions there so as to give the contributors a legal, moral, and political right to collect their pensions and their unemployment benefits. With those taxes in there, no damn politician can ever scrap my social security program. Those taxes aren't a matter of economics, they're straight politics.[13]

---

[11]   For more on the incidence of taxation, see Chapter 4.02.

[12]   Social Security Act, Pub. L. 74–271, 49 Stat. 620 (1935). For a history, see Larry DeWitt, *The Development of Social Security in America*, 70 SOC. SECURITY BULL. 1 (2010).

[13]   U.S. National Archives, *Congress and the New Deal: Social Security*, https:// www.archives.gov/exhibits/treasures_of_congress/text/page19_text.html (last visited May 1, 2018).

Funding benefits with a payroll tax can create an equivalent of purchased insurance or be viewed as a revenue source for government-provided insurance. Possibly a distinction only a lawyer can love, the competing views create a tension that has arisen many times in the program's history when policymakers seek to amend the program. The amount that a beneficiary can receive differs depending upon the answer to this policy choice. If payouts are the result of contributions, the amount a person is entitled to receive is set at retirement. However, if the tax is only a revenue source, the appropriate amount to be paid is subject to political debate. No definitive answer to the historical policy choice is known, and the current interpretation varies depending upon who is asked.

Social Security began taxing wages in 1937, and it was originally planned that the system would not begin paying out benefits until 1942, when the fund was expected to be solvent. However, payments of the tax reduced the amount of money in circulation so much that Congress decided to begin payouts in 1940. Since that time, Social Security has remained sacrosanct in American politics. Indeed, Congress has reduced other entitlement programs' budgets from time to time, but Social Security has consistently grown as a percentage of federal spending.

The disability portion of the Social Security program was not added until 1956, signed into law by President Dwight D. Eisenhower.[14] The program began providing targeted relief to disabled workers aged between 50 and 65. Over time, the program expanded significantly. The Supplemental Security income part of the disability program was added in 1974 under President Richard Nixon.[15] Although the government has generally resisted introducing or expanding disability benefits, in the 1980s mental illness and pain management began to be recognized as disabilities, ushering in a more expansive program.[16]

(b) Calculating Payments

The amount of a worker's monthly Social Security benefits depends upon the worker's earnings record and on the age at which the retiree chooses to begin receiving benefits.[17] The average benefit

---

[14]   For more on the history of disability insurance, see John Kearney, *Social Security and the "D" in OSDI*, 66 Soc. Security Bull. (2006).

[15]   Soc. Security Office of Retirement and Disability Pol'y, Supplemental Security Income Program Description and Legislative History, Annual Statistical Supplement (2012).

[16]   David Autor & Mark Duggan, *The Growth in the Social Security Disability Rolls*, NBER Working Paper No. 12436 (2006).

[17]   For a full description of benefits, see Soc'l Sec. Admin, Understanding the Benefits (2017).

in 2018 for a retired worker is $1,404 per month and for a retired couple is $2,808. All workers paying FICA or the self-employment equivalent for at least 40 quarters on at least $1,320 per quarter as of 2018 are eligible for full retirement at ages 65, 66, or 67 depending on the worker's year of birth. For those born before 1937, full retirement began at age 65; for those born after 1960, full retirement begins at age 67. Choosing to begin receiving payments earlier (but no earlier than at age 62) reduces benefits, and delaying receipt until age 70 increases benefits.

Entitlement to retirement benefits (and benefits for surviving spouses, former spouses, children, and the disabled) is a complex calculation and only partially described here. The effect is a progressive payout structure. Benefits are calculated using a retiree's average indexed monthly salary over the highest earning 35-year period. Therefore, a person bases their entitlement on 35 years of earnings and not their entire working life. If they worked more years, the highest earning years are used; if they worked less they receive a $0 allocation for unworked years as long as they worked 40 quarters. This index of salary is allocated among three salary brackets that adjust annually with inflation. The retiree's total monthly benefit is a percentage of each bracket. Specifically, an individual receives 90% of the lowest level of wages, then 32%, and 15% of the highest wages.

Brackets for 2018 (of monthly earnings)[18]		
Lowest bracket	90% times	income up to $895
Middle bracket	32% times	income between $895 and $5,397
Highest bracket	15% times	income between $5,397 and $10,700

These percentages weight heavily for lower income wages. Additionally, the income a person earns above FICA's ceiling, $128,400 in 2018, is not considered in this calculation (but is also not taxed). The progressive payment means that Social Security is a good wage substitute for lower-wage workers but a poor wage substitute for higher-wage workers.

In addition to traditional Social Security benefits provided to those who surpass an age threshold, the Social Security system also contains the largest of several federal disability programs. This disability relief is also funded with a portion of FICA tax revenue. Technically, there are two distinct disability programs operated through Social Security: Social Security Disability Insurance (SSDI),

---

[18]   SOC. SEC. ADMIN., PRIMARY INSURANCE AMOUNT (2018).

for those who worked long enough and paid Social Security taxes, and Supplemental Security Income (SSI), which pays based on financial need. Either program only applies if a person cannot work because of a severe medical condition that is expected to last at least one year or result in death, although the amount of benefits is not tied to the severity of the disability. The medical condition must significantly limit the person's ability to do basic work activities, such as lifting, standing, walking, sitting, and remembering. This is a more strict definition of disability than used for many other programs.

In 2017, the disability programs made payments to almost 8.7 million beneficiaries, although only about 35% of applications received that year were approved.[19] The large number of recipients largely stems from a 1984 congressional loosening of the screening process for qualifying for disability benefits.[20] The result has been an increase in the number of applications and awards.[21] Since the Social Security Disability Reforms Act of 1984, the Social Security Administration is required to place more weight on applicants' reported pain and discomfort and to relax the screening of mental illness. Additionally, applicants' doctors are to receive greater credence in the application process, which has since been made "controlling weight." The effect has been a shift in claimants to low-mortality disorders, such as mental illness and back pain.

Similar to Social Security, payments from SSDI are based on average past earnings. In 2018, the average monthly disability payment for workers was $1,197, and total benefits paid from the Disability Insurance Trust Fund in 2016 was $142.7 billion.[22] Payments of SSI are tied to income and, in 2017, more than 8 million people averaged $526 per month. Unlike Social Security, disability benefits are not automatically awarded; an application takes time before a successful award can be made. In 2017, there were almost 2.2 million applications (down from a peak of over 2.9 million in 2010).[23] No time limit is set for the Social Security Administration to approve or deny claims, but estimates are that applications take 30 to 90 days to receive and can take up to eight months to review, plus additional time if an applicant wants a denied application further

---

[19]   Soc. Sec. Admin. Selected Data From Social Security's Disability Program, https://www.ssa.gov/oact/STATS/dibStat.html (last visited May 1, 2018).

[20]   Social Security Disability Benefits Reform Act of 1984, Pub. L. No. 98–460, 98 Stat. 1794.

[21]   Autor & Duggan, *supra* note 16.

[22]   SOC. SECURITY ADMIN., MONTHLY STATISTICAL SNAPSHOT, MAY 2017; SOC. SECURITY ADMIN., ANNUAL BENEFITS PAID FROM THE DI TRUST FUND (2017).

[23]   SOC. SECURITY ADMIN., ANNUAL STATISTICAL SUPPLEMENT TO THE SOCIAL SECURITY BULLETIN, 2016, Table 6.C7, 2.F9 (2017).

reviewed. Nationwide, 32% of applications are approved, down from a peak of 53% in 1967 but similar to the rates of the early 1980s.[24]

Certain family members may qualify as survivors or for disability benefits based on another person's work. For Social Security benefits, the other person must have worked long enough to qualify for benefits; disability will pay if the other person qualifies as disabled. Potentially qualifying family members include a spouse whose age is past a threshold; a spouse caring for the person's child if the child is younger than 16 or is disabled; an unmarried child younger than 18; an unmarried child with a disability if the disability started before age 22; and in limited circumstances the parents of a deceased person.

Social Security works primarily as an intergenerational and a catastrophic disability insurance plan. It socializes the responsibility to care for the elderly and for disabled in need, at least for those employed long enough to qualify. It is estimated that Social Security keeps approximately 14.5 million elderly Americans above the poverty level.[25] Social Security is, in essence, an annuity rather than an asset; providing a guaranteed level of lifetime income for the beneficiary that cannot be sold, borrowed against, or inherited. Because lower-income earners have shorter life expectancies on average than higher-income beneficiaries, they may receive smaller cumulative benefits than the structure intends. In other words, low-income earners' shorter lives reduce the progressive effect of their relatively larger annual payments. The lack of inheritability arguably makes Social Security less progressive and more like a social safety net.

(c) Structural Critiques

Critics of the Social Security system have argued that the system is both not generous enough and is too generous. Which critique resonates depends upon one's view of what the system is intended to do. As currently structured, Social Security and the other payments that come out of FICA operate as forced savings and as social insurance. The dual, sometimes conflicting, objectives drive structural critiques, especially when evaluations focus on one or the other objective.

For example, the Social Security payout structure is progressive and intended, at least by some, to raise people out of poverty, a hallmark of social insurance. Moreover, payouts are only indirectly tied to contributions unlike traditional forced savings. Each dollar of

---

[24] *Id.*, at Table 6.C7.

[25] Paul Van de Water & Arloc Sherman, *Social Security Keeps 21 Million Americans Out of Poverty*, CTR ON BUDGET & POL'Y PRIORITIES (2012).

contribution does not count the same in terms of calculating benefits. On the other hand, the highest wages are carved out from the tax base. If the cap were removed on the amount of earned income subject to Social Security, it would further align Social Security with social insurance unless the contributions were entitled to benefits. Most proposals to remove the cap do not provide details of any changes to payouts; however, if the goal is to increase the amount of tax revenue available to pay to low-income recipients, it is unlikely these new contributions would entitle wealthier contributors to greater benefits.

If Social Security is to be viewed as a social safety net rather than as government-structured insurance, de-linking Social Security and insurance may make sense. In that case, eliminating the cap on wage earnings makes the tax more progressive as well as increasing the revenue that can be re-distributed. However, once spending through the program is disconnected from its revenue source, spending would be contained only through political limits. Although recipients are often a strong interest group, Social Security would also face reduction in a time of deficit spending if the program were viewed as an unfunded expenditure.

Regardless of the proper role of Social Security as insurance or a safety net, the current connection between taxes and benefits is tenuous. For example, Social Security benefits currently enjoy a cost of living adjustment to ensure the value of the payments is consistent with prior contributions. These adjustments are made even though contributions are not invested to earn a return. However, there is nothing to prevent Congress from abolishing the adjustment if it chooses. Congress also has the power to increase or reduce a recipient's benefits even after he retires.

Congress's power over benefits results from a Supreme Court ruling that, despite paying the payroll tax, taxpayers do not have an accrued property right to Social Security benefits. In *Fleming v. Nestor*, Ephram Nestor was not a U.S. citizen and was deported for having been a member of the Communist Party.[26] In that case, there was no dispute that Nestor had paid Society Security taxes for long enough to qualify for benefits, but the Court held that these tax payments did not give him any right to receive benefits. Today, a related political issue arises because many employers and employees pay Social Security taxes on the wages of undocumented workers, notwithstanding these workers' inability to collect benefits unless

---

[26] Fleming v. Nestor, 363 U.S. 603 (1960).

their legal status changes.[27] The Social Security Administration estimates these payments exceed $12 billion per year.[28]

Although recipients' benefits are protected only by politics, Social Security is generally off the chopping block. Because of the system's political popularity, one unintended consequence is that American poverty has been converted from a problem of the elderly to a problem for children.[29] As children are not voters, they are least able to demand benefits, and the political necessity of increasing payroll taxes to pay for Social Security benefits imposes its cost on workers, many of who are raising children. Therefore, not only do most payments go to the elderly, the revenue is often taken from those with dependents.

On the other hand, the elderly could argue that their benefits are not enough given their high costs. Current indexing rules for Social Security benefits increase payments at the same rate as average earnings, hence benefits' cost of living adjustment. However, costs to the elderly rise at a higher rate than the average cost of living because of their increased medical costs. Even with the current payout structure, the elderly are growing relatively poorer.[30]

In addition to these big picture consequences, some structural complaints focus on parts of the Social Security program. For example, the structure of Social Security taxes and the calculation of benefits are arguably unfair for some married couples and to single individuals. Some spouses or divorced spouses (the latter married for more than ten years before the divorce) pay into the system but are not paid out for those contributions and other spouses or former spouses receive benefits without making any contributions to the program. These outcomes occur because spouses are entitled to 50% of their spouse's benefit when that amount is greater than the benefit available based on their own earnings. Coupled with the bracket structure described above, this payout structure results in certain low-income, one-earner married couples receiving total Social Security benefits of 135% of the earner's salary and higher-income two-earner couples receiving benefits of 43% or less of the couples' salaries.[31]

---

[27]   For more on the interaction of immigration and taxation, see Chapter 16.01(b).

[28]   Stephen Goss et al., *Effects of Unauthorized Immigration on the Actuarial Status of the Social Security Trust Funds*, ACTUARIAL NOTE NO. 151 (2013).

[29]   Bernadette Proctor et al., *Income and Poverty in the United States: 2015*, CENSUS BUREAU 13 (2016).

[30]   Gary Engelhardt & Jonathan Gruber, *Social Security and the Evolution of Poverty*, NBER WORKING PAPER 10466 (2004).

[31]   For more on the impact marriage has on the labor supply, see Shinichi Nishiyama, *The Joint Labor Supply Decision of Married Couples and the Social*

Not only is this 50% of a spouse's benefit only possible if a person chooses to marry, some spouses pay into Social Security but their benefits are no greater than if they had made no such payment. This benefit imposes a cost on couples' lower earning spouses (often wives) who find their Social Security payments calculated by their spouse's higher wages. Their take-home income is reduced by the Social Security payroll tax, but they never receive a benefit for paying that tax. This should reduce their reward for working, causing some to remain out of the work force.

Narrow problems are also identified for disability insurance, but these problems are often tied to the qualifications for benefits. Although people find it difficult to lie to the government about their age, a person may find it relatively easier to lie about a disability. This puts the onus on the system to determine whether a disabled person has truly lost the capacity to work. This is a moral hazard problem in that people may prefer these benefits than to work. Evidence shows that a number of factors influence the number of applications for disability benefits, and that in most years application rates vary with unemployment rates.[32] Therefore, as unemployment rates increase, so do applications for disability making it appear susceptible to abuse.

(d) Solvency

Questions of the best and most equitable structure of Social Security benefits are often overwhelmed by concerns whether the system will survive. In other words, people frequently focus on Social Security's solvency rather than its optimal structure. In 2018, 44% of respondents to a Gallup poll personally worried about the Social Security system a great deal.[33] The government has repeatedly stated that the Social Security system is solvent but that it will run a shortfall, most recently estimated to be by 2034.[34] Disability insurance is in a worse financial position. Insolvency was averted in late 2016 only by reallocating revenue from regular Social Security to the SSDI trust funds.[35] Issues of fund solvency do not necessitate reducing benefits but call into question the source of funds for paying

---

Security Pension System, MICH. RETIREMENT RES. CTR. WORKING PAPER WP 2010–229 (2010).

[32]　BUREAU OF LABOR STATISTICS, ANNUAL STATISTICAL SUPPLEMENT TO THE SOCIAL SECURITY BULLETIN, Tables 2.A30, 4.C1, 6.C7 (2005).

[33]　GALLOP, ADULTS NEARING RETIREMENT WORRY MOST ABOUT SOCIAL SECURITY, http://news.gallup.com/poll/232172/adults-nearing-retirement-worry-social -security.aspx (last visited May 1, 2018).

[34]　SOC. SECURITY ADMIN., THE 2017 ANNUAL REPORT OF THE BOARD OF TRUSTEES OF THE FEDERAL OLD-AGE AND SURVIVORS INSURANCE AND FEDERAL DISABILITY INSURANCE TRUST FUNDS (2017).

[35]　Bipartisan Budget Act of 2015, Pub. L. No. 114–74, 129 Stat. 584.

future benefits. The government can fund benefits from general revenues to the extent that it can afford to do so.

Concerns over the program's solvency have existed for many years.[36] In 1970, Social Security was no longer separately reported from the rest of the government budget but included in a "unified budget" until it was taken off again in 1990. At the time, the issue was presented as how to measure the overall economic health of the program and the national budget. In the late 1970s, continuing concern over the long-term financial projections for Social Security prompted Congress to increase Social Security tax rates. Then, in 1984, Congress increased the age to receive full benefits and created the Social Security Trust Funds to hold surplus tax revenue.

One reason for the program's perceived financial crisis is its funding mechanism. In 2015, approximately 169 million people paid Social Security taxes and 60 million people received benefits.[37] The two sides of the program's obligations (revenue and payments) are linked because current year benefits and other expenses are paid from current year Social Security tax revenues. Therefore, the tie is in the current year and not over the life of a particular taxpayer.

Tax revenue in excess of current benefits is deposited in trust funds, both Social Security and Disability Trust Funds. The federal government is permitted to use these deposits as long as it issues to the Trust Funds low-risk, non-marketable U.S. Treasury securities. Therefore, workers stockpile money in the trusts and the government spends from the stockpile rather than borrowing on the public market but must repay the money as it is needed to fund benefits.

The Social Security Trust Fund was thought necessary because the Baby Boom generation is so much larger than later generations. The alternative would have allowed the Baby Boomers' contributions to Social Security to increase payouts for those already retired. Therefore, the money was saved to limit government largess to pre-Baby Boom retirees and to serve as a reminder of their contributions when Baby Boomers need the funds. Under this understanding of the Social Security Trust Fund, it was not intended to be a permanent feature of the Social Security system. Instead, the Trust Fund is at most a temporary feature to provide financial support for funding retirement benefits to the large group of perspective beneficiaries

---

[36] For more on the history of the Social Security Trust Funds, see Sita Nataraj & John Shoven, *Has the Unified Budget Undermined the Federal Government Trust Funds?*, NBER WORKING PAPER NO. 10953 (2004).

[37] For more on the state of the Trust Funds' financial health, see 2016 ANNUAL REPORT OF TRUSTEES OF THE FEDERAL OASDI TRUST FUNDS, H.Doc. No. 115–145, at 2 (2016).

that began to retire in 2011. Therefore, the Trust Fund is intended to phase down to $0.

Requiring the Trust Funds to invest in U.S. Treasury securities has unintended consequences. By purchasing U.S. government debt, the Trust Funds indirectly finance federal spending and become creditors of the federal government. This dynamic can obscure the size of the federal government's spending relative to its revenue and it can obscure the financial health of Social Security. The cumulative amount in the Trust Funds was over $2.8 trillion at the end of 2016 but that the government, rather than a private borrower, will repay the securities may confuse people. In 2016, Social Security expenditures were $922 billion and the Trust Fund's income was $957 billion, of which $88 billion was interest owed by the government on the Trust Fund's bonds. From the perspective of the Trust Fund, the securities are a good asset and the interest is legitimate income no different than if paid by a less financially secure bank.

Because of the deficit of Social Security tax revenue relative to program expenditures, in 2016 at $53 billion, Social Security now relies on the Trust Funds and ultimately on the federal government's payment of interest on Treasury securities to fund benefits. This result was intended when the Trust Funds were created. However, the economic result is that Social Security is now being partially supported by the federal government's general expenditure on interest and principal. Each time the government pays interest or principal on the securities held by the Trust Funds, the payments must be reallocated from other government activities or be financed through public borrowing. This impacts taxpayers rather than the system's beneficiaries.

According to the Trust Fund's trustees, Social Security's costs exceeded its income from taxes in each year since 2010. Using complicated (and, to some, controversially pessimistic) estimates of future demographic, economic, and program-specific conditions, this relationship is projected to continue through 2023 and beyond. The estimates are built on many assumptions. For example, they assume that national economic growth will average 1.8% over the next twenty years, that there will be no increase in immigration, and that there will be no growth in wages.

Although the Trust Funds operate as planned, the trustees also expect to deplete the Trust Funds and be unable to pay full benefits without using general government funds by 2034. This means that the government will not owe the money because of its prior borrowings from the Trust Funds, but too much will be owed from the Social Security system relative to current and prior Social Security taxes. In 2016, the trustees suggested that to keep Social Security self-financing for 75 years (1) revenues would need to be increased through a 2.58% increase in payroll taxes to 14.98% (in addition to the 2.9% for Medicare); (2) scheduled benefits would need a 16% reduction for all, including current recipients, or 19% if only for those eligible in 2016 and later; or (3) some combination of the two.[38] The political reality is that cutting benefits is unlikely because the elderly compose a well-organized and well-financed interest group that has proven itself capable of protecting their current benefits, if not always winning increased benefits.

Social Security's need for general government funds will arise, in part, because people are living longer today than people did in 1932 when the system was created. The benefit system could be altered to respond to this change but that would be perceived as a decrease in benefits. Lives are longer for purposes of Social Security benefits in two ways. First, people at age 65 expect to live a number of years longer than people reaching 65 in 1932 would. This increase in longevity increases the length of time each retiree will receive benefits. For example, men attaining age 65 in 2015 expected to live for 18 years compared to 12.7 years for men attaining age 65 back in 1940.[39]

The bigger issue is that the number of people, both absolutely and as a percentage of the population, who live to age 65 has increased dramatically since 1932. For example, in 1940 less than 54% of the men who reached adulthood expected to reach 65, whereas in 1990 over 72% would. Likewise, the number of people over age 65 in the U.S. has increased from 9.0 million, or 6.8% of the population, in 1940 to 40.3 million, or 13% of the population, in 2010.

If people are retiring at the same age but living longer, they will spend a larger proportion of their lives in retirement. These retirees will either have to save more for retirement privately or through increased Social Security taxes, accept having lower incomes in retirement, or receive more redistributed wealth from future generations.

A second concern about the long-term viability of Social Security arises from the declining number of workers that support retirees. In 1940, there were more than 159 workers for each beneficiary; by 2013 there were only 2.8 workers.[40] However, if workers' wages rise

---

[38]   *Id.*, at 5.

[39]   CTR FOR DISEASE CONTROL, LIFE EXPECTANCY AT BIRTH, Table 15 (2016); SOC. SEC. ADMIN, LIFE EXPECTANCY FOR SOCIAL SECURITY, https://ssa.gov/history/life expect.html (last visited Sept. 27, 2017).

[40]   Soc. Security Admin., Ratio of Covered Workers to Beneficiaries, https://www. ssa.gov/history/ratios.html (last visited Sept. 27, 2017).

sufficiently more than inflation, the system can support a reduced number of workers. With increased productivity, each worker performs more valuable work and his wages increase accordingly. So long as workers' wages stay below the inflation-adjusted $128,400 cap, increasing workers' wages also increase the Social Security taxes they pay and, therefore, the revenue the Social Security system receives. Moreover, because of the progressive payout structure, the system is financially better off with one worker earning $100,000 than with four workers earning $25,000. More tax revenue is received from the one worker with a smaller percentage paid out on her retirement.

(e) Privatization

Concerns about the Social Security system's long-term viability and the Trust Fund's long-term solvency have prompted proposals to privatize Social Security.[41] There have been many different proposals, most of which are not detailed enough to be meaningfully evaluated. In general, privatization proposals would permit workers to invest a required amount of savings within a group of designated assets that are expected to provide greater returns than Treasury securities but still remain relatively low-risk. Plans generally do not permit workers to invest in whatever they choose from a paternalistic concern that workers would lose their money in risky investments and be left with nothing for retirement.

The hope is that privatization would provide retirees a larger return than the current cost of living adjustment and also provide capital to businesses instead of being invested in Treasury securities. However, there is no guarantee these positive results would occur. For example, while Chile's pension privatization resulted in significant short-term economic growth, it has since been criticized for low returns; and the United Kingdom's privatization resulted in a $20 billion payout to citizens who were defrauded by investment advisors.[42]

The risks of privatization are well documented, and they can only be partially mitigated through planning. Among the potential risks, privatization increases the risk a retiree will not have enough money over the course of retirement. Today, the risk lies entirely with the federal government. The federal government could default on its

---

[41]　For example, Ryan Sager, *Time to Privatize Social Security*, CATO INSTITUTE (1998).

[42]　Michael Hiltzik, *Chile's Privatized Social Security System, Beloved by U.S. Conservatives, Is Falling Apart*, LA TIMES, Aug. 12, 2016; 49 INT'L STUDIES Q. 273 (2005); Elizabeth Tedrow, *Social Security Privatization in* Sarah Brooks, *Interdependent and Domestic Foundations of Policy Change, Other Countries*, 14 ELDER L.J. 35 (2006).

securities, lack the funds to pay benefits, or change the benefit structure. In a private system, the risk is in the issuers of the securities in each retiree's portfolio. Some of these investments may turn out to be a total loss, and many others may generate returns no better than the interest on Treasury securities. Even though the U.S. markets have historically risen over the long-term, during the 2008 financial crisis the Dow Jones Industrial average fell by 33.8%, the S&P 500 dropped by 38.5%, and the NASDAQ fell 40.5%.[43] Under a privatized system, a person who retires during one of these periodic downturns in the market may have little for retirement, and in some cases he may not have sufficient income for life.

Moreover, there is only so much total growth in investments that investors can realize. Market returns are unable to grow at a greater rate than the economy, so there is a cap on the returns investors as a group can make, although the cap can grow with the economy. How the growth is divided among investors is impossible to predict with privatization whereas it is allocated according to the payout structure with Social Security. Privatization of Social Security and the individual investment choices that come with it is likely to result in payouts being widely varied among recipients and significantly less progressive than under today's program.

Furthermore, private managers will likely charge higher administrative fees than the government requires, which means that private investments will need to outperform Treasury securities to provide the same amount of income for retirees. Today the administration of Social Security is relatively inexpensive, at 0.7% of the program's budget; disability is higher at 1.9%.[44] Comparatively, private managers average more than 1% a year on the value of the money they hold.[45] Therefore, a risk-averse retiree who invests in nothing but Treasury bonds will receive a lower effective return than the Trust Funds do on the same investment.

A second risk of privatization occurs in the transition to this type of program. The transition to a private program could result in significant federal liquidity problems and excessive short-term investment in retirement. First, current workers would fund their own private retirement accounts. Second, the government would need to disperse money accrued to workers to their private accounts or continue to pay Social Security benefits. This government

---

[43] Alexandria Twin, *Wall Street: Bring on '09*, CNN MONEY, Dec. 31, 2008.

[44] SOC. SECURITY ADMIN., SOCIAL SECURITY ADMINISTRATIVE EXPENSES, https://www.ssa.gov/oact/STATS/admin.html (last visited Sept. 27, 2017).

[45] Advisory HQ, Average Financial Advisor Income Per Client, http://www.advisoryhq.com/articles/financial-advisor-fees-wealth-managers-planners-and-fee-only-advisors/#Average-Advisor-Income-Per-Client (last visited Sept. 27, 2017).

obligation would exist despite the government not receiving new Social Security tax revenue.

Therefore, a transition requires the government to find a new revenue source until all of the accrued benefits have been paid. Congress could divert money from other expenditures, raise non-retirement taxes, or borrow to finance this burden. If the money were currently distributed to beneficiaries, twice the amount of money would go into the retirement system as long as there are accrued benefits. This obligation poses a risk to the federal budget, and it is uncertain whether sufficient investments with reasonable returns are currently available to absorb all this retirement capital.

Finally, privatization of Social Security risks its progressive payout structure and might result in poverty for many of the nation's elderly. Under the current system, lower-income workers receive a disproportionately large amount of future payments because the determination of payments is not proportional to the taxes paid. Because privatization creates a property interest in what is purchased with the taxes paid, under most proposals higher-income workers would have a property interest in this forced savings that they currently do not have. The result would reduce provision for lower-income workers that is currently hidden through Social Security's progressive calculation of benefits.

§ 10.03   Medicare Taxes

Medicare was enacted in 1965 to provide health care for the elderly.[46] Generally, persons 65 years of age or older who have been legal residents of the U.S. for at least five years are eligible for Medicare. Younger persons with disabilities or certain other medical conditions may also be eligible. Medicare has four parts. Part A covers hospital insurance, inpatient care, skilled nursing facility care, home health care, and hospice care; it is this portion that is paid for with the payroll tax. Part B provides medical insurance. Part C provides a public supplement option, popularly branded Medicare Advantage. Part D is for prescription drugs. In 2016, Part A cost $285.4 billion, but payroll taxes and fees raised $290.8 billion; and Parts B and D cost $389 billion but brought in $419.4 billion.[47] In 2016, about 37% of Medicare was funded with payroll taxes. What is not paid for with payroll taxes and fees is paid from general government revenue.

---

[46]   Social Security Amendments of 1965, Pub. L. 89–97, 79 Stat. 286.

[47]   2017 ANNUAL REPORT OF BOARDS OF TRUSTEES OF THE FEDERAL HOSPITAL INSURANCE AND FEDERAL SUPPLEMENTARY MEDICAL INSURANCE TRUST FUNDS 10 (2017) [hereinafter HI ANNUAL REPORT].

There are funding concerns with Medicare, as Part A's Trust Fund is expected to be depleted by 2029. Expenditures for Part A have exceeded income since 2008. One reason is that Medicare's enabling statute does not permit administrators to consider the cost of medical care when evaluating particular treatments.[48] This adds budgetary pressure when medical technology is both effective and expensive. To fund Part A, FICA requires each employee and employer to pay taxes of 1.45% of all wages earned. A wage cap equal to that for Social Security was eliminated in 1993, so that Medicare's total 2.9% is applied to 100% of wages in order to help balance Medicare's budget. In 2013, as part of the Patient Protection and Affordable Care Act, an additional employment tax of 0.9% was added for individuals earning more than $200,000 and for married couples earning more than $250,000.[49] Therefore, Medicare taxes are less forced savings than a source of funding for a social safety net.

More than $70 billion is paid to doctors each year for treating Medicare patients, and the fees paid for particular services are based on advice from the American Medical Association.[50] Medicare pays out according to a fee schedule and sets rates based on an estimate of the relative value of services. Prices take into account the amount of time a doctor is expected to spend and the amount of mental and physical efforts and skill required to perform the service compared to other services.

Additionally, more than 55 million people are covered by Medicare, and Medicare expenses constitute over 15% of the federal budget.[51] Medicare paid for 20% of total national health spending in 2016. In the aggregate and per capita, the growth in Medicare spending has slowed to about 3.6%, less than its historical average annual growth rate of 7.5%.[52] Growth in spending is not expected to stay this low in the near future, despite the Patient Protection and Affordable Care Act seeking to reduce costs, increase revenues, and combat fraud and abuse. Although total expenditures in 2016 were $679 billion, they are expected to increase faster than aggregate workers' earnings or the economy. As a percentage of GDP, Medicare

---

[48] Jacqueline Fox, *Medicare Should, But Cannot, Consider Cost*, 53 BUFF. L. REV. 577 (2005).

[49] I.R.C. § 3101(b)(2). Congress also enacted a 3.8% surtax on unearned net investment income, such as investments in stocks, to help fund Medicare. I.R.C. § 1411.

[50] U.S. GOV'T ACCOUNTABILITY OFFICE, GAO-15-434, MEDICARE PHYSICIAN PAYMENT RATES (2015).

[51] OFFICE OF MGMT. & BUDGET, HISTORICAL TABLES, Table 3.1; HI ANNUAL REPORT, *supra* note 47, at 7.

[52] HI Annual Report, *supra* note 47, at 180.

expenditures are estimated to account for between 6% and 9.1% by 2090.

Although funded by the federal government, in part with payroll taxes, Medicare is administered through private insurance companies. In other words, some companies have arrangements with the government to insure qualified recipients. Like other private insurance, Medicare often does not pay for all of a beneficiary's covered medical costs, and many medical costs are not covered at all. According to the Kaiser Family Foundation, Medicare covers on average about half of the health care costs of its enrollees.[53] Also like other private insurance, program premiums, deductibles, and coinsurance can differ substantially. One difficulty for those covered by Medicare is choosing the best policy for their future (perhaps unpredictable) medical needs.

Medicare should not be confused with Medicaid, which is the largest source of funding for health-related services for low-income citizens and legal residents. Medicaid is not paid for out of payroll taxes but is funded using federal and state general funds. Medicaid is a means-tested program funded in cooperation between states and the federal government, with states tasked with determining eligibility.[54] Over 75% of Medicaid recipients use managed care programs that are private health plans, the other 25% use fee for service programs.[55] Including the federal match, Medicaid composes an average of 19.7% of states' budgets.[56]

The Patient Protection and Affordable Care Act extended Medicaid coverage to a larger group of people, raising the maximum income for eligibility to 138% of the poverty line.[57] For 2018, this means coverage is available for a single person at $16,642 or for a family of three at $28,179. Eighteen states have not adopted Medicaid expansions and, of those, seventeen have no eligibility for Medicaid for those without children.[58] The Supreme Court held in *National Federation of Independent Business v. Sebelius* that states choosing not to adopt the congressional increase in Medicaid coverage

---

[53] Juliette Cubaski et al., *How Much Is Enough? Out-of-Pocket Spending Among Medicare Beneficiaries,* KAISER FAMILY FOUNDATION (2014).

[54] Social Security Amendments of 1965, Pub. L. 89–97, 79 Stat. 286.

[55] CTR FOR MEDICARE AND MEDICAID SERVICES, MEDICAID MANAGED CARE ENROLLMENT AND PROGRAM CHARACTERISTICS, 2014, at 17 (2016).

[56] MACPAC, MEDICAID'S SHARE OF STATE BUDGETS, https://www.macpac.gov/subtopic/medicaids-share-of-state-budgets/ (last visited Feb. 17, 2019).

[57] Although the Affordable Care Act states the threshold is 133% of the poverty line, the AGI is modified by adding 5%. I.R.C. § 2002(a)(1)(14)(*l*)(i).

[58] Kaiser Family Foundation, *State of State Action on the Medicaid Expansion Decision* (last visited Feb. 17, 2018).

do not lose their previously established levels of federal Medicaid funding.[59]

Annual Medicaid expenditures per person are large, particularly for the elderly. In 2014, the average cost of Medicaid per enrolled person was $5,736, but the cost per senior (in addition to Medicare) was $13,063.[60] For the elderly who anticipate significant medical costs, such as long-term managed care, there is a financial incentive to qualify for Medicaid to help defray these costs. To satisfy Medicaid's means-based requirements, some people have given their valuables to family members to preserve the value in the family while also qualifying for Medicaid. In response, Congress enacted a complicated 5-year claw back of gifts from people who become eligible for Medicaid.[61] In other words, the government can take back the gift and use it to reimburse expenses covered by Medicaid. The argument is that people should use their own assets to cover their medical expenses before relying on assistance intended for the poor.

Medicare (and more so Medicaid) is plagued by complaints that people game the system, although less often so than with disability insurance. Medicare and Medicaid face claims of moral hazard, which means that people make choices likely to increase the cost of their health care because they do not bear the full brunt of those costs. Smoking and driving a motorcycle without a helmet are often given as examples. However, there is conflicting evidence whether medical coverage affects these choices.[62] It is more likely that people who are covered choose more costly medical care than they otherwise would.

§ 10.04 Unemployment Taxes

FUTA is intended to cover the federal government's share of the cost of state-administered unemployment insurance and job service programs.[63] Additionally, FUTA pays 50% of the cost of extended unemployment benefits during periods of high unemployment. Under state-specific unemployment insurance, eligible unemployed workers are generally entitled to 40% to 50% of their previous pay for six months as long as they have become unemployed through no fault of their own. For a short period starting in 2010, Congress extended benefits for workers who had exhausted their benefits to 99 weeks of

---

[59] 567 U.S. 519 (2012).

[60] Kaiser Family Foundation, Medicaid Spending Per Enrollee, http://kff.org/medicaid/state-indicator/medicaid-spending-per-enrollee/ (last visited Feb. 17, 2018).

[61] Deficit Reduction Act of 2005, Pub. L. 109–171, 120 Stat. 4.

[62] Dhaval Dave & Robert Kaestner, *Health Insurance and Ex Ante Moral Hazard*, NBER WORKING PAPER 12764 (2006).

[63] For more on the workings of federal unemployment insurance, see Wayne Vroman & Stephen Woodbury, *Financing Unemployment Insurance*, 67 NAT'L TAX J. 253 (2014).

coverage, but states have since reduced the standard period to 26 weeks.[64] Unemployment benefits are subject to the income tax.[65]

The payroll tax to fund these benefits is paid by employers and calculated as a 6.0% tax on the first $7,000 of gross earnings per worker per year.[66] The total possible tax is $420 per employee. Although a small tax, it can raise a significant amount of revenue. For example, in 2016 Ohio had over 5.3 million workers covered; this means Ohio could collect up to $2.2 billion in revenue.[67] The amount paid to each unemployed worker varies with former salary and the number of dependents. In Ohio, an unemployed person could receive from $128 to a possible $598 for those earning $1,196 per week or more with three or more dependents.[68]

If a state meets all of its unemployment obligations to its unemployed, a state's employers may be entitled to a credit of up to 5.4% of the tax.[69] The credit reduces the rate of tax on employers, possibly to only $42 per employee. This reduces the amount of revenue that is raised on the theory that it is not needed. Thus, states with low unemployment are likely to have a lower FUTA tax rate.

On the other hand, if states are unable to cover their unemployment insurance obligations to the unemployed, states can borrow from the Federal Unemployment Account (FUA) to make their payments. If a state has an advance from the FUA that remains unpaid for two years, the state's credit against the unemployment tax is reduced. This costs employers the credit who end up paying more in tax. For example, in 2017, California and the Virgin Islands each lost 2.1% of their credit, requiring employers pay more of the full statutory FUTA rates for the year.[70]

There are debates regarding the effect of unemployment insurance, in particular whether it creates a moral hazard in the same way claimed for disability insurance and health insurance. The concern is that the insurance might encourage unemployment and discourage unemployed workers from finding and taking jobs. One economist claimed unemployment benefits raise the unemployment

---

[64] American Recovery and Reinvestment Act, Pub. L. 111–5, 123 Stat. 115 (2009).

[65] I.R.C. § 85.

[66] I.R.C. § 3301, § 3306.

[67] Ohio Dept. of Job & Family Services, *Quarterly Census of Employment and Wages*, https://data.bls.gov/cew/apps/table_maker/v4/table_maker.htm#type=0&year =2016&qtr=A&own=0&ind=10&supp=1 (last visited Feb. 17, 2018).

[68] OHIO DEPT. OF JOB & FAMILY SERVICES, OHIO UNEMPLOYMENT COMPENSATION BENEFITS CHART—2018 (2018).

[69] I.R.C. § 3302.

[70] U.S. DEPT. OF LABOR, HISTORICAL FUTA CREDIT REDUCTIONS, https://oui. doleta.gov/unemploy/futa_credit.asp (last visited Feb. 17, 2018).

rate 2%.[71] On the other hand, another economist claimed that the "vast majority" of the unemployed were without jobs because of "demand shocks" for goods and services, which reduce the need for workers and are outside workers' control.[72]

Government-provided unemployment insurance also protects against adverse selection: The workers with the highest probability of unemployment have the highest demand for unemployment insurance. As a result of adverse selection, reasonably priced private insurance is unlikely to emerge absent government intervention. Therefore, the lack of a private market arguably exists because of a market failure and, according to that theory, the government should step in to fill the void.

§ 10.05   Withholding

Federal and state withholding is used to pay estimated income and payroll taxes as wages are earned. In essence, withholding is a prepayment of taxes that are ultimately calculated on an annual basis. Amounts withheld are later credited on employees' tax returns, and overpayments are refundable. Accordingly, the amount withheld from paychecks is merely an estimate and does not necessarily match the taxes that will later be owed when the annual return is prepared.

For employees, withholding is required, and the computation of the amount to be withheld is based on representations made by the employee on Form W-4.[73] People sign their W-4s under penalties for perjury, so falsely claiming exemptions is punishable. Thereafter, employers must remit payments to the government either every month or every two weeks. Employers must also file quarterly reports with each applicable state and at the federal level. Technically, self-employed workers are not subject to withholding because they have no employers. However, the self-employed must file quarterly returns and make estimated payments of the tax that will later be due.[74] Too small estimated payments may result in penalties.

The penalty for failing to make appropriate withholding and proper payment of payroll taxes is high. For employees, the result of

---

[71]   Robert Barro, *The Folly of Subsidizing Unemployment*, WALL ST. J., Aug. 30, 2010.

[72]   Jesse Rothstein, *Unemployment Insurance and Job Search in the Great Recession*, NBER WORKING PAPER No. 17534, Oct. 2011.

[73]   I.R.C. § 31. For more on withholding obligations, see IRS, Employer and Employee Responsibilities, Employment Tax Enforcement, https://www.irs.gov/uac/employer-and-employee-responsibilities-employment-tax-enforcement (last visited Sept. 27, 2017).

[74]   For more on self-employed obligations, see IRS, SELF-EMPLOYED INDIVIDUALS TAX CENTER, https://www.irs.gov/businesses/small-businesses-self-employed/self-employed-individuals-tax-center (last visited Sept. 27, 2017).

under-withholding is often the underpayment of taxes.[75] If an employer does not pay federal payroll taxes as they become due, the employer faces a penalty ranging from 2% to 10% at the federal level, and penalties also apply at the state and local levels.[76] Additionally, employers face a penalty of up to 100% of the amount actually withheld from employees that is not paid over to the IRS. This employer penalty can be assessed against the employer entity as well as any persons having control or custody of the funds that should have been paid over to the government. This latter penalty means that the limited liability normally enjoyed by owners of corporations or LLCs does not shield those with control over withheld funds.

There has historically been debate about the usefulness and value of withholding.[77] Withholding was introduced during World War II in response to the concern that as more people became subject to the income tax, a system had to be implemented to ensure regular payment. A concern was that workers would fail to save to pay their taxes at the end of the year. Withholding does improve payment rates as withheld income has a 98% compliance rate.[78] Withholding also accelerates payments to the government, increasing the amount that the government can spend in the short term. This also evens out payments over the course of the year so that the government has less need to borrow to meet short-term spending obligations.

On the other hand, not only is withholding equivalent to an interest free loan to the government, withholding may prevent workers from being fully cognizant of their tax burdens. By eliminating the physical requirement of paying taxes, withholding reduces the salience of the tax. This is evidenced by the economically irrational desire 58% have to receive a refund.[79] A refund due to withholding is truly a return of the taxpayer's earnings. More than Social Security or Medicare, withholding operates as forced savings.

§ 10.06   Employee Versus Independent Contractor

Employees pay 50% of payroll taxes and employers pay the other 50%; self-employed workers pay an equivalent of both parts through a self-employment tax. This makes the distinction between employees and independent contractors important because the latter are self-employed for tax purposes. If no one makes required payroll

---

[75]   For more on underpayment penalties, see Chapter 2.02(b).

[76]   I.R.C. § 6672; I.R.C. § 7202.

[77]   *See* Leandra Lederman, *Statutory Speed Bumps: The Roles Third Parties Play In Tax Compliance*, 60 STAN. L. REV. 695 (2007).

[78]   For more on compliance rates, see Chapter 2.03.

[79]   Kit Yarrow, *Why We're So Irrational When It Comes to Tax Refunds*, TIME, Mar. 18, 2013.

tax payments, penalties accrue, but who is liable for the tax and penalties depends on the affected worker's status as either an employee or an independent contractor. The worker's status is determined based on all the facts and circumstances only after the taxes are due. A 2000 study by the Department of Labor found that between 10% and 30% of employers misclassify employees as independent contractors at a cost of $1.6 billion in tax revenues; the cost was updated to $2.72 billion for 2006.[80]

The distinction between an employee and independent contractor is hard to police. Employers are the ones who often decide the status and, in practice, their choices receive little scrutiny from the IRS.[81] Congress prevents the IRS from reclassifying workers or from collecting back taxes from an employer who misclassifies employees as independent contractors if (1) the classification follows judicial precedent or IRS rulings; (2) the classification is based on long-standing industry practice; or (3) the employer was audited in the past without being assessed for the misclassification even if the issue did not arise in the audit.[82]

The choice of label is often made at least partially for non-tax reasons. Employers often prefer to categorize workers as independent contractors because independent contractors are typically not entitled to costly employee benefits, such as health insurance. And all other things being equal, workers prefer to be employees in order to qualify for these benefits. Because of these competing incentives, the parties could be expected to negotiate over proper classification. However, workers are often the weaker party in the negotiation so that the employer's choice might dominate even if it does not reflect the economic reality.

Therefore, the determination of a worker's status for tax purposes is based on the facts and circumstances of the relationship. Workers who provide services and can control their hours, wages, supply of tools, or other work conditions are likely (although not certainly) to be independent contractors. Conversely, workers who have little to no control over their hours, wages, or work conditions are likely to be employees.

---

[80] LALITH DE SILVA ET AL., INDEPENDENT CONTRACTORS: PREVALENCE AND IMPLICATIONS FOR UNEMPLOYMENT INSURANCE PROGRAMS, Prepared for the U.S. Department of Labor Employment and Training Administration (2000); GOV'T ACCOUNTABILITY OFFICE, GAO–09–717, EMPLOYEE MISCLASSIFICATION (2009).

[81] U.S. Dept. of Labor, Contingent Workers, COMMISSION ON THE FUTURE OF WORKER-MANAGEMENT RELATIONS (1994).

[82] Revenue Act of 1978, § 530, Pub. L. 95–600, 92 Stat. 2763.

As seen by debate over the classification of Uber drivers, the importance of this classification is unlikely to subside.[83] Businesses are likely to continue to use, or even increase their use of, independent contractors. A Government Accountability Office report concluded that 40.4% of the 2010 labor force has alternative work arrangements, with 12.9% of the workforce being independent contractors.[84] The largest sector of these workers was in clerical or office work followed by industrial work. An Oxford Economics project showed that 83% of those executives who were questioned felt that companies are increasingly using contingent workers, in part because of their lower cost.[85] Notwithstanding employers' recognition of their cost savings, although 18.8% of independent contractors had a family income of less than $20,000, only 9.4% said they would prefer a different type of employment.[86]

---

[83]   Uber settled two class action lawsuits for as much as $100 million to permit its classification as independent contractors rather than employees. Mike Isaac & Noam Scheiber, *Uber Settles Cases with Concessions, but Drivers Stay Freelancers*, N.Y. TIMES, Apr. 21, 2016.

[84]   GOV'T ACCOUNTABILITY OFFICE, GAO–15–168R, CONTINENT WORKFORCE (2015).

[85]   Oxford Economics, *The Contingent Workforce*, *in* WORKFORCE 2020: THE LOOMING TALENT CRISIS (2014).

[86]   GOV'T ACCOUNTABILITY OFFICE, *supra* note 85.

Chapter 11

TAXATION OF BUSINESSES

Table of Sections

The tax system recognizes the importance of business to the nation, and the Internal Revenue Code contains numerous provisions intended to encourage or facilitate business endeavors. Nevertheless, there are limits on these favorable provisions, often responding to the perception of taxpayer abuse. The result is a veritable maze for businesses, but one whose complexity depends upon the taxpayer's desire for tax reduction. Business taxes are most complex for those seeking to maximize their tax reduction.

A key concept underlying the taxation of business is the phrase "trade or business."[1] The phrase is a term of art that generally includes selling goods or performing services for a livelihood or to make a profit. That does not mean the business must actually provide one's livelihood or a profit; there only needs to be a good faith effort to do so. The taxpayer's intent and the regularity of the activity are important elements that distinguish a business from a hobby or an investment.[2]

§ 11.01 Business Structure

Business income is generally taxable. The type of entity the business uses determines who owes the tax. Some entities, including sole proprietorships, partnerships, and S corporations, have their business income taxed directly to the business's owners. For traditional corporations, the entity itself is taxed on its income. Tax rates and tax-planning opportunities may differ depending on the

---

[1]   For example, see I.R.C. §§ 62, 162, 163(h)(2), 164.

[2]   Hobbies have less favorable treatment of losses and expenses. I.R.C. § 183. Investments also have limited deductibility of expenses. I.R.C. § 67; 212.

entity type. This makes the choice of business entity one of the most important tax decisions a businessperson makes. Nevertheless, the proper selection from the menu of entities created by state law depends on many factors, only some of which are tax considerations.

(a) Sole Proprietorships and Disregarded Entities

A sole proprietorship is a business owned and controlled by a single individual. That individual is liable for all of the business's debts, including the business's tax liabilities. As far as the tax system is concerned, the business and the person are one and the same.[3] The owner includes the business's income and deductions on Schedule C of her personal federal income tax return. Therefore, the business's net income is taxed at individual income tax rates, although potentially with a new deduction discussed in Chapter 11.01(e). Because the tax system ignores most distinctions between the person and the business, there are generally no tax consequences when the owner contributes money to the business or receives distributions of the business's earnings.

A disregarded entity shares many characteristics with a sole proprietorship. To be disregarded, a single member LLC must not elect to be taxed as a corporation.[4] The tax effect of being disregarded is simply that—the entity is ignored. The owner is taxed on the business's income. Individuals, pass-through businesses, and corporations can own disregarded entities, the latter as subsidiaries. The objective of creating a disregarded entity is often to limit liability or for other business planning opportunities.

(b) Corporations

A corporation is a legal entity formed under state corporate law. Management of a corporation is vested in a board of directors, and the owners of the corporation (its shareholders) do not participate directly in the management of the corporation unless they are also directors. Generally neither management nor shareholders are liable for a corporation's debts. There are two primary types of corporations for tax purposes: corporations governed by subchapter C of the Internal Revenue Code are traditional corporations and corporations governed by subchapter S are called S corporations. There are also special corporate entities for tax purposes, such as banks and insurance companies, that are governed by special tax rules.

---

[3]   Treas. Reg. § 301.7701–2(a).

[4]   Treas. Reg. § 301.7701–3(b)(1).

(i) C Corporations

A C corporation is governed by subchapter C and is a separate entity from its owner(s) for tax purposes. This means that a C corporation files its own tax return and pays its own taxes. Because of the separation between owner and business, there is double taxation of corporate income.[5] First, corporations are taxed on their earnings and on any appreciation on the sale of their assets; and, second, shareholders are taxed on most distributions they receive from the corporation and on any appreciation in the stock's value when shareholders sell their stock.

The corporate-level income tax is an excise tax on the privilege of doing business in corporate form. Until 2018, the statutory corporate income tax was mildly progressive but, as of 2018, is a flat tax at 21%.[6] Unlike the 2017 changes to individual tax rates, this rate change was structured as a permanent change, partly because a permanent corporate rate cut was less expensive than a permanent individual rate cut. The temporary change to individual tax rates cost $1.2 trillion whereas the permanent change to corporate tax rate cost $1.3 trillion.[7] In addition, it is often politically difficult to win corporate tax rate reduction, so politicians might have preferred to make this change permanent for fear of renewal debates in eight years.

Until the 2018 change, the top marginal corporate income tax rate had been static for the prior two decades. A 1% corporate income tax was enacted in 1909, four years before the individual income tax, and by 1986 the top marginal corporate rate had crossed 50%, largely in response to the Cold War and wartime revenue need.[8] Since 1986, the top marginal corporate income tax rate was 34%/35%, until replaced by a 21% tax in 2018.

---

[5]　For more on double taxation, see Chapter 11.01(d).

[6]　I.R.C. § 11. Corporate tax rates are progressive from 15% to 35% but an addition to tax eliminates the lower rates for high-income corporations.

[7]　For a breakdown of the cost of tax provisions, see Joint Ctte on Tax'n, Estimated Budget Effects of the Conference Agreement for H.R. 1, JCX–67–17 (2017).

[8]　For the history of the corporate income tax, see STEVEN BANK, FROM SWORD TO SHIELD: THE TRANSFORMATION OF THE CORPORATE INCOME TAX, 1861 TO PRESENT (2010); Marjorie Kornhauser, Corporate Regulation and the Origins of the Corporate Income Tax, 66 IND. L.J. 53 (1990).

Top Corporate Income Tax Rate

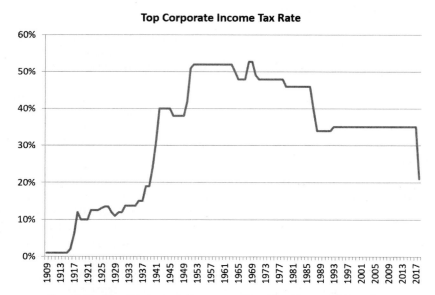

Tax Pol'y Ctr, Historical Corporate Top Tax Rate and Bracket:
1909–2016 (2017).

The second part of the double tax is the taxation of the shareholder on the shareholder's share of corporate earnings. This taxation is deferred until the shareholder receives distributions from the corporation or sells shares in the corporation. At that time, the shareholder is likely to enjoy favorable taxation of the dividends or any gains on the stock.[9] Since 2003, Congress taxes some dividends at favorable capital gain rates of 0%, 15%, or 20%, through a formula that generally ensures the rate is less than the taxpayer's ordinary income tax rate. However, a dividend on stock that has been recently acquired or of a corporation that has moved overseas is still taxed at ordinary income rates. In 2015, the individual income tax on dividends could have raised no more than $143 billion, and likely less because of the progressive rates.[10]

The tax cut enacted in 2017 was only at the corporate level. Much of the political argument for the corporate level rate reduction was in response to the perceived disadvantage the previous top 35% tax rate imposed on American businesses. For example, according to the conservative Tax Foundation, the U.S.'s statutory rate was the

---

[9]   I.R.C. § 1(h). For more on capital gains, see Chapter 7.03.

[10]   In 2015, there were $260 billion ordinary dividends, taxable at a highest 39.6% rate, and $203 billion qualified dividends, taxable at a highest 20% rate. IRS, SOI Tax Stats, PUBLICATION 1304, at 20 (2015).

highest rate in the OECD.[11] This was partially misleading. The combined rate used in its study was the top statutory rate of national plus state income taxes, ignoring the deductibility of the latter from the former. Additionally, the U.S. system contains a greater number of exclusions, deductions, and credits than most other countries, which reduces the income that is subject to tax.[12] The result is a significantly lower average tax rate than the corporate income tax's statutory rate.

However, because corporate tax preferences are not evenly distributed across all corporations, the average, or effective, tax rate that applies to corporate income as a whole varies widely depending upon the type of business. For example, AT&T's effective tax rate is 6%; Kroger's, a grocery store chain, is 23%.[13] The Congressional Research Service estimated that the overall U.S. effective corporate tax rate was 27.1%, which was slightly lower than our national competitors.[14] Despite relative stability in U.S. statutory rates until 2018, effective rates have declined over the past 25 years.[15]

Notwithstanding declining rates, over the last decade, the corporate income tax has raised between 9% and 13% of federal tax revenues. In 2017, the corporate income tax yielded approximately $297 billion, down from $343 billion in 2015.[16] The corporate income tax yields relatively little compared to the individual income tax, which yielded between 41% and 47% of federal revenue throughout the decade. However, the difference is the result of congressional politics rather than the limits of the tax's capacity. Before 1941, the corporate income tax produced more revenue than the individual income tax and, before 1968, raised more than payroll taxes (the latter recently tending between 33% and 40% of federal revenue). Corporate taxes have been reduced as other taxes have been raised.

Differences between corporate and individual income tax rates have sometimes encouraged, and other times discouraged, use of the corporate form. At times the corporate tax rate has been higher and other times lower than the individual income tax rate, often without Congress commenting on the disparity as it changes one or the other's rates. There is also no connection between a corporation's tax

---

[11]   Kyle Pomerlaeau & Andrew Lundeen, *The U.S. Has the Highest Corporate Income Tax Rate in the OECD*, TAX FOUNDATION (2014).

[12]   JANE GRAVELLE, CONG. RESEARCH SERV., R41743, INTERNATIONAL CORPORATE TAX RATES COMPARISONS AND POLICY IMPLICATIONS (2014); George Yin, *How Much Tax Do Large Public Corporations Pay?*, 89 VA. L. REV. 1793 (2003).

[13]   David Johnson, *Is Your Tax Rate Right Than Walmart's?*, TIME, Apr. 15, 2015.

[14]   GRAVELLE, *supra* note 11, at 4.

[15]   Scott Dyreng et al., *Changes in Corporate Effective Tax Rates over the Past 25 Years*, 124 J. FIN. ECON. 441 (2017).

[16]   Office Mgmt. & Budget, *Historical Tables*, Table 2.1 (2018).

rate and the tax rates of its shareholders. There can be low-tax shareholders of a high-tax corporation or high-tax shareholders of a low-tax corporation. This lack of connection in rates can create incentives to shift money into and out of corporations.

The recent reduction in the corporate income tax rate is likely to cause some corporations to retain earnings in corporations so their shareholders can avoid the shareholder level tax, but those retained earnings may be subject to an accumulated earnings tax or the personal holding company tax.[17] Originally enacted to dissuade shareholders from retaining corporate earnings in a lower-taxed entity and selling their shares for capital gains, Congress imposed a 20% tax on retained earnings that are deemed to exceed the corporation's ordinary and reasonable business needs. Additionally, the personal holding company tax is a 20% penalty on undistributed passive income if more than 50% of the value of a corporation's outstanding stock is held by five or fewer individuals and the corporation receives at least 60% of its income from passive sources. These taxes are in addition to the regular corporate income tax. When either of these other taxes applies, the effect is to force corporations to distribute earnings to be taxed to shareholders instead of letting the earnings grow after only the lower corporate income tax.

(ii) S Corporations

Not all corporations are subject to double taxation. Congress enacted subchapter S in 1958 to provide a single layer of taxation for businesses with limited liability. In order to be taxed as an S corporation, an entity must start as a corporation subject to double taxation and file an election for S corporation status.[18] Subchapter S was enacted before states created the limited liability company (LLC), which can accomplish many of the same goals with taxation as a partnership. However, subchapter S provides for taxation similar, but not identical, to partnerships, with simplified rules that restrain shareholder activities. Thus, S corporations have no double taxation but less flexibility than do partnerships. S corporations are popular business entities, in large part because of how relatively easy they are to operate. In 2013, more than 72% of corporations filed their tax returns as S corporations.[19]

---

[17]   I.R.C. § 531; § 542.

[18]   An LLC can elect to be an S corporation but, in the process, elects double taxation if it ever fails to satisfy the S corporation requirements. Treas. Reg. § 301.7701–3(c)(1)(v)(C).

[19]   SOI Tax Stats—Integrated Business Data, Table 1, https://www.irs.gov/statistics/soi-tax-stats-integrated-business-data (last visited Feb. 18, 2018). *See also*

The key feature of S corporations is that, unlike C corporations but like LLCs, S corporations are not taxable entities. Their income is taxed in the year it is earned to their shareholders. Shareholders are taxed on their pro rata share of income and can deduct their pro rata share of an S corporation's deductions. Because S corporations' shareholders are taxed as the business earns income, they are generally not taxed on distributions from the business and only on previously untaxed appreciation when they sell their shares. Therefore, S corporations are not subject to double taxation.

But electing to be taxed as an S corporation is not a perfect entity choice. For example, an S corporation's limited liability does not satisfy all of the same objectives as C corporation status. An S corporation, unlike a C corporation, cannot operate as a "blocker" entity. Therefore, S corporations status does not (1) prevent non-U.S. investors from having U.S. taxable income and having to file U.S. tax returns when they invest in the U.S. or (2) prevent tax-exempt investors from having "unrelated business taxable income," on which tax-exempts must report and pay tax.[20] Additionally, some states treat S corporations as taxable entities, imposing a second layer of taxation not imposed by the federal government.[21]

Finally, despite decades of liberalization, the eligibility requirements for S corporation status remain restrictive.[22] If an S corporation messes up even one of these eligibility requirements, the entity loses its status under subchapter S and defaults to taxation under subchapter C, which is double taxation. To be taxable as an S corporation, the business must:

- Be a state law corporation;

- File a special election;

- Have only one class of stock outstanding;

- Have no more than 100 shareholders, although all members of the same family are treated as one shareholder;

- Have as shareholders only individuals, estates, or certain trusts or tax-exempts or, alternatively, a single

---

David Denis & Atulya Sarin, *Taxes and the Relative Valuation of S Corporations and C Corporations*, 12 J. APPLIED FIN. 7 (2002).

[20]   For the UBTI provisions, see I.R.C. § 511 et seq.

[21]   For example, California and New York City impose a franchise tax or corporate income tax. *See* https://www.ftb.ca.gov/businesses/structures/s-corporations.shtml; http://www1.nyc.gov/site/finance/taxes/business-general-corporation-tax-gct.page   (last visited Sept. 27, 2017).

[22]   I.R.C. § 1361.

S corporation (thus corporations and partnerships cannot own shares); and

- Have only shareholders who are subject to U.S. taxation either because of their citizenship status or because of their residency in the U.S.; they cannot be nonresident aliens.

Notwithstanding these restrictions, there is no limit on the size of an S corporation, measured either by income or assets. An S corporation can be a small Mom-and-Pop store or a large multi-state enterprise.

The value of subchapter S has been debated because of the existence of other business forms.[23] Having choice adds to the tax system's complexity, and S corporations may be redundant because of the creation of LLCs, which also provide limited liability and a single layer of taxation to the owners. However, there are strategic advantages to S corporations that might make the S corporation preferable to an LLC in certain circumstances. Although adherence to the S corporation rules can be difficult and generally requires a shareholder agreement to ensure no one violates the rules, the operation of its pass-through taxation is simpler than a partnership because of subchapter S's pro rata allocations to shareholders. Additionally, S corporations may be able to maximize shareholder level business-income deductions and minimize Medicare taxes. An issue is whether these benefits are worth the added complexity of having another business form.

(c) Partnerships

Entities classified as partnerships for tax purposes are taxed pursuant to subchapter K of the Internal Revenue Code. All that is required to be a partnership for tax purposes is for two or more people or entities to work together with a profit motive.[24] Partners do not even have to be aware of their partnership status. There are numerous state law entities that fit this definition, and many, but not all, entities labeled as partnerships under state law are taxed as such. For most tax purposes except for the business's liabilities, it does not matter whether the entity is a state law general partnership, limited partnership, or limited liability company.[25]

---

[23] David Sicular, *Subchapter S at 55—Has Time Passed This Passthrough By? Maybe Not*, 68 TAX LAWYER 185 (2014); Roberta Mann, *Subchapter S: Vive le Difference!*, 18 CHAP. L. REV. 65 (2014); Walter Schwidetzky, *Integrating Subchapters K and S, Just Do It*, 62 TAX LAWYER 749 (2009).

[24] Treas. Reg. § 301.7701–1(a)(2).

[25] Depending upon whether liabilities are recourse or nonrecourse, liabilities may be treated differently depending on the form of the partnership. *See* I.R.C. § 752; Treas. Reg. § 1.704–1(b)(2)(iv)(c).

The underlying theory of partnership taxation is that, for most purposes, a partnership is an aggregate of its partners and not a separate entity. Similar to S corporations, partnerships receive pass-through taxation so that each partner reports her share of the partnership's income, gain, loss, deductions, and credits on her individual return, with the partnership's income also potentially offset by a business-income deduction. This pass-through taxation requires a complex tracing of tax items to owners, particularly when partners own limited interests in only part of the partnership.

Unlike with S corporations, businesspeople have significant flexibility when they structure their businesses to be taxable as partnerships. Partnerships are able to provide priority returns to partners for their invested capital or for their services without issuing different types of interests. The partnership agreement can allocate more to one partner than another as long as the allocations have substantial economic effect.[26] Partners are also able to determine the priority of operating distributions and, within limits, of distributions on liquidation. Most partnerships do not make full use of the flexibility available in subchapter K because the underlying business deals do not demand such flexibility.

Consider a partnership between two partners: Monroe (the rich money man) and Ida (the struggling entrepreneur). Monroe contributes cash and other forms of capital and Ida contributes her idea and entrepreneurial skills. With or without the income tax, Monroe would likely demand first priority for a return of the capital that he has invested and Ida would likely demand some form of compensation for her efforts. Allocation of income and gain satisfying these preferences will be respected for tax purposes unless something else is going on.

For example, the deal might produce an allocation schedule such that (1) Ida gets the first $30,000 of gross income each year, (2) then Monroe gets a return of his invested capital from the partnership's net profit, if any exists, and (3) the partners split any remaining net profit equally. Allocations (1) and (2) are generally permissible special allocations if incorporated into the partnership agreement. On the other hand, if the partnership allocates its tax deductions to higher-income Monroe to increase his economic return (by shielding from tax his income from other sources), the tax system ignores this special allocation because the only purpose of allocating tax deductions is to reduce taxes and does not have any other business justification.

---

[26]　Substantial economic effect is a defined, and complicated, term. I.R.C. § 704(b).

These special allocations are only possible for partnerships and not for S corporations. Although special allocations give taxpayers flexibility, complying with the requirements of subchapter K adds significantly to taxpayers' complexity. All partnerships face the same requirements because partnerships are so often used in tax shelters. Because of partnerships' role in tax planning, and government responses to the planning, partnership taxation has been called a "distressingly complex and confusing" area of law.[27] Accepting that few people choose to, or are able to, comply with the rules that govern special allocations, the special allocations may ultimately be counterproductive for the tax system.[28]

(d) Double Taxation

The double taxation of U.S. business income only occurs for businesses in the corporate form that do not elect to become S corporations. Sole proprietorships and partnerships do not face double taxation, in which both the entity and, later, the owner are taxed on business earnings. The double taxation of corporations has long been controversial. However, in 1986, Congress enacted an alternative minimum tax (AMT) for corporations to ensure a greater number of corporations owed the corporate level tax. This AMT was repealed in 2017. Congress also reduced the rates of tax on corporate dividends in 2003, arguing doing so would reduce the impact of double taxation.

(i) Arguments for Double Taxation

Advocates of the corporate income tax originally justified the tax on the grounds that the corporation was a separate entity from its owners and deserved to be taxed as such. However, much of modern academic theory holds that corporations are merely bundles of relationships between shareholders, employees, and customers and therefore are not, in reality, separate entities. Challenging this, Professor Reuven Avi-Yonah argues that corporations are separate in that they are under the control of corporate management.[29] According to this argument, those who manage corporate resources have tremendous economic and political power, so that the corporate

---

[27]   Judge Arnold Raum in Foxman v. Comm'r, 41 T.C. 535, 551 n.9 (1964).

[28]   *See Hearings on Select Revenue Measures Before Comm. on Ways and Means,* 99th Cong. 58–65 (1986) (statement of Joel Rabinovitz).

[29]   Reuven Avi-Yonah, *Corporations, Society and the State: A Defense of the Corporate Tax,* 90 VA. L. REV. 1193 (2004). *See also* Terrence Chorvat, *Apologia for the Double Taxation of Corporate Income,* 38 WAKE FOREST L. REV. 239 (2003); Hideki Kanda & Saul Levmore, *Taxes, Agency Costs, and the Price of Incorporation,* 77 VA. L. REV. 211, 229–31 (1991).

income tax may be justified as a tax to reduce the power of corporate management.

Additionally, even if a corporation is merely a composite of individual shareholders, some shareholders are not taxed on corporate earnings; therefore, the corporate income tax is the only tax on this income.[30] For example, tax-exempt and non-U.S. shareholders are not taxpayers in the traditional sense. Limited exceptions to these shareholders' exclusion from tax, such as withholding or the unrelated business income tax, are either not tied to the corporation's income or are not generally applicable.

A second argument views the corporate income tax as a way of taxing owners of corporations additionally because, as a group, they are wealthy. In 2010, Americans with the top 10% of net wealth held 81% of all stocks.[31] Because ownership of corporate stock tends to be concentrated in the hands of high-income taxpayers, eliminating the corporate income tax would be a tax cut for the wealthy. An additional concern is that, without this indirect tax, corporate owners could shelter income from tax by earning it in corporate form. While income is in corporate form, it would benefit from tax deferral, but only taxpayers with the right types of income-providing assets could enjoy this benefit.

However, this tax burden may be borne by many different groups of people. The corporate income tax might be borne by shareholders, workers, or consumers if the rate of return for investment, wages, or prices to customers is adjusted as a result of the tax. Unfortunately, it is inconclusive as to who bears the corporate income tax. Even if the tax is borne by shareholders, as is likely intended, on its face this taxes the income from corporations more heavily than income from other sources and other business forms. However, the corporate tax may be borne by all investors to the extent it depresses the rate of return throughout the economy.

Finally, the corporate income tax raises revenue, even if its share of federal revenue has declined in recent decades. In 1952, the corporate income tax raised approximately 32% of federal revenue; in 2017, the percentage was down to about 10%.[32] Despite the percentage, the amount of revenue was more than $297 billion in 2017, and in 2015 was over $343 billion, and would need to be replaced. Professor Jeffrey Kwall argues that eliminating the corporate income tax should only be considered in conjunction with a

---

[30] *See* LEONARD BURMAN & KIMBERLY CLAUSING, IS U.S. CORPORATE INCOME DOUBLE-TAXED? (2016).

[31] Edward N. Wolff, *Who Owns Stock in American Corporations*, 158 PROCEEDINGS OF AM. PHILOSOPHICAL SOC'Y 372 (2014).

[32] OFFICE OF MGMT. & BUDGET, HISTORICAL TABLES, Table 2.1 and 2.2 (2018).

proposed alternative that would replace its revenue.[33] In other words, if the alternative is a worse tax, the corporate income tax should not be repealed even if it is suboptimal in the abstract.

(ii) Arguments Against Double Taxation

Double taxation likely distorts the proper allocation of economic resources as owners plan around it. This distortion is the result of three separate biases double taxation produces: (1) in favor of debt financing (because of a corporate level deduction for interest payments) as opposed to equity financing (which does not have a deduction for dividends paid)[34]; (2) in favor of corporations retaining earnings because they are not double taxed as opposed to making distributions which are double taxed; and (3) against corporate as opposed to noncorporate (and not double-taxed) forms of business. Thus, the argument is that people make business choices to reduce taxation and not for well-reasoned non-tax objectives.

Second, double taxation may cause the tax system to be more complex than it otherwise would be. Taxpayers structure corporate activities to avoid double taxation, which often produces congressional reaction to minimize the gains from these structures. As a result, both the Internal Revenue Code and enforcement are more complex than if the corporate income tax were not in place; although this is the same as saying people would not plan around taxes if there were no tax. If Congress repealed the corporate income tax, a complex regime would likely be needed to ensure people did not hold all income-producing property in non-taxed corporations.

This planning is illustrated by the case of, and subsequent congressional response to, *General Utilities & Operating Co. v. Helvering.*[35] General Utilities located a buyer for some of its appreciated property. If General Utilities sold the assets directly, there would have been a taxable gain at the corporate level, and a dividend of the proceeds would have also been taxable to its shareholders. To avoid the corporate level tax, General Utilities distributed the appreciated assets to its shareholders with the understanding (but no legal commitment) that they would sell the assets to the prospective buyer. Four days later, the shareholders sold the assets on the same terms negotiated by General Utilities.

---

[33]   Jeffrey Kwall, *The Uncertain Case Against Double Taxation of Corporate Income*, 68 N.C. L. REV. 613 (1990).

[34]   In 1987, tax-exempt entities held 50% of corporate bonds, for which the corporate interest deduction was not offset by a tax on creditors; no tax was paid on these corporate earnings. Michael Graetz, *The Tax Aspects of Leveraged Buyouts and Other Corporate Financial Restructuring Transactions*, 42 TAX NOTES 721 (1989).

[35]   296 U.S. 200 (1935).

The Supreme Court accepted the taxpayer's argument that the corporation recognized no gain on this series of transactions because the distribution was not a sale to the buyer of the assets. This eliminated the first layer of the double tax regime. Surprisingly, Congress responded by codifying the result, encouraging corporations to distribute appreciated assets rather than cash as dividends.[36] After an assault on federal revenue, Congress repealed this position and now requires corporations recognize gain, but denies them a loss, on nonliquidating distributions of property.[37]

Congress could reduce complexity with double taxation but retain two layers of tax; however, complexity will always exist if taxpayers can plan around a type or level of taxation. When Congress enacted favorable tax rates for qualifying dividends, it reduced some transactional complexity.[38] Taxing gains and dividends at the same rate (whether or not favorable compared to ordinary income rates) eliminated a planning opportunity between selling stock and receiving dividends. When dividends were taxed at higher rates than long-term capital gains, there was a significant amount of tax planning to convert dividend payments into sales of shares or to disguise dividends as the corporate redemption of some of the shareholder's shares. That incentive was eliminated when tax rates were aligned.

(iii) Corporate Shareholders

Unlike individual shareholders, corporate shareholders do not have a favorable dividend or capital gain rate. However, corporate shareholders are partially exempt from tax on the dividends they receive because Congress enacted a partial or full deduction offsetting those dividends.[39] The percentage of the dividend that is deductible depends upon the recipient corporation's ownership interest in the paying corporation. This deduction may change corporate shareholders' preference for dividends over the sale of corporate stock.

The more a corporate shareholder owns of the distributing corporation the larger the percentage of the deduction. As of 2018, the percentages are 50%, 65%, or 100% of the dividend, reducing the middle layer of tax. The percentages on the deduction for a recipient corporation were larger, a tradeoff of revenue in order to finance the lower corporate tax rate.

---

[36]   I.R.C. § 311 (1954).

[37]   Tax Reform Act of 1986, Pub. L. No. 99–514, § 631, 100 Stat. 2086, 2269 (1986).

[38]   For more on capital gains and qualifying dividends, see Chapter 7.03.

[39]   I.R.C. § 243.

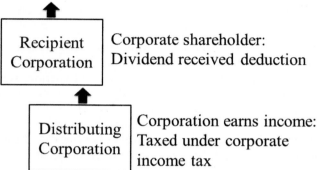

Individual shareholder:
Dividends taxed at capital gain rates

Recipient Corporation

Corporate shareholder:
Dividend received deduction

Distributing Corporation

Corporation earns income:
Taxed under corporate income tax

If a distributing corporation is taxed when it earns income, a corporate shareholder is taxed on receipt of dividends from that income, and the recipient corporation's own shareholders are taxed on distributions from that income, this produces three (and sometimes more) layers of tax. The deduction for the corporate shareholder in the middle reduces the levels of tax owed.

(iv) Eliminating Double Taxation

Double taxation could be eliminated through the integration of the individual and corporate income taxes, but no one agrees on the best method of integration. The options discussed below use a numerical example to illustrate pros and cons of each. For this example, a one-shareholder corporation earns $1,000 of ordinary income; the corporation pays tax (if any are owed) and distributes its remaining earnings; and the corporate income tax rate is 21%, the individual ordinary income tax rate is 37%, and the individual dividend rate is 20%.

As a baseline, the current double tax system requires the corporation pay $210 in tax ($1,000 corporate income times 21% corporate rate), and the shareholder receives a $790 distribution ($1,000 corporate income minus $210 in corporate tax) and pays $158 in taxes ($790 distribution times 20% dividend rate). A total of $368 is paid to the government. Without the favorable dividend rate, $292.30 is raised in taxes from the shareholder, for a total of $502.30 in taxes from the $1,000 earned.

The simplest form of integration eliminates the corporate level tax, as currently applied to partnerships. The $1,000 of ordinary earnings is taxed to the shareholder, whether or not distributed, at the 37% ordinary rate, raising $370 in tax. This integration method raises $2 less than double taxation with a favorable dividend rate. This example ignores the complications of allocating income and loss among large numbers of publicly traded shares or for corporations with many different types of income (such as ordinary, capital, passive, foreign, domestic, etc.).

Another method of integration retains the corporate income tax as withholding for the corporation's shareholders. Similar to wage withholding, the $210 of corporate tax is paid on behalf of the shareholder, and the shareholder owes an additional $160 of tax on her individual return because the total tax owed is the 37% individual rate times the $1,000 of corporate earnings. Withholding increases compliance with the shareholder's tax. Among this method's complications are the allocations of corporate income among many shareholders plus potential complications if a shareholder is in a lower tax bracket than the corporation, although this latter is less problematic with a flat rate corporate tax.

A similar, but simpler, alternative excludes dividends from the shareholder's income and leaves only a corporate level income tax. The $1,000 earned by the corporation is taxed at the corporation's 21% rate and distributions are tax-free to shareholders. This creates an incentive for high-income individuals to incorporate their assets to be taxed at lower corporate rates, unless corporate rates are equalized with individual rates. Additionally, low tax bracket shareholders lose a relative tax advantage they currently enjoy because of progressive individual capital gain rates.

A last alternative allows corporations a dividend-paid deduction similar to the current interest-paid deduction. The payment of a $1,000 dividend reduces corporate income to $0, and with current favorable dividend rates the shareholder owes taxes of 20% times the $1,000 corporate income, or $200. If the favorable dividend rate is repealed, corporate income is taxed at ordinary rates, the same result as if the corporation were not a separate entity unless the corporation retains earnings. If a corporation retains earnings, the corporation owes a double layer of tax under this latter integration method.

COMPARISON OF EXAMPLES				
	Corporate tax	Shareholder tax	Total tax owed	After-tax amounts
Double taxation with favorable dividend rates	$210	$158	$368	$632
Double taxation with ordinary dividend rates	$210	$292.30	$502.30	$497.70
Repeal corporate income tax	$0	$370	$370	$630
Corporate tax as withholding	$210	$160	$370	$630
Exclusion of dividends for shareholder	$210	$0	$210	$790
Dividend-paid deduction and favorable dividend rate[40]	$0	$200	$200	$800

Despite numerous proposals to integrate the corporate and individual income tax systems, integration has not occurred.[41] Professors Jennifer Arlen and Deborah Weiss argue that the failure to act results from conflicts within the business community.[42] Whereas shareholders want integration, managers do not. Shareholders want a reduction of tax on their current diversified holdings in many corporations, which integration would achieve. Managers want job security and to promote the growth of their own business, which integration would not achieve. Instead, managers prefer tax reduction focused on future investment, and they benefit from trapping earnings within the corporation so that the earnings can be invested even in suboptimal investments.

If adopted, integration may not fix the distortion caused by double taxation because the price of stock may reflect a discount for the double tax. If current prices correct for the tax, current shareholders would receive a windfall if double taxation were eliminated. The value of current stock would increase for no reason

---

[40]   Retained earnings would significantly increase the amount of tax and reduce the after-tax amount.

[41]   For example, *Integrating the Corporate and Individual Tax Systems Hearing Before Senate Finance Comm.*, 114th Cong. (2016); JANE GRAVELLE, CONG. RESEARCH SERV., R44638, CORPORATE TAX INTEGRATION AND TAX REFORM (2016).

[42]   Jennifer Arlen & Deborah M. Weiss, *A Political Theory of Corporate Taxation*, 105 YALE L.J. 325 (1995).

other than tax reduction. This benefit would come at the cost of over $297 billion in federal revenue (or 10% of the federal budget), meaning that federal expenditures would either need to be cut or the revenue would need to come from another source.

Finally, eliminating the corporate income tax may exacerbate the lock-in effect trapping wealth in corporate form. If income accumulates in a corporation without a corporate tax but is subject to tax on distribution, there is little desire to make distributions. One means of addressing this lock-in is a separate tax to encourage distributions, such as the accumulated earnings tax. These taxes are often more complicated than the corporate income tax. For many businesses, accumulated earnings taxes operate as an additional layer of tax because of legitimate business needs to retain earnings.

(e) Qualified Business Income Deduction

Congress enacted a business-income deduction that applies from 2018 through 2025 to offset some of the income of some pass-through entities and sole proprietorships. Although this tax cut was often touted as for small businesses, only some small businesses qualify. For example, the deduction does not apply to shareholders of businesses taxable as C corporations. Costing $414.5 billion over ten years, owners have a steep learning curve before claiming the deduction. The statute itself is complicated, and much additional complexity is expressly left for the Treasury Department to sort out.

Under the new deduction, pass-through income is taxed at regular individual income tax rates, but new section 199A provides up to a 20% deduction to offset some of a business's ordinary, non-investment income. This reduces the effective rate of taxation for business income, for example the 37% ordinary income rate is reduced to 29.6%.[43] As with all deductions, the greatest benefit is for those in top tax brackets.

Availability of the 20% deduction depends on the type of payment the owner receives. The deduction does not apply for salaries or guaranteed payments to partners. Also, any remaining eligible income can be deducted only up to the lesser of (1) 20% or (2) the greater of 50% of wages paid to employees or 25% of wages paid plus 2.5% of the cost of tangible depreciable property. For example, if Jane's LLC has $250,000 of qualified business income and pays $50,000 of W-2 wages to an employee, her deduction is limited to 50% of the $50,000 wages, or $25,000, because that is less than $250,000 times 20%, or $50,000. When available, the deduction applies to all partnerships, including publicly traded partnerships, unless the

---

[43] $(100\% - 20\%) \times 37\% = 29.6\%$.

partnership is a designated service-providing partnership, including doctors, lawyers, performing artists, athletes, those in the financial industry, and a trade or business whose principal asset is the owner's reputation or skill.

However, the limits of the prior paragraph only apply if the owner's total taxable income is above a threshold: $315,000 for joint filers and $157,500 for individual filers. In the prior example, if Jane's LLC had only $150,000 of income, she would be entitled to the 20% times the $150,000, or a $30,000 deduction. Therefore, lower-income professionals may benefit but are probably not in a position to hire the lawyers and financial advisors to make sure they are planning effectively. The purpose of the phaseout was "to deter high-income taxpayers from attempting to convert wages or other compensation for personal services to income eligible" for the deduction.[44] The new law provides a 20% penalty if taxpayers make more than a 5% error in claiming this deduction.

This targeted tax reduction may encourage people to structure their activities as independent contractors through entities that can pay salaries to themselves, namely S corporations. However, forgoing employee status has nontax risks, such as less likelihood of employer-provided benefits plus fewer labor law protections. Businesses hiring independent contractors not only avoid paying workers benefits, they also do not owe payroll taxes; independent contractors must pay employees' and employers' shares. In response, workers might negotiate higher wages but need a strong negotiating position to do so. Additionally, classification for tax purposes is uncertain and risks its own penalties.

(f) Medicare Taxes

Returns from businesses may be subject to additional tax imposed as of January 1, 2013, by the Patient Protection and Affordable Care Act to help fund Medicare. The Act imposes a 0.9% tax on earned income and a 3.8% tax on net investment income for taxpayers whose modified AGI exceeds certain thresholds.[45] The threshold for single taxpayers in 2018 is $200,000 and for joint filers is $250,000. Consequently, for these taxpayers, the top ordinary rate is 37.9% and the top capital gain rate is 23.8%.

Although these taxes might seem small, business owners can partially plan around these taxes in some instances. According to some tax advisors, if a shareholder of an S corporation materially participates in the business, the shareholder can partially avoid

---

[44]   H. Rep. 115–466, at 37.

[45]   I.R.C. § 1411; § 3101(b)(2).

these taxes. If the shareholder receives a reasonable salary, the salary is subject to the 0.9% tax. However, the portion not allocable to salary, but is a return on the shareholder's investment in the S corporation, is arguably subject to neither Medicare tax.

(g) Choice of Entity

No particular business entity is a perfect form, yet having a choice increases the tax system's complexity even as it increases taxpayer flexibility. However, just because a business owner wants a particular tax form does not mean the business necessarily gets it. The Internal Revenue Code and Treasury regulations set parameters for whether a particular business arrangement is taxed as a corporation, partnership, or is disregarded. The default for a single owner entity is to be disregarded from its owner for tax purposes, and the default for an entity with more than one owner is a partnership unless the entity is incorporated under state law.[46]

In 1997, the Treasury Department adopted a simple check-the-box system that permits taxpayers to file Form 8832 indicating their entity's tax choice from a menu of options.[47] This check-the-box system replaced a complex common law and regulatory system that evolved from the statutory definition of a corporation as an "association." Regulations implementing the common law had generally been pro-partnership because the Treasury Department focused on professional service providers, such as lawyers and doctors, unable to incorporate under state law but who attempted to form entities classified as associations for tax purposes in order to make use of the fringe benefits and retirement plans available to employees and, at that time, unavailable to partners.

Since the 1997 change to regulations, taxpayers have been able to elect business form but, even with the check-the-box rules, there are limits on taxpayers' choices. For example, partnerships must have two or more partners. Entities incorporated under state law are taxable as corporations. Certain non-U.S. business forms are designated as corporations for U.S. tax purposes. Once an election is made, taxpayers cannot change their classification for five years. When permitted, changing classification may have the effect of liquidating the business and reforming it for tax purposes.[48]

But even with its limitations, the check the box rules offer greater planning opportunities than had existed under the common law. International organizations often try "hybrid branch" or "hybrid

---

[46]   The regulations governing choice of entity are Treas. Reg. §§ 301.7701–1, –2, and –3.

[47]   Treas. Reg. § 301.7701–2(a) (pre-1997); Reg. § 301.7701.3(c).

[48]   *See, e.g.,* Rev. Rul. 99–5, 1996–6 I.R.B. 8.

entity" strategies that use different classifications in different countries to maximize tax and business planning opportunities.[49] That the Treasury Department, not Congress, created this planning opportunity means that the rules are alterable without congressional action. Because of their susceptibility to abuse and because they have little basis in statute, some argue the check-the-box rules are invalid.[50] Nevertheless, courts have consistently upheld them.[51]

An example illustrates the potential economic impact of the choice of business form, although it is based on many simplifying assumptions. If $100,000 of taxable income is earned by a single person's sole proprietorship and taxed at top individual rates of 37% and the 20% deduction does not apply (for example if the owner has significant other income), $63,000 is left for the proprietor. If the business is taxable as a pass-through entity and the partner is entitled to the full 20% deduction for the $100,000, $80,000 is taxed at 37% (for comparability; the top rate for single taxpayers earning $100,000 is 24%) so that $70,400 is left, a savings of 7.4%.[52] If a corporation earns the $100,000, it is taxed at 21%, leaving $79,000 after-tax; however, the shareholder will be taxed on receipt of the money, potentially at a 20% dividend rate (assuming the top tax bracket).[53] When the $79,000 is taxed, it leaves $63,200 for the shareholder.

	Sole-proprietorship (37% rate assuming no deduction)	Pass-through (37% rate and assuming 20% deduction applies)	Corporation (21% rate with distribution at 20%)
Earnings	$100,000	$100,000	$100,000
Taxes	$37,000	$29,600	$36,800
Income after-tax	$63,000	$70,400	$63,200
Effective tax rate	37%	29.6%	36.8%
Savings from sole proprietorship	--	$7,400	$200

---

[49]   Diane Ring, *One Nation Among Many*, 44 B.C. L. REV. 79 (2002).

[50]   *See* WILLIAM MCKEE ET AL., FEDERAL TAXATION OF PARTNERSHIPS AND PARTNERS 3–102 (3d ed. 1997); Gregg Polsky, *Can Treasury Override the Supreme Court?*, 84 B.U. L. REV. 185 (2004).

[51]   *See* McNamee v. U.S., 488 F.3d 100 (2d Cir. 2007); Littriello v. U.S., 484 F.3d 372 (6th Cir. 2007), *cert. denied*, 128 S.C. 1290 (2008); Stearn & Co., LLC v. U.S. 499 F.Supp.2d 899 (E.D. Mich. 2007); L&L Holding Co., LLC v. U.S., 101 AFTR2d 2008–2081 (W.D.La. 2008); Medical Practice Solutions, LLC v. Comm'r, 132 T.C. No. 7 (2009).

[52]   80% × 37% = $29.6% goes to taxes.

[53]   The 3.8% Medicare tax would also need to be added.

§ 11.02　Business Incentives

The American tax system extends significant tax privileges to businesses. The most important is that the system is a net income tax. Net income taxation, as opposed to gross income taxation, reduces taxpayers' taxable income by the expenses of earning it, with the goal of taxing only real increases in wealth.[54] Additionally, Congress has enacted benefits to favor businesses, such as accelerated depreciation deductions that recover the investment in business assets faster than the assets are worn out.[55] These can be contrasted with the narrow, limited deductions and credits for some personal expenditures. For example, caregivers of children may receive limited tax benefits only if they comply with significant restrictions.[56] Business deductions tend to be easier to claim although not without limitation.

(a)　Net Income as Opposed to Gross Income

First, the existence of a net income tax system benefits the production of income. The income tax is based on the idea that only net increases in wealth are taxable, and the alternative would likely cause some businesses to fail. Businesses that operate with small margins are at greater risk under a gross tax. In other words, denying deductions for expenses might make otherwise beneficial activities prohibitively expensive; it is not the tax or tax rate per se that threatens these businesses but a tax base ignoring the cost of doing business. Without a business expense deduction, most businesses with a low profit margin could never earn a profit because the tax on revenues would exceed their net earnings.

For example, grocery stores typically have low profit margins of about 1%.[57] They may net $1 on every $100 of revenue because they have $99 of expenses. Accepting these facts, grocery stores could not pay a 5% tax on revenues. To do so, they would lose $4 for every $100 earned ($100 earned minus $99 expenses minus $5 taxes, equals a negative $4). However, grocery stores could pay a 5% tax on a net basis, or 5% of the $1, or $0.05. In a gross tax system, prices would need to adjust upwards for the tax or grocery stores would no longer be profitable purely because of the tax expense. Thus, a gross, as opposed to a net, tax may drive grocery stores and other low margin

---

[54]　For individual owners of sole proprietorships and entities with pass-through taxation, net income taxation is accomplished through unlimited above-the-line deductions for most trade or business expenses. I.R.C. §§ 162; 62.

[55]　I.R.C. §§ 167, 168, 197.

[56]　I.R.C. § 21.

[57]　Russell Huebsch, *What is the Profit Margin for a Supermarket?*, SMALL BUSINESS CHRONICLE, http://smallbusiness.chron.com/profit-margin-supermarket-22467.html (last visited Sept. 27, 2017).

businesses out of business if the market does not respond adequately to incorporate the cost of taxes.

Not all profit-seeking activities are currently taxed on a net basis. Many investment activities have a profit motive but, as of 2018, their expenses are disallowed as miscellaneous itemized deductions. Before 2018, the first 2% of this type of expense was disallowed and the deductions phased out for higher-income taxpayers.[58] The denial of deductions means that some profitable activities are not undertaken by some taxpayers.

(b) Depreciation and Expensing

In addition to a net tax system, Congress enacts other tax benefits to encourage specific business decisions. For example, Congress has decided that investment in new equipment is sufficiently beneficial to warrant targeted tax reduction. Thus, Congress has made a political calculation the designated activity is worth congressional spending through tax reduction.[59]

Traditionally, assets that generate income in more than one year were not currently deductible. Instead, businesses could deduct a portion of the cost each year as the asset wore out. The system was for taxpayers to match the income of the asset with its wear and tear consistent with a net tax system. However, Congress has long since given up any obligation to measure wear and tear. Under widely applicable accelerated depreciation, Congress has created artificially short recovery periods and doubled the depreciation rate for most property that is not a building or similarly long-lived property, ostensibly to encourage businesses to invest in these middle-life assets.[60]

In the Tax Cuts and Jobs Act of 2017, Congress eliminated the requirement of wear and tear to encourage investment in short-term assets. Congress permitted all businesses, regardless of business form, to currently deduct all of the cost of short-lived capital investments, such as machinery and equipment.[61] This benefit, called "bonus depreciation," when coupled with a deduction for interest, makes investment in machines extremely attractive. However, this provision begins phasing out in 2023. Even when bonus depreciation expires, Congress increased the amount that can be currently expensed for all but large businesses. In 2017, Congress raised the small business expensing cap to $1 million spent on these non-real

---

[58]   I.R.C. § 212, § 67(a).

[59]   For more on using tax expenditures to correct market failures, see Chapter 17.02(a).

[60]   I.R.C. §§ 167, 168, 197.

[61]   I.R.C. § 168(k).

property assets with a phase out of the expensing benefit starting at $2.5 million of such assets.[62] Although a hope may be that these investments increase workers' productivity, the tax benefits may encourage purchases of machines at the expense of investment in the labor force.

(c) New Limitations

Although the Tax Cuts and Jobs Act provided many tax benefits for businesses, it offset some of the cost with narrow tax increases. For example, Congress capped business interest deductions for certain businesses. From 2018 through 2025, when a business pays interest on debt, net interest is only deductible to the extent that interest is no more than 30% of the business's earnings before interest, taxes, depreciation, and amortization (EBITDA).[63] After 2025, interest is only deductible up to 30% of earnings before interest and taxes (EBIT).[64] Interest that is not deductible can be carried forward indefinitely. Raising government revenue, this provision should also decrease demand for leveraging, particularly by multinational corporations using the U.S. entity to borrow, popularly called earnings stripping.

This limitation applies to both corporations and partnerships. Certain businesses have been excluded from this limitation, including real property trade or businesses or those involved in furnishing or selling energy, water, or sewage disposal. Certain small businesses were also excluded from the limitation, defined as those with average gross receipts not over $25 million for each of the three prior taxable years.

Additionally, Congress limited businesses' ability to deduct net operating losses (NOLs), the term for ordinary business losses.[65] First, Congress eliminated the carryback of non-farm-related NOLs. Businesses had previously been able to amend tax returns for the prior two years and possibly claim tax refunds. This change will make it harder for distressed businesses that might have used tax refunds generated from a NOL carryback to finance restructuring. The new law also provides indefinite NOL carryforwards (previously limited to 20 years after which NOLs expired); however, Congress limited NOLs to 80% of taxable income. Therefore, profitable businesses cannot use NOLs to completely avoid tax. For example, if a business has a $150,000 NOL in 2018 and has $100,000 of income in 2019, the

---

[62]   I.R.C. § 179.

[63]   I.R.C. § 163(j). EBITDA can roughly be equated with cash flow and is always greater than EBIT.

[64]   EBIT can roughly be equated with operating income and is always less than EBITDA.

[65]   I.R.C. § 172.

business can only use $80,000 of the NOL to offset the 2019 income and must pay tax on $20,000. The remaining $70,000 of NOL carries forward. Historic NOLs continue to be deductible against 100% of income because the limit does not apply.

(d) Indirect Benefits

Even some tax expenditures that do not purport to be pro-business may have that effect. For example, the largest form of income redistribution to the poor, the EITC, is tied to a person's participation in the labor market.[66] The result is that lower-income workers are required to earn wages but not too much income in order to maximize their tax credit. As a result, the credit may drive down the cost of unskilled labor. By providing a pool of workers, the credit shares the cost of labor with employers. Then, many of these same employers of low-cost labor sell their consumption items to those whom it has employed.

(e) Small Businesses

The extent to which pro-business expenditures accomplish their intended objective is ultimately unknowable and, although much of the justification is to help small businesses, it is unknown exactly how many small businesses there are or how best to help them. The congressionally-created Small Business Administration's Office of Advocacy argues that there were 27.9 million businesses with fewer than 500 employees in 2010.[67] Looking at tax returns reporting business income or losses, there may be 30.9 million taxpayers, or approximately 22%, who are small business owners, although some of these are likely reporting passive investment income.[68] About 72% of these taxpayers also report wage income, so that they are receiving income as a worker in addition to owning a business. Almost 74% of taxpayers with business income have adjusted gross income below $100,000 and about 1% have annual income over $1 million.

A common justification for the focus on small businesses is a sense of their entrepreneurial activity and job creation. These are some reasons Professor Mirit Cohen proposes additional tax assistance to help small businesses overcome the hurdles of competing with large businesses.[69] In the 1980s, research found that small businesses were the primary creators of jobs; however, recent research finds they create only slightly more jobs than larger

---

[66]   I.R.C. § 32.

[67]   U.S. SMALL BUSINESS ADMIN., FREQUENTLY ASKED QUESTIONS (2012).

[68]   THOMAS L. HUNGERFORD, CONG. RESEARCH SERV., R42043, AN ANALYSIS OF THE "BUFFETT RULE" (2012).

[69]   Mirit Eyal-Cohen, *In Defense of Intrapreneurship*, U. of Ala. Legal Stud. Res. Paper 2867611 (2016).

businesses.[70] New startups are the biggest creator of jobs but also the biggest creators of job destruction as most fail within five years and about 40% of their jobs disappear from business failure.

§ 11.03   Executive Pay

Congress uses the tax code to influence many business choices, including the size and composition of executive compensation. Although paying executives is an ordinary and necessary business expense and, therefore, generally deductible, Congress has repeatedly enacted limits on the deductibility of certain forms of executive compensation. These statutory restrictions contain numerous loopholes; and they do not seem to have limited the size of compensation packages, although they may have changed their structure.

First, Congress limits trade or business deductions to "reasonable compensation," but this term has never been adequately defined.[71] The IRS rarely denies deductions for payments to highly paid employees. Once the IRS successfully denied a $46,000 deduction for payments to a bookkeeper on the grounds that a reasonable salary would have been $13,000.[72] Pivotal to the Tax Court was that the increased salary resulted from wartime demand and not the employee's actions. More often courts consider either the return non-executives receive from the perspective of a hypothetical investor or a list of factors, such as qualifications and prevailing rates for comparable positions, attempting to create objective factors to determine whether compensation is reasonable, although application of either test is far from certain.[73]

Noting the failure of the prior limitation, in 1993 Congress enacted a provision potentially denying publicly-held corporations deductions for salaries exceeding $1 million if the recipient is one of the corporation's five highest paid executives.[74] Until 2018, only if the salary was based "on the attainment of one or more performance goals" was the deduction allowed, but outside directors could develop these goals as long as a majority of the corporation's shareholders approved them. As of 2018, no deduction for salaries greater than $1 million is permitted if paid by a publicly-held corporation to its CEO, CFO, or three other highest paid employees. No attempt was made

---

[70]   JANE GRAVELLE, CONG. RESEARCH SERV., R41392, SMALL BUSINESS AND THEE EXPIRATION OF THE 2001 TAX RATE REDUCTIONS: ECONOMIC ISSUES 8–11 (2010). *See also* John Haltiwanger et al., *Who Creates Jobs?*, NBER WORKING PAPER NO. 16300 (2010).

[71]   I.R.C. § 162(a).

[72]   Patton v. Comm'r, 168 F.2d 28 (6th Cir. 1948), aff'g, 6 T.C.M (CCH) 482 (1947).

[73]   Exacto Spring Corporation v. Comm'r, 196 F.3d 833 (7th Cir. 1999).

[74]   I.R.C. § 162(m).

to limit salaries of other employees or of any employees of private businesses or of publicly-traded partnerships.

It is unlikely all of an executive's compensation is salary. Many high-income CEOs and other executives have choice regarding their compensation packages, including deferring salary or bonuses or taking them in the form of stock. If executives defer compensation and meet certain statutory requirements, these taxpayers do not owe tax until the amounts are actually paid even if already earned.[75] Many others receive more in stock options than cash, but these payments are now subject to the $1 million deduction limit. Despite options' favorable tax treatment for some recipients, one empirical study found that tax law favorable to options was unlikely to have caused the explosion in stock options as a form of compensation.[76]

Finally, when payments are made to an executive leaving the business following a merger or an acquisition of the business, special tax rules may apply. Deductions for golden parachutes or other payments to executives displaced following mergers were limited in 1985 but only if those payments are found to be "excess parachute payments."[77] The term is poorly defined and has been interpreted so that the rules only come into play when the payment is contingent upon a corporation's change in control as defined by the statute. Moreover, the limit only caps deductions for payments to certain officers, shareholders, or highly compensated employees at three times the person's average annual compensation for the five prior years. Even then there are exceptions. In the limited instances where the provision applies, the deduction is lost and the recipient owes a 20% excise tax in addition to standard payroll taxes and income taxes.[78]

§ 11.04　Employee Benefits

Many employee benefits are given preferential tax treatment that exclude the benefits from gross income, such as section 132 for fringe benefits, section 119 for lodging provided as a condition of employment, section 79 for group life insurance, sections 105 and section 106 for accident and health benefits, section 129 for dependent care assistance, and section 401 for qualified retirement plans. For a benefit to be excluded from gross income, Congress must

---

[75]　I.R.C. § 409A.

[76]　Brian Hall & Jeffrey Liebman, *The Taxation of Executive Compensation*, 14 TAX POL'Y & ECON. 1 (2000).

[77]　I.R.C. § 280G. For more see on the impact of the golden parachute rules, see Andrew Lund, *Tax's Triviality as a Pay-Reforming Device*, 57 VILL. L. REV. 571 (2012).

[78]　I.R.C. § 4999.

have created a statutory exception. Congress reduced many of these benefits beginning in 2018.

Employers love giving employees non-taxable benefits. Because employees do not have to include these benefits in gross income, these employee benefits are worth more than cash to employees in terms of after-tax value. For example, if an employer gives an employee a discount worth $100, the employee enjoys $100 worth of value; however, if the employer gives the employee cash equal to $100 after tax, the employer must give the employee more than $100. If the employee is in a 25% tax bracket and only receives $100 cash, the employee is left with $75 after taxes because $25 is owed in taxes. Thus, with excludible benefits, employers can give employees after-tax value at a lower before-tax cost.

Because taxpayers love tax-free benefits, employers and employees have been creative in structuring perks for employees. For example, Google reportedly provides breakfast, lunch, and sometimes dinner; free company bus rides to and from work; and massages.[79] If these items are excluded from taxable income, less government revenue is raised and what is raised is inequitable across employers. Congress has limited the deductions that businesses may claim when providing these benefits and the recipients' exclusion of the benefits.

One problem with extending tax preferences to these benefits is that they may be unfair. For example, wealthier workers receive more of them than poorer workers. Even though statutory exclusions often prohibit employers from giving benefits only to highly compensated employees, these types of benefits tend to be available more often to higher-income workers. Moreover, because exclusions reduce taxable income, they are worth the value of the exclusion multiplied by the taxpayer's tax rate. This means they are worth more to higher tax bracket taxpayers.

Additionally, these tax preferences distort the market and thereby create economic inefficiencies. An exemption from tax makes the benefit worth more than cash compensation of an equal amount. Consider again the example of the employee in a 25% tax bracket who receives $100 of benefits that are not subject to tax. To purchase that benefit with after-tax dollars, the employee would have to earn $133, pay $33 of tax, and use the remainder to purchase the benefit.[80] Even if the benefit is not worth $100 to the employee, it is likely the employee would still prefer it to a cash payment. For example, if the

---

[79]   Jillian D'Onfro, *An Inside Look at Google's Best Employee Perks*, INC.COM, Sep. 21, 2015.

[80]   The equation is: $x - 0.25x = \$100$, or more simply as $x = \$100 \div 0.75$.

employee were willing and able to pay $90 for the benefit, doing so would require $120 of pre-tax wages. So the employee should prefer the $100 untaxed benefit compared to wages up to $120. This creates a strong incentive for employers to convert cash compensation to tax-preferred benefits. As a result, it leads to distortions in labor markets and creates inequities among employers based on their ability to provide these benefits.

As a specific example, the exclusion for employer-provided health insurance has been blamed for creating the existing healthcare system.[81] Spending on healthcare is no less in the U.S. than in many other countries, but how the money is spent differs with lots of money spent on some and almost none on others. Private actors manage the American healthcare system with indirect financial support from the government through tax deductions and exclusions, primarily tied to employment. Moreover, that employees do not have to pay tax on the value of their employer-provided health insurance likely contributes to the existence of Cadillac insurance plans that may provide greater coverage than the taxpayer would otherwise purchase.

Particular tax-preferred benefits often result from lobbying efforts, but some benefits result from concerns about administering the tax system. For example, airline employees won the right for their parents to receive free stand-by flights as a result of airline employees' lobbying.[82] This unusual provision shows a small segment of taxpayers changing the law in their favor. Alternatively, the IRS announced in 2002 that it would not seek to tax the frequent flyer miles that taxpayers received as a result of work-related travel but used for personal travel.[83] Although not fully explaining its reasoning, the IRS's stated motivation was a combined concern over valuation of the miles and enforcement.

Because Congress perceives that employee benefits have been abused, Congress enacts exclusions with tremendous statutory nuance. Therefore, employers must structure their programs to fit within narrowly defined limits. Otherwise compliant taxpayers may struggle to follow these rules whereas noncompliant taxpayers are likely to pay under the table or more fragrantly avoid their requirements.

---

[81]   JACOB HACKER, THE DIVIDED WELFARE STATE: THE BATTLE OVER PUBLIC AND PRIVATE SOCIAL BENEFITS IN THE UNITED STATES (2002).

[82]   Joel Newman, *Fly Me, Fly My Mother*, 35 TAX NOTES 291 (1987).

[83]   Announcement 2002–18, 2002–1 C.B. 621.

§ 11.05   Not Quite a Business: Hobbies, Home Offices, and Entertainment

A tension exists within the American tax system between the deductibility of trade and business expenses and the non-deductibility of personal expenses.[84] Because personal expenses are not deductible, taxpayers often try to mask their personal expenses as deductible business expenses. For expenses that could be either, taxpayers originally claimed the deduction and then litigated the proper classification. In response, Congress enacted detailed statutes to narrowly permit this type of deduction.

This problem of classification often arises when a hobby generates revenue, people work at least some time from home, and someone tries to live off of business dinners. The question for Congress is whether to permit or deny deductions associated with these hybrid activities. Because of perceived taxpayer abuse and the need for revenue, Congress limits the ability to claim these deductions. Therefore, taxpayers are often denied deductions for hobbies, home offices, and entertainment expenses.

(a) Hobbies

Hobbies are activities that are not engaged in for the purpose of earning a profit, although they may generate one.[85] For example, a taxpayer may keep horses as a hobby but sell one horse at a profit. To qualify as a hobby, it is not enough that owners love engaging in the activity; Treasury regulations list nine objective factors.[86] For example, the regulations question whether the taxpayer has particular expertise in the activity, any expectation the assets used in the activity will appreciate, the amount of time or effort spent on the activity, and the existence of prior success. Thus, whether an activity is engaged in for profit is based on the taxpayer's particular facts and circumstances. For example, an inherited farm in a residential area with substantial losses is a hobby, but an unsuccessful farm operated by a taxpayer in a fairly serious fashion is not; dog and horse breeding by a soft drink retailer is a hobby, but wells owned by an independent oil and gas wildcatter are not.[87]

Before 2018, hobby expenses were partially deductible against hobby income according to fairly complicated rules; however, these expenses are not deductible at all between 2018 and 2025. The political concern for initially limiting these deductions was that

---

[84]   I.R.C. §§ 162, 262.

[85]   I.R.C. § 183.

[86]   Treas. Reg. §§ 1.183–1, –2.

[87]   Treas. Reg. § 1.183–2(c), Examples 1–6.

wealthy people who breed horses for fun or who have large estates and a couple cute chickens would be able to use the expenses of their hobbies to offset their wages or investment income. Permitting deductions would also reduce the cost of expensive hobbies for those wealthy enough to enjoy them, possibly distorting their choices. Despite eliminating the deduction for hobby expenses as of 2018, the income from hobbies remains taxable.

(b) Home Offices

Congressional limits on the deductibility of home office expenses respond to perceived abuse and the need for revenue. *Forbes* reported that 26 million Americans have a home office; however, even before the 2018 limit on the deduction only 3.4 million taxpayers claimed a home office deduction.[88] The reason for the relatively few claimants is that the rules often deny the deduction because of the difficulty of policing when space in a home is really used for work and how much should be deductible. Congress enacted stringent rules limiting taxpayers' ability to deduct their living expenses in the name of their home office and, between 2018 and 2025, denies the deduction completely except for those who are self-employed.[89]

When otherwise deductible as a business expense, a home office must be used exclusively and on a regular basis as the principal place for the taxpayer's business. Alternatively, space is deductible if it is used to meet with patients, clients, or customers in the normal course of work. However, taxpayers cannot claim the deduction if they also have an office at work. Finally, the home office deduction only exists for offices used in a trade or business. Home offices that are used in profit-seeking activities, such as investing, are never deductible. All of this adds up to a lot of restrictions that make it hard for people to deduct home office expenses. Partly in response, in 2013, the IRS created a form to simplify the calculation and recordkeeping requirements for claiming the deduction, although the form will need to be revised in light of the denial of the deduction for employees.[90]

Even when a home office is deductible, the deduction is limited. This deduction can only offset income from the business and is applied after other available deductions. So the home mortgage interest deduction and deductions for property taxes are first applied. This limit of what can be offset reduces the likelihood a taxpayer can use the deduction. For many, the deduction, even when allowed, goes unused.

---

[88]   Richard Eisenberg, *Secrets of Claiming a Home-Office Deduction*, FORBES, Feb. 8, 2013.

[89]   I.R.C. §§ 280A(a); 67(g).

[90]   Rev. Proc. 2013–3, 2013–1 I.R.B. 113.

(c) Business Entertainment

A final example of the fuzzy line between business and personal expenses involves business entertainment. For many decades, taxpayers exploited the idea that entertainment was the social lubricant of business in order to deduct their personal entertainment expenses. For example, in *Sanitary Farms Dairy, Inc. v. Commissioner*, the Tax Court allowed the president and controlling shareholder of a dairy to deduct the cost of an African big game hunt as a business expense because it was advertising for the dairy.[91] *Cohan v. Commissioner* also permitted taxpayers to approximate their expenses if they did not keep records.[92] The *Cohan* rule made administrative policing of these deductions almost impossible. Congress has since limited or denied these entertainment expense deductions and demanded substantiation.

In 1962, Congress first limited entertainment deductions in large part because these benefits are more often enjoyed by highly compensated employees than by low-wage workers. For decades the amount of deduction was capped at a percentage of expenses, 50% as of 2017. As of 2018, Congress denies any deduction for entertainment, amusement, or recreation expenses for entertaining clients. On the other hand, holiday parties remain 100% deductible, meals when employees travel remain 50% deductible, and business meals provided for the convenience of the employer are now 50% deductible, although the latter are fully disallowed as of 2025 unless Congress takes further action. In many ways, these expenses are now seen as more personal than business.

§ 11.06   Hedge Funds and Private Equity Funds

Investment funds allow investors to pool their capital. Generally, hedge funds invest in securities and other liquid investments and private equity funds invest in the equity of operational businesses. Private equity funds can be divided into sub-groups: venture capital funds invest in businesses at relatively early stages of development; LBO (leveraged buy-out) funds invest in more established companies with sufficient cash flow to pay down or pay off the debt used to acquire them; angel funds help pure start-ups; distressed securities funds invest in financially troubled corporations; mezzanine funds provide capital shortly before an IPO (initial public offering). There are also real estate funds, geographically targeted funds, and many more.

---

[91]   25 T.C. 463 (1955).
[92]   39 F.2d 540 (2d Cir. 1930).

Over $2.4 trillion is invested through hedge funds and $2 trillion through private equity funds.[93] The funds share many similarities but also possess important differences in investment strategies. Although hedge funds were originally known for hedging (or reducing the risk of) investments, today hedge funds are often aggressively managed, highly leveraged, and make use of derivatives in a wide range of markets. Nevertheless, hedge funds almost always invest in liquid assets that are bought and sold frequently. On the other hand, private equity funds invest money raised from investors and from borrowings in the equity and debt of private operating companies, called portfolio companies. Private equity funds tend to hold investments in portfolio companies for several years. Typically a single private equity firm manages a series of distinct funds that each invests in different portfolio companies. Private equity managers often raise a new fund every three to five years.

Because of securities laws, interests in both types of funds are generally sold only to sophisticated or accredited investors (defined terms under federal securities law) and cannot be offered to the general public. These limits mean that only investors with significant assets can invest in these types of funds. As a result of the limited offering, these funds often avoid direct regulatory oversight by the Securities Exchange Commission (the SEC). Instead, these funds often impose their own requirements on their investors. Hedge funds are often structured as open-ended funds that allow investors to deposit or withdraw funds on a monthly or quarterly basis; private equity funds are typically for a fixed term of years during which investors cannot withdraw money.

(a) Structure of Funds

The structure of funds is relatively consistent across the market but with notable variations. Funds normally have onshore (meaning U.S.) and offshore (meaning non-U.S.) components. The onshore component is generally a limited partnership (LP) or a limited liability company (LLC). The offshore component is an entity taxable as a corporation for U.S. tax purposes set up in a low-tax jurisdiction, such as the Cayman Islands. Either the two components feed into a master fund or are operated side by side. Generally the master-feeder structure has reduced trading and administrative costs and guarantees consistent returns to the feeders because only the master invests. On the other hand, an offshore fund may be subject to U.S. withholding on dividends if it invests in a U.S. master, and

---

[93]   Brett Nelson, *Hedge Funds: How They Invest Their $2.4 Trillion War Chest*, FORBES, Jun. 30, 2013; THECITYUK, PRIVATE EQUITY, Jul. 2012.

differences among investors' preferences might make different strategies more appropriate for different funds.

The offshore component is primarily to mitigate concerns regarding U.S. tax for non-U.S. taxpayers and U.S. tax-exempts. An offshore component acts as a "blocker" corporation to prevent U.S. filing and taxpaying obligations. Blocker corporations are in low-tax jurisdictions because they provide little benefit except for their role in blocking U.S. tax obligations. The concerns of non-U.S. taxpayers and U.S. tax-exempts are related but different. Non-U.S. taxpayers worry that the fund's investments will produce income that is effectively connected to a U.S. trade or business, which if held directly by a non-U.S. taxpayer or indirectly through a pass-through entity would produce taxpaying and tax filing obligations. Non-U.S. taxpayers do not want to risk becoming subject to the U.S.'s worldwide tax regime.[94] U.S. tax-exempt investors (such as pension funds and charities) worry the investments will create unrelated business taxable income (UBTI).[95] If a U.S. tax-exempt has UBTI, the tax-exempt must report this income and pay tax on it as a U.S. taxpayer.

Investors investing through offshore blocker corporations must worry about U.S. withholding. Most countries require the payers of dividends and royalties to foreign recipients to withhold income tax from the payments. Although the U.S. does not tax gains from portfolio investment activities, dividends from the U.S. are generally subject to a 30% withholding tax unless the rate is reduced in a tax treaty.[96] Additionally, some countries, including the U.S., require a purchaser of real property to withhold. Under the Foreign Investment in Real Property Tax Act (FIRPTA), the U.S. imposes a 10% withholding tax on the gross sales price of U.S. real property unless advance IRS approval is obtained for a lower rate.[97] Withholding in these contexts is not the same as wage withholding; withholding on funds leaving the U.S. is the tax and is not offset by deductions or credits or used to pay some other amount owed.

On the other hand, U.S. taxpayers investing abroad, for example in a non-U.S. master fund, should worry that the fund is taxed as a passive foreign investment company (PFIC).[98] PFICs are a subset of pooled investments registered outside the U.S. and often include non-U.S. mutual funds, hedge funds, and pension plans. An investor in a PFIC can choose either current taxation or deferral of income but

---

[94]   For more on the U.S.'s worldwide taxation, see Chapter 12.01(b).
[95]   For more on UBTI, see Chapter 14.04.
[96]   Treas. Reg. § 1.1441–2.
[97]   I.R.C. § 1445.
[98]   I.R.C. § 1297.

with an interest payment to the U.S. government. Congress's goal with PFICs was to equalize the tax treatment of investors in offshore funds with investors in U.S. funds. Additionally, a PFIC's income, including capital gains, is generally taxed as ordinary income and taxed at the highest marginal rate and not the taxpayer's personal rate; and a PFIC's capital losses cannot be carried forward or offset other capital gains. The result is that it does not make sense for most Americans to invest in non-U.S. mutual funds or hedge funds or even to hold certain foreign bank accounts.

A tax concern for all investors in private equity funds that have gone public and so are available for purchase on a public exchange is double taxation. Ordinarily, publicly-traded partnerships (or PTPs[99]) are taxable as corporations and, therefore, PTPs face double taxation. Funds need to qualify for an exception to PTP status. One exception is if a partnership holds a sufficient amount of passive income, which includes interest and dividends. When Blackstone Group went public in 2007, it argued that the investments they actively managed fell within the literal language of this exception.[100] Thus, despite the funds being actively managed and traded, Blackstone's assets are sufficiently passive so that the funds do not qualify as PTPs.

Some politicians, including Senators Max Baucus (D-MT) and Chuck Grassley (R-IA), have argued that not requiring double taxation is a loophole and that funds traded on stock exchanges should be taxed as corporations. The Treasury Department declines to endorse that theory. In 2014, Representative David Camp (R-MI) proposed to tax all publicly-traded equity funds as corporations except those involved in the energy sector, a move that the Joint Committee on Taxation estimated would raise $4.3 billion over 10 years.[101]

(b) Managers' Fees

U.S. fund managers manage approximately 70% of global fund assets.[102] How they are paid has important tax considerations. Funds typically pay their investment manager an annual management fee (historically 2% of the fund's assets) and a performance fee

---

[99]   PTP can mean two different things. First, as discussed here, it is a partnership subject to double taxation as a C corporation pursuant to § 7704. Second, PTP may refer to a partnership that is traded on a securities market regardless of how it is taxed.

[100]   Securities and Exchange Commission, The Blackstone Group L.P., Form S-1, Mar. 22, 2007, https://www.sec.gov/Archives/edgar/data/1393818/0001047469070020 68/0001047469-07-002068-index.htm (last visited Sept. 27, 2017).

[101]   Victor Fleisher, *The So-Called Blackstone Bill, Resurrected*, N.Y. TIMES, Feb. 27, 2014.

[102]   THECITYUK, HEDGE FUNDS (2012).

(historically 20% of the increase in the fund's net asset value during the year). The performance fee is intended to be the primary form of payment and is popularly called the "carried interest" or the "carry."

The management fee is taxed as payment for use of the fund's infrastructure. For large funds, the standard 2% is often considered excessive to cover costs, and there is downward business pressure on this percentage. Regardless of the amount, management fees are taxed to the managers (often the management LLC) as regular business income at ordinary rates. The fee is also a deductible business expense by the fund. This aspect of managers' payment is not controversial from a tax perspective.

The tax treatment of the carry is more complicated, and there can be a lot of tax revenue at stake. The top twenty-five hedge fund managers were reported each to earn at least $130 million in 2016, with the top earner earning $440 million, and this was considered a bad year for hedge funds.[103] Earnings at the top are far higher than in any other sector of the financial industry. Of course, many managers are not getting paid a carry at all.

Not all carries are the same; their structure varies as part of a waterfall of the fund's earnings. The waterfall determines who receives shares of the fund's growth and in what order. One typical feature is a hurdle, which subordinates the manager's return to the investors. A hurdle gives investors a timing advantage, which may be important if a fund is successful but not too successful. With a hurdle, the investors are entitled to the first bite of the fund's gains up to a certain percentage but, after that success, the manager catches up by receiving the next share of gains equal that given to the investors.

For example, the waterfall of a fund's earnings could go, first, to the investors until they recover their invested capital; second, to the investors until they recover the amount the fund spends on fees and expenses related to their investment; third, to the investors until they recover their share of the fund's losses and expenses on prior sales, if any occurred; fourth, to the investors until they receive a 5% hurdle return times the sum of the first through third; fifth, to the manager until the manager recovers an amount equal to the fourth; and sixth, 80% to the investors and 20% to the manager. This waterfall makes the investors whole for their capital contribution, share of expenses, and prior losses and then gives them 5%. Only if the fund is able to make all of these payments to the investors does the manager receive anything, and then up to a 5% share. If the fund

103   Stephen Taub, *The 2017 Rich List of the World's Top-Earning Hedge Fund Managers*, INSTITUTIONAL INVESTOR'S ALPHA, May 16, 2017.

does well enough to make all of those payments, everything else is split 80/20.

Alternatively, the fund could be structured to provide investors a true preferred return. In that case, the investors receive back their investment plus some amount. To the manager, a preferred return is like paying interest on a debt funded by the investors. Managers only participate in the fund's gains once its investments' gains exceed the preferred return and then only to the extent of the excess. For example, the waterfall could go, first, to the investors until they recover their invested capital; second, to the investors until they recover the amount the fund spends on fees and expenses related to their investment; third, to the investors until they recover their share of the fund's losses and expenses on any prior sales; fourth, to the investors until they receive 5% times the sum of first through third; and fifth, 80% to the investors and 20% to the manager. The difference between the hurdle and preferred return is the elimination of the fifth step in the hurdle waterfall that allows the manager to catch up to the investors.

Waterfalls may be more complicated for private equity funds. Private equity funds often have clawback provisions that partially adjust for the distortions caused by these funds' longer-term investment strategies. The timing of gains and losses may distort the economic bargain if gains or losses are triggered consecutively. Managers are often paid when gains exceed losses over a designated period, but they are only intended to benefit if aggregate gains exceed aggregate losses. If losses precede gains, gains reimburse losses before the managers receive a carry distribution. However, if gains precede losses, managers may receive a distribution based on the gains. With a clawback, managers are required to return all or a portion of the carry already distributed if there are subsequent losses, and these returned amounts are distributed to investors.

From a tax perspective, private equity fund managers prefer carry to fees because their carry may benefit from long-term capital gain rates if the fund generates long-term capital gains rather than ordinary income. Permitting the character of managers' compensation to flow through the fund to align the financial interests of management with investors. In the process, however, it taxes private equity fund managers' chief compensation, or what is effectively salary normally taxed at ordinary income rates, at preferential rates. The Tax Cuts and Jobs Act limited this flow-through benefit to only those managers with a 3-year holding period, if the payment is received in connection with the performance of services for the fund.[104] This narrow change was only for capital gains and not the receipt of dividends taxable at favorable capital gain rates.

That private equity managers may enjoy a conversion of ordinary income into capital gain is not new or unusual. The deferral and lower tax rate occurs because the tax system ignores the manager's receipt of the right to 20% of the fund's growth. There is no current taxation even though the receipt is compensation for the manager's future efforts for the fund. The receipt is ignored because the IRS issued a rule in 1993 that provides that the receipt of a profits interest, or an interest in a partnership's future earnings, is not subject to current taxation in most circumstances.[105] To qualify for this deferral, the partnership and the manager must agree to treat the manager as a current member of the partnership and not claim a deduction for compensation when the manager's interest vests. Therefore, the fund gives up a deduction in return for the manager not being currently taxed on income. This generally applicable partnership rule exists because it is hard to value an interest in future profits yet to be earned.

In 2008, Professor Victor Fleischer published a law review article, *Two and Twenty: Taxing Partnership Profits in Private Equity Funds*, triggering a strong public reaction to this perceived abuse of carried interests.[106] Politicians and academics have criticized the carry's tax benefits, which are created by the partnership form, resulting in the change for 2018. Other proposals would require current taxation of allocations to managers even if money is not distributed or would require a current valuation of the carried interest when it is received; others would require the carried interest be taxed as ordinary income when the income is allocated. The difficulty with most proposals, as raised by the Treasury Department, is that they alter generally applicable partnership law for a single industry.[107] Drawing the line around which partnerships and which types of preferred returns would be subject to a new rule is difficult.

In the face of legislative proposals, fund managers have proven resilient in their tax planning. As a group, they are extraordinarily wealthy and well-advised taxpayers. For example, the Emergency

---

[104]   I.R.C. § 1061. In 2005, the Treasury Department issued proposed regulations that would apply to these types of compensatory partnership interests when, and if, the regulations are finalized. Notice 2005–43, 2005–1 C.B. 1221.

[105]   Rev. Proc. 93–27, 1993–2 C.B. 343.

[106]   Victor Fleischer, *Two and Twenty*, 83 N.Y.U. L. REV. 1 (2008).

[107]   *Testimony of Treasury Assistant Secretary for Tax Policy, Eric Solomon, Before Senate Finance Committee on the Taxation of Carried Interest*, 110th Cong. (2007).

Economic Stabilization Act of 2008 eliminated managers' ability to defer the 20% carry in offshore funds and requires managers take existing deferrals into income by 2017.[108] Private equity fund managers' response was the creation of a "mini-master" fund structure that uses a U.S. master fund with fees changed to allocations to preserve some deferral and to maximize other tax advantages. Similarly, hedge fund managers have funded 401(k)s with their carries so that appreciation on their interest is never taxed.[109] Another strategy is for managers to operate a reinsurance company in Bermuda as the capital base for investment in a hedge fund.[110] By stapling the reinsurance business to the fund interest, fund profits are deferred from U.S. taxation. To date, no specific proposals target these individual planning techniques.

(c) Crowdfunding

Crowdfunding is a relatively new process of asking a large number of people for small amounts of money to fund a business or other activity. Crowdfunding has become popular in the last decade as people have recognized the utility of the Internet for widely disseminating pleas for funding. Most limits on crowdfunding are imposed outside of taxation. For example, federal securities laws limit many businesses' ability to issue securities in return for Internet funding, although a limit that has loosened in recent years.[111] As alternatives, some enterprises offer meetings with those seeking the funds or advance copies in return for funding.

The proper tax treatment of contributors or recipients of crowdfunded donations has not been definitively decided. The IRS has issued no formal guidance and no litigated cases have involved these issues. Unless Congress takes a position, the taxation of crowdfunding is likely to be complicated because of the many models that crowdfunding takes.[112] That assumes, of course, that the IRS pursues crowdfunding, in which case the issue will almost certainly go to court.

For those who contribute to crowdfunding, the tax treatment of small amounts of cash contributions should have no tax effect.

---

[108]   Pub. L. No. 110–343, § 801, 122 Stat. 3765 (Oct. 3, 2008) (adding I.R.C. § 457A).

[109]   Jonathan Wiseman, *Romney's Returns Revive Scrutiny of Lawful Offshore Tax Shelters*, N.Y. TIMES, Feb. 7, 2012.

[110]   Zachary Mider, *A Hedge Fund Tax Dodge Uses Bermuda Reinsurers*, BLOOMBERG, Feb. 21, 2013.

[111]   Gary Ross, *Crowdfunding and the New SEC Rules*, ABOVE THE LAW, May 19, 2016.

[112]   Paul Battista, *The Taxation of Crowdfunding: Income Tax Uncertainties and a Safe Harbor Test to Claim Gift Tax Exclusion*, 65 U. KAN. L. REV. 143 (2015).

However, significant cash contributions or contributions of appreciated or depreciated assets would likely have income tax or gift tax consequences for contributors. To the extent contributions are of appreciated or depreciated property, the contributor would recognize the gain or loss if the contribution is not from the donor's detached and disinterested generosity.[113] If the contribution were deemed to be a gift for tax purposes, the transfer would not be subject to income tax but would be subject to the gift tax if in excess of the annual exemption and unified credit.[114] In either case, large transfers may subject contributors to tax. Contributors are also likely subject to tax on anything they receive in return for contributions, although with current practical limits on returns the tax should be minimal.

The larger concern is the taxation of recipients, particularly if large sums are raised. The person who creates a campaign and collects more than $20,000 in 200 or more transactions will receive a Form 1099-K reporting these amounts, alerting the IRS to the fundraising. In this case, the difference in tax treatment is more extreme. If the transactions are determined to be gifts, the recipient would not need to pay tax on the receipt.[115] However, if contributors made contributions in return for a reward, the contributions are a purchase, and the crowdfunding is taxable to the recipient. If that were the case, successful campaigns may generate a large tax bill.

§ 11.07   Illegal Businesses

Everyone must pay the taxes they legally owe on their income even if their income is earned in an illegal business. Failure to pay those taxes would be another illegal act. Al Capone learned this the hard way; he was incarcerated for tax evasion.[116] The Supreme Court has not accepted a Fifth Amendment defense to tax filing, that reporting one's illegal income on a tax return is equivalent to a forced confession.[117] Additionally, the Court recognizes, but is not persuaded by, the fact that paying taxes means a thief will have fewer resources to pay back the lawful owner of stolen goods.[118]

For some but not all illegal activities, owners can deduct their expenses and pay tax on net income, the same as legal businesses do. For example, a person engaged in securities fraud was permitted to deduct the cost of his legal defense as an ordinary and necessary

---

[113]   Comm'r v. Duberstein, 363 U.S. 278, 285 (1960).

[114]   For more on the gift tax, see Chapter 9.02.

[115]   I.R.C. § 102.

[116]   Capone v. U.S. 56 F.2d 927 (1931), *cert. denied*, 286 U.S. 553 (1932); U.S. v. Capone, 93 F.2d 840 (1937), *cert. denied*, 303 U.S. 651 (1938).

[117]   U.S. v. Sullivan, 274 U.S. 259 (1927); Garner v. U.S., 424 U.S. 648 (1976).

[118]   James v. U.S., 366 U.S. 213 (1961), *overruling* Comm'r v. Wilcox, 327 U.S. 404 (1946).

business expense.[119] However, businesses are not able to deduct fines for illegal activities or bribes to U.S. government officials.[120] Similarly, in response to a Tax Court case regarding a drug dealer who successfully claimed a deduction for his home-office, packaging expenses, and the scale to weigh his drugs, in 1982 Congress prohibited deductions for expenses associated with the business of trafficking in illegal drugs.[121] Congress chose to narrowly target drug trafficking rather than all illegal activities.

The rule denying business deductions for illegal drug businesses is currently being applied to marijuana businesses in the thirty states and District of Columbia that permit the sale of the drug, some limited to medical purposes.[122] Therefore, these businesses are taxed on a gross, and not net, basis except for the cost of buying their inventory. They must report all of their income without deducting the other costs of producing that income. In response to several states requesting the IRS stop enforcing this prohibition, the IRS responded that Congress would need to change the law.[123]

---

[119] Comm'r v. Tellier, 383 U.S. 687 (1966).

[120] I.R.C. § 162(c), (f).

[121] I.R.C. § 280E; Edmondson v. Comm'r, T.C. Memo. 1981–623.

[122] Olive v. Comm'r, 791 F.3d 1146 (2015); Californians Helping to Alleviate Med. Problems, Inc. v. Comm'r, 128 T.C. 173 (2007).

[123] Andrew Keyso, Deputy Associate Chief Counsel, IRS, *Letters* (Dec. 16, 2010), https://www.irs.gov/pub/irs-wd/11-0005.pdf (last visited Sept. 27, 2017); IRS CCA 201504011 (Dec. 10, 2014).

Part C

WHERE TO TAX

Chapter 12

INTERNATIONAL TAXATION

Table of Sections

International taxation governs the taxation of income and profits as they flow around the globe. When income enters or leaves a country, that country must decide whether the income will be taxed there, left to be taxed in the other country, or, possibly, be taxed by both countries. The issues are relatively simple in a binary world of Country A and Country B. Once many nations with different tax regimes and different political demands are considered, conflicts and confusion mount. Nations have different incentives with respect to their tax regimes, and there is no referee to ensure that any nation complies with the few international norms that exist.

§ 12.01   Worldwide Versus Territorial Taxation

Both individuals and corporations may have income subject to tax by different nations. For example, a person who works part of the year in one country, has a permanent residence in another, and has investments in a third country must determine which country is able to tax some or all of the person's income. Most countries ascribe to the notion that double taxation, or the taxation of the same income, asset, or financial transaction by two nations, is unjust and inefficient.[1] Therefore, double taxation is often reduced through tax treaties between countries, in which countries negotiate which country will tax particular types of income.

Concepts of double taxation are independent of considerations of worldwide or territorial taxation, which determines which country should impose the tax. In other words, double taxation can exist or be eliminated in either regime. The U.S. currently operates a partially worldwide tax system but minimizes double taxation. Worldwide taxation requires U.S. citizens, no matter where they are residing, and U.S. residents, no matter where they are citizens, comply with the Internal Revenue Code by reporting and paying tax

---

[1]   Double taxation has many different usages in taxation, although all revolve around the idea that the same income is being taxed twice.

on their worldwide gross income, but the U.S. uses deductions and credits to reduce double taxation.

Worldwide taxation is relatively unusual today. Of the thirty-four nations in the Organization for Economic Cooperation and Development (OECD), fewer than ten have worldwide taxation.[2] The alternative to the worldwide tax system is a territorial tax system. Territorial taxation only requires residents, ignoring citizenship, to report and to pay tax on the income earned in the country. Nowhere are worldwide or territorial systems pure; instead each adapts to concerns about double taxation or tax avoidance.

(a) The Theory of International Taxation

The economy has grown increasingly global, although in the U.S. most consumed goods are still produced domestically. Exports plus imports have risen steadily, from 9% of the U.S.'s GDP in 1960 to 28% in 2015.[3] Additionally, U.S. private assets abroad in relation to GDP have increased from 0.20 in 1976 to 1.39 in 2013. Despite the relative size, one should not discount the importance of international business. For example, companies that operate in the U.S. but are majority foreign owned directly contributed $869.1 billion to the U.S.'s GDP in 2014, a 3.2% increase from 2013.[4] They also employed 6.4 million workers.

Most American investment abroad is not direct but is through portfolio investment. In other words, most people invest in stock and bonds of companies that are located abroad rather than opening their own companies offshore. These indirect investments comprised 18% of U.S. residents' portfolios in 2013. U.S. companies directly investing overseas have only increased from 0.12% of GDP in 1976 to 0.42% in 2013.[5] The JCT estimated that as of August 31, 2016, the amount of money earned offshore by foreign subsidiaries of U.S. parent corporations was $2.6 trillion.[6]

Much public attention on international trade focuses on the extent to which U.S. corporations have shifted their headquarters or their employees overseas. Although it is unknown how many

---

[2]   Thornton Matheson et al., *Territorial v Worldwide Corporate Taxation*, INT'L MONETARY FUND WORKING PAPER WP/13/205 (2013).

[3]   THE WORLD BANK, TRADE (% of GDP), http://data.worldbank.org/indicator/NE.TRD.GNFS.ZS (last visited Sept. 27, 2017).

[4]   U.S. BUREAU ECON. ANAL., WORLDWIDE ACTIVITIES OF U.S. MULTINATIONAL ENTERPRISES (2016).

[5]   JANE GRAVELLE, CONG. RESEARCH SERV., RL34115, REFORM OF U.S. INTERNATIONAL TAXATION: ALTERNATIVES (2015).

[6]   PRESS RELEASE, HOUSE WAYS AND MEANS CTTE, JOINT COMMITTEE ON TAXATION ESTIMATES EVEN MORE FOREIGN EARNINGS FROM U.S. COMPANIES STRANDED OVERSEAS (Sep. 29, 2016).

multinational corporations (MNCs) have left the U.S. for tax reasons, some companies have purportedly done so, including Budweiser, Frigidaire, and Purina. Since the American Jobs Creation Act was enacted in 2004, which first targeted corporate inversions, the U.S. has lost 44 company headquarters from the Fortune 500 list.[7] For example, in 2014 Burger King acquired Tim Horton's and moved its global headquarters to Canada, saving as much as $275 million in U.S. taxes, although the company claimed the decision was "not tax-driven—it's about global growth."[8] Similarly, the U.S. Department of Commerce shows that U.S. MNCs reduced their U.S. workforce by 2.9 million in the 2000s and increased their employment overseas by 2.4 million.[9]

When goods, services, and other payments flow between countries, either country could potentially tax the flow. Competing theories justify taxation by either country. First, the taxpayer's residence could provide the basis of taxation. Taxing the consumer or recipient of income allows the government to more accurately assess that taxpayer's ability to pay taxes, and the income does legally belong to that person. Second, the source of the purchased good or service could provide the basis of taxation. Source-based taxation reflects the reality that the source country provides the infrastructure necessary to generate the income. Therefore, taxation based on source permits the country that generates income to recoup its costs. The source country may also be in a better position to know of the income's existence.

Today, theorists of international taxation generally accept that income has one source nation, and the source of income should determine where the income is taxed. However, in practice the process is often a hybrid of source- and residence-based taxation. Put most simply, the source of income is where the income is considered to be generated, and hence where income is first taxed, and other countries have a lesser authority to tax the income. The source country gets the first bite out of the tax apple, but countries with residence-based systems can also tax the income secondarily.

The source of income is generally determined based on the type of income. For example, wages are generally classified as arising where the services are performed; interest and dividends are generally treated as arising where the payer resides; rent for real property is generally treated as arising where the property is

---

[7]   William McBride, *How Best to Prevent the Corporations from Leaving?*, TAX FOUNDATION (2014).

[8]   Kevin Drawbaugh, *Burger King's Move to Canada Could Save Its $275 Million in Taxes*, HUFF. POST, Feb. 10, 2015.

[9]   David Wessel, *Big U.S. Firms Shift Hiring Abroad*, WALL ST. J., Apr. 19, 2011.

situated; royalties are generally treated as arising where the property is used. Source can be contested, and conflicts are often addressed in tax treaties.

A nation's view of sourcing is influenced by its objectives for international taxation. These objectives are generally classified according to one of four theories. These theories prioritize neutrality among a set of variables because it is impossible to be neutral among all variables. In other words, each theory has a goal and recognizes that, in order to achieve that goal, other principles or objectives must be sacrificed. A country could conclude international taxation should not affect a home country's investors' incentives to invest abroad or should encourage domestic investment. No tax regime can accomplish both. A choice of either domestic investors or domestic investment must be made.[10] The adoption of a theory shapes the choices political leaders make.

First, policymakers can focus on domestic investment and encourage foreign investment in the home market. To do so, countries engage in capital import neutrality. Capital import neutrality imposes the same tax on local businesses regardless of their home countries. With capital import neutrality, all investment in Country A pays the same rate of tax regardless of whether the investor lives in Country A, Country B, or Country C. It also means that all savers receive the same after-tax return, regardless of their residence. Foreign investors are not disadvantaged by being taxed more. This theory is generally associated with territorial taxation.

Second, policymakers can level the playing field for domestic investors. Often termed capital export neutrality, the government applies the same rate of tax to the country's residents regardless of where they invest and to the country's businesses regardless of where they are located. This theory underlies much of the U.S. tax system. The nation's taxpayers pay the same tax on all income regardless of where it is earned so that they are not discouraged from investing abroad. Capital export neutrality removes domestic taxation as a factor for choosing between domestic and foreign investment. An investor choosing between investing in Country A, Country B, or Country C should choose the nation with the highest pre-tax return because the tax consequences are neutralized. When income is earned in another country, the foreign government is the source country, and the taxpayer receives foreign tax credits for payments to that government.

---

[10] Facilitating investment abroad increases returns to domestic investors over time whereas domestic investment funded by money from abroad will send returns out of the country as they are paid to investors.

Third, policymakers can focus on the nation's welfare by focusing on the nation's total return on investment. This system, termed national neutrality, differs from capital export neutrality in that only taxes to the home country are treated as improving welfare so that taxes to foreign countries are a cost of production. This theory provides a domestic deduction for all taxes, including those to a foreign government, to ensure that foreign and domestic after-tax returns are equal. Thus, national neutrality replaces capital export neutrality's foreign tax credit with a deduction. Otherwise, foreign investment is disincentivized where foreign countries impose tax. With the deduction, investors are indifferent between the pre-tax return on domestic investments and post-tax returns on foreign investments.

Finally, policymakers can adopt capital ownership neutrality, which focuses on the growth in portfolio investment. It attempts to neutralize taxation's influence on who owns assets in order to maximize productivity. In one sense capital ownership neutrality may simply require a consistent international tax regime so that any business is as competitive as any other. Alternatively, to prevent taxation from distorting ownership, capital ownership neutrality may combine capital import neutrality with deductions for domestically incurred expenses attributable to earning the exempt foreign income. Doing so shrinks the domestic tax base because capital ownership neutrality is not simply neutral as between investments but encourages the flow of investment around the world.

Underlying these theories is an assumption that people invest where taxes are lowest because these countries provide a higher return to investors. This assumption itself is debatable. First, it assumes that taxes are a significant cost of production, large enough to influence choices and outweigh other factors such as workforce and transportation costs. Second, it ignores other, immeasurable factors for investors such as convenience and familiarity that might cause investors to make irrational choices with respect to taxes.

Policymakers, some unfamiliar with tax theory, must choose among these theories of international taxation even if they do not do so explicitly.[11] And policymakers make these choices in the face of other nations who may change their policies in anticipation or in reaction to changing international events. Thus, the tax system is not static, as businesses and countries adapt to new rules and new circumstances. Ultimately, the building of a country's international tax regime is as much international relations as it is tax policy.[12] The

---

[11]   David Weisbach, *The Use of Neutralities in International Tax Policy*, 68 NAT'L TAX J. 635 (2015).

[12]   *See* Diane Ring, *International Tax Relations*, 60 TAX L. REV. 83 (2007).

goals of tax policy, namely equity, efficiency, and simplicity, are more elusive because of the infinite number of players and factors in international policymaking. Moreover, however much policymakers seek to plan through tax policy, it remains only one variable among many.

(b) Worldwide Taxation

The U.S. has an impure worldwide tax system in which U.S. citizens and residents must report their worldwide income to the IRS and, potentially, pay U.S. tax on that income. In reality, U.S. taxpayers frequently do not owe U.S. tax on the income they earn outside the U.S. There are complex rules created by tax treaties and several subparts of the Internal Revenue Code to minimize double taxation by the U.S. and foreign countries; however, the Tax Cuts and Jobs Act added new provisions governing payments or transfers of assets to a multinational corporation's subsidiaries located outside the U.S.

(i) Theoretically

First, when functioning properly and among relatively equal taxing countries (neither premise is guaranteed), a worldwide tax system should work as a worldwide information system with credits for taxes paid to foreign governments so that the home country only taxes domestically produced income. The system is more complicated because of different national tax rates and different positions regarding the repatriation of income. Repatriation simply means bringing income earned in a foreign country to the headquarter's home country.

Consider MNC Inc., with its headquarters in Country A and also operating in Country B. MNC Inc. earns $100 in each country. Country A has a 50% tax rate and Country B has a 10% tax rate. Additionally, Country A offers a tax credit for the taxes paid in Country B, and MNC Inc. repatriates all income earned in Country B to Country A.

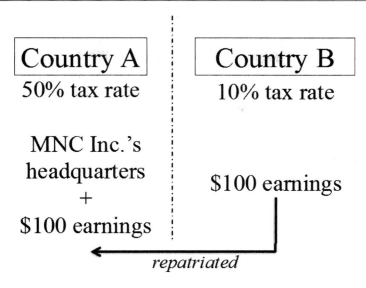

Under these facts, Country B would impose $10 in taxes on the $100 earned in that country. With repatriation of the remaining $90, Country A would tax all $200 worldwide income times its 50% rate, or $100, minus a $10 credit for taxes paid to Country B, for a total tax paid to Country A of $90. Therefore, MNC Inc. pays a total of $100 in taxes, retaining $100 in after-tax income. With repatriation, the government of Country B receives its full amount of tax and Country A receives the excess as though its higher rate were imposed globally.

The foreign tax credit offers a complete offset for the taxes paid to another country; a smaller offset is provided if a country offers a tax deduction for taxes paid to another jurisdiction instead of a credit. If Country A offers a deduction for the taxes paid to Country B, $10 is still paid to Country B but Country A reduces the amount of income subject to tax by $10. Therefore, Country A subjects $190 (rather than $200) to its 50% tax rate, so $95 is owed in tax. MNC Inc. pays a total of $105 in taxes, and MNC Inc. retains $95 after taxes. With the deduction rather than the credit, $5 less is available after taxes.

The tax results change if the worldwide system permits deferral when an MNC does not repatriate income back to its home country. Taxing foreign income only when it is repatriated creates significant incentives to shift income outside the home country's borders. Shifting this money overseas allows the MNC to benefit from the time value of that money because it is not subject to the home country's higher rates until the money is brought home. If the MNC waits to repatriate the income until the home country offers a tax holiday and imposes low or no tax, the income may go untaxed forever. A MNC may shift income by changing the location of activities generating income or by shifting income to foreign subsidiaries.

Using the above example, if the earnings in low-tax Country B remain in Country B, with deferral Country A only taxes the $100 earned in Country A. The amount earned in Country B is deferred from Country A's taxes. Therefore, $10 is paid to Country B and $50 is paid to Country A until repatriation. This leaves MNC Inc. $140 in post-tax dollars. The $40 deferred in taxes will be owed if the Country B income is ever repatriated to Country A.

(ii) The U.S. System

The U.S. system operates with foreign tax credits, adopted by the U.S. after World War I in part to encourage foreign investment to help rebuild Europe.[13] Technically, there is the choice between a deduction and a credit for foreign taxes paid; however, as shown by the example, the credit normally proves favorable.[14] Foreign tax credits reduce the amount of U.S. tax owed by anyone with foreign-source income by the amount of taxes paid to a foreign government. In 2004, U.S. MNCs paid to the federal government only $18.4 billion on foreign source income, for an effective tax rate of about 4%.[15] However, even the IRS website notes these rules are complex.

When applying the U.S. foreign tax credit system, the same rules apply for individuals and businesses and for residents and nonresidents. Source is determined for each item of income, and expenses and deductions are allocated to the income. Where the foreign tax rate of the country in which the income is taxed is greater than in the U.S., no U.S. liability is generated. However, if the U.S. tax rate is greater than the foreign tax, U.S. businesses owe residual tax to the IRS on their foreign earnings equal to the difference.

With the U.S.'s tax credit system for taxes paid to source countries, the real cost of worldwide taxation to U.S. taxpayers has been (1) the system's complexity and (2) their inability to profit from holding money and assets in low-tax jurisdictions. Tax credits generally prevent U.S. taxpayers from owing double tax on their income; however, credits are not available for income that has

---

[13] For more on the history of the foreign tax credit see, Reuven Avi-Yonah, *All of a Piece Throughout*, 25 VA. TAX REV. 313 (2005). *See also* Daniel Shavioro, *The Case Against Foreign Tax Credits*, J. LEGAL ANALYSIS 65 (2011).

[14] I.R.C. § 901; Treas. Reg. §§ 1.901–1(a), 1.901–1(d). The choice to claim foreign tax credits is an annual election.

[15] PRESIDENT'S ECONOMIC RECOVERY BOARD, THE REPORT ON TAX REFORM OPTIONS 82 (2010); GOV'T ACCOUNTABILITY OFFICE, GAO–08–850, U.S. MULTINATIONAL CORPORATIONS: EFFECTIVE TAX RATES ARE CORRELATED WITH WHERE INCOME IS REPORTED (2008).

avoided tax. With the U.S.'s corporate tax and taxes as a share of GDP below the OECD average for OECD countries, the real investment opportunities MNCs and wealthy individuals want to maximize through the repeal of worldwide taxation is the use of tax havens.[16]

Nevertheless, concerns persisted that U.S.-based MNCs were not repatriating income that would otherwise be invested in the U.S.[17] The argument was that there is money abroad that was taxed at lower rates than U.S. corporate rates and would be bought home as long as bringing it home is free from tax. Some commentators do not discuss what the repatriated money will be used for; others argue it will be invested in U.S.-based businesses to create U.S.-based jobs.

To encourage repatriation, in 2004 Congress enacted a repatriation tax holiday.[18] In a tax holiday the government offers low or no tax for designated activities. In 2004, U.S.-based MNCs could bring overseas profits back to the U.S. and pay a 5.25% tax rather than the normal 35% marginal rate. In total, $312 billion was repatriated and was estimated to cost $3.3 billion in government revenue over ten years.[19] Of the repatriated money, 77% came from OECD-labeled tax havens, such as the Bahamas and Cayman Islands, so the money had been parked in low-tax jurisdictions.

Studies have shown that the repatriation did not stimulate domestic economic growth.[20] Just fifteen companies were responsible for over 50% of total repatriations, including Pfizer, Inc., Merck & Co., Hewlett-Packard, and Johnson & Johnson. Some used repatriated money to repurchase their own stock and pay bigger dividends to shareholders; some of these firms laid off workers and decreased domestic research and development as they paid their dividends.[21] Professor Thomas Brennan found that since 2007 firms

---

[16]   JANE GRAVELLE, CONG. RESEARCH SERV., R41743, INTERNATIONAL CORPORATE TAX RATE COMPARISONS AND POLICY IMPLICATIONS (2014); OECD.Stat., REVENUE STATISTICS—OECD COUNTRIES, http://stats.oecd.org/Index.aspx?DataSetCode=REV (last visited Sept. 27, 2017). *But see* PwC & WORLD BANK, PAYING TAXES 2017 (2017) (finding U.S. corporate rate is 27.9% and OECD average only 15.9%).

[17]   For example, in early 2017 President Trump planned a 10% tax on more than $2.6 trillion held offshore, waiving additional corporate taxes. Jennifer Jacobs & Sahil Kapur, *Trump Plans to Seek 10% Tax on Offshore Earnings, Official Says*, BLOOMBERG, Apr. 25, 2017.

[18]   American Jobs Creation Act of 2004, P.L. 108–357, 118 Stat. 1418 (2004) (codified as § 965).

[19]   Kristina Peterson, *Report: Repatriation Tax Holiday a 'Failed' Policy*, WALL ST. J., Oct. 10, 2011.

[20]   Melissa Redmiles, *The One-Time Dividends-Received Deduction*, 27 STAT. INCOME BULL. 102 (2008).

[21]   SENATE PERM. SUBCOMM. ON INVESTIGATIONS, COMM. ON HOMELAND SECURITY AND GOVERNMENTAL AFFAIRS, REPATRIATING OFFSHORE FUNDS, MAJORITY STAFF REPORT 8 (2011).

anticipate a second holiday and have shifted profits overseas, increasing deposits in tax havens, as they wait for lower U.S. tax rates.[22]

Adopting a new approach, the Tax Cuts and Jobs Act of 2017 moved the U.S. further from a worldwide system but not in a simple way.[23] Congress established a limited participation exemption for certain types of businesses, at a cost of $224 billion between 2018 and 2027.[24] Under the new regime, certain foreign corporations can pay dividends of foreign-source income tax-free to a U.S. corporate shareholder that owns 10% of the dividend-paying corporation. However, to claim this offsetting exemption, the domestic corporation must have held the stock on which the dividend is paid for 366 or more days during the prior 731-day period.

Congress did not establish the exemption as a full participation exemption, which would have been a more complete move to a territorial tax system. Dividends received by non-corporate shareholders or by less than 10% corporate shareholders remain fully taxable (with the potential for foreign tax credit relief). Additionally, the exemption generally does not apply to gains from the sale of shares. Thus, there are planning opportunities as 10% corporate shareholders may choose to sell foreign assets and derive exempt dividends as compared to selling their stock.

The post-2017 system also retains other worldwide elements. Not only must taxpayers report their worldwide income, domestic corporations are taxed at a reduced rate of 10.5% on "global intangible low-taxed income" (referred to as GILTI) until 2025 and 13.125% thereafter because of changing deduction amounts; individual shareholders owe tax at their full individual rate on this income.[25] Because of complicated statutory definitions, qualifying U.S. shareholders of foreign corporations with relatively high interest expense, corporations with little basis in depreciable property, such as service corporations, and corporations with high-value intangibles may find that most of the foreign corporation's income is treated as GILTI. Continuing worldwide taxation, this tax on GILTI reduces the incentive to relocate to low-tax jurisdictions as any tax savings may be partially offset by an increase in taxes to the U.S. shareholders.

Additionally, Congress imposed a minimum tax, called the Base Erosion Anti-Abuse Tax or "BEAT," on U.S. corporations' taxable

---

[22]   Thomas Brennan, *What Happens After a Holiday?*, 5 NW. J. L. & SOC. POL'Y 1 (2010).

[23]   Pub. L. No. 115–97, 131 Stat. 2054.

[24]   I.R.C. § 245A.

[25]   I.R.C. § 951A.

income, ignoring certain payments made to foreign affiliated corporations.[26] The tax ensures that large U.S. corporations with average annual gross receipts of at least $500 million for the three preceding taxable years that make significant outbound payments to foreign affiliates of 3% or more of all of their deductions pay a minimum amount of U.S. tax. The minimum tax rate is 5% in 2018, 10% in 2019 through 2025, and 12.5% in 2026 and later years. This narrow tax is intended to discourage transferring assets to affiliates in low-tax jurisdictions.

On the other hand, a lower than the 21% statutory rate of only 13.125% tax rate (increased to 16.41% in 2026 and later years) applies to a domestic corporation's "foreign-derived intangible income" (or FDII, because international tax is replete with acronyms).[27] This favorable rate is for income related to services provided and goods sold by a domestic corporation for foreign use and is intended to encourage businesses to bring offshore intangibles back to the U.S. However, this targeted tax reduction is likely to be subject to objection by the World Trade Organization (WTO), of which the U.S. is a member, as an impermissible export subsidy.

These many changes in the Tax Cuts and Jobs Act strike a balance that partially eliminates the need for deferral for qualifying U.S. shareholders. Before 2018, when a business was operated in a foreign subsidiary that was a separate entity recognized in the U.S. as a foreign corporation, the income was generally subject to U.S. tax only when dividends were paid to the U.S. parent entity. Playing on the sourcing rules, some MNCs chose to locate different subsidiaries in nations with favorable tax rates. After strategic placement, MNCs only faced U.S. tax when they repatriated the income and then benefited from foreign tax credits. For shareholders qualifying for the post-2017 exemption, tax is never owed and not merely deferred.

However, to help fund the adoption of the exemption and prevent abuse, Congress adopted the new rules discussed above and imposed a one-time tax on many U.S. shareholders of foreign corporations, even some who will not benefit from the exemption. The tax on the shareholder's pro rata share of undistributed earnings accumulated offshore between 1986 and 2017 at rates of 8% and 15.5% for corporate investors (for earnings invested in tangible assets versus cash) and 9.05% and 17.54% for investors taxed as individuals and subject to the highest marginal rate.[28] The deemed repatriations can generally be paid over 8 years. This one-time tax masks the long-term cost of the exemption and effectively unlocks income that has been

---

[26]   I.R.C. § 59A.

[27]   I.R.C. § 250.

[28]   Revised I.R.C. § 965.

stashed overseas and permits its future tax-free return to the U.S. at an estimated cost to taxpayers of $339 billion over 10 years.

Congress also disallowed certain planning techniques that had been used to reduce MNCs taxable income. Beginning in 2018, corporations are disallowed deductions for payments of interest or royalties to a non-U.S. corporation related under the same common parent in a "hybrid transaction" or to a "hybrid entity."[29] These hybrids exist if the payment would otherwise generate a deduction in the U.S. but not be included in income in the other country.

Finally, Congress liberalized laws that discourage the shifting of income or assets to low-tax jurisdictions. For example, Congress made it more likely that taxpayers will be subject to the controlled foreign corporation (CFC) rules, which require certain shareholders of certain foreign corporations to currently report for U.S. tax purposes certain of a CFC's passive income (rents and royalties) and investment income (interest and dividends).[30] In other words, the CFC rules minimize deferral by requiring current U.S. taxation but only for 10% U.S. shareholders of certain foreign corporations, although as of 2018 the complex rules attributing ownership among people make it more likely a taxpayer is treated as owning significantly more than he directly owns.

Together these new rules will influence how MNCs choose to allocate income and expenses among member entities in a process known as transfer pricing. U.S. transfer pricing rules generally require related parties charge each other prices similar to what unrelated parties would charge.[31] Rules prescribe methods for testing whether prices meet this standard. The rules generally require a comparison of the related party transaction to similar transactions of unrelated parties. When there are insufficient comparable unrelated party transactions, surrogates may be permitted using comparable uncontrolled transaction prices, resale prices based on comparable markups, cost plus a markup, or an enterprise profitability method. Needless to say, transfer pricing is complicated and a big business for accounting firms and MNCs.

Thus, in 2017, Congress encouraged repatriation to the U.S. of money stashed overseas as it strengthened rules that should discourage businesses from shifting income and assets overseas in the future. News reports indicate that some businesses, such as Comcast, reported windfalls as others, such as Goldman Sachs, took

---

[29]   I.R.C. § 267A.

[30]   I.R.C. § 957.

[31]   I.R.C. § 482.

hits in its fourth quarter earnings.[32] It is impossible at this early date to conclude whether the new provisions will help the economy in the long-term or how businesses will respond.

(c) Territorial Taxation

Many American politicians have proposed adopting a territorial tax regime, often without discussing the particulars of what this system entails.[33] As compared to worldwide taxation, a territorial tax regime taxes only the income earned in the taxing country. Therefore, income earned in foreign countries is left to be taxed, or not, by foreign jurisdictions. Put simplistically, a territorial regime divides the world into fiefs where each country is able to tax the transactions that go on within its borders. However, no advanced country operates a pure territorial tax system but, instead, operates a hybrid with features of worldwide taxation.

For example, MNC Inc. has its headquarters in Country A, a country with pure territorial taxation. Country A has a 50% tax rate and in which MNC Inc. earns $100. MNC Inc. also earns $100 in Country B, and Country B has a 10% tax rate. After paying tax in Country B, MNC Inc. has $90 of post-tax income in Country B. That income is not taxable in Country A, which taxes only the $100 earned in Country A. Therefore, MNC Inc. owes $10 of tax to Country B and $50 of tax to Country A, for a total of $60 in tax. This leaves $140 in post-tax income. These tax results do not change whether or not MNC Inc. repatriates the income earned in Country B to Country A.

Although a territorial system only taxes income earned in the source country, such a system can operate in many ways. The system need not be as complex as a worldwide system because the international flow of income can be ignored, but ignoring international transfers encourages tax evasion. A territorial tax system could also become as complex as a worldwide system if the territorial system polices attempts to illegally portray income as earned in a low-tax jurisdiction. To facilitate policing, territorial taxation could allocate income with methods as complex as any worldwide system.

In practice, most countries attempt to reduce tax evasion and their territorial tax regimes are not pure. Most countries adopt some form of exemption system under which foreign source income is reported to the home country but mostly exempt from tax. For

---

[32]   Shawn Tully, *How Tax Reform Makes Goldman Sachs a Winner—And a Loser*, FORTUNE, Jan. 30, 2018.

[33]   *See* Derek Thompson, *A Comprehensive Guide to Donald Trump's Tax Proposal*, THE ATLANTIC, Apr. 26, 2017; Allison Burke, *How the Presidential Candidates Plan to Tackle Tax Policy*, BROOKINGS INST. (2016).

example, the home country may provide a 95% exclusion for foreign earnings so that the earnings are reported but the bulk of them are not subject to tax. The exemption helps offset the fact that the home country does not grant deductions for the cost of earning foreign income.

Moving from a worldwide to an impure territorial system would likely reduce tax revenue. Unless the domestic economy increases significantly in size as a result of a change in tax regimes, the cost of the switch could be substantial. The amount of revenue depends upon how the system is structured. In other words, a government could strengthen regimes that decrease the shifting of domestic profits overseas to bolster domestic source revenue as it accepts less revenue from foreign sources. Estimates if the U.S. government converted ranged from costing $130 billion to raising $76 billion over ten years.[34] Those making these estimates cannot know for certain how businesses will respond.

Within the U.S., arguments for territorial taxation are more prevalent during times of economic recession or after prominent businesses relocate their headquarters offshore. Supporters of territorial taxation argue that limiting the U.S.'s taxing powers will improve the domestic economy. In doing so, they frequently assume, although the assumption has not been proven, that territoriality would improve the competitiveness of American-based businesses. Therefore, businesses will retain or possibly establish headquarters in the U.S. because MNCs, as well as individuals, would not be taxed in the U.S. on that portion of their income not earned in the U.S. or that is shifted to other markets.

This argument accepts that businesses merge abroad, such as Burger King's merger into Tim Horton's, in order to avoid the U.S.'s worldwide taxation. Under this theory, the drag of worldwide taxation is sufficient to overcome any benefit offered by being headquartered in the U.S. Therefore, territorial taxation does not require that the U.S. reduce its domestic corporate income tax rates to offset this particular drag, although its proponents also tend to favor this policy.

In another sense, however, territorial taxation may force the U.S. government to decrease domestic tax rates. Territorial taxation may force the American government to make better use of its resources in order to compete for investment. Because worldwide taxation increases the cost of investing and producing abroad to equal domestic tax rates, domestic taxes can be artificially high. By

---

[34] PRESIDENT'S ECONOMIC RECOVERY BOARD, THE REPORT ON TAX REFORM OPTIONS 90 (2010).

removing tax impediments to investing abroad, in other words by being neutral as to the location of investment, territorial taxation forces the domestic government to reduce taxes in order to compete. A risk of this approach, however, is that money will flow out of the U.S. as domestic producers find that they cannot be more efficient faced with domestic constraints and are now free to invest in low-tax jurisdictions.

One reason to worry about decreasing the relative cost of U.S. investment abroad is if there is a limited amount of investment dollars. With finite investment, increasing investment abroad necessarily decreases domestic investment. However, investment is unlikely to be finite. Two studies show that foreign and domestic investment are compliments and not substitutes.[35] Professors Mihir Desai, Fritz Foley, and James Hines, Jr., found that 10% greater foreign investment is associated with 2.6% greater domestic investment, and that $1 of new foreign investment is associated with $3.50 of new domestic investment. Although this finding does not mean that increasing foreign investment would necessarily increase domestic investment because there are too many variables at play, it does suggest that foreign investment would not starve its domestic counterpart.

Regardless of territorial taxation's economic results, proponents of territorial taxation sometimes claim that the U.S. government has no right to tax or know about what a U.S.-based corporation does outside its borders. This desire for privacy supports a claim that what goes on beyond a nation's borders is beyond the nation's informational reach. However, even countries with territorial tax systems often seek global information if only to ensure that domestically produced income is taxed.

If taxpayers in territorial systems are able to source income to a low- or no-tax jurisdiction, that income is never taxed even if it is repatriated to a high-tax jurisdiction. This creates an absolute gain for taxpayers, whereas under the worldwide system this shifting is generally a timing advantage. In other words, a territorial system is more prone to income shifting because territorial taxation not only defers U.S. tax but also completely excludes such income from taxation. Consequently, serious problems of corporate profit shifting and tax evasion worsen under territorial regimes, which necessitates retention of many of the same rules and compliance tools as exist under worldwide taxation.

---

[35]   Mihir A. Desai et al., *Domestic Effects of the Foreign Activities of U.S. Multinationals*, 1 AM. ECON. J. 181 (2009); Madanmohan Ghosh & Weimin Wang, *Does FDI Accelerate Economic Growth? The OECD Experience Based on Panel Data Estimates for the Period 1980–2004*, 9 GLOBAL ECON. J. 4 (2009).

Anti-abuse rules to prevent evasion can turn a territorial system into something akin to a worldwide system. For example, Japan revised it corporate tax system in 2009, and the new regime is often labeled territorial.[36] However, the income of foreign subsidiaries of a Japanese MNC that faces less than a 20% effective tax rate on its foreign profits or headquarters of an MNC in a jurisdiction with no income tax is subject to Japan's domestic corporate income tax rate. Soon thereafter, Japan strengthened its anti-avoidance and income shifting measures as well as it CFC rules. To deter income shifting, companies must now maintain better documentation, and they have less ability to make interest bearing inter-company loans.

Similarly, in October 2016 the European Union (EU) launched a system of formulary apportionment that aims to ensure income earned in the EU is taxed to some EU country.[37] In March 2018, an EU Parliament approved, although the EU Council and Commission must still act, the Common Consolidated Corporate Tax Base that would require a MNC operating in more than one European country to apportion its income according to a formula that uses assets, labor force, and sales (the same factors traditionally used by U.S. states for state-level apportionment). These factors of production are harder to hide or shift between countries than intellectual property. This changes the consideration of intercompany transactions. Countries would then tax their allocable share at their domestic tax rates.

The retention of domestic rates for taxing domestic earnings, without a global allocation scheme, means that territorial taxation retains existing incentives to earn income in low-tax rather than in high-tax jurisdictions. Consequently, the U.S. should not expect significant domestic growth from a change in regimes and probably a drain in the corporate income tax. If a goal of changing tax regimes is to be neutral as among investment locations, a result may be that all else being equal the lowest-tax jurisdiction wins.

Finally, because of its potential for increasing tax competition, territorial taxation might harm poorer countries to the extent it changes their incentives for their domestic tax policies. Under worldwide taxation, poorer countries have less pressure to cut domestic tax rates because the advantage is timing in that repatriated income is eventually taxed at higher-income countries' rates. With the complete exemption of foreign-source income through

---

[36]   Ruud de Mooij & Ikuo Saito, *Japan's Corporate Income Tax*, IMF WORKING PAPER WP/14/138, at 11–12 (2014).

[37]   EUROPEAN COMMISSION, CORPORATE TAX REFORM PACKAGE (2016), https://ec. europa.eu/taxation_customs/business/company-tax/corporate-tax-reform-package_en _en (last visited Sept. 27, 2017).

territorial taxation, MNCs may care even more about host countries' taxation, which may push down poor countries' tax rates.

(d) Tax Treaties

Tax treaties (also called double tax agreements) exist between many countries on a bilateral or multilateral basis. The goal is to prevent the double taxation of income, profit, capital gain, or inheritance by the different governments. To this end, treaties provide definitions of key terms that are specific to the countries involved and adopt rules for sourcing. Treaties also adopt information sharing measures to ensure compliance. Thus, a fundamental purpose of tax treaties is to build better working relationships between taxpayers and tax collecting agencies in the relevant countries.

Taxpayers enjoy benefits from working in countries that are linked with tax treaties. Most treatises reduce rates of taxation on dividends, interest, and royalties between taxpayers of the respective countries. Additionally, they tend to limit each country's ability to tax business profits. Finally, they often have "tie breaker" clauses for conflicts between residency rules that make resolving disagreements over double taxation easier for their taxpayers.

From the governments' perspective, negotiating a treaty is often time consuming and costly, and tax treaties confer some degree of recognition on the treaty partner. Therefore, developed countries have a large number of tax treaties, and developing countries have significantly fewer. For example, the U.S. has treaties with 68 countries and the United Kingdom has treaties with more than 110 countries and territories.[38] If a country is regarded as a tax haven, it is unlikely to have many, if any, treaty partners. The Cayman Islands has no double tax treaties.

Since the League of Nations adopted a 1928 model bilateral income tax treaty, many countries begin negotiations from a model tax treaty.[39] However, because treaties are heavily negotiated, no two treaties are the same. This increases complexity and the planning opportunities in the international market because parties must pay attention to the treaties between respective countries. To reduce panning opportunities, many treaties prohibit their use by residents of a third country who do not meet additional tests. These attempts

---

[38]   U.S. income tax treaties are available at: https://www.irs.gov/businesses/international-businesses/united-states-income-tax-treaties-a-to-z. Additionally, treaties are updated at U.S. DEPT. TREAS., TREATIES AND TIEAS, https://www.treasury.gov/resource-center/tax-policy/treaties/Pages/treaties.aspx.

[39]   UNITED NATIONS, ST/ESA/PAD/SER.E21, MODEL DOUBLE TAXATION CONVENTION BETWEEN DEVELOPED AND DEVELOPING COUNTRIES, at xvi (2011).

to limit treaty shopping may focus either on objective characteristics or on a transaction's subjective purpose.

(e) Global Taxation

Global taxation differs from worldwide taxation. Global taxation has been proposed to collect taxes by a central, international revenue service.[40] The revenue that is raised would be used to address global problems, such as climate change, AIDs, or poverty and hunger. Because of administrative concerns, a global tax would likely be imposed on a narrow group of activities such as airline tickets or foreign currency transactions.

One argument in favor of a global tax is that charitable donations have proven insufficient and unreliable to cure global problems. Additionally, wealth remains highly segregated between countries, and much of the segregation was built on years of exploitation through slavery and colonialism. This latter point paints a global tax as a form of international reparation. In a practical sense, global taxation could be structured to reduce the value of MNCs engaging in tax avoidance or using tax havens.

Underlying an acceptance of global taxation is an acceptance of some notion of inter-nation equity. Do nations have claims against other nations, and should nations be able to object when other nations' tax policies cause them harm? And if different nations have different senses of taxation and equity, how can these senses be reconciled internationally? As global reparations, global taxes risk national sovereignty. Tax policy has traditionally been a matter of local government; global taxation creates an overarching taxing power that may reduce a local government's ability to tax.

To date, there is no mechanism in place to allocate any funds raised. Even if operated through the United Nations, which does not yet have such administrative capacity, there is no assurance that the money would not be siphoned off to oppressive leaders in countries with desperate need. Often ignoring the mechanics of such a regime, countries that expect to benefit directly support the global tax, and those who expect to pay may perceive a global tax as a way for the United Nations "to rob from wealthy countries and, after taking a big cut for itself, send what's left to the poor countries."[41] As a result, a

---

[40]   For example, Fidel Castro proposed a tax on financial transactions and that the United Nations administer the tax. FIDEL CASTRO RUZ, WORLD CONFERENCE AGAINST RACISM, RACIAL DISCRIMINATION, ZENOPHOBIA, AND RELATED INTOLERANCE, Sept. 1, 2001, http://www.un.org/WCAR/statements/0109cubaE.htm (last visited Sept. 27, 2017).

[41]   Ron Paul, *International Taxes?*, TEXAS STRAIGHT TALK (March 6, 2006).

global tax is likely to be strongly resisted by many countries, including the U.S.

§ 12.02 International Tax Planning

Individuals, businesses, and countries all engage in tax competition. What they hope to gain differs. Both individuals and corporations generally seek lower effective tax rates; whereas countries use tax competition to attract residents and businesses. The push and pull of tax competition ensures that it will never go away, even when there is a concerted international effort to decrease its prevalence. International tax competition makes possible the tax planning that reduces MNCs' and some individuals' taxes.

One concern stemming from this competition is that businesses, and possibly individuals, are not being required to pay their fair share of taxes or even enough to compensate their host countries for expenses directly related to them. There may also be a race to the bottom of lowering tax rates. Because of continuing competition, no nation may raise its tax rates for fear of losing the residents and businesses that the low tax rate attracted. A minimal tax rate may be locked in even when most of the country's constituents agree that some greater amount of tax revenue is necessary.

(a) Tax Havens

There is no definitive list of tax havens, and countries do not even agree what makes a tax haven. In a 2008 report, the U.S. Government Accountability Office listed the characteristics of tax havens as nil or nominal taxes; a lack of transparency regarding tax information to foreign tax authorities; a lack of transparency in the operation of legislative, legal, or administrative provisions; no requirement for a substantive local presence; and self-promotion as an offshore financial center.[42] Although most countries agree that a 0% rate with privacy laws would constitute a tax haven, what makes a rate low or nominal is not agreed upon; and it is not always agreed whether the determinative rate should be the effective or marginal rate.

Some organizations, such as the OECD, have generated lists of tax havens. Lists enable member governments to apply coordinated pressure to force listed countries to comply with the organizations' standards. Because some member countries were included in early tax haven lists because they had low tax rates, the current focus is

---

[42] GOV'T ACCOUNTABILITY OFFICE, GAO–09–157, INTERNATIONAL TAXATION (2008).

on the exchange of information.[43] In other words, providing information to a home country is the critical element for staying off tax haven lists.

Currently, the OECD maintains three separate lists of relative compliance with its standards.[44] The white list includes countries that have implemented agreed-upon standards. Countries on the gray list are those that agree to the standards but have not yet met them. Finally, there is a black list of countries that have not committed to the standards. Since 2009 no country has been on the OECD's black list. The lists have a political component as member nations object to their inclusion or of friendly countries.

Additionally, the EU creates a blacklist of the worst international tax havens, identified by member states as being non-cooperative on tax. Ten member countries must complain for a country to be included on the EU list. As with the OECD list, the goal is to pressure listed countries to change their domestic practices. But listing often leads to complaints rather than change. For example, in 2015 Guernsey complained of being included on the list, attempting to justify its 0% tax rate.[45] According to Guernsey's chief minister, only nine countries complained of Guernsey; one additional country complained of Sark, part of the same grouping of islands in the English Channel but a separate crown dependency. Of course, as Sark has only 600 or so residents, it outsources its financial and corporate regulation to the larger Guernsey. A unified EU list, published in December 2017, does not include Guernsey, which was listed as committed to addressing concerns by 2018.[46]

Reports of international tax evasion through the use of tax havens range from a doubtful $32 trillion to a more realistic $7.6 trillion.[47] A Congressional Research Service report found that 43% of foreign corporate earnings are currently held in five offshore tax preferred or tax haven countries but these companies have only 4% of their workforce and 7% of their investment located in those

---

[43]   When lists include low rates as a key factor of tax havens, Delaware is often included. Investors in Delaware can avoid the federal withholding tax on payments of dividends and interest to treaty partners and the state does not impose its income tax on payments for intangible assets, such as royalties.

[44]   OECD, LIST OF UNCO-OPERATIVE TAX HAVENS, http://www.oecd.org/countries/monaco/listofunco-operativetaxhavens.htm (last visited Mar. 2, 2018). The OECD has 34 member countries and is very influential in international tax, particularly its models for treaty negotiations and studies on various tax topics.

[45]   Simon Bowers, *For Pete's Sark!*, GUARDIAN, June 22, 2015.

[46]   Council of the European Union, *The EU List of Non-Cooperative Jurisdictions for Tax Purposes*, 15429/17, Dec. 5, 2017.

[47]   *Revealed: Global Super-Rich Has At Least $21 Trillion Hidden in Secret Tax Havens*, TAX JUSTICE NETWORK, Jul. 2012; Gabriel Zucman, *Taxing Across Borders*, 28 J. ECON. PERSPECTIVES 121 (2014).

countries.[48] Notably, an estimate in 2012 based on sixty large U.S. companies found that $166 billion was held in offshore accounts that sheltered over 40% of these corporations' profits from U.S. corporate taxation.[49]

The existence of these accounts is subject to many criticisms. First, some complain that tax havens may result in the accumulation of idle cash in countries that have little investment potential. Because of worldwide taxation, it can be expensive and inefficient to repatriate accumulated cash to the U.S. where the cash can be used, although the cash could be invested in other countries with territorial taxation. Thus, tax havens may benefit businesses in the short term but lead to wasted opportunities.

Second, wealthy businesses and individuals are more likely to benefit from tax havens than low-income taxpayers. As a result, a greater proportion of the world's tax burden is imposed on the poor. Additionally, the loss of government revenue from this tax evasion means that developed countries cannot provide as robust of a social safety net as they could if those countries had the tax revenue. Finally, tax havens may facilitate illegal tax evasion or be connected to fraud, money laundering, and terrorism.

On the other hand, arguments can be made for tax havens. Professor Andrew Morris argues that offshore tax havens actually provide a form of regulatory and tax competition that is beneficial.[50] If a domestic government is oppressive, unjust, or lacks institutions that support banking or the money supply, a tax haven with financial secrecy might be the only means of building wealth and a domestic middle class. Additionally, offshore tax havens may encourage onshore efficiency by pressuring politicians to lower domestic tax rates. In the process, offshore havens develop their own internal infrastructure in order to compete with other havens, potentially creating tools for further economic growth.

There are ways countries can discourage their taxpayers from using tax havens to shelter income. For example, Congress enacted the Foreign Account Tax Compliance Act of 2010 (FATCA) to force the disclosure of information regarding U.S. taxpayers' foreign bank accounts so that the IRS can prosecute tax evasion.[51] Additionally,

---

[48]   MARK KEIGHTLEY, CONG. RESEARCH SERV., R42927, AN ANALYSIS OF WHERE AMERICAN COMPANIES REPORT PROFITS 4–5 (2013).

[49]   Scott Thurm & Kate Linebaugh, *More U.S. Profits Parked Abroad, Saving on Taxes*, WALL ST. J., Mar. 10, 2013.

[50]   Andrew Morriss, *The Role of Offshore Financial Centers in Regulatory Competition, in* OFFSHORE FINANCIAL CENTERS AND REGULATORY COMPETITION 102 (2010).

[51]   Pub. L. 111–147, 124 Stat. 71, 97–117.

developed countries could coordinate a response that taxes passive and productive income leaving their countries. Professor Reuven Avi-Yonah argues that the coordinated imposition of withholding taxes on international portfolio investments where the money is invested and the taxation of goods and services where they are consumed would preserve progressive income taxes.[52]

However, in 1984, the U.S. stopped imposing a withholding tax on payments of interest to international lenders because of its need to finance deficit spending and because of then-popular treaty shopping. Since 1984, no major capital-importing country has been able to impose a withholding tax on interest for fear of driving investment to another country. Therefore, interest paid on debt is not taxed at the source under most treaties and it is not taxed in the recipient country if the country has a territorial system. Similarly, most countries do not tax productive income earned and taxed in other countries for fear of losing corporate headquarters. Thus, today, much income avoids taxation at the source.

(b) Tax Competition

Different countries tend to be havens for different types of business activities. Primary tax havens are countries where taxpayers deposit money or intellectual property in order to accumulate profits with tax-free deferral. Semi-tax havens are countries in which taxpayers produce goods for export and that offer free trade zones, tax holidays, or territorial taxation. Finally, there are conduit tax havens that act as a go between where income from extraterritorial sales is collected and distributed to another entity. Depending on a person's or business's needs, it uses one or more of the different types of havens. Therefore, the use of a particular tax haven or international tax plan for one business might not work for another business. Moreover, one business might develop a legal plan of international tax avoidance that is pushed further by another business into tax evasion.

Much of this tax competition is not hidden. Countries advertise their tax advantages to companies, and as long as businesses accurately report the activities that occur in each country, it generally remains lawful tax avoidance. For example, Luxembourg advertises that it is a great place to locate a headquarters because there is no tax on headquarters located there or anything allocated to its headquarters.[53] Ireland has long been a haven for intellectual

---

[52] Reuven Avi-Yonah, *Globalization, Tax Competition, and The Fiscal Crisis of the Welfare State*, 113 HARV. L. REV. 1574 (1999).

[53] LE GOUVERNEMENT DU GRAND-DUCHÉ DE LUXEMBOURG, COMPANY HEADQUARTERS, http://www.luxembourg.public.lu/en/investir/sieges-entreprises/index. html (last visited Mar. 2, 2018).

property, although it has recently closed some loopholes.[54] Other countries have tax holidays for the production of goods.[55]

The ability to use many of these planning techniques is dependent upon the ability to shift income among a MNC's subsidiaries. In order to do so, corporations rely on transfer pricing. Therefore, transfer pricing is important regardless of whether a country has worldwide or territorial taxation because it divides a MNC's profits among its subsidiaries in order to ensure proper tax is paid to each jurisdiction. However, because payments are among affiliated businesses, the allocation is to some extent arbitrary.

When income is shifted to low-tax jurisdictions, taxpayers can avoid or defer tax, at least as long as the money stays there. When MNCs report vast profits in tax havens such as the Cayman Islands, Luxembourg, Switzerland, and Ireland, there is concern that this income is taxed nowhere. Under a worldwide tax system, when, and if, these revenues are repatriated to the home country the MNC owes the home country's tax because revenues enjoy an artificially low rate in the foreign jurisdiction and therefore are entitled to fewer foreign tax credits. This home country tax may be waived if there is a repatriation holiday.

Because international tax planning requires shifting income offshore, not every corporation can engage in these planning activities. Generally corporations that do not rely upon intellectual property or have transferable property are taxed at significantly higher effective domestic rates because their income is not susceptible to these devices. For example, CVS Health paid a 30.8% effective rate whereas Microsoft had only 16.5%; the average of the ten most profitable American companies was 26.7%.[56]

A downside to tax competition is that countries must plan their domestic taxes in relation to other countries' planning, so that no country can apply its optimal tax but must compromise in anticipation of other countries doing the same. This may increase antipathy to international investment and decrease fairness among businesses with international versus only domestic markets. Investment and business activity may be poorly allocated internationally, especially if tax planning has a large influence in a particular business. Finally, addressing concerns of the evasive

---

[54]   Jim Puzzanghera & Paresh Dave, *Ireland to Close Corporate Tax Loophole Used by Google and Others*, L.A. TIMES, Oct. 14, 2014.

[55]   For example, PWC, People's Republic of China Corporate—Tax Credits and Incentives, http://taxsummaries.pwc.com/ID/Peoples-Republic-of-China-Corporate-Tax-credits-and-incentives (last visited Mar. 2, 2018).

[56]   Christopher Helman, *What America's Most Profitable Companies Pay in Taxes*, FORBES, Apr. 18, 2017. *See also* note 56 infra regarding Google's low tax rate.

shifting of income may increase administrative costs both for businesses and governments.

Many countries have lost significant revenue because of tax base erosion as money and investment flow to low-taxed jurisdictions. For example, Oxfam South Africa reported to the United Nations that South Africa's reduced tax base has caused an increase in poverty, inequality, and unemployment. The group blames the 400,000 registered companies that do not pay taxes.[57] Developing countries often compete by lowering their tax rates and shrinking their tax bases, possibly below sustainable levels.

The OECD produced detailed reports in a tax base erosion and profit sharing (BEPS) project.[58] The goal of the BEPS project is to tackle "transfer mispricing" and to create a coordinated response to base erosion. The action plan, published in July 2013, contained fifteen separate action points and was endorsed by G20 leaders.[59] In October 2015, the OECD published over 1,600 pages of final reports. It will take time for the recommendations to be fully applied, although some proposals, such as those to model transfer pricing guidelines, should be more rapidly implemented. A multilateral instrument, known as Action 15, was signed by more than 100 jurisdictions to permit nations to adopt the new procedures without renegotiating their bilateral agreements. The signing took place November 24, 2016.

The U.S. has targeted much of this tax competition with changes implemented by the Tax Cuts and Jobs Act of 2017. Congress enacted carrots and sticks to encourage businesses to retain or return assets to the U.S. rather than move them to a low-tax jurisdiction. How effective these changes will be remains to be seen.

(i) Hypothetical

Using a web of tax havens maximizes tax reduction for a MNC as long as the MNC does not repatriate the income to a country with worldwide taxation. Consider Import Co. that does not engage in tax planning and is located in a high-tax jurisdiction. Import Co. buys $10 of raw materials, applies a special patented process to turn them into Widgets, and sells Widgets in its home jurisdiction for $50 with no additional costs. In this scenario, Import Co. pays tax on $40 of taxable income because the $50 proceeds is reduced by the $10 cost

---

[57] UN, Countries' Experience Regarding Base Erosion and Profit Shifting Issues—South Africa, http://www.un.org/esa/ffd/tax/Beps/CommentsEJNandOxfam SA_BEPS.pdf (last visited Sept. 27, 2017).

[58] OECD, BASE EROSION AND PROFIT SHARING, http://www.oecd.org/tax/beps/ (last visited Sept. 27, 2017).

[59] The G20 was founded in 1999 as an international forum of governments and central banks from 20 major economies, including the U.S.

of goods sold. In this scenario, the company has not used tax havens to reduce its tax burden.

Alternatively, Import Co. places its patent in a tax haven subsidiary and performs much of the production in a subsidiary located in a country offering a tax holiday. Payment for the use of the patent is taxable but in a zero or low-tax jurisdiction. Similarly, production of the goods are taxable but at a 0% rate because of the holiday. Because Import Co. must pay its subsidiaries for these expenses under the rules of transfer pricing, Import Co. receives a tax deduction in its high-tax jurisdiction for those ordinary and necessary business expenses. This reduces the profit reportable in the high tax jurisdiction. If a sufficient percentage of profit is allocated to low-tax jurisdictions, little or no profit generated in the high-tax home jurisdiction is taxable until repatriated.

(ii) Double Irish and Dutch Sandwich

Tax planning often results in complex business structures that exist for no reason other than tax reduction. As a real world example, Google has used the "Double Irish with Dutch Sandwich" to reduce its global effective tax rate to 2.4%, and in 2015 alone Google saved $3.6 billion in taxes around the globe.[60] Google funneled its global corporate income through Ireland, which has a territorial tax system, and from there to a shell corporation in the Netherlands where the income was transferred to Bermuda. Bermuda has no corporate income tax so the income was never subject to tax. The Irish government shut down this strategy prospectively on January 1, 2015; however, companies using the strategy were given until 2020 to find another tax plan. The Tax Cuts and Jobs Act has attempted to limit U.S. corporations' ability to profit from this device with limits on deductions for payments to offshore affiliates and with a minimal tax.[61]

The Double Irish gains its name because it relies on two Irish companies. In step 1, the American company transfers its intellectual property (IP) to an Irish subsidiary that then, in step 2, sub-licenses the IP to a Dutch subsidiary that sub-licenses it to a second Irish subsidiary that sub-licenses it to the U.S.

---

[60]   J. Drucker, *The Tax Haven That's Saving Google Billions*, BUSINESS WEEK (2010); Jeremy Kahn & Martijn Van Der Starne, *Google Lowered 2016 Taxes*, BLOOMBERG, Dec. 21, 2016.

[61]   See Chapter 12.01(b)(ii).

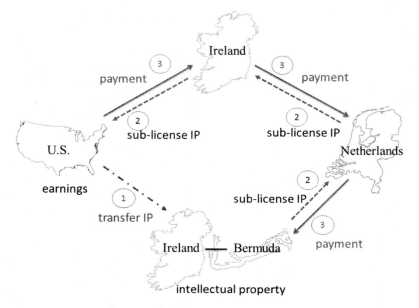

When, in step 3, the U.S. company pays royalties for the use of the IP, it generates U.S. deductions for those expenses, reducing its income taxable in the U.S. To get the income out of Ireland because Ireland charges a 12.5% corporate tax, the Irish company pays royalties to a Dutch subsidiary and receives a deduction so that no Irish taxes are owed to the top company in the chart. The Dutch subsidiary has no employees and so is not subject to Dutch taxation. The Dutch subsidiary then pays royalties to the second Irish subsidiary that holds the IP. Ireland disregards this subsidiary because it is controlled from Bermuda and, under pre-2015 law, is taxed at Bermuda's 0% tax rate. There is no Dutch withholding on the transfer because, from the Dutch perspective, the transfer is an inter-EU payment. In 2006, Google received blessing from the IRS for this transfer pricing plan with an advanced pricing agreement for IP existing before 2003.

       Ireland and Apple are each appealing an EU order to collect over $14 billion in taxes from Apple, which used a similar tax planning strategy, even though Apple has agreed to pay pending the appeal.[62] Apple has reported all European profits through Ireland and, using shell companies, had a 1% effective tax rate. The EU Competition Commissioner ordered Apple to pay Ireland on the gross underpayment of taxes from 2003 through 2014. Ireland's defense is that the technique was not unfair competition because all

---

[62]   Nick Statt, *Apple Agrees to Pay Ireland $15.4 billion in Back Taxes to Appease EU*, THE VERGE, Dec. 4, 2017.

corporations had the same ability to engage in this form of tax planning.

(iii)　Earnings Stripping

Another frequently used method of international tax planning is popularly called earnings stripping. With earnings stripping, a corporation in a low-tax jurisdiction makes a loan to a subsidiary or sister corporation in a high-tax jurisdiction. Both companies are all part of the same consolidated group, so the loan poses no business risk. As with all loans, the loan itself has no tax effect. However, when the high-tax company pays interest to the low-tax company, the payments are deductible to the high-tax company, reducing its taxable income.[63] Through the interest payments, earnings have been shifted from the high-tax to the low-tax jurisdiction.

The Treasury Department targeted earnings stripping in 2016 by issuing regulations that treat related-party debt that does not finance new investment in the U.S. as stock.[64] This converts the payments into dividends for tax purposes, which are not deductible, instead of interest, which is deductible. However, the regulations have been controversial. The Business Round Table complained the proposed regulations did not comport with the Administrative Procedure Act's required effective date and that businesses did not have sufficient time to comply.[65] Partially in response, the Treasury Department delayed the effective date for compliance with the documentation requirements until 2019.[66] Additionally, there are debates whether the Internal Revenue Code provides statutory authority for these regulations. The IRS's associate chief counsel expects the rules to withstand legal challenge.[67]

In the Tax Cuts and Jobs Act of 2017, Congress limited corporations' ability to profit from earnings stripping by capping interest deductions at 30% of an income measure.[68] Additionally, many new provisions deny U.S. deductions for outbound payments to discourage this type of tax planning. We have yet to see if these provisions will prove effective.

---

[63]　I.R.C. § 163.

[64]　Treas. Reg. § 1.386–3, T.D. 9790, 81 Fed. Reg. 72,858–01.

[65]　Business Round Table, BRT Comment Letter on Treasury Department Proposed 385 Regulations, July 7, 2016. *See also* Brant Goldwyn, *Witnesses Attack Earnings Stripping Regulations at IRS Hearing*, CCH TAX DAY REPORT, Jul. 15, 2016.

[66]　Notice 2017–36.

[67]　Kat Lucero, *IRS Official: Controversial Treasury Rules Should Survive Legal Challenge*, THE HILL, Oct. 28, 2016.

[68]　For more on the interest limitation, see Chapter 11.02(c). For more on the 2017 changes to U.S. international tax law, see Chapter 12.01(b)(ii).

(iv) Corporate Inversions

A corporate inversion occurs when a corporation relocates its headquarters to a low-tax country with the goal of tax reduction.[69] This is often accomplished without moving its material operations from high-tax jurisdictions. Senior officers may also remain in the high-tax jurisdiction despite the headquarters having been moved. The first inversion occurred in 1982, but this tax reduction scheme gained notoriety with very public transactions in the late 1990s. Since then the Treasury Department and Congress have responded by condemning and sometimes making this form of tax avoidance more difficult.[70]

Early inversions occurred when a corporation created a new parent entity in a low-tax jurisdiction that was a figurehead at the top of the corporate structure. In 2004, Congress enacted legislation that denied preferred tax results to these simple inversions and limited a U.S. corporation's ability to merge into a foreign company to accomplish similar results. The 2004 rules prevent merger inversions unless a significant amount of business is conducted in the new headquarters' country. In particular, the statute targets inversions when a U.S. corporation merges into a foreign corporation if the foreign acquirer's shareholders do not retain a meaningful stake, defined as 60% of the voting and 80% of the value, in the new foreign parent corporation.[71]

Nevertheless, corporations continue to plan around the rules to invert overseas. In 2014, Pfizer, Walgreen, and Medtronic each proposed high-profile inversions. Although the transactions were deemed unpatriotic, Congress failed to act. The Treasury Department issued controversial regulations in 2016 that alters the interpretation of the ownership thresholds.[72] These rules make it less likely that a U.S.-based company will be recognized as inverting if into a smaller foreign company by creating a three-year lookback rule to ensure that the foreign company did not increase its size to avoid the statutory inversion threshold. This agency action is not surprising given the political reaction against American corporations moving offshore; the issue is the statutory basis of these regulations.

---

[69]   *But see* Rita Gunn & Thomas Lys, *The Paradoxical Impact of Corporate Inversions on U.S. Tax Revenue* (2016), https://papers.ssrn.com/sol3/papers.cfm?abstract_id=2596706. For more on corporate inversions see CONG. BUDGET OFFICE, AN ANALYSIS OF CORPORATE INVERSIONS (2017).

[70]   Bret Wells, *Corporate Inversions and Whack-a-Mole Tax Policy*, 143 TAX NOTES 1429 (2014).

[71]   I.R.C. § 7874.

[72]   T.D. 9790, 81 Fed. Reg. 72, 858–01.

The regulations have been vacated in one District Court, although it is under appeal, but still apply in the other districts.[73] The Chamber of Commerce had filed the lawsuit in Texas seeking to block the inversion regulations as exceeding the Treasury Department's statutory authority. The District Court presiding over the case sided with the Chamber and granted summary judgment that the rule violated the APA. Despite this taxpayer resistance, in the short-term the Treasury Department's strategy was successful. The Pfizer deal was called off, with the company stating that the decision "was driven by the actions announced by the U.S. Department of Treasury."[74]

The Tax Cuts and Jobs Act also punished corporate inversions. Any corporation that engages in a corporate inversion between 2018 and 2028 is subject to a 35% tax, with no reduction for foreign tax credits, on the entire amount of the deemed repatriation for the corporation.[75] Moreover, dividends from corporations that have inverted are denied the favorable dividend unless the corporation is deemed to be a domestic corporation and taxed at domestic tax rates.[76]

(v) Renouncing Citizenship

Individuals can also avoid tax by renouncing citizenship in high-tax jurisdictions. A growing number of U.S. citizens have renounced citizenship each year for a number of years, although the number remained only 5,411 in 2016.[77] Notably, Eduardo Saverin did so in 2012 following Facebook's initial public offering.[78] Brazilian-born Saverin had become a U.S. citizen in 1998 but had been living in Singapore since 2009. And dual-citizen Boris Johnson, former mayor of London, finally did so, after being outraged that he was taxed on the sale of his London house.[79]

Americans are not the only people who renounce citizenship in order to avoid taxes. Complaining of a 75% top marginal income tax rate, Gérard Depardieu renounced French citizenship and took up residence in Belgium, although he insisted it was not purely for tax

---

[73]   Chamber of Commerce of the U.S.A. v. IRS, 2017 WL 4682050.

[74]   Press Release, Pfizer Announces Termination of Proposed Combination with Allergan (Apr. 6, 2016).

[75]   I.R.C. § 965.

[76]   I.R.C. § 1(h).

[77]   For the list of the quarter ending December 31, 2017, see Quarterly Publication of Individuals Who Have Chosen to Expatriate, as Required by Section 6039G, 83 Fed. Reg. 5,830 (Feb. 9, 2018).

[78]   Hayley Tsukayama, *Facebook Co-Founder Saverin Under Fire For Renouncing U.S. Citizenship*, Wash. Post, May 17, 2012.

[79]   Charles Riley, *Boris Johnson Has Given Up His U.S. Citizenship*, CNN.MONEY, Feb. 9, 2017.

reasons. Nearly 6,300 French renounced citizenship between 2001 and 2010 or about 630 per year.[80]

Renouncing U.S. citizenship is not without difficulties. The federal government requires citizens go to an embassy or consulate, pay a fee, and sign an oath or affirmation that they intend to renounce citizenship.[81] After two appearances and interviews, they must demonstrate that they have complied with U.S. tax obligations for the prior five years. Once they meet these requirements, it may take over six months to receive the official certification. The names of those who renounce citizenship are published quarterly in the Federal Register with the objective of shaming them publicly. This law, enacted in 1996, also bars entry to any listed individual, although there is no known case of the bar being enforced.

Moreover, some citizens must pay a tax before they are permitted to renounce citizenship. For taxpayers whose net worth is greater than $2 million (not adjusted for inflation) or whose average annual income for the prior five years is $165,000 (as of 2018), there is a tax imposed on expatriation that is calculated as though the person sold all of the person's property the day before the person renounces.[82] This tax is imposed even if the person continues to own the property and has liquidity problems because the person has wealth but not enough cash to pay the tax. Net capital gains are taxed as long-term capital gains but with a $713,000 exemption (as of 2018). U.S. heirs may also owe tax equal to the U.S. estate tax on assets received from an expatriate.[83]

(vi) Unreported Bank Accounts

Some individuals and businesses have hidden money and assets in foreign countries and not declared their associated earnings on U.S. tax returns. Because of the U.S.'s worldwide tax system this omission amounts to tax evasion, an illegal activity. The problem for tax purposes is not the existence of the accounts but the failure to report them.

Thus, nothing in worldwide taxation prevents U.S. taxpayers from having foreign bank or investment accounts. U.S. taxpayers are, however, obligated to report, and possibly pay U.S. tax on, foreign income if the foreign country's effective tax rate is lower than the U.S.

---

[80] Carol Matlack, *Depardieu Will Give Up French Citizenship Over Taxes*, BLOOMBERG.COM, Dec. 12, 2012.

[81] 8 U.S.C. § 1481(a)(5). For more on renouncing citizenship, see U.S. DEPT. OF STATE, BUREAU OF CONSULAR AFFAIRS, RENUNCIATION OF U.S. NATIONALITY ABROAD, https://travel.state.gov/content/travel/en/legal-considerations/us-citizenship-laws-policies/renunciation-of-citizenship.html (last visited Sept. 27, 2017).

[82] I.R.C. § 877A.

[83] I.R.C. § 2801.

rate. In 2002 the IRS estimated that as many as 1 million people had unreported offshore accounts, with an estimated $14.8 billion in total asset value in Swiss bank UBS alone.[84]

Some foreign countries have confidentiality laws that have made it difficult for the IRS to discover unreported offshore accounts when U.S. taxpayers illegally withheld the information. In 2009, the IRS struck a groundbreaking deal with UBS for the bank to pay $780 million in penalties and to provide the IRS a list of Americans holding assets through UBS.[85] At times foreign bank activities, including those of UBS, have gone beyond withholding information. Credit Suisse took a guilty plea and paid a record $2.6 billion fine for facilitating U.S. taxpayers' tax evasion.[86]

Additionally, Congress enacted FATCA, a law focused on information gathering.[87] It requires foreign banks with branches in the U.S. to disclose to the IRS all Americans' accounts holding over $50,000. Institutions that refuse risk being excluded from U.S. markets and their accounts face a 30% withholding penalty, meaning 30% of payments to those accounts from U.S. sources are paid to the U.S. government. Over eighty nations, including Switzerland, the Cayman Islands, and China, and over 77,000 financial institutions have agreed to comply with FATCA, although some banks stopped serving U.S. clients because of an inability or unwillingness to comply.[88] Because of FATCA's phased in requirements, the usefulness of the information to be supplied by these institutions has yet to be proved.

The amounts of revenue at issue are not trivial. For example, after Congress enacted a new federal whistleblower law that permits large payouts to those reporting others' tax evasion, ex-UBS banker Bradley Birkenfeld blew the whistle on how that bank provided U.S. taxpayers with vehicles to hide $20 billion in assets.[89] For his information, Birkenfeld was paid $104 million in 2012, although he was also sentenced to 40 months in jail and charged a $30,000 fine for abetting tax evasion.

---

[84]   U.S. DEPT. TREAS., A REPORT TO CONGRESS IN ACCORDANCE WITH § 361(B) OF THE USA PATRIOT ACT 6 (2002).

[85]   U.S. DEPT. JUSTICE, UBS ENTERS INTO DEFERRED PROSECUTION AGREEMENT (2009).

[86]   U.S. DEPT. JUSTICE, CREDIT SUISSE PLEADS GUILTY TO CONSPIRACY TO AID AND ASSIST U.S. TAXPAYERS IN FILING FALSE RETURNS (2014).

[87]   Pub. L. 111–147, 124 Stat. 71, 97–117 (2010).

[88]   Eyk Henning, *Deutsche Bank Asks U.S. Clients in Belgium to Close Accounts*, WALL ST. J., May 2, 2014.

[89]   David Kocieniewski, *Whistle-Blower Awarded $104 Million by I.R.S.*, N.Y. TIMES, Sept. 11, 2012.

U.S. taxpayers failing to report foreign accounts can be subject to criminal and civil penalties. Willful failure to file the annual Report of Foreign Bank and Financial Accounts (FBAR) is a felony punishable by up to five years in prison and a fine up to $250,000.[90] If the taxpayer files a tax return and fails to indicate on Schedule B that he owned or had control of a foreign account, the taxpayer may also be guilty of the felony of filing a false return.[91] If the IRS finds the violation was willful, the civil penalty is the greater of $100,000 or 50% of the highest account balance in each year there is a violation.[92] Thus, a $100,000 account yielding pennies of interest may generate a $50,000 penalty, tied to the balance rather than the amount of unreported income.

(c) Backlash to Tax Avoidance

Even lawful avoidance may generate negative publicity that can cost taxpayers. For example, a backlash followed disclosure of 2012 Republican presidential candidate Mitt Romney's Swiss and Cayman Islands accounts, even though they were properly reported on his U.S. tax return.[93] More recently, Starbucks faced investigation in Europe after its low global tax rate became public: All of Starbucks's coffee is bought by a Swiss subsidiary and sold at a 20% markup to Starbucks around the world to reduce profits in high-tax jurisdictions.[94] The public backlash could have been triggered by the recession, in which case Starbucks can renew its tax planning in better economic times. Or the backlash could result from disclosure of the elaborate planning techniques. The former suggests the public is only interested in limited circumstances; the latter suggests that interested parties need to shed light on tax planning to gain attention. It may be a combination of the two.

Despite most companies lawfully engaging in avoidance, rather than evasion, public sentiment is against them. Particularly in the EU, the recent exposure of MNCs who are paying little or no tax resulted in public outcry.[95] To reduce international tax avoidance, many have called for shaming businesses that engage in this form of planning. Shaming may work in certain instances. For example, Starbucks stated that it did not believe it owed more tax to the U.K.

---

[90]   31 U.S.C. § 5322.

[91]   I.R.C. § 7206.

[92]   31 U.S.C. § 5321(a)(5).

[93]   Josh Hicks, *Did Romney Avoid Taxes with Swiss Bank Accounts and Cayman Investments?*, WASH. POST, Aug. 29, 2012.

[94]   Tom Fairless, *Huge Profit Stokes Concerns Over Starbucks's Tax Practices in Europe*, WALL ST. J., Apr. 6, 2015.

[95]   Vanessa Barford & Gerry Holt, *Google, Amazon, Starbucks: The Rise of "Tax Shaming,"* BBC, May 21, 2013.

but nonetheless paid more in response to public pressure.[96] If aggressive tax avoidance damages a brand's image, it may result in less aggressive tax planning. Particularly with the growth of social media, shaming may be a means of maintaining public awareness of these issues.

Countries can also be shamed, but the effectiveness of this punishment is less clear. Awareness of major tax avoidance activity can affect a country's international reputation. This disclosure has not led to fines or other punishment. Some countries have been listed as tax havens, although no powerful countries for political reasons. For example, 340 international companies secured secret deals with Luxembourg to reduce their taxes to other nations yet had little presence in the duchy. The International Consortium of Investigative Journalists found in its investigation of LuxLeaks, as it is popularly called, that some companies paid tax rates of less than 1% on the profits shifted to Luxembourg.[97] The disclosure helped create the BEPS project. Nevertheless, Luxembourg has disclosed an additional 715 rulings were signed in 2014 and 726 in 2015, but the content remains private, although the European Union has contested some of Luxembourg's tax rulings.[98]

---

[96]   Rob Davies, *Starbucks Pays UK Corporation Tax of £8.1m*, GUARDIAN, Dec. 15, 2015.

[97]   Leslie Wayne et al., *Leaked Docs Expose More than 340 Companies' Tax Schemes*, HUFF. POST, Nov. 5, 2014.

[98]   European Commission, *Tax Rulings*, http://ec.europa.eu/competition/state_aid/tax_rulings/index_en.html (last visited Feb. 24, 2018); Jean-Michel Hennebert, *726 "Rulings" Traités en 2015*, PAPERJAM, Apr. 26, 2016, http://paperjam.lu/news/726-rulings-traites-en-2015.

Chapter 13

STATE AND LOCAL GOVERNMENTS

Table of Sections

State and local governments collect their own taxes; the three big sources of state and local tax revenue are property taxes, income taxes, and sales taxes. The federal government indirectly subsidizes those taxes. As of 2018, property taxes plus either a state income or sales tax is deductible up to a $10,000 cap for purposes of the federal income tax. In addition, the federal government makes direct payments to state and local governments. From their revenues, states and localities provide significant services for their residents. The amount of tax revenue raised and the choice of services vary greatly among the states.

§ 13.01 Sources of Revenue

The U.S.'s federalist system of government divides responsibilities between the levels of government. Not only do federal, state, and local governments provide different services, they also have different tools for raising revenue to pay for those services although their revenue sources may overlap. State and local tax sources have not always been great revenue providers. In 2009, sales tax revenue was 17% lower and state income tax revenue was 27% lower than the year before.[1] Cumulative budget shortfalls for state and local governments were estimated at more than $500 billion over the Great Recession. Forty states responded by enacting tax and fee increases; other states responded with tax cuts in the hopes of ending the recession quickly. To help these lower levels of government, the federal government increased its spending on state and local governments but not enough to make up the shortfall.

---

[1]   Tracy Gordon, *State and Local Budgets and the Great Recession*, BROOKINGS (2012).

(a) Federal Revenue

In 2010, 37% of states' revenue and 38% of local governments' revenue came from inter-governmental transfers, the great bulk from the federal government.[2] Although the amount spent by the federal government fluctuates as a share of federal spending, these expenditures generally constitute 17% of the federal budget and 4% of GDP.[3] The amount transferred often increases in times of disaster. For example, FEMA provided an additional $16.9 billion to New York and New Jersey after Hurricane Sandy in 2012.[4]

Some amount of federal spending has strings attached. Congress can tie federal grants to particular activities. Sometimes the requirement is to encourage states to change or adopt new local laws. For example, the federal government makes its funding for Medicaid dependent upon states' compliance with Medicaid rules that the states are otherwise free to ignore under the federal system. Similarly, starting in 1986 the federal government made funding for highways dependent upon states increasing their drinking age to 21. Louisiana was one of the last states to comply, and in 1996 its supreme court almost cost the state $17 million in highway money when it initially declared the higher drinking age a form of unconstitutional age discrimination.[5]

Other federal funding for states or local governments takes the form of general revenue sharing or block grants. General revenue sharing has the fewest federal restrictions on the use of funds; block grants permit local levels of government to decide priorities for spending within categories, such as community development, public health, or law enforcement. Allocation of this funding is often arbitrarily divided among states, whether according to population or political weight. Using these methods, the federal government helps fund state and local objectives. This also permits experimentation among states and responds to their different needs and priorities. On the other hand, it is often difficult to measure the results of this form of federal spending and whether other types of funding could more effectively accomplish society's larger goals.

---

[2]   Tax Policy Center, *State and Local Tax Policy, in* THE TAX POLICY BRIEFING BOOK, http://www.taxpolicycenter.org/briefing-book/state-local/revenues/state_revenue. cfm (last visited Sept. 27, 2017).

[3]   CONG. BUDGET OFFICE, FEDERAL GRANTS TO STATE AND LOCAL GOVERNMENTS (2013).

[4]   FED. EMERGENCY MGMT AGENCY, NR–013, FEMA AID REACHES $16.9 BILLION FOR NEW YORK'S HURRICANE SANDY RECOVERY (2015).

[5]   Manuel v. State, 692 So.2d 320 (1996).

The federal government also exempts from federal income tax the interest on most bonds that state and local governments issue.[6] The tax-free return to investors makes it cheaper for these levels of government to issue debt because taxpayers should be willing to take a lower interest rate than they would for taxable bonds. If a taxable bond yields 10% and an equivalent state tax-exempt bond yields 8%, the investor voluntarily forfeits 20% of the yield (2% less interest received divided by the 10% rate on taxable bonds) in order to avoid taxation.[7] This 20% is the public return on state and local government bonds' tax exemption because the government can issue bonds at 20% less than a taxable party. Based on a study of the yield of tax-exempt bonds, Professor Calvin Johnson argues that these tax incentives are extremely inefficient.[8]

Using the example's 20% lower interest rate, purchasing these particular tax-exempt bonds would only make sense for someone whose marginal tax rate equals or exceeds 20%. Someone who does not owe any federal income tax would lose 20% of her yield without an offsetting tax benefit. On the other hand, if a taxpayer in the 35% tax bracket purchases a $1,000 tax-exempt bond with 8% interest, the federal government loses $28 in foregone revenue ($80 taxable interest times 35% tax rate). The state benefits to the extent of the $20 in interest saved as compared to paying on a 10% interest rate taxable bond. The remaining $8 of lost government revenue delivers no public benefit. Johnson argues that the difference between taxable and tax-free bond rates has been dropping because state and local bonds' interest rates are rising. The benefit to the public is at times even lower than the lowest statutory tax bracket of 10%. To the extent this persists, tax-free bonds are a poor funding mechanism.

Finally, Congress permits deductions from the federal income tax for taxpayers' payment of some state and local taxes. This is another indirect source of federal funding. Currently, business taxes are always deductible. If individuals elect to itemize their below-the-line deductions, they can deduct up to $10,000 of (1) state and local personal property taxes and (2) either state and local personal income or sales taxes. Even before Congress expanded the standard deduction starting in 2018, less than one-third of taxpayers itemized, so the deduction for all but business-related taxes was worth nothing for the majority of taxpayers. For those who itemize, although the uncapped deduction provided the greatest benefit to high tax states because those states' taxpayers receive larger deductions, with the

---

6   I.R.C. § 103.

7   These percentages were arbitrarily chosen to illustrate the concepts.

8   Calvin Johnson, *Thermometer for the Tax System*, 56 SMU L. REV. 13 (2003).

cap, the deduction will be worth significantly less than most itemizers pay in high-tax states.

Although a popular deduction, any deduction for state and local taxes is regressive. High-income taxpayers receive the largest federal deduction because they are in higher tax brackets. Despite having limited applicability, before the cap in 2017 this deduction was estimated to cost approximately $1.27 trillion in federal revenue over ten years.[9] The JCT lumped the savings from the reduction caused by this deduction with other personal deductions.

Professor Kirk Stark argues against the federal deduction for state and local taxes because, to the extent that state and local taxes fund services provided to residents, there is no need for a deduction.[10] According to this interpretation, state and local taxes are equivalent to spending for private consumption, which is normally not deductible. Stark argues that the public market for services is as efficient as the private market because people move to the location that meets their needs. This mobility limits redistribution to the poor by state and local governments because of the potential selective emigration of residents desiring less redistribution.

Stark's study is part of fiscal federalism. Fiscal federalism studies the relation between state and federal levels of taxation. Theorists examine which level of government can best raise government revenue and provide any desired income redistribution. This study of the vertical and horizontal relations between units of government is a subset of public finance. When establishing this field, Professor Richard Musgrave argued that the federal government should promote economic stability and the distribution of income, and states and localities should allocate resources.[11] Decentralization may decrease planning and administrative costs and promote competition to favor innovation. However, there is a risk that state and local governments lack qualified staff and accountability for these types of allocation decisions.

(b) Property Tax

All fifty states impose property taxes. In 2016, states and localities collected $540 billion in property taxes, most of it at the local level.[12] Property taxes made up approximately 50% of state and local revenues in 2016, even more when focused only on local

---

[9] U.S. TREAS. DEPT., TAX EXPENDITURES (2017).

[10] Kirk Stark, *Fiscal Federalism and Tax Progressivity*, 51 UCLA L. REV. 1389 (2004).

[11] RICHARD MUSGRAVE, THE THEORY OF PUBLIC FINANCE (1959).

[12] CENSUS BUREAU, NATIONAL TOTALS OF STATE AND LOCAL GOVERNMENT TAX REVENUE, Table 1 (2017).

governments for which they were approximately 75%. As for states, New Hampshire has the highest dependency on property taxes at 66% of its tax revenue and the only state over 50%, whereas North Dakota's tax revenue from property taxes is less than 12% of its revenue.[13] The amount of revenue raised from this source has increased since the beginning of the Great Recession if revenue is not adjusted for inflation. Most of the tax's revenue comes from real property, such as land, office buildings, and housing; however, most states also tax at reduced rates personal property, such as machinery, furniture (often limited to that used in business), and business supplies. Thus, property taxes apply to both residential and commercial property. In most instances, the property tax is applied to the fair market value of property, and the owner on the date set by the government is liable for the tax.

The property tax is notable for being a relatively stable and reliable source of revenue because the tax base, at least when it is real property, is immobile. As another advantage, property tax revenue grows with no rate change as long as property values rise. However, the normally stable revenue source proved unstable with recent declines in real property values. Consequently, many states suffered significant budget shortfalls. Much of the time tax jurisdictions increase their property tax rate to balance the budget, although some are prohibited from doing so. Because of the perception of abuse or a dislike of rising taxes, some states limit localities' freedom and set the rates. Even jurisdictions with the authority to increase rates found raising rates politically untenable during the Great Recession.

Administering property taxes is sometimes difficult because of the need to determine fair market values.[14] Because owners may hold properties for a long time, the value must often be estimated. There are many different methods for this estimation, such as looking at comparable sales or depreciated cost, but all have problems of equity. Significant problems have plagued the assessment process. Homes may be assessed at more or less than the fair market value. Homeowners who disagree with the assessed value can file a challenge and, potentially, win an abatement.

From a study of the New York City assessment of property taxes, Professor Andrew Hayashi examines the extent to which

---

[13]   TAX POLICY CENTER, PROPERTY TAXES AS A PERCENTAGE OF STATE AND LOCAL TAXES (2017).

[14]   Stewart Sterk & Mitchell Engler, *Property Tax Reassessment: Who Needs It?*, 81 NOTRE DAME L. REV. 1037 (2006); Justin Ross, *Assessor Incentives and Property Assessment*, 77 SO. ECON. J. 776 (2011).

homeowners with high assessments challenge those assessments.[15] Although challenges do not always succeed, they offer an opportunity for tax reduction. Because challenges are not evenly dispersed throughout the city, the failure of some groups to challenge their assessments arguably shifts the property tax burden from those who do challenge assessment to those who do not. Hayashi finds that racial minorities, immigrants, and working families with children are the least likely to challenge their assessments, in part because their mortgages pay their property taxes from an escrow making the taxes less salient to these taxpayers than to those who pay the tax directly.

When rates or assessment increases, the tax is particularly burdensome for individuals whose home is their only or primary asset. If people cannot pay their property taxes, the burden generally attaches to the property and in rare instances can lead to forced sales. The government can provide a homestead exemption that controls rates or assessment values for those unable to pay property taxes on their homes. For example, gentrification of a community could prompt a revaluation of property that results in significant increases in property assessments, so a local government could control for this for its longer-term residents by not applying the higher assessment.

Even in the best of economic times, the property tax tends to be unpopular among taxpayers.[16] The tax can be visible, may result in different assessments for similar properties, and may burden fixed-income property owners in high-growth areas. In recent decades, many states have limited property tax rate growth, property tax revenue, or increases in assessed property values. For example, California's Proposition 13 limits the tax rate to 1% of a property's value and annual assessment increases to 2% until a property is sold.[17] A problem with limiting this revenue source, however, is that state and local budgets are often dependent upon it to meet changing needs.

Despite general opposition to property taxes, special assessments are often more popular, if only because they are tied to particular projects. Special assessments are levied against properties or neighborhoods when the government recognizes those properties are especially benefited from a specific project. For example, if streets are paved or a sidewalk is laid out, homes or businesses adjacent to these improvements may be taxed to cover part of the cost of the

---

[15] Andrew Hayashi, *The Legal Salience of Taxation*, 81 U. CHI. L. REV. 1443 (2014).

[16] The property tax's unpopularity extends internationally. *See* John Norregaard, *A Fair Assessment*, INT'L MONETARY FUND (2013).

[17] CAL. CONST. Art. XIII.

improvement. Municipalities may create special districts for businesses to provide merchants additional services, including extra street cleaning or trash pickup. These special assessments capture for the government some of the increase in the adjacent property's market value that result from the project. Payments of special assessments, similar to payments for a private benefit, are not deductible against federal income taxes.[18]

Alternately, states and local governments can abate property taxes for particular properties or neighborhoods. For example, several states have industrial development districts that can selectively reduce taxes. As one of these, the Michigan Economic Development Corporation is a public-private partnership granted by the state an Industrial Property Tax Abatement that abates 50% to 100% of property taxes to encourage manufacturers to build, expand, and renovate in designated areas.[19] Thus, states can use taxes and relief from taxes to encourage development.

(c) Sales Tax

Forty-five states impose a general sales tax, and all states impose at least one selective sales tax.[20] General sales taxes apply to all types of goods and services, and selective sales taxes typically focus on particular activities or goods, such as alcoholic beverages, gas, and tobacco products. In 2016, general sales taxes raised $282.8 billion and selective sales taxes raised $150 billion.[21] Overall, sales taxes raise approximately 35% of state and local government tax revenue, and an even larger percentage when looking at states alone. Sales taxes do vary greatly in importance among states. Washington raised almost 80% of its state tax revenue with sales taxes; Oregon less than 14%.[22]

What is taxed in states with a general sales tax also varies. Only seven states fully tax food sales, and four of those states allow a rebate or an income tax credit to offset the burden on poor households.[23] Six states tax food at a lower rate than other goods, and the remaining thirty-two states exempt food completely. Some localities in states that exempt food impose their own, local level tax. Some states also apply the sales tax to services; however, taxed

---

[18]   I.R.C. § 164(c).

[19]   MICH. ECON. DEV. CORP., INDUSTRIAL PROPERTY TAX ABATEMENT (2016).

[20]   For more on sales taxes as a type of consumption tax, see Chapter 8.02(a).

[21]   U.S. CENSUS BUREAU, STATE GOVERNMENT TAX COLLECTION 2016 (2017).

[22]   U.S. CENSUS BUREAU, 2016 ANNUAL SURVEY OF STATE GOVERNMENT TAX COLLECTIONS BY CATEGORY (2017).

[23]   Eric Figueroa & Samantha Waxman, *Which States Tax the Sale of Food For Home Consumption in 2017?*, CTR ON BUDGET & POL'Y PRIORITIES (2017).

services are frequently limited to event admissions, utilities, and lodging.

Additionally, several states have a number of special purpose districts that impose limited sales and use taxes. With only broad limits, states and local governments can define the amount and breadth of the tax as they prefer. For example, many states have transportation improvement districts that levy sales or property taxes to coordinate and finance transportation infrastructure programs. Alternately, districts can abate taxes in ways similar to, but for longer periods than, sales tax holidays. For example, Texas's Development Corporation Act of 1979 authorizes cities to adopt sales or use taxes to raise funds for development, and the state also has enterprise zones that exempt qualified expenditures from state sales and use taxes.[24] The goal in both cases is to increase capital investment and to create jobs.

Sales taxes, whether general or selective, raise significant amounts of revenue in small amounts, making the tax less objectionable to the taxpaying public. Thus, instead of requiring a large payment at year-end, revenue is raised with countless little payments over the year. Moreover, because sellers undertake compliance, the tax may not be salient to customers as they make their purchases.[25] This should mean that the tax has less effect on people's purchases and, therefore, be economically efficient. However, this may also mean that taxpayers do not respond to its economic signals. Finally, sales taxes are generally regressive, as are most consumption taxes. This means that low-income taxpayers are paying a disproportionately larger share of their incomes in sales taxes.

However, the sales tax is only regressive because low-income taxpayers tend to consume a greater percentage of their incomes. To the extent that people choose what they purchase, sales taxes can be thought of as optional. At least in the states that exempt food and clothing, people do not have to make most taxed purchases. Taxpayers can also evade the sales tax, for example by having goods shipped out of state. Refraining from purchases or evading taxes are forms of price discrimination in that those who object the most to the tax are most likely to avoid it. Unfortunately, restraint may impose a hardship and evasion may breed contempt for the tax system.

The way a sale tax operates arguably conscripts sellers as revenue collectors. Although a burden on businesses, compliance

---

[24]   GLEN HEGAR, TEXAS COMPTROLLER OF PUBLIC ACCOUNTS, TAX-RELATED STATE AND LOCAL ECONOMIC DEVELOPMENT PROGRAMS (2016).

[25]   For more on the effect of consumption taxes, see Chapter 8.

with the sales tax is generally practically easier than income tax compliance. However, little research has tested sales tax compliance levels.[26] A state audit of Chicago found that 27% of gas-station operators pocketed at least some of the state and local sales tax that was to be remitted to the government.[27] In California, the problem has been said to cost approximately $2 billion.[28] Compliance rates are likely lower than with withholding for the income tax because the sales tax suffers from a lack of third party information reporting to verify the taxes owed.

To comply with the sales tax, businesses remit sales taxes to the appropriate state or locality. To decrease costs and improve efficiency, many states permit online submissions after businesses obtain a certificate (almost a de facto issuance) from the state registering the business as a sales tax payer. Failure to pay over these taxes, when they apply, is likely to result in civil or even criminal penalties. Businesses have been formed to assist other businesses comply with sales taxes.

Not all businesses have to comply with a state's sales tax. In *Quill Corp. v. North Dakota*, the Supreme Court held that a business must have a physical presence (in legal speak, a nexus) in a state for the state to be able to require the business collect a sales tax.[29] This requirement arises from constitutional Dormant Commerce Clause jurisprudence, which is intended to prevent undue burdens on interstate commerce. North Dakota required a Delaware e-commerce seller to collect the North Dakota sales tax; however, the requirement was declared unconstitutional. The Dormant Commerce Clause's current interpretation creates a significant pro-interstate commerce result. However, the Supreme Court has indicated a willingness to revisit the issue; one case to be heard in the 2018 term.[30]

The physical presence requirement means that states cannot force the collection of sales tax at the point of sale for those conducted over the Internet. The revenue loss is substantial. States lose an estimated $23 billion per year in uncollected sales taxes from ecommerce.[31] It also means that businesses should plan their physical presence in order to reduce the number of states in which

---

[26]   P. Cary Christian, *Why Evasion Under a National Sales Tax Would Explode the Tax Gap: Lessons Learned from the States*, IRS RES. BULL. 141 (2013).

[27]   *Cracking Down on Sales-Tax Fraud*, CHI. TRIBUNE, Apr. 30, 2012.

[28]   CAL. STATE BOARD OF EQUALIZATION, NR 156–14–G, BOE NOTIFIES CALIFORNIA RETAILERS OF UPCOMING VISITS (2014).

[29]   504 U.S. 298 (1992).

[30]   Direct Marketing Ass'n v. Brohl, 135 S.Ct. 1124 (2015); South Dakota v. Wayfair Inc., 901 N.W.2d 754 (2017).

[31]   Greg Stohr, *Amazon Rejected by U.S. High Court on New York Sales Tax*, BLOOMBERG, Dec. 2, 2013.

they must comply with sales taxes. If the obligation were permitted, it is unclear how businesses, particularly smaller ones, would comply with the many different state and local tax systems. To date no national solution to the collection of sales tax has gained political traction.[32]

All states that impose a sales tax have a complimentary use tax that is intended to address ecommerce and other out of state purchases. A use tax is imposed on residents when a resident makes purchases in states that do not impose a sales tax at least as high as that applied in the consumer's home state. For example, Ohio taxpayers are obligated to pay a use tax on items purchased out of state in locations that impose a lower sales tax than that imposed by Ohio. Most use taxes, including Ohio's, are collected via the consumer's state income tax return. However, compliance with, and enforcement of, use taxes are notoriously poor. One study from the University of Cincinnati found that although 60% of households in Ohio made at least one on-line purchase in 2010, less than 1% of state income tax returns included the use tax.[33] The study claimed the evasion resulted in a revenue shortfall of more than $200 million in 2011 and a total of $1.1 billion for the years 2007 through 2012.

The failure to tax on-line purchases gained widespread public attention with Amazon's success, and some states reacted by trying to force Amazon to collect sales/use taxes. Although Amazon delivers goods in all fifty states, it was not until April 1, 2017, that Amazon agreed to collect sales tax nationwide.[34] In 2008, when Amazon did not collect sales tax for New York, New York enacted an expansive "Amazon law" that required on-line businesses to collect sales tax if they used in-state affiliates.[35] The goal, said the law's proponents, was to level the playing field for in-state retailers. At the time, Amazon contracted with websites based in New York to display click-through advertisements for Amazon's site, and the owners of the websites received a portion of any sales generated. New York argued this created a sufficient nexus to force Amazon to collect tax on purchases from the site by New York residents. In 2013, the New York Court of Appeals, New York's highest court, rejected Amazon's arguments allowing the law to remain effective, and the U.S.

---

[32]   CONG. BUDGET OFFICE, ECONOMIC ISSUES IN TAXING INTERNET AND MAIL-ORDER SALES (2003).

[33]   UNIV. CINC. ECONOMIC CENTER, ECONOMIC ANALYSIS OF TAX REVENUE FROM E-COMMERCE IN OHIO (2011).

[34]   Darla Mercado, *The Holiday Is Over: Amazon Will Collect Sales Taxes Nationwide on April 1*, CNBC, Mar. 24, 2017.

[35]   N.Y. TAX LAW § 1101(b)(8)(vi) (McKinney's 2017).

Supreme Court denied certiorari.[36] Amazon now collects taxes in New York.

Other states took steps to collect taxes for online purchases, similarly focusing on Amazon; however, they generally have not been successful. Some states, such as California, negotiated with Amazon to move past bitter fighting over tax collection. Before 2011, Amazon refused to pay or collect California tax but also had no fulfillment centers in the state. In 2011, California coupled collection of the sales tax with specific tax benefits for an Amazon fulfillment center in the state.[37] Bitter fighting has occurred throughout the country with states facing tremendous pressure to grant tax advantages to online companies.

Instead of a piecemeal state-level response, an alternative is a national law. In 1998, Congress enacted the Internet Tax Freedom Act to provide and preserve the commercial, educational, and informational potential of the Internet.[38] It prohibited Internet-only taxes but did not exempt sales made on the Internet from taxation. Thus, Congress's first position deferred the issue of state sales tax enforcement. Since 1998, Congress has considered several bills on this issue: some would permit states to collect their taxes from Internet providers and others would impose the sales tax nationally and remit the revenue to the states.

Most bills have not made it out of conference. In May 2013, the Marketplace Fairness Act made it out of the Senate, which would have allowed states to collect sales taxes for online purchases, but died in the House of Representatives.[39] Because resistance is often framed around the complexity of the thousands of taxing jurisdictions, since 2005 twenty-four states have voluntarily adopted the Streamlined Sales and Use Tax Agreement that seeks to simplify sales tax collection.[40]

(d) Income Tax

Forty-three states impose individual income taxes, and all but two states impose a corporate income tax, franchise tax, or gross receipts tax, although the latter could be classified as a type of sales tax. These state income taxes are a major source of revenue for the

---

[36]   Overstock.Com, Inc. v. NY State Dept. of Tax'n & Finance, 20 N.Y.3d 586 (2013); Amazon.com, LLC v. New York State Dep't of Taxation & Fin., 571 U.S. 1071 (2013).

[37]   Marc Lifsher, *Free Ride is Over—Amazon.com Collecting California Sales Tax*, L.A. TIMES, Sep. 15, 2012.

[38]   Internet Tax Freedom Act, Pub. L. 105–277, 112 Stat. 2681 (1998).

[39]   H.R. 684; S.336 (2013); S. 743 (2013).

[40]   For updates, see Streamlined Sales Tax Governing Board, Inc. at http://www. streamlinedsalestax.org.

states that impose them, approximately 23% of revenue from taxes.[41] Although each is an income tax, no two states impose exactly the same tax. Instead, there is tremendous variety in how states implement their income taxes.

First, what constitutes taxable income varies by state, although most states generally follow the federal definition. Some states mirror other features of the federal income tax, while others are more independent. For example, New Hampshire and Tennessee only tax interest and dividends rather than the broader definition of income used in the federal tax.[42] Some states require taxpayers use the same filing status as they use for the federal tax return, whereas some give their residents a choice. Some states index exemptions or other features of their systems for inflation and others do not. Some states tie their standard deduction and personal exemption to the federal ones, others set their own, and still others have none.

Second, the progressivity of income tax rates also varies among states. Eight states apply a flat tax to all individual incomes, while the rest have progressive rates that are still relatively flat compared to the federal individual income tax. In 2017, states' top marginal individual income tax rates ranged from 3.07% in Pennsylvania to 13.3% in California; and, in thirteen states, localities may impose an income tax in addition to the state's tax. Top marginal corporate income tax rates varied from 3% in North Carolina to 12% in Iowa.[43] On average corporate income taxes raised less than 5% of states' tax revenue.

After most states reduced their number of tax brackets in the 1980s, some states have reversed that trend. Focused on the highest earners, some states have imposed "millionaire's taxes," with new brackets for high-income taxpayers. For example, California approved a temporary millionaire's tax in 2013 that taxes incomes over $1 million an additional 1%, and several other states imposed similar but lesser taxes.[44] For example, Maryland had such a 6.25% tax on incomes of more than $1 million per year between 2008 and 2011. The anti-tax group Change Maryland found the state's millionaire tax caused 31,000 residents to leave the state between

---

[41]   U.S. Dept. of Census, *State and Local Government Finances By Level of Government*, American FACTFINDER (2017) (last visited Sept. 27, 2017).

[42]   Dan Dzombak, *The States Have No Income Tax*, USA TODAY, Apr. 26, 2014.

[43]   Morgan Scarboro, *State Corporate Income Tax Rates and Brackets for 2017*, TAX FOUNDATION (2017).

[44]   Cal. Proposition 30 (2012); Cal. Proposition 55 (2016).

2007 and 2010 and cost Maryland $1.7 billion in lost tax revenues, although these conclusions have been contested.[45]

The effects of the tax on the highest earners in a state is uncertain, although most research suggests it does not actually result in significant emigration of the wealthy. A 2016 study examined administrative tax returns for all million-dollar income earners in the U.S. over a period of thirteen years and found that millionaire tax flight occurs but only at the margins of statistical and socioeconomic significance.[46] A 2003 study estimated that a 10% increase in personal income tax rates in neighboring states induces a *decrease* of less than 1% in the tax rate of the home state.[47] The study also found that few workers move across state lines to reduce the income taxes they pay, hence relative rate discrepancies have little political effect on state income taxes.

State and local income taxes have many of the some pros and cons as the federal income tax.[48] This tax has the potential to raise significant revenue for the states. To raise that revenue, taxpayers must complete a separate income tax return (in addition to their federal one), often applying somewhat different rules. The income tax is best able to be based on people's ability to pay taxes as it is commonly defined; although nine states have flat tax rates, some because their state constitutions require flat rates.[49]

When states impose an income tax, they must allocate income between the states that have a claim to tax the income. Doing so is as difficult for states as it is for countries in the international market. U.S. states do not have an equivalent of transfer pricing with its arm's length transaction requirement. Instead, states apportion income. Apportionment is generally considered less expensive to operate than transfer pricing and a more accurate reflection of business reality. On the other hand, apportionment can lead to double or zero taxation of the same income when states fail to agree on the formula used to determine each state's share of taxable income.

Although states do not need to agree with each other regarding apportionment, states are constitutionally limited in how they

---

[45]   Robert Frank, *In Maryland, Higher Taxes Chase Out Rich*, CNBC, Jul. 9, 2012. This finding is contested. *See* INST. ON TAX'N & ECON. POL'Y, FIVE REASONS TO REINSTATE MARYLAND'S "MILLIONAIRE'S TAX" (2011).

[46]   Cristobal Young et al., *Millionaire Migration and Taxation of the Elite*, 81 AM. SOCIOLOGICAL REV. 421 (2016).

[47]   Jonathan C. Rork, *Coveting Thy Neighbors' Taxation*, 56 NAT'L TAX J. 775 (2003).

[48]   For more on the income tax, see Chapter 7.

[49]   Reboot Illinois, *Flat Income Tax? Progressive Tax? No State Income Tax? A Nationwide Overview*, HUFF. POST, Sept. 18, 2013.

apportion income. The limits are not bright line rules. In *Complete Auto Transit, Inc. v. Brady*, the Supreme Court declared that a state may tax a corporation if (1) there is a sufficient nexus between corporate income and the state, (2) there is a fair apportionment of the income between the relevant states, (3) the tax does not discriminate against or for domestic or interstate activity, and (4) the tax reflects a fair relationship to the state's services, such as police and roads.[50] The case upheld the Mississippi tax that applied to all businesses in the state including an interstate transporter of cars. This tax was not applied to discourage interstate commerce, which would violate the Dormant Commerce Clause of the U.S. Constitution.

Defining substantial nexus for purposes of the *Complete Auto* test, some states continue to tax out-of-state businesses. In 2016 in *Crutchfield Corp. v. Testa*, the Supreme Court of Ohio upheld the application of the state's commercial activity tax (CAT) on out-of-state e-commerce businesses without a physical presence in Ohio.[51] The court likened the CAT to a corporate income tax imposed for the privilege of doing business in Ohio. The tax only applies to out-of-state businesses with more than $500,000 in gross sales receipts in Ohio in order to establish the substantial nexus. Ohio was the first state to adopt the bright-line test to subject out-of-state businesses to the local tax, a test that other states have since adopted.

To reconcile the state supreme court's conclusion with *Quill*, the court distinguished the sales/use and income/privilege taxes and applied a different test for substantial nexus in each. The court narrowly limited *Quill's* physical presence requirement to the use tax. In its stead, the court argued that the CAT is in the same constitutional category as an income tax, which it argues has traditionally not had a physical nexus requirement. If *Crutchfield* had come out the other way, e-commerce businesses would not only avoid sales tax but also business-level tax.

Reaching these businesses is important to states because states can only tax the in-state portion of income. The Uniform Division of Income for Tax Purposes Act, adopted by about half the states, bases the apportioned percentage of a business's multi-state income on a three-factor formula of property, payroll, and sales within the state to that of the business overall.[52] Because it is hard to game the apportioned percentage, states have historically tried to increase the

---

[50] 430 U.S. 274 (1977).

[51] 88 N.E.3d 900 (2017).

[52] For more on the history of the Uniform Division of Income for Tax Purposes Act, see Arthur D. Lynn, Jr., *The Uniform Division of Income for Tax Purposes Act*, 19 OH. ST. L.J. 41 (1958).

apportionable tax base to be multiplied by their percentage in order to increase revenue. In other words, if a state is only entitled to tax 25% of a business's income, the state would want to make the amount of income larger.

Today, however, some states weight the formula and other states use a single factor formula to adjust the apportioned percentage to reduce the corporate income tax for businesses located in the state. The trend is towards focusing on sales over the other factors.[53] It is generally accepted that sales alone may not accurately depict a company's activity in a state. Property and payroll may be better indicators; however, taxing based on those factors may discourage local investment in order to minimize taxation. Therefore, the goal of recent changes is not a more accurate determination of fair apportionment but to encourage local investment by extending hidden tax relief.

Individuals have a different method of accounting for multi-state income. States must offer a credit for the taxes individuals who generate income in different states pay to other states. These credits are similar to foreign tax credits, in which U.S. credits are awarded for taxes paid to other governments to ensure there is no double taxation of income. In *Comptroller v. Wynne*, the Supreme Court held that Maryland's policy of not granting its residents credits for taxes paid to other states was unconstitutional.[54] This policy of taxing all income based on residency was held to violate the Constitution's Dormant Commerce Clause because it double taxed only that income earned in interstate commerce.

(e) Targeted Tax Reduction

Much as states impose taxes, they can reduce taxes, offer income tax credits, or even provide cash payments to their residents. States might do so to encourage taxpayers either to engage in certain behaviors or to stop doing something. These tax breaks can also be distributed selectively. For example, a city may offer a property tax abatement to encourage people to purchase homes downtown or to local businesses to move to less desirable neighborhoods. Some programs are limited by the recipient's income but some are generally applicable.

States and local governments often narrowly target tax reduction to convince businesses to relocate, hire, or invest within the state or locality. Significant amounts of tax revenue are involved. One estimate found that states give businesses $80 billion per year

---

[53]   Michael Mazerov, *The "Single Sales Factor" Formula For State Corporate Taxes*, CTR ON BUDGET & POL'Y PRIORITIES (2005).

[54]   135 S.Ct. 1787 (2015).

in targeted tax reduction.[55] This tax reduction for property, sales, or income taxes may be useful or necessary to spur economic growth by signaling to businesses a pro-business environment that makes the location more attractive.

On the other hand, these benefits are often distributed indiscriminately and, because businesses must locate somewhere, businesses have every reason to encourage this competition to reduce taxes. Thus, these benefits may not influence where a business ultimately locates. State and local taxes average only about 1.8% of a business's costs.[56] Factors other than taxes likely drive decisions regarding location, such as workforce, infrastructure, and proximity to market. This makes these tax breaks a windfall to the business. They are a form of corporate welfare tied to negotiating position rather than need or merit.

Nevertheless, states may have become so used to handing out these types of benefits that they have become path dependent.[57] This behavior has arguably created a race to the bottom for all state and local governments as each state tries to outdo others with larger packages. In doing so, this competitive tax reduction permits states and localities to poach businesses from other states and localities; in doing so they are not creating new growth. Focusing efforts (and tax revenue) on improving infrastructure and the labor force would permit states and localities to compete while adding value.

Additionally, despite their cost, states and localities are notoriously bad at measuring the returns on these tax expenditures. For example, in 2013, one think tank complained that Ohio tax expenditures amounted to over $7.7 billion, and yet there was no systematic review of their efficacy.[58] Even if attempted, it is difficult to measure returns because it is impossible to know what would have happened in a counterfactual world; whether the business would have relocated without the benefit. Some states limit their expenditures or attempt to measure their results. For example, Connecticut created a Business Tax Credit and Tax Policy Review Committee in 2005 to annually review the performance of all tax credits; and the state of Washington imposes a maximum 10-year sunset on provisions unless renewed, and each tax break package

---

[55]   Louise Story, *As Companies Seek Tax Deals, Governments Pay The Price*, N.Y. TIMES, Dec. 1, 2012.

[56]   INST. ON TAX'N. & ECON. POL'Y, TAX INCENTIVES: COSTLY FOR STATES, DRAG ON THE NATION (2013).

[57]   For more on tax incentives, see Chapter 17.

[58]   Policy Matters Ohio, Breaking Bad: Ohio Tax Breaks Escape Scrutiny (2013). Earlier in 2011, it was reported Ohio was spending $1. 4 billion to prepare industrial parks for which there were no tenants. Dennis Cauchon, *Ohio is Spending $1.4 Billion to Attract Jobs. Will It Work?*, USA TODAY, Apr. 25, 2011.

must include a statement of legislative purpose and spell out goals and metrics for measuring their achievement.[59]

Anecdotal evidence illustrates some concerns and potential gains with targeted tax reduction. For example, following bidding by thirty states, in 1993, Alabama offered a $253 million package of tax incentives to entice Mercedes-Benz to locate a plant in Tuscaloosa County that was expected to create 1,500 jobs.[60] The cost per job was $169,000. Because of the incentives, Mercedes-Benz spent only $100 for the plant. Ten years later, the city in which the plant was located had attracted a hotel, medical clinic, and a bank. The state had to borrow from its pension to meet its obligations and, partly in response, the governor was voted out of office. Whether the investment has netted a long-term benefit to the state is still debated. Some taxpayers are angry that other businesses did not get comparable tax cuts and have lost talented employees to the plant.

Targeted tax reduction's results may be no worse than when governments provide more direct aid. Even indirect aid may leave taxpayers to foot the bill. For example, Rhode Island guaranteed $75 million in bonds for Curt Schilling's video game company, 38 Studios, at a time when the company had not yet released a game.[61] The business failed. The state settled for $20.4 million to be paid to investors from tax revenue and, in 2017, the Rhode Island Commerce Corporation settled with the Securities and Exchange Commission for a $50,00 civil penalty in response to charges the parties knew the financing was insufficient to complete the project.

When states or localities offer these tax packages, taxpayers have few means to challenge them. Their origin is in the political process, and they are removed from most legal challenge. In 2006, Ohio and Michigan taxpayers sued after DaimlerChrysler was awarded $280 million in tax incentives. The taxpayers argued that it was unfair for one taxpayer to get tax cuts not available to others. In *DaimlerChrysler v. Cuno*, the Supreme Court held that the taxpayers did not have standing to challenge the state's expenditures in federal courts.[62] Without recourse to federal courts, the only possible pursuit is through the state judiciary pursuant to state constitutions.

---

[59]   2005 Conn. Acts 251 (now Conn. Gen. Stat. ch. 208, section 12–217z); Wash. Rev. Code section 41.236.045(1). For more on the Washington system, see http://www.citizentaxpref.wa.gov/.

[60]   For more on this story, see *Ten Years After Mercedes, Alabama Town Still Pans For Gold*, SAVANNAH NOW, Oct. 09, 2002.

[61]   Matt Bai, *Thrown for a Curve in Rhode Island*, N.Y. TIMES, Apr. 20, 2013.

[62]   547 U.S. 332 (2006).

§ 13.02   Expenditures

The sometimes difficult task of raising revenue at the state and local level, often limits their expenditures. Many lower levels of government are required to balance parts of their budgets so that the amount received in taxes directly corresponds to the amount spent. This also means that when tax revenue falls, there is tremendous pressure to reduce government services.

(a) Budgeting

State and local governments provide a significant amount of services from their revenue, including funding public education and emergency services. To provide these services, state and local governments employ almost 15% of the nation's workers and the spending comprises 12% of GDP.[63] To organize their spending, lower levels of government often have two interrelated budgets, although an allocation to one or the other can be somewhat arbitrary. Operating budgets keep track of the day-to-day delivery of services, such as city maintenance, police officer patrols, filling potholes, and teachers' salaries. Capital budgets track long-term investments for the improvement, construction, and purchase of assets that have a life of more than one year, such as police cars and school buildings.

Every state other than Vermont has state constitutional restrictions on deficit spending; however, the precise requirements of balanced budget provisions vary and they usually only apply to operating budgets. Capital budgets can normally run a deficit. Transfers between the budgets are generally prohibited so that states cannot increase operating funds by reducing capital spending. As a result, in tough financial times, either operating revenue must be raised or services cut to keep that budget balanced.

Illustrating this problem, despite declining state and local revenues in the midst of the Great Recession, enrollments for Medicaid, unemployment, and higher education increased rapidly. Ignoring the increased demand, most states cut spending in education, health, and social services because they are the biggest parts of state and local budgets. Also, state and local payrolls were trimmed to cover shortfalls. Overall, state and local public sector employment fell by 624,000 in the four fiscal years following August 2008.[64]

Because of balanced budget requirements, state and local governments face almost constant funding problems, particularly for

---

[63]   Tracy Gordon, *State and Local Budgets and the Great Recession*, BROOKINGS INST. (2012).

[64]   *Id.*

government employees' pensions. Pensions are a large, often unfunded obligation of state and local governments. One estimate found a $1.26 trillion deficit nationally at the end of 2009, which translates into aggregate pension systems only being 78% funded.[65] In 2000, over half the states had fully funded pension systems, but by 2009 it was only two states. In eleven states, more than one-third of the pension obligation was unfunded, including Illinois that was 49% unfunded. These numbers do not include healthcare or other non-pension benefits promised to public employees, for which nineteen states have funded none of these future financial responsibilities.

The structure of public pensions almost ensures they are large financial burdens. Eighty-nine percent of public employees have defined benefit plans that guarantee a certain payment on retirement, whereas only 19% of private employees do.[66] Private pensions tend to have defined contribution plans, which set aside a certain amount of money, which results in greater pre-payment. Even as many states are changing their retirement plans because of cost, many states have legal protections for current employees that limit governments' ability to adjust the benefits without negotiating with the parties. Therefore, most of the changes made since the Great Recession are for future employees. Since 2008, 74% of state plans and 57% of large local plans have cut benefits or raised contributions. The most common reduction has been to the cost of living adjustment.[67]

To pay for large projects or to withstand financial crunches, state and local governments often borrow.[68] Washington D.C. has the most debt per capita at over $18,000; Idaho has the lowest at less than $4,000. State and local debt can be short-term or long-term. In the third-quarter of 2010, there was $2.39 trillion of state and local debt outstanding, almost 95% of which was long-term. Short-term debt is usually intended to even out the budget cycles in anticipation of tax payments. Long-term debt is generally incurred to finance major capital outlays, such as the construction of bridges and new water systems. Some long-term debt has a private purpose, such as financing a sports stadium. The latter composed almost 20% of state

---

[65] PEW CTR. ON THE STATES, THE WIDENING GAP (2011).

[66] CTR FOR STATE AND LOCAL GOV'T EXCELLENCE, ISSUE BRIEF: DEFINED CONTRIBUTION PLANS IN THE PUBLIC SECTOR (2014).

[67] Jean-Pierre Aubry & Caroline Crawford, *State and Local Pension Reform Since the Financial Crisis*, CTR FOR RETIREMENT RES., BOSTON COLLEGE (2017).

[68] For more on state and local debt, see STEVEN MAGUIRE, CONG. RESEARCH SERV., R41735, STATE AND LOCAL GOVERNMENT DEBT (2011).

and local long-term debt in 2012.[69] Not all of this debt is backed by the full faith and credit of the government, meaning that taxpayers are not always on the hook for state and local liabilities. Some forms of state and local debt are only payable from designated revenue sources.

Servicing debt can be a strain on state and local governments' finances. Although debt is generally classified as operational or capital according to its use, interest payments on all debt is payable through the operational budget. The payment of this interest may be from designated sources of funding, such as sewer fees or water, or from general funds. When payments come from general funds, they are part of the balanced budget. In addition to the cost of servicing the debt, debt levels can affect a state's or local government's debt rating and, therefore, its ability to borrow in the future and at what interest rate. Despite widespread worry about heavy debt burdens, between 1970 and 2009, there have been only 54 municipal bond defaults.

To help insulate certain projects from operating budget woes, state and local governments can designate certain taxes or tax increases as raising revenue for particular purposes, a process called earmarking.[70] In 2005, almost one-quarter of state and local expenditures were earmarked, ranging from a limited 4.4% in Rhode Island to 84% in Alabama.[71] However, unless the designation is in the state constitution, lower levels of government are generally not legally required to follow them. For example, money can be moved from one purpose to another within general funds.

Despite earmarking's limited power to override politics, earmarking can be politically popular. Designating the use of tax revenue may provide greater political transparency on government operations and justify increases in taxes to people who otherwise find tax increases unpopular. In other words, the public may be more willing to authorize tax increases if they feel they control how the money is spent. This is one reason referendums are popular to raise earmarked taxes. Referendums may be used to indicate public support and deflect blame from elected officials. Referendums are also sometimes required by state constitutions or local government structures.

For those who support the earmarked purpose, earmarking creates a presumption of spending even if elected officials are not

---

[69]   Jared Walczak, *Where Does Your State Stand on State & Local Debt Per Capita?*, TAX FOUNDATION (2015).

[70]   Earmarking is different from special assessments. For more on special assessments, see Chapter 13.01(b).

[71]   Arturo Perez, *Earmarking State Taxes*, NAT'L CONF. OF STATE LEGIS. (2008).

bound to comply. In doing so, it targets funding and improves the predictability of that revenue supply. However, earmarking may actually cost a project government revenue because other spending may be redirected from the intended project. Therefore, projects funded with earmarked funds may receive less general government revenue once a revenue stream is secured.

Earmarking may also limit overall tax increases. To the extent taxpayers feel they can pick and choose which increases they sanction, they may not approve increases to general funds. This risks underfunding necessary, but less popular, government projects, such as road repair or pensions. Additionally, it limits the ability of elected officials to fulfill their functions, one of which is choosing between projects. Finally, earmarking taxes increases the cost of raising and dispersing funds and decreases state and local governments' flexibility when revenue is reduced or priorities change. Thus administrative costs are generally higher and response to changing circumstances generally slower in heavily earmarked systems.

(b) Rainy Day Funds

Because of states' and local governments' operating budget constraints, almost all states set aside revenue in budget stabilization or "rainy day" funds, although their labels for these funds vary. The nation's first rainy day fund was established by Florida in 1959 in recognition of the state's slow summer months and the effects of crop freezes.[72] The amount of contributions and the ability to withdraw from these funds vary by state. Most states finance their funds with year-end surpluses. Others use specific appropriations or dedicated sources of revenue. Some states allow withdrawals for any purpose deemed appropriate by the governor or the state legislature; others allow withdrawals only if the deficit is due to a revenue shortfall; and others allow withdrawals only if the deficit is caused by unexpected expenditures. Some states require the funds be repaid, ranging from the current year to after undefined upturns in the economy.

Despite twenty-five states capping the amounts deposited in rainy day funds, funds that are deposited may be insufficient in periods of need. The objective of the cap is to prevent the build-up of funds that might necessitate unnecessary taxes. However, although the fifty states collectively had about $60 billion set aside in 2008 (California and Wisconsin had $0 and Alaska had nearly 150% of its

---

[72]   For more on rainy day funds balances, see Justin Marlowe, *What's the Point of Rainy Day Funds*, GOVERNING.COM (2013).

annual expenditures), they faced a combined shortfall of nearly $117 billion in 2009.[73]

Since the recession, several states have made alterations to their funds, including increasing the amount that can be contributed and diverting specific revenue sources into the funds. Some states have changed the focus of their funds. Utah created a special rainy day fund focused on education; Oklahoma now permits the use of $10 million of its fund to support manufacturing when it faces a downsizing of its workforce.

(c) Education

Much of state and local funding goes to education. An estimated $1.15 trillion was spent nationwide at all levels of education for the 2012–2013 school year, and approximately 92% of elementary and secondary education funding was from non-federal sources (the remaining is primarily paid for by the federal government).[74] Although still a big number, the amount of money spent on education has been declining. In 30 states, total state and local funding was less in 2014 than in 2008.[75] Despite the overall decline, affluent schools continue spending, in what Professor Laurie Reynolds terms a luxury spending spree that, compared to international schools, fails to achieve educational success.[76]

Because local property taxes fund the bulk of most schools' budgets, districts have significant disparities in their funding. Striking differences in funding cross state lines. Alaska and New York spend two and a half times what is spent by Utah and Idaho. This amounts to $20,206 per pupil in New York compared to $6,575 per pupil in Utah.[77] Within the states, wealthy districts outspend poorer districts by a factor of two or three. States can counterbalance local spending. Delaware, Massachusetts, Minnesota, and New Jersey are unusual in that they have high funding levels and provide significantly more funding to low-income districts.[78] With the money they do spend, 21 states are regressive in that they provide less funding to low-income districts. In Nevada, for example, a high poverty district receives only 59 cents to the dollar as a wealthy district.

---

[73] Pew Charitable Trusts, Building State Rainy Day Funds (2014).

[74] U.S. Dept. of Educ., The Federal Role in Education (2017).

[75] Michael Leachman et al., *Most States Have Cut School Funding, and Some Continue Cutting*, Ctr on Budget & Pol'y Priorities (2016).

[76] Laurie Reynolds, *Skybox Schools*, 82 Wash. U.L. Q. 755 (2004).

[77] U.S. Census Bureau, Public Education Finances: 2015, Table 20 (2017).

[78] Bruce Baker et al., *Is School Funding Fair?*, Educ. L. Ctr (6th ed. 2017).

Significant litigation has developed over school funding, in particular the appropriateness of using the property tax as the primary source of funding. Protestors lost their litigation over this funding in *San Antonio Independent School District v. Rodriguez*.[79] The Supreme Court held that the plaintiffs had not proven education was a fundamental right and, therefore, basing school financing on property taxes does not violate the Fourteenth Amendment's equal protection clause. Litigants did better, but still failed to achieve much, when basing their arguments on equality or the requirement for adequate education under state constitutions.[80]

Several states have begun redressing disparate spending on the assumption that more spending in poor districts would help equalize educational opportunities.[81] Some states have enacted revenue caps. Colorado, for example, has a system that freezes per-pupil funding by local governments but permits additional levies to provide limited amounts of additional revenue. The state increases the budgets for lower income districts, making it the largest item in the state's budget. Other states have enacted levy caps. Washington's localities tax at a uniform rate and turn the revenue over to the state, so effectively creating a statewide property tax. Some states have adopted Robin Hood systems. Texas and Vermont take from wealthier districts and give to poorer districts, without providing additional state aid. Finally, some states have equalization models. Kansas and Wyoming have adopted standards in addition to equitable financing. Although likely decreasing inequality in spending, these changes have not achieved equalization of spending or of outcomes.[82]

---

[79]   411 U.S. 1 (1973).

[80]   For more on school funding litigation, see Lauren Gillespie, *The Fourth Wave of Educational Finance Litigation*, 95 CORNELL L. REV. 989 (2010).

[81]   States' websites offer a lot of information about their stated spending priorities but often gloss over their programs' shortcomings.

[82]   Despite Kansas's equalization model, its state supreme court held that it does not spend enough on the education of lower-income students. *See* Mitch Smith & Julie Bosman, *Kansas Supreme Court Says State Education Spending Is Too Low*, N.Y. TIMES, Mar. 2, 2017.

Chapter 14

CHARITABLE ORGANIZATIONS

Table of Sections

Most people think of tax-exempt organizations as 501(c)(3) organizations—the traditional religious, scientific, and educational charities—but there is a much more diverse system of tax exemption. As of 2009 there were over 1 million charities in the U.S.[1] There are also 500,000 more organizations that are exempt from tax, such as social welfare organizations, labor organizations, fraternal societies, and political organizations. Tax exemption means that the organization itself is not subject to tax. This exemption can be at the state or federal level; at times, entities exempt from tax at one level of government are not exempt at another. Additionally, some contributors to a subset of tax-exempt organizations, namely 501(c)(3) charities, are entitled to a federal tax deduction for their contributions.

§ 14.01   Tax-Exempt Status

All tax exemption means is that an entity does not pay tax on its taxable income. Many types of entities may be tax-exempt, and their tax treatment does not depend upon the tax treatment of their donors. On the other hand, the tax treatment of donors does depend upon the classification of the entity because only some tax-exempts entitle donors to deductions for contributions. Therefore, it is important to know where a particular entity fits within the rubric of tax-exempt status.

---

[1] NAT'L CTR FOR CHARITABLE STATISTICS, NUMBER OF NONPROFIT ORGANIZATIONS IN THE UNITED STATES, 1999–2013, http://nccs.urban.org/sites/all/nccs-archive/html/PubApps/profile1.php?state=US (last visited May 1, 2018).

(a) Types of Exemption

Tax exemption can be enjoyed for federal, state, or local purposes. Although it may be possible to enjoy exemption from multiple layers of government, it is not assured. Instead, different levels of government target different activities with exemption and place different restrictions on parties seeking to eliminate their tax burdens.

The type of entities people generally associate with tax-exemption can be classified into three groups: nonprofits, tax-exempts, and charities. Classification as a nonprofit, tax-exempt, or charitable organization entails increasingly restrictive requirements. Nonprofit status is a state law concept but one that, alone is not tax-exempt. This status requires the organization use any surplus revenue to further its mission rather than distributing the surplus to owners or directors. Founders can be rewarded with salaries for their work but not dividends from their success. Thus, nonprofit status does not mean that there is no intent to make a profit, only that the profit is reinvested in the organization. Without more, nonprofits are not tax-exempt.

To be tax-exempt under the federal Internal Revenue Code, nonprofits generally must seek recognition of their tax-exempt status. Although most people think of 501(c)(3) organizations, section 501 alone has twenty-seven other tax-exempt, but not charitable, classifications. The federal application for tax-exempt status requires disclosure to ensure that the entity meets certain requirements, such as an acceptable purpose and limitations on spending. Tax-exempts include chambers of commerce, teachers' retirement funds, and mutual insurance companies.

Finally, charitable organizations, popularly known as 501(c)(3)s, are a subset of tax-exempts that, in addition to not being subject to tax themselves, entitle their donors to a tax deduction for contributions. Requirements for forming charitable organizations vary by state, but the ability for donors to claim a deduction requires the contribution be made to a corporation, trust, community chest, fund, or foundation that has specific objectives, namely religious, charitable, scientific, literary, or educational purposes, fostering national or international amateur sports competition, or for the prevention of cruelty to children or animals.[2]

To illustrate the maze of classifications, consider a donor who establishes a nonprofit under Ohio state law to distribute food at a reduced price to the poor. Any profit that is generated is spent buying

---

[2]   I.R.C. § 170.

more food for the poor. Until the federal paperwork is completed, the nonprofit owes federal income tax on any profit that it generates. After completing the necessary paperwork, this nonprofit becomes tax-exempt and likely qualifies as a 501(c)(3) charity. If it becomes a charity, donors to this nonprofit receive a tax deduction for their contributions. On the other hand, donors do not receive a deduction for donating to a tax-exempt nonprofit that is not a charity, such as the NHL or a trade union.

Foundations are a final type of tax-exempt entity. They abound for targeted projects. A private foundation is any domestic or foreign 501(c)(3) that is not a public charity or a supporting organization for a public charity. Thus, nongovernmental, nonprofit organizations that receive contributions from a few sources, as opposed to the wider public, are private foundations. To make things more complicated, foundations can be classified for tax purposes as private operating foundations, exempt operating foundations, and grant-making foundations, each with different distribution requirements and donation deduction limitations.

Foundations share characteristics with charities but have important differences. A private foundation is subject to the same operational rules as a charity; and contributions to both are generally tax deductible. Also like charities, private foundations must file annual informational tax returns and are generally considered tax-exempt; however, unlike charities, there is a 1% or 2% excise tax on most domestic private foundations' net investment income. This excise applies to a foundation's earnings from investment assets that are contributed from a few sources and used to fund the foundation's annual expenditures. To remain a private foundation, the entity must annually distribute 5% of its income for charitable purposes, although what constitutes a charitable purpose is broadly interpreted. Additionally, there are limits on the assets that foundations can hold and on self-dealing with their substantial contributors.

There are several very large foundations and public charities but most are relatively small. Nevertheless, the concern about these tax exempts' market power and their influence is one reason that there are significant restrictions on what they can and cannot do, some of which are conditioned upon the entity's size. There is also concern that private foundations and other tax-exempts remove a significant amount of income from the tax base. For example, the Bill & Melinda Gates Foundation has over $41 billion in assets that generates millions of income annually.[3] On the other hand, approximately two-

---

3   BILL & MELINDA GATES FOUNDATION, CONSOLIDATED FINANCIAL STATEMENTS, Dec. 31, 2016.

thirds of the more than 84,000 foundations filing in 2009 had less than $1 million in assets.[4]

The reason for the different classifications is not for complexity's sake but to create a system that tailors tax benefits to the extent organizations further approved goals. In other words, because the government is partially funding contributions, the government wants to ensure only contributions to those entities working for the public good receive exemption or their donors receive deductions. A question remains whether the public has sufficient understanding of the rubric or whether the government undertakes proper review to ensure compliance. The complicated regime may simply increase the administrative costs of those who want to comply while justifying their disregard by those who do not.

Similar distinctions apply at the state and local levels, and the economic impact of state and local exemptions may be greater than their federal counterpart. For example, in 2014, the University of Pittsburgh Medical Center's tax exemption was worth an estimated $20 million in annual property tax on its $1.6 billion worth of property and a large share of its $500 million in profits.[5] In 2014, 190 owners of previously tax-exempt land in Alleghany County became taxable, raising over $1,000,000 in local revenue.[6] Thus, state and local tax exemptions are significant both to the organizations and the governments. In fact, the exemptions might have a greater impact on the latter than at the federal level because of the relative size of the exemption to the available tax base.

Finally, just because an organization is exempt from income, property, or sales taxes does not exempt it from employment taxes. In almost all instances, tax-exempt organizations that pay wages must pay payroll taxes. The rationale is that these workers need the same safety net provided by payroll taxes as other workers. Payroll taxes do not apply to unpaid volunteers or to ministers who have taken a vow of poverty or who apply for an exemption on the grounds that they are opposed to public insurance for religious or conscientious reasons.[7] But their income generally remains subject to the individual income tax.

---

[4]   King McGlaughon, *Think You Know Private Foundations? Think Again*, STAN. SOC. INNOVATION REV. (2014).

[5]   Robert Zullo, *UPMC, City Drop Legal Fight Over Taxes*, PITTSBURGH POST-GAZETTE, Jul. 29, 2014.

[6]   Sean D. Hamill, *Small Non-Profit Groups Losing Property-Tax Exemptions in First Wave of County's Review*, PITTSBURGH POST-GAZETTE, Feb. 15, 2015.

[7]   For the IRS's interpretation, see IRS, TOPIC 417 EARNINGS FOR CLERGY, https://www.irs.gov/taxtopics/tc417.html (last visited Jul. 11, 2017).

(b) Paperwork

Recognition as a tax exempt entity requires submission of an application, generally Form 1023, with a user fee. The application requires significant information, including three or four years of projected financial data. The amount of the fee depends upon the organization's average annual gross receipts but is either $400 or $850. One goal of the application is to gather information. As described on the IRS's website, the hope of requiring this information is to detect tax avoidance.[8] The most common forms of tax avoidance for these purposes are improper business dealings, excessive compensation, fundraising abuses, and the receipt of prohibited foreign grants.

(i) General Processes

The IRS generally processes applications as they are received. The average processing time of a Form 1023 is 191 days. A Form 1023-EZ is available for organizations with $250,000 or less of assets and $50,000 or less of annual gross receipts. The Form 1023-EZ has an average 13-day processing period.[9] After review, a ruling or determination may be granted confirming an entity's exemption, but the result can be revoked or modified. An adverse ruling can be appealed to the Appeals Office within thirty days of an adverse determination letter. In 2016, the IRS reviewed 92,129 applications for tax-exempt status, approving almost 94%.[10]

Requests that the IRS expedite review of an application can be made, but there must be a compelling reason for expediting the application.[11] Acceptable reasons include the risk of losing a grant without which the organization might not be able to operate or because the organization is to provide disaster relief. There has been a lot of press about delays in granting applications. In most cases, it is impossible to tell whether the delay is because too little or inaccurate information was supplied to the IRS or if, as critics charge, the agency stonewalled groups it did not support.

An organization has successfully litigated over the delay in consideration of its application. In 2015, *Z Street v. Koskinen*, a non-profit organization dedicated to Israeli issues sued the IRS on the

---

[8] IRS, PUBLICATION 557, TAX-EXEMPT STATUS FOR YOUR ORGANIZATION, https://www.irs.gov/publications/p557/ch01.html (last visited Sept. 27, 2017).

[9] Alistair Nevius, *Form 1023-EZ: First-Year Results Are In*, J. OF ACCOUNTANCY, Mar. 1, 2016.

[10] IRS, DATABOOK 52 (2017).

[11] IRS, APPLYING FOR EXEMPTION: EXPEDITING APPLICATION PROCESSING, https://www.irs.gov/charities-non-profits/applying-for-exemption-expediting-application-processing (last visited Sept. 27, 2017).

grounds that the IRS undertook more rigorous review of its internal policies than other non-profits as a result of President Obama's Middle East policies.[12] The District Court had concluded that this litigation was not to restrain "the assessment or collection of a tax but to prevent the IRS from delaying consideration of an application for tax-exempt status."[13] The D.C. Circuit Court agreed that Z Street had no other remedy. Although Z Street could wait and pursue administrative remedies, those remedies only apply to the organization's qualification for tax-exempt status. Here the issue was the timing of consideration, not the result.

Tax-exempts must also file annual information returns. Although considered onerous by some charities, the forms are intended to ensure continued compliance with the requirements for tax exemption. Penalties for the failure to file these annual returns are $20 per day (indexed for inflation) for each day the failure continues.[14] These penalties are capped at a maximum of the smaller of $10,000 or 5% of the organization's gross receipts for the year. Penalties may, however, be higher for organizations with more than $1 million of gross receipts.

(ii) Religious Organizations

Religious organizations are charitable organizations for which the normal application process is waived.[15] In other words, religious organizations do not have to apply to be granted a tax exemption or for donors to claim tax deductions for their contributions. Religious organizations are supposed to report their annual spending, but the filing is often waived. Additionally, there are special restrictions on the IRS's ability to audit religious organizations to confirm whether they are religious organizations.[16]

These exceptions derive, in part, from the desire to protect religious freedom and the concern that the government could target a religious minority. However, there is also the risk to the IRS of bad publicity and public or political backlash for undertaking a review of a religious organization. For example, the IRS revoked the Church of Scientology's tax exemption in the 1960s on the grounds that the church was a commercial enterprise. The church fought the IRS's

---

[12] Z Street v. Koskinen, 791 F.3d 24 (D.C. Cir. 2015).

[13] *Id.*, at 31.

[14] I.R.C. § 6652.

[15] *See* Nicholas Mirkay III, *Losing Our Religion*, 17 WM. & MARY BILL RTS J. 715 (2008); John Witte, Jr., *Tax Exemption of Church Property*, 64 SO. CAL. L. REV. 363 (1991). For the IRS's information, see IRS, TAX INFORMATION FOR CHURCHES AND RELIGIOUS ORGANIZATIONS, https://www.irs.gov/charities-non-profits/churches-religious-organizations (last visited Sept. 27, 2017).

[16] I.R.C. § 7611.

denial of the exemption by filing approximately 200 lawsuits against the IRS, and over 2,000 individual members similarly sued the IRS over deductions. They depleted the IRS litigation budget. In 1993, the IRS restored the tax exemption.[17]

The privilege for religious organizations could arguably violate the separation of church and state by privileging religious organizations. The concern is that by sharing the cost of contributions through deductions and less oversight, the government aids religion. In the process, the exemption significantly erodes the tax base. In 1970, the Supreme Court upheld the constitutionality of their benefits to the extent they are shared by other charities. In *Walz v. Tax Commission of the City of New York*, the Court held that an exemption for all houses of worship from property taxes is the some as that given to other tax-exempt nonprofits.[18] The government's decision that these entities foster moral or mental improvement to a similar degree as other nonprofits was not seen to be the endorsement of religion. The Court did not address exemptions enjoyed only by religious organizations.

(c) Abuse of Exemption

Congress defined the organizations that deserve tax exemption in the Internal Revenue Code; however, qualification under these rules is not always consistent with the public's perception of charity. In part this arises from the legal distinction between tax-exemption and 501(c)(3) charities. Additionally, some entities claim tax-exemption even when they are not legally entitled to do so. Thus, there is abuse that is consistent with the law but not public perception and there is tax evasion when the claim is inconsistent with the law itself.

First, some organizations successfully use the law to avoid tax on their business profits. The rules of section 501 focus on the public good element of the organization, but public good is often interpreted broadly. Ranging from university bookstores to the PGA Tour, organizations that claim tax-exempt status may well be commercial enterprises. For example, the $10 billion a year NFL was a tax-exempt entity until 2015 when it voluntarily waived the status.[19] The NFL claimed that the issue had become a distraction. To be fair, the football teams were never tax-exempt, just the collective equivalent to a trade association.

---

[17]   Rev. Rul. 93–73, 1993–34 I.R.B. 7; Joe Childs & Thomas Tobin, *Scientology*, TAMPA BAY TIMES, June 21, 2009.

[18]   397 U.S. 664 (1970).

[19]   Jonathan Clegg, *NFL to End Tax-Exempt Status*, WALL ST. J., Apr. 28, 2015.

Second, some entities claim to be tax-exempt even when there is no justification under the law. This is tax evasion using the tax-exempt form. For example, in its 2006 List of Dirty Dozen Tax Scams, the IRS listed charity Type III support organizations.[20] Legitimate support organizations can be donor advised and, therefore, not controlled by the charity. In the referenced scam, the donor gives what is nominally a support organization money in return for a deduction, and the organization gives it back to the donor's family either through offshore investments or interest-free loans. Through this circuitous route the income escapes U.S. taxation but returns to the donor. Although not naming them, the IRS revoked 72 such organizations' tax-exempt status within a five-year period.[21] These cases of abuse are different, but with the same effect, as a charity using its funds to pay officers exorbitant salaries or to fund extravagant dinners and trips.

Political and theoretical challenges to the charitable tax exemption have persisted since the enactment of the Code but currently take issue with much of charities' activities and question whether they are in the public interest.[22] The exemption (and possibly a deduction) costs a significant amount of government revenue that is spent according to the desires of private donors rather than elected representatives. Therefore, elected officials may object if charities are not fulfilling what they perceive as a worthy goal. Targeted opposition arises from time to time; however, no significant effort has been made to eliminate the privilege. Nevertheless, organizations that stray from the charitable basis that initially justified the tax exemption may be problematic for the organization or, possibly, the future of tax-exempt status.

§ 14.02 Donation Deductions

People who contribute to charities are often entitled to a tax deduction for those contributions.[23] However, contributions to all tax-exempts do not qualify for the deduction, neither do all contributions to charities. As with tax-exempt status, numerous rules limit these deductions. Sometimes people claim deductions for donations even when they are not entitled to do so. Perhaps more troubling, in 2016, the IRS warned about groups "masquerading as charitable

---

[20] IRS, IR–2006–25, IRS ANNOUNCES "DIRTY DOZEN" TAX SCAMS FOR 2006 (2006).

[21] Stephanie Strom, *IRS Takes on Abuse By Charity Support Groups*, N.Y. TIMES, Feb. 14, 2011.

[22] For example, see Nicholas Mirkay, *Is It "Charitable" to Discriminate?*, 2007 WISC. L. REV. 45; Lloyd Mayer, *Grasping Smoke: Enforcing the Bank on Political Activity byCharities*, 6 FIRST AMEND. L. REV. 1 (2007).

[23] I.R.C. § 170.

organizations" to gain contributions.[24] In those cases, not only do good organizations not receive the funds but the contributors do not receive deductions. Tax deductions are generally only available for certain types of contributions to 501(c)(3) organizations. Two types of 501(c)(4)s also qualify for charitable donation deductions: Veterans organizations with 90% war veteran membership and volunteer fire departments.

(a) Entitlement to the Deduction

Although 65% of the general population and 98.4% of high net worth households give to charity, a much smaller percentage of taxpayers claim a tax deduction on their income tax returns for doing so.[25] The federal tax deduction for charitable donations was reported in 2014 on 36.2 million returns at a cost of $210.6 billion in federal revenue.[26] Only those individuals who itemize deductions on their returns can claim these deductions. For the 66% of individuals who claim the standard deduction, there is no charitable deduction.

Despite the significant amount of government revenue that is at stake, the deduction remains easy to claim, even if taxpayers claim it erroneously. All that is required is claiming a deduction on a tax return. Compliance with the many rules of the deduction is ensured only on an audit of the taxpayer, although some of that auditing can be completed electronically.

Error may occur because of the numerous rules for proper deductibility.[27] First, the deduction is only available for contributions actually paid to charities; a pledge is insufficient to generate a deduction. Second, although deductions are permissible for contributions made in cash and in property, the contributions must be substantiated and, if of valuable property, the property must generally be appraised.[28] Third, there is a ceiling as to the amount of deduction a taxpayer can claim: 60% of an individual's adjusted gross income for cash contributions and 50% for contributions not in cash. Lower caps are applied for contributions to certain organizations, such as private foundations, and for contributions of capital gain property. Deductions for corporate donors are capped at 10% of a corporation's taxable income. Therefore, taxpayers are unable to give away all of their income and avoid taxes. Deductions disallowed because they exceed the ceiling may be carried forward and deducted

---

[24] IRS, IR–2016–20, FAKE CHARITIES ARE A PROBLEM AND ON THE IRS "DIRTY DOZEN" LIST OF TAX SCAMS FOR 2016 (2016).

[25] U.S. TRUST & LILLY FAMILY SCHOOL OF PHILANTHROPY AT IND. UNIV., THE 2014 U.S. TRUST STUDY OF HIGH NET WORTH PHILANTHROPY at 6 (2014).

[26] IRS, INDIVIDUAL COMPLETE REPORT, PUBLICATION 1304, Table 2.1 (2017).

[27] I.R.C. § 170.

[28] There are special rules regarding bargain sales to charities. I.R.C. § 1011(b).

in the succeeding five years. If the deductions cannot be claimed within five years, the deductions are lost forever.

To further limit what is done with deductible funds, Congress limits what types of entities can receive deductible contributions. Deductions are only allowed for contributions to qualified recipients, and this list is not as broad as all tax-exempts. The list of qualified recipients in 501(c)(3) includes educational, religious, art, and scientific organizations. The organization must be organized and operated exclusively for a permitted purpose; no private shareholder or any individual can receive the benefit of the organization's net earnings. Additionally, the organization's lobbying and political activities must be limited.

Notwithstanding those limitations, the charity or the group benefited does not have to reside in the U.S. Under current law, a 501(c)(3) must be a U.S. entity but is allowed to conduct operations outside the U.S. However, a contribution to such a 501(c)(3) is only deductible if the organization uses the contribution and is not a conduit or agent for another organization. Contributions to a foreign charity are only deductible if made deductible in a federal treaty, and currently the U.S. has established this relation only with Canada, Mexico, and Israel.[29] These treaties also require the U.S. taxpayer have income in the country in which the charity resides. In other words, a donation to a Canadian charity is only deductible if made by a person with Canada-sourced income.

Another limitation on donation deductions is that donors may not claim a deduction for a donation if they expect a specific benefit from their donation. Permitting donors a benefit plus a tax deduction would double the benefit. For this disqualification to apply, motive matters. For example, a private school requested that the parents of children enrolled in the school contribute $400x for each child, and parents who did not make the contribution were required to pay $400x in tuition. The IRS did not allow a deduction for the $400x contribution because the contributions were not the result of disinterested and detached generosity.[30] It is for this reason that purchasing tickets to charity events generally state the cost of the dinner because that portion of the ticket price is not deductible as a specific benefit.

Policing the limit on the receipt of benefits from charities has not been easy. For example, many universities require alumni make ostensibly charitable donations to the university for the opportunity

---

[29]   IRS Publication 526, https://www.irs.gov/publications/p526/ar02.html (last visited Sept. 27, 2017).

[30]   Rev. Rul. 83–104, 1983–2 C.B. 46.

to buy tickets to sporting events. Historically, the tax treatment of donations in excess of ticket prices caused confusion.[31] Donors are not detached or disinterested because the payments are a gateway cost to purchasing coveted tickets. Nevertheless, the payments were initially allowed to be deducted, until, in 1984, Congress denied all of these deductions. Then, in 1986, Congress permitted deductions for payments to the University of Texas and Louisiana State University, who likely rewarded their representatives for a job well done. In response to outrage from other institutions, in 1988, Congress enacted a special rule allowing taxpayers to deduct 80% of contributions made for the privilege of buying tickets until, in 2017, Congress against eliminated the deduction.[32] Eliminating the deduction was estimated to raise $2 billion between 2018 and 2027. Any part of the contribution for the tickets themselves was never deductible.

Finally, because of the incentive for tax avoidance through charitable contributions, today the Internal Revenue Code imposes substantiation requirements by which taxpayers are to prove that they made a charitable donation.[33] For contributions over $250, a contemporaneous written receipt must be received from the charity, and it must state that no goods or services were provided in exchange for the contribution. The Durdens learned this the hard way when they claimed a deduction for a $22,517 donation to their church and received a letter acknowledging the contribution. When the IRS denied the deduction for the missing language stating that they had not received goods or services in return, the Durdens obtained a new letter from their church but it was not contemporaneous with the donation. The Tax Court disallowed their deductions.[34]

(b) Consequences of the Deduction

It is because of the combined limits on the deduction that Professor Lilian Faulhaber questions whether the charitable deduction is hypersalient, causing taxpayers to make charitable donations on the assumption that they receive a deduction they never claim.[35] The deduction is public knowledge; the limitations

---

[31]   For more on the development of this tax policy, see GILBERT GAUL, BILLION-DOLLAR BALL 43–70 (2015); Richard Schmalbeck, *Ending the Sweetheart Deal Between Big-Time College Sports and the Tax System* (2014), https://papers.ssrn.com/sol3/papers.cfm?abstract_id=2559886 (last visited Sept. 27, 2017). Even after I.R.C. § 170(*l*)'s enactment, the IRS struggled in its application. For example, see Rev. Rul. 86–63, 1986–17 I.R.B. 6; I.R.S. Tech. Adv. Mem. 2000004001 (Jul. 7, 1999).

[32]   I.R.C. § 170(*l*).

[33]   I.R.C. § 170(f)(8).

[34]   Durden v. Comm'r, T.C. Memo. 2012–140.

[35]   Lilian Faulhaber, *The Hidden Limits of the Charitable Deduction*, 92 B.U. L. REV. 1307 (2012).

restricting the deduction are not. And charities have reason to exaggerate the availability of the deduction, increasing the hypersalience. This hypersalience may distort taxpayer behavior by causing people to give more than they would if they understood the tax results.

Although the goal of the deduction is to facilitate contributions to charities focused on the issues listed in the statute, which includes helping the poor, there are class-based effects of the donation deduction. It is impossible to measure all of the effects because there is no complete measure of who makes charitable contributions. The *Chronicle of Philanthropy* found that households making at least $100,000 per year give an average of 4.2% of their discretionary income to charities while those that make between $50,000 and $75,000 give on average 7.6%.[36] This information is based on income tax returns, which cannot show the entire picture. Because deductions phase out and because of the alternative minimum tax, some higher-income taxpayers may not be able to claim deductions for the donations they make. They may also make donations as part of estate planning which would not show up on annual returns. Additionally, because lower income taxpayers tend not to itemize, it is impossible to see their charitable giving based on their tax returns.

As a deduction rather than a tax credit, the charitable donation deduction should be worth more to taxpayers in higher tax brackets than in lower ones but that is not always true. For example, a $100 deduction to a taxpayer in a 25% tax bracket is worth $25 but to a taxpayer in a 10% tax bracket is worth only $10. Moreover, those claiming the standard deduction receive no benefit from this itemized deduction. On the other hand, the exclusion from the alternative minimum tax for higher-income taxpayers may limit its value. Thus, donors need tax advice to learn the true value of the deduction based on their complete personal tax situation.

For all of those who claim the deduction, the taxpayer is no worse off for the portion of the contribution that would have been paid to the government in taxes. In other words, the government pays a portion of the contribution through reduced tax revenue. The justification is that Congress defines the worthy causes for which deductions can be received in 501(c)(3). Taxpayers are allowed to choose among these qualifying charities, producing a more efficient and effective selection than the government might make.

To illustrate the government's partnership in the contribution, consider a simplified hypothetical of taxpayer Tom with a flat 40%

---

[36] Emily Gipple & Ben Rose, *America's Generosity Divide*, Chron. of Philanthropy, Aug. 12, 2012.

tax rate, $500,000 of income, and a $50,000 contribution to a qualified charity. If the government does not allow a charitable deduction, Tom is taxed $200,000 ($500,000 times 40%), and he makes the $50,000 contribution with after-tax dollars. Alternatively, if Tom is given a deduction for the contribution, he reduces his taxable income by the $50,000; so only $450,000 is taxed at 40%, raising $180,000 in taxes. With the deduction Tom owes $20,000 less in taxes because of the contribution so Tom is really only paying $30,000 for the contribution. The government pays the other $20,000. The higher the tax rate, the less of the contribution Tom actually pays. Instead, he diverts a portion of his taxes to a cause of his choice.

The contribution of appreciated property generates even larger tax benefits and shifts more of the cost of the contribution to the government because taxpayers can deduct the full fair market value of contributed property without including its appreciation in income.[37] In other words, donors never owe tax on the donated item's built-in gain. Despite this benefit, contributions of appreciated assets are less than one-third of the value of contributions claimed on tax returns.[38] When claimed, these types of contributions are prone to abuse, with the Treasury Inspector General for Tax Administration estimating that 60% of those claiming deductions for contributions of property did not comply with reporting requirements and that $3.8 billion of potentially erroneous deductions were claimed at a potential cost of $1.1 billion in taxes.[39] Charities have opposed attempts to remove this tax benefit.[40]

Continuing the earlier example, if instead of cash Tom contributes stock worth $50,000 for which he paid $3,000, Tom receives a $50,000 deduction. However, there was $47,000 of untaxed appreciation in the stock at the time of the contribution. Under current rules, Tom is never taxed on that $47,000 of built-in gain. If he had sold the stock and contributed the cash, he would owe tax on the $47,000 gain and then receive a $50,000 deduction, a net benefit of only $3,000. Therefore, contributions of appreciated assets give

---

[37]   Limits may apply. For example, a 30%-of-AGI limit was imposed for contributions of appreciated property. If the property would produce ordinary income (such as a contribution of inventory), limitations restrict the donor's deduction to the cost of the property. I.R.C. § 170(b)(1)(C).

[38]   IRS, INDIVIDUAL COMPLETE REPORT, PUBLICATION 1304, Table 2.1 (2017).

[39]   TAXPAYER INSPECTOR GEN. OF TAX ADMIN., 2013–40–009, MANY TAXPAYERS ARE STILL NOT COMPLYING WITH NONCASH CHARITABLE CONTRIBUTION REPORTING REQUIREMENTS (2012).

[40]   For example, Americans for the Art, Charitable Giving & Tax Reform, http://www.americansforthearts.org/by-program/reports-and-data/legislation-policy/legislative-issue-center/charitable-giving-tax-reform (last visited Sept. 27, 2017).

donors a double tax benefit—an exclusion of gain from income plus a deduction.

To be clear, Tom contributes an asset that is worth $50,000 and his net worth declines by this amount. The issue, however, is that the tax system never recognized $47,000 of that asset. So unlike the contribution of cash from wages that has been taxed, with the contribution of appreciated property some amount escapes taxation. If the $50,000 deduction reduces Tom's taxable income to $450,000, he saves $50,000 times his 40% tax rate, or $20,000. Thus, the contribution saves him $20,000 in taxes. Without the double benefit (and ignoring issues of capital gains taxation), Tom would save only $3,000. With the contribution of the appreciated stock, Tom no longer has the stock but he has a larger share of his salary.

Contrasted with the favorable treatment of contributions of appreciated assets, no deduction is currently allowed for the contribution of uncompensated services. If Tom contributes his time that is worth $50,000, the contribution is ignored for tax purposes. The alternative would provide a substantial benefit to service providers, although arguably no greater than for the contribution of appreciated assets. If a taxpayer sells his services, the taxpayer has gross income and, when the taxpayer contributes the cash received as payment, he receives a deduction. The income and deduction generally offset. If the deduction were permitted without requiring the inclusion of income, the taxpayer would get a double tax benefit and be in a better tax position because of the ability to offset other income with the deduction.

The availability and limits of the charitable donation deduction incentivizes some individuals to donate large sums in certain forms, more often as estate planning than annual giving because of the ability to maximize the tax savings. The government is arguably creating a win-win for the wealthy and society by encouraging private spending (supplemented with decreased tax revenue) for purposes the government has deemed worthy.

On the other hand, this is an expensive deduction. Congress's Joint Committee on Taxation estimates that the deduction will cost approximately $777 billion between 2017 and 2026.[41] In comparison, the United Way testified before the Senate Committee on Finance that a cap on charitable donation deductions could lead to a reduction in giving of $2.9 to $5.6 billion each year, for a maximum of $28

---

[41]   U.S. TREAS. DEPT., TAX EXPENDITURES, Table 1 (2017). The JCT did not isolate the revenue effects of increasing the percentage limit for contributions of cash from 50% to 60% in 2017.

billion in the same 10-year period.[42] The loss in tax revenue from the deduction is much greater than the potential loss to charities if it is eliminated because not all giving is driven by tax savings.

A persistent question is whether society should assist charities through donors' tax reduction. In other words, should the public pay for music halls, ballets, or food banks, and, if so, should taxpayers decide which activities to sponsor through their tax deductible donation or should the government fund these activities directly? On one hand, by allowing taxpayers to choose with their contributions, only a portion of the cost is paid in lost tax revenue, and the act of giving increases civic involvement. On the other hand, the deduction reduces the revenue available for programs established by the nation's elected representatives.

Other means could be adopted to accomplish similar objectives as the deduction, although the alternatives may pose their own problems. For example, some countries do not provide tax deductions but match taxpayers' contributions. This makes the government's portion of the contribution more clearly government spending. Consequently, matching programs are more likely subject to the same political pressures as other spending programs. For example, in 2013 the U.K. launched, and renewed in 2016, a £120 million three-year program to match donations to international charities.[43] Additionally, through a program called Gift Aid, British charities can claim 25p every time a person contributes £1.[44] Thus, taxpayers can contribute pre-tax amounts with the tax that is owed going to the charity. As a result, someone in the 20% bracket pays £12 and the charity receives £15 and a 40% taxpayer gives £9 and the charity gets £15. For this latter program, the result is the same as with the deduction but with different optics and fewer planning opportunities.

§ 14.03 Tax Planning Using Charities

Charities are often used in tax planning, although in most instances a philanthropic objective must exist because the tax savings does not exceed the contribution. This planning can be over the course of a taxpayer's life or as estate planning. Contributing appreciated assets is one means of tax planning; and contributing retirement assets, such as individual retirement accounts, carves the account out of the taxable estate plus earning a tax deduction. In

---

[42] *Tax Reform Options: Incentives for Charitable Giving Hearing Before Senate Comm. on Finance*, 112th Cong. 55 (2011) (testimony of Brian Gallagher).

[43] PRESS RELEASE, U.K. DEPT. FOR INTERN'L DEVEL., U.K. AID MATCH £120 MILLION BOOST FOR BRITISH CHARITIES, Sept. 29, 2013.

[44] U.K. GOV., GIFT AID: WHAT DONATIONS CHARITIES AND CASCS CAN CLAIM ON, https://www.gov.uk/guidance/gift-aid-what-donations-charities-and-cascs-can-claim-on (last visited Sept. 27, 2017).

addition to these simple techniques, Congress and estate planners have created many tools for effective planning using tax-exempt entities.

This type of tax planning has several possible objectives. Often the use of charities in estate planning is intended to reduce the tax base for purposes of the estate tax. Any money given to a charity is fully deductible from a decedent's estate. Therefore the gross amount goes to the charity and not a lesser net amount after taxes. Another goal may be to transfer appreciated assets or those with lots of untaxed gain so that the tax-exempt can sell the asset without the donor triggering the tax. For these purposes, charities are ideal partners because the contributions permit the transfer of the property with a deduction to offset other income.

There are ways to maximize the tax savings from charitable donations. For example, Congress established the charitable remainder trust (CRT).[45] The primary tax benefit of the CRT is that the donor is entitled to a charitable deduction when the trust is created based on the present value of an amount going to a charity years later. This current deduction is granted even though nothing may go to the charity for a long time. That deduction reduces taxes on other income, and with the time value of money the savings can exceed the present value of the contribution. Additionally, as a tax-exempt entity, the trust can sell appreciated assets with fewer tax consequences than if they were sold directly by the donor.

Many rules govern a CRT's operation. A CRT is as an irrevocable trust meaning that once it is established its creator cannot change the trust. Additionally, the CRT annually distributes a fixed percentage based on the trust's assets to someone not tax-exempt (the beneficiary). At the expiration of some period, such as when the donor dies, the remaining balance in the trust is distributed to a charity. Per federal statute, the percentage going to the beneficiary must be at least 5% but no more than 50% of the trust's assets and, as of the formation of the trust, at least 10% of the trust's assets must be expected to go to a charity.

Donors' objective for these planning tools may be philanthropic or to create a family dynasty. From society's perspective, the alternative would likely be more tax revenue but also more concentrated wealth. One question is whether a sufficient amount of the assets are put to charitable purposes to justify the tax benefit? Another question is, even if the assets are used for noble purposes, is

---

[45]   I.R.C. § 664. For more on CRTs, see Justin Ransome & Vinu Satchit, *Charitable Remainder Trust Update*, J. ACCOUNTANCY, Oct. 1, 2009.

the complexity it adds to the tax system worth it? Significant planning goes into the creation of tax efficient donations.

§ 14.04   Tax on Tax-Exempts

Congress has long been concerned that tax-exempt entities can produce goods or services that compete with tax-paying businesses.[46] At issue is whether this competition is unfair in some sense. All else being equal tax-exempts have greater capacity for predatory pricing because they have fewer costs since taxes are not included. Therefore, tax-exempts can sell at a lower price than businesses that have to pay taxes. However, this reasoning ignores that tax-exempts are choosing among investments for which all returns are exempt from tax, and tax-exempts have little incentive to engage in price-cutting. A tax-exempt could charge the same as a tax-paying business and retain the profits for its tax-exempt activities.

Nevertheless, in recognition of the perceived advantage that tax-exempts have over taxpayers, Congress enacted rules and restrictions on tax-exempts engaged in business. As a result, a tax-exempt may owe tax on its net investment income and a tax on the failure to distribute income; and if a tax-exempt has "substantial" unrelated business income, it is possible for the tax-exempt to lose its tax-exempt status.[47] Substantial is not defined for this purpose; regulations threaten the loss of status if the unrelated business constitutes 5% or more of a tax-exempt's activities. However, the IRS failed to invoke this provision in at least one instance in which the unrelated business constituted 75% of a tax-exempt's activities.[48]

Additionally, income from activities unrelated to the tax-exempt's purpose is taxable in the same way it would be taxed if earned by a taxable business. This requirement arose after New York University School of Law operated a subsidiary, the Mueller Macaroni Company, and no income tax was owed on profitable macaroni.[49] The IRS and Tax Court both objected that the macaroni business was not an exempt purpose, but the Third Circuit disagreed about the interpretation of the tax-exempt law, permitting the tax-exempt to avoid tax on all of its activities. Congress responded in

---

[46]   Gov't Accountability Office, GGD–87–40BR, Competition Between Taxable Businesses and Tax-Exempt Organizations (1987). This is of particular concern for tax-exempts, see Gene Takagi, *Fair or Foul? A Review of Federal Tax Laws Governing Unfair Competition*, Nonprofit Quarterly, Oct. 28, 2014.

[47]   Indiana Retail Hardware Assn v. U.S. 366 F.2d 998 (Ct. Cl. 1966). These rules apply particularly to private foundations; however, 501(c)(3)s also have UBTI if they use debt-financing for passive investing.

[48]   Reg. § 1.501(c)(3)–1(b)(3)(i); Rev. Rul. 57–313, 1957–2 C.B. 316.

[49]   C.F. Mueller Co. v. Commissioner, 190 F.2d 120 (1951). NYU also operated other taxable businesses. *See* Michael S. Knoll, *The UBTI: Leveling an Uneven Playing Field or Tilting a Level One?*, 76 Fordham L. Rev. 857, 862 (2007).

1950 by enacting a tax on these unrelated businesses. NYU Law kept running the business (and paying tax) until it was sold in 1976 for $115 million.

The 1950 tax continues to apply and is called the unrelated business income tax (UBIT).[50] The UBIT applies to income, termed unrelated business income (UBI), derived from a regularly carried on trade or business that is not substantially related to the tax-exempt's purpose. In other words, the business is a real profit-seeking business that is not the tax-exempt's purpose. That the income is used to further the exempt purpose does not qualify the income as related. The income itself must be earned in the course of furthering an exempt purpose.

Despite the existence of the special UBIT, not all tax-exempts' income is UBI. An important exclusion from UBI is revenue generated in a passive manner, such as interest, dividends, or royalties; however, this income may have its own tax consequences. Additionally, one-time sales are generally excluded from UBI on the grounds that the tax-exempt is not regularly carrying on the activity. Business activities are deemed regularly carried on only if the activities are pursued in a manner similar to comparable taxable commercial activities.

UBI is generally taxed at general corporate income tax rates, except for certain tax-exempt trusts that are taxed at trust rates. In 2013, almost 23,000 tax-exempts paid tax on UBI and almost an equal number of organizations filed the requisite form but had offsetting deductions and so owed no tax.[51] Nearly two-thirds of these were 501(c)(3) charities. They reported over $400 million in tax. In 2007, charities reported almost $600 million in tax. An intensive audit of 34 universities found an additional $90 million in UBIT, with 70% of their returns being adjusted.[52]

To the extent tax-exempts comply with the UBIT, it places tax-exempts and for-profits on an equal tax field. However, this ignores that a tax-exempt has alternate investments so that the proper theoretical focus should be on an investment's rate of return. The investment's rate of return must be comparable to alternative investments whether for a tax-exempt or a for-profit for either to engage in the activity. Therefore, the better frame for comparison,

---

[50] Knoll, *supra* note 50; Henry Hansmann, *Unfair Competition and the Unrelated Business Income Tax*, 75 VA. L. REV. 60 (1989).

[51] IRS, SOI TAX STATS, EXEMPT ORGANIZATIONS' UNRELATED BUSINESS INCOME TAX STATISTICS, Table 2 (2013); IRS, UNRELATED BUSINESS INCOME TAX 2012 ONESHEET (2013).

[52] IRS, COLLEGES AND UNIVERSITIES COMPLIANCE PROJECT FINAL REPORT 2 (2013).

not addressed by the UBIT, is the entity's rate of return as among the entity's investment opportunities rather than UBTI's focus as between entities.

Consider a $1 million investment that is being considered by a tax-exempt and a for-profit. The tax-exempt has a 0% tax rate and the for-profit has a 35% tax rate. If the investment generates $100,000 each year, the tax-exempt would retain it all and the for-profit would retain $65,000 after tax. Thus, the investment generates a 10% return for the tax-exempt and a 6.5% return for the for-profit. Although this appears to favor the tax-exempt, this investment must be compared to alternate investments. The for-profit is indifferent between this investment and any other that yields 6.5%, whereas the tax-exempt's comparable investments yield 10%. Thus, investors consider their own return on investment and not that of other investors. If an alternate investment yields 8% post-tax for either investor, the for-profit would prefer the alternate to this investment but the tax-exempt would not.

Taxes may play a part in the relative attractiveness of an investment for tax-exempts and taxpayers if different rates apply to different investments. If a particular investment is more heavily taxed than the prevailing rate, its return is lowered for the for-profit but not for the tax-exempt who, in the absence of the UBIT, does not care about taxes. If the investment's tax is lower than comparable investments, its return is increased for the for-profit but not for the tax-exempt. Moreover, if either entity can increase the investment's yield more than the other can, it affects their relative returns and the desirability of entering into the business.

Despite tax-exempts' and taxpayers' different focus, tax-exempt investment theoretically threatens the corporate tax base. Without the UBIT, tax-exempts have a higher rate of return for many investments that may crowd out for-profits but only if an unlimited amount of money can flow into tax-exempts. This was evidenced by NYU Law's entry into the noodle business. Even if the tax does not raise significant revenue, it is impossible to know if tax-exempts would engage in more unrelated businesses if they were untaxed.[53] Anecdotally it appears they did before 1950. It is also impossible to know whether the amount of tax-exempt money available for investment is capped.

On the other hand, the UBIT adds significantly to tax-exempt entities' complexity. What constitutes UBI is not always clear. For example, a museum applied for a private letter ruling from the IRS

---

[53]   Because the UBIT raises revenue, consideration of its repeal should include a relatively better revenue source.

to learn whether the sale of reproductions of artwork and the operation of a gift shop constituted UBI. The organization was formed to encourage and develop the study of art, the application of art to manufacture and practical life, and the advancement of general knowledge of art. The IRS said the sale of reproductions and of artistic utilitarian items and clothes was substantially related to the museum's purpose but the sale of original artwork was not. Consequently, the former was not UBI and the latter was. The sale of mugs, ashtrays, and towels with the museum's logo and not reproductions was also UBI.[54] Thus, the rules are complex, and the penalties for violating them are severe.

Finally, because the UBIT taxes this income even if it is spent on the tax-exempt's purpose, the tax can be seen to hamper the tax-exempt's ability to accomplish its mission. Because the business's proceeds are used on the tax-exempt's purpose, the ability to reap higher profits furthers the tax-exempt's objectives. Perhaps because the tax decreases their rate of return, a study has found that tax-exempts are unlikely to produce UBI unless the entity is in financial need.[55] The UBIT makes investments that are tax-exempt relatively more attractive to tax-exempts than UBI by increasing their return relative to taxable businesses. It is also possible that a tax-exempt operating an unrelated business would unacceptably divert attention away from the charity's purpose or risk alienating the public. Therefore, tax-exempts might choose not to undertake these activities even without the tax.

§ 14.05   Social Enterprises

Recently, entrepreneurs have begun creating business hybrids that use taxable businesses to create "good products," such as clean water or clean energy. These hybrids generally have a charitable objective as their primary purpose; profit-making is secondary. Nevertheless, the entity is permitted to distribute post-tax profits to shareholders, unlike tax-exempts. An open question is whether 501(c)(3)s that receive tax-deductible donations should be able to fund these new businesses with grants. These grants might be the most efficient way of accomplishing the tax-exempt's objective; however, using these grants in profit-seeking businesses may create an uneven playing field with taxable entities that do not have access to tax-exempt investment. To date, the IRS sees no distinction between these businesses and traditional for-profits.[56] Therefore,

---

[54]   I.R.S. Tech. Adv. Mem. 8326008 (1983); I.R.S. Tech. Adv. Mem. 8328009 (1983).

[55]   James R. Hines, Jr., *Non-profit Business Activity and the Unrelated Business Income Tax, in* TAX POLICY AND THE ECONOMY, vol. 13, at 57 (James Poterba, ed. 1999).

[56]   For example, see Family Trust of Mass. Inc. v. U.S., 722 F.3d 355 (2013).

these entities cannot receive the charities' investments without the charity risking its status, despite the business being substantially related to the public good.

Despite the lack of tax benefits, states have created several special types of entities to permit the consideration of social good over profit. The low-profit limited liability company (L3C) was first created by Vermont in 2008 but is enacted in eight states as of April 2018.[57] North Carolina had an L3C statute but repealed the provision in 2013 in order to simplify its general LLC act without significant public response.[58] To qualify as an L3C, the entity's charter generally must have a profit-seeking objective plus another charitable objective. The existence of this other objective shields the company and management from lawsuits that they did not maximize profits as required under general corporate law.

A goal of the L3C form is to permit private foundations to contribute to for-profits despite the tax rules that normally prevent foundations from doing so. Foundations are limited in their activities to program-related investment (PRI) so most state statutes require L3Cs conform to the PRI rules.[59] The IRS proposed regulations in 2012 that makes these investments more likely.[60] Nevertheless, foundations remain reluctant to invest for fear of losing their own tax-exempt status.

A similar entity is the benefit corporation. Maryland authorized the first benefit corporation in 2009, and as of April 2018 thirty-four states have statutes establishing them.[61] Although taxed in the same manner as a for-profit corporation, these entities must have a purpose of creating a general public benefit, normally focusing on society and the environment. However, unlike L3Cs, benefit organizations do not have to narrowly pursue charitable goals as long as they consider the impact of their decisions on society and the environment as well as on shareholders. Most enabling statutes impose reporting obligations as a form of self-audit on how well the benefit corporation accomplishes its goals. Although these restrictions permit benefit corporations to distinguish themselves to investors as having a social conscience, benefit corporations are

---

[57] For a description of L3Cs, see Daniel Kleinberger, *A Myth Deconstructed: The "Emperor's New Clothes" on the Low Profit Limited Liability Company*, 35 DEL. J. CORP. L. 879 (2010). For the tally, see InterSector Partners, L3C, http://www.inter sectorl3c.com/l3c (last visited May 1, 2018).

[58] Anne Field, *North Carolina Officially Abolishes the L3D*, FORBES, Jan. 11, 2014.

[59] J. William Callison & Allan Vestal, *The L3C Illusion*, 35 VT. L. REV. 273 (2010).

[60] 77 Fed. Reg. 23429, 23430 (2012).

[61] BENEFIT CORPORATION, STATE BY STATE STATUS OF LEGISLATION, http://benefitcorp.net/policymakers/state-by-state-status (last visited May 1, 2018).

generally unable to receive grants from a tax-exempt as an L3C might.

Finally, since 2012 California has authorized the Social Purpose Corporation (formerly the Flexible Purpose Corporation).[62] This entity form retains the primary objective of traditional corporations, seeking a profit, but also has a special purpose that can be a charitable purpose or just to minimize adverse effects on employees, the community, or the environment. As with the other new hybrid forms, the state offers liability protection for businesses that consider their special purpose in addition to shareholder profits. Social Purpose Corporations seek traditional capital market investment.

Hybrids can raise revenue for social welfare projects, with only some of the funding at the cost of federal revenue. These investments are attractive to donors who want a return (rather than to make a charitable contribution) but are not seeking to maximize that return. In other words, investors may be willing to take a smaller profit on a social or environmental investment because of the potential public good. In the process, hybrids help market a company's social commitment, thereby increasing funding for, and awareness of, their societal aims. To the extent one likes charitable giving, hybrids enhance the likelihood of that giving.

On the other hand, expanding the ability to use tax-exempt money to invest in profit-seeking enterprises comes with risks. These organizations have fundamentally conflicting purposes of social goals plus profit-seeking. As hybrids struggle with this conflict, they risk charitable assets and tax subsidies being misused. If these organizations succeed in raising more funds, they also risk crowding out funding for pure charities that are unable to create a marketable good or service around the problem they try to address. Moreover, hybrids' "halo effect" may be a good marketing tool but possibly distort the market because the public may not be savvy about the different forms of these entities.

Finally, there is no assurance hybrids will use their investments wisely. To date there is no proof that for-profits are more efficient or otherwise better equipped to accomplish social welfare purposes than are tax-exempts. Congress placed restrictions on tax-exempts' use of funds because tax-exempts act with government subsidies. Loosening the restrictions for hybrids removes those protections for the use of those subsidies. Donating to a hybrid entity may give contributors greater control over the business than they can have over a charity; however, that limited control is a congressionally enacted tool to

---

[62]   CAL. FRANCHISE TAX BOARD, WHAT IS A CALIFORNIA SOCIAL PURPOSE CORPORATION?, https://www.ftb.ca.gov/Archive/professionals/taxnews/2015/September/All_About_Business.shtml (last visited Feb. 21, 2018).

isolate nonprofits from the personal greed or motivations of individual persons. Hybrids risk favoring personal goals over charitable autonomy.

§ 14.06 Lobbying

The Internal Revenue Code strictly limits tax-exempts' activities to ensure they pursue a congressionally defined public good. Those limits include capping the amount of political lobbying and campaigning, unlike for-profit businesses that are generally unlimited in their political activities since *Citizens United v. FEC* was decided in 2010.[63] In *Citizens United*, the Supreme Court permitted unlimited corporate and union spending in political elections. For corporations, lobbying does not affect their tax status, but tax-exempts may lose their status if they lobby. Nevertheless, since *Citizens United*, tax-exempt entities have doubled their political spending although their spending has lessened since the 2012 election cycle.[64]

Political spending by tax-exempt entities raises concerns about the advantage given to those who lobby through tax-exempts with pre-tax dollars. Those operating outside of a tax-exempt must use post-tax dollars to do so. Rules respond to this concern by limiting, if not eliminating, the lobbying efforts of tax-exempt entities if they are to retain their tax-exempt status. In other words, if a tax-exempt engages in prohibited lobbying, it may lose its tax-exempt status.

Statutory and regulatory limits on lobbying apply differently to the many types of tax-exempts. These rules evolved in response to perceived abuse, and they have grown increasingly complex. Additionally, different rules exist for political activities for particular candidates versus activities for particular legislation. Thus, there is a maze of rules that a tax-exempt must learn, and it is hard to generalize how much lobbying a tax-exempt may do.

For example, charities are prohibited from participating in any partisan political activity for particular candidates, but they may engage in limited amounts of lobbying to influence legislation. These limitations do not extend to truly nonpartisan activity, such as voter education and voter participation activities, unless it is evidenced by bias favoring or opposing a candidate. However, even permitted lobbying is limited. Lobbying for legislation may not be a substantial part of a charity's total activities. Although the test itself is vague, many tax-exempts can elect to use an expenditure test to gain greater

---

[63]   558 U.S. 310 (2010).

[64]   CTR FOR RESPONSIVE POLITICS, DARK MONEY BASICS, https://www.open secrets.org/dark-money/basics (last visited Sept. 27, 2017).

certainty regarding the threshold.[65] Going over the threshold can result in fines, penalties, or back taxes. Additionally, the IRS claims the right to revoke tax-exempts' status for abuse of this limit.[66]

As charities, churches cannot retain their 501(c)(3) status or donors receive tax deductions if churches advocate for or against particular politicians. Thus, churches are not singled out with this prohibition but held to the generally applicable rule for charities. This has become a political issue as churches seek to influence their congregations before elections.[67] Although the IRS often turns a blind eye on this advocacy, in *Branch Ministries, Inc. v. Rossotti*, the D.C. Circuit Court upheld the revocation of a bona fide church's tax-exempt status because it sponsored a series of newspaper ads urging people not to vote for Bill Clinton.[68] Despite the existing prohibition on advocating for or against candidates, churches may engage in limited lobbying for particular pieces of legislation. Moreover, churches may engage in any of the prohibited or limited activities through segregated taxable organizations not funded with tax-deductible donations.

President Donald Trump signed an executive order singling out churches by critiquing the limitation on charities.[69] Despite the rhetoric, President Trump's order is unlikely to change the implementation of the law in the short term. His order merely calls for the Justice Department to develop rules for the "executive branch to vigorously enforce Federal law's robust protections for religious freedom" and instructs the IRS not to take "adverse action" for political speech "not ordinarily . . . treated as participation or intervention in a political campaign." Eliminating these limits only for churches likely violates the separation of church and state as required by the First Amendment; repealing it more broadly would diminish campaign finance rules.

Rules regarding the lobbying activities of social welfare organizations organized under section 501(c)(4) are murkier. The

---

[65]   I.R.C. § 501(h).

[66]   IRS, Lobbying, https://www.irs.gov/charities-non-profits/lobbying (last visited Sept. 27, 2017). Organizations that do not file their information returns for three consecutive years automatically lose their tax-exempt status. IR.C. § 6033(j).

[67]   IRS, *Charities, Churches and Politics*, https://www.irs.gov/uac/charities-churches-and-politics (last visited Sept. 27, 2017). The issue is not new. For example, in 2008 pastors made political sermons to challenge the law. PEW RESEARCH CTR, PASTORS TO PROTEST IRS RULES ON POLITICAL ADVOCACY, http://www.pewforum.org/2008/09/19/pastors-to-protest-irs-rules-on-political-advocacy/ (last visited Sept. 27, 2017).

[68]   211 F.3d 137 (D.C. Cir. 2000). *See also* Regan v. Taxation with Representation, 461 U.S. 540 (1983); Jimmy Swaggart Ministries v. Board of Equalization, 493 U.S. 378 (1990).

[69]   Exec. Order No. 13,798, 82 Fed. Reg. 21,675 (May 4, 2017).

Internal Revenue Code defines 501(c)(4)s as tax-exempt civic organizations "operated exclusively for the promotion of social welfare." Some courts interpret the 501(c)(4) provision as permitting only insubstantial political activity, but the Treasury Department's regulation interpreting this statutory requirement requires that they be "operated primarily for the purpose of bringing about civic betterment and social improvements."[70] Per the statute, campaign activities are not social welfare activities; therefore, the difference between exclusivity, substantiality, and primarily is critical. The Treasury Department's looser standard has been interpreted as allowing up to 49% of a 501(c)(4)'s money to be spent on politics.[71] The IRS provides as an example that a tenant group for an apartment complex would not qualify as a 501(c)(4) but one for all tenants in a community would qualify.[72] Lobbying for particular legislation to obtain the organization's objective is permissible; however, campaigning for a candidate cannot be the organization's primary activity.

As political actors, 501(c)(4)s have an additional benefit over other tax-exempts in that they are not required to disclose the identities of their donors because their donors do not receive tax deductions. This can make them powerful political actors. For example, Carolina Rising spent 97% of its almost $5 million advertising for Senator Thom Tillis in 2014.[73] Almost all of its money came from one person, thought to be Art Pope but this is not known for certain. As a result of its many advantages, 501(c)(4)s' political spending increased from $1.26 million in 2006 to $257 million in 2012, although this spending has subsequently declined to $145 million in the 2016 election cycle.[74]

There have been difficulties for some who seek to establish 501(c)(4)s. Although these organizations were not required to apply for tax-exempt status before 2016, reviewing applications that were submitted proved difficult and fraught with political consequences.[75]

---

[70]   *See* Treas. Reg. § 1.501(c)(4)–1(a)(2)(ii); Vision Serv. Plan v. U.S., 265 Fed. Appx. 650, 651 (9th Cir. Cal. 2008); Amer. Ass'n Christian Sch. Vol. Emp. v. U.S., 850 F.2d 1510, 1515–16 (11th Cir. 1988); Mutual Aid Ass'n of the Church of the Brethren v. U.S., 759 F.2d 792, 796 (10th Cir. 1985).

[71]   *See* Roger Colinvaux, *Political Activity Limits and Tax Exemption: A Gordian's Knot*, 34 VA. TAX REV. 1 (2014).

[72]   IRS, Social Welfare Organizations, https://www.irs.gov/charities-non-profits/other-non-profits/social-welfare-organizations (last visited Sept. 27, 2017).

[73]   Robert Maguire, *Political Nonprofit Spent Nearly 100 Percent of Funds to Elect Tillis in '14*, CTR FOR RESPONSIVE POLITICS, Oct. 20, 2015.

[74]   CTR FOR RESPONSIVE POLITICS, DARK MONEY BASICS, https://www.open secrets.org/dark-money/basics (last visited Sept. 27, 2017).

[75]   A 501(c)(4) organization must notify the IRS within 60 days of its establishment. Consolidated Appropriations Act of 2016, § 405, Pub. L. 114–113, 129 Stat. 2242, 3118.

Evidence shows that groups with Tea Party, Occupy, and some other likely-political signifiers in their name were subjected to special scrutiny.[76] It is probable a concern was that groups with political names were more likely to engage in too much political activity to qualify as 501(c)(4)s. Evidence does not prove a particular partisan preference in the review. In other words, both sides were subjected to scrutiny that caused delay. Nevertheless, the delay sparked protest from people who saw it as a partisan attack on conservative groups.

In response to political backlash, in 2013 the Treasury Department issued proposed regulations to help define 501(c)(4)s' permissible political activity.[77] One new limit would prohibit public communications within 60 days of a general election that identify a candidate or political party. The Treasury Department's proposed regulations generated more than 150,000 written comments, the most ever received for a proposed regulation. The rules did not mollify the public or Congress. These issues were discussed in congressional hearings and resulted in calls for the IRS Commissioner's impeachment. A 2015 law prohibited the Treasury Department from finalizing regulations on this issue in 2016 and no further action has been taken.[78]

---

[76]   TREAS. INSPECTOR GENERAL FOR TAX ADMIN., 2017–10–054, REVIEW OF SELECTED CRITERIA USED TO IDENTIFY TAX-EXEMPT APPLICATIONS FOR REVIEW (2017); TREAS. INSPECTOR GENERAL FOR TAX ADMIN., 2015–10–025, STATUS OF ACTIONS TAKEN TO IMPROVE THE PROCESSING OF TAX-EXEMPT APPLICATIONS INVOLVING POLITICAL CAMPAIGN INTERVENTION (2015).

[77]   Notice of Proposed Rulemaking, "Guidance for Tax-Exempt Social Welfare Organizations on Candidate Related Political Activities," 78 Fed. Reg. 71, 535 (Nov. 23, 2013). One Representative sued the IRS to get it to draft new rules. Gregory Korte, *Democratic Congressman Sues IRS Over Political Rules*, USA TODAY, Aug. 21, 2013.

[78]   Consolidated Appropriations Act of 2016, § 127, Pub. L. 114–113, 129 Stat. 2242, 2433.

Part D

WHO IS TAXED?

Chapter 15

TAXATION OF THE FAMILY

Table of Sections

The tax system treats the family as somehow different than other groups of people. Based on an understanding that people are not autonomous beings, Congress has always recognized some groupings as affecting members' ability to pay taxes. Congress chose to limit those groups to families. Because the grouping both benefits and burdens its members, Congress does not make the group voluntary. Instead, Congress assigns people to groups with only limited choice. This imposes a definition of family in taxation that may or may not be widely accepted over time.

The tax system cares about the taxpayer's family status for two reasons. First, taking care of others may decrease a person's ability to pay taxes, and the system reduces taxes in response to some of the financial burdens of caring for one's family members. Second, taxpayers are most likely to work with those they trust to avoid taxes, making families natural allies in tax avoidance. For this latter reason, tax authorities closely scrutinize families. Thus, there is a push and pull of family status in taxation.

§ 15.01 Marriage

The tax system struggles with the concept of marriage. The federal income tax defaults to treating each individual as a separate economic unit, except for married individuals. Married couples are recognized as a single economic unit unless spouses choose not to be. Recognition as an economic unit is currently constrained by state law marriage; either couples are legally married or they are not. If individuals are married under state law they are an economic unit for tax purposes, and if they are not married they are not part of a unit. The classification is regardless of couples' personal economic realities. For payroll and sales taxes, individuality pervades.

(a) Filing Unit

Every unmarried person with more than approximately $11,000 of income (the threshold amount is adjusted for inflation and marital status) must file a tax return, but not all must file alone. The U.S. income tax system has four filing statuses for individuals: as individuals, married filing jointly, married filing separately, and as heads of household. Marital status and care for dependents place people within categories, so choice is not unlimited. The filing status determines whose income is reported on a tax return and is also called the person's tax unit.

(i) Classifications

A taxpayer's tax unit is often directed by statute and not by choice. As part of an economic unit, married couples are to file a single income tax return and, if they choose not to be part of a unit, each spouse is still treated as half of the couple for some purposes. People married under state law cannot file as individuals or heads of households. Unmarried people can file as individuals and, if they have certain financial dependents, as heads of households. Thus, the choice of tax unit is determined by decisions with much broader consequences than tax filing.

Married couples are often pressured into filing jointly. If married couples choose to file separately, they may lose tax credits because many tax credits require married couples file jointly. For example, the earned income tax credit, the dependent care tax credit, and education benefits are not available to spouses who file separately. But not all couples are legally able to file jointly. Joint filing is not possible if either spouse is a nonresident alien. Additionally, if one spouse refuses to sign the joint return, the other spouse cannot file jointly. Finally, because marital status is determined as of the last day of the year, a couple that divorces on December 31 cannot file a joint return that year; but in that case each would file for the year as a single individual.

Nevertheless, spouses have a choice whether to file jointly or separately. This provides some couples a planning opportunity and increases the tax system's complexity. For example, couples might choose to file separately if certain deductions constitute a large proportion of one spouse's, but not both, adjusted gross income and the deduction would not be permitted for the collective. Unreimbursed health care costs are one such deduction that is only deductible if they exceed 7.5% or 10%, depending upon the tax year, of the taxpayer's adjusted gross income. It is not uncommon for these expenses to exceed the threshold for one spouse's adjusted gross income but not for the couple's combined incomes. These couples may choose to file separately in order to claim these deductions when the deductions would otherwise be lost.

The tax unit that often receives the least attention is for heads of households. By 1951, tax rates for single taxpayers was higher than during World War II, and political pressure mounted for tax relief for certain especially "worthy" groups, such as widows and widowers who were raising dependent children.[1] Congress responded to these concerns by enacting a heads-of-household schedule, which gave certain qualified single persons with dependents one-half of the tax advantage enjoyed by married couples.[2]

(ii) Income-Shifting

To limit taxpayers' ability to reduce taxes by shifting income from high-tax to low-tax taxpayers, courts developed rules determining who is taxed on income from different sources.[3] These rules are particularly important within the confines of the family. First, income is taxed to the taxpayer who earns the income. In *Lucas v. Earl*, a high-bracket taxpayer was not allowed to direct his employer to pay wages or other benefits to his low-bracket spouse.[4] Second, income from property is taxed to the person who owns the property. In *Helvering v. Horst*, the taxpayer could not assign away income from his property unless he also gave away that property.[5] These rules make it harder for taxpayers to shift income to reduce their collective taxes.

The need for the rules is because of potential collective tax savings for taxpayers that feel themselves part of a single economic unit. For example, families might be indifferent as to who receives income if receipt by particular members reduces their collective tax bill. When a family member in a 40% bracket shifts taxable income to another member in a 15% bracket, the family collectively saves 25%. That reduction is only for the higher bracket taxpayer and the collective. In the example, the 15% taxpayer has an increase in taxes offset by increased wealth and the higher income member has lower taxes but less wealth. The family might be willing to accept this shifting if each member enjoys some of the tax savings or is indifferent as to ownership.

---

[1] *See also* George F. James, *The Income of Married Couples: Is the Knutson Bill Justice?*, 26 TAXES 311, 366 (1948); F. M. Ryan, *Tax Treatment of the Family*, 33 MARQ. L. REV. 1–24 (1949).

[2] Revenue Act of 1951, Pub. L. No. 82–183, Title III, sec. 301, 65 Stat. 452, 480–83 (Oct. 20, 1951).

[3] The incentive for shifting exists because of progressive rates; if the income tax had a flat rate with no exemption, there would be less incentive for income shifting.

[4] 281 U.S. 111 (1930). *See also* Helvering v. Eubank, 311 U.S. 122 (1940) (holding an insurance agent assigning commissions on the renewal of insurance contracts is taxed on the income).

[5] 311 U.S. 112 (1940). Compare with Rev. Rul. 54–599, 1954–2 C.B. 52; Siegel v. U.S., 464 F.2d 891 (1973).

These standard rules apply differently to married couples than for other taxpayers because of states' marital property rules. For example, some states' community property laws alter the standard no-assignment rule. Under this marital property regime, half of all income earned during marriage is deemed to be owned by each spouse and not solely by the earner. Consequently, in *Poe v. Seaborn*, the Supreme Court held that each spouse was taxable on half of the couple's earnings.[6] This permits community property couples to split their income for tax purposes in a way impermissible to couples in common law states.

This splitting is no longer necessary for married couples because of the modern joint return. In 1948, Congress enacted the modern joint tax return for married couples that treats couples as each owning half of their property even if they do not.[7] Congress did so largely in response to family tax avoidance and differences in the tax treatment of couples resulting from different state marital property regimes. Thereafter, filing jointly meant that half of a couple's collective income was taxed, and the tax owed doubled. Because of progressive tax rates, double tax on half the income was often less than the tax on the whole. This was a tax break for many couples but also meant that there are fewer planning opportunities as between spouses.

(b) Alternatives

Perhaps the most popular alternative to the existing regime is to ignore marriage for tax purposes. Under this alternative, everyone would file individually. This alternative recognizes that married couples do not always pool their resources or otherwise act as an economic unit. Therefore, individual filing ignores marriage because everyone is a person but not every couple is an economic unit. The individual system may also further equality between spouses by recognizing that each is a separate person.[8]

Another alternative would permit spouses to choose whether to file as individuals or jointly. Taxpayer choice allows taxpayers to file using the status that minimizes their individual or collective taxes. However, this choice increases the complexity of the system and in tax filing. There is also little theoretical justification for optional joint filing other than to permit a subset of married couples to minimize their taxes.

---

6   282 U.S. 101 (1930).

7   Revenue Act of 1948, Pub. L. No. 80–471, §§ 301–303, 62 Stat. 110, 114–16 (1948).

8   To recognize each spouse requires that each spouse complete a tax return and not delegate the task to the other spouse.

A third alternative would broaden the unit beyond married couples to families or larger self-classifying groups. The larger the unit, the greater the division of income and the greater the ability for some groups to benefit or suffer based on the group's specific characteristics.[9] If the grouping is mandatory, its expansion could decrease some tax avoidance from income shifting. However, if expanded to more than well-defined groups, this type of system would be difficult or impossible for the government to audit.

Mandatory individual filing prevails in much of the world. For example, the United Kingdom changed to individual filing from a joint return system in 1998.[10] One stated goal was to improve the economic position of the country's wives. However, although transfers of income generally benefit women, there are instances when British husbands have transferred interests with sufficient restrictions to secure income tax savings but without transferring control. A larger concern with the British conversion is that wealthy taxpayers have adopted a variety of tactics to reduce their collective taxes. In *Arctic Systems*, a married couple successfully transferred half of a husband's business to his wife to reduce their taxes.[11]

There are concerns unique to the U.S. in adopting an individual-based tax regime because of the country's federalist system. Individual filing, or any of the variants of individual filing, would likely result in different tax treatments of couples living in different states because the states have different marital property regimes. Before 1948, the Supreme Court permitted couples in the community property states to split their income and file individually whereas couples in common law regimes could not.[12] A return to individual filing may re-create the situation in which couples have different tax results based in part on the labels given to their different property regimes.

Adopting an individual-based system might also produce different taxes for couples within a single state based on couples' relative tax planning. Historically, the easiest means for couples to reduce their collective taxes was for one spouse to sell or to make a gift of income-producing property to the lower-income spouse. With a return to individual filing, couples could again engage in this form of tax avoidance behavior. Doing so might advance some notion of

---

9   For more on marriage bonuses and penalties, see Chapter 15.01(c).

10   *See* Stephanie Hunter McMahon, *London Calling: Does the U.K.'s Experience with Individual Taxation Clash With the U.S.'s Expectations?*, 55 ST. LOUIS U. L.J. 159 (2010).

11   Jones v. Garnett, [2007] UKHL 35 (H.L.) [28]–[31].

12   Poe v. Seaborn, 282 U.S. 101 (1930); Lucas v. Earl, 281 U.S. 111 (1930).

fairness to the extent the transfers increase the wealth and relative power of the lower-income spouse, if at the expense of tax revenue.

Less empowering in the pre-1948 period was the use of trusts or family partnerships to effectuate this shifting of income to lower-income spouses. Often the goal was to create a relationship that transferred taxable income but as little power over the underlying assets as possible. President Franklin D. Roosevelt reported that one family had established 197 trusts to divide family income and have it taxed at lower rates and that gifts were used to reduce a $100 million estate to $8 million two years prior to one man's death.[13] Partnerships were popular but risked having their favorable tax treatment denied on the ground that they were not *bona fide*. Ultimately, family partnerships were found invalid in 65% of the cases brought to test their income-shifting ability because they were found not to be real partnerships.[14]

More generally, individual filing would require Congress make many choices that might prove less equitable than joint filing. In particular, Congress would need to devise administrable rules to divide a couple's income, deductions, and credits. For example, some couples jointly earn income but perhaps not 50-50. How should the income be divided on tax returns? How should a couple divide their children's exemptions: equally, to the caregiver, or to whichever spouse saves the most in taxes? A couple's deductions and credits might need to be doubled or halved, like the home mortgage interest deduction. Each choice poses the opportunity for tax cuts, tax increases, or the shifting of tax burdens.

To make an individual-based system administrable, Congress would need to make choices with respect to each credit or deduction and decide whether some sense of equity or administrability should triumph. An unintended consequence would be that the IRS must investigate tax avoidance or abdicate control over spousal income shifting. Unfortunately, there may be too many taxpayers for the government to make a meaningful attempt at enforcing an ownership-based system with complex ownership structures. If so, removing structural restrictions on income-shifting tax avoidance would shift the taxes onto those who earn wages because they cannot be shifted under *Lucas v. Earl*, those who choose to comply with the tax law, and those few who are targeted for audit.

Another unintended consequence of moving to individual filing is its threat to head of household status. Heads of household are those

---

[13]   *Press Conference Number 225 July 31, 1935, in* 6 COMPLETE PRESIDENTIAL PRESS CONFERENCES OF FRANKLIN D. ROOSEVELT 64, 67, 69 (1972).

[14]   Carolyn C. Jones, *Split Income and Separate Spheres: Tax Law and Gender Roles in the 1940s*, 6 LAW & HIST. REV. 259, 278 (1988).

individuals with children or other dependents, a growing segment of society. This status allows filers more advantageous tax brackets and standard deductions than are available to single taxpayers. It is possible that if individual filing were adopted, this benefit would be lost. Comparable benefits could be transferred to other child-based programs or taken out of the tax system. Thus, the question is whether new benefits would remedy the loss.

Finally, optional or mandatory individual filing cannot accomplish all of the tax system's goals. Unfortunately, there is no way to accomplish everything policymakers might want. One principle often sought in the tax system is that it be neutral as to marriage in that taxes should neither encourage nor discourage people from marrying. A second principle is that married couples with the same income should pay the same amount of tax regardless of how the income is divided between spouses. The goal of equality between equal earning couples aims to treat couples with equal incomes the same. A third principle is that the tax should be progressive even if that progressivity is only a basic personal exemption. These three principles cannot be achieved at the same time. To make a tax system progressive requires the choice of a filing unit and the choice must be between equal earning taxpayers or marital status.

(c) Marriage Bonuses and Penalties

The tax benefit created by the 1948 joint return only existed for married couples when one spouse earned disproportionately more than the other spouse.[15] This benefit soon drew criticism from single taxpayers who felt disadvantaged. In 1969, in response to single taxpayers complaining about their tax burden relative to this segment of joint filers, Congress capped the tax benefit for joint returns at 120% of individual filers.[16] This created different rate tables depending upon filing status that persists today.

Because joint filing brackets are no longer twice as wide as filing as a single person, some married couples enjoy a bonus as opposed to filing as two single individuals and other couples suffer a marriage penalty. The labels, "marriage bonus" and "marriage penalty," rhetorically capture the economic advantages and disadvantages created by joint filing. When a wealthy earner marries a low-earner, the wider rate brackets result in reduced taxation, a marriage bonus. On the other hand, when two relatively equal earning people marry,

---

[15]   Because not all couples can file jointly, for example if one chooses not to sign the joint return, Congress has always permitted spouses to file separately. Today, the status of married filing separately has rate brackets which are half that of joint filing.

[16]   Tax Reform Act of 1969, Pub. L. No. 91–172, § 803, 83 Stat. 487, 678–85 (1970).

they find their tax rates increase from when they were single. This increased rate of taxation on two-income married couples is a marriage penalty. Thus, although capping single taxpayers' disadvantage vis-à-vis joint filers was meant to restore equity between single and married taxpayers with the same combined incomes, it had the effect of causing some spouses to face higher tax rates upon marriage.

For example, in 2018, to be in the 37% bracket joint filers must have at least $600,000 of taxable income; married filing separately at least $300,000 (half of the joint filing threshold); and single individuals at least $500,000. Therefore, two single people who each earn $450,000 are not taxed at 37%, but if they choose to marry they will have $300,000 taxed at 37%, a marriage penalty. On the other hand, if a single person earning $599,999 marries a person with no income, the person will go from having $99,999 taxed at 37% to having none taxed at that rate, a marriage bonus.

Before 1969, married couples could only have a bonus but that was only if one spouse earned disproportionately more income than the other. At the time, that distribution of earnings was the reality for most married couples and most people married. Subsequent legislative changes that have altered the relative taxation of different types of couples reflect the political environment at the time of their enactment. When the marriage penalty was created in 1969, there were significantly fewer relatively equal earning couples or unmarried cohabitating couples than today. The changes in behavior likely have little to do with income taxation, although it raises questions whether the tax system should respond to this change.

To be clear, couples do not choose a marriage penalty or a marriage bonus; their status depends on spouses' earnings relative to each other. Married couples with relatively equal incomes experience a marriage penalty, and married couples with unequal incomes experience a marriage bonus. Because the penalty only affects relatively equal earning spouses, this may create a bias against the spouse earning secondary wages, discussed below. Couples with one spouse not in the paid labor market are most likely to enjoy bonuses.

There are marriage bonuses and penalties throughout the Internal Revenue Code in addition to the tax brackets. Many marriage penalties and bonuses are in tax deductions and credits. For example, the home mortgage interest deduction applies to the interest on up to $750,000 in home mortgages paid by either a single individual or a married couple and on up to $550,000 of mortgages if paid by a married person filing separately.[17] Thus, getting married costs one spouse's deduction if the couple has a large enough mortgage. Adding a penalty further to marriage, courts have decided that if two unmarried people live together in the same house and enter into a mortgage together, they can claim interest deductions on twice the value as compared to a married couple because each taxpayer can claim the deduction.[18]

Sometimes penalties only apply to part of the calculation of a deduction or credit. For example, the student loan interest deduction has a penalty in the amount of the deductible interest.[19] Although the phase-out range for the deduction for a married couple is twice that of a single taxpayer, potentially creating a marriage bonus, the amount of deductible interest is the same $2,500 regardless of marital status. This cap on interest also means there is no possibility of a marriage bonus.

From a study of the 105th and 106th Congresses, both major political parties supported elimination of the marriage penalty, although few agreed how to do so.[20] The most recent changes targeting the marriage penalty/bonus occurred in 2001 and 2003. Congress widened the standard deduction and 15% tax bracket for married couples to double those of a single person.[21] This eliminated the marriage penalty for couples in those brackets while increasing marriage bonuses.

For example, in 2018, the 10% tax bracket for joint filers applies to taxable income under $19,050; for married individuals filing separately the threshold is under $9,525; and, finally, for single individuals it is under $9,525. Thus, at the low end of the income spectrum, the single and filing separately brackets are the same and exactly one-half of those filing jointly, so there is no penalty regardless of filing status. However, there are marriage bonuses. If a single person with $18,000 of income marries someone with no income and files jointly, all of the income becomes taxable at 10%, rather than having the excess over $9,525 taxed at 12%. This change did little for higher income taxpayers who still suffer significant marriage penalties.

---

[17]   I.R.C. § 165(h)(3).

[18]   Sophy v. Comm'r, 796 F.3d 1051 (9th Cir. 2015), rev'g 138 T.C. 204 (2012).

[19]   I.R.C. § 221.

[20]   Ann Thomas, *Marriage and the Income Tax Yesterday, Today, and Tomorrow*, 16 N.Y.L. SCH. J. HUM. RTS. 1 (1999).

[21]   Economic Growth and Tax Relief Reconciliation Act of 2001, Pub. L. 107–16, 115 Stat. 38 (2001); Jobs and Growth Tax Relief Reconciliation Act of 2003, Pub. L. 108–27, 117 Stat. 752 (2003).

For the 5% of married couples who file separately, separate filing does not prevent marriage penalties. For example, if two $400,000 unmarried income earners choose to marry and file jointly, they have a marriage penalty. If they file separately, each uses brackets half that of the joint return so each still faces the penalty. For each spouse, $100,000 is subject to the 37% bracket because of their marriage, none of which was taxed at that rate if they had had remained unmarried.

The marriage bonus/penalty issue pervades the tax system and would be difficult to eliminate, even with a flat tax. Under most flat tax proposals, the tax would have an exemption or standard deduction, often a substantial one. An exemption creates a simplified progressive structure. Income below the exemption level is taxed at 0%; all other income is taxed at the flat rate. The existence of the exemption creates marriage penalties or bonuses. If the couple does not receive double a single person's exemption some couples would suffer a penalty; and, if couples receive double the exemption, some couples receive a bonus. The only way to eliminate the marriage penalty is to treat the couple as two single people, for example by adopting individual filing, which creates significant marriage bonuses for some couples.[22]

(d) Joint and Several Liability

Only spouses filing jointly are liable for another person's taxes. In fact, their liability for the couples' taxes is joint and several.[23] Consequently, either spouse may be held liable for all of the tax owed on the income reported, or failed to be reported, on a joint return even after divorce and even if the income was earned and spent by the other spouse. Congress specifically enacted joint and several liability in 1938 for "administrative reasons" and for the "privilege of filing such joint returns."[24] Married filing separately eliminates this risk of joint filing.

Joint and several liability arguably facilitates administration of the income tax.[25] Much as the joint return reduces the number of tax returns that need to be processed and audited, joint and several liability reduces the cost of collection. Joint and several liability reduces the number of people against whom the IRS must collect and discourages some amount of tax avoidance if only because one spouse fears liability.

---

[22]   For more on individual filing, see Chapter 15.01(b).

[23]   I.R.C. § 6013(d)(3); Treas. Reg. § 1.6013–4(b).

[24]   H.R. Rep. No. 1860, 75th Cong. 3d sess., 29–30 (1938).

[25]   Stephanie Hunter McMahon, *What Innocent Spouse Relief Says About Wives and the Rest of Us*, 37 HARV. J. L & GENDER 141 (2014).

When joint and several liability was adopted, Congress concluded that spouses assumed this liability in return for the privilege of filing jointly. In a way it was the cost of reducing the paperwork of tax filing and couples' need to divide assets and income for tax purposes. Without joint and several liability, some couples would have more paperwork, and a non-earning spouse could be unjustly enriched when the spouse enjoys the benefit of income that is owed but not properly paid to the government in taxes. With joint and several liability, a non-earning spouse who pays taxes on income that the other spouse earns has a state law right of contribution from the other spouse.[26] This places the burden on the couple, as opposed to the government, to equitably divide taxes.

Critics question the appropriateness of joint and several liability because of the lopsided power structure within many families.[27] Because the joint return provides economic benefits only to couples with disparate incomes, when joint and several liability is imposed on a non-earner, the liability is almost invariably born by the relatively poorer spouse. Thus, the poorer spouse is taxed on another's income, while the system ignores the poorer spouse's ability to pay the tax. To the extent that the joint return is justified by the concept of marital unity between wealthier and poorer spouses, if that unity does not exist then it is reasonable to call for removal of the liability that underpins the regime.

Potential inequity and tax avoidance can be seen in the classic cases of *Scudder v. Commissioner* and *Ohrman v. Commissioner*.[28] In *Scudder*, a husband embezzled from his wife's family business, yet she was initially held liable for tax on the embezzled funds as a joint filer. The Sixth Circuit reversed the Tax Court on the grounds that the husband must have fraudulently completed the return. In *Ohrman*, a couple was legally separated but remained living together when the husband transferred more than $782,000 in property to his wife one week after the IRS sent the couple a letter stating their tax deficiency. Under the separation agreement, the husband retained only his personal belongings. The Ninth Circuit held the couple tried to use state law to transfer assets for the avoidance of tax and held her liable.

---

[26] The Uniform Contribution Among Tortfeasors Act § 1.

[27] *See* Lily Kahng, *Innocent Spouses*, 49 VILL. L. REV. 261 (2004); Amy Christian, *Joint and Several Liability and the Joint Return*, 66 U. CIN. L. REV. 535 (1998); Richard Beck, *The Innocent Spouse Problem*, 43 VAND. L. REV. 317 (1990).

[28] 405 2d 222 (6th Cir. 1968), *rev'g*, 48 T C. 36 (1967); 157 F3d. Appx. 997 (2005), *aff'g* T.C. Memo. 2003–301.

Not everyone who is jointly and severally liable ultimately pays the tax; tax relief is available for some spouses.[29] Congress enacted limited statutory forms of relief because spouses may have equitable claims to have innocently signed the return while being lied to, abused, or manipulated. This relief effectively undoes joint and several liability, and the relief is not tied to the other spouse paying the taxes owed. Although often called "innocent spouse" relief, innocence is generally not required. Relief is not, however, available in all circumstances.

There are three avenues for a spouse to claim relief from a joint return's joint and several liability. Traditional relief applies when a couple failed to report income, reported it incorrectly, or claimed improper deductions or credits. The tax deficiency must be solely attributable to the non-requesting spouse's erroneous items. Second, separation of the liability permits the IRS to allocate taxes between spouses. To qualify, the spouses must have separated as of the time of the request and the requesting spouse must not have had actual knowledge of the item at the time of the filing. Finally, equitable relief is the broadest form of relief, and it also permits relief when taxes were properly reported but not paid. For equitable relief to apply, a requesting spouse must demonstrate that it would be unfair to require payment of the tax, often based on existing economic hardship, history of abuse, or lack of control over family finances.

Innocent spouse relief is an escape hatch for the joint and several liability regime. However, the relief is arguably over- and under-inclusive by not offering relief to all spouses or former spouses who are unable to assess the validity of their returns but offering relief to some who both knew and helped orchestrate the tax evasion. This result is costly for taxpayers, estimated to have been $1.4 billion in section 6015's first decade, but so is the relief's indirect cost as one of the IRS's top ten litigated issues.[30] It also puts the federal government in a different position than other lenders. Most lenders do not provide an innocent spouse exception. On the other hand, the relationship between taxpayers and the government is much more complex than borrow-lender.

An alternative to joint and several liability is transferee liability, which also exists with respect to taxes.[31] Transferee liability permits the IRS to collect from a recipient of transferred property in limited circumstances. This liability was introduced in 1926 when taxpayers

---

[29]   I.R.C. § 6015. Community property couples may avail themselves of I.R.C. § 66 if community property is being used to pay a tax debt.

[30]   JOINT COMM. TAX'N, JCX–51–98, ESTIMATED BUDGET EFFECTS OF THE CONFERENCE AGREEMENT RELATING TO H.R. 2676 (1998).

[31]   I.R.C. § 6901.

tried to avoid collection by transferring assets away, and it has since been a separate method for collecting taxes that are owed. Transferee liability is administratively difficult. To win a claim of transferee liability, the government must prove that the recipient of transferred property did not provide adequate consideration for the transfer. This is hard within marriage because relinquishing spousal claims might suffice.[32] Additionally, the person who earned the income generally must be insolvent for the government to collect against the recipient, and the government must first exhaust legal remedies against that income-earner. All this raises the cost of collection. It does make it more likely that the financial arrangement finalized in a divorce is not altered after the fact.

A separate issue from innocent spouse relief is an injured spouse claim, which is for an allocation of a joint refund.[33] Through injured spouse relief, the IRS allocates refunds in a way it generally will not allocate liability. This relief ensures that a person's refund is not applied to satisfy the other spouse's financial obligations. For example, if one spouse owes child support or on a student loan, that person's tax refund can be garnished to make the payment. An injured spouse can ensure that his portion of the joint tax refund is not used for that purpose.

(e) Secondary Earner

The joint return arguably discriminates against a family's secondary earner because the secondary earner is psychologically taxed at the primary earner's highest tax rate.[34] Consequently, the value of secondary wages is discounted within the family. For most couples, the wife is the lower-earning spouse. In other words, spouses may stack wives' income on top of their husbands' income to see what tax rate applies to each spouse's income, causing wives to be psychologically taxed at higher rates.

Studies show that marriage penalties in tax credits have an especially large impact on low-income taxpayers.[35] These marriage

---

[32]   Stephanie Hunter McMahon, *An Empirical Study of Innocent Spouse Relief*, 12 FLA. TAX REV. 629, 702 (2012).

[33]   I.R.C. § 6402(d)(3)(B). Injured spouse relief is made on Form 8379.

[34]   *See* Martha McCluskey, *Taxing the Family Work*, 21 COLUM. J. GENDER & L. 109 (2011); Shari Motro, *A New "I Do,"* 91 IOWA L. REV. 1509, 1532 (2006); Wendy Richards, Comment, *An Analysis of Recent Tax Reforms from a Marital-Bias Perspective*, 2008 WIS. L. REV. 611 (2008); Lora Cicconi, Comment, *Competing Goals Amidst the "Opt-Out" Revolution*, 42 GONZ. L. REV. 257 (2007).

[35]   *See* Dorothy A. Brown, *The Tax Treatment of Children: Separate But Equal*, 54 EMORY L.J. 755, 826–8, 832 (2005); Stacy Dickert-Conlin and Scott Houser, *EITC and Marriage*, 55 NAT'L TAX J. 25, 26 (2002). David Ellwood, *The Impact of the Earned income Tax Credit and Social Policy Reforms on Work, Marriage, and Living*

penalties may affect choices to work and how much to work and whether or not to marry. The effect, although real, is not large. Studies are inconclusive, but it is likely that less than 2% of secondary earners' decisions to enter the market are affected by taxation.[36] The CBO reported that joint taxation leads the lower-earning spouse to work between 4% and 7% less than she otherwise would.[37] A British study found that structuring tax credits to encourage low skilled and low wage mothers to work in order to eradicate poverty among children is not determinative of their pathway choice and that paid work does not always lead to more opportunities.[38]

Not everyone agrees that wives can be categorized as secondary wage earners. Many couples do not have the luxury to consider either spouse's labor as secondary in a way that implies the labor is optional.[39] Additionally, at the higher end of the income spectrum, both spouses are increasingly entering and remaining in the paid labor market regardless of the tax penalties. As of 2013, 53% of all married couples in the U.S. had two earners, and this is increasingly true for wealthier couples who are more likely to face marriage penalties.[40] Thus, any psychological stacking of income that occurred before is less true for couples today.

For five years, Congress provided partial tax relief to secondary earners. From 1981 until 1986, two-earner couples could claim a deduction for 10% of the lower-earning spouse's earned income.[41] The maximum deduction allowed was $3,000. This meant that only a fraction of a secondary spouse's income was offset, a small fraction for high-earning spouses. Congress chose this option over eliminating joint filing because its primary concern was secondary earners, and Congress did not want to increase marriage bonuses for single-earner couples. The estimated cost of the deduction was to be $37.5 million

---

Arrangements, 53 NAT'L TAX J. 1063, 1087–1100 (2000), finds some changes in behavior but finds it "small and ambiguous."

[36] Nada Eissa & Hilary Williamson Hoynes, *Taxes and the Labor Market Participation of Married Couples: The Earned Income Tax Credit*, 88 J. PUB. ECON. 1931 (2004).

[37] CONG. BUDGET OFFICE, FOR BETTER OR FOR WORSE: MARRIAGE AND THE FEDERAL INCOME TAX 12 (1997).

[38] Kitty Stewart, *Employment Trajectories for Mothers in Low-Skilled Work*, 43 SOC. POL'Y & ADMIN. 483 (2009).

[39] Lawrence Zelenak, *Marriage and the Income Tax*, 67 S. CAL. L. REV. 339, 348–54 (1994); Dorothy A. Brown, *Race, Class, and Gender Essentialism in Tax Literature: The Joint Return*, 54 WASH. & LEE L. REV. 1469, 1508–11 (1997).

[40] U.S. BUREAU OF LABOR STATS., REPORT NO. 1059, WOMEN IN THE LABOR FORCE: A DATABOOK 3 (2015).

[41] Economic Recovery Tax Act of 1981, Pub. L. 97–34, § 103, 95 Stat. 172, 187–88 (1981); Tax Reform Act of 1986, Pub. L. 99–514, § 131, 100 Stat. 2085 (1986).

over five years, a relatively small part of the overall $251 billion tax cut enacted in 1981.[42]

The two-earner deduction was not a perfect fix. The two-earner deduction did not eliminate the marriage penalty for all couples because of its low cap. It was also structured to grant relief only for earned income and not investment income. Therefore, some spouses with relatively less investment property might be discriminated against through the marriage penalty. At the same time, the deduction increased the marriage bonus for couples in which one spouse earned just enough to secure the deduction, which created new inequities between single persons and one-worker couples and between nonworker couples and one-worker couples. This attempted legislative fix illustrates that inequities always exist between different classifications of taxpayers, and even eliminating the classification will not solve taxing problems for people in different economic circumstances.

The two-earner deduction was quietly repealed because it did not have strong women's support. According to Congress, the marriage penalty was "reduced sufficiently" by tax rate cuts to eliminate the need for the two-earner deduction. The rate cuts' structure also increased marriage bonuses, but they received no press for doing so. Although the secondary earner bias affects more women than men, it never became a gendered issue possibly because of women's divergent economic interests.[43] In other words, there is no women's position because women do not compose a single interest group with respect to taxes. On this issue, women compose three groups—singles; those in one-earner marriages; and those in two-earner marriages. Men are also members of each of these groups even if their position remains more often as the couple's primary rather than secondary earner. Because interests diverge, there is no way for the tax system to please everyone all of the time.

(f) Planning on Divorce

Much as marriage can offer a tax break for couples, so can divorce. If divorcing couples engage in tax planning, some may reduce their collective taxes. If they either do not or cannot plan effectively, couples will have a tax increase relative to couples who use divorce as a tax planning opportunity. This result has long been a feature of the Internal Revenue Code, although not all divorcing couples are

---

[42] JOINT COMM. ON TAX'N, JCS–71–81, GENERAL EXPLANATION OF THE ECONOMIC RECOVERY ACT OF 1981, at 33–37 (1981).

[43] Stephanie Hunter McMahon, *Gendering the Marriage Penalty*, *in* CONTROVERSIES IN TAX LAW 27 (Anthony Infanti ed., 2015).

aware of this possibility. Additionally, not all couples are in a financial position to benefit from this planning.

Three types of payments may occur in a divorce: alimony (or support payments), transfers of property, and child support. In 2018, each payment type is taxed differently. Although scheduled to change for divorces executed after 2018, alimony is currently taxed to the recipient and deductible by the payer, which permits income shifting from wealthy payers to poorer recipients.[44] Transfers of property allow deferral of any tax otherwise due on appreciation until the recipient sells the property, and the recipient then owes tax on any gains that accrued when the property was owned by the transferor. This treatment of property transfers permits income shifting and deferral.[45] By shifting the taxation of alimony and of gain on property, the person who receives and controls the property pays the tax. Finally, child support is taxable to the payer and excluded by the recipient, therefore securing neither income shifting nor deferral.[46] The existence of three different tax results opens the door for careful tax planning if divorced spouses are in different tax brackets and are willing to structure their divorce settlement to decrease their taxes.

In the Tax Cuts and Jobs Act of 2017, Congress prospectively changed the tax treatment of alimony so that the payer of alimony will pay the tax and the recipient is expected to receive the funds tax-free. This was the law before 1944 but had been changed because of concerns that payers of alimony in high tax brackets might unduly suffer after paying the tax and payment. This change is not scheduled to go into effect until 2019, giving Congress another year to consider the loss of income-shifting. Nevertheless, an estimated $6.9 billion in revenue for years 2018 and 2027 was used to offset tax cuts enacted in the 2017 law.

Additional tax planning opportunities exist for divorcing couples with children. Although a child's child tax credit defaults to the custodial parent, parents can agree that the noncustodial parent may claim these tax benefits.[47] Some states' family courts treat these tax benefits as tradable property that can be allocated between parents at the discretion of the court.[48] On the other hand, neither parents nor courts may transfer the ability to claim a child for purposes of

---

[44]   I.R.C. § 71, § 215.

[45]   I.R.C. § 1041.

[46]   I.R.C. § 71(c).

[47]   I.R.C. § 152(d). The same transferability rule applies to a child's personal exemption when in effect.

[48]   Thirty-five states' courts routinely exercise their power to allocate exemptions and may direct the custodial parent to execute the necessary written declarations to transfer children's exemptions. NAT'L TAXPAYER ADVOC., ANNUAL REPORT TO CONGRESS FY 2001, at 110–117 (2001).

head-of-household status (which has favorable rate brackets and a favorable standard deduction compared to filing as a single individual) or for the earned income tax credit; Congress defined who might claim these benefits.

These planning opportunities help ensure that divorce does not increase couples' taxes. Divorce is a difficult time financially for many spouses; in fact, 22% of women who had divorced in the prior 12 months were in poverty.[49] Arguably the government should not make divorce more financially difficult by eliminating the tax reduction available to married couples. If less of the couple's collective income goes to the government, more income is left for the spouses to divide.

On the other hand, not all divorcing couples can benefit from this tax savings. The receipt of tax savings on divorce is contingent upon spouses being in different tax brackets because they have different amounts of taxable income. Thus, the only couples who receive tax reduction are those with a wealthy and poor spouse because it permits income shifting. Couples with two poor spouses or two wealthy spouses gain nothing under the current regime. Thus, under current law, tax reduction is not tied to need but to tax planning and the relative tax positions of the divorcing spouses.[50] More targeted tax relief to divorcing spouses in need might be a more cost effective and equitable system than current law.

(g) Other Relationships

The joint return has been criticized because not all couples can file jointly. In an era when the law recognizes a growing number of relationships and the percentage of the population that is legally married is declining, a tax preference for this group may be less justifiable. As of 2012, only 48% of all households were that of married couples and only 66% were family households.[51] Single-person households composed over a quarter of the population, family households headed by a woman with no husband present were over 13%, and family households headed by a man with no wife present were 5%. Unmarried couple households were over 5% of the population, as were all other multi-person households.

The Supreme Court's ruling in *Obergefell v. Hodges*, that the Fourteenth Amendment guarantees a right to same-sex marriage,

---

[49] U.S. CENSUS BUREAU, MARITAL EVENTS OF AMERICANS: 2009, at 9 (2011).

[50] Stephanie Hunter McMahon, *Should Divorce Be More Taxing?: Structuring Tax Reduction to Reduce Inequality*, 3 IND. J. L. & SOC. EQUALITY 74 (2015).

[51] Jonathan Vespa et al., *America's Families and Living Arrangements: 2012*, CENSUS BUREAU 4 (2013).

permits some same-sex couples to file jointly.[52] However, only those legally married can do so. In fact, married same-sex couples must now file jointly or married filing separately and may not file as individuals. This may change the tax treatment of approximately 170,000 couples.[53]

But what of other, equally committed relationships? Common law married couples must file as married, but according to the Treasury Department couples who enter into civil partnerships are not permitted to file jointly.[54] Similarly prohibited from filing jointly are cohabitating couples, polygamists, best friends, brothers and sisters. These other relationships, regardless of any economic unity, are unable to file joint tax returns. That also means that the termination of these relationships is not governed by divorce-related taxation so that dissolving relationships must comply with the tax rules for payments between third parties.

If Congress expands the list of those entitled to file a joint or combined return beyond legally married couples, Congress would need to decide what limits, if any, should be imposed on the economic groups entitled to do so. Moreover, the IRS would be required to police those relationships. Without an easily enforced black line rule, those who shift the tax burden for income but do not shift other attributes of ownership would only be caught on tax audit, which is currently less than 1% of individual taxpayers. If no limits are imposed of who can file together, those who are interested in tax avoidance could reduce their tax burdens by expanding their tax unit. However, forming these tax unions would likely have risks. In other words, depending upon how the tax regime was structured, signing joint tax returns could create legal liability among those seeking tax reduction.

§ 15.02   Children

Raising children is expensive. Keeping children out of poverty in 2018 costs $4,320 per child.[55] Without the personal exemption, the tax system no longer directly covers this amount. A child's $2,000 partially refundable child tax credit covers a portion of this cost for most taxpayers. However, not only do these tax benefits presuppose parents have taxable income, they are significantly lower than the amount the average family spends per child. Parents spend on average $233,610 (fluctuating from $253,770 for the urban Northeast

---

[52]   576 U.S. ___, 135 S.Ct. 2584 (2015).

[53]   D'Vera Cohn, *How Many Same-Sex Married couples in the U.S.?*, PEW RESEARCH CENTER (2015).

[54]   Rev. Proc. 2013–17, 2013–11 I.R.B. 612; T.D. 9785, I.R.B. 2016–38.

[55]   U.S. DEPT. OF HEALTH & HUMAN SERV., POVERTY GUIDELINES (2017).

to \$193,020 in rural areas) on each child before they turn eighteen.[56] Tax benefits offset only some of these expenses. These benefits are seen by some as entitlements; others propose eliminating all tax benefits for children.

(a) What Are Children for Tax Purposes?

The appropriate tax treatment of children largely depends upon the function of children in society. Are children their parents' personal consumption items? Or are children born and raised for society's good? Congress could decide that global overpopulation and scarce societal resources make the decision to have a child a personal choice that parents should pay for, much as a new car or a house. As personal consumption, there is no need for the tax system to provide for children. On the other hand, children are future members of society, workers, and its leaders. As a societal good, society should defray some of the cost of caring for a child, at least as much as other favored expenses.

The existing tax system does not answer these questions directly. In many ways the tax system classifies lower- and middle-class children differently from the children of upper-class households. For those in lower- and middle-class families, children are more likely to be recognized as societal goods in that tax provisions exist for their basic well-being and education. Because most of these provisions phase out, children in higher income households are largely treated as consumption for tax purposes.

At both ends of the income spectrum, the tax system is less favorable to the costs of raising children than it is to the costs of engaging in business. Almost all business expenses are deductible if they are reasonable; but no general deduction exists for caring for children.[57] Although business expenses generally need less justification than children's expenses, those business expenses that are partially personal expenses are often subject to additional limits.[58] Consistent with these latter expenses, children's expenses may be seen as a hybrid of consumption and societal good that deserves some assistance but not complete subsidization.

Alternatively, Congress could classify children as claimants on political and societal resources. This would have broader implications than the tax system. According to Professor Jens Qvortrup, children are often improperly treated as part of a feudal system and are not

---

[56] U.S. DEPT. OF AGRIC., EXPENDITURES ON CHILDREN BY FAMILIES, 2015, MISC. REPT. NO. 1528–2015 (2017).

[57] I.R.C. § 162.

[58] For more on home office and entertainment expenses, see Chapter 11.04.

granted immediate rights.[59] Instead of being viewed as autonomous citizens, children are subsumed by the household in which they live. This classification threatens the legitimacy of redistribution to benefit children.

For tax purposes, the classification of children as claimants would mean that they are more than a source of credit for their parents. Instead, children should be viewed as individuals, possibly as individual taxpayers. Reclassification as a claimant might not dictate which tax policies are appropriate for children; however, it would force reconsideration of the structure of tax benefits created on children's behalf and whether they should be directed to children. Under current law, Congress may choose to funnel resources to children, but access to resources is not guaranteed because children lack economic and political power. This would necessarily change if children were seen as claimants. Pursuant to this theory, assigning their tax benefits to parents or custodians may be problematic to the extent children are legitimate claimants in their own right.

Because of the unresolved nature of children's role in society, many tax policies forge an uneasy compromise or else ignores the issue. For example, the Internal Revenue Code ignores child support as long as it is so labeled but allows parents to choose the label.[60] Similarly, payments to pregnant women who have not yet had the child are ignored for tax purposes. Without a paternal obligation under state law, the tax treatment of earlier payments can be classification as gifts, compensation, or possibly child support.[61]

Determining the proper classification of children for tax purposes is particularly difficult because of their many living arrangements. Some live with both parents, some with one, and some with none. Some are adopted; some are fostered. The tax system recognizes these relationships to a degree. The law generally provides that adopted children are to be treated for tax purposes the same as biological children. Stepchildren, however, may only be treated as a taxpayer's children if they are adopted. Children that reside in a taxpayer's household without a legal relationship are often ignored for tax purposes.

---

[59] JENS QVORTRUP, CHILDREN AS LEGITIMATE CLAIMS MAKERS ON SOCIETAL RESOURCES (2004), available at http://s3.amazonaws.com/zanran_storage/www.ciimu. org/ContentPages/43033530.pdf.

[60] I.R.C. § 71(c). Because parents have an obligation to support their own children, payments on children's behalf are not deductible or credited. This eliminates some tax planning opportunities but often reduces the amount available for the care of children if a higher-income parent pays to a lower-income parent.

[61] See Shari Motro, Preglimony, 63 STAN. L. REV. 647 (2011).

Arguably, the tax system encourages some people to care for their own children, but the system expects this care will occur without encouragement for wealthier families and distrusts that it will be extended far beyond one's biological children. Moreover, for many purposes even biological or adopted children need to reside with the parent for the parent to be able to claim a tax benefit. For example, taxpayers may not claim a child for purposes of the EITC if the child resides outside the U.S., even if the taxpayer provides all of their financial support.[62] This tension over which children are counted for tax purposes arises in large part because of the uncertain justification for their recognition in the Code.

(b) Federal Aid

Although Congress has failed to devise a generally accepted theory of why and to what extent the tax system should provide for children, Congress has recognized children in several provisions. Tax provisions account for 39% of government spending on children, and spending on children is roughly 10% of the federal budget.[63] These tax provisions are not consistent about when children should be recognized or for what purposes, making these provisions difficult for parents to navigate. In a simplifying move in 2004 Congress created a single definition of child for purposes of tax provisions.[64] Nonetheless, different provisions retain different age limits at which a particular tax benefit is lost.

Adding to the complexity, different persons may claim different tax benefits based on the same child. In some cases, benefits are available to custodial parents; in other cases, benefits are transferrable between parents; others are based on levels of financial support. This chapter discusses some of the most commonly claimed tax benefits associated with children, but there are more.

(i) Adding a Child

Congress recognizes some of the costs of adding children to a family but not all. The traditional method of having a biological child may produce deductible medical expenses but only to the extent those costs are more than 10% of the taxpayer's adjusted gross income.[65] Similarly, medically assisted fertilization, such as in vitro or other treatments, may be deductible if unreimbursed by medical insurance. However, potential medical expenses are only deductible if paid on behalf of the taxpayer, the taxpayer's spouse, or dependents.

---

[62] I.R.C. § 32(c)(1)(A)(ii)(I).

[63] Sara Edelstein, *Kids' Share 2016*, URBAN INSTITUTE (2016).

[64] Working Families Relief Act of 2004, Pub. L. 108–311, § 201, 118 Stat. 1166, 1169–75 (2004).

[65] I.R.C. § 213.

Therefore, the cost of purchasing an egg or the costs of a surrogate are not currently deductible regardless of the amount, even for male same-sex couples who could not otherwise have biological children.[66]

Additionally, Congress has enacted specific tax benefits for fostering or adopting a child. Foster care payments are nontaxable income on the theory that the money is to be spent on the child's support and not on the caregiver.[67] Congress also enacted a tax credit for qualified adoption expenses and a limited exclusion from income for employer-provided adoption assistance.[68] The adoption credit is nonrefundable with a five-year carry forward and is capped at $13,840 per child for 2018. This is less than the total average cost of a domestic adoption, which is between $8,000 and $40,000 depending upon the type of adoption.[69] The adoption credit also phases out for high-income adopting parents.

(ii) Personal Exemptions

In 2017, Congress temporarily suspended personal exemptions for tax years 2018 through 2025. Although Congress increased the standard deduction in the same law, the standard deduction does not adjust for the number of children. Before 2018, once a child was in the family, a child's custodian who paid for more than one-half of the child's care was entitled to a personal exemption, which, in 2017, was $4,050 and the amount was indexed for inflation.[70] This exemption amount was the same for children as for adults, and the number of personal exemptions increased with the number of children, a benefit to large families. Over 83 million exemptions for children were claimed for 2014.[71] A child for this purpose was a person under the age of nineteen, under the age of twenty-four if a full-time student, or any age if permanently and totally disabled. Parents could not claim the exemption if the child provided more than one-half of his or her own support, was married, or if the government provided more than one-half of the child's financial support.

When codified in its current form in 1954, the personal exemption was intended to exclude from taxation roughly the amount required for a subsistence livelihood. In the 1913 income tax, the exemption had been much larger in real terms and prevented all but the wealthiest from paying an income tax. Regardless of amount,

---

[66]   *See* Morrissey v. U.S., 871 F.3d 1260 (11th Cir., 2017). *See also* Longino v. Comm'r, T.C. Memo. 2013–80; Magdalin v. Comm'r, T.C. Memo. 2008–293.

[67]   I.R.C. § 131.

[68]   I.R.C. § 23; § 137.

[69]   Geoff Williams, *The Cost of Adoption*, U.S. NEWS & WORLD REP., Oct. 2, 2014.

[70]   I.R.C. §§ 151, 152.

[71]   IRS, TAX STATS, ALL RETURNS: EXEMPTIONS BY TYPE AND NUMBER OF EXEMPTIONS, Table 2.4 (2015).

personal exemptions reduce taxable income against which tax rates are applied. Therefore, an exemption is really worth the amount of the exemption times the taxpayer's tax rate; to the extent exemptions are not phased out, this makes the exemption worth more to higher tax bracket taxpayers. However, the exemption phased out for most high-income taxpayers and did not apply to the alternative minimum tax.

(iii) Heads of Household

Unmarried custodians of children under the age of nineteen, under the age of twenty-four if a full-time student, or any age if permanently and totally disabled can file their tax returns using the head of household status.[72] Head of household status provides the taxpayer a favorable set of tax rate brackets and a larger standard deduction as compared to filing as a single taxpayer. This status is only available to a single filer who provides support for a dependent who resides with her for more than half the year. Support in this context includes paying for food, insurance, and the property taxes, mortgage interest, rent, utilities, and repairs and maintenance on the dependent's residence. Perhaps counter-intuitively, support does not include the cost of education, clothing, vacations, or transportation. This calculation can make it hard for taxpayers to know for certain if they can legally claim the status. It is likely most custodians just assume that they can.

The benefit of head of household status does not increase with the number of children, which maximizes its benefit for small families. Furthermore, it is not eliminated for higher-income taxpayers, except for those subject to the alternative minimum tax. In 2014, over 22 million taxpayers, of which 7 million owed tax, filed as heads of household.[73] Despite its prevalence, there has been little public policy debate about the head of household status.

(iv) Earned Income Tax Credit

A refundable earned income tax credit (the EITC) provides a credit against the taxes owed by low-income wage earners. The amount of the credit increases if the taxpayer is the custodian of and supports children.[74] Twenty-six states and Washington D.C. also offer a state-based EITC.[75] The federal EITC increases in amount with the number of children but is capped at three children.

---

[72] I.R.C. § 2(b).

[73] DEPT. TREAS., INDIVIDUAL INCOME TAX RETURNS 2014, Publication 1304, at 49 (Rev. 08–2016).

[74] For more on the EITC, see Chapter 16.02(b).

[75] Erica Williams, *States Can Adopt or Expand Earned Income Tax Credits to Build a Stronger Future Economy*, CTR ON BUDGET & POL'Y PRIORITIES (2017).

Therefore, there is no increase in benefit for four or more children. For purposes of the federal EITC, children are the same as those who qualified for exemptions and permit the head of household status.

The EITC is intentionally progressive so that its aid is targeted to lower-income taxpayers. It is available only for low-income taxpayers and only those receiving wages. The credit phases out the more income that a taxpayer earns and phases out more quickly if the taxpayer has unearned income, such as interest or dividends. In 2016, over 27 million families claimed the credit, costing approximately $67 billion in government revenue.[76]

Determining eligibility for the EITC is complex, particularly when more than one person can claim a particular dependent. For some custodians, the determination of who properly claims a child depends upon potential claimants' relative adjusted gross income. Therefore, taxpayers need to share information to properly calculate the EITC. As a result of its complexity and taxpayer abuse, it is estimated that in 2015 the IRS overpaid as much as $18.1 billion in EITC, or almost 25% of payments.[77] At the same time, about 15% of households entitled to the EITC do not claim the credit.

(v) Child Tax Credit

As of 2018 but only through 2025, a $2,000 child tax credit is available for each child, although the credit phases out for those taxpayers with high incomes.[78] The thresholds were significantly increased in 2017 to joint filers with $400,000 of income and singles with $200,000. When enacted in 1997 the credit was set at $1,000 but began to phase out for single taxpayers at $75,000 of income (neither the amount of the credit nor the phaseout amounts were adjusted for inflation). Thus, today more people can claim a larger credit.

Because the child tax credit is not indexed for inflation, its value will erode each year. This credit's amount is the same for all qualifying children, unlike in some other countries where the amount of assistance increases with the child's age in recognition that costs increase with age. Unlike the head of household status, this credit only applies for qualifying children who are under the age seventeen and are U.S. citizens, U.S. nationals, or U.S. resident aliens with Social Security numbers. Additionally, in 2017 Congress enacted a

---

[76] IRS, STATISTICS FOR TAX RETURNS WITH EITC, https://www.eitc.irs.gov/eitc-central/statistics-for-tax-returns-with-eitc/statistics-for-tax-returns-with-eitc (last visited Sept. 27, 2017).

[77] GOV'T ACCOUNTABILITY OFFICE, GAO–16–475, REFUNDABLE TAX CREDITS 28 (2016).

[78] I.R.C. § 24.

$500 nonrefundable credit for each of the taxpayer's dependents who are not also qualifying children.

As a partially refundable credit, Congress gets to determine the amount that can be refunded, and Congress capped the refund at $1,400 per child and only if the taxpayer has more than $3,000 in earned income. In 2013, the total cost of the credit was $55.1 billion, of which $27.9 billion was refunded.[79] It was estimated to protect 3.1 million people from poverty, including about 1.7 million children, and reduced the severity of poverty for another 13.7 million people, including 6.8 million children.[80] The changes to the child tax credit, including the creation of one for other dependents, are estimated to cost $543.6 billion in federal revenue between 2018 and 2017.

(vi) Dependent Care Credit

Congress partially recognizes the cost of child and dependent care when parents are at work.[81] Congress enacted a tax credit for the care of dependent children younger than thirteen years or those who are physically or mentally incapable of self-care. The dependent care credit is nonrefundable so it provides no benefit to those who otherwise owe no tax. Additionally, it only covers between 20% and 35% of up to $3,000 in expenses per child, with a cap of $6,000 in expenses for two or more children. Therefore, at most $1,050 may be received as a credit for one child's expenses. The national average for childcare for children younger than five is over $9,000 annually per child.[82] Consequently, a significant portion of these expenses is not offset with the credit.

The dependent care credit is larger for low-income taxpayers but does not phase out completely at high incomes as do many other child-related benefits. The more adjusted gross income the parent in a one-parent household or both parents in a two-parent couple has, the lower the percentage of expenses that can be credited. As a result, a wealthy couple's maximum credit for one child's care is $600, as compared to the $1,050.

For all claimants, the expenses must be incurred to enable the taxpayer to work and cannot exceed the earned income of the taxpayer or, if married, the lower-earning spouse. An effect of the phase-down is that the credit is worth less to families who are likely

---

[79] GOV'T ACCOUNTABILITY OFFICE, GAO–16–475, REFUNDABLE TAX CREDITS 8 (2016).

[80] CTR ON BUDGET & POL'Y PRIORITIES, THE CHILD TAX CREDIT, available at http://www.cbpp.org/files/policybasics-ctc.pdf (last visited Sept. 27, 2017).

[81] I.R.C. § 21.

[82] Lynda Laughlin, *Who's Minding the Kids?: Child Care Arrangements*, U.S. CENSUS BUREAU (2011).

to pay more for childcare. It may also send the message that the labor of secondary earners in high-income couples is valued less than their labor in low-income couples. Thus, wives in low-income couples should work but wives in high-income couples should not. This illustrates how, in tax matters, gender issues may conflict with class-based advocacy.

Aside from the class element, the dependent care credit addresses the costs of couples with two earners versus one earner. Care for children by a stay-at-home caregiver creates imputed income that is not taxed. In other words, the couple is better off for having children cared for, which produces income in the economic sense, but the income is not subject to tax. On the other hand, two-income parents must pay tax on their income before they can purchase the equivalent childcare of the stay-at-home spouse. Using after-tax dollars increases the cost of that care.

For example, consider a couple with two children. The couple has two earners and so must pay someone to provide care. If the care costs $20,000 per year, the second earner of the two-income couple must earn significantly more than $20,000 to pay for the childcare. If the two-income couple is in a 30% tax bracket, the childcare costs $28,571.43 before income taxes and even more with payroll and state income taxes. Ignoring these other taxes, if the second earner cannot earn more than $28,571.43, the couple is in a better financial position if the second earner does not work outside the home. Even if the person can earn $27,000, which is more than the $20,000 market value of the care, it is not a wise short-term financial choice for the family. Addressing this lost employment, the dependent care credit closes the gap between the pre-tax and after-tax cost of childcare.[83]

The cost of childcare and its impact on wives' work has received a lot of attention, but few politically viable solutions have been developed.[84] The focus is often on the gendered impact of the cost of childcare as women remain the larger group of stay-at-home spouses. An alternative to the credit that would equalize treatment between families is to treat childcare as a deductible business expense because, without the care, there could be no business.[85] This would allow parents an above-the-line deduction for the full cost of reasonable childcare. Another alternative would tax stay-at-home parents for the imputed income that they earn from caring for their

---

[83]   *See* Chapter 7.02(b)(2) for more on imputed income. The portion of the credit exceeding the imputed income reduces the cost of care itself.

[84]   For a tax professor who got an op-ed selected by the N.Y. Times on the issue, see Lilian Faulhaber, *How the I.R.S. Hurts Mothers*, N.Y. TIMES, Apr. 3, 2013.

[85]   Childcare has not been deductible as a business expense since a 1939 lower court decision. Smith v. Comm'r, 40 B.T.A. 1038 (1939).

children. This would burden some parents who could not afford to pay the tax and could force some mothers into paid employment who otherwise would not choose to leave the home. With each alternative, families would be in equivalent after-tax positions; although only the former equalizes those with children against those who do not.

(vii) Combination of Benefits

Through a combination of ad hoc benefits, Congress has responded to the existence of children by recognizing a societal obligation for the support of children living in lower-income families. However, as their custodians' income rises, children become consumption items and the societal burden disappears even for these children's basic care. For example, there is no tax support for the care of the children of a wealthy, married, one-income couple.

Existing tax benefits have been shown to produce some good results, but whether equal or better results could be achieved in other, less costly ways is unclear. Research suggests that low-income families do not fully understand the details of the child tax credit or the EITC; however, they understand that there is a connection between working and significant tax benefits.[86] Additionally, research finds that an increase in family income is associated with an increase in children's test scores and college enrollment rates.[87]

That the many different tax benefits involving children are structured differently creates complexity for those with children. Between different age limits and different income limits, complying with the law, much less legal tax planning, is difficult. In addition, the complexity and lack of enforcement arguably increases the opportunity for tax fraud. Some of the opportunities have been reduced with computer matching and information reporting but not all. For example, when the IRS began requiring Social Security numbers to claim a child's personal exemption in 1987, it was said that 7 million children went missing.[88]

Additionally, the current structure for phasing out the EITC and the child tax credit and the phase-down of the dependent care credit imposes marriage penalties and marriage bonuses. Consider two

---

[86]   Ruby Mendenhall et al., *The Role of Earned Income Tax Credit in the Budgets of Low-Income Families*, 86 SOC'L SERV. REV. 367 (2012); SARAH HALPERN-MEEKIN ET AL., IT'S NOT LIKE I'M POOR (2015).

[87]   RAJ CHETTY ET AL., NEW EVIDENCE ON THE LONG-TERM IMPACTS OF TAX CREDITS (2011), available at http://www.irs.gov/pub/irs-soi/11rpchettyfriedman rockoff.pdf; Gordon Dahl & Lance Lochner, *The Impact of Family Income on Child Achievement: Evidence From The Earned Income Tax Credit*, 102 AM. ECON. REV. 1927 (2012); Greg J. Duncan et al., *Does Money Really Matter?*, 47 DEVELOPMENTAL PSYCH. 1263 (2011).

[88]   Jeffrey Liebman, *Who Are the Ineligible ETIC Recipients?*, 53 NAT'L TAX J. 1165, 1171 (2000).

single taxpayers who each has a qualifying child and $15,000 of taxable income. If these taxpayers marry, their combined income of $30,000 exceeds the EITC's threshold for joint filers and begins to phase out the credit. If they remain single, each taxpayer is entitled to the full credit. This imposes a marriage penalty. On the other hand, if one single taxpayer has two qualifying children and $24,000 of taxable income and another taxpayer has no income and no children, they benefit by marrying. As a single taxpayer, the EITC phased down for the higher-income taxpayer. When married, their combined income is less than the joint filing phase-out so they would be allowed the full credit for both children. This provides a marriage bonus.

Tax reduction based on children is easier to justify politically if the money saved in taxes is spent on the children. This may often be Congress's expectation; for example, it is the basis for the exclusion of foster care payments. However, it is unknown the extent to which tax savings are spent on children, although discretionary spending is a small percentage of most low-income taxpayers' budgets and evidence does show that the amount spent on children and family stability items is significant.[89] The U.S. ties much of its child-based benefits to earning income rather than the provision of childcare, although many benefits are also dependent upon the custodial relationship. Alternatively, in Australia and Canada, tax credits are paid to nominated caregivers and, while their amount generally declines depending on joint incomes, these credits are not directly tied to work.[90] In each case, payments are to enable custodians to make choices for their children. Nonetheless, there remains a tension between parental autonomy and society's desire to ensure that its tax aid is being spent for the intended purpose.

(c) Tax Treatment of Education Savings

To the extent that Congress recognizes a societal obligation for children, the focus is heavily on their education. Tax benefits for education are numerous but generally capped in some form. They are also primarily for post-secondary education, almost ignoring the uneven dispersal of quality lower-level public education. Together, education-based tax provisions create a labyrinth for parents seeking tax reduction for educational costs.

Currently, there are two primary education tax credits: the American opportunity tax credit and the lifetime learning tax

---

[89]   Lauren Jones et al., *Child Cash Benefits and Family Expenditures*, NBER WORKING PAPER NO. 21101 (2015).

[90]   Patrick Nolan, *Tax Relief for Breadwinners or Caregivers?*, 8 J. COMP. POL'Y ANALYSIS 167 (2006).

credit.[91] These credits only apply for qualified educational expenses at qualified post-secondary educational institutions and phase out for higher-income taxpayers. Additionally, these credits are only available for the educational expenses of the taxpayer, the taxpayer's spouse, or the taxpayer's dependent. It is unlikely many people pay the costs of a non-family member's education, and if they do it is not offset with a credit. The credits also do not cover all permitted educational expenses. The American opportunity tax credit is capped at $2,500 and is partially refundable, whereas the lifetime learning credit is capped at $2,000 and is nonrefundable. Only one of these credits can be claimed in any given year for a child.

Other tax benefits exist related to children's educational expenses, making it necessary for taxpayers to allocate their expenses among the various programs. For example, a taxpayer may deduct up to $4,000 in tuition and fees for the higher education of the taxpayer, spouse, or dependent, although the expenses cannot be the same ones used to claim a credit.[92] Additionally, taxpayers with less than $80,000 in modified adjusted gross income may deduct the interest paid on loans used to finance higher education.[93] Finally, employees and the self-employed may be able to itemize certain work-related educational expenses, although this deduction is subject to numerous limitations.[94]

Much less federal tax assistance is offered to those who seek to save for primary and secondary education. One is a tax-advantaged investment account, the Coverdell savings account, which can be used for early education.[95] Coverdell accounts are limited in amount and have strict income limits for contributors. No more than $2000 can be contributed per student per year and any excess is subject to penalties. Contributors may not have adjusted gross income above a capped amount: $110,000 for individual filers and $220,000 for those filing a joint return. The accounts' tax benefit is that contributions grow tax-free and its proceeds can be withdrawn without tax as long as they are used for qualified educational expenses. Thus, deposits are not deductible by contributors but then appreciate without taxation. Potential appreciation is limited, however, by the caps on contributions. Distributions must be made by the time the

---

[91]   I.R.C. § 25A. The American opportunity credit is an expansion of the Hope scholarship credit, made permanent in 2015, so the federal Hope credit has been subsumed.

[92]   I.R.C. § 222.

[93]   I.R.C. § 221.

[94]   I.R.C. § 67. For more on the IRS's take on the deductibility of these expenses, see IRS, Topic 513: Work-Related Education Expenses, at https://www.irs.gov/tax topics/tc513.html (last visited Sept. 27, 2017).

[95]   I.R.C. § 530.

beneficiary turns 30, and distributions in excess of qualified educational expenses are subject to a penalty.

The only education benefit without a means-tested component is 529 plans.[96] Therefore, parents of any income level can claim a tax benefit by saving for the cost of their children's education, but this only benefits parents if they are otherwise planning on paying for this expense. These plans are operated by a state or educational institution, and they provide tax advantages and potentially other incentives to make it easier to save for college and other post-secondary training for a designated beneficiary. Like Coverdell plans, earnings generated on investments in a 529 plan are not subject to federal tax and generally are not subject to tax when used for the qualified educational expenses of the designated beneficiary, such as tuition, fees, books, and room and board. Thus, contributions to a 529 plan are not deductible, so an after-tax amount is invested but then allowed to grow tax-free and the distribution is generally tax-free. As of 2018, $10,000 per year of a 529 plan can be used to pay tuition for elementary or secondary education.

And if pre-funding fails, some taxpayers may be relieved of their student loans without tax if their student loans are forgiven or canceled, despite the fact that the discharge of other types of loans generally produces taxable income.[97] A complication is that some loan forgiveness programs are taxable and others are not. In order to have student loans discharged without tax consequence, the student must generally be employed in public service for a number of years and make 120 payments on their loans or have the discharge on account of the student's death or disability. For those employed, permitted professions include teaching, healthcare, military service, law enforcement, social work in a public agency, and public interest law. For other former students who have their loans discharged, they owe tax on the benefit of not having to repay the loan.[98]

At times, taxpayers have choices as to which provision to use. The mix of tax benefits for educational spending requires taxpayers make savvy choices in how they want to classify their educational expenses for tax purposes. Although there are multiple benefits, the law does not allow taxpayers to claim multiple benefits for the same expense. Attempts have been made to consolidate the various provisions; however, the attempts have failed. This failure is likely due to the various qualifications making different provisions preferable to different groups.

---

[96] I.R.C. § 529.

[97] I.R.C. § 108(f).

[98] I.R.C. § 61(a)(12).

(d) The Kiddie Tax

Children are not only consumers of family resources but, historically, they have been used for tax planning. Parents and grandparents have relied on their close relationship with their children and grandchildren to shift taxable income to the next generation while the children are lower-taxed family members. By shifting income from parents in higher tax brackets to children in lower tax brackets, collective taxes can be reduced in the same way spouses could shift income before the 1948 changes to the joint return. As parents in higher tax brackets found their tax obligations going down, their children's were likely to go up, but not by as much as their parents saved. It is the difference in relative tax brackets that encourages intra-family income shifting.

To reduce this planning opportunity, Congress enacted the "kiddie tax" in 1986.[99] Regardless of the existence of the kiddie tax, if a child earns sufficient income to be taxed, the child is taxed as an individual; the kiddie tax adds a catch regarding the applicable tax rate for unearned income on investments. Between 2018 and 2025, children under the age of 24 who are full-time students and who do not earn more than one-half of their support or children not yet 19 have their unearned income taxed at rates applicable to trusts and estates, which has fewer rate brackets and the top 37% rate applies at only $12,500.[100] Reducing its impact, the kiddie tax does not negate preferential capital gain rates; however, the tax does determine which of the favorable capital gain rates applies.

The kiddie tax is complicated. For example, because the kiddie tax does not apply to wages or self-employment, it is sometimes necessary to allocate a child's income between earned and unearned to ensure that the kiddie tax only applies to the appropriate portion. The tax may be more complicated if more than one child in the family is subject to the kiddie tax. The kiddie tax can be paid in one of two ways: (1) the child's investment income can be reported on the parents' return; or (2) the child can file a separate return using a special form. The tax owed on the child's income will be the same regardless of the filing mechanism; and the child is liable for the tax.

The complication is arguably necessary to target the tax to its narrow purpose. The kiddie tax is to reduce the economic incentive for shifting income to children. In other words, it targets tax planning by wealthy parents and grandparents so that its focus on unearned

---

[99]   Codified as I.R.C. § 1(g).

[100]   Before 2018 and after 2025, the applicable tax rate was the parents' highest rate bracket which required parents share information with each other and their children.

income limits it generally to investment income, such as interest, dividends, and capital gain. Congress likely expected that parents or grandparents purchased these investments and, at the time of the transfer, desired for its income to be reported by lower tax rate children. In 2010, about 50% of payers of the kiddie tax were college students, 40% between 14 (the original age limit in 1986) and 18, and 10% were younger than 14.[101]

Nonetheless, the tax applies even when tax avoidance cannot be the motive, such as for inherited property, and it fails to prevent all income shifting but may push taxpayers to be more creative. For example, the tax creates an incentive for parents with a trade or business to hire their dependent children to work for the business to reduce their tax costs. Of course, the amounts that can be transferred this way and not face significant payroll taxes are limited. Thus, even if successful as a backstop for progressive taxation, the kiddie tax adds complexity and its own costs to affected taxpayers.

---

[101] PRESIDENT'S ECONOMIC RECOVERY ADVISORY BOARD, THE REPORT ON TAX REFORM OPTIONS (2010).

Chapter 16

TAXATION OF RACE AND CLASS

Table of Sections

Issues of race and class are politically sensitive topics generally, and combining these issues with the Internal Revenue Code does not abate that sensitivity. Despite the potential for heated conflict, these debates are often oblique because much of the intersection of race, class, and taxation remains invisible to the public. Critical race and class scholars work to shed light on how discrimination arises within the tax system. Although the issues are presented in this chapter in isolation, they are best considered as overlapping issues, often exacerbating each other.

§ 16.01 Race and National Origin in Taxation

Although race is not mentioned directly in the Internal Revenue Code, scholars have documented how tax law affects people of different races and national origins. Negative effects have been found for African Americans and documented and undocumented immigrants despite today's tax system itself being color-blind and the rules generally being adopted for legitimate, nonracial objectives. In fact, rarely is race mentioned in tax discussions in Congress or the Treasury Department. Nevertheless, critics focus on the disparate harms perpetrated by the tax system.

(a) African-Americans

Because race is not explicitly referenced in the Code, the issue of race comes up surreptitiously when Code provisions impact people of different races differently. Sometimes the difference may benefit minorities but more often the Code disadvantages them. Therefore, despite a prevailing perception that tax is neutral with respect to race and that any disadvantage is not planned, its discrimination may nevertheless have a lasting impact on the public. This impact has been studied for African Americans, although not all scholars agree on the results.

(i) Prejudiced Preferences

Critical race theorists argue that the existing tax system discriminates against African Americans. Professors Beverly Moran and William Whitford conclude that enacted tax preferences systematically favor whites over blacks even when they control for income.[1] According to their study, deviations from a comprehensive tax system, which would tax all income equally, have a racially disparate impact even if worded without reference to race. Consequently, current tax policies violate horizontal equity between the races, with the primary cause being differences in the races' lifestyles as consumers of different types of goods.

As examples of this disparate impact, Moran and Whitford note the favored tax status enjoyed by wealth and wealth transfers that they conclude favors whites and Asians and disadvantage African Americans and Latinos. The exclusion of gifts from income, the failure to tax appreciation at death, the capital gain preference, the requirement for realization before taxation, and tax-free financing through the deductibility of interest and accelerated depreciation deductions all favor the wealthy and savers over the poor and consumers.

Not only do African Americans own fewer assets and fewer appreciated assets in particular than whites, the assets African Americans own tend to be the wrong kinds of property to enjoy tax preferences. According to Moran and Whitford, African Americans are more likely to hold consumption items and less likely to hold financial and investment assets. Similar disparities exist for home ownership, which enjoys a longstanding tax preference. All races spend approximately the same percentage of their income for housing, but a smaller percentage of African Americans own their home and their homes tend not to appreciate in value to the same extent as the homes of other races.[2]

Using the metaphor of a black Congress enacting new tax legislation, Moran and Whitford suggest ways to change the law to eliminate existing preferences. For example, the home mortgage interest deduction could be replaced with a credit that declines to $0 as adjusted gross income exceeds $50,000. Also, because African Americans tend to own fewer investment assets, the professors propose repealing favorable capital gain rates and taxing

---

[1]   Beverly Moran & William Whitford, *A Black Critique of the Internal Revenue Code*, 1996 WIS. L. REV. 751 (1996).

[2]   U.S. CENSUS BUREAU, CB17–55, QUARTERLY RESIDENTIAL VACANCIES AND HOMEOWNERSHIP, FIRST QUARTER 2017 (2017).

appreciation as it accrues on investments in publicly traded securities and nonresidential real estate.

Professor Lawrence Zelenak engages in a critical exchange with Moran and Whitford over their article.[3] First, Zelenak criticizes the baseline used for determining what is a tax preference intended to favor taxpayers. If, instead of an income tax, a consumption tax were posited as the ideal, their results would differ. Most of the tax provisions Moran and Whitford find favor whites exclude savings from current taxation, a cornerstone of consumption taxation. Thus, the preferences that favor others over African Americans also make the system more like a consumption tax. To the extent this is true, a consumption tax is likely to be racially disparate in its impact.

Second, Zelenak challenges Moran and Whitford's evidence on the grounds that they chose provisions from the Code most likely to support their hypothesis. In particular, he contests the exclusion of the EITC, which benefits the working poor. Moreover, he argues that they used a faulty data set of social science studies and tax returns. In particular, data from tax returns cannot be perfected for this purpose because returns are not coded by race. It is impossible to know for certain who claims a particular tax preference.

Additionally, although Professors Moran and Whitford attempt to control for income, their sample size is small and their findings might be more indicative of class rather than race.[4] Thus, preferences may favor wealthier taxpayers and affect African Americans similarly to the less well off of other races. Furthermore, the professors' proposals to redress the discrimination focus largely on issues that would favor all lower-class taxpayers, and the proposals retain the same color-blind trappings of the current Internal Revenue Code.

Any shift in policies to address provisions' racial impact would change how the tax system influences taxpayers' behavior. Congress enacts most tax preferences, such as favoring investment assets, in order to get taxpayers to do what it wants. Thus, the discrimination may result from some taxpayers responding to these economic incentives more than others. In other words, some people are more elastic in their behavior than others and they get the tax reduction. Those who do not do what Congress thinks is best for them and society pay the price in higher taxes.

---

[3]   Lawrence Zelenak, *Taking Critical Tax Theory Seriously*, 76 N.C. L. REV. 1521 (1998); William C. Whitford, *Remarkable*, 76 N.C. L. REV. 1639 (1998); Beverly Moran, *Exploring the Mysteries: Can We Ever Know Anything About Race and Tax?*, 76 N.C. L. REV. 1629 (1998).

[4]   Wilton Hyman, *Race, Class, and the Internal Revenue Code*, 35 CAP. U. L. REV. 119 (2006).

Focusing on incentive effects accepts the merits of the policies, such as that taxpayers should hold investment assets. Moreover, to be convinced by this argument, policymakers must accept the policy goals regardless of their racial impact. However, applying an across-the-board incentive may mean that African Americans are incentivized too little and non-minorities are rewarded for actions they would take regardless of the tax consequences. If this is the case, incentives are spent to reward without a corresponding change in behavior.

Not only potentially wasteful, racially disparate tax preferences may harm African Americans without a corresponding gain for other races. The price of investment assets may already incorporate existing tax preferences, which would mean they are sold at a higher price because of the tax benefit they can command. If that is the case, there is no current benefit to owners of these assets. The ones who benefited were the owners when the tax preference was enacted. Nevertheless, there is harm to African Americans and other current purchasers or users of assets who are personally unable to reap the reward of the tax preference. They are forced to pay more for the use of these assets without the offsetting tax benefit, which was captured by initial owners.

For example, housing prices may be higher because of widespread use or expectation of the use of the home mortgage interest deduction. To the extent that African Americans as a group do not claim the deduction because they claim the standard deduction instead, they must pay higher prices for homes without the offsetting tax benefit.[5] Furthermore, if African American communities generally do not claim the home mortgage interest deduction, it may help explain their lower housing prices. These lower prices are partially based on the assumption that buyers will not claim the deduction; and they would create a windfall to those who buy into these neighborhoods who do benefit from the deduction.

At other times a racial disparity may result from the workings of tax penalties and bonuses that impact African Americans more negatively than whites. For example, Professor Dorothy Brown notes how the marriage penalty particularly burdens African American couples and that few enjoy the marriage bonus.[6] Because couples with a dominant income earner enjoy the bonus, African American couples, who are more likely to have relatively equal earning spouses, lose relative to other couples. On the other hand, because African

---

[5]   Dorothy A. Brown, *Shades of the American Dream*, 87 WASH. U. L. REV. 329 (2009).

[6]   Dorothy Brown, *The Marriage Bonus/Penalty in Black and White*, 65 CINN. L. REV. 787 (1937).

Americans disproportionately raise children in nontraditional families, the loss of the head of household status possibly resulting from adopting individual taxation would likely be economically severe.

The existence of tax preferences that do not benefit the American population equally or of tax penalties that do not burden equally raises questions of equity. Should the nation have a home mortgage interest deduction if some groups are more likely than others to be advantaged by the deduction? As a deeper question, should the tax system encourage certain behaviors, such as savings, if doing so punishes other behaviors, such as consumption? What if different groups of people self-identify with one or the other of those behaviors? These choices regarding the allocation of the tax burden could be labeled political choices and dismissed. However, that would ignore the very insidious nature of the racial discrimination critical legal scholars condemn.

(ii) Reparations and Incarceration

Those studying racism in America may question if and how the government uses the tax system to address the painful legacy of slavery and racial discrimination. In the aftermath of the Civil War, Congress did not award freed slaves forty acres and a mule.[7] Although the House of Representatives apologized for slavery and subsequent discriminatory laws in 2008, Congress has never seriously debated direct reparations to the descendants of slaves.[8] Nevertheless, scholars have examined the likely tax treatment of reparations if they were ever paid.[9] Unless Congress specifically excludes reparations from taxation, direct payments would be taxable to the recipient.

The lack of reparations for African-Americans and their default taxation can be compared to reparations made to compensate Japanese Americans for internment during World War II.[10] In 1988, Congress enacted the Civil Liberties Act, apologizing for the internment and authorizing $20,000 to each camp survivor. More than $1.6 billion was paid to 82,219 internees.[11] The $20,000

---

[7]   Special Field Orders, No. 15 (series 1865) (William Tecumseh Sherman).

[8]   H. Res. 194, 110th Cong (2008).

[9]   Andre Smith & Carlton Waterhouse, *No Reparation without Taxation*, 7 PITT. TAX REV. 159 (2010).

[10]   ALFRED BROPHY, REPARATIONS PRO AND CON (2006); David Gray, *A No-Excuse Approach to Transitional Justice: Reparations as Tools of Extraordinary Justice*, 87 WASH. U. L. REV. 1043 (2010).

[11]   The financial ramifications of slave reparations would differ from reparations to the Japanese internees. The 82,219 recipients from Japanese internments were of the approximately 120,000 U.S. citizens and residents who were relocated and

payment was only to surviving internees; the only way heirs received payment was if the internee died after requesting payment. Congress legislated that these payments to internees were tax-free. This increased the value of the awards because recipients might otherwise have had 28% of their awards, as the top marginal rate at the time, claimed by the government paying them.

Although Congress has not awarded reparations for slavery, many people annually claim an unauthorized tax credit in the name of reparations. In 2004, the IRS notified taxpayers, promoters, and tax return preparers that claiming such a credit was a frivolous position with no merit.[12] Not only is the credit disallowed, the IRS seeks to recover erroneously issued refunds in addition to assessing interest and, perhaps, penalties on any unpaid tax due to the claim.

Separate from reparations but nonetheless disproportionately affecting African Americans are payments for wrongful incarceration. People of all races can be wrongfully convicted; but of the 324 DNA exonerations, 63% of those exonerated were African-American and a further 7% were other minorities.[13] In 2015 Congress enacted a provision that excludes payments for wrongful incarceration from taxation, thereby privileging some civil damages in the tax system.[14] Before 2015, payments for wrongful incarceration would be taxable unless the recipient could show that they related back to a physical injury or sickness. The new provision is partially retroactive. The new provision does not apply to exclude from income payments for derivative suits, such as for the loss of consortium by a spouse.

(iii) Litigation Awards

All successful civil rights litigants who receive damages are taxed on those payments unless the payment is for wrongful incarceration or the damages stem from physical injury or sickness.[15] The inclusion in the event of non-physical effects had been ambiguous until 1996, when Congress amended the Internal Revenue Code to make clear that a portion of settlements and damage payments were to be taxed. This creation of a dichotomy between physical injury or sickness and everything else applies to all personal litigation. Payments because someone breaks your nose are

---

interned. Although 388,000 Africans were brought to the U.S. in the slave trade, the number of slaves reached 4 million before the end of the Civil War.

[12]   Rev. Rul. 2004–33, 2004–1 C.B. 628.

[13]   David Love, *Dealing With the Racial Nature of Wrongful Convictions*, HUFF. POST, Feb. 22, 2015.

[14]   I.R.C. § 139F.

[15]   I.R.C. § 104.

not taxed but payments because of a non-physical racial, sexual, or rights violation are taxed.

Consequently, a payment for a civil rights violation that results in physical harm is not taxable, but equal payments without the physical harm are taxable. This causes some odd results. Payments for lost wages or pain and suffering may be taxable or not depending upon their cause, and the tax consequence has nothing to do with the severity of the damage beyond a threshold physical injury. This bifurcation of payments is not limited to issues of race but is a generally applicable rule.

Applying the bifurcation consistently produces a theoretical justification for excluding internment reparations but not hypothetical slavery reparations. Payments for internment were only paid to those physically interned and for the consequences arising therefrom because each recipient had been moved and forced to live in a camp. This creates a nexus with the physical injury component. Reparations for slavery that ended over a hundred and fifty years ago are for past physical deeds or for today's non-physical effects of that legacy. Thus, these payments have no nexus to a current physical injury.

Despite the application of general exclusion rules with respect to damages, civil rights litigation does receive a tax preference in that attorney fees paid in pressing this type of claim are always deductible.[16] Attorneys' fees in most personal litigation are a miscellaneous itemized expense, which between 2018 and 2025 are completely not deductible but before were subject to a 2% floor. Therefore, many personal awards are taxable on a gross basis.[17] Civil rights litigation, on the other hand, was granted its special exception in 2004 and is taxed on a net basis.

(b) Immigrants

In 2015, an estimated 43.3 million immigrants lived in the U.S., or almost 13.5% of the total U.S. population.[18] Immigrants can be classified as lawful permanent residents (or green card holders), nonimmigrant visa holders (tourists), those with temporary protected status (those with a pending application), or undocumented residents. All U.S. citizens and U.S. residents (regardless of their status) are required to comply with American tax laws, including the

---

[16]   I.R.C. § 62(a)(20).

[17]   Most settlements are deductible by the payers of damages; however, in 2018 Congress denied deductions for payments related to a sexual harassment or sexual abuse if the payments were subject to a nondisclosure agreement.

[18]   Jie Zong & Jeanne Batalova, *Frequently Requested Statistics on Immigrants and Immigration in the United States*, MIGRATION POLICY INSTITUTE (Mar. 8, 2017).

income and payroll taxes. Immigrants face unique consequences if they fail to comply with the tax laws in addition to the civil and criminal punishments faced by U.S. citizens.[19] Immigrants can be deported from the U.S. for failing to file tax returns or for misrepresentations on their returns. These punishments, coupled with the complaints listed by Moran and Whitford, are critiqued by critical race scholars.[20]

These consequences may apply even though all immigrants in the U.S., whether documented or not, pay some amount of tax. The CBO estimates that between 70% and 80% of undocumented immigrants pay federal, state, and local taxes.[21] An empirical study of undocumented immigrants' impact on the U.S. tax system indicates that they contribute more in taxes than they cost in social services.[22]

For example, documented and undocumented immigrants pay sales taxes on their purchases of goods and pay property taxes on their residences. Estimates are that almost 3.5 million undocumented workers, or 31%, own homes on which they pay property taxes.[23] If they do not own their homes directly, undocumented workers pay property taxes indirectly through their payment of rent. The Institute on Taxation and Economic Policy found that, in 2014, 11.1 million undocumented immigrants paid a total of $11.74 billion in state and local taxes, of which $3.6 billion was in property tax and more than $7 billion was in sales and excise taxes.[24] If these immigrants were legalized, the amount they would pay in tax would increase by an estimated $2.18 billion per year.

In addition to sales and property taxes, undocumented workers are estimated to pay $12 billion into Social Security each year.[25] Despite these payments, undocumented workers are ineligible for distributions from the program unless their status changes. Instead, earnings paid on a Social Security number that does not match

---

[19]   For more on generally-applicable civil and criminal penalties, see Chapter 2.

[20]   Leo Martinez & Jennifer Martinez, *The Internal Revenue Code and Latino Realities*, 22 U. FLA. J.L. & PUB. POL'Y 377 (2011); Mylinh Uy, [Note], *Tax and Race: The Impact on Asian Americans*, 11 ASIAN L.J. 117 (2004).

[21]   CONG. BUDGET OFFICE, THE IMPACT OF UNAUTHORIZED IMMIGRANTS ON THE BUDGETS OF STATE AND LOCAL GOVERNMENTS (2007).

[22]   Luis Larrea, *Taxation Inequality and Undocumented Immigrants*, 5 WM. MITCHELL L. RAZA J. 2, 3 (2013–2014).

[23]   MIGRATION POL'Y INST., PROFILE OF THE UNAUTHORIZED POPULATION, http://www. migrationpolicy.org/data/unauthorized-immigrant-population/state/US (last visited Sept. 27, 2017).

[24]   INST. TAX'N & ECON. POL'Y, UNDOCUMENTED IMMIGRANTS' STATE AND LOCAL TAX CONTRIBUTIONS (Mar. 2, 2017).

[25]   Stephen Goss et al., *Effects of Unauthorized Immigration on the Actuarial Status of the Social Security Trust Funds*, SOC'L SEC'Y ADMIN. (2013).

anyone on record go into an Earnings Suspense File until someone can prove that the wages are theirs. Even if a person's status changes, only in limited circumstances can the person claim past Social Security contributions.[26]

Finally, all U.S. residents must comply with the federal income tax. To do so, most documented immigrants can receive a Social Security number to use for tax filing. Until 1996 undocumented workers were also granted Social Security numbers, but then the Social Security Administration limited their issuance to U.S. citizens, lawful permanent residents, and immigrants with a work visa. In response, the IRS created individual taxpayer identification numbers (ITINs) to comply with the Internal Revenue Code's requirement that taxpayers have identifying numbers for their tax filings. ITINs enable undocumented immigrants to file tax returns and open interest-bearing bank accounts. ITINs do not, however, change an individual's immigration status, authorize work in the U.S., or provide eligibility for Social Security benefits. In 2010, over 3 million people used an ITIN when filing their tax returns, more than half of which were filed by undocumented immigrants, paying over $870 million in income tax.[27]

Because ITINs do not authorize work, undocumented workers have difficulty when filing income tax returns. Undocumented workers may face complications because of a mismatch between their lawful ITIN and the Social Security number they use to obtain work. After working with a false Social Security number, the undocumented worker would need to (1) file a tax return with the illegal Social Security number but doing so constitutes document fraud which could have future immigration consequences or (2) file a tax return with an ITIN but attach a W-2 with an illegally obtained Social Security number. The IRS permits this mismatch, even with electronic filing, and the IRS is statutorily prohibited from sharing this information with other government departments; but undocumented workers may not trust this segregation of information.[28]

When undocumented workers use illegally obtained Social Security numbers to file tax returns, they pay their federal and state income taxes through withholding. If they then fail to file a tax return, they violate the Internal Revenue Code but doing so often

---

[26]   A process of reconciliation can permit a person to claim their prior earnings. Luz Arévalo, *Who Said Your Immigrant Client Cannot Get Credit for Social Security Payments?*, 19 BENDER'S IMMIGR. BULL. 1181 (2014).

[27]   AM. IMMIGR. COUNCIL, THE FACTS ABOUT THE INDIVIDUAL TAX IDENTIFICATION NUMBER (Apr. 5, 2016).

[28]   I.R.C. § 6103.

constitutes a windfall to the federal government. Many non-filing immigrants would receive a refund if they filed their returns because for low-income earners withholding often results in overpayments of income tax. Workers must file returns within three years or forfeit their refund.

Before 2018, one reason undocumented workers were often entitled to tax refunds was their ability to claim some tax credits. For example, undocumented workers were permitted to claim all of the child tax credit if they satisfied its requirements; however, the Tax Cuts and Jobs Act of 2017 requires taxpayers provide a Social Security number for each qualifying child in addition to being resident in the U.S. for half the year in order to receive the refundable portion of the child tax credit. This requirement is expected to save almost $30 billion between 2018 and 2027. In 2011, the Treasury Inspector General reported $4.2 billion in child tax credit refunds to individuals who were not authorized to work in the U.S., up from $924 million in 2005.[29]

Similar to the new limitation on the child tax credit, undocumented immigrants and U.S. citizens married to undocumented immigrants are not permitted to claim the EITC.[30] To claim the ETIC, the taxpayer must include both spouses' Social Security numbers, and ITINs do not suffice for this purpose. If a U.S. citizen or lawful immigrant with a Social Security number uses an incorrect filing status, either head of household or single, to claim EITC benefits because the person's spouse is not eligible, the filing constitutes fraud.

Despite often owing little to no tax, there are many reasons immigrants fail to file income tax returns. First, their low incomes may be less than tax filing thresholds. Immigrants are more likely to be low-income than native-born citizens. One study found that 10% of U.S. born families and 13% of legal immigrants lived in poverty, compared to 32% of undocumented immigrants.[31] The poverty guideline for 2018 for single individuals was $12,140 and for married couples was $16,460, slightly above and below the tax filing thresholds. Thus, some in poverty are required to file income tax returns. One study found that the average undocumented families' income in 2007, before the Great Recession, was $35,000 and $38,000

---

[29]   TREAS. INSPECTOR GEN. FOR TAX ADMIN, 2011–41–061, INDIVIDUALS WHO ARE NOT AUTHORIZED TO WORK IN THE U.S. WERE PAID $4.2 BILLION IN REFUNDABLE CREDITS (2011).

[30]   For more on the EITC, see Chapter 16.02(b).

[31]   MIGRATION POL'Y INST., *supra* note 21.

depending upon their length of time in the U.S., but significantly below U.S.-born residents' $50,000 median income.[32]

Second, immigrants may struggle to obtain the ITINs necessary to file tax returns. To receive an ITIN, the taxpayer, the taxpayer's spouse, and each of the taxpayer's dependents must supply personal information and original (or certified copies of) passports or birth certificates to establish their identity and non-citizen status. Moreover, to the extent undocumented immigrants do not have computer access or a residence at which they regularly receive mail, they may find it difficult to request an ITIN even if they have the necessary documentation.

Third, many immigrants face literacy issues. An estimated 49% of undocumented workers have not completed high school and 32% have less than a ninth grade education.[33] This often results in the use of paid return preparers. Back in 2001, less than 3% of taxpayers prepared their own returns if they used an ITIN.[34] The IRS acknowledges the widespread problem of preparer fraud, extending beyond immigrant communities, and that these are taxpayers who are often unaware of the false exemptions, credits, or deductions shown on their tax returns.[35] The lack of literacy is compounded because not all countries have a similar taxpaying culture as does the U.S. For example, 60% of Mexican workers live in the informal, nontaxpaying economy; and not all countries have an individual income tax or one that requires the person to file a return.[36]

When an immigrant fails to file a tax return or files a fraudulent tax return, the consequences may include the inability to become a U.S. citizen or becoming subject to deportation. These collateral consequences arise because immigrants must have a finding of "good moral character" to naturalize, and that finding may be precluded for a person who fails to file accurate tax returns.[37] In 2012, in

---

[32]   Jeffrey Passel & D'Vera Cohn, *Social and Economic Characteristics, in* A PORTRAIT OF UNAUTHORIZED IMMIGRANTS IN THE UNITED STATES (Pew Hispanic Organization 2009).

[33]   Francis Lipman, *The "Illegal" Tax*, 11 CONN. PUB. INT. L.J. 93, 119 (2011); Francine J. Lipman, *Taxing Undocumented Immigrants: Separate, Unequal, and Without Representation*, 59 TAX LAW. 813 (2006).

[34]   U.S. TREAS. DEPT., THE INTERNAL REVENUE SERVICE'S INDIVIDUAL TAXPAYER IDENTIFICATION NUMBER CREATES SIGNIFICANT CHALLENGES FOR TAX ADMINISTRATION 13 (2004).

[35]   IRS, FS–2009–7, HOW TO CHOOSE A TAX PREPARER AND AVOID PREPARER FRAUD (2009).

[36]   Krista Hughes, *Mexico Aims to Bring Shadow Economy Into the Light*, REUTERS (Jun. 26, 2013).

[37]   One question on the Naturalization Application (Form N-400) is whether the applicant has "ever not filed a Federal, State or local tax return since you became a Permanent Resident?"

Kawashima v. Holder, the Supreme Court upheld a deportation order for a Japanese couple.[38] The couple had lawfully operated restaurants in California for over ten years before pleading guilty in 1997 to underpaying their taxes by nearly $250,000. The couple was thereafter subject to deportation as aliens convicted of aggravated felonies. The Court's minority did not think that tax crimes were sufficiently serious to merit deportation.

The government warns of scams that pray on people's fear of deportation. In 2016, the government claimed to have stopped one scam that caused at least 15,000 individuals to pay more than $300 million.[39] In this scam, people telephoned immigrants posing as tax or immigration agents and threatened arrest or deportation unless money was sent. In that case, 61 defendants were charged in connection with the India-based call center.

§ 16.02   Class in Taxation

Unlike race, class is ubiquitous in the Internal Revenue Code.[40] In one poll, 60% of respondents said that the tax system favors the wealthy; 22% said it favors the non-wealthy or treats them equally.[41] People may complain "wealthy folks pay less" and that the "rich do not pay their fair share and should pay more."[42] However, identifying class-based provisions is not always easy. The use of progressive tax rates expressly recognizes that taxpayers with more income should pay more in taxes. On the other hand, the standard deduction does not have a different face value depending on income. Many Code provisions couple class elements with other objectives. For example, the EITC encourages paid employment and couples it with a phase-out to target those incentives to lower-income taxpayers. In this way class is prevalent throughout the Code but not always in a measurable way.

(a) General Principles

The federal tax system is generally a progressive tax system, although its component parts are more or less progressive. Therefore, the government raises disproportionately more money from higher

---

[38]   565 U.S. 478 (2012). *See also* Joshua Blank, *Collateral Compliance*, 162 U. PA. L. REV. 719 (2014).

[39]   AP, *In Call Center Scam, Threats of Arrest and Deportation*, CBS.COM (Oct. 27, 2016).

[40]   For a discussion of whether the tax system should be used for income redistribution, see Chapter 18.02.

[41]   Ariel Edwards-Levy, *America's Tax System is Widely Seen as Favoring the Rich, Poll Shows*, HUFF. POST (Jan. 29, 2015).

[42]   Alain Sherter, *Skinning America*, CBS MONEY WATCH (Apr. 15, 2010); Dan Berger, *Tax Code Skewed in the Rich's Favor*, US NEWS & WORLD REPT (Dec. 16, 2011).

income taxpayers but only when the tax system is examined as a whole. It was popularly reported in 2015 that the top 20% of all taxpayers paid 87% of all federal income taxes and the bottom 50% received a refund.[43] The conservative Tax Policy Center found that only 12.1% of households in the bottom quintile pay any federal income tax, which should be unsurprising because of the EITC and the child tax credit. These numbers for the lower-end of the income spectrum reflect that much of the federal welfare system now operates through the income tax system. On the other hand, 57.4% of the households who do not pay income tax do pay payroll taxes.[44]

These numbers reflect the complexity of what the tax system must accomplish. Traditionally, the tax system focused on raising revenue that was distributed through other parts of the government. In such a regime there is little to be done for low-income people other than to exempt them from tax. Even if a person lived in poverty and was not subject to the income tax, low-income workers were expected to pay payroll taxes on every dollar that was earned, sales tax on much of what they bought, and property taxes on what they owned.

The current tax system continues most of those tax realities except that the current federal income tax disperses significant amounts of government largesse to the public. Under this regime, low-income tax filers can receive a lot through the tax system. Most provisions favoring low-income taxpayers are tax credits that phase down or out as a taxpayer's income rises.

Although there has been a change in the tax treatment of the poor, the wealthy have always been selectively aided by the tax system. Several income tax provisions benefit activities most often engaged in by wealthier taxpayers. Moreover, the wealthy only pay payroll taxes on up to $128,400 of wages in 2018. Therefore, less has changed in how Congress taxes the wealthy.

Perhaps ironically, the tax system helps the wealthy and the poor at the same time through targeted provisions. Increasing the system's complexity, this possibly conflicting dispersal of federal tax preferences is more reflective of congressional politics than well thought out tax policy. Politicians can point out favorable tax provisions to each of their constituents. The ones harmed by this system are those who have difficulty figuring out how to claim their

---

[43]   Catey Hill, *45% of Americans Pay No Federal Income Tax*, MARKETWATCH (Apr. 18, 2016).

[44]   TAX POLICY CENTER, HOW DOES THE FEDERAL TAX SYSTEM AFFECT LOW-INCOME HOUSEHOLDS, http://www.taxpolicycenter.org/briefing-book/how-does-federal-tax-system-affect-low-income-households (last visited Sept. 27, 2017).

tax benefits and anyone who falls into the cracks between special provisions.

A structural question for evaluating class-based tax issues is whether a person's class should be determined by looking at the person in isolation or as part of a group. In other words, should the EITC or other tax benefits or narrow tax penalties be tied to family income or individual income? Particularly with the expansion of family types, a person's economic resourfces often depend on a group larger than the person alone and possibly not limited to legal marriage. Family or other networks may be invaluable buffers for events that would otherwise result in changes to a person's class. However, because networks are so personal, it may not be administrable to factor this reality into the tax system.

(b) Earned Income Tax Credit

The tax system currently administers the largest income redistribution program in the U.S.: the earned income tax credit (EITC).[45] In 2016, over 27 million families claimed the credit at a cost of $67 billion in revenue.[46] While no other antipoverty program reduces the poverty rate as much as the EITC, the EITC's beneficial effects are concentrated for those who are close to the poverty line and for those with children.[47] Understanding Congress's underlying motives for the EITC would help analyze the program's success; however, that information is not available. Two objectives for the EITC can be teased out of its legislative history; Congress did not make clear which was paramount when enacting or subsequently amending the provision.[48] First, the EITC might be an income supplement that is intended to raise people out of poverty. If that is the case, its tie to earnings is less persuasive because those of comparable incomes who do not work are no less poor, unless Congress felt the earnings component was a necessary long-term solution to poverty.

---

[45]   For more on the EITC, see Sara Sternberg Greene, *The Broken Safety Net: A Study of Earned Income Tax Credit Recipients and a Proposal for Repair*, 88 NYU L. REV. 515 (2013); Anne Alstott, *Why the EITC Doesn't Make Work Pay*, 73 LAW & CONTEMP. PROB. 285 (2010); David Weisbach & Jacob Nussim, *The Integration of Tax and Spending Programs*, 113 YALE L.J. 955 (2004).

[46]   IRS, STATISTICS FOR TAX RETURNS WITH EITC, https://www.eitc.irs.gov/eitc-central /statistics-for-tax-returns-with-eitc/statistics-for-tax-returns-with-eitc (last visited Feb. 21, 2018).

[47]   Temporary Assistance for Needy Families (TANF) and the Supplemental Nutrition Assistance Program (SNAP, formerly the Food Stamp Program) are more targeted to those at the very lowest incomes.

[48]   Dennis Ventry, *The Collision of Tax and Welfare Politics*, 53 NAT'L TAX J. 983 (2000).

Second, the EITC might be an offset to employment taxes for those at the bottom end of the income spectrum. Payroll taxes are regressive as a larger component of low-income taxpayers' income, and that regressivity may be redressed through the offsetting credit. As currently structured, the EITC can offset burdensome payroll taxes without reducing the person's accumulated earnings for purposes of qualifying for future Social Security payments.

The argument that the EITC is to "make work pay" exists in the legislative history, but Congress does not state this was the primary motivator or even a motivation shared by most in Congress. The credit's maximum benefit is available to someone who earns slightly more than full-time work at the national minimum wage. Therefore, changes to the minimum wage may lead to significant adjustments in the EITC depending upon how Congress sees the interrelation of the wage law and the tax benefit.

However, the credit's effectiveness at motivating people to enter paid employment or to work more hours has yet to be proven.[49] One study shows that the EITC significantly increases the work effort of its recipients, particularly of single mothers with young children and mothers with little education.[50] A second study found that the EITC increased single mothers' employment by 7% following a credit increase in 1996.[51] A third study found no correlation between the EITC and the number of employment hours worked.[52] It is possible that the credit simply shifts labor among participants. In other words, one spouse might work more but the other less. Additionally, the credit may encourage labor but, in the process, push down wages in low skilled labor markets. The result would decrease the working poors' earnings and reduce their employment opportunities even as it ties government aid to that employment.

The calculation of the EITC is complex, but its structure generally maximizes the credit amount for those working poor who financially support children.

---

[49]   Nada Eissa & Hilary W. Hoynes, *Behavioral Responses to Taxes: Lessons from the EITC and Labor Supply*, in TAX POLICY AND THE ECONOMY, at 73, 94 (2006). *But see* Kartik Athreya et al., *Single Mothers and the Earned Income Tax Credit*, IZA DP. No. 811 (2014).

[50]   Bruce Meyer, *The Effects of the Earned Income Tax Credit and Recent Reforms*, *in* NBER BOOK SERIES TAX POLICY AND THE ECONOMY (Jeffrey Brown ed. 2010).

[51]   Bruce D. Meyer & Dan T. Rosenbaum, *Welfare, the Earned Income Tax Credit, and the Labor Supply of Single Mothers*, NBER WORKING PAPER No. 7363 (1999).

[52]   Maria Cancian & Arik Levinson, *Labor Supply Effects of the Earned Income Tax Credit*, NBER WORKING PAPER No. 11454 (2005).

number of qualifying children claimed[53]			
0	1	2	3 or more
maximum amount of credit			
$520	$3,468	$5,728	$6,444
required earned income to begin credit			
$6,800	$10,200	$14,320	$14,320
income at which EITC starts to phase out			

	0	1	2	3 or more
Single; head of household	$8,510	$18,700	$18,700	$18,700
Married filing jointly	$14,200	$24,400	$24,400	$24,400

income at which EITC is completely phased out				
Single; head of household	$15,310	$40,402	$45,898	$49,298
Married filing jointly	$21,000	$46,102	$51,598	$54,998

If a person owes income tax, the EITC reduces the taxes owed. If a person does not owe tax, the EITC is a refundable credit so that recipients can receive a payment of some amount of their credit.

The credit is not a flat amount per taxpayer but phases in and out depending upon a person's earnings. The amount of the credit increases as people earn money up to a plateau and then declines as earnings continue to rise. With enough earnings the credit is reduced to $0.

---

[53]   The amounts provided are for the 2018 tax year. The amounts are adjusted annually for inflation. The 2018 inflation-adjusted amounts are available at Revenue Procedure 2017–58.

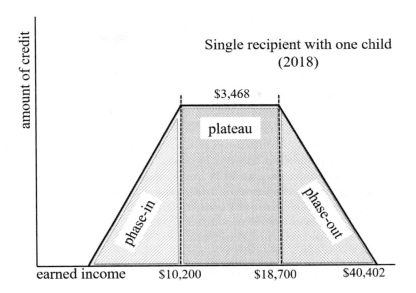

Single recipient with one child
(2018)

amount of credit

$3,468

plateau

phase-in

phase-out

earned income $10,200 $18,700 $40,402

In the phase-in range, the structure of the credit incentivizes work. In the phase-out range, earning more income causes a decrease in the credit. The disincentive would be greater if the phase-down was not gradual. Thus, that the EITC phases out rather than falls off reduces the cliff effect if all the credit were lost at once.

Nevertheless, the phase-out retains the complicated incentives for workers that all phase-outs have. Taxpayers in the phase-out range face a potentially high marginal tax rate. The collective tax on each new dollar earned is the rate of lost benefits plus the income and payroll taxes owed. For example, in 2018 the credit begins phasing out at $24,400 for joint filers with one child. These joint filers are in the 12% tax bracket. Therefore, of each additional dollar earned, 12¢ in income tax is owed plus payroll taxes plus an incremental amount of the EITC is lost. The taxpayer pays more taxes and receives a smaller credit. Other income-based benefits may also be lost, further disincentivizing additional work.

To the extent that the credit affects behavior, recipients should decrease the number of hours they work as they enter the plateau or phase-out range in the EITC. That result has not been found empirically. The reasons for this failure may be varied: workers may not be able to vary their hours easily, they may incorrectly measure their hours reported, or they may not understand their marginal tax rates. Nevertheless, policymakers should understand that a credit to encourage behavior might produce complicated or unintended results.

One unintended consequence of the EITC may be that it encourages low-income taxpayers to have more children because the amount of the credit increases with the number of children. Although capped at three children, the difference between children and three children is significant: a $5,808 difference. Almost half of that jump is from no children to one child.

Moreover, the EITC's economic incentives may affect choices other than whether or not to work, for example whether or not to marry. The earnings schedule is almost the same for singles and couples, creating both marriage bonuses and marriage penalties. Because of this structure, the EITC encourages couples with a single earner to marry but discourages two-earner couples from marrying. Based on most real economic situations, the EITC should discourage marriage overall because of the labor patterns of low-income couples. Nevertheless, most studies find little or no effect on the choice to marry.[54]

The credit may also create the incentive to lie. In the lowest, phase-in range, the EITC constitutes a negative income tax. Its benefits increase more than any associated tax increase (the increase primarily being payroll taxes). Therefore, someone who is not currently working could claim to be self-employed and receive a 40% credit in exchange for paying a Social Security tax of 15.3%, a net gain for the claimant, although there is a timing issue in that Social Security payments are due quarterly. However, by paying the Social Security tax, the person also receives credit toward future Social Security benefits.

There are important distinctions between the EITC and other U.S. welfare programs. Although people may claim most other welfare programs for a limited number of years, the EITC can be claimed for a worker's entire career as long as its requirements are satisfied. And whereas most welfare programs take into account the recipient's accumulated wealth, the EITC is an income-based program that ignores wealth. As a result, low-income persons with substantial wealth that is not generating current income can receive the EITC.

The EITC is also operationally different from other welfare programs. Unlike programs that provide aid quickly once proof of need is shown, the EITC is not designed to respond quickly to need. The EITC is retroactive aid, in that it is calculated at the end of a tax period, and payable annually. Between 1979 and 2010, it was possible to collect the EITC as advance payments over the course of

---

[54] *See* Chris Herbst, *The Impact of the Earned Income Tax Credit on Marriage and Divorce*, 30 POPL. RES. POL'Y REV. 101 (2011); Stacy Dickert-Conlin & Scott Houser, *EITC and Marriage*, 55 NAT'L TAX J. (2002).

the year but the program had a 3% take up rate and low compliance.[55] Nevertheless, annually may not be the best period of time to measure income in order to determine the recipient's need or end of the tax year be the best time to make disbursements, coinciding with other tax refunds.

Possibly because the EITC is calculated on the tax return as opposed to requiring appearance at a government agency, the EITC has higher participation rates than other welfare programs but also higher noncompliance rates. This means that 80% of those who are eligible for the EITC claim the credit but 24% do so incorrectly.[56] In 2016, the Treasury Department reported that over $15.5 billion in claims were paid out in error.[57] Other programs tend to have low participation rates but also low rates of noncompliance. Despite the inaccuracies and publicity of noncompliance, the federal EITC rarely comes under serious political attack; the 26 state and Washington D.C. EITCs have faced opposition although most states have increased their EITCs in recent years.[58]

Most errors associated with the EITC are unlikely the result of lying but due to confusion. The credit's complexity contributes to the EITC's relatively high error rate, along with taxpayers' high turnover of eligibility so that people eligible in one year may not be in the next. Instructions for the EITC are a dense thirteen or fourteen pages depending upon the tax year. If more than one person qualifies to claim a child for the EITC, eligibility may depend on relative adjusted gross income; information that is not always available to a potential claimant. Many claimants of the EITC seek help filing their tax returns. Currently, almost 60% of returns claiming the EITC use commercial preparers.[59]

That more than one person may claim a child for purposes of the EITC can result in delayed refunds. The first person who claims the EITC is generally awarded the credit, possibly including a refund. If a second filer should have received the credit, that filer cannot submit an electronic return and will not receive a refund based on the EITC until after an audit. In the audit, the IRS will apply the tiebreaker

---

[55] GOV'T ACCOUNTABILITY OFFICE, GAO–16–475, REFUNDABLE TAX CREDITS 5–6 (2016).

[56] TREAS. INSPECTOR GEN. FOR TAX ADMIN., 2015–40–009, THE INTERNAL REVENUE SERVICE IS WORKING TOWARD COMPLIANCE WITH EXECUTIVE ORDER 13520 REPORTING REQUIREMENTS (2014).

[57] U.S. TREAS. DEPT., AGENCY FINANCIAL REPORT 49 (2016).

[58] For example, Michigan recently faced challenges to its EITC and in 2016 Oklahoma made its EITC nonrefundable.

[59] *IRS Actions to Reduce Improper Payments Before H. Comm. on Oversight and Government Reform, Subcomm. on Government Operations*, 113th Cong. (Jul. 9, 2014) (statement of John Koskinen, IRS Commissioner).

rules Congress established.[60] Nevertheless, during the delay, the government is left in the unenviable position of refereeing between claimants of a child.

Despite the EITC's imperfections, that this subsidy to the working poor is distributed through the tax code instead of through another agency may be advantageous. Using annual tax filing, the EITC reduces recipients' poverty in a way that may have less social stigma than traditional welfare payments. Unfortunately, in the process it adds to the complexity of tax returns and adds to the IRS's administrative burdens. It may also limit relief to some who need it. As part of the income tax system, the EITC is not particularly accessible to transients or those who have few other ties to the income tax regime.

(c) Phase-Outs

For those on the other end of the income spectrum, Congress generally finds it difficult to increase tax rates. A politically easier way to make aspects of the Code more progressive is to phase down or phase out tax benefits because these changes' impact is relatively hidden. Thus, many deductions and credits, like the child tax credit, phase out at higher income levels, eliminating any benefit for high-income taxpayers. This targets many tax expenditures' benefits to lower- and middle-income taxpayers and limits the amount of government revenue that is lost.

Despite prior political appetite for phase-outs, many were reduced in the Tax Cuts and Jobs Act of 2017, if only for the period between 2018 and 2025. For example, the phase-out of the standard deduction was eliminated, despite the phase-out of it and the personal exemption having been estimated to save almost $90 billion in government revenue between 2016 and 2020.[61] Some phaseouts, such as that of miscellaneous itemized deductions, were eliminated because the deductions themselves were disallowed. The limited duration of the repeal may have been more for budgetary concerns rather than a desire to see phase-outs resurrected.

Although targeting higher-income taxpayers, the use of phase-outs to increase progressivity only affects those who would otherwise be entitled to existing preferences. For example, Congress encourages retirement savings through the tax system; however, higher-income taxpayers do not receive the same encouragement as

---

[60]   IRS, QUALIFYING CHILD OF MORE THAN ONE PERSON, AGI AND TIEBREAKER RULES, https://www.eitc.irs.gov/tax-preparer-toolkit/faqs/tiebreakers/qualifying-child-of-more-than-one-person-agi-and-tiebreaker (last visited Sept. 27, 2017).

[61]   JOINT COMM. TAX'N, JCX–3–17, ESTIMATES FOR FEDERAL TAX EXPENDITURES FOR FISCAL YEARS 2016–2020, at 37 (2017).

middle-income taxpayers.[62] Thus, phase-outs are not an across the board tax increase and operate to increase the taxes of those who are engaging in the socially beneficial behavior or with the hardships or costs that Congress has chosen to recognize. This targeting of tax increase might raise revenue but at the cost of discouraging otherwise privileged behavior or penalizing otherwise compensated loss.

For example, before 2018, personal exemptions and most itemized deductions, a subset of deductions that are available in lieu of the standard deduction for taxpayers with significant specified expenses, such as charitable contributions, home mortgage interest, and state and local taxes, all phased out for higher-income taxpayers. The Pease limitation on these deductions, named after former congressman Donald Pease (D-OH), eliminated many of these deductions for wealthy taxpayers.[63] About one-third of taxpayers itemize their deductions and, of those, about 13% had to calculate the Pease reduction.[64] However, certain specified below-the-line deductions, such as the deduction for medical expenses, were carved out of the phase-out, increasing their tax value but also the system's complexity.

Congress could be acting according to many theories when adopting phase-outs. First, phase-outs contain a provision's cost. If only a limited amount of money can be spent, targeting the benefit to taxpayers who would otherwise need assistance may make financial sense. In the process, phase-outs reduce the opportunity for tax gamesmanship by wealthier taxpayers who are better able to change their behavior to minimize their taxes.

Operating largely as a surtax, phase-outs have also proven less politically objectionable than a tax rate increase. Theoretically, hiding tax increases for the wealthy is no different than hiding sin taxes and payroll taxes that disproportionately affect the poor. If Congress needs to raise more revenue and is unable to do so through higher tax rates, phasing out benefits contains the cost of a preference while targeting the preference to low-income taxpayers.

Additionally, Congress might expect high-income taxpayers to undertake a favored behavior without needing a financial incentive. If the wealthy are, in fact, savvy, the phase-out makes good financial sense overall. Of all groups in society, high-income taxpayers can provide for their own livelihoods, educations, and retirements. They

---

[62]　For more on retirement savings, see Chapter 17.01(e).

[63]　I.R.C. § 68.

[64]　THOMAS HUNGERFORD, CONG. RESEARCH SERV., R4196, DEFICIT REDUCTION: THE ECONOMIC AND TAX REVENUE EFFECTS OF THE PERSONAL EXEMPTION PHASEOUT (PEP) AND THE LIMITATION ON THE ITEMIZED DEDUCTIONS (PEASE) 6–7 (2013).

have the financial means and, generally, the acumen to act in ways Congress thinks is long-term economically rational. The system also provides for those wealthy who fail to do so, but only once they deplete their own incomes and wealth.

On the other hand, taxpayers may not fully understand how or why benefits are reduced through phase-outs. Therefore, they may not adjust their behavior in economically rational ways in response to congressional limits. Although general phase-outs tied to income levels operate as a surtax, specific phase-outs reduce the benefit of the activity, so that the wealthy may undertake an activity expecting a tax benefit they cannot claim. Perhaps worse, they may change the market for everyone by assuming tax results that do not exist. For example, taxpayers may buy a home or price homes assuming a mortgage interest deduction they will not claim. This complication is made worse because Congress frequently changes these provisions. Although a problem for tax preferences generally, the lack of assurance where a phase-out will fall should change marginal behavior.

Phase-outs also add other complexities to the Internal Revenue Code and the administration of the Code. Phase-outs are not uniform and often require different formulas for determining when the phase-out is reached; some benefits phase down while others phase out completely; some are indexed for inflation and some are not. Some phase-outs reduce credits, thus having the same tax effect for all affected taxpayers. Others reduce deductions, in which case their effect depends on the taxpayer's marginal tax rate: the higher the rate, the greater the loss. Many contain significant marriage penalties or bonuses because the phase-out range for married couples is less than twice that of single filers. In addition to taxpayers' difficulty in fully appreciating the incentive effects intended by Congress, all of this complexity makes compliance difficult for taxpayers and administration difficult for the IRS.

Within the complexity, taxpayers have clusters of lost preferences. Some phase-outs are triggered by roughly the same threshold amount, causing taxpayers to lose multiple tax benefits at the same time. Additionally, some phase-outs, like the deduction for higher education, have pronounced cliffs, which means the tax benefit is reduced in large increments when a taxpayer's income exceeds a threshold. These effects should impact a taxpayer's choice between work and leisure and their incentive to engage in tax planning to avoid the phase-outs.

Finally, phase-outs may inequitably fall on a small subset of wealthy taxpayers. Although by definition these are wealthier taxpayers, that a subgroup may be selectively punished violates norms of horizontal equity. Moreover, Congress may not be fully aware of the potentially narrow impact of certain phase-outs. For example, in 2013, 45% of the taxpayers who had to calculate the personal exemption phase-out claimed exemptions for dependents.[65] Of this 45%, about half had their tax liability affected by the exemption phase-out; the other half were unaffected primarily because of the alternative minimum tax. Of all the taxpayers affected by the exemption phase-out, each taxpayer with no dependent exemptions was projected to pay $1,400 more in taxes; each taxpayer with dependent exemptions was projected to pay $4,900 more in taxes.[66] Consequently, people with dependents paid a large share of the $9 billion raised from the phase-out of exemptions, and Congress may not have intended this effect.

Thus, not all wealthy taxpayers are affected evenly by phase-outs and phase-downs. Phase-outs and phase-downs affect those within an income band because once preferences phase down to $0, the surtax no longer applies because the higher rate prevails. The level of income at which this occurs depends on the particular phase-out. For income above the phase-out, any surtax declines as a percentage of income and makes the impact of the phase-out less relevant to the affected taxpayer.

(d) Alternative Minimum Tax

Individual taxpayers at the higher end of the income spectrum are also generally subject to the alternative minimum tax (AMT).[67] Congress enacted this second tax calculation intending to affect wealthy taxpayers. The AMT is close to a flat tax because there are only two brackets with 26% and 28% rates on income above a larger exemption than applies for the regular income tax. To raise revenue, the AMT taxes a larger tax base by denying many deductions that were not phased out under the regular income tax. In 2017, the AMT was estimated to raise $38 billion, or 2.5% of individual income tax revenue, from approximately 4 million taxpayers.[68] For 2018 through 2025, the AMT exemption has been raised significantly, to $109,400 for married taxpayers filing a joint return and the phase-out threshold increased to $1 million for these taxpayers. Therefore, many fewer taxpayers should be subject to the tax, at an expected cost of $637 billion between 2018 and 2027.

---

[65]   *Id.*

[66]   *Id.*, at 9–10.

[67]   I.R.C. §§ 55–58. A 20% corporate AMT was repealed in 2017.

[68]   TAX POL'Y CTR, HOW MUCH REVENUE DOES THE AMT RAISE?, http://www. taxpolicycenter.org/briefing-book/how-much-revenue-does-amt-raise (last visited Sept. 27, 2017).

Congress enacted the AMT in 1969 largely because a group of 155 millionaires were front-page news of the *New York Times* for not paying any federal income tax.[69] It was widely believed that wealthy taxpayers were using tax preferences to unfairly reduce their tax obligations. Therefore, Congress sought "to ensure that no taxpayer with substantial economic income can avoid significant tax liability by using exclusions, deductions, and credits."[70]

Despite Congress's narrow focus, the AMT applies to anyone for whom the elimination of targeted preferences applies. The Klaassens learned this the hard way.[71] In 1995, the family of twelve had $83,056.42 of adjusted gross income and did not calculate their AMT. Following an audit, the couple was held liable for $1,085.43 pursuant to the AMT and that liability was upheld through the Tenth Circuit. The Klaassens were taxed because their personal exemptions, state and local tax deductions, medical expense deductions, interest deductions, and charitable contribution deductions were disallowed under the AMT.

Under the AMT, no deduction is allowed for state and local taxes; the standard deduction and personal exemptions are eliminated; and certain stock options are taxed as realized even if they are not. Accelerated depreciation deductions must often be recalculated and other add-ons must be made. Therefore, those in high tax states, with many dependents, large charitable donations, and many deductible (but not trade or business) expenses might find themselves unexpectedly hit by the AMT. Perhaps worse, they may be subject to AMT under-withholding penalties because withholding is tied to regular income tax liabilities.

The number of taxpayers unexpectedly hit with the AMT was greatly reduced in 2012, and again in 2017, when Congress raised the exemptions.[72] Before 2012, Congress would annually or biannually enact a patch to raise the exemption from its 1969 level. Those patches were generally only good for a year, maybe two. This put millions of taxpayers at risk for the AMT each year.

Notwithstanding its revenue-raising potential, the AMT sometimes fails to tax the wealthy, its stated goal. Many people earning millions a year are not subject to the AMT for much of their income because, since 1986, the AMT has the same favorable capital gain rates as the regular income tax. Thus, for taxpayers whose income is primarily composed of capital gains, they retain favorable

---

[69]   *Treasury Secretary Warns of Taxpayers' Revolt*, N.Y. TIMES, Jan. 18, 1969, at 15.

[70]   H.Rep. No. 99–426, 99th Cong. 1st sess., pp. 305–06.

[71]   Klaassen v. Comm'r, 182 F.3d 932 (10th Cir. 1999).

[72]   I.R.C. § 55(d).

rates rather than apply the floor created by the AMT. In this way, the AMT taxes high wage earners but not the wealthy earning their income from investments.

Additionally, the AMT is extremely complex, entails relatively high effective tax rates, and is essentially a flat rate tax without public acceptance or understanding of these features. The AMT disproportionately burdens those living in high tax states or who have second mortgages, possibly incurred in part on the belief that the interest on these mortgages would be deductible. The tax may require taxpayers maintain a second set of records, such as different versions of depreciation or tax carry forwards. Some of these criticisms target specific parts of the AMT, while others take exception to its additive nature to the income tax. Instead of maintaining the AMT, it might be better to confront issues within the regular income tax.

Nevertheless, the AMT is a source of revenue from those most capable of paying the tax. The tax generally falls on those making more than $100,000 per year; therefore, raising revenue in a progressive way. To repeal the tax would require reducing expenditures or raising revenue from another source, and the revenue loss is not insubstantial. In 2016, the loss of revenue from repealing the individual AMT was estimated to be $412.8 billion over 10 years.[73]

(e) General Benefits with Specific Appeal

Unlike tax increases that may raise additional revenue from the wealthy, some tax benefits disproportionately benefit the wealthy. This favoritism may or may not be by congressional design. It is often impossible to tell whether a tax preference that has the effect of benefiting the wealthy had that as its congressional goal. With most preferences having limited legislative history, the history that exists often focuses on alternate objectives for the preference.

For example, the top 1% of income earners enjoy 68% of the benefit from the favorable capital gain rate.[74] This concentration of the benefit exists even though nothing structurally targets capital gain benefits to high-income taxpayers and capital gains face a higher tax rate at higher income levels. Nevertheless, the capital gain preference is estimated to cost the U.S. Treasury $690 billion over

---

[73]   Jim Nunns et al., *An Analysis of Donald Trump's Revised Tax Plan*, TAX POL'Y CTR. 7 (Oct. 18, 2016).

[74]   For more on the taxation of capital gains, see Chapter 7.03.

five years, and taxpayers with incomes in the bottom 80% will receive only 7% of that tax savings.[75]

The concentration of tax benefits may result from causes other than naked congressional greed. The concentration of preferences may result from wealthy taxpayers' desire or ability to achieve Congress's political objectives for preferences, such as increasing investment in capital assets. A secondary question then arises whether members of Congress, many of whom are wealthy taxpayers, are biased in establishing tax preferences consistent with their personal choices.

Concentration of benefits may also occur because of structural issues in the economy. For example, the capital gain preference may be concentrated because the wealthy can best afford capital assets or value them more. Similarly, the favorable tax treatment of hedge funds' and private equity funds' carried interest is only enjoyed by those in limited, and often highly paid, professions. A follow-up question is whether deeper changes to these payments need to be made than to the tax result.

Wealthier taxpayers are also the primary recipients of more innocuous tax benefits, such as the home mortgage interest deduction. This deduction cost $64 billion in 2017.[76] That reduction can only be enjoyed by the one-third of American taxpayers who itemize their deductions and produces greater tax savings for those in higher tax brackets. In 2008, about one-third of taxpayers making $50,000 to $75,000 claimed the mortgage interest deduction with an average tax savings of $179. Almost three-quarters of homeowners with incomes exceeding $200,000 claimed the deduction and received an annual tax benefit of more than $2,221.[77]

---

[75]   CONG. BUDGET OFFICE & JOINT COMM. TAX'N, THE DISTRIBUTION OF ASSET HOLDINGS AND CAPITAL GAINS 8 (2016).

[76]   U.S. TREAS. DEPT., TAX EXPENDITURES 23 (2016).

[77]   Dean Stansel & Anthony Randazzo, *Unmasking the Mortgage Interest Deduction*, REASON FOUNDATION POLICY STUDY 394 (2011).

Part E

USES OF TAXATION

Chapter 17

INCENTIVES AND
DISINCENTIVES

Table of Sections

As Congress taxes a particular activity or source of income, or refrains from taxing it, Congress changes activities' relative tax rates. Focusing on the relative rates, incentives and disincentives are shown to be the inverse of each other. Which label Congress adopts, and hence how it frames the tax, depends upon whether Congress seeks to privilege or punish a given activity, but the economic results are generally the same. Despite these frames having existed since the first tax, the impact of tax incentives and disincentives on the economy remains uncertain as their effectiveness at targeting specific behavior is often hard to quantify.

§ 17.01   Tax Incentives for Favored Activities

A tax incentive, or tax subsidy, can be broadly described as any tax provision that is not necessary to define net income and that is intended to encourage, recognize, or reward behavior. By most accounts, tax incentives include such things as accelerated depreciation deductions, the capital gain preference, child and dependent care credits, and student loan interest deductions. Tax incentives' structure varies: They can be exclusions from income, deductions, credits, preferential rates, or deferrals of taxation. As targeted tax reductions, they are not intended to be evenly distributed throughout the population but focus, instead, on particular activities or items. It has been popularly reported that the top 1% of income earners earn 17% of U.S. income before taxes but 27% of its tax breaks.[1]

(a) Taxing as Spending

The federal government can provide monetary assistance in many ways, including with direct payments, loans (possibly at below

---

[1]   Susanne Wooley, *How the IRS Helps the Rich Get Richer*, BLOOMBERG, Sep. 29, 2016.

market interest rates), guarantees of private loans, or tax incentives.[2] With each form, the government provides financial assistance to the recipient. Thus, tax incentives are comparable to government spending in that they are government subsidies. Tax incentives either reduce the taxes recipients owe or entitle recipients to a tax refund. The economic result is the same in that Congress favors certain behaviors over others for reasons unrelated to the tax system.

Granting taxpayers tax incentives is often politically popular. The federal government disperses twice as much revenue through tax incentives as it does through discretionary spending programs. Their use is wide ranging from family policies to environmental initiatives. For example, in 2009 the IRS issued notices explaining how to claim tax credits for coal facilities and gasification projects.[3] Professor Edward Kleinbard noted the odd paring of the Department of Energy and the IRS, a "bureaucratic odd couple," as joint evaluators of applications.[4]

However, not everyone recognizes the connection between targeted tax reduction and government spending. Tax incentives are not always salient, in that many people are unaware of incentives if they do not personally benefit and many people do not understand the incentives that they claim. Proponents of a particular tax incentive may rhetorically claim that the income which belongs to the taxpayer is simply being retained by the taxpayer. This argument can be politically useful as it utilizes the illusion that tax subsidies are not equivalent to government spending. Nonetheless, as a selective decrease in taxes rather than an across the board decrease, tax incentives have a disparate impact as between taxpayers.

Recognizing tax expenditures as a substitute for government spending frames taxation as taxpayer versus taxpayer in that a taxpayer's tax burden is examined comparatively with other taxpayers' burdens.[5] On the other hand, most people view taxation as taxpayer versus the government in that one taxpayer's burden is evaluated only as what that taxpayer pays or does not pay. Under the former framing, when one taxpayer is selectively relieved of taxation, other taxpayers are paying relatively more in taxes than the person relieved. In other words, tax reduction is not borne by an

---

[2]   Stanley S. Surrey & Paul R. McDaniel, *The Tax Expenditure Concept and the Budget Reform Act of 1974*, 17 B.C. L. REV. 679 (1976).

[3]   Notice 2009–23 and Notice 2009–24, 2009–16 I.R.B. 802, 817.

[4]   Edward Kleinbard, *The Congress Within the Congress*, 36 OHIO N. U.L. REV. 1, 2 (2010).

[5]   For more on fairness between taxpayers and as against the government, see Chapter 4.02.

amorphous government but by others who make up the deficit or face reduced spending. In this sense, not only is government revenue reduced but taxpayers in similar situations may no longer be taxed equally, possibly without the public's recognition of that fact.

The increased use of tax incentives has changed how many people pay taxes and what taxes people pay. In 2016, the Tax Policy Center reported that less than 56% of American households paid income taxes.[6] This frames the issue around the payment of tax and ignores the expansion of social spending, such as the ETIC and the child tax credit, through the tax system. In other words, a larger percentage would pay income tax but for having these taxes reduced to $0 because of tax incentives. The statement also ignores the payment of other federal taxes. As Congress increases the use of social welfare and economic stimulus policies through the income tax system, we should expect to see a smaller percentage of income taxpayers but a possible expansion of other tax burdens.

(b) Measuring Tax Incentives

Much like tax loopholes, what constitutes a tax incentive is in the eye of the beholder. Thus, although a broad conceptual sense of tax incentives is relatively easy to grasp, creating a list is difficult. The difficulty stems, in large part, from the lack of a generally accepted baseline against which incentives should be measured. For example, if the baseline is a comprehensive definition of income (such as the original Haig-Simons definition), anything not required for a broad-based, net income tax is a tax incentive. Therefore, deductions for 401(k) savings plans and child tax credits are tax incentives. On the other hand, if the proper baseline is a consumption tax, 401(k) deductions are not incentives but part of what makes the income tax more consumption-based; child tax credits would still be incentives. Thus, the baseline is critical to determining whether something is properly viewed as a tax incentive.

Despite the difficulty of defining tax incentives, a federal list is maintained. In 1968, Stanley Surrey as the first Assistant Secretary of Tax Policy laid the groundwork for the Tax Expenditure Budget when his book convinced many policymakers that anything funded with a tax incentive could be funded directly.[7] Six years later, Congress passed the Budget Act of 1974 to quantify the money spent in this way to improve its budgeting process.[8] When establishing the

---

[6]   Roberton C. Williams, *A Closer Look at Those Who Pay No Income or Payroll Taxes*, TAX POL'Y CTR, Jul. 11, 2016. For more on class issues in taxation, see Chapter 16.02.

[7]   STANLEY SURREY, PATHWAYS TO TAX REFORM (1968).

[8]   Budget Act of 1974, Act of July 12, 1974, Pub. L. No. 93–344, 88 Stat. 297.

tax expenditure budget, Congress adopted the term "tax expenditures" as deviations from the "normal income tax." However, the plan did not define a normal income tax. Despite this omission, the budget moved Congress towards equating tax funding with appropriations.

Since 1974, the CBO and the President annually present estimates of the revenue cost of existing tax expenditures. In practice, the JCT creates the list.[9] The list generally contains estimates for a rolling five years of the cost of over 150 tax expenditures. To make it onto the list, an expenditure must be estimated to cost more than a threshold of $50 million.

The list of tax expenditures is generally dominated by a big ten: The ten largest expenditures account for roughly two-thirds of the budgetary impact of all tax expenditures.[10] This means that they released from tax more than $900 billion or 5.7% of GNP in 2013 and are estimated to be over 8% in 2018.

Top 10 tax expenditures (estimates for 2016–2020 in billions)[11]	
$1,208.3	Exclusion from income of net pension contributions and earnings
$863.1	Exclusion from income of employer-sponsored health insurance
$677.7	Preferential rates on capital gains and dividends
$373.4	Earned income tax credit
$369.8	Itemized deduction for certain state and local taxes
$357.0	Itemized deduction for home mortgage interest payments
$313.4	Itemized deduction for charitable contributions
$270.5	Child tax credit
$213.8	Exclusion from income of a portion of Social Security and Railroad Retirement benefits

---

[9]   JOINT CTTE ON TAX'N, JCX–3–17, ESTIMATES OF FEDERAL TAX EXPENDITURES FOR FISCAL YEARS 2016–2020 (2017).

[10]   CONG. BUDGET OFFICE, THE DISTRIBUTION OF MAJOR TAX EXPENDITURES IN THE INDIVIDUAL INCOME TAX SYSTEM 1–2 (2013); CONG. BUDGET OFFICE, THE BUDGET AND ECONOMIC OUTLOOK: 2017 TO 2027, at 24 (2017).

[11]   JCX–3–17, *supra* note 9.

| $179.4 | Exclusion from income of capital gain on assets transferred at death |

Although the tax expenditure budget is maintained, its value in the budget process remains limited. First, tax expenditures are not expressly included in the annual budget but are assumed into the revenue baseline. Hence, revenue estimates include existing tax expenditures. This makes the tax expenditure budget purely informational; its value depends upon policymakers' recognition of its import.

That tax expenditures remain hidden as a baseline in budgeting privileges them over direct appropriations. Appropriations may be cut to balance the budget but tax expenditures must be legislated out of existence.[12] Therefore, tax subsidies are procedurally privileged over direct appropriations. The exclusion from budgetary restrictions makes the tax system a preferred method of funding new programs even if use of the tax system would otherwise be suboptimal.

Second, the tax expenditure budget has limited value in budgeting because the decision of which tax provisions are included in the tax expenditure budget is political, even if no one intends it to be. The Government Accountability Office (GAO) and the JCT have debated the proper criteria for classifying a provision as a tax expenditure, and neither has created a generally accepted definition.[13] The JCT references a "normal income tax structure" to determine what is a tax expenditure. Therefore, the JCT only considers the income tax, not excises or employment taxes. Additionally, provisions that have the purpose of "enforcing general tax rules, or to prevent the violation of other laws" are not treated as tax expenditures even if they result in a decreased tax burden. The GAO, on the other hand, lists provisions according to their intended purpose and monitors the success of expenditures based on the accomplishment of their purpose or net benefit to society.

Finally, to date, despite a movement toward dynamic scoring for other budget information, the government does not include in its measure of tax expenditures taxpayers' responses. Therefore, the government does not recognize that tax cuts may increase government revenue or indirectly reduce revenue. Instead, the focus is linearly on the cost of the provision in what taxpayers will not pay directly as a result. Coupled with this limitation is the budget's focus

---

[12]   For more on budgeting, see Chapter 18.01.

[13]   U.S. GOV'T ACCOUNTABILITY OFFICE, GAO–13–167SP, TAX EXPENDITURES (2013); JOINT CTTE TAX'N, JCX–15–11, BACKGROUND INFORMATION ON TAX EXPENDITURE ANALYSIS AND HISTORICAL SURVEY OF TAX EXPENDITURE ESTIMATES (2011).

on tax reduction with only incomplete information on penalties that increase tax revenue. Therefore, the tax expenditure budget is incomplete as an informational tool. For example, although incorporated into the estimate of the tax cost of losses, the budget does not differentiate the tax increase from limitations on the ability to deduct losses. Because the costs and the benefits are unlikely to flow to the same group of taxpayers, this information would be useful.

(c) Structural Choices Regarding Incentives

Tax incentives are little different than gifts from the government. Therefore, the government can structure them as it pleases unless the incentive discriminates against a protected group in a way that courts recognize as discriminatory.[14] Incentives are generally structured as deductions, favorable tax rates, exclusions from tax, or credits against tax. Not only does the choice of structure affect the amount of benefit a taxpayer receives, the structure also determines whether a particular tax incentive accomplishes its purpose. Thus, despite Congress's freedom in structuring tax incentives, some structures may be more effective at accomplishing Congress's objectives.

Deductions have an indirect effect on the amount of taxes that are owed. They reduce the amount of taxable income to which tax rates are applied, which, in turn, determines the amount of tax owed. For example, the deduction for home mortgage interest reduces a homeowner's income that is subject to tax so that a smaller amount is multiplied by the tax rate.[15] Because the value of deductions depends upon a taxpayer's tax rate, deductions of the same face value vary among taxpayers in the amount they decrease taxes. To target deductions for particular purposes, deductions can be complex in structure, either limiting who can claim a deduction or what warrants a deduction.

As a simplified example, Alice, a 50% tax bracket taxpayer, has $100,000 of income. For Alice, a $1,000 deduction is worth the tax owed without the deduction ($100,000 times the 50% bracket, or $50,000) minus the tax owed with the deduction ($100,000 minus $1,000, or $99,000, times the 50% rate bracket, or $49,500). The result is that the $1,000 deduction decreases the amount Alice owes by $500.

Compare Alice to Bert, a 20% tax bracket taxpayer, with $50,000 of income. For Bert, a $1,000 deduction is worth the tax owed without the deduction ($50,000 times the 20% bracket, or $10,000) minus the

---

[14]   White v. U.S., 305 U.S. 281 (1938).

[15]   For more on deductions, see Chapter 7.01(c).

tax owed with the deduction ($50,000 minus $1,000, or $49,000, times the 20% rate bracket, or $9,800). The result is that the $1,000 deduction decreases the amount Bert owes by $200.

Finally, Candice, a 10% tax bracket taxpayer, has $500 of income. For Candice, a $1,000 deduction is worth only $50 because she reduces her taxes owed from $50 without the deduction ($500 times 10%, or $50) to $0 with the deduction ($500 minus $1,000, which can only be brought down to $0, times 10%). The result is that the $1,000 deduction has significantly less value to Candice than to Alice or Bert.

This example demonstrates that a deduction (and similarly an exclusion or preferential tax rate) is worth more to a higher tax bracket taxpayer. This is an upside-down subsidy in that wealthier taxpayers receive more benefit than low-income taxpayers. Because deductions and exclusions are tied to taxable income, the amount of benefit increases with the recipient's income that is subject to higher progressive tax rates. On the other hand, the reduced amount of income reflects real changes in the taxpayer's wealth that Congress chooses to tax.

Similar to a deduction, an exclusion from income of a payment or benefit is an indirect reduction of the taxes owed; preferential tax rates are only slightly more direct tax reductions. With an exclusion, Congress provides that certain income is simply not reportable to, or taxable by, the government. With preferential rates, Congress provides that the income is taxed less than other types of income. Consequently, these benefits only benefit those who would otherwise owe tax. For example, the exclusion of employer-provided frequent flyer miles only matter if the value of the miles, coupled with the taxpayer's other income, would be taxable. Recipients of these benefits, particularly exclusions, also benefit in that they have few filing obligations to claim the benefit. They also tend to be simpler provisions and easier for taxpayers to understand. For example, taxpayers do not have to keep track of or report frequent flyer miles that are not taxable.

Unlike deductions, exclusions, and preferential rates, credits directly reduce the amount of tax that is owed. After taxpayers calculate their initial amount of tax owed (in other words, they apply their tax rates to their taxable income), they reduce that amount by any allowable tax credits. For example, a parent can subtract the child tax credit from their taxes due. As a direct reduction of the tax owed, in most instances the value of a credit is equal among recipients.

Affecting credits' value for low-income taxpayers is whether the credit is nonrefundable or refundable. Nonrefundable tax credits reduce a taxpayer's tax liability; however, they cannot reduce tax liability below $0. If a taxpayer owes no tax, the taxpayer receives no benefit from being eligible for a nonrefundable credit. Alternatively, refundable credits can reduce a taxpayer's liability below $0 so that, if the taxpayer owes no more tax for a taxable year, the amount of any excess credit is refunded to the taxpayer. The taxpayer receives a refund for a part or full amount of any remaining refundable credit.

Because credits are not a taxpayer's right but Congress's largess, Congress can impose almost limitless restrictions on credits and the amount that can be refunded. As a result, refundability varies significantly among credits. Only fully refundable credits are worth the same in nominal amounts to all taxpayers. If credits are not refundable, they provide no benefit to low-income taxpayers who owe no tax due to other tax credits or insufficient income.

In the above example, if instead of a deduction there was a $1,000 credit, the credit would reduce Alice's tax owed from $50,000 to $49,000, or by $1,000, and would reduce Bert's tax owed from $10,000 to $9,000, or by $1,000. The value of the $1,000 credit to Candice depends upon whether the credit is refundable. If the credit is not refundable, the credit is worth only $50 to Candice because she only owes $50 in tax. If the credit is fully refundable, it is worth $1,000 to Candice, as it is to the other taxpayers. If the credit is partially refundable, it is worth some amount between the $50 tax reduction and the full $1,000 credit. Thus, unlike a deduction that is not worth the same to all taxpayers, a credit can be worth the same to all taxpayers; however, this equivalence depends upon the type of credit.

Especially with a refundable feature, credits can be viewed as differing for taxpayers in different income brackets. As a flat nominal amount they comprise a larger percentage of low-income taxpayers' income. Therefore, unlike deductions, exclusions, or favorable rates, credits may be progressive. As a percentage of income the refundable credit is worth more to the low-income taxpayer ($1,000 of Candice's $500 income is 200%) than it is to high-income taxpayers ($1,000 of Bert's $50,000 of income is 2% and $1,000 of Alice's $100,000 income is 1%). Policymakers can target benefits even more precisely to low-income taxpayers by phasing out credits for high-income taxpayers. To the extent that the political goal is to give more benefit to low-income taxpayers, combining the credit structure and phasing it out is an effective means.

Because deductions and credits have a different impact on taxpayers of different income levels, a knowledgeable Congress will choose which to use depending upon who it seeks to target with tax reduction. Additionally, when choosing a structure, Congress must remember the relative costs of different structures and their potential political spin. A $1,000 deduction and a $1,000 credit would not cost the same amount of government revenue. A credit of the same face value as a deduction would decrease tax revenues significantly more because the credit decreases taxes dollar for dollar. Deductions only decrease revenue by the tax rate times the deduction amount. Therefore, credits in smaller nominal amounts than deductions produce the same net government expenditure and the same tax savings. Nonetheless, the different amounts produce different optics and may be interpreted as different values by the public.

In addition to the type of incentive, Congress must consider the period of time for which the incentive will operate. Some incentives are long-term additions to the Code, like the home mortgage interest deduction or the charitable contributions deduction. Other tax incentives lapse, requiring Congress renew them after a year or so. The former may become entrenched and difficult to repeal even if their justification no longer exists; the latter may make it difficult for taxpayers to respond to their short-term incentive effects. For example, tax incentives that require an initial investment, such as the first time homebuyer credit, requires an initial savings that may take years to accumulate.

Also, Congress must decide whether the incentive will be a one-time payment or a periodic subsidy to taxpayers. The form depends upon Congress's larger objective; different periodization produce different taxpayer responses. A periodic subsidy might produce greater long-term changes in behavior but, to the extent the payments are smaller because spread over time, they may have less initial power to overcome taxpayers' inertia. To make these choices even more difficult, they are part of larger budgetary metrics and cannot be made in the abstract.

(d) Effectiveness of Tax Incentives

Although it may be difficult for the public to determine many tax provisions' underlying purposes, the purpose of a tax incentive is more obviously to reward or change particular behavior. Congress is effectively paying for a result it desires. If the public does not respond by changing or by continuing its behavior, the provision fails. Although many incentives are operated through the tax system, use of the tax system to distribute subsidies may not be the best method to achieve Congress's desired objective. A difficulty for policymakers is the inability to quantify whether changes in behavior directly result from a tax incentive.

When evaluating an incentive's effectiveness, effectiveness may include an analysis of the incentive's efficiency. If so, the answer will change depending upon how one defines efficiency.[16] Tax incentives cannot be efficient when efficiency is defined as not altering taxpayer behavior, unless it corrects a market failure. In other instances, Congress is purposefully tipping the scales in taxpayer choices. Most economists worry that influencing taxpayer choices in this way results in a bad allocation of resources.

In a different sense, however, tax expenditures may be efficient at accomplishing their congressional objective by costing less government revenue than other means to the same end. Efficiency in this latter sense is difficult or impossible to measure. To measure whether behavior is changed, it is necessary to estimate what behavior would be without the tax provision.

Application of economic theory to tax incentives is made harder because it is impossible to know from the label alone if a tax incentive distorts the market or corrects for a market failure. At times Congress favors activities or products to reward their owners simply because it likes the activity or the taxpayer and for no other reason. At other times, Congress responds to an inefficient provision of goods and services, possibly as a result of information asymmetries or the existence of public goods or externalities. In this latter context, tax incentives can be used to help reduce these market failures. Understanding this purpose helps in the evaluation of the incentive.

(i)   Choice of Tax System

To evaluate a tax incentive, Congress can restrict its evaluation to the incentive itself or include the incentive's impact on the tax system as a whole. More likely Congress chooses a hybrid approach whereby policies are considered on their own merits, including some thought of their administration. However, incentives cannot be completely isolated when first considered by Congress because of their budget effects. A policy choice's budget effects may determine its viability but often does not determine whether the policy is administered through the tax system or by some other agency. The choice of who administers a particular policy is the result of political forces rather than an unalterable feature flowing from a policy's labeling.

According to some, framing a policy as a tax expenditure rather than direct spending is a question of institutional design that should

---

16   For more on efficiency, see Chapter 4.01(b).

focus on each particular policy as it arises. Professors David Weisbach and Jacob Nussim note that, because there is no normative tax base, the real issue is how best to meet the needs of the proposed program.[17] This approach considers that any burden that operating the incentive puts on the tax system is a cost to be weighed in the choice of structure.

Similarly, Professor Edward Zelinsky argues in favor of legislating through the tax process, which favors use of tax incentives.[18] He contends that tax committees and tax agencies are more competitive and more visible than those who administer spending programs. This heightened competitiveness exists because tax institutions have more numerous and diverse constituencies than specialized committees. As a result of a lack of competing interests, specialized committees may more easily become captured by those they are regulating than may tax committees. Therefore, the Madisonian ideal of diverse and conflicting groups fighting it out in the government is better secured in the tax code.

However, it is possible that interest groups have already captured the tax system, so Zelinksy's competitive ideal is a myth. Moreover, if policymakers treat the tax system as a bottomless bag from which to dispense treats, no one has to compete for their attention. Balanced budget restrictions may minimize this result; however, with large legislative bills a single provision may receive little attention.

Consider one particularly notorious tax expenditure: the Louis B. Mayer amendment.[19] As part of the second restatement of the Internal Revenue Code, Mayer received a personalized tax perk estimated to have saved him $2 million in taxes in 1954, or over $18.4 million in 2018 dollars. The savings was effectively on his future compensation. Mayer had been the studio executive of MGM until he was ousted from power in 1951, although he remained an employee. In 1954, Congress enacted a provision to the revised Code believed to apply to only two people, Mayer and one other executive at MGM. The new provision, although framed in general terms, provided capital gain tax rates rather than ordinary income rates for amounts he, as an employee of more than twenty years, received from releasing his rights to a percentage of MGM's future profits. To limit the applicability of the provision, a claimant's contract for future profits had to have been in effect for at least twelve years.

---

[17]   David Weisbach & Jacob Nussim, *The Integration of Tax and Spending Programs*, 113 YALE L.J. 955 (2004).

[18]   Edward Zelinsky, *James Madison and Public Choice at Gucci Gulch*, 102 YALE L.J. 1165 (1993).

[19]   I.R.C. § 1240 (1954). Discussed in SURREY, *supra* note 6, at 1147, n4.

A more recent example of the moneybags approach has been the repeated extension of a 2004 special provision permitting NASCAR racetrack owners to deduct depreciation on their tracks over a seven-year period.[20] The standard deduction period is 39 years for nonresidential property and 15 years for improvements of that property, such as fences and roads. By decreasing the deduction period, track owners may claim larger deductions and reduce their income subject to tax in earlier years. This narrowly tailored tax incentive costs the government an estimated $78 million over ten years.

By structuring government benefits as tax incentives, their costs will always be hard to predict accurately because it is hard to know how effective incentives will be at changing behavior. These expenditures are intended to reward or alter taxpayer behavior, but it is impossible to know how many taxpayers will respond as desired. And it takes time for those costs to be determined, unlike with a rolling application process for appropriations. The reporting period is the end of the tax year; therefore, revenue costs are unknowable for significant periods after the law is in force. Consequently, tax incentives are generally open-ended costs that risk unpredictable amounts of revenue in a structurally hidden way.

However, this revenue cost is exactly what is intended. Tax incentives should cost more revenue the more successful they are. Moreover, it is possible tax incentives are less expensive than administering a direct appropriations program for the same goal. They may also change behavior with less government interference on taxpayers. Of course, tax expenditures do not necessarily have to demand less oversight or compliance than direct spending. Congress could create tax expenditures with similar compliance requirements as direct spending programs. Nevertheless, in practice Congress tends to structure tax incentives with less restrictive procedures for claiming the benefit.

Less supervision of tax incentives may stem from the IRS's own operational limitations even more than congressional design. For example, the IRS has a limited enforcement budget and most of its oversight is retroactive rather than before the grant of benefits. Even in its retroactive review, the IRS has a limited ability to procure the information needed to evaluate a taxpayer's qualification for many expenditures without an extensive audit.[21] Consequently, placement

---

[20]   Robert Pear & Mary Pilon, *Auto Racetrack Owners Keep Coveted Tax Break*, N.Y. TIMES, Jan. 4, 2013.

[21]   The IRS tried a pre-certification program for the EITC, but it has been discontinued. For more on pre-certification, see Lawrence Zelenak, *Tax or Welfare? The Administration of the Earned Income Tax Credit*, 52 UCLA L. REV. 1867 (2005).

of government spending in the tax code generally necessitates a lesser ability to audit compliance with the rules that are enacted.

(ii) Incentives as Part of the Tax System

As parts of the Internal Revenue Code, tax incentives are part of the larger tax system. Widespread use of tax incentives may compromise the tax system's primary function: raising government revenue. Tax incentives complicate the Code and increase the IRS's policing functions. Adding far-reaching provisions that are hard to police increases the IRS's role in society, but Congress may enact these provisions without increasing the IRS's budget. Moreover, because tax incentives reduce revenue, Congress often enacts complicated rules to contain their cost. Implementing these dense provisions, the IRS must identify taxpayer errors and fraud. Thus, despite calls to reduce tax complexity, tax incentives work in the opposite direction. Perhaps worse, they force the IRS to administer substantive programs over which it has no particular expertise, diverting attention from its primary task of fairly raising revenue.

For example, the first-time homebuyer credit, available between 2008 and 2010, was worth up to $8,000 for the purchase of a home but resulted in significant fraud that was difficult for the IRS to detect.[22] The Treasury Inspector General for Tax Administration estimated that the IRS issued at least $513 million in erroneous refunds as a result of the credit.[23] Problems included claims by single incarcerated prisoners (who are unable to purchase a home), purchases completed before the credit was enacted, and multiple claims for the same house. Even IRS employees were found to have made fraudulent claims. Congress had estimated that the credit would cost $13.6 billion and the JCT had estimated it would cost $4.3 billion; however, the credit ended up costing $22 billion.[24]

(iii) Repealing a Provision

Tax incentives may be particularly hard to repeal even if the incentive's original justification no longer exists. Because tax incentives are included in budgetary baselines, their cost is hidden relative to direct appropriations. Therefore, the political initiative necessary to repeal an incentive is greater than cutting the funding for something that requires annual appropriations. The costs of repeal are also concentrated, potentially motivating recipients to

---

[22] I.R.C. § 36.

[23] U.S. TREAS. INSPECTOR GENERAL FOR TAX ADMIN., 2011–41–35, ADMINISTRATION OF THE FIRST-TIME HOMEBUYER CREDIT INDICATES A NEED FOR IMPROVED CONTROLS OVER REFUNDABLE CREDITS (2011).

[24] GOV'T ACCOUNTABILITY OFFICE, GAO–10–1025R, USAGE AND SELECTED ANALYSIS OF THE FIRST-TIME HOMEBUYER CREDIT (2010).

fight for the incentives' retention. To the extent that people respond as Congress wanted but no longer receive the benefit, people risk being stuck in behavior that is suboptimal for themselves without the tax savings. The difficulty and cost of repeal should be considered when a tax incentive is first enacted because understanding that a benefit is likely to become entrenched should affect estimates of its long-term cost.

Many of those who would be negatively affected by repeal may not have directly benefited from a longstanding tax incentive. These taxpayers may have come to a market with prices that include the value of the preference. For example, tax expenditures favoring home ownership, especially the home mortgage interest deduction, are reflected in the price of housing because they lower homeownership's after-tax cost.[25] In other words, houses today likely cost more than they would without the existence of tax benefits. As a perverse result, most current homeowners, even those that claim the deduction, benefit little from these current tax expenditures; owners at the time the deduction was enacted or those building new homes reap the benefit of the expenditure by charging more on the sale of their homes. Nevertheless, all homebuyers pay for the benefit in higher home prices. Eliminating the benefit would likely reduce home prices and would hurt those selling homes even if they had not benefited from the incentive.

Second, eliminating established tax expenditures may disrupt markets, even if the expenditure itself creates economic distortion. For example, in 1981, Congress created a large tax incentive for holders of real estate by accelerating depreciation.[26] Thereafter, owners of buildings were able to deduct depreciation faster than they had before, and those deductions could offset other income. Taxpayers who owned real estate in 1981 enjoyed windfalls of these deductions, and others who had previously not invested in real estate became attracted to it. The result was a building boom driven by tax savings.

Too much building resulted from this accelerated depreciation but the provisions' repeal was not a perfect solution. With the benefit, people left empty buildings throughout the country, built for tax benefits and not market need. Congress responded by limiting the ability to claim the depreciation deductions by enacting the passive activity loss rules.[27] These rules prevented most taxpayers from using these depreciation deductions to offset their earned income.

---

[25]   Margery Austin Turner et al., *How Would Reforming the Mortgage Interest Deduction Affect the Housing Market?*, URBAN INSTITUTE (2013).

[26]   Economic Recovery Tax Act of 1981, sec. 201, Pub. L. No. 97–34, 95 Stat. 172.

[27]   I.R.C. § 469. For more on the passive activity loss rules, see Chapter 5.01(e).

Consequently, the value to investors of commercial real estate declined. As investors no longer flocked to commercial real estate investments, real estate prices declined, and people could no longer service their mortgages. This partly caused the savings and loan (S&L) crisis because many S&Ls had invested heavily in commercial real estate mortgages.[28]

(e) Savings Plans

A long-standing and economically important group of tax incentives favors savings. Backed by a concern that Americans do not save enough, Congress has enacted several tax-preferred savings plans. Savings plans target a wide range of activities, from retirement to education to healthcare.[29] There are dozens of these different plans. Tax-preferred plans are intended to negate the disincentive to saving caused by the income tax taxing wages and then taxing the earnings on savings. This combined tax decreases the return to saving. That there are so many plans means that efficient savers must navigate their different, often complicated, eligibility, contribution, and distribution rules.

Much of American savings are in tax-preferred retirement plans. Since Congress first enacted Individual Retirement Accounts (IRAs) in 1974 and the Treasury Department promulgated the 401(k) regulations in 1981, they have become major sources of retirement savings. According to one estimate, 70% of retirement savings are in IRAs, self-employed plans, and employer-based defined contribution plans for those who have such plans, which is almost 50% across all demographic groups.[30] However, these accounts compose only 11.5% of their holders' total wealth.[31]

Globally most governments use tax incentives to encourage savings. One pre-recession study found that the U.S.'s savings rate is average at about 25 cents per dollar earned and about 1.1% of GDP.[32] To encourage these savings, these plans cost a lot in terms of government revenue. The JCT estimates that over a five-year period they cost $1.2 trillion.[33] One hope is that savings will grow the

---

[28]   Discussed in Robert S. McIntyre, *The Hidden Entitlements: 1. Accelerated Depreciation*, CITIZENS FOR TAX JUSTICE (1996).

[29]   For more on education savings plans, see Chapter 13.02(c).

[30]   Craig Copeland, *Individual Account Retirement Accounts*, EMPLOYEE BENEFIT RESEARCH INST. ISSUE BRIEF NO. 406 (2013).

[31]   James Poterba et al., *The Composition and Drawdown of Wealth in Retirement?*, 25 J. ECON. PERSP. 95 (2011).

[32]   Kwang-Yeol Yoo & Alain de Serres, *Tax Treatment of Private Pension Savings in OECO Countries and the Next Tax Cost Per Unit of Contribution to Tax-Favoured Schemes*, OECD ECON. STUD. NO. 39 (2004).

[33]   JCX–3–17, *supra* note 8.

economy and counterbalance the lost revenue. The revenue that is lost to the government is disproportionately from sophisticated or wealthy savers rather than low-income taxpayers less likely to save for their retirement. The CBO found that two-thirds of the incentive goes to the top fifth of income earners.[34]

Despite their cost and Congress's intent, the little evidence available shows that savings incentives have minimal success at increasing savings. One study based on experience in Denmark found that each dollar of spending on tax-preferred savings generated only one cent in new savings.[35] In part this was because the study found that 85% of savers were passive with respect to tax incentives and tax savings. Another study found that people respond in small, but statistically significant, ways to changes in the after-tax price of contributing.[36] But some people who respond simply shift amounts they would otherwise save into more tax-preferred options.

Retirement savings plans in particular are structured to encourage long-term investing and take away some of savers' choices. Their tax incentives for savings are coupled with penalties on taxpayers who withdraw their savings before retirement. For example, if taxpayers withdraw the funds in an IRA for any purpose that is not legislatively sanctioned before they reach the eligible age for distribution (age 59½), the taxpayer owes a 10% penalty on the income portion of the early distribution in addition to the regular tax owed on the total distribution. There are statutory exceptions that allow taxpayers to withdraw funds without the penalty but not without the ordinary tax. For example, taxpayers can withdraw funds without penalty because of disabilities and certain hardships.

Despite widespread use of tax-preferred savings plans, it is unknown the extent to which investors meaningfully differentiate between the plan options. Most people do not fully understand their choices in plans; and many people do not respond rationally to the tax incentives or their accompanying penalties for violating the rules. For those who use retirement savings accounts, one estimate found that approximately 18.5% of gross distributions in any given year were to recipients before they reached age 55. Of these, 21% was subjected to a penalty for doing so.[37]

---

[34]   CONG. BUDGET OFFICE, THE DISTRIBUTION OF MAJOR TAX EXPENDITURES IN THE INDIVIDUAL TAX SYSTEM (2013).

[35]   Raj Chetty et al., *Active vs. Passive Decisions and Crowd-Out in Retirement Savings Accounts*, 129 Q. J. OF ECON. 1141 (2014).

[36]   Bradley Heim & Ithai Lurie, *The Effect of Recent Tax Changes on Tax-Preferred Saving Behavior*, 65 NAT'L TAX J. 283 (2012).

[37]   Robert Argento et al., *Early Withdrawals from Retirement Accounts During the Great Recession*, 33 CONTEMPORARY ECON. POL'Y 1 (2015).

Some confusion exists because of the many options that are available. Consider, for example, Roth and regular IRAs.[38] Both accounts provide investors the advantage of the principal growing tax-free until distribution. However, regular IRA contributions are made with tax deductible dollars and appreciation is taxed on distribution whereas Roth IRA contributions are made with already taxed money and then appreciation is not taxed on distribution. These differences can have no effect or profound economic effects depending upon a taxpayer's relative tax rates at contribution and distribution.

Thus, the choice between a regular and a Roth IRA generally depends upon a taxpayer's expected rate of return and whether the taxpayer expects applicable tax rates at the time of the contribution to be higher or lower than at the time of the distribution. If the tax rate is higher at the time of contribution, it generally makes more sense to contribute to a regular IRA and postpone taxation until the taxpayer is in a lower tax bracket. Alternatively, if the taxpayer expects to have a higher rate at the time of the distribution than contribution, it generally makes sense to choose a Roth IRA and pay the tax upfront.

The breadth of choices requires taxpayers to guesstimate their future tax situations, perhaps decades in advance. Relative tax rates at the time of the investment and the time of distributions can vary depending both on a person's earnings and congressional action so people cannot know the rates with certainty. Uncertainty often empowers those in the financial industry. Those who seek advice from financial experts may find that their experts are conflicted because of their own money-making agenda. Receiving advice from sources that are conflicted because of their fee and commission structures costs investors roughly 1% lower returns each year.[39] Others who save through work-based plans give employers a large say in the design of their retirement savings, despite employers' motivation being to attract workers and not their retirement.[40] There is a risk that employers will magnify workers' myopia and other behavioral problems. The existence of uncertainty and choice leads some people to save less for retirement. Overwhelmed, they do not save for fear of making the wrong choice.

---

[38]   There are many varieties of IRAs. For example, there is the SEP-IRA (simplified employee pension) in § 408(k) and SIMPLE IRAs (savings incentive match plan for employees of small employers) in § 408(p).

[39]   COUNCIL OF ECON. ADVISERS, THE EFFECTS OF CONFLICTED ECONOMIC ADVICE ON RETIREMENT SAVINGS (2015).

[40]   Ryan Bubb et al., *A Behavioral Contract Theory Perspective on Retirement Savings*, 47 CONN. L. REV. 1317 (2015).

Not all are overwhelmed, and some taxpayers have learned to exploit these choices to their advantage. In particular, some use IRAs to shelter large amounts of economic growth from taxation, as illustrated by 2012 Republican presidential candidate Mitt Romney's $102 million IRA.[41] More recently, Max Levchin, co-founder of PayPal, invested in Yelp through a Roth IRA.[42] Wealthy investors can invest low value assets, such as shares in a private equity fund or privately held company, in the hopes that the shares will dramatically increase in value. If planned appropriately, that appreciation is never subject to income tax. Although not consistent with the intent of these retirement plans, these strategies currently fit within the law.

§ 17.02   Tax Penalties to Discourage Behavior

It is a necessary consequence of tax preferences that non-preferred items or activities are relatively more heavily taxed. This lack of preference is, in effect, a penalty for not being something Congress prefers. Additionally, there are more explicit deterrents in the tax system.[43] These occur when Congress uses the tax system to punish behavior. These punishments remain relatively rare but are likely to grow as more social policies are deployed through the tax system. This chapter focuses on three specific tax penalties: the healthcare mandate, sin taxes, and carbon taxes. These taxes are to discourage taxed behavior and, in some cases, to encourage alternative behavior. To date, the cost of relative tax burdens is not quantified.

(a)   Use as Punishment

Tax incentives are carrots to entice taxpayers into the desired behavior; tax penalties are sticks to discourage them. The best use of carrots and sticks depends, in large part, on one's measure of human psychology and people's response to the obligation to pay taxes. Are taxpayers customers of the government who should be wooed with rewards or is there a Spartan obligation to comply with congressional demands and failure to do so warrants punishment? Use of sticks has a different psychological impact on taxpayers than the use of carrots.

---

[41]   William D. Cohan, *What's Really Going on With Mitt Romney's $102 Million IRA*, THE ATLANTIC, Sept. 10 2012.

[42]   Dan Caplinger, *Here's How the Rich Use Their IRAs*, USA TODAY, Mar. 5, 2017.

[43]   For more on tax penalties for late or underpayments of taxes owed, see Chapter 2.02(c).

People are averse to loss and sticks take away what a person has because they do not act as the government wants.[44]

There are also important operational differences between tax carrots and sticks. Unlike carrots, sticks take from the affected person rather than give to that person. This may change the relative distribution of wealth between those who do and do not comply with the government's wishes. Depending upon the size of the stick and who is hit with it, the change in relative wealth could be significant. In the process, sticks generally increase government revenue even if they are no easier to police.

Academics are divided over the use of sticks in tax policy. For example, Professor Dennis Ventry argues that tax regulation should be based on cooperation, information sharing, and interest convergence rather than the use of penalties.[45] Focusing on resource and information asymmetries between the government and taxpayers, Ventry argues that optimal penalties are impossible. On the other hand, Professor Brian Galle argues sticks are generally preferable to carrots, although when issues of salience come into play people's responses to complex issues may increase the value of carrots.[46] Only if people are aware of penalties and rewards can Congress predict their relative impact.

Sticks' effectiveness at deterrence depends on how people respond. However, policymakers cannot know whether people will respond to tax penalties. The human element makes it difficult to know if and, if so, how people will respond to disincentives operated through the tax system.

A unique risk of imposing tax penalties unrelated to tax filing is that it may magnify dislike of the tax system despite the targeted behavior not being tax-related. A negative association with the penalty might stick to the tax system rather than Congress or the targeted behavior. An effect might be further noncompliance with taxes in general. For example, a dislike of the healthcare mandate may justify to a particular taxpayer overstating his exemptions or deductions either out of general frustration, an attempt to minimize or avoid the mandate, or to show dislike of the federal government. In a tax system based on voluntary compliance, this could negatively affect revenue and the future health of the tax system.

---

[44]   Per Engstrom et al., *Tax Compliance and Loss Aversion*, 7 AM. ECON. J. 132 (2015); Edward McCaffery & Jonathan Barron, *Thinking About Tax*, 12 PSYCHOLOGY, PUB. POL'Y, & L. 106 (2006).

[45]   Dennis Ventry, *Cooperative Regulation*, 41 CONN. L. REV. 431 (2008).

[46]   Brian Galle, *Carrots, Sticks, and Salience*, 67 TAX L. REV. 53 (2013).

Despite the risks, there are many types of sticks in the Code. For example, one could view phase-outs or phase-ins as a punishment for having wealth above or below the threshold. Their limits can be interpreted as penalizing those who are unable to claim the tax benefit. More direct penalties are relatively rare but sin taxes are as old as the country.

One reason for the rarity of tax penalties is that in the early decades of the twentieth century the Supreme Court interpreted the Commerce Clause as limiting the taxing power in ways that made it difficult to enact tax penalties. For example, in *Bailey v. Drexel Furniture Co.*, a tax on child labor was held to impermissibly regulate commerce.[47] The Constitution permitted Congress to tax in order to raise revenue; taxes aimed at changing behavior were to be struck.

By 1936, the Supreme Court had changed course and broadened the taxing power to permit taxes as penalties. In *United States v. Butler*, the Court held that the power to tax is an independent power, although it struck down the particular tax at issue as a usurpation of state power.[48] The power to tax has since been broadly interpreted. For example, in *United States v. Kahriger*, the Court upheld an occupational tax on persons involved in gambling enacted to discourage the behavior.[49] Unless tax penalty provisions are extraneous to any tax revenue need, they are likely to be upheld by the Court today.

(b) Healthcare Mandate

Until repealed in 2017 for tax years beginning in 2019, the Patient Protection and Affordable Care Act imposed a financial penalty on a taxpayer if the taxpayer failed to purchase or otherwise hold health insurance.[50] The mandate, enacted in 2010, was first required in 2014 with reporting on a taxpayer's federal income tax return. Although the prospective repeal was widely reported in the press, the mandate operates in 2018, and the IRS has said it will not accept electronic returns that do not report insurance coverage, an exemption, or submit payment.[51]

The amount of the penalty varied depending upon income and family status. The fee was calculated either as a percentage of household income or per person, with the larger of the two being due. In 2018, the percentage of household income is a maximum 9.56%

---

[47]   259 U.S. 20 (1922).

[48]   297 U.S. 1 (1936).

[49]   345 U.S. 22 (1953).

[50]   Pub. L. No. 115–97, sec. 11081, 131 Stat. 2054 (2017); Pub. L. No. 111–148, sec. 1501, 124 Stat. 119 (2010). *But see* E.O. 13,765 (Jan. 20, 2017).

[51]   Notice 2017–74.

but with a cap at the yearly premium for a designated insurance plan. Thus, the mandate is not unlimited for high-income taxpayers. The average per person amount in 2016 was $667 per filer who owed a penalty.

The constitutional permissibility of using a tax penalty to force taxpayers to act was subject to heated debate. In *National Federation of Independent Business v. Sebelius*, the Supreme Court upheld the mandate in a 5–4 decision.[52] In doing so, the Court ruled that the penalty was a tax and yet was not a tax; it depends on the purpose of the inquiry. First, the penalty was not a tax for the purpose of determining the Court's ability to rule on the case. The federal Tax Anti-injunction Act prevents courts from reviewing tax provisions before the IRS enforces them. In other words, taxpayers cannot challenge a tax law until the government tries to collect the taxes the law says are owed. Two former IRS commissioners, Mortimer Caplin and Sheldon Cohen, filed an amici curiae brief arguing that the Anti-Injunction Act prevented early judicial review of the mandate.[53] The Supreme Court disagreed and decided the case, finding that the penalty was not a tax for purposes of the anti-injunction statute because the label provided in the statute, a "penalty," was controlling.

Second, the Supreme Court decided that the penalty was a tax for constitutional purposes. Chief Justice John Roberts wrote that the financial penalty for failing to carry insurance possesses "the essential feature of any tax," which is producing revenue for the government. As a tax for this purpose, the mandate was permitted by what is now an almost limitless taxing power in Article I, section 8. The Court needed to call the penalty a tax for constitutional purposes because the Court held that the penalty could not be upheld under the Commerce Clause. The majority likely found that upholding the mandate under the Commerce Clause would remove any meaningful limit on federal power to require individuals to engage in specific activities. However, upholding the mandate under the taxing power opens the door for a financial penalty for failing to do whatever Congress demands.

Many arguments were made for and against the penalty as a tax. The General Welfare Clause gives the federal government the power "[t]o lay and collect taxes, duties, imposts and excises. . . ."[54] To fall within this taxing power, the Supreme Court requires that a tax raise revenue; and the mandate does so. The CBO estimated that

---

[52]   567 U.S. 519 (2012).

[53]   Discussed in Steve R. Johnson, *The Anti-Injunction Act and the Individual Mandate*, 133 TAX NOTES 1399 (2011).

[54]   U.S. CONST., Art. I, sec. 8.

the mandate would raise $17 billion by 2019.[55] That is much more than the revenue raised by penalties the Court has permitted in the past. In *Sonzinsky v. United States*, the Court upheld a tax designed to regulate firearms dealers that raised $5,400 in 1934, approximately $90,000 in today's dollars.[56]

The second part of the clause requires that a tax must "pay the debts and provide for the [nation's] common defense and general welfare." This requirement is often interpreted broadly, so the conclusion that better health coverage promotes general welfare is not unreasonable. Those who pay the penalty rather than acquire insurance help pay for federal health insurance subsidies. Professor Edward Kleinbard reframes the issue: The penalty is not a tax on not doing something but on self-insurance.[57] Not having insurance has economic consequences, and the federal government can tax that choice because, if the self-insurer proves unlucky, the government will ultimately absorb a substantial portion of the cost.

That Congress has as an objective to punish and discourage behavior does not negate tax status, although taxes are not allowed to violate individual rights or be a criminal penalty in disguise. In *United States v. Sanchez*, the Supreme Court upheld a $100-per-ounce tax on marijuana.[58] The Court stated that "a tax does not cease to be valid merely because it regulates, discourages, or even definitely deters the activities taxed." The Court permits the revenue objectives to be secondary as compared to the regulatory objective.

If the mandate is a tax, it could then be challenged as a direct tax. However, this argument was ultimately unsuccessful before the Supreme Court. Professors Steven Willis and Nakku Chung argued that the penalty was an unapportioned direct tax and, therefore, unconstitutional.[59] Article 1 Section 9 requires that direct taxes be apportioned according to state population, meaning that the total amount of revenue collected each year from each state must be proportional to each state's population. This is not politically tenable because each state would have a different tax rate depending upon its population and their wealth.

It was always unlikely that the mandate would be struck as a direct tax if only because so few taxes are considered direct. The Constitutional Convention did not define direct taxes, and it has

---

[55]   CONG. BUDGET OFFICE, COST ESTIMATE FOR THE AMENDMENT IN THE NATURE OF A SUBSTITUTE ADDRESSED TO NANCY PELOSI (Mar. 20, 2010).

[56]   300 U.S. 506 (1937).

[57]   Edward Kleinbard, *Constitutional Kreplach*, 128 TAX NOTES 755–762 (2010).

[58]   340 U.S. 42 (1950).

[59]   Steven Willis & Nakku Chung, *Constitutional Decapitation and Healthcare*, 128 TAX NOTES 169–195 (2010).

remained an open issue ever since.[60] To remove confusion, courts tend not to find something to be a direct tax. Moreover, although the healthcare mandate is a tax imposed per person, the amount of the penalty is tied to income levels that are nationally applied.

Studies did not conclude whether the penalty influenced behavior or if this approach will be adopted for other congressional purposes. A precedent has been established of using a tax stick to encourage specific activity, and there is nothing to prevent this type of penalty from being used more broadly. Nevertheless, there should be concern about its administrability. In 2014, nearly 8.1 million taxpayers paid almost $1.7 billion in the healthcare mandate, over 6% of taxpayers, but about 5.1 million failed to state their coverage, claim an exemption, or pay the fine.[61] The Treasury Department estimates that about 300,000 paid the mandate were likely mistaken because they qualified for an exemption.[62]

(c) Sin Taxes

"Sin taxes" are excise taxes that operate like a selective sales tax. These taxes are often levied on commodities, such as tobacco and alcohol, or activities, such as gambling. As the name implies, sin taxes are imposed on things that at the time the tax was enacted were objects of widespread disapproval. These targeted taxes continue to be tolerated because a large enough portion of the population still feels there is something immoral or bad about the items themselves. Thus, as all taxes operate as a disincentive to engage in the taxed behavior, sin taxes are to decrease the sinful behavior.

Sin taxes have a long history in the U.S. In 1791, Congress enacted an excise tax on whiskey as one of the government's first revenue measures to help pay down the debt incurred in the Revolutionary War.[63] For a time, these excise taxes raised about 5% of federal revenue. However, whiskey was not just for imbibing, it was used as a currency on the currency-poor western frontier because it did not spoil as grains do and was easier to transport. The tax's unpopularity with these farmers led to the Whiskey Rebellion in 1794. President George Washington led 13,000 militiamen to suppress the uprising, demonstrating the new government's power in

---

[60]   For more on direct taxes, see Chapter 3.01(a).

[61]   IRS, STATISTICS OF INCOME—2014, INDIVIDUAL INCOME TAX RETURNS, PUBLICATION 1304 (Rev. 08–2016).

[62]   The IRS did not have sufficient information from exchanges to determine how much of the $4.4 billion in credits paid to 1.4 million returns were correct. TREAS. INSPECTOR GEN. FOR TAX ADMIN., 2015–43–057, AFFORDABLE CARE ACT (2015).

[63]   For more on the Whiskey Rebellion, see THOMAS P. SLAUGHTER, THE WHISKEY REBELLION (1988).

a way critically important in the constitutional era—enforcing its power to tax.

Today, most sin taxes are imposed as a stated amount per unit or as a percentage of the consumer's cost. For example, Congress imposes a specified number of cents in tax per package of cigarettes but a tax of 52.4% times the sales price on small cigars. Their rates tend to increase with political and financial need. For example, to fund an expansion of the State Children's Health Insurance Program (SCHIP) in 2009, Congress raised the federal tax rate on cigarettes from $0.39 to $1.01 per pack.[64] This tax increase is in addition to state level taxes. As of January 2018, states tax cigarettes from $0.17 in Missouri to $4.35 in New York.[65] Chicago has the highest taxes in the country, at a total of $7.17 in federal, state, and local tax per pack.

Although tobacco has been taxed since the Civil War, more recently sin taxes have been proposed to combat obesity, often on the grounds that obesity, like smoking, increases healthcare costs. Medical costs related to smoking are estimated to be $170 billion per year and to obesity, between $147 and $210 billion per year.[66] Currently, 15.1% of American adults smoke and more than 33% of American adults are obese with more than 66% either overweight or obese.[67] Taxing behaviors is likely to curb smoking and the growth in obesity. Tax is not, however, the only way to reduce people's consumption. For example, New York City passed the U.S.'s first ban of oversized sugary drinks in 2010 which was struck by New York's highest court in 2014.[68]

Sin taxes also raise revenue; for example, cigarette taxes have long been an important revenue source for both federal and state governments. States added their own taxes to the federal tax starting with Iowa in 1921. By 1969, all states taxed cigarettes. In 2012, cigarette taxes raised over $17.6 billion nationally; from a high of

---

[64]   Children's Health Insurance Program Reauthorization Act of 2009, sec. 701, Pub. L. No. 111–3, 123 Stat. 8 (2009).

[65]   Campaign for Tobacco-Free Kids, State Cigarette Excise Tax Rates and Rankings, https://www.tobaccofreekids.org/research/factsheets/pdf/0097.pdf (last visited Feb. 26, 2018).

[66]   Xu X et al., *Annual Healthcare Spending Attributable to Cigarette Smoking: An Update*, 48 AM. J. PREVENTIVE MEDICINE 326 (2015); E.A. Finkelstein et al., *Annual Medical Spending Attributable to Obesity*, 28 HEALTH AFFAIRS 822 (2009).

[67]   Ahmed Jamal et al., *Cigarette Smoking Among Adults—United States, 2005– 2015*, CTR. FOR DISEASE CONTROL, 65 MORBIDITY AND MORTALITY WEEKLY RPT. 1205 (2016); Cynthia Ogden et al., *Prevalence of Obesity Among Adults and Youth: United States, 2011–2014*, CTR. FOR DISEASE CONTROL, NCHS DATA BRIEF NO. 219 (2015).

[68]   NY Statewide Coalition of Hispanic Chambers of Commerce v. NYC Dept. of Health & Mental Hygiene, 23 NY3d 681 (2014).

almost $1.7 billion in New York and a low of $26 million in South Carolina.[69]

Similarly, sodas have been targeted because public health officials estimate that Americans consume an average of 40 gallons of sugary soda per person per year.[70] The CBO estimates that a tax of 3¢ per ounce of sugary beverage would generate over $24 billion in revenue over four years.[71] In 2016, Philadelphia enacted a 1.5¢ tax per ounce of sugary and diet beverages, the constitutionality of which will be considered by the states' supreme court. The city expected to generate $91 million annually and earmarked that spending for universal childhood education, parks and libraries, and 20% for other programs and employee benefits.[72] In its first year, the tax raised close to $79 million but less than estimates.

Other sources of obesity have also been targeted with special taxes with varying success. Maine enacted a 6% snack tax in 1991 because of a budget crisis.[73] The state's obesity rates increased by 7.3% before the act was repealed in 2001. That tax was unpopular in part because its definition of a snack seemed arbitrary. Despite the failure, the state made most snacks subject to the state sales tax in 2016 whereas other foods are exempt. Some local governments have failed to enact these taxes. For example, in 2005, Detroit's mayor proposed a 2% tax on fast food to fill a $300 million budget hole; it was not enacted.[74] The tax would have taxed everything sold at a fast food restaurant, regardless of its health value.

As a revenue source, sin taxes can raise tax revenue to offset the costs produced by the targeted behavior, to fund other measures, or to decrease the behavior by making it more expensive. For example, soda tax revenue can fund general government expenditures or things that would improve health, such as nutrition education, grocery stores in food deserts, parks and places for physical activity. Some evidence has shown the reduction in targeted behavior. For example, studies show that increased cigarette taxes reduce smoking

---

[69]   Tax Policy Center, *Tobacco Tax Revenue 1977 to 2014*, available at http://www.taxpolicycenter.org/taxfacts/displayafact.cfm?Docid=403&Topic2id=80 (last visited Sept. 27, 2017).

[70]   Leslie McGranahan & Diane Schanzenbah, *Who Would Be Affected By Soda Taxes*, CHICAGO FED. LETTER (2011).

[71]   CONG. BUDGET OFFICE, BUDGET OPTIONS VOLUME 1: HEALTH CARE (2008).

[72]   Maria Amante, *Philadelphia's Soda Tax Generates More Publicity Than Revenue*, FORBES, Jun. 30, 2016.

[73]   Lindsay Tice, *Sneaky Food Tax Gives Maine Heartburn*, BDN ME, Mar. 15, 2017.

[74]   Greg Levine, *Detroit Mayor Eyes Fast-Food Tax*, FORBES, May 9, 2005.

rates, especially for teenagers for whom every 10% increase in price leads to an overall drop in use of about 7%.[75]

On the other hand, these taxes have negative side effects. Sin taxes involve the government in what are arguably private matters, and this paternalism is regressive in its effect. Low-income taxpayers are disproportionately the consumers of these items so the government is disproportionately involved in their affairs. Sin taxes may even target particular groups within society if they are more likely to engage in the behavior. For example, in the Progressive Era taxes on alcohol were often recognized as a tax on Irish and German Catholics who were thought to drink more than other members of society, even among those of equivalent economic levels.

Sin taxes are also economically regressive because they take up a larger proportion of low-income taxpayers' income than high-income taxpayers' income even if both groups consume equal amounts of the targeted item. All excise taxes, as long as they have a flat rate and are imposed on goods consumed by the poor, will be regressive in this sense. A study conducted on behalf of the New York State Department of Health revealed that smokers in households making under $30,000 spent an average of 23.6% of their annual household income on cigarettes compared to 2.2% for smokers in households making over $60,000.[76] Attempts could be made to make these taxes less regressive, for example, by exempting lower income households from the tax. However, this would decrease revenue and beneficial health effects.

Although taxed equally, targeted behavior may also not be equally bad for all people. Some people may make a rational choice to engage in the targeted behavior. For example, a person may understand the risks of smoking and decide the risks are outweighed: a cancer victim smoking marijuana, a dying person smoking a cigarette, or a college student planning to quit before experiencing negative health effects. Perhaps morosely, some have argued that cigarettes and alcohol result in younger deaths that may decrease healthcare costs.[77] Thus, these paternalistic taxes penalize a person for using a product or engaging in an activity, possibly without a rational basis for doing so.

---

[75]   F.J. Chaloupka et al., *Tax, Price, and Cigarette Smoking* (2002), http://tobaccocontrol.bmj.com/content/11/suppl_1/i62.full (last visited Sept. 27, 2017); WORLD HEALTH ORG., TOBACCO ATLAS (2002).

[76]   Matthew Farrelly et al., *The Consequences of High Cigarette Excise Taxes for Low-Income Smokers* (2012), available at http://journals.plos.org/plosone/article?id=10.1371/journal.pone.0043838#top.

[77]   For a study in Sweden that found a moderate decrease in costs, see Jari Tiihonen, *The Net Effect of Smoking on Healthcare and Welfare Costs*, 2 BMJ OPEN 1 (2012).

In fact, sin taxes produce their own social harms, such as smuggling and black markets. Tobacco's global black market is estimated at 11.6% of the world's cigarette consumption, leading to significant international crime and the creation of unregulated counterfeit cigarettes.[78] In some U.S. cities, up to 40% of cigarettes are illegally trafficked at a cost of $680 to $729 million in revenue.[79] Sin taxes may also change consumers' behavior to more dangerous alternatives. For instance, when the per-pack tax is raised, cigarette taxes may increase smokers' propensity to smoke high-tar, high-nicotine cigarettes, which are less healthy and lead to higher healthcare costs.[80]

Finally, sin taxes create perverse incentives for the government. Some state budgets are based on sin taxes. Sin taxes are the biggest revenue item in Rhode Island, Nevada, West Virginia, New Hampshire, and Delaware. Pennsylvania made over $2.7 billion of its tax revenue from sin taxes.[81] If sin taxes reduce the behavior, they decrease funding for state programs that rely on such funding. For example, economist Gary Becker argued cigarette taxes will produce a 10.6% decrease in unit sales, which the National Tax Foundation estimated will lead to a $1 billion loss for the states.[82] Ironically, states may find that they cannot afford to discourage behavior that is such a large source of revenue.

(d) Carbon Tax

Driven by concerns of global warming, many countries have adopted taxes on fuels' carbon content. Carbon is present in every hydrocarbon fuel, such as coal, petroleum, and natural gas, and is released as carbon dioxide when burned. According to environmentalists, carbon dioxide is a heat-trapping greenhouse gas that leads to global warming. To reduce the production of carbon dioxide, carbon taxes may be imposed on energy products and motor vehicles or carbon emissions directly. According to sympathetic economists, the tax on goods is necessary to fix a market failure in that the gas is a negative externality not properly reflected in the price of the goods that produce it. Thus, the carbon tax is a form of

---

[78]   Keith Humphrey, *Why the Massive Black Market Trade in Cigarettes Affects You Even If You Don't Smoke*, WASH. POST, June 25, 2014.

[79]   Kevin Davis et al., *Cigarette Trafficking in Five Northeastern Cities*, TOBACCO CONTROL, 2013.

[80]   Richard Williams & Katelyn Christ, *Taxing Sin*, MERCATUS CTR AT GEORGE MASON UNIV. (2009), available at http://mercatus.org/publication/taxing-sin (last visited Sept. 27, 2017).

[81]   Commonwealth Foundation, *How Does Pennsylvania's Tax Burden Compare?*, Aug. 25, 2016.

[82]   Brad Schiller, *Obama's Poor Tax*, WALL ST. J., Apr. 1, 2009.

carbon pricing that makes finished products more expensive because of their environmental impact.

An alternative to a tax model is cap-and-trade. Under a cap-and-trade regime, pollution levels are capped and permits covering such pollution are either allocable to prior polluters (in other words, current polluters are grandfathered) or auctioned off. The result is a market in emission permits so that polluters can trade some or all of their permits. Government revenue is only raised under the cap-and-trade regime on an initial auction, which reduces its value as a revenue source. Additionally, there is a risk that banks and investment funds will create their own revenue source by controlling the after-market sale of permits.

Support for a carbon tax or cap-and-trade relies on acceptance of the science behind greenhouse gases. Those who do not accept the environmental concern are unlikely to accept the need for a carbon tax. Those that accept the environmental concern may nonetheless worry that businesses will respond to these measures by relocating to countries with fewer environmental controls. Not only would current employees lose their jobs, greenhouse gases and other environmental degradation might increase in a less regulated country. Additionally, both carbon taxes and cap-and-trade risk having limits or tax rates be set politically rather than scientifically focused on the externality.

Carbon taxes also raise concerns, as with all taxes, about who bears the cost of a tax that is reflected in the higher price of finished goods. Carbon taxes are likely to be passed on to consumers and, as a result, carbon taxes would be regressive. Because those with lower incomes consume a larger proportion of their incomes, a larger proportion of their income would be spent on carbon taxes. This effect exists with all generally applicable consumption taxes.

If the value of environmental protection triumphs, carbon taxes have some advantage over cap-and-trade.[83] Carbon taxes are a cost-effective means of reducing greenhouse gasses with any economic upside of the regulation remitted to the government as opposed to being captured by the polluter. Taxing something that produces this negative externality corrects for the inefficient market by forcing its producers to pay the environmental cost. A cap-and-trade regime, on the other hand, simply limits production, which might force up prices if the number of items is reduced and for which producers then

---

[83] *See* Reuven Avi-Yonah & David Uhlmann, *Combating Global Climate Change: Why a Carbon Tax is a Better Response to Global Warming than Cap and Trade*, 28 STAN. ENV'T L.J. 3 (2009).

capture the benefit of this reduced supply without owing any offsetting tax.

Coupled with the efficiency and benefit rationale, a tax-based system should be easier to police than cap-and-trade. Both systems require the correct measuring of pollution; however, cap-and-trade or any command and control regulation, such as that imposed by the Environmental Protection Agency, also requires establishing standards for the amount that can be produced. Because of an underlying uncertainty in the science as to appropriate levels, this opens regulations to significant debate before enforcement can commence. The tax regime can more simply start taxing from the first emission. Additionally, to the extent that cap-and-trade models impose rules for meeting the appropriate levels, it reduces the market's ability to find better solutions, although this is not a necessary part of cap-and-trade. Under a tax regime, producers have an incentive to decrease pollution in any way they can.

Therefore, not only should a carbon tax result in less consumption, it should stimulate investment in more environmentally friendly energy sources because final products can be sold at higher prices. The relative advantage of not being taxed makes wind, sunlight, hydropower, and other non-carbon based power sources more competitive, especially when coupled with targeted tax incentives.[84] Congress would be purposefully un-leveling the field to shift taxpayer preference through cost mechanisms. The increased investment in less damaging energy sources are likely to reduce their cost so that they can eventually compete on an equal playing field with carbon-based fuels.

However, while carbon taxes would increase the cost of carbon-based fuels, Congress has already enacted tax incentives for carbon-based energies that might negate any incentive effects of a carbon tax. For example, Congress permits current deductions for the cost of drilling to encourage investment in oil and gas production.[85] Additionally, as these resources are mined, producers are permitted to claim a depletion deduction for the shrinking reserves.[86] Congress even exempted investments in certain oil and gas interests from the passive investment loss limits so that investors can use expenses and costs to offset their unrelated income.[87] In total, there are significant tax benefits for carbon-based energy sources. In 2013, federal tax

---

[84]   Congress extended an investment tax credit and production tax credit for renewable energy products in 2015 but the credits phase out. I.R.C. § 45, § 48.

[85]   I.R.C. § 263(c).

[86]   I.R.C. § 613A.

[87]   I.R.C. § 469(c)(3).

incentives for energy were estimated at $23.3 billion, of which 20.4% were for fossil fuels.[88]

To date Congress has not enacted a carbon tax or considered repeal of its pro-carbon incentives; however, some states and localities have adopted a carbon tax with varying success. For example, in 2006, and renewed in 2015, Boulder, Colorado voted for the first municipal carbon tax, its Climate Action Plan.[89] It taxes electricity consumption through utility bills. Deductions are awarded for using electricity from renewable sources. The goal of the Climate Action Plan was to reduce carbon emissions to those outlined in the Kyoto Protocol, requiring a 7% reduction from 1990 levels. Although the tax failed to achieve this goal, tax revenues of approximately $1.8 million annually have been used by the city's Office of Environmental Affairs to fund programs to reduce greenhouse gas emissions.

---

[88]   MOLLY SHERLOCK & JEFFREY STUPAK, CONG. RESEARCH SERV. R41953, ENERGY TAX INCENTIVES (2015).

[89]   City of Boulder, CO, *Climate Action Tax*, https://bouldercolorado.gov/climate/climate-action-plan-cap-tax (last visited Sept. 27, 2017).

Chapter 18

WHAT TO DO WITH
TAX REVENUE?

Table of Sections

From many different sources, governments at the federal, state, and local levels raise a tremendous amount of revenue. In 2017, the federal government raised $3.3 trillion in total revenue; state and local governments raised $2.92 trillion.[1] Together, this $6.2 trillion constituted over 30% of the country's GDP. Elected officials have tremendous say over how this money is spent, although politics often make it hard to reach consensus.

§ 18.01 Advanced Budgeting

Despite raising significant amounts of revenue, the different levels of government do not have complete freedom to disperse the money. Instead, there are limits on their spending power.[2] The limits on the way the different levels of government allocate money are not the same. Unlike state and local governments, the federal government does not have capital and operating budgets.[3] Instead, the federal government divides its spending into mandatory, discretionary, and net interest on debt. Not included in the budget is spending through tax expenditures in the Internal Revenue Code, which was more than $1.6 trillion in 2017, or more than all discretionary spending that year.

---

[1]   DEPT. OF COMM., BUREAU OF ECONOMIC ANALYSIS, NATIONAL INCOME AND PRODUCT ACCOUNTS, Federal Receipts: Table 3.2, State Receipts: Table 3.20, Local Receipts Table 3.21 (2018).

[2]   For more on the budget process, see Chapter 1.01(b).

[3]   For more on state and local budgeting, see Chapter 13.02.

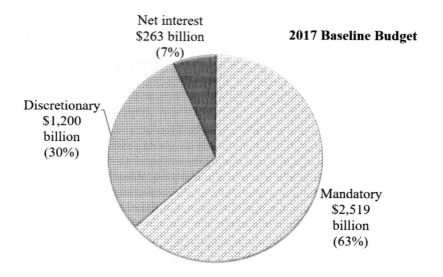

OMB, Historical Tables, Tables 8.5 and 8.7 (2018).

The labels discretionary and mandatory imply that the former are flexible whereas the latter are not; however, the terms really reflect only the process for their funding. Mandatory spending is set by existing law and is not annually appropriated. Discretionary spending is annually determined through the appropriations process. Thus, mandatory spending is provided in laws other than appropriations. For example, the Social Security Act creates the spending regime for Social Security, so it is mandatory spending. The IRS's budget is set annually through the appropriations process, so its budget is discretionary. Consequently, a simple way to think of the distinction is that mandatory spending, sometimes referred to as entitlements, are programs on autopilot whereas discretionary spending requires annual funding.

Although in many ways the division between mandatory and discretionary spending is semantic, there are some important distinctions. One effect of the source of spending is that in the event of a government shutdown or hitting the debt limit, discretionary spending suffers greater reduction. For example, reduction under the 2011 Budget Control Act disproportionately focuses on discretionary spending. Mandatory spending is projected to be reduced by less than $0.2 trillion from fiscal year 2012 to 2021 whereas discretionary spending is expected to be reduced by $1.5 trillion.[4]

---

[4]   GRANT DRIESSEN & MARC LABONTE, CONG. RESEARCH SERV., R42506, THE BUDGET CONTROL ACT OF 2011 AS AMENDED: BUDGETARY EFFECTS (2015).

Because statutes outside of the tax code determine mandatory spending levels, they are generally only adjusted by direct congressional action. Therefore, as with discretionary spending, mandatory spending can be reduced; however, mandatory spending is only reduced if Congress specifically acts. So either group of spending can be congressionally adjusted, but discretionary spending is at risk by the debt ceiling and is politically easier to reduce as part of the annual budget. Mandatory spending requires amending another act, making it more conspicuous to interested parties.

Today, mandatory spending comprises more than 60% of the federal government's spending. Because this spending is tied to bills originating in committees other than the budget committees, they are not linked to budgeting resolutions or to reconciliation.[5] Under most mandatory regimes, such as Social Security, the government must pay out to everyone who qualifies unless Congress changes the process of determining the entitlement.

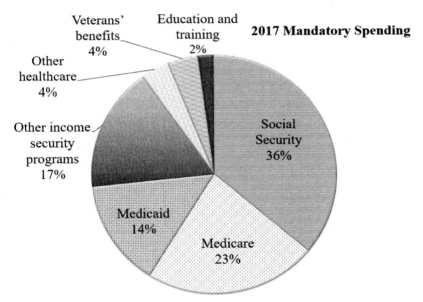

OMB, Historical Tables, Tables 8.5 (2018).

The two largest mandatory items are Medicare and Social Security. These two items together account for almost 60% of the federal budget. With Medicaid these are 73% of mandatory spending. Income security programs, including SNAP and unemployment compensation, account for 17% of mandatory spending.

---

[5]   For more on reconciliation, see Chapter 1.01(a).

Mandatory spending's revenue does not necessarily come from a different source than does discretionary spending. However, revenue for mandatory spending may also come from earmarked taxes, for example payroll taxes funding Social Security and unemployment. Earmarks do not cover all of mandatory spending, and the revenue raised does not currently limit the amount spent.

On the other hand, discretionary spending is annually appropriated through the budgeting process. Each house of Congress has a committee on appropriations with twelve subcommittees, and each subcommittee is responsible for the spending on its group of activities.[6] Thus, spending is generally through twelve smaller discretionary budgets. Activities within each subcommittee's purview compete with each other for funding. When allocating within the smaller budgets proves too difficult, Congress enacts a large omnibus appropriation bill for the entire discretionary budget.

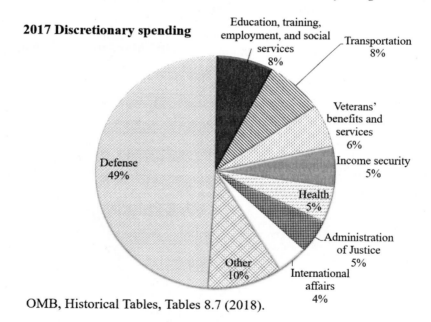

2017 Discretionary spending

Education, training, employment, and social services 8%

Transportation 8%

Veterans' benefits and services 6%

Income security 5%

Defense 49%

Health 5%

Administration of Justice 5%

Other 10%

International affairs 4%

OMB, Historical Tables, Tables 8.7 (2018).

There are three types of appropriations: regular, continuing (when Congress does not act by its October 1st start of a new fiscal year), and supplemental (for spending on national emergencies that

---

[6]   The 12 subcommittees are: agriculture, FDA, and related agencies; commerce, justice, science, and related agencies; defense; energy and water development; financial services and general government; homeland security; interior, environment, and related agencies; labor, health and human services, education, and related agencies; legislative branch; military construction, veterans affairs, and related agencies; state, foreign operations, and related programs; and transportation, housing and urban development, and related agencies.

are not part of the regular budget process).[7] In only four years since 1977 have all appropriations been completed in the regular process; all other years required continuing appropriations.

Supplemental appropriations are exempt from the normal budgetary caps, but it is not always easy to get the designation. The Senate, for example, generally requires a super-majority vote. Supplemental appropriations generally arise after the fiscal year has begun, and generally about 60% of these late appropriations are designated as for an emergency. For example, much of the war in Iraq and Afghanistan and certain stimulus measures and earmarks are from these special appropriations.

Categories within the budget are not always clearly demarcated in practice. For example, military spending is a catchall for many different types of spending. These include the cost of military personnel, research and development, and procurement of military equipment. Additionally, although spending is divided within categories, most agencies' budgets are partially mandatory and partially discretionary. For example, the Department of Defense, Department of Education, and Department of Veterans Affairs all have significant parts of their budget in both categories. In popular discussion, the classification of a particular program depends on where the majority of funding comes from and that often depends on which committee initiates a particular project.

A final category of spending is for interest on the government's debt. Currently, the federal government spends 6% of its budget on interest on federal debt. This spending is required and must be paid in regular intervals because of prior government borrowing. In 2017, these payments were approximately $457 billion and, as discussed below, are expected to grow as a percentage of the budget. It is possible for this percentage to shrink if the government reduces its future borrowing from the public or increases revenue from other sources.

As shown by the budget, a large percentage of federal money is designated for particular activities as part of mandatory spending. This has not always been the case. Before the adoption of the Social Security system and Medicare, most spending was discretionary. Before the 1930s, mandatory spending was very little of the federal budget and still less than 30% before enactment of Medicare and Medicaid in 1962.[8]

---

[7]   After the money has been appropriated, it must then be authorized. Authorization occurs when Congress permits the money to be spent.

[8]   MINDY LEVIT ET AL., CONG. RESEARCH SERV., RL30074, MANDATORY SPENDING SINCE 1962 (2015).

The federal budget also shows that most money is spent domestically, and much of federal spending is on politically popular items. Studies show how hard it is for people to designate where cuts should be made.[9] Often when people want to shrink government spending, they target foreign spending. In particular, the public focuses on international affairs that are not international security assistance, as international security is included with defense. However, as of 2017, this spending, including international humanitarian aid, is less than 1% of the federal budget.

§ 18.02 Redistribution

Redistribution takes income or wealth from some and gives it to others; it does not matter whether the transfer is paid through discretionary or mandatory spending. Moreover, redistribution can occur either through taxing or spending or through both. In the U.S., some aspects of the tax system are regressive but, overall, the system is generally agreed to be progressive so that more income is transferred to lower income taxpayers rather than away from them.[10] The proper amount of, and justification for, redistribution remains open to debate.

In a progressive tax system, the government takes income from the haves. Therefore, even with equal spending to every member of society, income is redistributed because the haves pay more than the have-nots or the have-lesses. In a progressive spending regime, redistribution can be accomplished with equal taxation by spending more money on the have-notes and have-lesses. On the other hand, in a regressive regime, the government takes from the have-lesses and gives it to the have-mores.

(a) Defining the Have-Nots

To redistribute to the have-nots, Congress must define who should fit within that group. Being poor can be defined in an absolute or relative sense. As an absolute measure, the government created the poverty line, a complicated balance of poverty thresholds and poverty guidelines. The threshold is used by the Census Bureau to issue a poverty report stating who is below the threshold and how income is distributed. This report measures many significant factors such as family type, race, ethnicity, age, gender, and region in addition to the numbers of household members. Additionally, the U.S. Department of Health and Human Services creates poverty

---

[9]   Edward McCaffery & Jonathan Baron, *The Political Psychology of Redistribution*, 52 UCLA L. REV. 1745, 1773–80 (2005).

[10]   For a fascinating take on progressivity in the income tax, see Jason Oh, *Are Progressive Tax Rates Progressive Policy?*, 92 N.Y.U. L. REV. (forthcoming 2017).

guidelines as a simplified version of the thresholds that tell the amount of money required to be out of poverty based on family size.

The poverty guidelines were established in the 1960s as part of the Great Society movement. In 2018, the poverty line in the forty-eight contiguous states is $12,140 for single persons and $16,460 for a family of two. This amount is significantly below the average household income, found by the CBO in 2013 to be $86,000 plus $14,000 of government transfers, or $100,000 before an average of $20,000 of taxes.[11] Using a different measure, the Census Bureau found the median income in 2016 was $59,039.[12] Congress often ties government benefits to the poverty line or some multiple of it, such as 150% of the poverty line. In 2016, 12.7% of the public, or 40.6 million people, lived below the poverty line. During the period between 2009 and 2012, approximately 34.5% of the population had at least one spell of poverty lasting two or more months while 2.7% were in chronic poverty during all 48 months.[13]

For purposes of this federal measure, the only amounts that count as income are earnings and support not received in kind. The focus is on pre-tax cash income. Therefore, food stamps, rent controlled housing, or other benefits that are not cash equivalents do not count towards income for the purpose of applying the poverty guidelines. The measure also ignores any incremental expenses incurred in earning that income.

The poverty guidelines themselves are based on a series of studies undertaken in the 1960s for the Social Security Administration. The poverty threshold was determined by estimating the cost of a nutritionally adequate diet for various family groups. This amount was then multiplied by three on the assumption that low-income families spent approximately one-third of their income on food. This assumption was supported by surveys at the time. Although there was some criticism, the index was widely accepted. Since the 1960s, neither the basket of food nor the proportion of the budget expected to be spent on food has been changed. These amounts are annually adjusted for the consumer price index.

The use of the 1960s diet with the 1960s percentage of income spent on that diet might be inaccurate because of a dramatic change in American lifestyles. Thus, the measure may no longer reflect the

---

[11]   CONG. BUDGET OFFICE, THE DISTRIBUTION OF HOUSEHOLD INCOME AND FEDERAL TAXES (2013).

[12]   U.S. CENSUS BREAU, INCOME AND POVERTY IN THE UNITED STATES: 2016 (2017).

[13]   U.S. DEPT. OF COMM., INCOME AND POVERTY IN THE UNITED STATES: 2015 (2016).

real level of poverty. The proportion of our incomes spent on food decreased from 32.5% in 1950 to 19.4% by 1986 and more people consume cheaper food than is in the basket the poverty guidelines use.[14] On the other hand, we now spend more on housing and transportation than we did in the 1960s. Additionally, other items may now be considered necessary (such as computers and cell phones) that were rare or did not exist in the 1960s. Finally, if society has raised the standard as to what is minimally necessary, the gap widens between what is needed to emerge from poverty and what the average person consumes.

Another measure of the have-nots is as a relative measure focusing on those in lower economic classes. Classes are ambiguous categories that show relative position. There is no real definition of the term. However, classes can be defined operationally either by dividing the population into groups, often as quintiles, or less rigorously according to economic security. Using economic security measures, the middle-class is composed of professionals or business owners who share a level of relative security resulting from possession of a socially desired skill or wealth. The lower-class is the unemployable or those employed with little prestige or economic compensation who often lack high school educations and are relatively disenfranchised from society.

Depending upon the class model that is used, the middle-class includes anywhere from 25% to 66% of households. The lower-class is generally the bottom quintile of incomes, of which 13% is the working poor and 12% is an underclass. Middle-class incomes range from $35,000 to $100,000; lower-class incomes are anything below $35,000. Historically, most Americans self-identified as middle-class. The share that identified themselves as lower-class in 2011 was 8.4%, the highest level in forty years.[15]

Furthermore, classes can be defined in terms of income or wealth, although income and wealth are substantially different measures of economic prosperity. Income is the amount a person receives in a given period; for most purposes the government measures income per year. Wealth is commonly measured in terms of net worth as the sum of an individual's assets, including the market value of real estate, minus her liabilities. Unlike incomes that are generally determined annually, wealth is generally defined cumulatively.[16] There may be a high correlation between income and

---

[14]   David Johnson et al., *A Century of Family Budgets in the U.S.*, MONTHLY LABOR REV. 28 (2001).

[15]   Patrik Jonsonn, *US Poverty Rate Steady at 15 Percent, But 'Lower Class' Is Booming*, CHRISTIAN SCIENCE MONITOR, Sept. 17, 2013.

[16]   An alternate measure of wealth is the length of time that a person (or family) could maintain their current lifestyle without receiving compensation for performing

wealth, but they are not synonymous. Wealthy people generally (but not always) have high incomes, and those with high incomes do not always have wealth.

Income and wealth are both unevenly distributed in the U.S. According to the CBO, between 1979 and 2007 the incomes of the top 1% of Americans grew by an average of 275%; the incomes of the middle-class grew by 40%.[17] Of the post Great Recession recovery, 116% of the growth was enjoyed by the top 10% of the population. For the two-year period ending 2015, the incomes of the top 1% grew by nearly 20% while the incomes of the remaining 99% rose by only 6% (although that rate is better than the growth the 99% has had over the last decade).[18]

Wealth is similarly unevenly distributed. The top 1% now owns between 33% and 40% of the nation's wealth, depending upon the measurement used.[19] However, those between the top 1% and top 0.5% lost a significant share over the past fifty years; while the top 0.5% grew astronomically. Thus, it is at the very top of the income spectrum that wealth is growing exponentially.

The composition of wealth varies among the classes.[20] For 60% of Americans their home is their most valuable asset. This is not true of the wealthiest 1%, whose home is generally less than 10% of their assets, including liquid assets, pension assets, and debt. Ownership of financial assets is even more lopsided. In 2010, the top 5% of wealthiest households held approximately 72% of the nation's financial wealth and the bottom 80% owned 5%. Wealth is also unevenly distributed in relation to race, education, geographic location, and gender.

An explanation for some of the disparate wealth accumulation is the life cycle of savings hypothesis. This theory posits that individuals plan their savings and consumption over their life cycle. The life cycle requires people save during their peak earning years so that they can spend on their children (who do not earn) and on their retirement (when they do not earn). According to this theory, as Baby Boomers near retirement they should have saved tremendous amounts of wealth that they will begin to spend, decreasing

---

additional work. This measure illustrates many high consumption individuals' precarious financial position.

[17]   CONG. BUDGET OFFICE, TRENDS IN THE DISTRIBUTION OF INCOME (2011).

[18]   Neil Irwin, *Income Gains in the Obama Economic Recovery*, N.Y. TIMES, Sept. 28, 2014; Tami Luhby, *Top 1% Aren't As Rich As They Used to Be*, CNN.COM, Jul. 8, 2016.

[19]   Jesse Bricker et al., *Measuring Income and Wealth at the Top Using Administrative and Survey Data*, BROOKINGS INSTITUTE (2016).

[20]   EDWARD N. WOLFE, THE ASSET PRICE MELTDOWN AND THE WEALTH OF THE MIDDLE CLASS (2012).

concentrated wealth. This theory has not always been popular among economists, and the elderly do not consume as quickly or completely as the theory would suggest.[21]

In practice many measurements of income fail to incorporate important underlying facts about household types. For example, there are on average two wage earners in the top income quintile households, one earner in middle quintile households, and no wage earners in lower quintile households. Additionally, married earners report their income together on tax forms, so that their income is combined for most indices. However, two unmarried working adults living together and sharing expenses may report their income as if they were two separate households (this is not true for all purposes).

Finally, bottom quintile households may receive as much as 80% of their incomes in transfer payments that are not included in most income data, as they are not included in poverty calculations; other quintiles receive much smaller percentages of their income from transfer payments.[22] These structural differences may have a real impact on how people live, for example in their choice between work and leisure and the provision of child and elder care.

In the U.S., income mobility may be more important politically than measures of current inequality. To the extent that there is an unequal distribution of wealth but people are able to change income and wealth classes, Americans are generally less concerned about the initial inequality. However, there is debate about how much mobility actually exists. The PEW Charitable Trusts found significant upward mobility from the late 1960s, but most of the growth in total family income was attributed to the increasing number of women in paid employment since male earnings were relatively stable throughout this period.[23]

The group's research also showed that 43% of children in the lowest quintile remained there as adults, 70% remained below the middle, and only 4% made it to the top.[24] This does mean that 30% of those born in the lowest quintile moved up two quintiles or more in one generation. The Treasury Department found that roughly half who began in the bottom quintile in 1996 had moved to a higher group by 2005 and only 25% of the top 0.1% remained in that group.[25]

[21]   Angus Deaton, *Franco Modigliani and the Life-Cycle Theory of Consumption*, 58 BNL Q. REV. 91 (2005).

[22]   Scott Hodge, *Federal Transfer Payments to Low-Income Households Top $17,000*, TAX FOUNDATION (2007).

[23]   PEW CHARITABLE TRUSTS, PURSUING THE AMERICAN DREAM 12 (2012).

[24]   *Id.*, at 2.

[25]   U.S. TREAS. DEPT., INCOME MOBILITY IN THE U.S. FROM 1996 TO 2005 (2007).

Moving between quintiles was more frequent for the middle-class than for lower- and higher-class Americans.

(b) Measuring Inequality

A conception of have-nots requires a sense of the haves, and the difference between these groups is the degree of inequality. Several measures have been created to measure inequality, or the difference between groups' income or wealth. Although those citing these measures may do so in pursuit of their sense of fairness or to alleviate poverty, the measurements themselves do not define either. In other words, inequality may be fair or unequal societies may have no poverty, it depends how you define equality. These measures of inequality seek only to quantify the difference in how much different groups have in relation to other groups.

The value of measures of inequality is strictly tied to one's acceptance of how they define terms. Economist Emmanuel Saez has documented how income inequality has been increasing since the 1970s.[26] Based on his findings, inequality has reached levels equal to that immediately before the Great Depression. However, his study excludes most government transfer programs, including Social Security and unemployment compensation. Thus, his measure of inequality has a relatively narrow definition of income.

The most commonly used measure of inequality, the Gini coefficient, was developed in 1912. The Gini coefficient measures the extent to which individuals' or households' income deviates from a perfectly equal distribution across society. The range of the coefficient is normally between 0 and 1. Zero expresses perfect equality where everyone has the same income. One, or 100%, expresses maximum inequality where only one person has all the income and the others have none. In 2012, the U.S. had a pre-tax Gini index of 0.51 and after-tax Gini index of 0.39; the OECD averages was 0.46 for pre-tax income and 0.31 for after-tax income, showing that the U.S. had greater inequality than the average OECD nation.[27]

---

[26] EMMANUAL SAEZ, STRIKING IT RICHER: THE EVOLUTION OF TOP INCOMES IN THE UNITED STATES (UPDATED WITH 2015 PRELIMINARY ESTIMATES) (2016), https://eml.berkeley.edu/~saez/saez-UStopincomes-2015.pdf (last visited Feb. 28, 2018).

[27] OECD.STAT, INCOME DISTRIBUTION AND POVERTY (2017), available at https://stats.oecd.org/Index.aspx?DataSetCode=IDD (last visited Feb. 28, 2018).

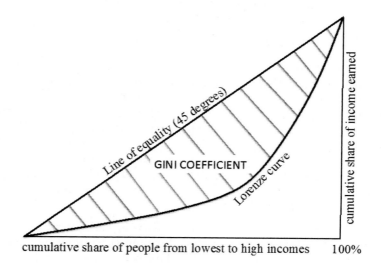

cumulative share of people from lowest to high incomes   100%

Although useful, the Gini coefficient does not always tell the whole story. The same coefficient number may result from many different distribution curves. Countries with aging populations, for example, generally experience an increasing pre-tax Gini coefficient. Even if the real income distribution for working adults remains constant, retirees generally do not earn the same income off their savings as working adults. Additionally, the coefficient of a poor country may be more equal because everyone is in poverty. In other words, the coefficient does not state how much the richest and poorest have. Finally, the Gini coefficient focuses only on income and ignores other important components of a person's wealth or happiness.

To provide more robust information, the United Nations developed the human development index (HDI).[28] The HDI is a composite statistic of life expectancy, education, and income indices. Originally the HDI measured potential human development as if there were no inequality. The greater the level of equality, the closer the nation's score is to 1. Since 2010, an inequality-adjusted HDI also measures inequality in the actual level of human development incorporating inequality. For 2015, the U.S. ranked 10th in HDI but 20th in the more comprehensive inequality-adjusted human development index.

---

[28]   UN DEVELOPMENT PROGRAMME, 2016 HUMAN DEVELOPMENT REPORT (2017).

Country	HDI	HDI rank	Inequality-Adjusted HDI	Inequality-Adjusted HDI rank
Norway	0.949	1	0.898	1
Australia	0.939	2	0.861	3
Switzerland	0.939	2	0.859	6
Germany	0.926	4	0.859	5
Denmark	0.925	5	0.858	7
Singapore	0.925	5	. . .	. . .
Netherlands	0.924	7	0.861	5
Ireland	0.923	8	0.850	10
Iceland	0.921	9	0.868	3
Canada	0.920	10	0.839	12
U.S.	0.920	10	0.796	20
UNDP, HUMAN DEVELOPMENT REPORT 2016, at 198, 206 (2016).				

Sometimes people interpret other measures as making statements about relative wealth when the measures are not really up to that task. For example, a popular, but not academically rigorous, measurement of the purchasing power parity between currencies is the Big Mac Index introduced by *The Economist* in 1986. The index charts the amount of money required in each country to buy a Big Mac. Therefore, this measures exchange rates more than relative wealth and ignores important differences in what a Big Mac means in different cultures. Fast food is cheap food in the U.S. but in many counties it is considerably more expensive than the food provided at local restaurants. Nevertheless, the U.S. was relatively expensive for a Big Mac on January 17, 2018.[29]

UBS Wealth Management Research went further and indexed the amount of time it would take an average worker in 71 cities around the world to work and earn the money to buy a Big Mac.[30] This measure incorporates more factors into the index, including local wage variances. Under this measure, in 2015, the American cities that were tested tied for the third fastest time, at 11 minutes.

Most measures focus on outputs, perhaps out of necessity. They measure income and wealth more readily than inputs in the economy,

---

[29]   D.H. & R.L.W., *The Big Mac Index*, ECONOMIST, Jan. 17, 2018.
[30]   UBS, PRICES & EARNINGS, https://www.ubs.com/microsites/prices-earnings/edition-2015.html (last visited Feb. 28, 2018).

such as quantity or quality of food and education. This does not negate the need for policymakers to decide where their focus should be in a world of limited resources. If Congress decides to reduce inequality, should it direct its attention to inputs or outputs? What if equalizing inputs does not equalize outputs? What if equalizing outputs frustrate production of inputs? These are complicated issues that go beyond tax policy as they reflect a sense of what society owes to its members.

(c) Theoretical Arguments over Redistribution

Not everyone accepts that redistribution through the tax system should be used to reduce income inequality. Redistribution is heavily debated under various theories of distributive justice, but no theory is conclusive. The premise of distributive justice is that money and resources ought to be distributed in such a way as to lead to a socially just society but even that contains its own ambiguity.

For example, a Rawlsian interpretation of distributive justice requires a truly fair society be organized in a manner benefiting the least advantaged, and inequality is permissible only to the extent that it benefits the least advantaged.[31] An alternative view of justice focuses on laissez-faire expressions of individual autonomy provided that those who do poorly for arbitrary reasons, such as lack of talents, receive compensation from those who do well.[32] Thus, distributive justice seeks ideals of justice but may define these ideals differently.

Under any definition of distributive justice, taxation is a tool that directly affects the distribution of income. Therefore, taxation can be a tool for achieving or frustrating distributive justice however it is defined. Nevertheless, although individuals may have an ethical duty to help those less fortunate, it may be morally impermissible to compel them to do so through the tax system without universal consent for redistribution.[33] Thus, the propriety of using the tax system is no more certain than the ideals of distributive justice.

In addition to focusing on after-tax justice, redistributive taxation can focus on the pre-tax distribution of property. According to this argument, the starting point of what a person "owns" is not what he "earns" because there is something suspect in what a person is able to earn. Historical discrimination, legislative capture, or theft played some role in the current distribution of wealth and income that can be redressed through current taxation.

---

[31]   *See* JOHN RAWLS, A THEORY OF JUSTICE 266 (1971).

[32]   ROBERT NOZICK, ANARCHY, STATE AND UTOPIA 33 (1974).

[33]   For more on morality versus ethical obligations to the tax system, see Chapter 4.01(a)(v).

Professors Liam Murphy and Thomas Nagel argue that the cause of wealth and income distributions does not matter because all pre-tax incomes are, in fact, morally insignificant.[34] People do not own anything except through property laws enforced by the state. Without state action, there is no property but a Hobbesian state of nature. Therefore, governments have the right to adjust property allocations as governments see fit in the process of creating property rights.

Under these theories that question pre-tax distribution of income or wealth, tax policy should be evaluated for its results for every American. Accordingly, tax policy is not a question of what is taken and given from any one person or group. If people have no particular moral claim to what they have, wealth can be redistributed as politically elected leaders choose subject to constitutional due process limits.

The premise of these arguments reject philosopher John Locke's (and others') defense of a natural right to property that has long been a bedrock principle in the U.S. Under Lockeean theory, civil society was created to protect property and people have a claim to what they have used their labor to create. Thus, the fruits of one's labor become one's own because of the work. However, even under Locke this strongly libertarian theory had limits. Wasting property was considered an offense against nature, and even accumulation without spoilage was only acceptable so long as "there was enough, and as good, left in common for others."[35]

Although it is possible to debate the philosophical underpinnings of redistributive taxation and its potential impact on the economy and the poor, the question for most people boils down to their personal sense of obligation to those who are less fortunate. Perhaps equally important is a sense of whether wealthy people have earned what they receive. Accepting the use of taxation to change these distributions is not deciding an individual moral obligation. Instead, it determines whether the government should be able to compel people to provide for those less fortunate in order to alleviate poverty or to reduce inequality. If so, to what extent should the government be able to engage in this compulsion? The answers to these types of questions are inherently personal and therefore likely to vary substantially within society.

These theoretical debates question the baseline against which a particular tax should be measured: Should a tax be measured against pre-tax income distributions or is the ability to earn income skewed

---

[34]   LIAM MURPHY & THOMAS NAGEL, THE MYTH OF OWNERSHIP 4 (2003).

[35]   JOHN LOCKE, TWO TREATISES ON GOVERNMENT, chapter V.

enough to make the pre-tax distribution suspect? In other words, should a tax be evaluated against a world without any tax or in a world with a 100% tax? The answer likely depends on a person's sense of the proper role of government. That starting position is likely to influence a person's evaluation of the tax as people anchor their analysis to their starting point.

(d) Pragmatic Arguments over Redistribution

Redistributive policies to reduce inequality can be debated over pragmatic concerns and not simply over a sense of justice. Both those for and those against redistribution claim an impact on economic growth and the welfare of those at the bottom end of the income spectrum. The weight of the evidence sides with those who seek to mitigate inequality. Thus, it is likely that inequality is more detrimental to the economy and society than it is a motivator for personal efforts, although there remains room for doubt. There is no answer as to how much redistribution is helpful to accomplish those goals or if there is a sliding scale of optimal redistribution.

First, research shows that less stratified economies enjoy greater economic growth. For example, a 2011 report by the International Monetary Fund found a strong association between lower levels of inequality and sustained periods of economic growth.[36] Developing countries with high inequality (such as Brazil and Jordan) have succeeded at high rates of growth for a few years, but longer periods of growth are robustly associated with more equal income distributions. Thus, arguably greater equality is necessary, if not sufficient, for long-term growth.

There are several ways which promoting redistribution may stimulate growth. This may be because a larger middle-class enables more people to be consumers, whose demand stimulates the production of goods and services. Additionally, more redistribution may take the form of, or result in, investing in human capital promoting future growth. A lower rate of redistribution may increase future inequality due to limited investment in both human and physical capital among lower-income members of society. Conversely, lack of redistribution may adversely affect growth as a cause of economic crises. To the extent redistribution reduces these inequalities it may reduce the threat to the economy and either prevent or ameliorate economic crises.

An alternate approach argues that it is better to grow the pie than redistribute it, with the implication that redistribution will reduce the pie or at least limit its growth. Often unstated, the

---

[36]   Andrew Berg & Jonathan Ostry, *Inequality and Unsustainable Growth*, INT'L MONETARY FUND (2011).

rationale is that redistribution reduces the work ethic of both higher- and lower-income individuals. Higher-income people might choose leisure to work if they expect to pay high taxes; the poor might choose leisure if they know that they will be taken care of through redistribution. Consistent with largely discredited Social Darwinism, in 1883, Yale professor William Sumner famously concluded that assistance to the poor weakens their ability to survive.[37]

Little evidence supports Sumner's conclusion or that taxes impair work ethic. Anecdotally and rhetorically people have made strong claims but generally fail to supply proof. One older study, finished in 1953 by the Harvard Business School, found that the wealthy had great variance in their reaction to taxation.[38] It found that few wealthy people would greatly reduce their production if their taxes increased because they, as with most people, have little ability to change their marginal effort. Some might retire earlier than otherwise, but others might work harder in order to earn a targeted after-tax amount. Similarly, the EITC should cause low-income people to reduce their employment as they phase out of the credit but evidence does not find this result.[39] Possibly people would become more economically rational with time; however, no evidence proves this will occur.

Problems resulting from inequality are not only economic. British researchers Richard Wilkinson and Kate Pickett demonstrate a correlation between income inequality and higher rates of health and social problems using statistics from twenty-three developed countries and the fifty U.S. states.[40] These problems include obesity, mental illness, teenage births, incarceration, child conflict, and drug use. Additionally, there are lower rates of social goods, namely life expectancy, educational performance, trust among strangers, women's status, social mobility, and number of patents issued. The authors' argument is that inequality produces harm because of the psychosocial stress that status anxiety creates. Critics of the study claim that attempts to duplicate the findings (standard in scientific inquiries) failed to find the correlation or that the authors conflated correlation with causation.[41]

---

[37] WILLIAM SUMNER, WHAT SOCIAL CLASSES OWE TO EACH OTHER (1883).

[38] Results were published in seven volumes. Of particular interest is J. KEITH BUTTERS ET AL., EFFECTS OF TAXATION: INVESTMENTS BY INDIVIDUALS (1953).

[39] For more on the EITC, see Chapter 16.02(b).

[40] RICHARD G. WILKINSON & KATE PICKETT, THE SPIRIT LEVEL (2009).

[41] See Karen Rowlingson, Does Income Inequality Cause Health and Social Problems?, JOSEPH ROWNTREE FOUNDATION (2011); Peter Robert Saunders, Beware False Profits, POLICY EXCHANGE, Aug. 7, 2010; CHRISTOPHER SNOWDON, THE SPIRIT LEVEL DELUSION (2010).

Finally, redistributive taxation may be justified as a form of insurance. For risk adverse individuals who face wage uncertainty, redistributive taxation insures against low wages. People earning high incomes owe large amounts of tax but if they fall on hard times their low incomes will produce little amounts of tax and provide social insurance. The need for this type of insurance may be particularly great if, as Professors Robert Frank and Philip Cook argue, the modern American labor market is a series of winner-take-all competitions.[42] A few workers take huge rewards while most win little or nothing.

Law school may be an example of the winner-take-all market. A few students graduate with large firm paychecks and secure economic futures, but many finish with significant debt and uncertainty over how to repay that debt. Because each person decides whether to enter law school (or any other winner-take-all profession) based on the expected payoff to one person, she is likely to be overly optimistic and unlikely to consider the negative externality her entrance to the job market poses to all other entrants. The more entrants, the more who fail. A progressive tax reduces this problem by reducing the size of the winnings. It should lessen the likelihood people enter the winner-take-all market.

(e) Means of Redistribution

To the extent that there is a desire to lessen inequality, redistribution can be accomplished through either taxing or spending. Social services can be provided equally to all but funded through progressive taxation. Alternatively, disproportionate spending on the poor can be funded with equal taxes. For example, a flat tax coupled with redistributive spending of the revenue that is raised would produce redistribution similar to progressive taxation with equal spending.

The choice of taxing or spending is only one of many questions that must be answered in order to formulate a redistributive system. Redistribution can be largely hidden from the public (such as Social Security's progressive payout structure) or widely salient (such as progressive tax rates). It may be easier to enact hidden progressivity but less salutary for those in need. Redistribution can be through cash payments or the provision of goods. While recipients may prefer to be given cash, programs that provide in kind benefits may be more palatable to taxpayers as they give society more control over how the redistributed funds are spent. Each set of decisions highlights the

---

[42]   ROBERT H. FRANK & PHILIP J. COOK, THE WINNER-TAKE-ALL SOCIETY (1995).

choices that must be made to create a redistributive system. Politics determines which form, and the level, of redistribution that is chosen.

The U.S. uses taxation, monetary policies, welfare and entitlement spending, and private charities to accomplish its redistribution. Thus, it is through a combination of direct and indirect government intervention that it provides for the have-nots. The government's commitment to redistribution also changes over time. Although no study traces the government's attempts to decrease inequality per se, the government is certainly more involved with these issues than it was at the time of the American Revolution in 1787 but possibly less involved than in the 1960s Great Society.

Direct government spending on redistribution is a large component of the federal government. In 2007, the federal government spent almost 50% of its total spending, or $1.45 trillion, on redistribution programs.[43] These programs ranged from means-tested entitlement programs like Medicaid, housing assistance, unemployment compensation, and food stamps to Medicare and Social Security, which are not means-tested but nonetheless transfer income on a mass scale and are generally justified on the grounds that they reduce poverty among the elderly.[44] That percentage increased modestly as a result of the recession. Although the numbers are contested, one conservative group found that America's lowest-income families receive $5.28 worth of federal, state, and local government spending for every $1 they pay in total taxes; middle-income families receive $1.48 in spending per tax dollar; the highest-income families receive $0.25 cents in spending per dollar of taxes paid.[45]

One effect of decreasing inequality through progressive taxation is that those with rising incomes contribute more to the government, providing more revenue with which to implement government projects. As people earn income faster than inflation, government revenue increases because more national income is taxed at the higher tax rates applicable to higher-income taxpayers. Therefore, although tax rates have largely fallen for each income quintile, overall more income is subject to tax at higher rates. This bracket creep means that more income is pushed into higher tax brackets but, because tax brackets are adjusted for inflation, only with real increases in income.[46]

---

[43] OFFICE OF MGMT. & BUDGET, FISCAL YEAR 2016 HISTORICAL TABLES BUDGET OF THE U.S. GOVERNMENT (2015).

[44] Jeffrey Miron, *Rethinking Redistribution*, 6 NAT'L AFFAIRS (2011).

[45] Gerald Prante & Scott Hodge, *The Distribution of Tax and Spending Policies in the United States*, TAX FOUNDATION (2013).

[46] For more on inflation adjustment, see Chapter 7.01(d).

However, it is possible that many government transfers are not from the rich to the poor but from the less unorganized (such as consumers and general taxpayers) to the more organized.[47] Those who are better organized include the elderly, farmers, and oil and steel producers. Under this theory, the most important factor in determining the pattern of redistribution appears to be political influence, not poverty. For example, of the $1.07 trillion in federal transfers in 2000, only about 29%, or $312 billion, was means tested.[48] The other 71% was distributed with little attention to need.

This favoring of the organized is evidenced by tax-preferred savings plans. Wealth inequality persists despite the availability of many tax-favored wealth-building tools. Congress enacted 401(k) plans and IRAs to favor savers, but those who benefit the most might be organized savers and financial institutions. These savings plans allow for pre-tax contributions of earned income to savings accounts. Although framed as aid to the poor, the bottom quintile of income earners rarely open these savings accounts.[49] Therefore, these tax expenditures do little to lessen inequality, one of the justifications for their creation.

§ 18.03   Pay Down the Debt?

Only once since 1787 when the Constitution was ratified has the U.S. been a nation without debt. In 1835, under President Andrew Jackson, a Senator made the big announcement: "Gentlemen . . . the national debt is PAID." The debt-free status lasted no longer than one year until the country, in a financial panic, headed into a massive depression. Since 1835 the federal government has always had debt, now issued to the public and its own trust funds, although the amount as a percentage of the nation's GDP has fluctuated greatly. Since the Great Recession, the national debt has grown rapidly, and it shows little sign of being reduced. One currently unanswerable question is what amount of debt is too much?

(a) Debt Versus Deficit

The national debt is not the same thing as the nation's budget deficit. The national debt measures the amount of money that the federal government owes, or more specifically the money that the government has borrowed in order to fund its spending. It is a cumulative measure of all unpaid borrowings. Alternatively, the

---

[47]   Dwight Lee, *Redistribution, in* THE CONCISE ENCYCLOPEDIA OF ECONOMICS (2008).

[48]   Robert Rector, *Means Tested Welfare Spending, in* POLICY RESEARCH AND ANALYSIS, HERITAGE FOUNDATION (2001).

[49]   Eric Toder & Karen Smith, *Do Low-Income Workers Benefit from 401(k) Plans,* CENTER FOR RETIREMENT RESEARCH AT BOSTON COLLEGE (2011).

deficit measures the annual difference between what the government takes in and what it spends. If the government borrows to fund the deficit, it increases the national debt. If there is a budget surplus, there is no addition to the debt even though the surplus may not significantly pay down the national debt.

The national debt is composed of outstanding Treasury securities issued by the Treasury Department or other agencies.[50] Not all agencies can issues securities, but Congress has given some agencies, such as the Federal Home Loan Bank and the Federal Farm Credit Bank System, specific authority to do so. All this debt can be divided into two types of federal debt: (1) national debt held by the public, either by individuals, corporations, the Federal Reserve System, or foreign governments; and (2) intragovernmental national debt, such as non-marketable Treasury securities held by the Social Security Trust Fund.

According to the Federal Reserve, at the end of the third quarter of 2017, national debt held by the public had surpassed $14.5 trillion or about 75% of the nation's GDP.[51] According to the CIA's World Factbook, this ratio ranks the U.S. the 43rd highest debt loaded country in the world.[52] Approximately 30% of the public debt was held by foreign investors, of which the People's Republic of China and Japan have particularly large holdings, although estimates of exactly how much a country holds is hard to verify because countries often hold through intermediaries. The publicly-held debt excludes the $5.5 trillion intergovernmental debt (such as the Social Security Trust Fund) and quickly growing $5.8 trillion state and local debt. Combined, the total federal debt (still excluding state and local debt) was $20.5 trillion or over 104% of GDP and, with state and local debt, this nation's total government debt exceeds 140% of GDP.

Measuring the federal deficit is similarly complicated. Although the federal government has only one budget, so that the deficit is most simply revenue minus expenses, in practice it is more complicated. Not everything is "on book" or "on budget," which means not everything is reported in the central budget. Being off book shields these items from some budget pressures but risks confusing people over how much revenue is raised or spent. The two biggest items off budget are the Social Security Trust Funds and the Postal Service. Other off budget items are independent agencies, such as the

---

[50]   For more on state and local debt, see Chapter 13.02(a).

[51]   For a breakdown of the federal debt, see FED. RESERVE BANK OF ST. LOUIS, ECONOMIC RESEARCH, FEDERAL DEBT: TOTAL PUBLIC DEBT, https://fred.stlouisfed.org/series/GFDEBTN (last visited Mar.1, 2018).

[52]   CIA, THE WORLD FACTBOOK, https://www.cia.gov/library/publications/the-world-factbook/rankorder/2186rank.html (last visited Mar. 1, 2018).

Federal Reserve, or items that are private in character, such as the funds managed for Native American tribes or the Federal Home Loan Banks. Most other expenditures and receipts are on budget.

The unified federal deficit is the sum of the on budget and off budget deficits. Since 1960, the federal government has run an on book deficit every year except for fiscal years 1999 and 2000, and total federal deficits in every year but fiscal years 1969 and 1998 through 2001. The CBO expects growing deficits in the 2017 to 2026 period.[53] Under current law, economic growth will be insufficient to cover increasing spending. The baseline for 2017 was a $559 billion deficit, or 2.9% of GDP, although this was less than the $587 billion 2016 deficit. However, the difference between 2016 and 2017 was primarily the result of the timing of income and expenses because the beginning of the 2017 fiscal year began on a weekend.

Therefore, although the terms national deficit and federal debt are the same as used in normal parlance, there are special definitions that cause the terms not to be transparent to those unfamiliar with their hidden meanings. For example, supplemental appropriations are outside the budget process and do not affect the federal deficit. Nevertheless, if there is insufficient offsetting revenue and the government has to borrow to fund the spending, supplemental appropriations will affect the national debt. It is, at least in part, the intricacies of these concepts that make it hard to know the government's financial position precisely.

(b) Limits on the National Debt

The Constitution gives Congress the power to borrow money; however, the ability to borrow requires that someone is willing to lend.[54] Currently, U.S. borrowing is to two groups: the public and to other government agencies. The first is marketable securities and the rest are non-marketable in that they cannot be sold. A debt ceiling caps the amount that the government can borrow from either source; however, the debt ceiling is a statutory limitation and not a constitutional requirement.

For federal debt that is sold to the public, the Treasury Department offers securities through auctions.[55] Competitive bidding sets the interest rate the government must pay its lenders. Individuals buy these securities through financial intermediaries,

---

[53] CONG. BUDGET OFFICE, THE BUDGET AND ECONOMIC OUTLOOK: 2017 TO 2027 (Jan. 24, 2017). As of March 1, 2018, the 2018 outlook had yet to be published.

[54] U.S. CONST. art. I, § 8.

[55] For more on the auction process, see TREASURYDIRECT.GOV, HOW TREASURY AUCTIONS WORK, https://www.treasurydirect.gov/instit/auctfund/work/work.htm (last visited Mar. 1, 2018).

such as banks, and have no direct influence on the bidding. Some countries and big buyers of government debt—pension funds, mutual funds, broker-dealers, and money managers—bid without the assistance of a financial intermediary. Direct bidders account for approximately 10% of the securities that are issued.

Most intragovernmental debt is a government account series of securities that is owed to government trust funds. This federal obligation was almost $5.5 trillion as of December 2017.[56] In reality, this debt is owed to the various programs' beneficiaries. For example, in the case of the Social Security Trust Fund, payroll taxes were deposited into the trust fund but the cash was spent for other purposes. If Congress does not have revenue from other sources to pay back the money it borrowed from the trust fund, Congress will need to issue debt to the public to do so. In other words, without new revenue sources, reduced government expenditures, or significantly increased GDP, Congress will need to exchange public debt for intragovernmental debt to enable the Social Security Trust Fund to make its required payments of retirement benefits.

The Treasury Department can borrow no more from the public or intragovernmentally than as permitted by the debt ceiling, a political device created in 1917.[57] The debt ceiling denies the Treasury Department the authority to pay expenditures after the limit is reached, even if the expenditures are congressionally approved. When the debt ceiling is reached, the Treasury Department can adopt only limited, extraordinary measures. These measures would not cover government operations for an extended period, and it is unclear if the Treasury could prioritize interest payments to avoid default on the national debt.

In the last half decade, Congress has repeatedly risked hitting the debt ceiling and suspended the debt ceiling for periods, for example between October 30, 2015 and March 15, 2017 and from September 8, 2017 until December 8, 2017. In 2011, there was a near default on public debt; the delay in raising the ceiling resulted in the first downgrade of the U.S.'s credit rating, a sharp drop in the stock market, and an increase in borrowing costs.[58] Another debt ceiling crisis arose in 2013 with a brief suspension of the ceiling after a

---

[56]   TREASURYDIRECT.GOV, INTRAGOVERNMENTAL HOLDINGS AND DEBT HELD BY THE PUBLIC, https://www.treasurydirect.gov/govt/charts/principal/principal_govpub.htm (last visited Mar. 1, 2018).

[57]   The debt ceiling has no direct effect on deficits. For more on how the law is made and the statutory limits on deficit spending, see Chapter 1.01(b).

[58]   U.S. Gov't Accountability Office, GAO–12–701, Analysis of 2011–2012 Actions Taken and Effect of Delayed Increase on Borrowing Costs (2012).

partial government shutdown. The Treasury Department was forced to take extraordinary measures in October 2013.[59]

The debt ceiling is affected by tax revenue, and tax cuts can threaten the ceiling. For example, new withholding tables created by the Tax Cuts and Jobs Act of 2017 resulted in less revenue paid into the government, and the Treasury Department's extraordinary measures to balance the books were expected to be exhausted by late March or early April 2018. These extraordinary measures included suspending sales of some series of Treasury securities, not making Civil Service retirement and Disability Fund investments, and not reinvesting other fund money so that it is available to pay U.S. debts.[60] Congress responded by suspending the debt limit until March 1, 2019, with spending caps and a continuing resolution for appropriations.[61]

Some federal obligations are excluded from calculations of the national debt. For example, the government's obligations to Fannie Mae and Freddie Mac are excluded even though they are government-sponsored enterprises under long-term federal conservatorship. Fannie Mae and Freddie Mac securitize home mortgages by buying them from banks and then selling interests in large groups of them to the public. Therefore, defaults by homeowners would result in these entities having to pay the buyers of their securities a significant amount without receiving the money to do so. If Fannie Mae and Freddie Mac cannot make their payments, the federal government would likely make payments for them as demonstrated in the housing crisis in 2009 when the federal government paid on Fannie Mae and Freddie Mac's behalf.

Additionally, unfunded obligations for mandatory programs, such as Medicare, Medicaid, and Social Security, are not included in government debt projections despite the recognition that they pose substantial future costs. The lack of any accounting for these programs ignores that payouts for these programs are almost certainly going to exceed tax revenues. The present value of these unfunded obligations was estimated in 2012 to be as much as $222 trillion.[62]

---

[59]   Jonathan Weisman & Ashley Parker, *Republicans Back Down, Ending Crisis Over Shutdown and Debt Limit*, N.Y. Times, Oct. 16, 2013.

[60]   U.S. Treas., Description of Extraordinary Measures (2017).

[61]   Bipartisan Budget Act of 2018, Pub. L. 115–123 (Feb. 9, 2018).

[62]   Mercatus Ctr., A Comprehensive Look at U.S. Debt, George Mason Univ., https://www.mercatus.org/system/files/debt-in-perspective-analysis.pdf (last visited Sept. 27, 2017).

(c) Effects of National Debt

Economists agree that the government's ability to incur debt is beneficial in times of economic recession. As tax revenues fall, government spending remains necessary to maintain infrastructure and unemployment insurance. Additionally, much as individuals borrow money to pay for capital investments and to smooth their economic cycles, so too can governments. The government must repay the principal amount of this debt plus interest, which is the cost a borrower pays in order to have the use of borrowed funds. This is a real cost that must be borne by the public, but the benefit of the use of the money may outweigh the cost.

A question without an answer is how much government debt is appropriate. Fiscal conservatives prefer that deficits be counterbalanced by budget surpluses in growth periods, so that long-term budgets are balanced. Alternatively, a balanced budget may not be necessary as long as the nation's GDP increases. If the government pays only the interest on its debt and leaves the debt outstanding, the debt amount remains constant. If GDP increases, the accumulated debt becomes a smaller percentage of GDP. Because GDP is a workable proxy for the tax base, as debt becomes a smaller percentage of GDP, a smaller proportion of the nation's taxing capacity is used to service the debt. Thus, the greater the growth in GDP, the more debt the nation can maintain.

Government borrowing may make particular sense when its interest rates are low. As of July 2016, the Treasury Department obtained a negative real interest rate on government debt because the inflation rate was greater than the interest rate owed on U.S. securities.[63] In other words, the market could not find better investments with sufficiently low risk as compared to the U.S. government so that the public was willing to lend to the government for very low interest payments. Moreover, certain insurance companies, pensions, and mutual funds are either required or choose to invest in U.S. securities to hedge against risk, driving down required rates. Some economists, such as Lawrence Summers, argue that when interest rates are low, borrowing actually saves taxpayer money and improves national creditworthiness.[64]

Debt must be considered with its alternatives. One alternative is to reduce spending, possibly by reducing redistribution. Another alternative is to print money, not expressly permitted in the

---

[63]   Craig Anthony, *Can Real Interest Rates Be Negative?*, INVESTOPEDIA (Jul. 26, 2016).

[64]   John Hilsenrath, *Summers: U.S. Should Gradually Shift to More Short-Term Debt*, WALL ST. J., SEP. 30, 2014.

Constitution but a necessary and proper power.[65] However, printing money comes with risks. Printing money does not increase economic output, and increasing the money supply risks causing inflation because each new dollar has less purchasing power.

On the other hand, debt to fund government spending has downsides. First, a portion of the nation's savings goes to purchases of debt, rather than investments in the market. Therefore, less money is going to productive capital goods such as factories and computers. This should lead to lower output and incomes. Reduced investment does not automatically occur because federal money can be spent on these activities. However, even if government investment is made wisely, it may increase the cost of money as public sector borrowing crowds out private borrowers. As a result, the private market may not be able to finance its own growth.

Evidence is mixed on national debt's effect on economic growth. In 2010, economists Kenneth Rogoff and Carmen Reinhart reported that among twenty developed countries, growth in average annual GDP was 3% to 4% when debt was relatively moderate or low, defined as under 60% of GDP. When debt was high, defined as above 90% of GDP, growth fell to 1.6%.[66] These conclusions were questioned when a coding error was discovered in their paper. After correcting the error, other economists found no evidence that debt above a specific threshold reduces growth. Rogoff and Reinhart maintain that a negative relationship between high debt and growth exists. One 2012 paper by two French economists countered that growth rates increased as the debt-to-GDP ratio passed 115%.[67] Other economists, including Paul Krugman, argue that it is low growth that causes debt to increase, although that might not matter if the effect is mutually reinforcing.[68]

One reason for this debate is that debt is not merely a proxy for spending but is also an asset to its holders. Future generations benefit from previously accumulated national debt to the extent they hold these assets. However, these assets are unlikely to be evenly distributed. Therefore, to the extent national securities are properly viewed as assets, only a subset of the future will benefit from debt incurred today. To the extent the debt is owed to foreign investors, payments on these assets are not directly received by future generations of Americans.

---

[65]   Knox v. Lee, 79 U.S. 457 (1871).

[66]   Carmen Reinhart & Kenneth Rogoff, *Growth in a Time of Debt*, 100 AM. ECON. REV. 573 (2010).

[67]   Alexandru Mineau & Antoine Parent, *Is High Public Debt Always Harmful to Economic Growth?*, AFC Working Papers No. 8 (2012).

[68]   Paul Krugman, *Debt and Growth*, N.Y. TIMES, May 31, 2013.

Issuance of government debt may also increase the influence of foreign countries who purchase the debt. As of February 2018, non-U.S. persons held almost $6.3 trillion in U.S. debt, which was approximately 30% of publicly-held debt.[69] The largest holders are China, Japan, and the European Union. If the federal government were to have difficulty paying on this debt, its holders would be in the position to negotiate for redress. Alternatively, these foreign holders could sell their interests, deluging the market and driving up the interest rates necessary to sell additional debt. The Secretary of Defense conducted a national security risk assessment of U.S. federal debt held by China and concluded that the "threat is not credible" because of the limited potential effect and that any action would likely be more harmful to China than to the U.S.[70]

Another potential downside of debt as a source of funds is that, if Congress has to increase marginal tax rates to pay interest costs, the incentive effects could damage national production. This concern is no different than the fear any time taxes are increased that workers will substitute untaxed leisure for more productive pursuits. However, in this context, the disincentive could be worse if the tax is seen as less equitable because it is used to fund prior spending. Although this is a theoretical risk, to date no evidence proves this fear.[71]

Rising interest costs could also force the reduction of government programs. This result is more likely if publicly-held debt grows, whose issuance may force higher interest rates. Intragovernmental debt does not pose this same problem of raising rates because the federal government is simply paying interest to itself, as long as the government does not need to issue public debt to repay the loans. The higher the interest rate, the more future interest will be owed to lenders. If interest grows as a percentage of the budget, less money is available for other spending and there may not be enough discretionary spending to cut. Therefore, entitlement programs, such as Social Security, Medicare, and Medicaid, may have to be reduced.

Regardless of the interest rate, government debt risks intergenerational equity. As the current generation receives the benefit of government programs funded with debt, future generations must pay the cost. However, to the extent the proceeds are invested to improve the long-term productivity of the economy and workers,

---

[69]   U.S. TREAS. DEPT., FOREIGN HOLDINGS OF U.S. DEBT, https://www.treasury.gov/resource-center/data-chart-center/tic/Pages/ticsec2.aspx (last visited May 1, 2018).

[70]   WAYNE MORRISON & MARC LABONTE, CONG. RESEARCH SERV., RL34314, REPORT ON CHINA'S HOLDINGS OF U.S. SECURITIES (2013).

[71]   For more on the economic theory of income substitution, see Chapter 6.01.

future generations may benefit from today's debt. Even spending on people's quality of life may equitably reflect their share of future economic growth. In the end, this is an issue of the allocation of the economic pie with the assumption that the pie is growing.

But the future may also have its own difficulties. When saddled with heavy debt burdens, policymakers have less ability to respond to recessions or economic slowdowns with government spending or tax reduction. The loss of these fiscal tools may affect the ability to overcome economic challenges. Continued growth in debt loads may even become unsustainable. In other words, if national debt is significantly greater than national GDP, it is possible that the government could not pay off the interest owed plus the debt itself.

There is no consensus on what amount of debt is sustainable or when it would become unsustainable. The International Monetary Fund's study of market-access economies concludes that a country's debt level warrants higher scrutiny if current or projected public debt exceeds 50–60% of GDP or if current or projected public gross financing needs exceed 10–15% of GDP.[72] These thresholds are higher than those set for low-income countries because market-access countries can generally sustain higher levels of debt than emerging markets.

The history of Greece is a good warning of rising national debt levels, as the nation suffers austerity measures and structural reforms imposed by its creditors.[73] Its domestic sovereignty is threatened as its economy continues to struggle. Having agreed to a third bailout on August 11, 2015 set to end in August 2018, Greece accepted harsh austerity measures in return for approximately $94.4 billion in aid. The first two bailouts totaled about $264 billion in aid, with much of the money paying off older national debt. As of the October of 2017, unemployment remained at 20.7% but had been as high as 27.9% in 2013. Public debt is approximately 180% of GDP.[74] Nations and the International Monetary Fund were hesitant to bail Greece out, in part because of the country's rampant tax evasion compounded by a large black market that makes it difficult for the government to pay its debt. For example, while Germany collects 67% of the VAT owed, Greece collects only 42%.[75]

If the U.S. government reaches the point that it cannot sustain its debt through tax increases, tough choices must be made. First,

---

[72]   INT'L MONETARY FUND, DEBT SUSTAINABILITY ANALYSIS FOR MARKET-ACCESS COUNTRIES (June 15, 2015).

[73]   For a timeline of Greek debt, see Greece Profile—Timeline, BBC NEWS, Jun. 19, 2017.

[74]   Greek Unemployment at 20.7 Percent in October, REUTERS, Jan. 11, 2018.

[75]   OECD, ECONOMIC SURVEYS: GREECE 2013, at 77 (2013).

Congress could default on national creditors, such as China, who loaned the government money. Second, Congress could default on the Federal Reserve, which holds much federal debt as the central bank of the U.S. Third, Congress could print money to pay its debts. Finally, Congress could reduce expenditures, such as by limiting Social Security and Medicare payments. Each solution is problematic. Defaulting on nations would likely lead to a global financial crisis. Defaulting on the public would create a currency crisis for the dollar and anyone who holds the dollar. Printing money would likely lead to massive inflation, problematic for everyone but especially the public, as witnessed in post-World War I Germany. Finally, reducing expenditures sufficiently to fix the problem would require a massive reduction in benefits.

A more appealing, but less predictable, solution would be for the national debt to shrink relative to GDP through significant growth in GDP. The U.S. has only run budget surpluses in four of the past forty years but has had several periods when the national debt as a percentage of GDP was reduced. If GDP grows in real terms (as opposed to through inflation) faster than debt is incurred, it is easier to service existing debt because the nation is wealthier. Higher productivity, discovery of the next power source, or some other means to grow the economic pie in ways that increase government revenue could avert problems if the national debt nears unsustainability.

Table of Cases

Table of Statutes

Table of Regulations

Table of Rules

Index

References are to Pages